Green Signals

Green Signals
Ecology, Growth, and Democracy in India

Jairam Ramesh

OXFORD
UNIVERSITY PRESS

Oxford University Press is a department of the University of Oxford.
It furthers the University's objective of excellence in research, scholarship,
and education by publishing worldwide. Oxford is a registered trademark of
Oxford University Press in the UK and in certain other countries

Published in India by
Oxford University Press
YMCA Library Building, 1 Jai Singh Road, New Delhi 110 001, India

ISBN-13: 978-0-19-945752-6
ISBN-10: 0-19-945752-2

Typeset in ITC Giovanni Std 9.5/13
by The Graphics Solution, New Delhi 110 092
Printed in India by Rakmo Press, New Delhi 110 020

Contents

Tables

A Note of Thanks

Varad Pande and Mohammed Khan have been close aides, colleagues, and friends for over five years. They are very gifted young men—the former an economist and the latter a lawyer—who were part of my office in the Ministry of Environment and Forests, and later moved with me to the Ministry of Rural Development. They contributed heavily to whatever I wrote between 2009 and 2011, a large part of which finds place in this book.

Vineel Krishna was my private secretary for over three years and played a key role influencing my thinking and actions on a wide range of issues, especially those relating to the role of the forest administration in the Maoist-affected areas and to the special development challenges faced in tribal regions of the country.

Ramakrishnan Ramesh was my additional private secretary for almost eight years and maintained records of my written output meticulously without which this book could not have materialized.

Mahesh Rangarajan encouraged me to put together this collection and facilitated the involvement of Oxford University Press. The originals of all the materials included in this book and much more are available for public use at the Nehru Memorial Museum and Library.

The Running Thread

This is a book about how an enviro-agnostic became an enviro-believer. But to tell that story I have to begin, well, at the beginning.

I

In the summer of 2009, after the United Progressive Alliance (UPA) was re-elected, Prime Minister Manmohan Singh offered me the position of Minister of State (Independent Charge) Environment and Forests—not quite a full Cabinet position but just a notch lower. This was an offer that, to be frank, surprised me since my background and experience had been in economic administration. I had previously held ministerial positions in commerce and power, and bureaucratic positions in the Prime Minister's Office, Ministry of Finance, Planning Commission, Ministry of Industry, and the Advisory Board on Energy.

This is not to say that I was unaware of or uninterested in issues related to the environment. I counted among my close friends quite a few environmental administrators, T.N. Seshan and Samar Singh, environmental scientists, T.N. Khoshoo and S.Z. Qasim, environmental activists, Anil Agarwal and Ashok Khosla, and academics, Madhav Gadgil and Mahesh Rangarajan. Besides, I had written about and spoken on some of these issues as well.[1]

Immediately after taking over I met with Prime Minister Manmohan Singh, who had recruited me to the Planning Commission back in

1986 and with whom I had worked closely both in government and in the Congress party. He told me that the environment ministry had acquired a reputation for corruption and I should introduce a culture of transparency and accountability. He said that while India cannot afford to ignore ecological concerns, we should not forget the urgent imperative for sustaining high economic growth rates. Finally, he advised me that on international climate change negotiations, India should be part of the solution even though we had not created the problem and that he expected me to give India a positive and constructive image in global negotiations.

II

The Prime Minister's three-point brief—ensuring transparency and accountability in the workings of the ministry, balancing high growth with environmental protection, and changing the global perception about India—needs to be understood in the context of the workings of the environment ministry prior to 2009.

It was Prime Minister Indira Gandhi who had set up a full-fledged Department of Environment in November 1980. She was extraordinarily passionate in her concerns for the environment and had been personally involved in the passage of several landmark laws and regulations of which the Wildlife (Protection) Act, 1972, the Forest (Conservation) Act, 1980, and the Air (Prevention and Control of Pollution) Act, 1981 were the most prominent.

Then in January 1985, Prime Minister Rajiv Gandhi expanded the scope of the department by transferring 'forests' from the Ministry of Agriculture and creating a separate Ministry for Environment and Forests. In his first address to the nation as an elected prime minister on 6 January 1985, Rajiv Gandhi announced the creation of the National Wastelands Development Board and a national programme to clean the Ganga river. Following the unprecedented Bhopal gas catastrophe in December 1984, the Environment (Protection) Act, 1986 came on the statute books.

That was in the late 1980s, when the face-off between the gross domestic product (GDP) growth-first advocates and the environmental lobby was still a long way off. That situation changed in the 1990s, with a slew of controversies surrounding the implementation of the green laws, especially as the momentum of new investment and economic growth picked up significantly. Over the next two decades, there emerged two clear strains of public perception about the ministry—at best, it had been reduced to a 'rubber stamp' and at worst, it functioned as what one newspaper described as 'an ATM' ministry. The general impression was that it could be 'managed'. Undoubtedly, this is what Prime Minister Manmohan Singh had in mind when he exhorted me to ensure that environmental regulations do not become a new form of industrial licensing, which he had boldly abolished in July 1991 with the full political backing of Prime Minister P.V. Narasimha Rao with a little help from sherpas like Rakesh Mohan and I.

III

There is much truth in century-old comment by US Supreme Court Justice Louis Brandeis that 'if the broad light of day could be let in upon men's actions, it would purify them as the sun disinfects'. I would learn over the next twenty-five months that sometimes in the Indian condition, sunlight could scorch and burn. But no matter how harsh the sunlight, I remain convinced that transparency is crucial not just for accountability but also for responsive and responsible policymaking and administration.

The first change I made was to install glass doors to my office, as I had done wherever I had been a minister before. But what substantive measures could I take to ensure transparency?

One distinctive feature of my transparency efforts emerged from a conversation with Harish Salve, the *amicus curiae* to the Forest Bench of the Supreme Court, who was among the first persons I met after assuming office. He made a remark that stuck in my mind. As I recall, he said something to the effect that if ministers were to clearly state the reasons for their decisions in writing and place them in the public domain immediately, controversies could well be avoided. This gave me the idea of the 'speaking order', normal in the judiciary but not prevalent in government. While it brought about a great measure of transparency, I must confess it did little to avoid controversies.

As I saw it, my job was to ensure that officers could exercise their professional judgement without fear or favour and I had to take a final view, giving my reasons clearly when I disagreed. I also felt that given the public interest in and gaze on environmental issues, making these 'speaking orders'[2] public proactively without waiting for Right to Information (RTI) queries and applications, would strengthen the forces of openness and accountability.

In these speaking orders, I set out the rationale for decisions, which on a couple of occasions set aside the advice and recommendations of experts after taking into account other factors—social, economic, and political. The first speaking order[3] imposed a moratorium on the commercial introduction of genetically modified brinjal, also known as Bt-brinjal.

A second route to transparency that I adopted was public advocacy. Most ministers usually read out anodyne speeches prepared by others. Since my approach to speeches was not in the traditional mould, and I did not have to depend on others for preparing my speeches, I thought that the 'bully pulpit' could be used productively to increase the understanding and awareness of my thinking on different subjects that were engaging public attention. Of course, having spent a lifetime drafting speeches for others, writing them for myself was a whole new experience, more so since I was habituated to speak extempore.

Often ministers are asked to make public addresses,[4] for me these became opportunities to introduce new ideas and concepts that were important departures from our traditional understanding of the mandate of the ministry and for making it responsive to the challenges facing a rapidly growing economy. The objective was to set out the 'big picture', to propagate the need to look at environment in wider terms than just preservation and conservation as well as draw out its linkages to public health, poverty alleviation, and ensuring sustained and inclusive growth.

My essential message was the need to adopt a 'middle path', avoiding the fundamentalism of the 'grow now, pay later' variety as also the fundamentalism of a large number of civil society activists who were instinctively hostile to the idea of high GDP growth rates. The two positions seem completely opposed with the protagonists talking at each other, instead of talking to each other.

Both sides, it often seemed, were deeply uncomfortable with the idea of pluralism that is the essential hallmark of a liberal democracy. The technocrats and experts thought there was one rational solution to every policy conundrum; hence, there was no need for debate, while the activists believed that there was an authentic popular will and sentiment, which they alone could discern and represent and, hence, there was no need for debate. My quest was to walk the middle path, knowing very well that there was a risk of being hit from both sides.

Public consultations were another form of public advocacy. To ensure wider participation, and to ensure that neither the ministry nor I influence the choice of participants, these consultations were organized and conducted by the Ahmedabad-based Centre for Environment Education (CEE). The first series of public consultations was on the commercial introduction of Bt-brinjal in January–February 2010 in Bengaluru, Hyderabad, Ahmedabad, Kolkata, Nagpur, Chandigarh, and Bhubaneshwar in which over 8,000 people took part. The second set of consultations was for finalizing the new coastal zone regulations and took place in Puri, Chennai, Mumbai, Goa, and Kochi, in which about 5,000 people participated. The third set of such interactions was on the Green India Mission and these were held in Guwahati, Pune, Dehradun, Jaipur, Bhopal, and Mysore. About 1,500 people took part in these meetings.

My objective in each of these meetings was to ensure that the government's thinking was made available to all stakeholders, even though they may be holding divergent points of view, and have that thinking subject to critical scrutiny. Getting divergent viewpoints together in the same forum could, no doubt, lead to cacophony as it sometimes did. But my goal was not to develop a sharp unanimity but to build a wider consensus.

Two other public stakeholder consultations proved to be groundbreaking and continue to resonate. The first was a public interaction held near Coonoor in February 2010 that led to the formation of the Western Ghats Expert Ecology Panel headed by Madhav Gadgil, whose recommendations created a sensation and evoked sharp reactions—both positive and negative. The second was a large interaction at Guwahati in September 2010 on the issue of developing the enormous, hydroelectric potential of northeastern states, particularly Arunachal Pradesh. My report to the Prime Minister suggesting a revisit of the hydroelectric power policy in the region created quite a stir but I thought it was important to sensitize my own government to different and opposing views.

A third route to ensuring transparency available to ministers in our system is that of active engagement with Parliament. Keeping members of Parliament (MPs) fully informed about public issues and arranging for debates on important subjects in both the Lok Sabha and the Rajya

Sabha are some of the ways by which this engagement can be pursued. The idea was to be proactive and not shy away from encouraging MPs to raise questions and call for discussions. I managed to create quite a few opportunities for such engagement.[5]

I knew that this would definitely open the doors to criticism of both my approach as well as actions and indeed it did. But then I felt it also gave me a great opportunity to state my case in arguably the most influential forum in the country, which would then not only get reported and commented upon widely, but also be part of the written records. It gave me a chance to take on board often divergent viewpoints and address misgivings so as to ensure a broad-based acceptance of policies and changes I sought to usher in. It was not just debates and discussions in Parliament. I wrote to MPs—sometimes to individuals, other times to groups of MPs and, on occasion, to all the MPs. On occasion, I wrote to my colleagues in the Council of Ministers seeking to sensitize them on issues related to the environment to ensure these issues merit consideration in their planning process, provide inputs, and involve them in the broader engagement on the environment question.

A final and important plank of my transparency and accountability drive was that of engagement with chief ministers and my counterparts in state governments. Our federal structure makes it incumbent on the central government to build consensus with the states. At the end of the day, the policy decisions have to be implemented by the state and local governments. Not taking the states on board in the decision-making process can lead to resistance in implementation, defeating the purpose of even the best policies. In many instances, the inputs of the state governments were essential to a decision as they were in a better position to make ground-level assessments of needs and attitudes.[6] Not all state chief ministers were happy with all my decisions,[7] but I did, wherever possible, seek to work out an effective balance that took on board their concerns without compromising the broader intent of the central government's policy or directives.[8]

IV

Transparency with the public was certainly one of the key anchors of my approach to decision-making. At the same time, I considered it necessary to engage the Prime Minister in a conversation on my priorities, approach, and decisions. This was not just because he was the prime minister but also because Dr Manmohan Singh, more than anybody else I knew, was not just steeped in concerns on economic growth but was also well aware of and sensitive to ecological priorities.

I wrote to him frequently. Each of my missives was graciously acknowledged and at times, follow-up actions were initiated, on the issues I had raised, by the Prime Minister's Office and the ministries concerned. Thus, my letter to him on hydroelectric power projects in the Northeast led the Ministry of Power to start talking in terms of cumulative impact assessments. My letter following the Fukushima nuclear disaster elicited a detailed response on the safety systems in place in our own nuclear reactors. My letter on 'go–no-go' areas for coal mining led to the creation of a Group of Ministers (GoM) headed by the-then finance minister, Pranab Mukherjee, to find a way forward.

For his part, the Prime Minister would also write to me when he received letters from chief ministers unhappy with my stance (for instance, on the Navi Mumbai Airport and on the Maheshwar hydroelectric power project) or from industrialists whose proposals got stuck because of some reason or the other but mostly because they adversely impacted the environment (like, the Mahan coal block in Madhya Pradesh) or from some of my ministerial colleagues who did not agree with my decisions (for instance, Sharad Pawar on Bt-brinjal). I would explain the rationale of my position to the Prime Minister and never once did he ask me to go against my convictions. But he did make it a point to tell me on more than one occasion that while ecological security is all very well, what India needs most is rapid economic growth. I did not disagree with him completely but put across my point of view that this rapid economic growth must also be sustainable. That he took my arguments seriously is borne out by the Twelfth Five Year Plan (2012–17), which has rapid, inclusive, and sustainable growth as its objective. The inclusion of 'sustainable' was a huge intellectual victory made possible by Dr Singh's own sensitivity to ecological concerns even as he kept talking about unleashing the 'animal spirits' of Indian entrepreneurs and enterprise.

V

Balancing ecological concerns with the imperative of high economic growth was to be a major challenge and proved to be contentious since it would involve making agonizing choices. The contest between the demands for environmental protection and conservation, on the one hand, and economic growth, on the other, is inevitable. Both ends are good and, therefore, the struggle would always be about maintaining a carefully calibrated balance to prevent what Isaiah Berlin described as the 'occurrence of desperate situations, intolerable choices'. This would prove to be the more difficult than I had anticipated.

My past profile in government and in the party as an advocate of unbridled growth and liberalization of the economy, was seen as a source of comfort to industry and growth advocates, while my intimate involvement with the National Advisory Council and my tenure in the commerce ministry—where I had focused relentlessly on the plantation sector—was cheered by environmentalists. I was not a doctrinaire environmentalist but had also strayed from the 'growth-first' path; this meant that I would work towards compromise.

With an eye on the Prime Minister's brief, and given my own understanding, I believed that contrary to received wisdom, the job of an environment minister was not that of merely protecting the environment and the country's forests. As a responsible member of the government, the environment minister must balance the task of environmental protection and conservation with the broader aims of the government, that of ensuring high economic growth and poverty alleviation. My task was to ensure that the goal of high economic growth was achieved in a manner that was ecologically sustainable—creating safeguards to ensure that the environment would be protected and to minimize the deleterious impacts of human and industrial activities on the environment.

This was not a new idea for me. The broad strokes of the environment minister's task had been laid out of by Prime Minister Indira Gandhi. At the first United Nations Conference on Human Environment in June 1972 at Stockholm, Indira Gandhi, who was the only head of government attending the meet (that is, other than host Sweden's Prime Minister Olaf Palme), said: 'We do not wish to impoverish the environment any further and yet we cannot for a moment forget the grim poverty of large number of people. Are not poverty and need the greatest polluters? The environment cannot be improved in conditions of poverty. Nor can poverty be eradicated without the use of science and technology.'[9] She was clear that growth and environment were not inimical to each other, instead 'the inherent conflict is not between conservation and development but between environment and the reckless exploitation of man and earth in the name of efficiency'.[10]

The practical conundrum that the late prime minister's words presented was driven home to me very early—to be precise, on my first day on the job. The day I took over as minister, the Genetic Engineering Approval Committee (GEAC), a statutory body of the ministry, was meeting to discuss a proposal for the commercial introduction of Bt-brinjal. The GEAC's recommendations would soon be sent to me for approval, prompting me to take a difficult decision on a complex issue. This was a decision that, in many ways, set the contours of the way I would execute my duties as minister. It would also earn me admirers as well as bitter critics across the world.

It was abundantly clear from the first day itself that my task as environment minister was not going to be easy, I would have to make some tough choices. I was, to use Berlin's words, 'doomed to choose, and every choice may entail an irreparable loss'. Every choice and decision made would contribute to the growth versus environment debate. India had travelled a long way since that day in Stockholm. The country was on a high-growth path, people's aspirations had increased manifold, as had their needs.

On the one hand, there were the demands of a growing economy, with an industry wanting faster access to natural resources and a government keen to create the jobs so needed to ensure that more and more people could be part of the growth story that India has come to essay. On the other hand, the livelihoods of a large section of the population is still intricately entwined with nature—be it the farmers, most of whom still depend on the monsoons for a good harvest or the tribal population that depends on non-timber forest produce and firewood from the forests.

It would be erroneous to believe that economic growth and development will not entail any environmental degradation. At the same time, it is a fallacy to think that environmental protection is an obstacle to economic growth. Ensuring economic growth that is both sustained and environmentally sound would require sacrifices by all. But these sacrifices would not be for personal gains nor would the sacrifices benefit a few. The sacrifices would form the bedrock of the choices, which would be made for a common good.

There is unfortunately no silver bullet to resolve the growth–environment debate. It is not an either- or choice between industry and environment. But that does not mean there isn't a choice to be made. It only means that there is no set pattern or formula, and that the choice will, more likely than not, be a compromise with neither side emerging completely victorious. I saw my task, to quote Henry Kissinger from a different context, as ensuring 'balanced dissatisfaction'. Indeed by the end of my tenure, it was precisely that. Growth zealots dubbed me as Dr No while the conservationists accused me of not being bold enough and not backing intent with action.

The pulls and pressures of our ever-changing world made one thing clear that environmental concerns could no longer be the also-ran in our relentless pursuit of higher GDP growth. Not only would environmental concerns have to be at the core of larger economic decisions but, sometimes, it would even have to be the driving force.

There were occasions when environmental concerns were overriding and decisions would appear to be tilted in favour of the environmental lobby, to the detriment of 'developmental' projects. I was, for instance, faced with the difficult decision of what to do with three hydroelectric power projects under construction on the Bhagirathi river. After much deliberation and in the face of opposition from politicians from Uttarakhand, I persuaded the Prime Minister to scrap these three projects on larger ecological (as well as, I should admit, on faith-related concerns) considerations, to stipulate a minimum environmental flow to be ensured by all hydroelectric power projects and to mandate cumulative basin-wide assessments of ecological impacts.

Sometimes, the question of balance was not just about environmental protection and growth. It was about mediating between the growth expectations of the present and ensuring growth prospects for the future. This tussle was starkly evident in the case of the Western Ghats. The Madhav Gadgil expert panel's recommendations were both hailed and condemned leading to the setting up of a review committee headed by K. Kasturirangan, whose recommendations too proved contentious. That new plant and animal species continue to be discovered in the Western Ghats has reinforced my belief that, criticisms notwithstanding, I was right.

Not all situations were as contentious, and solutions could be found to address the needs of the present in a manner that safeguarded the future. The Coastal Regulatory Zone Notification, 2011 was an example of collaborative effort at balancing the needs of environmental protection with economic growth. India's 7,000 km-long coastline is home to some 250–300 million people. The coastline is strategic and has to be protected as do the livelihoods it supports. The coastline is also an ecological and economic asset. Infrastructure had to be created in coastal areas, at the same time there was a need to create systems to deal with the incontrovertible adverse effects of climate change. The 2011 Notification created special dispensations for sensitive areas such as Mumbai, Kerala, and Goa, perhaps not to the extent demanded by the 'growth at all costs' constituency but certainly less restrictive than its predecessor regulation.

The quest for balance was not just a need to address legitimate demands from competing lobbies but a realization that disregarding environmental and ecological concerns would adversely affect the goal of eradicating poverty and putting the country on a sustained high-growth path. To this end, there was a need to redefine the debate, away from the growth versus environment paradigm. This debate is meaningless and, in its current framing, environmental protection and ecological security can never win.

There is a strong and unequivocal linkage between addressing environmental issues and poverty reduction. Environmental issues such as air and water pollution have obvious public health implications and with it issues related to productivity. There is a need to consider the implications especially as India is a latecomer to the high growth rate club. The need to pull millions of our people out of poverty means ensuring sustained high growth rates but that should not necessarily mean that we have to repeat the mistakes others countries have made.

VI

The challenges of administering and crafting policies related to the environment in a manner that balances competing demands, and the pulls and pressures of all hues are many. The risks and costs are too high, and the line between the right thing to do and a good decision often blur. I was conscious that the impact of my decisions, good and bad, would outlive my tenure as environment minister. Hence, it was incumbent on me to ensure that I was truly convinced of the efficacy and integrity of my decisions and actions.

The policies we formulate and the decisions we take are only as good as the inputs. Making space for different, sometimes even divergent, voices was, to my mind, essential. This would ensure that the instances when the 'evil that men do lives on' and 'the good men do is oft interred with our bones' is minimized, if not totally eliminated. But there was a more persuasive reason for guaranteeing the plurality of voices. Environment is, I wanted to convey, not an esoteric or techno-cratic issue of 'expert opinions' but an issue linked to people and their daily lives.

So I opened my doors to all. I made a concerted attempt to involve not just more experts (especially younger ones) but also activists, environmentalists, conservationists, academics, administrators, indus-try experts, and civil society representatives in the process of policy formulation. Committees and task forces, with clear and time-bound mandates, were set up to address a variety of issues, such as protecting the Indian elephant that was facing a crisis of attrition if not extinc-tion, reintroducing the cheetah (from the Sanskrit *chitraka*) the only mammal to have become extinct in India over two millennia, revamp-ing the Botanical Survey of India and the Zoological Survey of India, establishing new regulations for disposal of plastic waste, e-waste, and hazardous waste, reviewing high-profile and controversial projects such as Vedanta, Posco, and Lavasa, strengthening laws governing protection of wildlife, enforcing the laws enacted for the protection of biodiversity, and assessing the implementation of the Forest Rights Act, 2006.

It was not just 'experts' who were welcomed in the ministry. I have always believed that young people, with proper guidance and encour-agement, can contribute to government. They bring with them a pas-sion untainted by scepticism and experience. Two of my early mentors, Lovraj Kumar and Abid Husain, opened the doors of government to bright, inquisitive young minds and gave them the freedom to chal-lenge the establishment, and protected them as well. In keeping with this tradition, of which I had been a beneficiary, I started the Ministry of Environment and Forests Internship Programme, which attracted a number of young men and an even larger number of young women. The National Environmental Sciences Fellows Programme was another effort at building the next generation of human resources. It is generally

not known that the first two secretaries to the Government of India dealing with the environment were eminent scientists—the noted botanist
Dr T.N. Khoshoo and the well-known oceanographer Dr S.Z. Qasim.
But then, this post became the preserve of the Indian Administrative
Service (IAS) and science was relegated to the background. I was very
keen that the ministry's scientific capabilities be enhanced substantially.
The Fellows' programme launched in February 2010 was directed at
post-doctoral scholars, below the age of thirty-five, desirous of working
at the forefront of environmental sciences, engineering, and technology at selected academic institutions both in India and abroad. Ten
fellowships were to be awarded every year, each worth up to Rs 30 lakh
a year—a handsome amount by Indian standards. Through this initiative I hoped to build a cadre and network of top-class Indian scientists
who would inform our ecological agenda, ensuring that it is based on
rigorous science.

VII

Choices must be made on the basis of hard facts and information.
There was a need to ensure that assessments are made in a neutral and
fair manner. This required a change in approach—new institutions
were required. Building institutions requires time but decisions needed
to be made in the here and now. The speaking orders and public dissemination of all decisions through an active ministry portal allowed
all stakeholders to a project to access relevant information helped fill
the gap.

The merits and importance of these measures notwithstanding, it
was not the solution to the problem of ensuring that the factors that
went into taking decisions were based on scientific and empirical facts.
The majority of the proposals that would come to the ministry would
not require speaking orders. The question was how to ensure that
decisions are based on hard facts and how to ensure that conditions
laid out to protect, minimize, and address environmental fallouts are
adhered to?

In a bid to provide a solution that answered these questions, I
worked towards setting up a new institution—a permanent body for
appraising and assessing projects that were seeking environmental and
forest clearances. The Environment (Protection) Act, 1986 provides for

expert appraisals. However, these are ad hoc bodies, where experts met periodically to assess projects, decide which ones should be permitted and the conditions under which these projects would be permitted. The ad hoc nature of these committees and the large number of projects taken up at any particular meeting made proper assessment sometimes difficult, often requiring additional information to ensure a more informed decision, resulting in delays on decisions. There is also no system for continuous monitoring of projects, which often renders the conditions set out at clearance a mere formality.

For the better part of my tenure, I worked to put in place the framework for a professional and independent body, first conceived of as National Environment Protection Authority, modelled loosely on the Environmental Protection Agency in the United States, and later modified keeping in mind Indian conditions as National Environmental Assessment and Monitoring Authority, which would be tasked with assessing projects based on facts and continuously monitoring implementation. This, I believed, would usher in an era of predictability. An independent regulatory authority would do away the uncertainties, and the back and forth that have marked the implementation of environmental regulations. A framework for the proposed authority was put in the public domain for stakeholders and other interested individuals to discuss threadbare in order to develop a blueprint for a system that would deliver on its promise. Additionally, I set up an expert committee to suggest ways to improve the monitoring functions, which were unfortunately rather lax and ineffective.

Despite my best efforts, I was unable to see this plan through as I was moved to the Ministry of Rural Development as Cabinet minister in July 2011. An intervention by the Supreme Court in January 2014 made it imperative for the government to act on this plan in a time-bound manner.[11]

When choices are made, there are bound to be grievances. Redress is the cornerstone of any vibrant system. However, redress of real or perceived grievances cannot be such that the cure is worse than the disease. The Indian judicial system is overburdened and slow, therefore resolution of grievances take forever. This was another plank of my intervention—to create an appellate authority that would be independent, accessible, and speedy. After extensive consultations with stakeholders, a new institution was designed.

There was another aspect to the judicial situation. Our system was not without a modicum of appellate recourse—the National Environment Tribunal and the National Environment Appellate Authority—but these were confined to the specialized cases of accident or absolute liability. India stood judicially unable to litigate and adjudicate major environmental claims from large-scale accidents.

The idea of the National Green Tribunal emanated from the need to remedy this situation. This quasi-judicial body was to go beyond invoking liability to rectify a wrong; it was by design mandated to impose high costs for non-compliance; to make it financially unviable for violators to repeat the offence. This tribunal would be both authorized and expected to punish environmental violations by imposing significant monetary damages as well as issue salutary and remedial damages. The National Green Tribunal was to be a one-stop judicial forum where all substantial environmental disputes would be addressed.

The National Green Tribunal, set up in 2010 by an Act of Parliament, became the first judicial body in India that would observe the 'polluter pays' principle. My role in setting up the National Green Tribunal, notwithstanding, the fact that it has questioned some of my decisions[12] and castigated me personally is a testament to the fact that I succeeded in putting in place a system in which stakeholders could place their trust and faith for fair redress of their concerns and grievances.

VIII

Institutions need time, and in a boisterous democracy like ours it would entail discussion and debate. In the meantime, it could not be business as usual. It was one thing to talk about situating environment in the larger framework of economic growth in public addresses, lectures, and parliamentary debates but taking concrete steps at the administrative level was quite another. These measures were not just about signalling that the environment ministry was serious about implementing its mandate but also about putting in place systems that would ensure predictability of processes, reduce possibility of conflict and litigation, and create avenues for balancing the needs of environmental protection with the demand for economic growth.

Among my early executive actions was the controversial (definitely for the growth-at all-costs constituency, at least) circular of 2 August

2009, which logically flowed from the provisions of the Forest Rights Act, 2006.[13] This circular made it mandatory to produce written consent from the *gram sabha*s that their forest rights had been settled and they had no objection to the diversion of the forest area.[14]

The Environment (Protection) Act, 1986 gives the central government, under Section 5, the power to issue notices in case of violations. The provision had been used sparingly in the past, so much so it was almost forgotten. In an effort to ensure that environmental norms were not observed in the breach, I resorted to the use of this provision in cases of gross violations. Show-cause notices were issued to a number of industries discharging untreated effluents in the critically polluted 740 km Kannauj–Varanasi stretch along the Ganga, the Lavasa project in Maharashtra, the Jindal coal mining project in Chhattisgarh, and Adani's Mundra port in Gujarat. The process allows the project proponents to present their case and take corrective measures. While these actions drew a fair bit of flak, including opposition from the political class, I believe it helped restore some measure of integrity to the environment ministry and the administrative set up. It also sent a clear message that polluters must pay, and violations even by the powerful and connected would not be tolerated.

I was seen, particularly by those in the industry, as someone who was out to obstruct economic growth by throwing a green spanner in the works; while others saw me as some kind of a twenty-first century throwback to Miguel de Cervantes' literary creation, tilting away at windmills, and that it would not be long before I would give up and fall in line with the growth-first-and-foremost gang. Predictability of regulations was something that corporate and industry leaders consistently harp on. But predictability cannot be a one-way street. While business needs to know that rules and regulations will be applied fairly and equally across the board, it is also important for business and industry to know that violations will be dealt with the same predictability.

In a bid to reduce the grey areas in environmental regulations, I oversaw several changes in the clearance processes. The first was to ensure that project developers particularly in sectors allied to coal and mineral mining, such as power plants and steel, did not use an environmental clearance to force or influence a forest clearance. Fait accompli forest clearances had become something of a norm, where developers would cite expenses incurred on the basis of the environmental clearances to secure the diversion of forest land.

In part, the genesis of the problem was on account of the difference in time and the process for environmental and forest clearances. Environment clearance is given to the project developer, while forest clearance is given to the state government, which owns the forest land in which the project will be located. Forest clearance is given by the central government after the proposals have been examined by the state government concerned. This more often than not requires consultation and that can justifiably take time. The time lag was often being used to push through clearances. This situation was addressed through two sets of orders. The first required project developers to secure forest clearance for their projects before applying for an environment clearance. The second order made it incumbent on project developers to demonstrate that they had secured requisite clearances for the linked coal and/or mineral block from where the raw material or component would be sourced.

To strengthen the integrity of the clearance process, I introduced a system of mandatory accreditation of consultants preparing environmental impact assessment reports and environmental management plans. In many cases, these reports were of poor quality, often unintelligent 'cut and paste' jobs, making proper assessment by the expert appraisal committee difficult. The ensuing request for more information and clarifications also contributed to delays in clearances.

The project-by-project approach to clearances meant that some areas had reached the limit of their carrying capacity, necessitating the need for circumspection and a landscape-wide approach. It was not just river basins or certain fragile ecosystems such as the Western Ghats that faced this problem, industrial clusters were a prime example of areas where the environmental indicators were at a critical level. In 2009, the Central Pollution Control Board (CPCB) carried out a comprehensive environmental assessment of eighty-eight important industrial clusters. The assessment was based on the Comprehensive Environmental Pollution Index (CEPI) developed by a number of prominent academic institutions, led by the Indian Institute of Technology (IIT), Delhi, which were also associated with the field-level assessments. Of the eighty-eight industrial clusters, forty-three were identified as 'critically polluted' where the CEPI score was seventy or more.

To remedy the situation, on 13 January 2010, the ministry imposed a moratorium on environmental clearance for new projects (and expansion of existing projects) in these critically polluted industrial clusters. The idea was to stimulate environmental remediation activities by industry and the state governments concerned. The moratorium would be in place till there was a perceptible improvement in pollution levels in the area, which had been brought about by a remedial plan prepared by the state government, reviewed and approved by the CPCB and then implemented by the state and local governments. This would be a dynamic process; the intention was to ensure that environmental indicators were within manageable and acceptable limits. A moratorium was a good tool to ensure effective action.

Existing regulations did not always address new demands—the air quality norms were revised for the first time, fifteen years after they had been promulgated, bringing them at par with the stringent European Union standards. A single standard for industrial and residential air pollution was introduced and I was of the view that the Revised National Ambient Air Quality Standards would lead to the use of 'clean fuel' to lower emissions. For the first time, the revised norms included standards for ozone, dangerous volatile organic compounds, and for heavy metals as well. Regulations and norms are important but is equally necessary to ensure that these were responsive to current situation and needs. In this context, the revised ambient air quality norms also addressed a growing public health concern—the increasing incidence of respiratory diseases. It also fit in with India's need to stem the rise in emissions of greenhouse gases.

IX

The change in approach required was not just about how we understood environmental issues in the larger framework of the country's quest to move up on the developmental ladder. It had to be a change in the relationship between the ministry and the judiciary, in the manner it viewed and involved markets in tackling pollution, in how it incorporated science at the core of its functioning, and in evolving an understanding of the administration's role in preserving and conserving the country's forest cover.

For many years, it was the judiciary that offered effective protection against the repeated attack on our natural resources and ecosystems. Judicial activism—that has been at the core of the discourse on environmental protection since 1984—has been a natural consequence of the executive's lethargy and malfeasance. Over the years, in large measure because of the executive's neglect in implementing the laws passed by Parliament, the courts, while exercising the right of judicial review, gradually reduced the role of the executive. It was time to exert pressure on the executive to stand up and be counted.

Therefore, building a partnership with the judiciary, especially with the Supreme Court, became one of my early priorities. In 1995, the Supreme Court of India admitted a writ petition by a gentleman by the name of T.N. Godavarman Thirumulpad to prevent the unauthorized felling of forests in Kerala and Karnataka. This application, became a catch-all forum where all matters related to forests (and later) larger questions of environment were tagged and heard. I once enquired about the background of the original petitioner who had left behind such a rich legacy of litigation and I was informed that he had long ceased to play a role other than the loan of his name to a landmark judgment.[15]

The number of matters filed and attached to this case grew exponentially to the extent that the Supreme Court had to constitute a separate 'Forest Bench'—a three-judge court headed by the chief justice, which would convene, and still does, specifically on Friday afternoons to hear and decide matters related to environment and forests. Some issues were more complicated than others and the learned judges soon realized that experts would have to be drafted to counsel on matters that merited a more thorough enquiry. Thus the Central Empowered Committee (CEC) was born. This committee comprised three officers all of whom had a background in environmental and forest administration. By 2008, the breadth and reach of this bench and the CEC had extended into the realm of executive functions such as the grant of forest clearances, the most notable being the Stage I clearance given to Vedanta for bauxite mining in Odisha.

Within my first week of taking charge, I was keen to ensure this bifurcation of executive functions between the ministry and the judiciary should be harmoniously reconciled. I met with the CEC officers who shared a similar vision. Our first challenge was the revival of the idea of the Compensatory Afforestation Management and Planning Authority (CAMPA). In October 2002, the Supreme Court had directed that a CAMPA Fund be created in which all monies received from user agencies as compensation for use of forest land would be deposited. In April 2004, my ministry in the previous National Democratic Alliance (NDA) regime had constituted CAMPA and in May 2008, the United Progress Alliance government introduced the Compensatory Afforestation Fund Bill in the Lok Sabha to give statutory backing to CAMPA. But the parliamentary Standing Committee dealing with environment and forests rejected this legislation saying that it violated the legitimate rights of states. The Bill was passed in the Lok Sabha but could not be passed in the Rajya Sabha.

As a result, the fund languished in an escrow account created by the Supreme Court for over seven years. My colleagues and I met with Law Minister Veerappa Moily, the CEC, Attorney General G.E. Vahanvati, and the amicus curiae, to find a solution to how we could access these funds, lying locked in this account. My attention was drawn to a 5 May 2006 order of the Supreme Court, which had on the recommendations of the CEC, directed the constitution of an ad hoc CAMPA to collect funds (accumulated with the states post-30 October 2002). This body was intended to function till a statutory body was set up. By the time I took over as minister about Rs 10,000 crore had been accumulated in the CAMPA account.

Finally, on 10 July 2009 we filed an affidavit before the Forest Bench of the Supreme Court requesting that the ad hoc CAMPA committee be made operational on the basis of detailed guidelines that had been submitted. The Attorney General, who appeared on behalf of the ministry as well as the amicus curiae, urged the Court in independent submissions to accept the affidavit and the suggestions made by the ad hoc CAMPA, which were further endorsed by the CEC. As a result the Forest Bench allowed the prayer. A total of about Rs 1,000 crore was transferred to these states for purposes of regenerating natural forests and afforestation activities in 2009–10. This was a moment of great personal satisfaction because I had been able, within two months of taking over, to break a logjam that had lasted almost eight years to the satisfaction of all concerned.

X

The Indian economy had undergone a sea change during the nearly thirty years that the environment portfolio had existed as a separate entity. We moved from being a planned socialist economy, the shackles of the inspector raj gone forever, to an economy where markets have an important role and where the private sector is vibrant.

However, environmental regulation has largely not made the transition. India had left behind the era of 'command and control', yet it continued to be the default option in the area of environmental regulation. I believe that markets have a role in environmental regulation. The trick is to realize where markets can deliver and how to ensure that markets can be used effectively to deliver on a public good.

When I took over as the minister of environment and forests, it was clear to me that we were in a '1991 moment' on environmental regulation. We needed to adopt more innovative methods of regulating our environment. There were inbuilt limitations to the traditional 'inspector raj' model of regulating, not to mention the ever present risk of rent seeking. While India has some of the most progressive and comprehensive legislations in the area of environmental protection, what we needed were regulations that can be implemented with fewer inspectors. We needed to move towards systems that leverage technology and harness markets to ensure better compliance with environmental laws and regulations.

It is in this context, that I asked a team from the Massachusetts Institute of Technology (MIT) and Harvard University led by Esther Duflo (widely acknowledged as one of the world's most eminent economists) to prepare a blueprint for an emission trading system for addressing air pollution. The idea was to introduce a market-based mechanism of self-regulation among industrial units by putting a price on emission of pollutants. Each unit would have a 'cap' or limit on the amount of pollutants it was permitted to emit—and if its emissions exceeded the 'cap', it would have to buy emission credits from other units who managed to keep their emissions below their 'cap'. The pilots of domestic emissions trading scheme were introduced in Tamil Nadu, Gujarat, and Maharashtra. The real-time online emissions reporting that this system required, itself brings considerable transparency.

The plan drew on the US experience of dealing with acid rain—reducing sulphur dioxide emissions by 40 per cent and saving, in the mid-1990s, more than $1 billion annually, the emissions offsets trading programme for total suspended particulate matter in Chile in the early 1990s, and the emissions trading scheme for carbon dioxide in the European Union. While still under implementation, the emissions trading pilot helped us test the challenges in implementing a new approach, one using markets, for environmental regulation in India. The learnings from the pilots, I believe, will go a long way in paving the way for robust use of market mechanisms in environmental regulation in India in the future.

Here again, I ended up stirring up some controversy. Industry hailed it as a step forward and environmentalists shouted that I was abandoning regulations. I was at pains to point out that there could well be market-friendly ways of implementing regulations so that those being regulated are freed from the clutches of inspectors.

XI

If changing mindsets (and, more critically, set minds) had become the leitmotif of my efforts in the environment ministry, the issue of forests and forest conservation presented a unique challenge. The forest administration needed to change its attitude from considering itself as the sole defender of the country's forests and viewing everyone as an encroacher to realizing that there existed a huge community of people, especially tribal populations whose daily livelihoods depended on the forests. For the most part, with some honourable exceptions to be sure, I found that the forest bureaucracy did not see such people as partners in the protection and regeneration of natural forests. The other challenge was presented by the wildlife conservationists who, like the forest administration, viewed the local population as interlopers into the natural habitat of the tiger and other wildlife.

These two strains fed into another serious challenge that presented as the rising hold of Maoists in the forest areas, which were coincidentally also the most underdeveloped and home to some of the most marginalized sections of our society. The forest-rich areas, the mineral-rich areas, the Maoist affected areas, and the tribal areas converged in a number of states—Jharkhand, Odisha, Chhattisgarh, and

Andhra Pradesh. Indeed, the generally accepted view has been that the insensitive approach of the forest administration especially at the level of guards and rangers coupled with colonial era laws such as the Indian Forest Act, 1927 have given Maoist organizations the ammunition to spread their propaganda.

The way out was to ensure that both conservationists and forest administrators readjusted their approach to the ground realities of the country. My endeavour was to drag them, albeit kicking and screaming, into the twenty-first century. To this end, I initiated the amendments to the particularly irksome Section 68 of the Indian Forest Act, 1927 to reduce instances of unnecessary harassment and prosecution of forest dwellers and tribals for relatively minor offences, and literally forced the reclassification of bamboo as a non-timber forest produce, and the empowerment of the gram sabhas in its cultivation, transportation, and ultimate sale as well.

On bamboo, the initiative in Menda Lekha village of the Maoist-affected Gadchiroli district of Maharashtra proved to be a huge success and the annual income of the gram sabha soared to over Rs 1 crore and was acclaimed even by those who had been ambivalent about my tenure otherwise. Devaji Tofa, a local Gond leader, summed it up well when Maharashtra Chief Minister Prithviraj Chavan and I handed him the transit passbook for bamboo: '*Dilli, Mumbai mein hamari sarkar, Menda Lekha mein ham hi sarkar*' (In Delhi and Mumbai it is our government, in Menda Lekha we are the government.). I wrote to all chief ministers asking them to replicate this initiative to begin with in those areas where community forest rights were recognized under the Forest Rights Act, 2006. I did not have great success though. It was only in March 2013, when I was the rural development minister, that I was able to show progress: gram sabhas took control of bamboo trade in the Jamguda village of Kalahandi district of Odisha and in the Daddugula and Munasarapalli villages of Vishakhapatnam district of Andhra Pradesh.

There were other initiatives to deal with the Maoist challenge. Greater flexibility was given to states to establish social and other infrastructure in forest areas without necessarily having to get clearance under the Forest (Conservation) Act, 1980. I also engaged the chief ministers in order to get them to re-initiate the process of recruitment, wherever possible, from the local youth, at the cutting-edge levels, and in positions involving public interface of forest administration so that a new face of the forest bureaucracy could be visible to the people at large. After a gap of many years, a number of states recommenced recruitment to posts of forest guards, rangers, etc.

The examination for the Indian Forest Service (IFS) is conducted by the Union Public Service Commission (UPSC) only in English and is open only to science graduates. I felt these were anachronisms and took up the matter with the UPSC over the objections of my senior IFS colleagues. To my regret, this matter could, however, not be resolved during my tenure. But one thing I was able to get done was to persuade the finance minister to provide a special one-time grant of Rs 100 crore for the strengthening of the Indian Council of Forestry Research and Education (ICFRE) that had been languishing for many years. The ICFRE had been created with high hopes in 1986 and my objective was to breathe new life into it, like I attempted with the Botanical Survey of India established way back in 1890 and the Zoological Survey of India created in 1916.

XII

The difficulties that an environment minister who takes her or his job seriously faces was best evident on the issue of the go–no-go demarcation of forests when it came to clearing coal mining projects. Ironically, the idea was given to me by a former chairman of Coal India, who wanted a priori clarity on which projects would get approval and which would not be given the go-ahead. The demarcation, as the material included in this book will show, was not arbitrary but based on detailed analytical exercises carried out by joint expert teams. The problem arose because a large number of coal deposits are located in rich forest areas. Mining in degraded forest areas does not pose a dilemma but in forest areas with high tree cover and density it certainly does since dense natural forests once destroyed are gone forever. Man-made plantations can never be a substitute for natural forests, which apart from being repositories of valuable and irreplaceable biodiversity, act as a substantial carbon sink and help minimize global warming. I had got a study conducted that had estimated that our forest cover absorbs anywhere between 8 and 10 per cent of our annual greenhouse gas emissions.

Personally, the go–no-go issue caused me great anguish. Having served as junior minister in the Ministry of Power, and my prior interactions with the sector, I was aware of the need to massively augment power-generating capacity and that in the short-to-medium term, coal—of which India has the world's third largest reserves—was the only option. Yet, in good conscience, I had to take a tough stance not because I wanted to be contrarian or play to the enviro-gallery but simply because it seemed to me to be the right thing to do. I was also deeply conscious of the need to utilize our resources better, to conserve them for the future. I was also of the view that our coal mining companies needed to be more environment friendly and efficient in its production and needed to upgrade their technological capabilities.

I was on occasion able to accommodate the needs for coal mining, but my efforts to walk more than half way were not met by the coal and infrastructure lobbies. On occasion, companies that could not get the green light became implacably hostile to me—somewhat ironical, since many of them were my close personal friends and I had excellent relationships with them. These go–no-go debates that made me quite unpopular with my own colleagues are very much part of this book.

My stand on coal mining in forest areas was nuanced, but the nuance was mostly lost in the public discourse. Environmentalists bemoaned that I had not gone far enough and that at times I compromised. Industry asserted that I had caused grievous damage to the investment climate. The point I was trying to make—that it has to be case-by-case evaluation—just did not get through. This was an issue in which I was damned if I did and damned if I didn't. What made matters worse was the position I took on nuclear energy, which I have always believed is a red rag to the green bull. I was convinced that India had to increase the contribution of nuclear energy to its energy supply basket, up from the present level of 3.5 per cent or so to at least 20 per cent over the next two decades. The very same people who applauded my stance on Vedanta, for instance, condemned me for according clearance for the Jaitapur Nuclear Power Park at a time when the Fukushima catastrophe was dominating the headlines. I believed that public concerns about the safety of nuclear plants was not completely misplaced, but these concerns could be addressed through better public outreach and an independent regulator in whom the people could repose faith.

XIII

The constant attempt to achieve a precarious equilibrium between growth and environmental protection throws up an important question. How do we manage what we haven't measured? If we are to make a more robust case for environmental protection, we must be able to objectively quantify the costs of environmental degradation caused by our growth process (as well as quantify the benefits too arising out of interventions to protect the environment).

Economists traditionally estimate GDP as a broad measure of national income and net domestic product (NDP) accounts for the use of physical capital. However, there is no generally accepted system to convert GDP into 'green' GDP, which would reflect the use of depleting natural resources in the process of generating national income.

That is why in August 2010, I persuaded the Prime Minister to constitute an expert committee under the chairmanship of the distinguished Cambridge economist, and one of the gurus of environmental economics, Partha Dasgupta. The Dasgupta Committee, which also had other noted economists like Vijay Kelkar, Nitin Desai, Kaushik Basu, and T.C.A. Anant, was tasked with developing a framework for Green National Accounts, which would reflect environmental costs as part of the national macroeconomic accounting system. The Dasgupta Committee presented its report, with a robust framework and road map for implementation to the Prime Minister in April 2013.

The Dasgupta Committee report calls for including new types of 'capital' including 'human capital' and 'natural capital'—the nation's ecosystems, land, water, sub-soil resources, etc.—in our national accounts. The report proposes a new paradigm of economic growth—defining it as growth in 'wealth per capita', instead of the more popular growth in 'GDP per capita'. It is possible, for example, that in a forest-rich, timber-exporting country, GDP per capita is increasing, while its 'wealth per capita' is falling, because its natural capital (in this case its forests) is being razed, thereby fuelling its GDP growth. It argues that this new paradigm where we measure changes in the nation's wealth per capita provides a more robust measure of a country's welfare, compared to the traditional paradigm of GDP per capita. The Dasgupta Committee lays out the steps for being able to report Green National Accounts; the onus is now on the government to implement it.

XIV

It was clear to me that the issue of climate change, which was at the international centrestage in 2009, the year I took charge of the ministry, could not be straitjacketed as an issue discussed solely by negotiators and ministers every year at a United Nations conference. With two out of every three Indians dependent on agriculture for employment, and 250–300 million people living along the coast, climate change is a real issue for India. Over the past few years, countless scientific studies, including assessments by the Intergovernmental Panel on Climate Change (IPCC), have stressed and re-stressed the impact that climate change would have on water availability, food production and security, coastal areas, and livelihoods. The impact of climate change on monsoons, the rising sea level, the retreat of the Himalayan glaciers, and its impact on the health of our river systems, particularly the Ganga, the lowering of our carbon sequestration capacity with the increased rate of deforestation that accompanies our relentless need to extract more and more of our natural resources point to one simple fact—climate change is as much of a domestic issue as it is international. It is an issue of local livelihoods, as much as it is an issue of the global commons. To relegate climate change to just a matter of never-ending international negotiations is not just wrong but inherently harmful.

In a sense, I was questioning the climate change orthodoxy, which viewed the issue as one reserved for the realm of international negotiations. But how do you begin to address such complex issues? Especially given that most of the scientific research that was publicly available emanated from the West, done by researchers who were not always aware of Indian realities and compulsions? To my mind, the answer lay in building our scientific capability and putting their work out in the public domain, so that it could stand up and be counted when the decisions were being made. US President Harry Truman is believed to have said that decisions are made by those who show up. The Indian scientific community had not showed up, and even though India accounted for 17 per cent of the world's population, our voice was not to be heard in discussions on the vexed global problem of climate change and the science that guided it.

It is with the idea of ensuring that the Indian story would be reflected in the discussions that I set up the Indian Network on Climate Change

Assessment (INCCA), a network of scientists in India to be set up to publish peer-reviewed findings on climate change in India. The network brought together 250 scientists from 125 Indian research institutions and collaborated with international organizations.

I visualized the INCCA to operate as a sort of an Indian IPCC. It built upon existing piecemeal efforts in climate science in India and was significant in many ways. First, the programme was broad-based, covering every sector of the economy and every significant aspect related to climate change, including, for example, the study of black carbon and the impact of climate change on glaciers and on rainfall patterns. Second, it engaged a larger set of institutions and scientists, including those in the private sector and those outside India, so that the best available expertise could be brought under a unified knowledge network. Third, it would be an ongoing programme, not a one-off, the results of which will be made available in the public domain for peer review, discussion, and debate. Fourth, the programme would provide capacity building to create and nurture the next generation of climate change scientists and experts. It was my intent that the '3 Ms'—measuring, modelling, and monitoring—would become the essence of sound climate policymaking in India.

If highlighting the domestic aspect of climate change and questioning orthodoxies was seen by some as undermining India's negotiating position, then my approach to international negotiations was, to their mind, nothing less than heretical. The Prime Minister had made it clear right at the outset that though India's contribution to the problem of climate change was minimal, he wanted India to be part of the global solution.

I had been charged with effecting an image makeover for India. To move away from being the perpetual naysayer to the proactive participant in crafting a solution to this vexed global issue that had consumed scientists, bureaucrats, and political leaders for nearly two decades. A more positive and proactive role for India, while keeping eyes trained on our national interest, was not anathema to me. In fact, I was, and continue to be, of the view that negotiating positions cannot be carved in stone. Our negotiating stance should consistently be guided by and anchored in our national interests—the need to protect our economic growth and poverty eradication agenda, enhance and pursue domestic environmental policies, and use climate change negotiations as part of the arsenal to meet our foreign policy objectives. None of these have to be at the cost of the pursuing a global good—a vibrant and viable international effort to tackle the global problem of climate change.

I saw an opportunity for India to take leadership, and be proactive in fashioning the outcome of the international negotiations. In doing so, India would be able to protect its developmental space and foreign policy agenda even as it changed the global narrative on India from a naysayer in the international negotiations (this image transcended climate change negotiations) to a proactive solution seeker. This does not mean abdicating our negotiating position. It means that you need to walk on two legs. It means adjusting the negotiating position to reflect the changed circumstances without abdicating national interest. It means that India had to negotiate from a position of strength, which would come from working proactively on the domestic front, taking substantive policy action. We had the example of China and the US before us, countries that took 'rigid' positions in international negotiations while taking domestic measures to address climate change and its impacts. To my mind, India's straddling the two worlds—of the global high table of the big powers and that of poverty and deprivation that was comparable to Sub-Saharan Africa—need not be a weakness. It put India in a place that allowed it to find and champion an approach that would work for countries across the board. It gave India the advantage of being natural leaders. Now, it was for India to seize the opportunity.

But domestic understanding, in large sections of the media, influential civil society organizations, the political and official class, saw any changes in the negotiating stance and a proactive domestic agenda as a sign of capitulation. My first 'break' from the orthodox negotiation position came way ahead of the United Nations Framework Convention on Climate Change (UNFCCC) negotiations in Copenhagen in 2009. I was keenly aware of the growing pressure on developing countries— the emerging economies such as India (more so, China) to 'do more' to tackle climate change. With the global conversation focused on a climate deal in Copenhagen in December 2009, the focus was on advanced developing countries like ours.

In the international imagination, India and China would often be lumped together perhaps on account of their large populations, growing economic strength, and both countries were outsourcing destinations—albeit for different categories of products. In negotiations, we worked together with China under the G77 umbrella. But given that China was a larger economy and more advanced than ours, it often offered India a cover. But ahead of Copenhagen, I was fearful that Beijing would move ahead by forging a deal of its own, leaving India on its own. China had announced a 40–45 per cent reduction in the emission intensity of its GDP. New Delhi needed to be doing something or at least seen to be doing so. This is when I decided to activate the BASIC, a grouping of the four advanced developing countries—Brazil, South Africa, India, and China. The BASIC was till then active during negotiations, I sought to give it a pre-negotiation focus. The four countries, despite being in different places on the development curve, had common interests in protecting their development space.

It was not just the BASIC countries that I sought to build links with, I reached out to the South Asian Association for Regional Cooperation (SAARC) countries and sought to develop a platform for discussion for the region. To my dismay, the SAARC network didn't pan out in a satisfactory manner. However, the SAARC Coastal Zone Management Centre in the Maldives and the SAARC Forestry Centre in Bhutan were established at my initiative with Indian funding to launch them. Within the region, I was able to build links with Nepal over the Kailash-Mansarovar ecosystem but my effort to set up the Sunderbans Ecosystem Forum with Bangladesh didn't take off.

I was of the view that building stronger links with other developing countries didn't, and shouldn't, mean not building partnerships with developed countries. India is a member of the G20 and the Major Economies Forum (MEF), and keeping the dialogue open and building partnerships with the industrialized was important to ensure that India's needs and viewpoint were given due space. It is in this context that I worked actively to set up the US-India joint working group on issues relating to environment. This joint group focused on among other things reducing the use of refrigerant gases like hydrofluorocarbons (HFC). The issue had come up in the climate negotiations, and there were differences in viewpoints between India and countries like the US. This working group was a mechanism to address the differences and work together towards an acceptable solution.

My efforts were to put in place close and focused working relationships with other countries, both developed and developing. My attempt at the bilateral, regional, and multilateral levels at the UNFCCC negotiations at Copenhagen and then at Cancun were all part of an effort to reposition India, ensuring that New Delhi had a bigger say in the fashioning of a global approach while at the same time safeguarding its developmental space.

XV

I have to be honest and admit that twenty years ago, I was something of a zealot about putting GDP growth uncompromisingly ahead of everything else. I believed that the answers to India's problems lay in increasing GDP growth. I still believe in growth, but I no longer equate it solely with rising GDP, I believe that we should focus on increasing wealth. I still believe growth is absolutely essential but it is equally important to sustain growth, ensure that the benefits of growth accrue tangibly to all, and to pursue that rapid growth in a manner that is more mindful of its environmental impacts and consequences.

This book is a testament to that journey. It attempts to bring to the fore the various, often contradictory, pulls and pushes that confront India as it seeks to chart a path of sustainable development. I have included all my speaking orders, each representing choices that needed to be made and will be required in the future as India seeks to balance ecological interests with high economic growth. It also includes some of my speeches and public lectures, letters, and parliamentary debates that reflect the thinking that informed my decisions, and policy interventions.

My stint as the environment and forests minister was undoubtedly tumultuous, to say the least. It is still being either applauded or criticized. This book is not an exercise in self-defence or a reply to my many critics. This is by no means a complete account of my twenty-five month tenure there. It is selective and brings into focus those issues that created a stir and became controversial. It is, therefore, not a political memoir that seeks to settle scores and seeks to give me a halo. This book, I hope, throws light, to some extent, on why my ministerial term continues to evoke such strong responses—both positive and negative. But more than anything else, I hope that the book will help provide a better understanding of my decisions and actions as environment minister as well as the challenges that India faces as it seeks to grow. That issues relating to ecological security are now very much part of the mainstream of the nation's political agenda and of the developmental debate, is, I would like to think, in some measure due to my efforts and intervention as environment minister.

Notes

1. 'Globalization and Ecological Security', lecture organized by the Foundation of Ecological Security, October 2002, reproduced in Samar Singh (ed.), 2007, *Ecological Security: The Foundation of Sustainable Development*. New Delhi: Shipra Publications; 'The SHG Revolution; What Next?', Silver Jubilee Lecture at the Society for the Promotion of Wasteland Development (May 2007) and 'Bush Fires over Kyoto Protocol', *India Today* (25 June 2001), reproduced in Ramesh, Jairam, 2000, *Kautilya Today*, New Delhi: Research Press; 'Demand for a Statement and Discussion on Issues Arising Out of the United Nations' Climate Change Conference', 'Matters Raised with Permission', Rajya Sabha, 14 December 2005. The first one has been included in this volume.

2. Along with the speaking order, I also made public the reports, letters, and other materials that contributed to the decision.

3. In all, fourteen speaking orders were issued and all of them have been included in this book.

4. Over the two-year period, there were eight such public lectures and all of them are included in this book. I have also included my address to the Finnish Parliament—though I was minister of rural development at the time—since it deals with issues I grappled with as environment minister and is the outcome of the work I handled at the time, including my participation in the United Nations Secretary General's High-Level Global Sustainability Panel.

5. Debates in both Houses of Parliament under different Rules of Procedure took place during 2009–11 on a wide range of issues, such as environmental impact of big dams in the Northeast, state of the Ganga river, concerns about dwindling population of tigers, climate change and international negotiations, pollution in rivers and lakes, oil spill off the Mumbai coast, to mention a few of the subjects.

6. The response from the states contributed to my decision to impose a moratorium on the commercial introduction of Bt-brinjal. All chief ministers or their ministerial colleagues cutting across party lines wrote to me asking me not to allow the commercial introduction of Bt-brinjal.

7. The decision to reject forest clearance for bauxite mining in the Niyamgiri Hills did not please Chief Minister of Odisha Naveen Patnaik, nor did my decision to restrict private participation in redevelopment of urban areas in Mumbai earn encomiums from the Maharashtra chief minister. I managed to attract the

ire of both Congress and non-Congress chief ministers, contrary to allegations that I was playing party politics I was, what could be described as, 'an equal opportunity offense-giver'. Some Congress MPs were unhappy with my positions as they were related, for example, to the Western Ghats or coal mining.

8. Clearance for the Navi Mumbai Airport is an instance of hammering out a compromise between Mumbai's need for a new airport and the need to ensure ecological safeguards for the mangrove forests, which provide an important environmental service to the city by serving as a natural protection against rising sea levels, while protecting against coastline erosion.

9. 'Man and Nature', address to the first UN Conference on Human Environment, Stockholm, 14 June 1972.

10. Ibid.

11. After my exit from the ministry, the enthusiasm to set up an independent regulator seemed to have waned. In January 2014, the Supreme Court, in an order issued to enforce a 2001 judgment on the Lafarge mining case in Meghalaya, directed the Government of India to establish an environmental regulator by 31 March 2014. However, a regulator is yet to be appointed.

12. In March 2014, the National Green Tribunal castigated me for overruling the recommendations of the Forest Advisory Committee that were based on the policies that I had myself put in place and for approving coal mining projects in the rich forest area of Hasdeo–Arand in Chhattisgarh. My reasons for doing so were spelt out in detail in a speaking order dated 23 June 2011, which is included in this book.

13. Refers to the legislation—Scheduled Tribes and Other Traditional Forest Dwellers (Recognition of Forest Rights) Act, 2006.

14. This circular would play an important role in the decisions on Vedanta and Posco, speaking orders on which are included in this book. However, there is a need to acknowledge that implementing the order—in light of the provisions of the Forest Rights Act, 2006, which doesn't have a time limit on making claims—would present situations of conflict, because projects would have to be cleared in a time-bound manner. This needs to be refined, or the circular would be more in the nature of an advisory, and worse still observed more in its breach. The order was amended subsequently in 2013 exempting linear projects such as roads, highways, and power transmission lines from its purview.

15. *T.N. Godavarman* v. *Union of India* (Writ Petition 202 of 1995)

1 Expanding the Public Space

Over the years, the environment ministry had come to be viewed as a government agency that could be managed by industry, and for those most affected by its decisions it was yet another turret in Kafka's castle. For the environment ministry to shed this image, to become a place where everyone comes together and not be the preserve of a few, it was first necessary to create space for all stakeholders.

For me, it was important to reach out especially to the people whose voices were heard the least during the decision-making process. Not only would this help usher in transparency and accountability in the working of the ministry but would ensure responsive and responsible decision making.

On three key issues—commercial introduction of Bt-brinjal, new regulations governing the Coastal Regulation Zone (CRZ), and the Green India Mission—large-scale public consultations were held. These consultations provided inputs to the formulation of policy by flagging concerns, finding solutions to flashpoints, and turning the spotlight on issues that required further action and consideration. I believed that public debate, however messy, would lend to wiser decisions. These interactions also helped shape my approach to related and larger questions of policy. The Bt-brinjal consultations contributed in no small measure to the design of the proposed Biotechnology Regulatory Authority; regrettably the government made no progress towards setting up the authority. While the interactions on the CRZ regulations provided key inputs to the formulation of the Fisherman Livelihood Guarantee Bill, it also remained on the drawing board.

The multi-city public consultations apart, on occasion I engaged in deliberations with smaller groups when the focus was on regional issues—the public interaction in Guwahati on hydroelectric power projects in the Northeast, especially in Arunachal Pradesh, being a good example. It helped drive home something that we in far-away Delhi often forget—that the region is not homogenous, therefore, harnessing hydroelectric power in Arunachal Pradesh can have quite the adverse impact in Assam. Similarly, another small group interaction in Kotagiri in the Nilgiris in February 2010 with the Save the Western Ghats Movement led to setting up the Western Ghats Ecology Expert Panel under the chairmanship of ecologist Madhav Gadgil.

Sometimes, consultations meant getting stakeholders to the table to begin a dialogue, with the ministry and I playing the part of honest brokers. Environmental clearance for the Jaitapur Nuclear Power Park was one such occasion—meetings between the project developers Nuclear Power Corporation of India Limited (NPCIL) and the Konkan Bachao Samiti, a platform of civil society organizations working in the project area, were held in my office at Paryavaran Bhavan. The idea was to provide a neutral platform to address the concerns and questions of the residents and to enable NPCIL to provide full information that often got lost in the din of protests.

The value that wide-ranging consultations bring to formulating effective and responsive policies besides preventing unproductive standoffs was driven home in the case of the Guidelines to Identify Critical Wildlife Habitats or areas that would be free of human presence within national parks and sanctuaries. The ministry had prepared guidelines in February 2011. However, some provisions ran counter to the Forest Rights Act, 2006. This landmark legislation, which recognizes the rights of people living in forest areas, demanded a change in mindset in the forest administration. I held a meeting with forest rights and wildlife activists, scientists, social scientists, and officials of the tribal affairs ministry, and set a time frame of two months for drawing up fresh guidelines incorporating their suggestions.

Many of my ministerial colleagues opposed my decision on the Bt-brinjal, arguing that my decision would hurt Indian science and its prospects. Following the imposition of the moratorium, I met with the heads of the six science academies, along with Dr Kasturirangan to discuss and develop the road map for biotechnology in food crops in India. Through it all, I kept the Prime Minister informed, by way of both in-person briefings and letters.

Engagement and consultation with experts and stakeholders, which includes the public, is crucial to ensuring ecological security and inclusive growth. That is why I made it a point to write to chief ministers and state governments when I got to know that the public hearing for projects, a crucial step in the environment clearance process, was being disregarded. It is also the reason why I went the extra mile to ensure that local people in the project area of the South Korean major Posco's integrated steel plant in Odisha had been consulted and their rights respected. It is the same reasoning why—based on a letter drawing attention to the problem of deforestation to meet the charcoal needs of Meghalaya's ferro-alloy units—I wrote to the state government asking them to set up a committee comprising eminent persons in the field of environment, forests, industrial engineering, and representatives of local tribal communities to study the problem and recommend short-, medium-, and long-term measures.

Many critics felt that these public consultations were publicity stunts, or a way to force through my own views on the issue. As I saw it, consultations, particularly those that included the usually unheard voices, were about bringing in real-life inputs into the sometimes dry process of policy formulation. It was also about public advocacy, of reaching out and showing people that economic activity and development do not necessarily have to be anti-environment or anti-people. My high-profile consultations, I would like to believe, enthused people to step up and make themselves heard, putting forth their ideas to address issues relating to the environment.

This chapter deals with the efforts made to expand the public space, the opening up of the environment ministry to a variety of views and perspectives, from specialists, activists, and the wider public. The selection, I hope, will serve to strengthen the argument that it is only when we reach out to people and let them into the policy-making process, can we have responsive policies and laws, which will be observed, not in their breach but in letter and spirit. It is my deep belief that it only when we keep talking with each other, and not at each other, that we can achieve the balance between the equally urgent imperatives of faster economic growth and deeper environmental conservation.

Letter to Deputy Chairman Planning Commission Montek Singh Ahluwalia on the Need for a New Building to House the Ministry of Environment and Forests

5 OCTOBER 2009

I wrote to you on 29 September 2009 on the need for the Ministry of Environment and Forests to have a new building for itself… Right now we are situated in the midst of paramilitary forces complex surrounded by CRPF, BSF, ITBP, and CBI. This is a most inappropriate location for our ministry given that we have to deal with the public on a minute-to-minute basis. This location makes it extremely difficult for civil society organizations to access our ministry easily.

Responding to Rattan Singh Ajnala, Member of Parliament (Lok Sabha). He had written to the Prime Minister Seeking a Moratorium on GM Crops

7 JUNE 2009

This has reference to your letter dated 16 February 2009 addressed to the Hon'ble Prime Minister seeking a moratorium on genetically modified (GM) crops/food in general and Bt-brinjal in particular until there is an independent evaluation mechanism in our country and rights of consumers and farmers are squarely addressed.

The matter has been examined in the ministry and I have been informed that the existing bio-safety regulation in India is adequate to evaluate the bio-safety of GM crops. The bio-safety guidelines adopted by the Review Committee on Genetic Manipulation (RCGM) under the Department of Biotechnology and the Genetic Engineering Approval Committee (GEAC) under the MoEF follow the international norms prescribed by the Organization for Economic Cooperation and Development (OECD), CODEX Alimentarius Commission and International Plant Protection Convention (IPPC).

Our endeavour has always been to permit field trials on biotech crops that are needed for experiments for scientific evaluation that conform totally to a transparent set of safeguards and guidelines. I hope this clarifies your concerns.

Setting the Record Straight with Union Minister for Agriculture Sharad Pawar on the Role of the Statutory Advisory Body, GEAC

[Pawar was one of the most vocal supporters for permitting GM food crops, and the commercial introduction of Bt-Brinjal.]

21 January 2010

My attention has been drawn to some newspaper reports today that you have said that the GEAC's decision on the introduction of Bt-brinjal will be final and that the central government does not have any say in the issue. I beg to completely disagree with this view, if indeed, the newspaper reports have quoted you accurately.

GEAC may well be a statutory body but when crucial issues of human safety are involved, the government has every right and in fact has a basic responsibility to take the final decision based on the recommendations of the GEAC. I understand that my predecessor Shri T.R. Baalu gave the final nod to Bt-cotton in April 2002.

The GEAC recommendations on commercialization of Bt-brinjal came to me on 14 October 2009. Since Bt-brinjal will be the first genetically modified food crop and since I am very well aware of the concerns that have been raised on this issue, I decided that I will have public consultations in seven cities—Kolkata, Bhubaneswar, Ahmedabad, Hyderabad, Bangalore, Nagpur, and Chandigarh. I have also written to chief ministers of six important brinjal cultivating states—West Bengal, Odisha, Bihar, Maharashtra, Andhra Pradesh, and Karnataka. In addition, I have sought feedback from over fifty top scientists both from India and abroad.

By 20 February 2010, I will be in a position to take a considered view on GEAC recommendations regarding Bt-brinjal. I will then be sharing my final view with the Prime Minister as well as with you and the health minister.

I am sure that you will agree that in a democracy like ours, we have to take decisions that have far-reaching consequences with the greatest degree of caution, with the greatest degree of transparency and after ensuring that all stakeholders have been heard to their satisfaction. This is what I have sought to ensure ever since the GEAC recommendations reached me. I respect the GEAC and the work that it has done. However, as the minister concerned and as a concerned minister I am sure you will agree with me that when I say that I am personally entitled to take my own time arriving at a decision on what to do with the GEAC recommendations, I have no personal agenda whatsoever in this matter except to listen, to study, and then take a decision.

Speaking Order Imposing a Moratorium on the Commercial Introduction of Bt-brinjal

[This was preceded by extensive public consultation, and discussions with scientists, experts, civil society activists, farmer groups and other stakeholders.]

9 FEBRUARY 2010

The GEAC was set up in May 1990 under the Environment (Protection) Act, 1986. While it is a statutory body under Rules 1989 of the Environment (Protection) Act, 1986 and as such it is authorized to grant approval for large-scale trials and environmental release of genetically modified organisms, on the issue of Bt-brinjal the GEAC in its 97th meeting held on 14 October 2009 observed that '... as this decision of the GEAC has very important policy implication at the national level, the GEAC decided its recommendation for environmental release may be put up to the government for taking a final view on the matter.'

The GEAC, being located in the MoEF, sent its recommendations to me. After receiving the recommendations of the GEAC on Bt-brinjal, I communicated the following to the GEAC on 16 October 2009: 'I have just received the recommendations of the GEAC on Bt-brinjal. I have studied the recommendations and have decided on the following course of action: The report of the Expert Committee (EC-II) submitted to the GEAC on 8 October 2009 that formed the basis of the GEAC decision of 14 October 2009 is being made public with immediate effect. It is being uploaded straightaway on the website of the MoEF. All previous reports and studies on Bt-brinjal are already in the public domain. Comments on this report are being sought by 31 December 2009 and I encourage their submission. During January and February 2010, I propose to have a series of consultations in different places with scientists, agriculture experts, farmers' organizations, consumer groups and serious-minded NGOs who want to engage in a responsible manner. All points of view will be represented in these consultations. Strong views have been expressed on the Bt-brinjal issue, both for and against. My objective is to arrive at a careful, considered decision in the public and national interest. This decision will be made only after the consultations process is complete and all stakeholders are satisfied that they have been heard to their satisfaction.'

Between 13 January 2010 and 6 February 2010 public meetings on Bt-brinjal were organized by the Centre for Environment Education (CEE), Ahmedabad (a centre of excellence supported by the MoEF), in Kolkata, Bhubaneswar, Ahmedabad, Nagpur, Chandigarh, Hyderabad, and Bangalore... Almost 8,000 people from different sections of society participated enthusiastically in these seven public meetings.[1]

Letters were sent to the chief ministers of West Bengal, Odisha, Bihar, Maharashtra, Andhra Pradesh, and Karnataka since these are the major brinjal cultivating states accounting for 30 per cent, 20 per cent, 11 per cent, 6 per cent, 6 per cent and 4 per cent, respectively, of India's brinjal production.[2]

I should like to make clear at the very outset that my concern is with Bt-brinjal alone[3] and *not* with the larger issue of genetic engineering and biotechnology in agriculture. The issue before me is limited to what to do with the GEAC recommendation on the commercialization of Bt-brinjal.

All the states, which have written to me, have expressed apprehension on Bt-brinjal and have called for extreme caution. Because this is extremely important in our federal framework and agriculture is a state subject, I summarize below the views of the state governments that have been submitted in writing to me by the chief ministers/state agriculture ministers:

Andhra Pradesh: 'It is clear that the data generated, the tests conducted and the information disseminated by GEAC are not sufficient for suggesting the commercial release of Bt-brinjal ... Until safety parameters in terms of environment, human and animal health are clearly established, release of Bt-brinjal for commercial cultivation is to be deferred.'

Kerala: 'Considering all this, Government of Kerala has taken a decision to prohibit all environmental release of GMOs and keep the state totally GM free. We would request the Honourable Prime Minister to reconsider the policy of GM in a national scale and declare a moratorium at least for the next fifty years.'

Chhattisgarh: 'Before giving permission for commercial cultivation of Bt-brinjal, all tests to establish full impacts, including negative impacts, on human and animal health and on the environment should be carried out.'

Karnataka: 'The commercial release of Bt-brinjal should be deferred till the issue is thoroughly examined from all the angles by taking into account the views of all stakeholders and conducting a long-term research for its bio-safety and its consequent contributions to food security and farmers well-being.'

Bihar: 'The Rajya Kisan Ayog is not in favour of the introduction of Bt-brinjal in the state at this point of time. The recommendation of the Rajya Kisan Ayog has been considered by the state government and the state government fully endorses the view of the Ayog.'

West Bengal: 'I have got the report of the Expert Committee of the GEAC downloaded. I feel that the matter needs thorough examination by the experts in the field. I am requesting some members of the erstwhile State Agriculture Commission to examine the report and forward their views to the government to enable us to take a holistic view on the subject.'

Odisha: 'The Government of Odisha does not support the introduction of Bt-brinjal at this stage and until sufficient trials are made and interests of small and marginal farmers of the state are safeguarded.'

In addition, the chief minister of Uttarakhand has spoken to me and conveyed the decision to ban Bt-brinjal in that state. The chief secretary of Tamil Nadu has informed me that the state of Tamil Nadu is not in favour of commercialization of Bt-brinjal now. The Madhya Pradesh chief minister has told me that Bt-brinjal should be introduced 'only after all doubts and fears have been properly dispelled'. The Himachal Pradesh chief minister has told me that the Himachal Pradesh government will take a view after all trials have been completed and after the Government of India has decided.

Clearly, Bt-technology is not the only route for reducing pesticide use. That pesticide use can have deleterious public health impacts is already visible in places like Bhatinda—which as the chief minister of Punjab told me a couple of days back—has emerged as a major cancer-afflicted region. How to reduce pesticide use without compromising on food security at the macro-level and returns to farmers at the micro-level is an urgent public policy in our agriculture. In this connection, it is worth recalling that there are now close to 6 lakh farmers in Andhra Pradesh fully practising non-pesticide management (NPM) agriculture over an area of about 20 lakh (2 million) acres. I have myself been seeing this initiative over the past four years. The advantage of NPM is that it eliminates chemical pesticide use completely whereas Bt-technology only reduces the pesticide spray, albeit substantially.

Incidentally, one of the eight missions under the National Action Plan on Climate Change is the National Mission on Sustainable Agriculture of which NPM is an integral part. On 19 January 2009, much before I became minister for environment and forests, I had written to the agriculture minister on the need to evaluate the Andhra NPM experiment from the point of view of replicating it on a larger scale. The issue of safety tests has been raised repeatedly by critics of Bt-brinjal. The plant family *Solanaceae*, to which brinjal belongs, appears to be more problematic than others because it contains several natural toxins that can resurface when metabolism is disturbed. The kind of testing done, it is being said, is not specific or stringent enough to detect toxins. This is an important issue since brinjal is an item of almost daily consumption for most of us.

While there may be a debate on the nature and number of tests that need to be carried out for establishing human safety, it is incontrovertible that the tests have been carried out by the Bt-brinjal developers themselves and not in any independent laboratory. This does raise legitimate doubts on the reliability of the tests, doubts that I cannot ignore. The fact that brinjal is very largely a cross-pollinated crop, according to the generally accepted scientific consensus, makes the threat of contamination with the use of Bt-brinjal on other varieties a particularly worrisome issue.

Very serious fears have been raised in many quarters on the possibility of Monsanto controlling our food chain if Bt-brinjal is approved.[4] Indeed, it would not be an exaggeration to say that public concerns about Bt-brinjal have been influenced very heavily by perceptions of Monsanto itself. I have no bias whatsoever. Monsanto has made substantial investments in India, including in R&D [research and development]. Many Indian-origin scientists work in Monsanto. As a country, we must learn to derive full benefit of Monsanto's expertise and capabilities, without jeopardizing national sovereignty and also develop countervailing power to it. Unfortunately, we do not seem to have a large-scale publicly-funded biotechnology effort in agriculture. Had there been one, there would have been competition to Monsanto. It is true that Mahyco, an Indian company, is involved in the development of hybrid Bt-brinjal. But 26 per cent of Mahyco is owned by Monsanto itself.

It is also true that two government-owned agricultural universities—Tamil Nadu Agricultural University (TNAU), Coimbatore and University of Agricultural Sciences, Dharwad—have developed Bt-brinjal varieties.[5] But doubts have been raised on how Bt-related research in these two institutions has been funded. Further, the Material Transfer Agreement between TNAU and Monsanto in March 2005 has raised worrisome questions on ownership (both of products and germplasm) and what TNAU can do and cannot do.

Apart from being the world's largest producer of brinjal, India is undoubtedly the country of origin as far as brinjal is concerned, as testified by Vavilov in 1928. Data that has been made available to me by the National Bureau of Plant Genetic Resources of the Indian Council for Agricultural Research (ICAR) reveals that there are 3,951 collections in the bureau and the number of diversity-rich districts is 134. The bureau also points out that diversity-rich regions are likely to be affected by the introduction of Bt-brinjal due to gene flow. The loss of diversity argument cannot be glossed over especially when seen in light of the experience we have had in cotton where Bt-cotton seed has overtaken non-Bt seeds.

Bt-cotton is not comparable to Bt-brinjal no doubt but it is nevertheless necessary to review our experience with it. Undoubtedly, Bt-cotton has catapulted India into second position in the world as far as cotton production is concerned; up from number three after the new technology took root. Over 90 per cent of cotton farmers in India cultivate Bt-cotton. It is also true that many farmers in the public consultations vociferously expressed their support to Bt-cotton on economic grounds. But a number of farmers also expressed doubts. More than that, the Central Institute of Cotton Research, Nagpur, has done a comprehensive review of Bt-cotton in India and this review has thrown up a number of questions.[6] The director of the institute that has produced a Bt-cotton variety *Bikaneri Nerma* (whose seeds can be kept by farmers for planting during the next season unlike hybrids where farmers have to be buy seeds every year) while expressing his clear support for the Bt-brinjal technology, has said the following based on the Bt-cotton experience:

1. Resistance development is a very serious concern for monophagous pests. There is a need to develop baseline susceptibility data of Cry toxins on the fruit and shoot borer populations from all the brinjal-growing states in a government institute or laboratory known for its expertise in resistance management. The data available thus far is only from Mahyco. There is also a need to set up a main resistance monitoring laboratory to monitor the changes in baseline suscep-tibility changes of the fruit borer to Cry proteins after releasing the technology.

2. Resistance management strategies are essentially developed based on output profiles of stochastic models which integrate toxicologi-cal, ecological, genetic, and biological parameters. Stochastic mod-els for resistance should be developed to calculate resistance risk and devise proactive insect resistance management (IRM) strategies. The structured refuge strategy of 5 per cent conventional brinjal within the ecosystems of Bt-brinjal proposed by Mahyco is based on basic simplistic assumptions and not through defined algorithms and modelling.

3. There is a need for a consolidated report on ecology, biology, genet-ics, and population dynamics of insect pests of brinjal that are available thus far. Based on the ecology, biology, and population dynamics, simulation models should be developed so that appropri-ate strategies can be formulated to prevent the emergence of new pests and delay development of resistance in key pests.

This only points to the need for more tests that are well-designed, widely—accepted and independently conducted. The Bikaneri *Nerma* also demonstrates the importance of strengthening public good research.

A number of doubts have been raised on the integrity of the GEAC process itself, particularly by Dr P.M. Bhargava, one of India's eminent biotechnologists who arguably was amongst the earliest to coin the very term 'genetic engineering' and who is a nominee of the Supreme Court on the GEAC. He has provided a detailed point-by-point critique of the EC-II report that has formed the basis of GEAC's recommen-dation to commercialize Bt-brinjal. Dr Bhargava has claimed that the

Chairman of EC-II had agreed with his assessment that eight essential tests had not been conducted by Mahyco. Another fact brought to my attention is that an expert committee set up by the GEAC in 2006 (EC-I) had asked for several tests to be conducted but one-third of the EC-II members who were also members of EC-I chose to discard the need for these studies while evaluating Bt-brinjal as EC-II. I do not propose to do a post-mortem on the way the GEAC has functioned.[7] Many have called for an independent genetic engineering regulator. A National Biotechnology Regulatory Authority has been on the anvil for almost six years now but it has yet to come into being. Such an authority has to be professional and science-based, independent of the government, and that should have facilities for conducting all essential tests with integrity and impartiality. In the absence of such a body, arguments that have been made on the limitations of the GEAC cannot be ignored.

Many countries, particularly in Europe, have banned GM foods. I have spoken with my counterpart in China and he has informed me that China's policy is to encourage research in GM technology but to be extremely cautious when it comes to its introduction in food crops. In any case, China's Bt-cotton is entirely indigenously developed, in marked contrast to the case in India. China has a very strong publicly-funded programme in GM technology unlike India. True, Bt-corn and Bt-soya is widely available in the US but that is no great compulsion for us to follow suit.

Some scientists and civil society organizations have pointed out that the GEAC process has violated the Cartagena Protocol on Biosafety to which India is a signatory, particularly the provisions pertaining to public consultations prior to the release of GM food crops and also the broad principles governing risk assessment. It is pertinent to also recall Article 15 of the Rio Declaration on Environment and Development, which echoes the precautionary principle when it states 'where there are threats of irreversible damage, the lack of full scientific certainty shall not be used as a reason for postponing cost-effective measures to prevent environmental degradation'. Further, Section 45 of Codex Alimentarius 'Guideline for the Conduct of Food Safety Assessment of Foods Derived from Recombinant-DNA Plants' says, 'The location of trial sites should be representative of the range of environmental conditions under which the plant varieties would be expected to be grown. The number of trial sites should be sufficient to allow accurate assessment of compositional characteristics over this range. Similarly, trials should be conducted over a sufficient number of generations to allow adequate exposure to the variety of conditions met in nature. To minimize environmental effects, and to reduce any effect from naturally occurring genotypic variation within a crop variety, each trial site should be replicated. An adequate number of plants should be sampled and the methods of analysis should be sufficiently sensitive and specific to detect variations in key components.' It does appear that the current standards by which the GEAC has formulated the decision to approve Bt-brinjal do not match these global regulatory norms to which India is a party.

I have received a number of emails from scientists in the US, France, Australia, UK, and New Zealand raising very serious doubts on Bt-brinjal and also on the way tests have been conducted in India. Among them, I should mention communications received from (i) Professor G.E. Seralini from France, who in a detailed report has pointed out several flaws in the EC-II report and concludes that 'the risk on human and mammalian health is too high for authorities to take the decision to commercialize this GM brinjal'; (ii) Dr Doug Gurain-Sherman of the Union of Concerned Scientists, Washington, DC, who says that 'the record compiled over a thirteen-year period shows that the 4 per cent yield enhancement contributed by Bt-corn varieties constitutes only 14 per cent of overall corn yield increase'. Further, Dr Gurain-Sherman highlights serious flaws in the EC-II report on evaluation of gene flow risks from Bt-brinjal; (iii) Professor Allison Snow and Professor Norman Ellstrand of the Ohio State University, who identified several shortcomings in the EC-II report concerning gene flow from Bt-brinjal to wild and weedy relatives; (iv) Dr Nicholas Storer of Dow Agro Sciences (a private US company much like Monsanto), who says that Bt-brinjal does not pose unreasonable adverse risks to the environment or to human and animal health but calls for careful implementation of resistance management strategies and points out that Bt-technology should not be seen as a silver bullet to manage lepidopteron pests in brinjal; (v) Dr Jack Heinemann of the University of Canterbury, New Zealand, who questions the consistent yield increases claimed for Bt-cotton and says that the Bt-brinjal tests conducted in India would not meet careful international standards; (vi) Dr David Andow of the University of Minnesota, US, who says that his reading of the EC-II report is sufficient to lead him to question the adequacy of environmental risk assessment but it is not sufficient for him to conclude that the environmental risk assessment is erroneous; and (vii) Dr David Schubert of the Salk Institute of Biological Studies, US, who says that Bt-brinjal should definitely not be introduced in India since it poses serious environmental and health risks, will increase social and political dependence on private companies, and will entail higher costs at all levels of the food chain; and (viii) Dr Judy Carman of the Institute of Health and Environmental Research, South Australia, who has analysed Mahyco's biosafety dossier of 2008 in great detail and who says that her doubts and questions have not been answered at all in the EC-II report.

Some suggestions have been made that we could consider limited release of Bt-brinjal hybrids in limited areas and ensuring that its sale would be monitored through mandatory labelling. The president of the Indian National Science Academy, Dr M. Vijayan of the Indian Institute of Science, Bangalore, a noted microbiologist himself, has made the suggestion of limited release. My view is that while this offers a possible compromise route, it would be extremely difficult to ensure such 'quarantine'. Mandatory labelling is indeed required in countries such as the US but this is somewhat impractical here because our retail market is fundamentally different than that of the US and also because it is extremely difficult to monitor limited usage in practice. Another scientist, Dr N.S. Talekar, who has worked on the brinjal shoot and fruit borer at the World Vegetable Centre, Taiwan, and is now with the Mahatma Phule Krishi Vidyapeeth, while justifying the use of Bt-technology has strongly warned against the use of Bt-brinjal in its present form saying that the manner in which the proponents of the product are recommending to farmers to use this technology is faulty and unscientific, and would lead to disaster.

Some eminent Indian scientists have written expressing their support for the commercialization of Bt-brinjal. Prominent among them is Dr G. Padmanabhan of the Indian Institute of Science, Bangalore, who debunks several domestic and international criticisms of Bt-brinjal, makes a strong plea for commercialization but also makes the point that we need a statutory body with regulatory authority and R&D capabilities to govern all aspects of GM crop cultivation in the country once they are released for commercialization. Specifically, Dr Padmanabhan argues that such an autonomous institution should address issues such as: (i) choice of GM crops and traits relevant for commercialization in the country; (ii) registration of GM crops for a finite period and reassessment of their performance and the ground situation, before extending the registration for another finite period; (iii) inputs for determining the price of GM seeds sold to farmers; (iv) technical help and advice to farmers on a continual basis; (v) positioning of Bt crops with Integrated Pest Management (IPM) strategies and also handling of secondary infections; and (vi) education of the public on the pros and cons of the use of GM technology in agriculture.

The agenda sketched out by Dr Padmanabhan is both ambitious and necessary but will take time to implement in an effective manner. Another eminent scientist who has supported GEAC's decision to release Bt-brinjal for general cultivation is Dr Deepak Pental, vice-chancellor of Delhi University. But he has also said that the two realities must be understood—one, that as India is centre of origin of cultivated brinjal, transgenes can move to the wild germplasm though this should not unduly alarm us and, two, that we will not be able to differentiate between Bt-brinjal and non-Bt-brinjal, making labelling impossible. Dr Raj Bhatnagar of the International Centre for Genetic Engineering and Biotechnology, New Delhi, has sent a highly technical communication which, in simple language, implies that there is no health risk whatsoever by eating Bt-brinjal.

I have had a discussion with both the director-general of the Indian Council of Medical Research (ICMR) as well as with the Drug Controller to the Government of India. Both have recommended that chronic toxicity and other associated tests should be carried out independently. The parallel has been drawn with drugs where during the crucial clinical trials phase, independent testing is carried out on human beings instead of relying on just the data generated by the developer companies themselves. The director-general of ICMR told me that in the face of contradictory evidence of the health effects he would advocate more caution and further tests. Doctors for Food and Safety, a network of around hundred doctors across the country, have sent a representation on the health hazards related to GM foods in general and Bt-brinjal in particular. They have drawn attention to the recommendations made by the American Academy of Environmental Medicine that GM foods have not been properly tested for human consumption and that there are substantial risks associated with the use of GM foods. I have also been informed that the Indian Systems of Medicine, including ayurveda, siddha, homeopathy, and unani use brinjal as a medicinal ingredient, both in raw and cooked form, for treatment of respiratory diseases and that the entire brinjal plant is used in such preparations. There is a fear that Bt-brinjal will destroy these medicinal properties due to loss of synergy, differences in the alkaloids, and changes in other active principles. In the opinion of this network of doctors, these factors have not been considered by EC-II.

The Indian Council for Agricultural Research (ICAR) and the Department of Biotechnology have also given their unqualified support to Bt-brinjal. Some farmers' organizations such as the Bharat Krishak Samaj and Shetkari Sanghatana and farmers' spokespersons such as Bhupinder Singh Mann and Sharad Joshi have come out fully in support of Bt-technology [8] in general and Bt-brinjal in particular on the grounds that we should not be denying modern technology to farmers and that this will improve the income of farmers. As I have mentioned earlier, many farmers at the public consultations argued that Bt-cotton has been very profitable for them.

I have stressed the importance of public investment in biotechnology for agriculture. But Indian private investment in this area is already a reality. Mahyco is one example. Between 2007 and 2009, the GM crops approved for field trials by the GEAC included insect-resistant cotton and rice developed by Metahelix Life Sciences, Bangalore, and hybrid-rice developed by Avesthagen, Pune, both companies run by a new generation of Indian scientists. Clearly, such science-based companies launched by Indian entrepreneurs need to be encouraged and the regulatory process should not stymie such innovation.[9] Apart from this, even publicly funded institutions such as the Indian Institute of Horticulture Research, Bangalore, need encouragement since I have been informed that trials using a Bt-brinjal variety with the *Cry2A* Bt gene are at an advanced stage. Scientists at another publicly funded institution—the Indian Institute of Vegetable Research, Varanasi—have developed Bt-brinjal using *Cry1Aaa3* gene in their own cultivar IVBL-9. These public sector products need to be introduced first, if at all, going by the Bt-cotton experience.

I have had the benefit of extended conversations with Dr M.S. Swaminathan, MP, who is, without doubt, India's most distinguished and senior-most agricultural scientist and was one of the scientific architects of the Green Revolution. Dr Swaminathan, whose research foundation is working on GM technology, has said that we need to be concerned with three issues: (i) chronic toxicity since brinjal is an element of such frequent consumption in India; (ii) independent tests that command credibility and not depend only on data provided by the developers themselves; and (iii) the need to have an independent regulatory system that will be in a position to study all aspects of GM technology in agriculture and arrive at a measured conclusion. Dr Swaminathan has also agreed with the view since brinjal itself contains natural toxins, we have to be extra-careful on Bt- technology. In view of his great stature both in India and abroad, I would like to place below his most recent communication to me on this subject in full.

Dear Jairam,

I am glad you had wide-ranging consultations, and something useful should emerge from such unprecedented churning of minds and experience. Both benefits and risks are now well known. There are unquestionable benefits in the short term, but also potential risks to human health and our brinjal heritage in the long term. What is the way forward?

1. Conserve India's genetic heritage in brinjal: My postgraduate thesis at the Indian Agricultural Research Institute (IARI) in 1949 was on Brinjal and non-tuber bearing *Solanum* species. I have studied our rich genetic wealth in this wonderful crop. What will be the long-term impact of numerous local strains being replaced with one or two varieties with *CrylAc* gene from Monsanto? I suggest that during 2010, ICAR (the National Bureau of Plant Genetic Resources) along with Dr Anil Gupta of the Indian Institute of Management, Ahmedabad (he maintains a national data base on indigenous knowledge and farmers' innovations), should both collect, catalogue, and conserve the existing genetic variability in brinjal. Such a collection must be carefully preserved, before we permit the extinction of the gifts of thousands of years of natural evolution and human selection.

2. Assess the chronic effects of consumption of Bt-brinjal: The second step which needs to be taken is to ask the National Institute of Nutrition, Hyderabad, and the Central Food Technology Research Institute, Mysore, to undertake a careful study of the chronic effects of Bt-brinjal on human health. This is analogous to the studies carried out on the impact of tobacco smoking on the incidence of lung cancer in human beings.

It will be in national interest to complete these two steps before a decision on the release of Bt-brinjal for commercial cultivation and human consumption is taken.

It also bears mention that the Supreme Court has been hearing a public interest litigation (PIL) filed in early 2005 seeking to put in place a comprehensive, stringent, scientifically rigorous, and transparent biosafety test protocol in the public domain for Genetically Modified Organisms (GMOs)—for every GMO before it is sought to be released into the environment. The Supreme Court has given six orders so far in order to ensure transparency and accountability in the functioning of the GEAC. The PIL has yet to be finally disposed and the most recent order of 19 January 2010 asks the Union of India to respond in four weeks to the question of what steps have they taken to protect our traditional crops. Clearly, the decision on Bt-brinjal has to take note of this PIL that has already been filed. In addition, the Supreme Court has invoked the precautionary principle as a guiding instrument in environmental decisions (*A.P. Pollution Control Board* vs. *M.V. Nayudu* (1999(2)SCC718) by relying on the following:

> There is nothing to prevent decision-makers from assessing the record and concluding there is inadequate information on which to reach determination. If it is not possible to make a decision with 'some' confidence, then it makes sense to err on the side of caution and prevent activities that may cause serious or irreparable harm. An informed decision can be made at a later stage when additional data is available or resources permit further research.

I am also persuaded that the studies being demanded by responsible civil society groups before the release of Bt-brinjal should be conducted as a measure of our sensitivity to public opinion. A couple of scientists and civil society groups have also pointed out: (i) things that are problematic with the protocols of the studies already conducted; (ii) things that are problematic with the analysis of the data submitted; (iii) things that are problematic with the interpretation of the results; (iv) things that are problematic with the reporting by Mahyco; and (v) things that are problematic with the procedures adopted. It is incumbent upon us as an accountable and transparent administration to respond to these concerns in a serious manner.

Based on all the information presented in the preceding paragraphs and given that there is no clear consensus within the scientific community itself, there is so much opposition from the state governments, responsible civil society organizations, and eminent scientists have already raised many serious questions that have not been answered satisfactorily, the public sentiment is negative, especially when Bt-brinjal would be the first genetically modified vegetable to be introduced anywhere in the world, with no overriding urgency to introduce it here, it is my duty to adopt a cautious, precautionary, principle-based approach and impose a moratorium on the release of Bt-brinjal, till such time as independent scientific studies establish—to the satisfaction of both the public and professionals—the safety of the product from the point of view of its long-term impact on human health and environment, including the rich genetic wealth existing in brinjal in our country. A moratorium implies rejection of this particular case of release for the time being; it does not, in any way, mean conditional acceptance. This should be clearly understood.

This decision should not, however, be construed as discouraging the ongoing R&D in the areas of using tools of modern biotechnology for crop improvement and strengthening national food and nutrition security. Since issues of this kind have to be examined and decided necessarily on a case-by-case basis, I hope the moratorium period would be used to build a broader consensus so that as a country we would be able to harness the full potential of GM technology in agriculture in a safe and sustainable manner.

The moratorium period should also be used to operationalize the independent regulatory body in its entirety as being recommended by many scientists as well as civil society organizations. I also hope that in the moratorium period we give serious thought to the strategic importance of the seed industry, and how we retain public and farmer control over it even as we encourage private investment in agricultural biotechnology. I would also recommend that the moratorium period be used to have a detailed debate in Parliament and also a comprehensive discussion in the National Development Council (NDC) on this subject.

I believe the approach outlined above is both responsible to science and responsive to society. In arriving at this decision, I have also kept in mind what Prime Minister Dr Manmohan Singh himself had said on this subject in his speech at the Indian Science Congress on 3 January 2010 at Thiruvananthapuram:

> Developments in biotechnology present us the prospect of greatly improving yields in our major crops by increasing resistance to pests and also to moisture stress. Bt-cotton has been well-accepted in the country and has made a great difference to the production of cotton. The technology of genetic modification is also being extended to food crops

though this raises legitimate questions of safety. These must be given full weightage, with appropriate regulatory control based on strictly scientific criteria. Subject to these caveats, we should pursue all possible leads that biotechnology provides that might increase our food security as we go through climate-related stress.

I expect the GEAC to take follow-up action on the matter of further studies and tests with appropriate protocols and in appropriate laboratories. I also expect the GEAC to carefully study all the material I have received and am turning over to it. I would like the GEAC to engage and interact with all those scientists, institutions, and civil society groups that have submitted written representations to me. The GEAC should consult with scientists like Dr M.S. Swaminathan, Dr P.M. Bhargava, Dr G. Padmanabhan, Dr M. Vijayan, Dr Keshav Kranthi, Dr Madhav Gadgil, and others, to draw up a fresh protocol for the specific tests that will have to be conducted in order to generate public confidence. Under no circumstances should there be any hurry or rush. The moratorium will continue for as long as it is needed to establish public trust and confidence. Meanwhile, I also intend to change the name of the GEAC from Genetic Engineering Approvals Committee to Genetic Engineering Appraisal Committee.

In order to ensure complete transparency and public accountability, I am making my decision on the GEAC recommendation regarding commercialization of Bt-brinjal public right away.

Letter to the Prime Minister about My Meeting with Scientists on the Use of Biotechnology for Food Crops

29 MARCH 2010

On 19 March, Dr Kasturirangan and I spent two-and-half hours with the presidents of the six premier scientific academies of India—the Indian National Science Academy (INSA), National Academy of Science, Indian Academy of Science, National Academy of Agricultural Sciences, National Academy of Medical Sciences, and Indian National Academy of Engineering. Dr Kasturirangan organized the interaction at INSA, New Delhi, and Dr M. Vijayan, president of INSA, conducted it.

The objective of the interaction was to discuss biotechnology in food crops. I must inform you that all the six academies appreciated the manner in which I had arrived at the decision on Bt-brinjal. Some of them were not in agreement with the decision, while some others felt that under the circumstances it was the right decision to take. I must also tell you that all of them felt that it was ridiculous to accuse me, of all people, of being anti-science on the basis of the Bt-brinjal decision.

In response to a suggestion made by Dr Kasturirangan and me, the six academies have agreed to collectively prepare a detailed report covering all aspects of the subject of biotechnology in food crops and submit that report to Dr Kasturirangan in six months' time. The academies have also agreed to review the draft Biotechnology Regulatory Authority Bill and submit their collective views on it to Dr Kasturirangan in about three months. INSA will co-ordinate the preparation of these two reports.

Letter to Minister of State (Independent Charge) Science and Technology, and Earth Sciences Prithviraj Chavan on the Outcomes of the Discussions Held with Officials on the Biotechnology Regulatory Authority of India (BRAI) Bill, 2010

15 AUGUST 2010
I have just had a discussion with Dr M.K. Bhan, Secretary, Department of Biotechnology, regarding the BRAI Bill with a view to ensuring that the objectives of the Environment (Protection) Act, 1986, for the protection and management of the environment are not compromised. We have, after due discussions, come to the following understanding:

1. Section 26(1) of the BRAI Bill be modified to bring it in line with paragraph 3.11 of the Cabinet Note, along with other adjustments in the Cabinet Note to ensure that the Chairman and Member-Secretary of the Environment Appraisal Panel (EAP) are nominees of the MoEF
2. Section 25(2)(c) of the BRAI Bill and paragraph 3.10 of the Cabinet Note be modified so that the appointment of the expert member related to environment on the Product Ruling Committee is picked up from a roster of experts to prepared jointly by BRAI and MoEF.
3. The EAP shall be governed by the Environment Protection Act for implementing the provision for protecting and managing the environment. The Cabinet Note should be clear on this dimension.

4. The consultation with the public under Section 27(5) of the Bill be made mandatory and accordingly the word 'may' in the Section be substituted by the word 'shall'.

5. Paragraph 3.21 of the Bill be amended to clearly bring out the fact that the BRAI Bill is only for addressing the safety and efficacy aspects and that any decision on commercialization will have to be taken by the competent authorities under the relevant laws; and

6. The EAP will give its findings directly to the BRAI; in case of difference of opinion the BRAI will pass a speaking order. Accordingly the Cabinet Note and Section 27(4) of the Bill will reflect this.

Letter to Kerala Minister for Agriculture Mullakkara Retnakaran Explaining the Reasons of Approving Field Trials for GM Rubber

4 JANUARY 2011

… The Genetic Engineering Appraisal Committee (GEAC) has recently approved field trials of GM rubber, a non-food crop. The GM plant has been developed by the Rubber Research Institute of India (RRII), Kottayam, a research organization of the Rubber Board which is under the Ministry of Commerce. It incorporates the target gene (*MnSOD*) from rubber itself and not from any other species. Strictly speaking, therefore, this GM plant is not a transgenic in the normal sense of the word. The new gene is expected to impart increased tolerance to drought as well as tolerance to physiological disorders that significantly reduces rubber productivity. The field trials will be done in designated experimental sites inside research farms belonging to the RRII in Kerala and Maharashtra. The field trials will not be done in commercially cultivated holdings. The growth of these plants will be closely monitored by a multidisciplinary team of scientists. Without doing field trials, it would not be possible to say—with 100 per cent guarantee—if there would be any adverse effects to the ecosystem from GM rubber but laboratory studies seem to indicate that there are good reasons to expect favourable results from GM rubber plants.

The RRII is not a private research institute interested in making GM rubber and making money by selling it. All plants/clones produced will go to the rubber growers free of cost. There are no patents for RRII rubber clones that are not IPR [Intellectual Property Rights]-protected as far as Indian growers are concerned. In the past, RRII has produced and given to Indian rubber growers' highest-yielding clones anywhere in the world, making India No. 1 globally in terms of natural rubber productivity, although it ranks No. 4 in the production of natural rubber.

Extension of natural rubber cultivation to non-traditional areas such as Tripura, Assam, Meghalaya, Mizoram, and north Konkan will require development of new rubber varieties for which the GM approach is one option. The challenge of climate change, which has already led to longer dry periods for rubber cultivation, also necessitates the GM approach.

Commercial cultivation of GM rubber can be contemplated only on the basis of results obtained from the proposed field trials. The total duration of the field trials will be around fourteen years. A decision on commercial cultivation will be taken only after the field trials are completed fully, at which time the views of the state governments concerned will be given due consideration.

Finally, may I point out that the approval is for biosafety research level-1 (BRL-1) trials at first stage, to assess the efficacy, safety, and stability of the new GM rubber plant. This just cannot be compared with the Bt-brinjal case, which was for commercialization of a food crop.

Letter to Chief Ministers and Administrators of Coastal States and Union Territories Seeking Comments on the Swaminathan Report on Coastal Zone Management and Regulations

8 AUGUST 2009

As you may be aware, for the purpose of protecting the coastal environment the MoEF had issued CRZ Notification, 1991 under Environment (Protection) Act, 1986. This notification has undergone several amendments during the last seventeen years.

In order to examine the issues related to coastal zone management in a holistic manner, this ministry had constituted an expert committee under the chairmanship of Prof. M.S. Swaminathan in June 2004. The expert committee had submitted its report in 2005 and the ministry had initiated steps to implement the recommendations of the committee. One of the steps included, issue of the draft Coastal Management Zone (CMZ) Notification dated 1 May 2008 and it was reissued on 9 May 2008, inviting public suggestions and objections in accordance with

Environment (Protection) Act, 1986 within a period of sixty days from the date of issue of the notification.

The ministry had received large number of suggestions and objections on the above draft notification. Further, the ministry had also obtained the comments of the local communities through Centre for Environment Education who are assigned by the ministry. The majority of them, mainly the local communities, had strong reservations about the implementation of the draft CMZ Notification, 2008.

Keeping in view the above comments, the ministry constituted a four-member expert committee under the chairmanship of Prof. M.S. Swaminathan on 15 June 2009. The committee submitted its report on 16 July 2009 and the ministry accepted the recommendations of the report.

One of the main recommendations of the report is to let the Coastal Management Zone Notification, 2008 lapse and initiate steps to strengthen the Coastal Regulation Zone Notification 1991, including its implementation and enforcement. My ministry has already initiated steps to implement the recommendations of the above report.

In this regard, I would request you to get the report examined and send us your valuable comments and suggestions so that the same can be considered for incorporation while revising the CRZ Notification, 1991.

Letter to M.S. Swaminathan on Holding Multi-centre Consultations with Fishermen on the Proposed Coastal Zone Regulations

2 July 2009

Today I met with a multi-state delegation of the National Fishworkers' Forum. There were over ten people in the delegation. Basically, the delegation wants an opportunity to be heard. They feel that a consultative process needs to be adopted where differing opinions are heard and a chance is given for people to raise grievances on CMZ, 2008.

I explained to them that we are going to be allowing CMZ, 2008 to lapse by 23 July 2009 and that any modifications we will bring about will be using CRZ, 1991 as the basic framework. I have also reiterated that the interest of fishermen and their families would be fully protected and there is no question of carrying out any amendments that adversely affects their livelihoods.

I have also agreed to have five meetings of your committee at Mumbai, Goa, Kochi, Chennai, and Bhubaneswar by 31 August. The first consultation will be at Kochi and I will definitely attend. I will try and attend others as well.

Letter to Union Minister for Agriculture Sharad Pawar on Drafting the Fisherman's Livelihood Bill. A copy of the Swaminathan Report was also Sent for the Minister's Perusal

22 AUGUST 2009

As you may be aware, for the purpose of protecting the coastal environment the MoEF had issued CRZ Notification, 1991 under the Environment (Protection) Act, 1986. This notification has undergone several amendments during the last seventeen years.

In order to examine the issues related to coastal zone management in a holistic manner, this ministry had constituted an expert committee under the chairmanship of Prof. M.S. Swaminathan in June 2004. The expert committee had submitted its report in 2005 and the ministry had initiated steps to implement the recommendations of the committee. One of the steps included the issue of the draft CMZ Notification, dated 1 May 2008 and reissued on 9 May 2008, inviting public suggestions and objections in accordance with the Environment (Protection) Act, 1986 within a period of sixty days from the date of issue of the notification.

The ministry had received a large number of suggestions and objections on the above draft notification. Further, the ministry had also obtained the comments of the local communities through the Centre for Environment Education, Ahmedabad, who were assigned by the ministry to organize public consultations. The majority of them, mainly the local communities, had strong reservations about the implementation of the draft CMZ Notification, 2008.

Keeping in view the above comments, the ministry constituted a four-member expert committee under the chairmanship of Prof. M.S. Swaminathan on 15 June 2009. The committee submitted its report on 16 July 2009 and the ministry has accepted the recommendations of the report. I am enclosing a copy of the same for your perusal.

One of the main recommendations of the report is to let the CMZ Notification, 2008 lapse and initiate steps to strengthen the existing Coastal Regulation Zone Notification, 1991, including its implementation and enforcement. My ministry had already initiated steps to implement the recommendations of the above report.

Further, in para 7.2.3 of the report, the committee has recommended enactment of a separate legislation along the lines of the Traditional Forest Dwellers Act, 2006 for securing traditional fisherfolk rights by the relevant ministry.

Since the fisheries sector is listed under the Ministry of Agriculture as per the Allocation of Business Rules, I would like to seek your opinion as to which ministry would initiate drafting of above legislation to protect the livelihood and interest of the fisherfolk of the country. I have no problem in getting a first draft prepared for your consideration.

Letter to Prime Minister on the Fisherman's Livelihood Protection Bill, Forwarding a Draft of the Proposed Legislation for Perusal

17 SEPTEMBER 2009

As soon as I took over, I had appointed a committee headed by Dr M.S. Swaminathan to examine the entire issue of coastal zone regulations afresh ... One of the recommendations of the Swaminathan Committee, as also that of the earlier Standing Committee on Environment and Forests, related to legislation to protect livelihood security of fishermen. Considering the importance of this issue, I have got a draft legislation prepared, a copy of which I am taking liberty of attaching. Whether the MoEF should take this legislation forward or whether it should be done by the Ministry of Agriculture is for the government to decide. But I have got this draft prepared in order to get the discussion going on this very vital issue.

Responding to the Issues Raised by Union Minister for Agriculture Sharad Pawar on the Need for the Fisherman's Livelihood Bill. A Draft of the Proposed Bill was also Sent to Pawar

8 OCTOBER 2009

I write to you with reference to your letter regarding the enactment of a separate legislation for securing traditional fisherfolk rights along the lines of the Traditional Forest Dwellers Act, 2006.

The distinction you make is indeed valid. However, my suggestion is not to draft the proposed legislation as a law giving these fishermen certain rights over a particular fishing area. It is instead to provide certain basic benefits to facilitate their fishing activities so that these fisherfolk can protect their livelihood without fear of deprivation or exploitation.

As you may be aware that the fishermen, especially the traditional fisherfolk who are one of the most downtrodden communities inhabiting the coastline, are affected by various man-made and natural phenomena. The man-made impacts include constructions such as ports, harbours, tourism projects, etc., which involve active acquisition of land. In most instances, these communities are wantonly displaced (an action that gravely and prejudicially affects their livelihood). In such cases there exist no legislative safeguards to compensate and protect these fisherfolk directly.

There are also other developmental activities that have a direct impact on the livelihood of traditional fisherfolk. These include fishing by large vessels/mechanized trawlers in the coastal waters. This method, if unregulated (and currently it is), is highly unsustainable and depletes the fish and fisheries in particular areas by overfishing. In addition, there are discharges of waste and effluents into the waters, which destroy the fishing habitat along with shoreline changes caused due to construction activities, etc. Without any legislation to regulate these activities, all this translates into fewer opportunities for the traditional fisherfolk. These problems are compounded and aggravated by a lack of basic facilities for berthing of the boats and fish curing activities, etc.

The aim of the proposed law would be to protect the fisherfolk from such impacts. Further, a proposed Act would intend to raise the economic status of the traditional fishermen and to meet their economic aspirations by empowering them with technological and financial assistance from various state and central agencies. This would include training facilities, extension activities, and post fish-harvest technologies such as cold storage, cold chain, and transportation, including fair prices for their catch/products during marketing.

Furthermore, in case of natural hazards on the coasts, such as cyclones, floods, tsunami, storm surges, etc., the major victims are the families of these traditional fisherfolk, as they do not have *pucca* houses and live in close proximity to the waters. Hence, there is a compelling need to provide protection to these communities against such disasters as they are the most vulnerable to the same. The proposed Act provides for institutional measures to galvanize support to minimize the impacts of such disasters.

I agree with you that the issues relating to the forest dwellers and the traditional fisherfolk are different, but our intention here is to protect the most basic rights of the fisherfolk and provide a mechanism to uplift them from an economic and social angle, while simultaneously providing safeguards to minimize loss of life and property during natural disasters.

To obtain the views of the public on the coastal management approach in the country, I have been personally interacting with the fishing communities. My ministry had organized consultation meetings with these communities in Mumbai (12 August 2009), Chennai (19 August 2009), and Panjim (30 August 2009). In these meetings, about 800–2,000 people participated. I will also be meeting the fishing communities of Odisha, West Bengal, and Kerala during the latter part of this month.

During the above consultations, there has been an unwavering demand from these communities to enact legislation to protect the rights and livelihood of traditional fisherfolk along the lines mentioned.

I also feel strongly that there is a clear need to protect the rights and livelihood of these communities, which are currently extremely vulnerable. To that end I have taken the liberty to attach a draft version of a Bill titled the 'Traditional Coastal and Marine Fisherfolk (Protection of Rights) Act, 2009'. I would be highly obliged if you could review the same and give us the benefit of your insights on the issues contained therein.

Letter to Prime Minister Briefing Him on the Features of the Draft Coastal Regulation Zone Notification, 2010

17 SEPTEMBER 2010

I am pleased to inform you that we have put up the draft CRZ Notification, 2010, on our website. This is made available to the public for sixty days and thereafter the CRZ Notification, 2010 will be issued.

There are several new and innovative features in the CRZ Notification, 2010:

1. We are providing a special dispensation for Greater Mumbai. This includes rehabilitation schemes for slums (more than a million people will benefit); redevelopment of dilapidated, cessed, and unsafe buildings (half a million people will benefit); preservation of green spaces.

2. We are providing a special dispensation for Kerala, which is one of the most unique coastal environments, where more than 300 islands are located within its backwaters. These islands are densely populated and the existing CRZ Notification, 1991 has put severe constraints on development of dwelling units of these local communities.

3. We are providing separate provisions for Goa recognizing the need for ecological promotion and also for meeting infrastructure requirements for the livelihoods of traditional fishing communities.

4. We are including a special dispensation for Critical Vulnerable Coastal Areas like Sunderbans in West Bengal, Gulf of Khambat and Gulf of Kutchh in Gujarat, Bhitarkanika in Odisha, Malvan and Ratnagiri in Maharashtra and East Godavari and Krishna in Andhra Pradesh.

5. A separate Island Protection Zone Notification is being issued for islands of Lakshadweep, and Andaman and Nicobar Islands.

Letter to Prime Minister on the Features of the CRZ Notification, 2011 and Island Protection Zone Notification, 2011

7 January 2011

After an eighteen-month long process, the CRZ Notification, 2011 is being formally notified and published today. This replaces the CRZ Notification, 1991. In addition, for the very first time and in keeping with your directions at an Island Development Authority meeting, an Island Protection Zone Notification, 2011 is being notified and published covering Andaman and Nicobar Islands and Lakshadweep.

Both these new notifications reconcile three objectives: (i) protection of livelihoods of traditional fisherfolk communities; (ii) preservation of coastal ecology; and (iii) promotion of economic activity that have necessarily to be located in coastal regions.

Apart from codifying the twenty-five amendments that were made to CRZ Notification, 1991 between 1991 and 2009, the CRZ Notification, 2011 has several new features. It has special provisions for Goa, Kerala, Greater Mumbai, and critically vulnerable coastal areas (CVCAs) like the

Sunderbans mangrove area, Chilka and Bhitarkanika (Odisha), Gulf of Khambat and Gulf of Kutchh (Gujarat), Malwan (Maharashtra), Karwar and Kundapur (Karnataka), Vembanad (Kerala), Coringa, East Godavari and Krishna Delta (Andhra Pradesh), and Gulf of Mannar (Tamil Nadu). Clear procedures for obtaining CRZ approval with timelines have been stipulated along with post-clearance monitoring and enforcement mechanisms.

Water area up to 12 nautical miles in the sea and the entire water area of a tidal water body such as creek, river, estuary, etc., would now be included in the CRZ areas, without imposing any restrictions of fishing activities.

The concept of a Coastal Zone Management Plan (CZMP), to be prepared with the fullest involvement and participation of local communities, has been introduced.

The concept of a hazard line to be demarcated over the next five years has been introduced to protect life and property of local communities and infrastructure along coastal areas.

Measures have been put in place to combat pollution in coastal areas/coastal waters. The shorelines would be mapped through time-series satellite images with no foreshore development being permissible in high-eroding areas. The 'no development zone' is being reduced from 200 metres from the high-tide line to 100 metres only to meet increased demands of housing of fishing and other traditional coastal communities.

Over the past eighteen months, I have had public consultations on the new CRZ notification in Goa, Mumbai, Kochi, Chennai, and Puri. In addition, I have had five rounds of discussions with fishermen associations from across the country. The recommendations of an expert committee comprising Dr M.S. Swaminathan, Sunita Narain, Dr Shailesh Nayak, and Shri J.M. Mauskar submitted to the MoEF in July 2010 have also been incorporated. This new CRZ notification has been in the public domain in draft form since September 2010 and I have received a large number of suggestions that have been given due consideration.

I wish to state categorically that barring cases of fishermen families, violations of CRZ Notification, 1991 will not be condoned or regularized with CRZ Notification, 2011 coming into force. Directions are being issued early next week by the MoEF under Section 5 of the Environment

(Protection) Act, 1986 to all state/UT coastal zone management authorities to: (i) identify all such violations within a period of four months from today using latest appropriate maps, satellite imagery, and information technology; and (ii) initiate necessary action in accordance with the Environment (Protection) Act, 1986 within a period of four months thereafter. Details of all such violations and action taken will be listed on the website of the NCZMA [National Coastal Zone Management Authority] concerned as well as of the MoEF. Action already initiated in the cases where violations have been established will continue unimpeded.

An important recommendation of the expert committee headed by Dr M.S. Swaminathan is that the government should enact a law to protect the traditional rights and interests of fishermen and coastal communities. This law would be somewhat along the lines of the Forest Rights Act, 2006. Fishermen associations have supported this recommendation. The MoEF has already prepared such a draft law in this regard and put it in the public domain for comments and suggestions. I have also written to you in this regard seeking guidance as to whether the Ministry of Agriculture or the MoEF should take the matter forward.

The CRZ Notification, 2011 demonstrates that the MoEF is conscious of and alive to the need to bring about modifications in laws and regulations to ensure a demonstrably better balance between the equally urgent imperatives of faster economic growth and deeper environmental conservation.

Responding to the Issues Raised on the CRZ Notification, 2011 by Chairperson of the National Fishworkers' Forum Matanhy Saldanha

11 JANUARY 2011

This has reference to your letter regarding certain points which you claim have not been agreed to by the ministry while framing the CRZ Notification, 2011 that was issued on 6 January 2011.

As you may have seen in my response to your earlier mail, I had clarified each of the issues that has been raised by you and the justification for incorporating or not incorporating them in the notification.

All issues relating to housing of the fishermen communities have been addressed in a comprehensive manner in CRZ Notification, 2011 and in the Island Protection Zone Notification, 2011. These include:

1. Para 8(111) CRZ III(ii), wherein the earlier regulation of 33 per cent FAR [floor area ratio] restriction, including the doubling clause, was deleted to provide for more housing space within the fishing village for constructing dwelling units.

2. Para 8(111) CRZ III(ii) relaxation of 100m relaxation from earlier 200m of no development zone has been provided for undertaking dwelling units of fisherfolk and traditional coastal communities.

3. In para V(g) for the Koliwadas and fishing settlement as identified in the development plan of 1981 or any other records of the Government of Maharashtra, the Koliwadas will be declared as CRZ III even if located within CRZ II. Such Koliwadas will be developed as per local town and country planning regulations.

4. Reconstruction and repair works of fishing communities can be undertaken in accordance with local town and country planning regulations.

5. As per para 6(d) dwelling units of traditional fishing communities will be regularized even if they have been constructed in violation of CRZ Notification, 1991.

6. In the case of those fishing-dwelling units that fall within the hazard zone will be provided with necessary safeguards from natural disaster and will not be relocated until unless the situation warrants it.

I have tried to take into account all the issues raised by fishing communities and the notification has been drafted accordingly. Wherever there have been deviations from the suggestion made by the fishermen association, I have clarified the position earlier in my mail dated 10 January 2011 and the table that was enclosed.

I think we should now work cooperatively to ensure the success of the CRZ Notification, 2011. If there are mid-course corrections required, I would gladly consider them.

Letter to Chief Minister of Chhattisgarh Raman Singh informing Him about Irregularities in the Public Hearing Held for a Power Project in the Jangir Champa District

3 JULY 2009

I am sending you a copy of an email that I received from a gentleman saying that serious mockery is being made of the public hearing process in Jangir Champa district for a 1,200 MW thermal power plant by a company called D.B. Power Limited. I take the email seriously, as I am sure you also will after you have read it. I request you for your intervention in the matter so that a signal goes that public hearing cannot be taken for granted and should be conducted in all seriousness and transparency.

Letter to Prime Minister Updating Him on the Discussions to Address the Issues Raised by Civil Society Organizations About the Jaitapur Nuclear Power Park

[The second of the two meetings between the NPCIL and the Konkan Bachao Samiti was held on 13 July 2010. Subsequently, the Samiti wrote on 16 October 2010 expressing its dissatisfaction with the manner in which NPCIL shared information. It requested that clearance not be accorded to the project.]

16 JULY 2010
I have personally arranged for two rounds of discussions between the NPCIL and the Konkan Bachao Samiti on the Jaitapur nuclear power project. I was present in one of these meetings. Many serious questions have been raised by the NGOs, which the NPCIL has to clarify and answer. The interactions are to continue.

Actually, sir, I have no business getting involved in this manner but considering the strategic significance of Jaitapur, I decided to intervene and try and bring the two sides together. I cannot completely ignore what the Konkan Bachao Samiti is saying but at the same time I cannot be oblivious to the larger national imperative for getting Jaitapur going.

I have told the Department of Atomic Energy (DAE) and NPCIL to be less adversarial and contemptuous while dealing with serious-minded NGOs. Ideological differences cannot be bridged but technical questions relating to environmental impact assessment can surely be addressed in a collegial atmosphere. The same message I have given to the NGOs as well is that they must realize the developmental compulsions that make projects like Jaitapur necessary and that they should not question the motives and competence of the DAE and the NPCIL.

Letter to Prime Minister on the Apprehensions Raised by Groups in Assam About Hydroelectric Power Projects in the Northeast during Consultations Held in Guwahati

16 SEPTEMBER 2010

I was in Guwahati last week in response to a request made by a large number of civil society organizations in Assam. A public consultation had been organized on 10 September on the issue of big dams in the Northeast. Over a thousand people participated in the interaction, which extended over six hours. At the end of the interaction, I assured the audience that I would bring the sentiments expressed to the attention of both the Prime Minister and the Union Power Minister. The views expressed are as follows:

1. There is opposition building up in Assam to the 2,000 MW Lower Subanisiri hydroelectric power project being implemented by the NHPC in Arunachal Pradesh. The dominant view in Assam appears to be that this project will have serious downstream impacts in districts such as Lakhimpur, Dhemaji, Sonitpur, Sibsagar, Jorhat as well as in the Majuli river island. This demand being made, on the basis of an expert committee report prepared by a team from the Indian Institute of Technology, Guwahati, Guwahati University, and Dibrugarh University is for the project to be scrapped completely.

2. There is great concern on the downstream impacts already being felt in districts of Assam like Lakhimpur, Dhemaji, Marigaon, and Nagaon from existing hydroelectric power projects of the North Eastern Electric Power Corporation Limited (NEEPCO) like Ranganadi and Kopilli. There is also concern on the Kurichu hydroelectric power project executed by India in Bhutan and its downstream impacts in districts like Barpeta, Baska, Nalbari, and Kamrup.

3. There are over 135 dams of varying capacity being planned in Arunachal Pradesh for which memorandums of understanding (MoUs) have already been signed. These projects are being given the green signal without carrying out cumulative environmental impact assessment studies; comprehensive biodiversity impact studies; and comprehensive analysis of downstream impacts particularly in Assam.

4. The 1,750 MW Lower Demwe hydroelectric power project on the Lohit river will have serious downstream impacts till Dibrugarh in

Assam and should not be given forest clearance, although environmental clearance has already been given for the project. Similarly, the 1,500 MW Tipaimukh hydroelectric power project in Manipur should not be proceeded with till a comprehensive downstream impact assessment study has been undertaken.

5. Projects are being awarded in the same river basin in Arunachal Pradesh to different companies. This makes the task of environmental impact assessment very difficult. For example, three different companies are implementing three different projects on Subanisiri and three different companies are implementing different projects on Siang.

6. While signing the MoUs in Arunachal Pradesh, which has been done with the knowledge of the central government, the sentiments of the people of Assam have not been kept in view. The Assam Government should be a party to these MoUs, especially where downstream impacts are significant. Only one of the 103 projects for which MoUs have been signed by Arunachal Pradesh is a multipurpose project with a flood moderation component.

7. There should be a moratorium on any further clearances for hydroelectric power projects in Arunachal Pradesh till downstream impact assessment studies, cumulative environmental impact assessment studies, and biodiversity impact studies are completed.

8. The Northeast is a region of high seismicity and rich biodiversity. Both these factors have not been adequately considered by the Government of India in giving the clearance for hydroelectric power projects in the region. The entire approach to big dams in the Northeast needs to be looked at afresh. The environmental impacts of mega hydroelectric projects in Bhutan need to be studied better. The 720 MW Mangdechhu hydroelectric power project will impact the riverine ecology of the Manas river in Assam.

I made it absolutely clear to the audience that I am in no position to make any commitment on the existing Lower Subanisiri project, which is under implementation. The project is expected to be commissioned by December 2012. All I promised was that I would convey their sentiments and concerns to the Prime Minister and the power minister. I also expressed the view that NHPC would undoubtedly take steps to address the concerns of the people of Assam in a credible manner.

What I could assure the audience, of course, is that for projects not yet started, we will carry out cumulative environmental impact assessment studies as well as comprehensive biodiversity studies. I also assured the audience that in consultation with the Ministry of Power and the Ministry of Water Resources, we will undertake studies to analyse the downstream impacts of existing hydroelectric power projects and identify measures to be taken to mitigate such impacts.

I also explained to the audience the strategic significance of some of these hydroelectric power projects in Arunachal Pradesh, particularly the projects on the Siang. Interestingly there were some NGOs from Arunachal Pradesh that contested these views of mine and said that we should not make Arunachal Pradesh a pawn in the race between India and China. This NGO called the Adi Students Union (AdiSU) gave me a memorandum that was very critical of the large number of projects planned in Arunachal Pradesh.

I would request the Prime Minister to call a meeting of the Union Power Minister, Union Minister of Water Resources, and myself to discuss the issues that I have put down in this letter. These issues are bound to be the subject of agitation given that the elections in Assam are due in about six months' time. Even leaving aside elections, these issues are important in themselves and merit our serious consideration. Personally, I believe that some of the concerns that were expressed cannot be dismissed lightly. They must be taken on board and every effort made to engage different sections of society in Assam particularly and in other states in the Northeast as well. Right now the feeling in vocal sections of Assam's society particularly appears to be that 'mainland India' is exploiting the Northeast's hydroelectric resources for its benefits, while the costs of this exploitation will be borne by the people of the Northeast.

Note on Controversy over Identification of Core Areas in the Tiger Reserves and Critical Wildlife Habitats and the Forest Rights Act, 2006

[This note was an effort to set the record straight after reports that the ministry's guidelines ran counter to laws such as the Forest Rights Act.]

14 FEBRUARY 2011

Recently, there have been some newspaper reports that the Ministry of Environment and Forests is flouting the Scheduled Tribes and Other Traditional Forest Dwellers (Recognition of Forest Rights) Act, 2006 in tiger reserves and critical wildlife habitats. Such reports are false and misleading and as someone who has taken the lead in ensuring the proper and full implementation of the Forest Rights Act, 2006. I want to set the record straight.

Tiger Reserves

1. Section 38V of the Wildlife (Protection) Act, 1972 (as amended in 2006) explains the core or critical tiger habitat as well as the buffer or peripheral area of a tiger reserve.
2. A tiger reserve includes two parts:
   a. Core or critical tiger habitat (National Park or Sanctuary status).
   b. Buffer or peripheral area.
3. The phrase 'core or critical tiger habitat' is mentioned only in the Wildlife (Protection) Act, 1972 as a sequel to an amendment made to the Act in 2006. It is *not* defined in the Scheduled Tribes and Other Traditional Forest Dwellers (Recognition of Forest Rights) Act, 2006.
4. The phrase 'critical wildlife habitat' is defined only in the Scheduled Tribes and Other Traditional Forest Dwellers (Recognition of Forest Rights) Act, 2006, and *not* in the Wildlife (Protection) Act, 1972.
5. 'Core or critical tiger habitat' is different from the 'critical wildlife habitat'. Tigers are territorial big cats, hence, considering their social land tenure dynamics, the 'core or critical tiger habitat' has been viewed separately from the 'critical wildlife habitat', which is applicable to other wild animal species.
6. Based on deliberations with experts and simulation results from scientific data, it has been found that a minimum inviolate area of 800–1,200 sq km is required to sustain a viable population of tigers (20 breeding females).
7. Establishing the core/critical tiger habitat as 'inviolate' involves two steps as per the Wildlife (Protection) Act, 1972:
   a. Identifying the core or critical tiger habitat by establishing—on the basis of scientific and objective area—that such areas are

required to be kept as inviolate for the purpose of tiger conservation, without affecting the rights of the Scheduled Tribes or such other forest dwellers, and notified as such by the state government in consultation with an expert committee constituted for the purpose. Out of seventeen tiger states, sixteen have notified the core/critical tiger habitat following this process, and action is pending only from Bihar).

b. Establishing the identified core/critical tiger habitat as inviolate through voluntary relocation on mutually agreed terms and conditions, provided that such terms and conditions satisfy the requirements laid down in the Wildlife (Protection) Act, 1972. No Scheduled Tribes or other forest dwellers shall be resettled or have their rights adversely affected for creating inviolate areas for tiger unless:

i. The process of recognition or determination of rights and acquisition of land or forest rights of the Scheduled Tribes and such other forest dwelling persons is complete.

ii. The concerned agencies of the state government need to establish with the consent of the Scheduled Tribes and such other forest dwellers in the area, besides also consulting an ecological and social scientist familiar with the area, that the activities of the Scheduled Tribes and other forest dwellers or the impact of their presence on wild animals is sufficient to cause irreversible damage and shall threatened the existence of tigers and their habitat.

iii. The state government has to obtain the consent of the Scheduled Tribes and other forest dwellers and come to a conclusion (besides consulting an independent ecological/social scientist) that no coexistence options are available.

iv. Resettlement package needs to be prepared, providing for the livelihood of the affected individuals, while fulfilling the requirements of the National Rehabilitation and Resettlement Policy.

v. The informed consent of *gram sabhas* and affected persons has to be obtained for resettlement.

vi. The facilities and land allocation at resettlement area are to be provided, otherwise the existing rights of people shall not be interfered with.

8. The above provisions laid down in the Wildlife (Protection) Act, 1972 (Section 38V), subsequent to the 2006 amendment, are specific to tiger conservation, and are not only compatible but more stringent than the Scheduled Tribes and Other Traditional Forest Dwellers (Recognition of Forest Rights) Act, 2006.

9. Under the revised Centrally Sponsored Scheme of Project Tiger (2008), two options have been given to people:

Option-I: Payment of Rs 10 lakh per family in case the family opts so, without any rehabilitation or relocation process by the forest department.

Option-II: Carrying out relocation/rehabilitation by the forest department with the following per family norms out of Rs 10 lakh:

Table 1.1 Composition of the Compensation Package

(a)	Agricultural land procurement (2 ha) and development	35% of the total package
(b)	Settlement of rights	30% of the total package
(c)	Homestead land and house construction	20% of the total package
(d)	Incentive	5% of the total package
(e)	Community facilities (access road, irrigation, drinking water, sanitation, electricity, telecommunication, community centre, places of worship, and cremation ground)	10% of the total package

10. The cash option has been provided for catering to people who are not interested in resettlement and are prepared to establish themselves elsewhere under 'mutually agreed terms and conditions', as indicated in the Wildlife (Protection) Act, 1972. This has checks and balances as the money is provided through the district collector after the villager produces evidence of his procuring land, etc.

11. The relocation is voluntary, and is done only if people are willing to move.

12. Monitoring committees at the district as well as state levels are required to be constituted and detailed guidelines have been issued for handholding the people after relocation, besides ensuring the centrality of PRI institutions, while involving independent agencies.

13. Advisories have been issued to the states for complying with the Wildlife (Protection) Act, 1972, and the Scheduled Tribes and Other Traditional Forest Dwellers (Recognition of Forest Rights) Act, 2006.

Critical Wildlife Habitats

1. The Forest Rights Act had come into force in January 2007 and the MoEF had issued guidelines to the state/UT governments for notification of the critical wildlife habitats (CWLHs) in October 2007. During the last three years, not much headway could be made in notification of CWLHs. The state/UT governments have been expressing difficulties in notifying CWLHs on the basis of the 2007 guidelines. Accordingly, MoEF convened meetings with the chief wildlife wardens and officers of the Wildlife Institute of India, discussed the guidelines, and has now issued the revised guidelines, which are in consonance with the Forest Rights Act.

2. CWLHs are such areas of the national parks and sanctuaries that are required to be kept as 'inviolate' for the purpose of wildlife conservation as determined and notified by the MoEF, after an open process of consultation by an expert committee. Such areas are to be clearly identified on a case-to-case basis following scientific and objective criteria and only after settling the rights of tribals and other traditional forest dwellers.

3. The identification and declaration of CWLHs are two distinct processes. While the identification of an area required for betterment of wildlife conservation is purely a scientific exercise to be carried out by the forest departments on a case-to-case basis in consultation with the scientific institutions (the criteria for identification of CWLHs have to be site-specific), its notification is to be done only after extensive consultations (means consent) with the gram sabha and the affected persons/stakeholders.

4. The guidelines ensure that CWLHs are declared only with the voluntary consent of the affected people. It also gives ample scope to the state/UT governments to explore the possibility of 'coexistence'. If such a possibility is not practicable, the expert committee, which also includes the district tribal welfare officer and an NGO working in the field of tribal welfare, will have consultations with the gram sabha/affected persons for their relocation, during which the available options (Option-I for payment of Rs 10 lakh per family and Option-II for comprehensive rehabilitation by providing land, house with facilities, community rights, by the forest department) for voluntary relocation would also be explained. The relocation involves providing secure livelihoods to the persons to be relocated. In fact, they may choose the option most suited to them.

5. The guidelines for notification of CWLHs apply only to the national parks and sanctuaries and not to other forest areas.

The MoEF will take all the steps to ensure that the letter and spirit of Forest Rights Act, 2006 is respected and followed in all wildlife conservation programmes. If there is any violation anywhere and that violation is reported with full documentation and evidence, it will be prepared to intervene to ensure that the situation is rectified forthwith.

Letter to Sanctuary Asia Kids for Tiger Project Director, Forwarding a Message for the Students at Kendriya Vidyalaya, Hebbal, Bangalore

25 JANUARY 2010

Thank you very much for sending me the letter from the students of Kendriya Vidyalaya, Hebbal, Bangalore regarding practical solutions to fight the climate change. I am enclosing a message for the school children and would appreciate if the same is conveyed to them.

Dear Students,
It is really heartening to go through your letter and I appreciate the concerns voiced by you all to protect our biodiversity and tiger, besides saving our country from the climate change crisis. We, in the MoEF, are

collaborating with the states and civil society institutions to collectively address these challenges, besides taking steps for mitigating the climate change. I am confident, with the active support of future citizens like you, we will succeed in our efforts, even when the going is not all that smooth. I wish you all the best in life.

Letter to Chief Minister of Maharashtra Ashok Chavan about concerns raised by a ladies group in Mumbai about the Botanical Garden

30 MARCH 2010

I have received a letter from a group of ladies in Mumbai who are very much interested in biodiversity and environmental conservation. They have brought to my notice the environmental implications of the planned redevelopment of V.J.B. Udyan. Their main concern is that in the process of redevelopment into an expanded zoo, the Botanical Garden would get destroyed. Their suggestion is that the expanded zoo should be located outside the city precincts and not at V. J.B. Udyan ... Knowing the V.J.B. Udyan for as I do for so long, I find a lot of merit in the arguments being put forward by the Save Rani Bagh Botanical Garden Action Committee. I request you to please have this matter re-examined in light of the concerns that have been expressed by such a large cross-section of citizens of Mumbai city. Next year will mark the 150th anniversary of the Botanical Garden and it would really be a pity if the diversity in the Botanical Garden were to be destroyed in the name of zoo expansion.

Excerpts from Remarks Made at the Guru Jambeshwar Dham at a Convention of the Vishnoi Samaj in Maulisar, Churu, Rajasthan

12 APRIL 2011

I come here not as a minister but as a pilgrim and as a student of India's fascinating cultural and ecological history.

The late fifteenth century was an unusual period in Indian history. This was a period which saw the birth of a large number of social reformers who continue to inspire us even today—Purandaradasa in the south, Shankardev and Chaitanya Mahaprabhu in the east, Vallabhacharya in central India, Narsinh Mehta in the west, Guru Nanak, Mirabai, and Guru Jambeshwar in the northwest, Ravidass and Kabir in the north.

Guru Jambeshwar, who founded the Vishnoi sect, laid down twenty-nine rules for simple living and high thinking, eight of which have to do with environmental protection and biodiversity conservation. Some 363 of his followers led by Amrita Devi sacrificed their lives in Khejarli village near Jodhpur nearly 280 years ago protecting the *khejri* tree from the greed of the Maharajah of Jodhpur. Amrita Devi inspired Gaura Devi to lead a band of intrepid women to protect their trees in Reni village in Chamoli district of Uttarakhand in 1974 giving rise to the famous Chipko movement. Thus two women, Amrita Devi and Gaura Devi are the pioneers of the environmental conservation movement in our country. They deserve to be remembered by all of us. The MoEF will institute national awards in their name to recognize the contributions of communities, particularly women, to the cause of forest protection and regeneration.

The Vishnoi community has played a pioneering role in fostering ecological consciousness and its example must be emulated by others in our society. I congratulate the Vishnois for the role they played in apprehending Salman Khan and his friends. The Wildlife (Protection) Act, 1972 is now being amended to make punishment more stringent for offenders. Future Sansar Chands and Salman Khans cannot get away lightly. The amendments will be introduced in the Monsoon session of Parliament.

The Talchapper Blackbuck Sanctuary is an unusual sanctuary located as it is in a desert ecosystem. It is about 700 ha in area and it is being expanded by another 1,000 ha. Although blackbucks are the mainstay, the sanctuary is also a birdwatchers' delight with cranes coming all the way from Central Asia every year during winter. Talchapper must be brought on to the tourist circuit in a public–private partnership mode, perhaps clubbed with the Bharatpur Bird Sanctuary. Tourism will help in boosting incomes of local communities who must see an economic benefit to them from the preservation of such sanctuaries and protected areas.

Notes

1. Those who attended were farmers and farmer organizations, scientists, state agriculture department officials, NGOs, consumer groups, allopathic and ayurvedic doctors, students and housewives. A summary report prepared by the CEE based on these seven meetings is at Annex-I to the electronic version of this note available at www.moef.nic.in.

2. Copies of these letters to the chief ministers and the responses received were placed at Annex-II to the electronic version of the speaking order, which was made available on the ministry website. Letters from the state governments of Kerala, Madhya Pradesh, and Chhattisgarh ; the letter from the chairman of the committee of agriculture of the Lok Sabha and other political leaders including a former prime minister was also made public. Opinions were also sought from a number of scientists both from India and abroad. In addition, a very large number of emails from research institutes, NGOs, and concerned individuals were received. Opinions from scientists were made public in Annexe-III to the electronic version of the speaking order; a representative sample of emails from research institutes and NGOs was made available as Annexe-IV of the order, which was put up on the ministry website.

3. I leave aside the basic issue of 'why Bt-brinjal?' in the first place since there does not seem to be any overriding food security, production shortage or farmer distress arguments favouring the enormous priority that has been accorded to it by private companies.

4. At the Bangalore public consultation on 6 February, a former managing director of the Monsanto (India) came out strongly against Bt-brinjal on this ground and on the grounds that profits should not drive seed supply.

5. At the Bangalore consultations, Dr G.K. Veeresh, a former vice-chancellor of the University of Agricultural Sciences, Bangalore, a sister organization of University of Agricultural Sciences, Dharwad expressed strong opposition to the commercialization of Bt-brinjal.

6. The review was subsequently published in *Current Science*. At the time of the consultations an advance copy was made available to me, it was included as part of the Annex-III of the electronic version of the speaking order.

7. Dr S. Parasuraman, director of the Tata Institute of Social Sciences, Mumbai wrote to me saying that the questions he raised as member of EC-I were never answered.

8. However, there are farmers organizations like the Bharatiya Krishak Samaj and the Karnataka Rajya Raitha Sangha, and some in Tamil Nadu that have opposed the commercialization of Bt-brinjal.

9. I received a representation from the Bangalore-headquartered Association of Biotechnology-led Enterprises (ABLE) arguing for the commercialization of Bt-brinjal on various grounds.

2 The Trade-offs

I had spent most of my professional life, whether in the government or in the party, focusing on mainstream economic issues—the stuff that makes for high economic growth. I was more than an ardent proponent of the need to liberalize the economy and had played a role in the July 1991 'big bang' reforms episode. But this commitment to high growth does not mean undermining environmental concerns.

High growth is an imperative. We cannot ignore the overriding essentiality of growth in creating jobs, in generating revenues for investing in health, education, and infrastructure. At the same time, managing environmental risks must be integral to the growth strategy. The reverse is also true—the need for higher economic growth must be integral to environmental protection. Ecological security in a framework that promotes economic growth is what the country is looking for. We cannot forget that poverty is both a cause and consequence of environmental degradation. To take-off and logically extend from the then finance minister, Manmohan Singh's 1991 Budget speech, 'we cannot deforest our way to prosperity and we cannot pollute our way to prosperity.'

There is no running away from the fact that developmental and industrial activities can lead to environmental degradation. The trick, then, lies in how we balance the demands of today—high growth and its concomitant benefits with the imperatives of tomorrow—the impact and cost of ecological degradation. This balance is the essence of sustainable development. This balance can be achieved through interventions to minimize and limit adverse environmental impacts.

Just as nearly twenty-five years ago we realized the need to make economic reforms fiscally sustainable, the time had come to find ways to make high economic growth ecologically sustainable. I do not believe that there is a conflict between a high-growth strategy and ecological security, it is a matter of achieving balance. In the attempt to achieve this balance where environmental concerns are an input into economic decisions, I sought to move away from the binary approach to green clearances for projects to a three-way classification—'yes', 'yes, but', and 'no'.

Before I took over, 99.999 per cent of the clearances were in the 'yes' category. I increased the population of cases in both the 'yes, but' and 'no' categories. However, contrary to perception, the fact is that almost 95 per cent of the proposals for environmental clearances got the go ahead and 85 per cent of the proposals for forests projects received the green signal and on time. In striking the balance between ecological security and high growth, it is the 'yes, but' category that should concern us most because these form or should form the bulk of the clearances, and this is where the balance is precarious. The conditions under which the projects are given the go-ahead should be interventions that limit and minimize environmental damage, but these conditions must not stifle and strangulate.

Saying 'no' to bauxite mining in the Niyamgiri Hills was, therefore, logical—the total quantum of bauxite that could be mined would only form a fraction of the alumina refinery's requirement in its entire life cycle. While the Navi Mumbai Airport was a 'yes, but'—it was a case of balancing the need for a new airport to manage the growing air traffic and the need to ensure that the destruction of mangroves, which provide a natural barrier to Mumbai in the event of natural calamities, was minimal and that the course of the Mithi river was not altered so much as to adversely impact the city's natural drainage system.

Sometimes, the greater economic imperatives would override other concerns—permitting SAIL to develop the Chiriya mines, which are located in the dense sal forests of Saranda in Jharkhand—is an example. Allowing for mining in Saranda Forests was a difficult decision, but I had to balance it with SAIL's survival and the much larger economic impact of putting SAIL's health at risk. The steel major, got a 'yes, but' clearance with conditions imposed to ensure that the ecological impact is mitigated.

There has to be constant assessment of the benefits and costs to any project and intervention. In some cases, the toss of the coin will favour economic growth and in other cases, it will favour environmental control. This assessment needs to be both project-specific and area- or region-specific. It is in an effort to make ecologically and economically sustainable decisions, that I called for cumulative impact assessments of several river basins, including the Alaknanda and Bhagirathi rivers and ecologically fragile areas like the Western Ghats. There was no gain in overburdening an area beyond its carrying capacity. Such assessments have to become part of the normal course of the project clearance system.[1]

There is another aspect to achieving the much desired balance, and that is following the laws of the land in letter and spirit.[2] Our environmental legislations encapsulate this need for balance between growth and ecological security, but unfortunately these laws have been observed more in the breach. In many of the cases such as the Adarsh Housing Society, the development of the Lavasa township, and Vedanta's expansion of its refinery at Lanjigarh, it was a clear case of disregard for the laws of the land, which resulted in an imbalance. Rectifying the situation was seen as a step to stifle growth, when really it was about restoring balance.

The pressures to allow for short cuts in ensuring ecological security, in order to allow for economic and developmental activities will always be immense. At first glance, perhaps even in the short-run, economic growth and ecological security may seem at odds with each other. But on closer look, it is clear that environmental protection contributes to sustaining growth. I, therefore, increasingly came to the view that there is no real trade-off because economic growth that is environmentally not benign, and growth that is ecologically not secure is not sustainable.

This chapter addresses the environment-development debate. It brings together practical illustrations of the three-way classification of clearances highlighting that while there are trade offs, it possible to balance development with ecological security. In fact, more often than not ecological security and economic growth are not at odds with each other.

'Globalization and Ecological Security', Lecture Organized by the Foundation for Ecological Security, India International Centre, New Delhi

31 October 2002

I am not from the mainstream environmental sustainable development movement. And when I was asked what I would like to speak on, I suggested this somewhat controversial topic—globalization and ecological security—because the economic system is seen to be eroding ecological security.

The conventional wisdom on globalization and ecological security is that these are fundamentally conflicting goals and that globalization is actually eroding the infrastructure for ecological security. This is perhaps the most succinct and most eloquent description that I have ever read. It is also the most profoundly mistaken and wrong statement on the subject that I have read.

Let me begin by saying that there are two themes today, and it is only appropriate that we are discussing this in the background of the climate change conference that is going on because what has happened in the last few years is not just a question of globalization and ecological security but what we are seeing is the globalization of ecological security. That is really the issue that has sort of fixed in the public agenda of both the developing countries and the developed countries. We understand less the link between globalization and ecological security and we are preoccupied more with the issue of globalization of ecological security. And, I would like to make a distinction between the two, because it has its own economic and political consequences.

Many of the problems we associate with ecological insecurity—the over-exploitation of natural resources, the damage to the water system, the enormous increase in the pollution load in terms of air pollution, water pollution, land pollution, the deforestation taking place in the upper catchment areas, the degradation of forest lands—these all pre-date globalization. These are all processes that have been going on over the last few years. Perhaps, they have come into public focus in the last decade or so. But it is important to realize that the so-called romantic period of planned development that we had was actually a period in which great damage to the entire foundation of ecological security was done.

I make it a point not to criticize the past but to draw attention to the fact that very often we tend to make the assumption that market economies are environment-unfriendly and somehow planned economies are environment-friendly. The greatest environmental disasters that the twentieth century has seen were in Central Asia under the Communist regimes. In fact, Communist regimes in Europe and Central Asia have been the most environment-unfriendly governments the world has ever seen. The type of ecological disaster that has happened in the Aral Sea, for example, is something that could never be possible in a market-friendly environment. So, this is the conventional assumption that people make that somehow if you make the transition from a planned economy to a market economy, the casualty is the environment or ecological security, is not borne out by facts. There have been market economies in the world where the environment has been at a discount, there have been planned economies in the world where environment has been at a discount ... I think the issue is between countries that follow environmental policies that are integrated with the overall mainstream of development concerns and countries that do not really pay serious attention to the whole environmental dimension of what they were doing. In fact, the paradox is that—and we do not realize this—very often even in the market economies, many of the great environmental movements have actually been the result not of market forces but of judicial pronouncements or of regulatory instruments that have been adopted in response to popular pressure from civil society. So even in market economies, it is the interplay of regulation and technology and public pressure that has forced a certain pattern of environmental behaviour.

So, the first point I want to make is that we need to get out of this mindset of looking at the market economy as a villain and to romanticize the planned economy environment as a friend of ecological security.

Let me then move on to the second theme I want to talk about: To give some content to what is globalization because everything now comes under its rubric. It is a catch-all phrase under which anything can come. I would tend to argue that if you want to look at globalization and want to make some sense out of it, and look at the link with ecological security, you have to look at it in four different dimensions. There is trade globalization; there is globalization in finance—financial globalization; there is globalization in people, that is, the movement of labour both within countries and across countries; and then, of course, there is the broader issue of cultural globalization.

It is important to look at each component separately, because I believe to confuse the issues of the impact of trade globalization with the movement of capital, with the movement of people, and this broader issue of cultural globalization, does not do justice to the whole concept. The paragraph that I read from Dr Amrita Patel's lecture[3] really refers to the globalization of trade, that is, the opening up of markets, the movement of goods and services, the linking of producers in one country with the consumers in another country ... By and large, when we say globalization we are talking about the movements of goods and services both within geographical borders and across geographical borders.

I want to ask the question, what is the evidence, in fact, that this movement of goods and services is in the economic and ecological interest? I think one has to separate these issues. Clearly, if it is not in the economic interest of countries or communities, there is no worthwhile objective in pursuing this process. The question of ecological security then becomes secondary. But, if there is an economic benefit being obtained, then there is a trade-off between an economic benefit that may be obtained and an ecological cost that may be incurred. So, I think it is important to spend a few minutes trying to understand this whole question—a very controversial question—about the impact of globalization of trade in goods and services on the local economies.

If we take livelihoods as the base, then there could always be evidence to suggest that globalization has had both a positive as well as a negative impact. But here, I am going to use the country basically as the unit of analysis. I am not looking at local communities as a unit of analysis. If we take the country as a unit, there is enough evidence to actually suggest that actually globalization of trade makes the country's economy much more resilient and, in fact, leads to security of the most fundamental kind, which is employment security. There is no empirical evidence to suggest, except in the case of some African countries, which are a separate category, that the globalization of trade has actually led to weakening of a country's economic position. The reason why Africa is different is because Africa's agriculture is very fragile, most African economies are mono-crop or mono-product economies, and basically the starting point of Africa's diversification of economic structure never really took place, unlike other countries in Latin America and Asia.

So, when we look at the empirical evidence of the last twenty years and ask the question—which most people are beginning to ask—'has globalization made countries poorer or richer?', I think the evidence is clear; that globalization of trade, in terms of trade, in terms of opening up new markets, and integration with the international product markets have, in fact, made countries richer by creating more jobs at home. In the process, some livelihoods may have got lost. In the process, the employment structure may have got diversified—less people involved in agriculture, more people involved in industry, less people involved in industry, more people involved in services. We are not talking of individual cases, we are now talking of the broad macro economy. I want to reiterate that there is absolutely no empirical evidence to suggest, barring the unique case of Africa, that globalization in trade has actually led to a weakening of a country's economic security or employment security.

The two outstanding examples of this are basically India and China—China more dramatically than India. In the case of India's own experience during the past ten–fifteen years, all the evidence certainly suggests that the opening up of the Indian economy to trade has, in fact, made the Indian economy stronger and much more resilient and much less vulnerable to international shocks.

Now, I am not going to talk about globalization of finance, globalization of labour, globalization of culture, because I think that takes us into a completely different dimension and the links with ecological security are far less explicit ... the focus of my talk is exclusively on globalization of trade, on which really much of the debate is taking place in forums both within the country and outside.

The question is, 'has ecology become stronger or not?' That is really the question, whether in the process of globalization, in the process of integration, in the process of international relocation of labour and capital, the local ecological structures have in fact weakened. Here, it is necessary to note that we are not writing on a clean slate, that over the last thirty–forty years we have accumulated a set of problems, on account of development strategies that have been adopted. However, people ascribe water-logging in Punjab to the opening up of the World Trade Organization (WTO) but clearly there is no link between the WTO and water-logging in Punjab. Likewise, there is no clear link between deforestation that has gone on over the last thirty-five years and the integration of world trade, because if we look at the pattern of international trade for India, very little of our export trade is forest-based products or natural resource products, as we have diversified away from that structure. It could be true of Africa but certainly not true in India.

The question whether globalization of trade has, in fact, had a deleterious effect on ecological security is difficult to answer because of the accumulated set of problems that we have inherited on account of a certain pattern of development. And, this is where I think, one needs to distinguish between the stock and the flow. At a given point of time, there is a certain stock of problems that have accumulated, for example, the stock of accumulated greenhouse gases. The real question is: How is the flow?

Is the increment to the stock accelerating, decelerating, or is it constant? What is the globalization process doing to the accumulated stock of problems? That is the real issue that we have to come to grips with.

On the issue of economic integration, which Dr Amrita Patel has talked about—that the process of economic integration is leading—as she says, to adverse ecological and environmental consequences in areas where these resources are exploited, I would argue that the fundamental impact of globalization of trade, going by the evidence, has been less on the environment and more on employment. And a strategy of globalization that actually increases employment, in my view, strengthens the foundation of ecological security, because it could be argued and it has been argued in the Indian context, that most of our ecological problems arise out of poverty. Most ecological problems arise out of lack of access to economic resources and in empowering communities economically, the transition to a safer ecological regime is made automatically. Therefore, I would argue that globalization—by increasing opportunities for employment, by increasing opportunities for specialization of trade in the resource in which a country is surplus, namely labour—leads to increased employment, and certainly it is a strategy that has led to greater ecological security.

The fact of the matter is that India has not done very well in this regard compared to China. That has more to do with the fact that we have not been able to exploit the opportunities of globalization because of our own policies and less to do with the fact that globalization does not open up these opportunities. If we again compare India and China, look at India and China ten years ago and India and China today, most of the successes that China has had in terms of globalization of trade are precisely in those areas where India also had a comparative advantage—whether in textiles or labour-intensive manufacturing of consumer goods. These are all industries in which basically local jobs have been created. And the fact that China has been able to do this, and India has not, has to do more with the nature of domestic policy and less with the nature of external constraint. But we tend to blame the external world much more for our own failure, whereas the clear evidence is that there are other countries, which have been able to exploit these markets to good advantage.

I would say that the verdict today is that globalization of trade certainly creates far greater economic opportunities for countries that participate in the process of globalization. There is enough evidence to suggest that closed economies grow at slower economic growth rates and that economies that have opened themselves up to trade as opposed to capital—now I am making a distinction between financial globalization and trade globalization—that economies that participate in the process of integration of international trade are countries, which have increased economic wealth, and, therefore, they have increased their ability to deal with ecological security.

Now, from this it does not follow that a country that has become economically more resilient out of globalization automatically increases the strength of its ecological structure. I think nobody in his right mind—and if anybody has, in fact, argued that the he or she is wrong—would argue that there is an automatic link between economic development and ecological security. The question is: What are the safeguards and what are the instruments that one should adopt in order to ensure that goals of environmental and ecological protection and conservation are fulfilled while at the same time the objective of economic growth is also maximized?

I think there is a great belief in this country, particularly that a low-growth economy is more protective of the environment than a high-growth economy. Somehow, if you are growing at 7 or 8 per cent and industrializing faster, you are imposing a great cost on the environment, whereas if you had a low rate of economic growth you would have a low level of equilibrium with the environment. But I think we have enough evidence to show that this is really not the case. So, the real challenge in my view, in the years ahead—to shift this debate away from globalization versus ecological security to globalization and economic security—I think, is to recognize that globalization of trade has a positive effect on a country's economic position and it provides an opportunity for the country; then, to follow policies and instruments in order to meet the requirements of environment protection.

The second issue is of globalization of ecological security. It is only appropriate that we are meeting today in the background of the negotiations and discussions on climate change, because this is one of issues really that has come up in the public arena in the last ten or fifteen years, which epitomizes what I am trying to talk about—which is that ecological security has become more globalized.

What are the issues we have to be worried about in this arena? I think the most important issue is that there would certainly be attempts made to link trade with environmental concerns. There is a large community of people particularly among civil society organizations, certainly in Western countries, which believe that this link should exist, that, in fact, the only way to ensure ecological security is to impose trade sanctions. In fact, the entire debate on trade and environment in the context of the WTO is about this. Now, we have a large body of material, jurisprudence, law that we have accumulated to show the conflict that exists between the promotion of globalization of free trade to meet the objectives of environment.

The famous Shrimp–Turtle case in the international community, I do not know how many of you are familiar with it, is redefining the whole link between trade and environment. The US banned the import of shrimp from countries like India on the grounds that the way shrimp is caught in these countries kills turtles … The first ruling went in favour of India, Malaysia, and Thailand but subsequently the US went back to the appellate body in the WTO. The appellate body gave a ruling that seemed to justify the application of domestic environmental standards in what is essentially a matter of international trade. Now there is a big question mark whether, in fact, the WTO has sanctioned the use of environmental safeguards and the use of trade sanctions basically to meet domestic environmental goals.

So, I think the big issue is to what extent the trade sanctions would be used to enforce desirable patterns of environmental behaviour. We are seeing this not only in the area of environment but also in social areas ... There are important issues pending, for example, in Europe, where there is a move to ban import of leather from India on the grounds that tanning uses carcinogenic chemicals. ... There are a large number of instances where I think today there is a progressive move towards the use of trade sanctions in order to meet the objectives of ecological security.

Many people actually welcome this and say that the only way we are going to get environment integrated with the development process is if you start using trade sanctions. I think this is going to be a very contentious political issue—the use of trade sanctions to control market access. All I can say at this stage is that the next three–four years are going to be absolutely critical in the international negotiating process.

The second issue is of climate change. This again is a good case of globalization of ecological security and some of the principles I have been talking about. The whole Kyoto Protocol, which has been a subject of controversy, is based on the fundamental distinction between stock and flow. There are countries which have contributed to the stock of greenhouse gases and there are countries that are contributing to the flow of greenhouse gases. The first problem you really have to address is the responsibility of those countries, which have contributed to the stock and then address the problem of what is the responsibility of other countries that are contributing to the flow. I think this inability to have an equitable distribution, in the eyes of many countries, between those who contribute to the stock and those who are contributing to the flow has led to the political controversies over the Kyoto Protocol, but I am sure that this is something that is going to get resolved.

The key issue here, whether it is the WTO or the Kyoto Protocol, is that environmental/ecological security is becoming an instrument of protectionism. I think that is the real issue here. The real danger is that if ecological security is going to be raised to the level of godhood—as it should perhaps be and it certainly has—then the countries are going to use the environmental arguments, the ecological arguments basically as an instrument of neo-protectionism. I think that is the danger, that having seen the positive effects of globalization of trade, if ecological security is going to be used as a criteria for restricting market access and for actually making free trade un-free, then I think we are going to be denying many countries the benefits of the globalization process.

Therefore, to summarize, what I want to say is that ecological security really is a matter ultimately of domestic policy. Ecological security is a matter of economic policy, of agricultural policy, of how you deal with water, air, and land. I think the globalization process I have explained to you, largely in terms of globalization of trade, is basically an opportunity for specialization in capital, in labour, in factors of production, and basically an opportunity for a country to expand its presence in international markets, to create jobs at home, to increase its prosperity, which creates conditions for addressing these questions of ecological security.

As I said and I want to reiterate, it is not when countries have in fact become much more global then, automatically, ecological concerns become addressed. Ecological concerns need to be addressed as matters in their own right. And the real challenge for countries like India is to ensure that the globalization process moves in a manner that not only increases its economic wealth but also actually enhances ecological well-being. Therefore, I would say that contrary to what most people think, the objectives of globalization and ecological security are not, in fact, mutually exclusive and in fact can be reconciled in a proper economic framework, and I hope this is done sooner rather than later.

'The Two Cultures Revisited: Some Reflections on the Environment-Development Debate in India', Eleventh ISRO–JNCASR Satish Dhawan Memorial Lecture, Jawaharlal Nehru Centre for Advanced Scientific Research, Bangalore

28 September 2010

I am privileged to be delivering this prestigious lecture dedicated to a most remarkable Indian—an outstanding engineer-administrator, a great institution-builder, a most inspiring teacher, and an intellectual who demonstrated a profound commitment to the most sensitive and progressive of human values.

I never knew Professor Satish Dhawan personally but he was very much part of my growing up since my father and he were colleagues, although belonging to different institutions. Over the years, as I read more and reflected about him and talked with people who had worked with him, I was profoundly impressed by two uncommon traits of his. First, he was a true builder of men because of his willingness to stand up for his team and take the responsibility for failure, while generously giving away credit to others on occasions of success. This was most evident in the Satellite Launch Vehicle (SLV) saga and Dr Abdul Kalam has written about this movingly. Second, he was one mentor who did not become a tormentor. The bane of Indian science (and indeed, of industry, politics, and many other fields in this country) is the unwillingness and reluctance of charismatic trailblazers to call it a day when at the top, to train a new generation of successors, and, most importantly, to leave the successors free to do their job.

Since this lecture is co-sponsored by the Indian Space Research Organisation (ISRO), permit me to recall that I have consciously endeavoured to forge a close partnership between the Ministry of Environment and Forests and ISRO. India will launch its own dedicated satellite for monitoring greenhouse gas and aerosol emissions in 2012 and its own dedicated forestry satellite in 2013 to enable real-time monitoring of both deforestation and afforestation in our country. The MoEF is also co-financing the National Institute of Climate and Environment Studies being established by ISRO and working closely with the Space Applications Centre in modelling and monitoring the health of the Himalayan glaciers. One of the early decisions I took after becoming minister was to ensure that ISRO is an integral part of our climate science and climate change negotiations team because of the tremendous capability it has built up in this area.

II

Over half a century ago, while giving the Reith Lectures over BBC, the eminent British physicist-author C.P. Snow spoke of how the breakdown of communication between the 'two cultures' of modern society—the cultures of science and that of humanities—was becoming a hindrance to understanding and addressing pressing public issues. The lectures were later published as a book, which the *Times Literary Supplement* in 2008 included in its list of 100 books that have most influenced Western public discourse since World War II.

This afternoon, I wish to speak of a later-day facet of these 'two cultures' syndrome—the apparent gap between those espousing the case for faster economic growth and those calling for greater attention to protection of the environment. On the face of it, there should be no gap at all—who can argue against faster economic growth since that alone will generate more jobs and at the same time who can argue against the preservation of our rivers, lakes, mountains, and wonderful biodiversity in its myriad forms, since that alone will make for sustainable development. But I am afraid that the two groups are not talking to each other—they are talking at each other and with every passing day, the gap seems to be widening. It seems so for a number of reasons. For one, our growth aspirations themselves have changed perceptibly and anything less than an 8–9 per cent annual rate of real gross domestic product growth is deemed a 'slowdown'. For another, an energetic and exuberant environmental community has emerged with a very large number of well-educated youngsters in its vanguard. And, of course, our track record on environmental management certainly does not inspire much confidence.

III

When pushed, a growth protagonist will say 'there must be a proper balance between environment and GDP growth'. When pushed, an environmentalist will say 'there must be balance between GDP growth and environment'. Notice the slight shift in the sequence in the two statements. The first implies that a fetish is being made of the environment but in the final analysis a balance must indeed be struck. The second implies that a fetish is being made of economic growth but in the final analysis a balance must indeed be struck. Balance, therefore, is the key. Both sides will agree on the importance of faster economic growth. Both sides will also agree on the need to reflect and factor in ecological concerns in the fast growth process. So, where is the problem? So, why so much discord, instead of dialogue, why so much confrontation, instead of cooperation.

The problem lies when you go beyond 'balance' as a general philosophical concept and try and give it some operational meaning—when hard choices need to be made about large projects that are considered central to economic growth but are detrimental to the environment. Let us all accept the reality that there is undoubtedly a trade-off between growth and environment. In arriving at decisions to untangle the trade-off, three options present themselves—'yes', 'yes, but', and 'no'. The real problem is that the growth constituency is used to 'yes' and can live with 'yes, but'. It cries foul with 'no'. The environment constituency exults with a 'no', grudgingly accepts the 'yes, but' but cries foul with a 'yes'. Therefore, one clear lesson is this—maximize the 'yes, but', where this is possible.

The vast majority of environmental and forest clearances are in the 'yes, but' category but they do not hit the headlines like the 'yes' or the 'no' decisions do. Of course, as we gain experience, we must refine the 'but' in the 'yes, but' approach. The 'but' often takes the form of conditions that must be adhered to before, during the construction, and after the launch of the project. I believe that in laying down these conditions, we must strive for three things: First, the conditions must be objective and measurable, so that it is clear what is to be done and whether it has been complied with. Second, the conditions must be consistent and fair, so that similar projects are given similar conditions to adhere to. Finally, the conditions must not impose inordinate financial or time costs on the proponents (which would render them impractical).

This has indeed been our effort in the last fifteen months for the vast majority of the cases that have come before us. For instance, we allowed a power project in Ratnagiri in the face of non-governmental organization objections since it was already well-advanced in implementation. There is also the urgent need to enhance our ability to monitor compliance with the conditions we lay down—our current capabilities in this regard are completely inadequate. In upgrading these abilities, we will need to be innovative and think smart, going beyond traditional inspection-based systems, a theme I will come back to later.

One of the most interesting innovations introduced over the last decade relates to valuation of ecological cost of projects. This initiative, the entire credit for which must go to the Supreme Court, is the concept popularly known as 'CAMPA'. CAMPA, which stands for Compensatory Afforestation Management and Planning Authority, is an innovation ordered by the Supreme Court in 2002, according to which every party, whether government or private, that wishes to divert forest area for non-forestry purposes, has to deposit a certain sum equivalent to the total value of ecological benefits lost per hectare diverted for such purpose. The value of benefits lost is arrived at by taking into account the net present value (NPV) of benefits lost, the stipulated compensatory afforestation amount and the funds accrued under the catchment area treatment plans submitted. This approach has served us well—today we have almost Rs 11,000 crore available to state governments for reforestation and regeneration of natural forest cover. However, there is a need to periodically revisit the prescribed formula to ensure that the value of forest land diverted is based on calculations that reflect the true and accurate cost of such diversion. There is also a case to be made for the introduction of a similar levy for projects that have environmental costs, even when they do not involve diversion of forest land.

'Yes, but' cases aside, there will most certainly be instances, few and far between I should add, in the overall scheme of things, when a firm 'no' will be required. In such cases that have complex scientific, ecological, and social dimensions, my approach has been to make decisions in the most consultative and transparent manner possible. This is what we did in the case of Bt-brinjal and in the case of the Vedanta mining project in Odisha, where I consulted extensively, and shared a most detailed explanation for our decision with the public. I am convinced that the time has come to make trade-offs explicit and make the correct choice, however unpalatable that might be to some. This is exactly what Indira Gandhi did almost three decades back, if you will recall, when she said a decisive 'no' to the Silent Valley Hydroelectric Project in one of India's most ecologically sensitive regions. Her 'no' was not unilateral but it was unequivocal.

IV

Part of the problem arises from the fact that we do not have a system of 'green accounting'. Economists estimate GDP, which is gross domestic product, as a broad measure of national income and also estimate NDP or net domestic product, which accounts for the use of physical capital. But as yet, we have no generally accepted system to convert Gross Domestic Product into Green Domestic Product that would reflect the use of precious natural resources in the process of generating national income. Many years ago, the noted Indian environmentalist Anil Agarwal had advocated the concept of a Gross Nature Product to replace the usually estimated gross national product (GNP).

Economists all over the world have been at work for quite some time on developing a robust system of green national accounting but we are not there as yet. Ideally, if we can report both gross domestic product and 'green' domestic product, we will get a better picture of the trade-offs involved in the process of economic growth. Alternatively, as some economist have argued, we need alternative indicators to measure true welfare improvement, as Green GDP is not be the best indicator of sustainability or future increases in consumption or welfare—indicators such as 'Genuine Savings/Investment' and 'Genuine Wealth Per Capita' are being developed as alternatives. We do not need precise numbers. Even a broad-brush estimate will be a huge step forward to give practical meaning to the concept of 'sustainable development', which all of us swear by in theory.

This term 'sustainable development', incidentally, was first defined by the Indian economist Nitin Desai in the report of the World Commission on Environment and Development called *Our Common Future*, widely known as the Brundtland Report after the then Norwegian prime minister, who was the chairperson of the commission. The definition, beautifully clear yet intangible at the same time, runs thus— 'sustainable development is development that meets the needs of the present without compromising the ability of future generations to meet their own needs'.

In the last few months, I have tried to set the ball rolling so that by 2015 at least we can have a system of green national accounting. We will not be starting on a clean slate, of course. One of the world's leading authorities in this field is Professor Sir Partha Dasgupta at Cambridge University, and he has published extensively. In one of his seminal pieces published along with others including the Nobel laureate Kenneth Arrow, he has calculated that the 'genuine' domestic investment rate in India is around 2.3 percentage points lower than the normally reckoned domestic investment rate for the period 1970–2001 after taking into account environmental costs and both calculated as a proportion of GDP. He goes on to show that as against the estimated annual growth rate of India's per capita GDP of 2.96 per cent during this period, the growth rate of per capita genuine wealth, after taking into account environmental costs, works out to 0.31 per cent annually. Such analyses help put a number to the environmental cost of our growth process, making our trade-offs more explicit and, hence, must be mainstreamed.

Building on Professor Dasgupta's work, the World Bank has institutionalized a metric called the 'adjusted net savings'. This measures the 'true' rate of savings in an economy after taking into account investments in human capital, depletion of natural resources and damage caused by pollution. This is considered an indicator of the true wealth generation of the economy, and hence of its sustainable development potential. Adjusted net savings helps make the growth–environment trade-off more explicit, since countries that choose to prioritize growth today at the cost of the environment will have depressed rates of adjusted net savings. Just as an example, according to the World Bank data, India's Gross National Savings as a percentage of GDP was about 34.3 per cent in 2008, but its adjusted net saving in the same year was 24.2 per cent, the difference arising due to the depletion of natural resources and pollution related damages, in addition to conventionally measured depreciation of the nation's capital assets.

Another extremely interesting and valuable exercise of quantifying the economic benefits from ecosystems of various types and costs associated with their loss is being coordinated by Pavan Sukhdev. This is a global study called The Economics of Ecosystems and Biodiversity (TEEB) supported by the United Nations Environment Program, the German government, the European Commission, and other institutions. Already two volumes have been released. A TEEB study for India is to be launched with the support of the MoEF. This will demonstrate why prosperity and poverty reduction depends on maintaining the flow of benefits from ecosystems and why biodiversity conservation and protection is not a luxury but, in fact, is essential for achieving developmental objectives. Earlier, work done by Professor Kanchan Chopra of the Institute of Economic Growth, Delhi, helped in establishing the concept of net present value.

Let me suggest another way of handling this new 'two cultures' phenomenon. And this is to look at environment not as some sort of elitist or upper middle-class clean air or tiger protection issue per se but more as a public health issue. Even as India scales new heights of economic growth, it cannot afford to do so at the cost of the health of its population, its greatest asset. Recent reports show that people in different parts of India are raising serious concerns about a series of health issues due to air, water, and industrial pollution. Climate change is expected to exacerbate these already serious public health problems. From unprecedented industrial and vehicular growth to the dumping of chemical waste and municipal sewage in rivers, the build up to a public health catastrophe is already underway. India faces the prospect of a significant increase in cancers and respiratory illnesses. Most of urban India faces some form of toxic health threat due to the environment.

If environmental control is seen, managed, and sold as a public health enhancing intervention, then I would argue that much of this cacophony over 'environment versus development' would subside. That is why recently I have taken the initiative to bring the MoEF into a partnership with the Indian Council for Medical Research and the Public Health Foundation of India. Central to the objective of this initiative is the growth of environmental public health as an academic and practical discipline and creating a new cadre of trained professionals. Environmental public health as a formal discipline should ideally integrate streams of knowledge from diverse disciplines, integrating learnings and perspectives from life sciences, especially human biology, immunology and ecology; quantitative sciences such as epidemiology, biostatistics and demography; social sciences such as environmental health economics and policies; environmental toxicology; waste management; and occupational health.

One of the more visible and even successful environmental conservation efforts in India has been Project Tiger, launched under the leadership of Indira Gandhi in April 1973. True, there are just about 1,400–1,600 tigers left in the wild in our country today, although this accounts for around half of the world's tigers in the wild. There is an argument raging now, on why these Project Tiger reserves should be protected with such ferocity, especially when they come in the way of using our coal reserves, for instance, for generating electricity needed by a burgeoning population. Again, if the terms of the debate are posed thus—protection of tigers alone versus opening of new coal mines—I think we are headed nowhere. But when we highlight the fact that the thirty-nine Project Tiger reserves account for some 5 per cent of our forest areas and are home not only to tigers and other forms of biodiversity, but are also places from where many of our rivers originate, critical to our livelihoods, then I believe there is a greater chance of bridging the 'two cultures' gap.

Having said this, I want to return to the very formulation of this modern-day 'two cultures'. Is the debate really environment versus development or is it one of adhering to rules, regulations, and laws versus taking the rules, regulations, and laws for granted? I think the latter is a more accurate representation and a better way to formulate the choice. When an alumina refinery starts construction to expand its capacity from 1 million tonnes per year to 6 million tonnes per year without bothering to seek any environmental clearance as mandated by law, it is not an 'environment versus development' question, but simply one of whether laws enacted by Parliament will be respected or not. When closure notices are issued to distilleries or paper mills or sugar factories illegally discharging toxic wastes into India's most holy river, it is not a question of 'environment versus development' but again one of whether standards mandated by law are to be enforced effectively or not. When a power plant wants to draw water from a protected area or when a coal mine wants to undertake mining in the buffer zone of a tiger sanctuary, both in contravention of existing laws, it is not an 'environment versus development' question but simply one of whether laws will be adhered to or not.

India is fortunate to have strong, progressive legislations to safeguard its ecology. The Wildlife (Protection) Act of 1972, the Water Act of 1974, the Forest (Conservation) Act of 1980, the Air Act of 1981, the Environment (Protection) Act of 1986, and the most recent Forest Rights Act of 2006 have all been passed by Parliament after much discussion. The question before the country is very, very simple: Are these laws to be enforced or are they to just adorn the statute books, honoured more in their breach than in their observance? This is the more intellectually honest way of formulating Lord Snow's dialectic in the Indian context today.

I have to say that for too long, we have taken these laws and the discipline they enforce for granted. Industry has assumed that somehow these laws can be 'managed' and governments too have not insisted that the laws be implemented both in letter and spirit. We have now reached a crucial juncture when fait accompli will not do any longer. Gopal Gandhi put it to me recently in his own inimitable way—the thrill of circumvention must be replaced by the joy of compliance.

Of course, I would be the first to accept the need to relook at the ways in which regulations are enforced. Our traditional approach has been to automatically assume that tough regulations mean an army of regulators. There is a legitimate fear that this could end up being another source of what economists call 'rent seeking' or what ordinary human beings would call 'harassment' or 'corruption'. Of course with Right to Information (RTI), accountability of public agencies has increased manifold. But this may well not be enough. That is why I have been saying that we need to think of market-friendly instruments for enforcing regulations.

If you go look to the 1970s and see how the US dealt with the acid rain problem, you will find that while the US Environmental Protection Agency (EPA) set the standards, what ensured cost-effective success was an emissions trading system. Recently, I invited four leading economists from Massachusetts Institute of Technology (MIT) and Harvard to design the outline of a market-based system for us so as to enforce air quality standards more effectively. The team has prepared a concept paper, which is available on our website, and we are going to start with pilot programmes in Tamil Nadu and Gujarat. Online monitoring is clearly a pre-requisite for such an innovation to bear fruit.

I am also deeply conscious of the need to improve the system of environmental governance itself so as to enhance its credibility and integrity. This will go a long way in bridging the gap between the new 'two cultures'. Parliament has already passed the National Green Tribunal Act, 2010 and this specialized network of courts will come into being soon. We are now finalizing the establishment of a National Environmental Protection Authority (NEPA) that will be a permanent professional body to appraise projects and monitor compliance. Right now, these appraisals are done by ad hoc expert committees which have been plagued by a number of conflict of interest issues. NEPA will bring greater focus, objectivity, and professionalism in our environmental appraisal and monitoring process.

There is no doubt in my mind that India desperately needs to sustain a high growth trajectory for at least two–three decades. This is absolutely essential for meeting our pressing social objectives and also our key strategic objectives. At the same time, the 'growth first at all costs and environment later' approach is clearly unacceptable. India needs to press into its development all that modern science and technology has to offer. At the same time, the notion that we can impose technological fixes without caring for their larger ecological consequences and without addressing larger social concerns is clearly untenable anywhere, but even more so in an open, argumentative society like ours.

And, increasingly, these concerns are of the poor and the traditionally disadvantaged sections of society. This is giving a whole new dimension to the environment versus development debate. In fact, it is, in some ways, making the debate as formulated largely exaggerated. Sunita Narain puts it well when she says that India's environmental movement is about managing contradictions and complexities—and, to this, I would also add conflicts. This environmentalism of the poor, as she calls it, or livelihood environmentalism, as I would term it, as opposed to lifestyle environmentalism of the privileged sections, manifested itself on the national scene first in the mid-1970s with the birth and growth of the Chipko Movement in the hills of Uttarakhand. The women were asserting the rights of local communities over the use of local resources.

Such assertions are visible in different parts of the country today. We misread such assertions as the conflict between environment and development when they actually are about establishing a fundamental right to livelihood security and a fundamental right to determine the nature of what we call development that impacts their daily lives in a profoundly disturbing manner. Such assertions are also, I may add, a product of our boisterous democracy, which the growth-fundamentalists are uncomfortable with, and the empowerment it has engendered. Sustainable development, we need to remind ourselves every now and then, is as much of politics and involvement of local communities as it is of innovation and new technology. In a powerful new book distinguished Indian economist Bina Agarwal highlights the centrality of the presence and participation of women in institutions of local green governance so essential for achieving the goals of sustainable development.

I am now coming to the end of this lecture. Let me end as I started— by remembering Professor Satish Dhawan. His academic credentials were impeccable. He was steeped in modernity. Yet, he was never oblivious of the larger social context in which he operated. It is this spirit that we need to recapture—this spirit of public engagement cutting across disciplinary boundaries but with discipline and in a spirit of humility. This engagement is essential if we are to bridge the two cultures. I had spoken earlier of the breakdown of communications between the two sides. I saw this most vividly during the course of the public consultations I had on Bt-brinjal. Incidentally, the gap was at its vociferous peak in the two cities which pride themselves as representing the scientific and technological face of a new India, namely, Bangalore and Hyderabad. Here particularly, and in other cities, too, I found the scientific community unable to communicate in a language and in an idiom that is comprehensible to a larger public.

Democracy means the need to explain, the need to justify, the need to convince, the need to get people on board, the need to compromise. Speaking at the Jawaharlal Nehru Centre for Advanced Scientific Research (JNCASR) and recalling the memory of the man after whom the centre is named, I would urge the scientific community and the larger community of growth-fetishists that they have a special role to play in this regard. They need to engage the larger public in a more collegial and in a less condescending manner. I can do no better than quote from Indira Gandhi's famous speech at the UN Conference on the Human Environment delivered on 13 June 1972. The most famous one-liner from that speech that is still in wide use is 'poverty is the worst polluter', no matter that what she actually said was a more nuanced 'are not poverty and need the greatest polluters?' In that very seminal speech, she had also said—and this is really the essence of the message I wish to convey today—that 'the inherent conflict is not between conservation and development, but between environment and the reckless exploitation of man and earth in the name of efficiency'.

Speaking Order Rejecting the Proposal for Diversion of Forest Area Submitted by Odisha Mining Corporation Ltd for Bauxite Mining in the Niyamgiri Hills in the Kalahandi and Rayagada Districts, Odisha

[The mined bauxite was to be used exclusively by Vedanta at its alumina refinery in Lanjigarh, which is located in the foot of the Niyamgiri Hills]

Brief Background

On 28 February 2005, a proposal was forwarded by the state government of Odisha for the diversion of 660.749 ha of forest land for mining of bauxite ore in favour of the Odisha Mining Corporation (OMC) in Kalahandi and Rayaga districts.

The Forest Advisory Committee (FAC) in the MoEF met thrice thereafter and recommended 'in principle' approval on 27 October 2007 stipulating certain conditions like concurrent reclamation, minimum tree felling in phased manner modified wildlife management plan, etc.

Following this, the Supreme Court delivered its judgement on 23 November 2007. In this judgement the Supreme Court issued orders laying down certain conditions that were to be fulfilled by the company before forest clearance could be granted. One condition laid down was that Sterlite (SIIC) or OMC would be charged with the execution of the project while Vedanta, in all its forms, was not to be involved.

The Supreme Court delivered a second judgment on 8 August 2008, in which it held:

> For the above reasons and in the light of the Affidavits filed by SIIC, OMCL and State of Odisha, accepting the rehabilitation package, suggested in our order of 23 November 2007, we hereby grant clearance—to the forest diversion proposal for diversion of 660.749 ha of forest land to undertake bauxite mining on the Niyamgiri Hills in Lanjigarh. The next step would be for MoEF to grant its approval in accordance with law.

Subsequently, the MoEF formally issued the 'in principle' approval to the state government on 11 December 2008. It also bears mention that the Central Empowered Committee of the Supreme Court had submitted its report on this project on 21 September 2005, in which it expressed the view the diversion of forest land as envisaged should not be permitted. It had also recommended that the environmental clearance granted by the MoEF for the alumina refinery plant on 22 September 2004 be revoked and all work be stopped.

Stage-II Examination in the MoEF

On 10 August 2009, the state government applied for final clearance to the MoEF. The FAC considered the matter on 4 November 2009. In this meeting, the FAC recommended that final clearance be considered only after ascertaining community rights on forest land and after the process for establishing such rights under the Scheduled Tribes and Traditional Forest Dwellers (Recognition of Forest Rights) Act, 2006, also known as the Forest Rights Act, 2006 (FRA), is completed. The FAC also decided to constitute an expert group to carry out a site inspection. Thereafter on 1 January 2010, a three-member team composed of Dr Usha Ramanathan (a noted expert on tribal issues), Vinod Rishi (former director, Project Elephant) and J.K. Tiwari (Regional Conservator of Forests, MoEF, Bhubaneswar), was set up to consider and make recommendations to the MoEF on the proposal submitted by OMC. The team carried out site visits during the months of January and February 2010 following which it submitted three individual reports to the MoEF on 25 February 2010. These reports provided valuable field-level information. However, they also revealed the need for further detailed examination on various counts and also the need to look upon different issues of relevance in an integrated manner.

On 16 April 2010, the FAC met to consider these three reports. It recommended that a special committee under the Ministry of Tribal Affairs be constituted to look into the issues relating to the violation of tribal rights and the settlement of forest rights under the FRA, 2006.

Therefore, on 29 June 2010, keeping in mind the primary responsibility and obligation of the MoEF itself and also keeping in mind that on 13 April 2010, the MoEF and the Ministry of Tribal Affairs had already jointly set up a committee to look into implementation of the FRA, 2006, I decided to constitute a team—composed of specialists, which would be charged with looking into (i) settlement of the rights of forest dwellers and the 'Primitive Tribal Groups' (PGT) under the FRA, 2006; and (ii) impact on wildlife and biodiversity in the surrounding areas.

Accordingly, Dr N.C. Saxena, Dr Amita Baviskar, Dr Pramode Kant, and Dr S. Parasuraman, all of whom have impeccable professional credentials, were invited to join the committee. Dr Saxena is also the chairman of the joint MoEF–Ministry of Tribal Affairs committee to study and assess the impacts of the FRA, 2006. Dr Baviskar is also a member of the FAC. The terms of reference for this committee were drafted in a manner that would facilitate a holistic, rather than a piecemeal, investigation. The committee submitted its report to the MoEF on 16 August 2010 and the report was made available immediately on the ministry's website.

Salient Findings of the Saxena Committee

I wish to recall here the main findings of the Saxena Committee that have a bearing on the decision whether or not to grant final Stage-II approval:

Ecological Costs of Mining

1. Mining operations of the intensity proposed in this project spread over more than 7 sq km would *severely disturb this important wildlife habitat* that has been proposed as a part of the Niyamgiri Wildlife Sanctuary.
2. More than 1.21 lakh trees would need to be cleared for mining besides many lakhs more shrubs and herbal flora.
3. Mining in the PML [Proposed Mining Lease] will destroy the valuable 'edge effect' of the grassland-forest landscape and adversely affect wildlife in the area.
4. The grasses are breeding and fawning ground for four-horned antelope (*Tetracerus quadricornis*), barking deer (*Muntiacus muntjac*) as well as spotted deer (*Axis axis*). A rare lizard, golden gecko (*Callodactylodes aureus*), is found in the proposed lease area. The populations of all these species will decline if mining is allowed.
5. The value of Niyamgiri Hill forests as an important elephant habitat is well recognized by its inclusion in the South Odisha Elephant Reserve. Mining on the scale proposed in this habitat would *severely disturb elephant habitats, and threaten the important task of elephant conservation* in south Odisha.
6. The mining operations in the PML site involves stripping off more than 7 sq km of the Niyamgiri Hill top which would *drastically alter the region's water supply*, severely affecting both ecological systems and human communities dependent on this water.

Human Costs of Mining

1. The PML area is intimately linked, by way of economic, religious, and cultural ties, to twenty-eight Kondh villages with a total population

of 5,148 persons. The affected include about 1,453 Dongaria Kondh, which constitutes 20 per cent of the total population of this tribe.

2. If the economic, social, and cultural life of one-fifth of the Dongaria Kondh population is directly affected by the mining, it will threaten the well-being of the entire community.

3. Since the Dongaria and Kutia Kondh are heavily dependent on forest produce for their livelihood, this forest cover loss will cause a significant decline in their economic well-being. Landless Dalits who live in these villages and are dependent upon the Kondh will also be similarly affected.

4. Lands that the Dongaria Kondh cultivate lie in close proximity to the PML area. Mining-related activities such as tree-felling, blasting, the removal of soil, road building, and the movement of heavy machinery will deny them access to their lands that they have used for generations.

5. These activities will also adversely affect the surrounding slopes and streams that are crucial for their agriculture.

Violations of the Forest Rights Act

1. It is established beyond any doubt that the area proposed for mining lease and the surrounding thick forests are the cultural, religious, and economic habitat of the Kondh Primitive Tribal Groups. Discouraging and denying the claims of the Primitive Tribal Groups without the due process of law is illegal on the part of the district or sub-divisional committees. Since the provisions of the FRA have not been followed by the state government, and the legitimate and well established rights of the Kondh Primitive Tribe Groups have been deliberately disregarded by the district administration and the state government, the only course of the action open before MoEF is to withdraw the Stage-I clearance given under Forest Conservation Act for the said area.

2. From the evidence collected by the committee, we conclude that the Odisha government is not likely to implement FRA in a fair and impartial manner as far as the PML area is concerned. Since it has gone to the extent of forwarding false certificates and may do so again in future, the MoEF would be well-advised not to accept the contentions of the Odisha government without independent

verification. The Government of India should, therefore, engage a credible professional authority to assist people in filing their claims under the community clause for the PML area with the state administration.

3. In sum, the MoEF cannot grant clearance for diversion of forest land for non-forest purposes unless:
   a. The process of recognition of rights under the FRA is complete and satisfactory;
   b. The consent of the concerned community has been granted; and
   c. Both points have been certified by the *gram sabha* of the area concerned (which must be that of the hamlet being a Scheduled Area).

4. All of these conditions, not any one, must be satisfied. This is irrespective of the fact whether people have filed claims or not. In short, the circular of 3 August 2009, by the MoEF which lays down these conditions, has articulated the correct legal position.

5. If mining is permitted on this site it will not only be illegal but it will also:
   a. Destroy one of the most sacred sites of the Kondh Primitive Tribal Groups;
   b. Destroy more than 7 sq km of sacred, undisturbed forest land on top of the mountain that has been protected by the Dongaria Kondh for centuries as sacred to Niyam Raja and as essential to preserving the region's fertility;
   c. Endanger the self-sufficient forest-based livelihoods of these Primitive Tribal Groups;
   d. Seriously harm the livelihood of hundreds of Dalit families who indirectly depend upon these lands through their economic relationship with these primitive tribal groups; and
   e. Build roads through the Dongaria Kondh's territories, making the area easily accessible to poachers of wildlife and timber smugglers threatening the rich biodiversity of the hills.

Violation of Forest Conservation Act

The company is in illegal occupation of 26.123 ha of village forest lands enclosed within the factory premises. The claim by the company that they have only followed the state government orders and enclosed the forest lands within their factory premises to protect these lands and that they provide access to the tribal and other villagers to their village forest lands is completely false. This is an act of total contempt for the law on the part of the company and shows an appalling degree of collusion on the part of the concerned officials.

For the construction of a road running parallel to the conveyor corridor, the company has illegally occupied plot number 157 (p) measuring 1 acre and plot number 133 measuring 0.11 acres of village forest lands. This act is also similar to the above although the land involved is much smaller in extent.

Violation of the Environment Protection Act

The company M/s Vedanta Alumina Ltd has already proceeded with construction activity for its expansion project that would increase its capacity sixfold from 1 MTPA (million tonnes per annum) to 6 MTPA *without obtaining environmental clearance as per provisions of* EIA (Environment Impact Assessment) Notification, 2006 under the Environment Protection Act. This amounts to a serious violation of the provisions of the Environment (Protection) Act, 1986. This expansion, its extensive scale and advanced nature, is in complete violation of the EPA and is an expression of the contempt with which this company treats the laws of the land.

Violation of Conditions of Clearance Granted to Refinery

The refinery was accorded clearance under the Environment Protection Act on the condition that no forest land would be used for the establishment of the refinery. But now it is clearly established that the company has occupied 26.123 ha of village forest lands within the refinery boundary with the active collusion of concerned officials. Hence, the environmental clearance given to the company for setting up the refinery is legally invalid and has to be set aside.

Very Limited Relevance to the Expanded Refinery

The mining activities in the PML site will have limited relevance to the refinery now under a six-fold expansion as the 72 MT ore deposit here would last only about four years for the increased needs of the expanded refinery. In balance against this are the severe adverse consequences on the primitive tribal people, environment, forests, and wildlife that inhabit these forests.

Overall Conclusion of the Saxena Committee

In view of the above, this committee is of the firm view that allowing mining in the proposed mining lease area by depriving two Primitive Tribal Groups of their rights over the proposed mining site in order to benefit a private company would shake the faith of tribal people in the laws of the land. Since the company in question has repeatedly violated the law, allowing it further access to the proposed mining area at the cost of the rights of the Kutia and Dongaria Kondh, this will have serious consequences for the security and well-being of the entire country.

On 17 August 2010, the state government wrote to the MoEF expressing certain grievances with the findings of the Saxena Committee and requested an opportunity to be heard before any decision was taken on the committee's report. A copy of this letter was forwarded by the MoEF to the members of the committee to enable them to respond to the charges contained therein. Dr N.C. Saxena replied on 23 August 2010.[4] Dr Saxena stated that all findings of the committee were based on direct interactions with the state government officials.

Meeting with the Chief Minister of Odisha and State Government Officials

On 23 August 2010, I met with the chief minister of Odisha and the principal secretary of the state in New Delhi. The chief minister told me that since the Supreme Court had already granted 'in principle' approval subject to certain conditions and since the state government had already fulfilled those conditions, final approval should now be given by the MoEF.

Thereafter, on 24 August 2010, I met with a delegation of officers from the Odisha state government who reiterated the points made by the chief minister. In addition, these officers challenged the Saxena Committee on five specific grounds: (i) impact of hilltop mining and aquifers; (ii) impact of mining on vegetation and biodiversity; (iii) impact of mining on wildlife; (iv) customary rights of primitive tribal groups; and (v) the role of the gram sabha and other procedural issues relating to the implementation of the FRA, 2006. The state government officials were also very critical of the Saxena Committee's report for the observations made on their role in the implementation of the FRA, 2006.

Basis of the Final Decision on Stage-II Clearance

Clarification from the Attorney General of India

Before a decision on the merits of the case could be taken, there were some questions regarding the role and procedure to be followed by the MoEF. By virtue of the fact that the Supreme Court in its judgment dated 8 August 2008 had 'granted' clearance to the project, there were doubts raised as to what role that left for the MoEF to discharge.

By way of abundant caution, on 19 July 2010, I wrote to the law minister to solicit the opinion of the learned Attorney General of India on the matter. Shortly thereafter, on 20 July 2010, the learned Attorney General submitted his opinion to the Ministry of Law stating, among other things, that the MoEF was in no way restricted by the Supreme Court judgment of 8 August 2008, even if the MoEF chose to deny the clearance. The learned Attorney General stated that there was 'never any question that the clearance from the Supreme Court was meant to obviate the necessity of obtaining clearance from the central government'.

In direct response to my question as to whether the decision of the Supreme Court to grant forest clearance was final and binding or subject to approval and ratification by the MoEF, the learned Attorney General unambiguously answered in the negative and opined as follows:

> The MoEF is bound to apply its own mind and grant independent clearance to the project. Needless to say, if approval is to be granted then all the terms stipulated by the Supreme Court have to be incorporated. However, that question would not arise if it is decided that the approval is not to be granted, for cogent and valid reasons.

Observations of the Forest Advisory Committee, dated 23 August 2010

On 20 August 2010, the Saxena Committee's report was placed before the FAC in accordance with Section 3 of the Forest (Conservation) Act,

1980. The FAC noted that: 'The FAC has found compelling and significant evidence of prima facie violations of the following laws: Forest Rights Act, Forest Conservation and the Environmental Protection Act. Any clearance would thus be in contravention of the above legislation (sic)'.

The FAC also noted that it has the highest regard for the Hon. Supreme Court and is acting strictly in accordance with its ruling dated 23 November 2007. The FAC's report has recognized and recorded the following violations:

1. Violation of the FRA, 2006: The FAC has found that there has been a violation of section 3(1)(e) of the FRA, which relates to the rights of the Primitive Tribal Groups. The FAC found as follows—'As seen in the report of the Committee, it is apparent that there has been a serious failure to implement these specific provisions of the FRA to protect the culture, livelihood and rights, "including community tenure of habitat and habitation" as specified in the FRA, of people belonging to the Dongaria Kondh and Kutia Kondh tribes, which are both PTGs'.

   Relying on the Saxena Committee's reports the FAC concluded that the Primitive Tribal Groups were not consulted in the process of seeking project clearance.

2. Violation of the Forest (Conservation) Act, 1980: The FAC has relied on the findings of the Saxena Committee's report stating that M/s Vedanta Alumina Ltd to whom the bauxite extracted from the Niyamgiri mines is to be supplied, has illegally enclosed 26.123 ha of Gram Jogya Jungal (village forest) within premises of an alumina refinery set up at Lanjigarh, thereby denying access to the villagers. Similarly for construction of a road running parallel to the conveyer corridor, M/s Vedanta Alumina Ltd has illegally occupied plot number 157 (p) measuring 1.0 acre and plot number 133 measuring 0.11 acres of village forest lands.

3. Violation of the Environment (Protection) Act, 1986: The FAC has found that the project proponent M/s Vedanta Alumina Ltd has already proceeded with construction activity for its enormous expansion of its aluminium refinery project at Lanjigarh to increase its capacity sixfold from 1 MTPA to 6 MTPA without obtaining prior and complete environment clearance as per provisions of the EIA Notification, 2006 under the Environment (Protection) Act, 1986.

However, we are informed that 60 per cent of the additional construction has been completed.

4. Violation of the condition of clearance under the Environment (Protection) Act, 1986: The FAC has taken note of the Saxena Committee's findings that certain facts were concealed by the project proponent while seeking environmental clearance. On 16 August 2004, Vedanta Alumina submitted a proposal for diversion of 58.943 ha of forest land for setting up a refinery at Lanjigarh and for a conveyer belt, which included 26.123 ha of forest land for the refinery, and the rest for a conveyer belt and a road to the mining site. However, while filing environmental clearance on 19 March 2003, the company claimed that no forest lands were needed and that there was no reserved forest within 10 km of the proposed refinery. Later on, learning from the CEC that a proposal for diversion of forest land for setting up of the said refinery is pending before the ministry, the MoEF vide notice dated 23 May 2005 directed M/s Vedanta that further construction should be undertaken only after getting the requisite clearance under the Forest (Conservation) Act, 1980. Instead of obeying the orders of the MoEF, the company informed the MoEF that they did not need the use of 58.943 ha of forest land. They also continue to claim that the refinery project does not use any forest land. The refinery however, continues to occupy all the lands including the 26.123 ha of forest land, with the full knowledge of the district administration, which has allowed its continued illegal occupation. While the enclosure of village forests is in violation of the law, the incomplete and inaccurate information given by the project proponent is an equally grave matter. The FAC has recommended that this matter be investigated fully by the MoEF and acted upon as required under law.

5. Impact on biodiversity: The FAC has found that the high ecological and biodiversity values of the Niyamgiri Hills, upon which the Dongaria Kondh and Kutia Kondh depend, will be irretrievably damaged by mining. The FAC has gone on to observe that the area is home to species, which are listed in Schedule-I of the Wildlife (Protection) Act, 1972 such as the four-horned antelope. It has concluded that mining on this scale in this ecologically sensitive area will lead to the economic and cultural life of the dependent human population.

6. Very limited relevance of the proposed mining lease: The FAC has observed that the mining activity in the proposed mining lease site at Niyamgiri will have limited relevance to the Lanjigarh refinery now under six-fold expansion as the 72 MT ore deposit here would last only about four years for the increased needs of the expanded refinery.

7. Questionable sourcing of bauxite ore by the company: The FAC has expressed concern at the finding of the Saxena Committee that the current expansion plans rely on bauxite being sourced from questionable sources. Given the expansion sought to be undertaken the current supply of bauxite can only fuel the operations of the refinery for four years. The FAC noted it is 'a cause for concern that, as per the report, the bulk of the bauxite ore presently being used by the refinery is being sourced from fourteen mines, eleven of which do not have the requisite environmental clearance as per the latest available information'.

8. Recommendation of the FAC dated 23 August 2010: In the opinion of the FAC, the Saxena Committee report clearly indicates the lack of diligence in safeguarding the rights of the Primitive Tribal Groups in the adjoining forest areas and unless the state government provides evidence of their serious intent for following observance of due process of law, it appears to the FAC that this is a breach of law.

Based on this analysis, the FAC has found that this is a fit case for applying the precautionary principle to obviate irreparable damage to the affected people, and recommends for temporary withdrawal of the in-principle/stage-I approval accorded, in accordance with Section 2 of the Forest (Conservation) Act, 1980 by the MoEF for the diversion of 660.749 ha forest land in favour of the OMC for bauxite mining in Niyamgiri Hills in the Kalahandi and Rayagada districts of Odisha.

The FAC has further advised the ministry to consider suitable action under the law in respect of the violations pointed out vis-à-vis environmental clearance given or under consideration for the alumina refinery.

Before taking a final decision, the FAC recommended that the MoEF give an opportunity to the state government to be heard, a process that I have followed including hearing no less a person than the chief minister of the state himself.

Factors Dictating Decision on Stage-II Clearance

I have considered three broad factors while arriving at my decision:

Violation of the Rights of the Tribal Groups, Including the Primitive Tribal Groups and the Dalit Population

The blatant disregard displayed by the project proponents with regard to rights of the tribal and primitive tribal groups dependent on the area for their livelihoods, as they have proceeded to seek clearance is shocking. Primitive Tribal Groups have specifically been provided for in the FRA, 2006 and this case should leave no one in doubt that they will enjoy full protection of their rights under the law. The narrow definition of the project affected people by the state government runs contrary to the letter and spirit of the FRA, 2006. Simply because they did not live on the hills does not mean they have no rights there. The FRA, 2006 specifically provides for such rights but these were not recognized and were sought to be denied.

Moreover, the fate of the Primitive Tribal Groups needs some emphasis, as very few communities in India, in general, and Odisha, in particular, come under the ambit of such a category. Their dependence on the forest being almost complete, the violation of the specific protections extended to their 'habitat and habitations' by the FRA, 2006 are simply unacceptable.

This ground by itself has to be foremost in terms of consideration when it comes to the grant of forest or environmental clearance. The four-member committee has highlighted repeated instances of violations.

One also cannot ignore the Dalits living in the area. While they may technically be ineligible to receive benefits under the FRA, 2006, they are such an inextricable part of the society that exists that it would be impossible to disentitle them as they have been present for over five decades. The committee has also said on page 40 of their report that 'even if the Dalits have no claims under the FRA the truth of their de-facto dependence on the Niyamgiri forests for the past several decades can be ignored by the central and state governments only at the cost of the betrayal of the promise of inclusive growth and justice and dignity for all Indians'. This observation rings true with the MoEF and underscores the MoEF's attempt to ensure that any decision taken is not just true to the law in letter but also in spirit.

Violations of the Environmental Protection Act, 1986

1. Observations of the Saxena Committee and MoEF records: In addition to its findings regarding the settlement of rights under the FRA, 2006, the four-member committee has also observed—with reference to the environmental clearance granted for the alumina refinery—on page 7 of its report dated 16 August 2010, that:

   The company M/s Vedanta Alumina Limited has already proceeded with construction activity for its enormous expansion project that would increase its capacity six-fold from 1 MTPA to 6 MTPA without obtaining environmental clearance as per the provisions of the EIA Notification, 2006 under the Environment Protection Act. This amounts to a serious violation of the provisions of the Environment Protection Act. This expansion, its extensive scale and advanced nature, is in complete violation of the Environment Protection Act and is an expression of the contempt with which this company treats the laws of the land.

2. Case before the NEAA by Dongaria Kondhs: After the grant of environment clearance, the local tribal population and other concerned persons, including the Dongaria Kondhs, challenged the project before the National Environment Appellate Authority (NEAA)— *Kumati Majhi and ors* vs. *MoEF, Srabbu Sika and ors* vs. *MoEF, Prafulla Samantara* vs *MoEF and ors* Appeal Nos. 18, 19, 20, and 21 of 2009.

   It is brought to my attention that this is the first time that the Dongaria Kondhs have directly challenged the project in any court of law. The appeals highlighted the several violations in the environmental clearance process. Some of the key charges raised were that the full environment impact assessment report was not made available to the public before the public hearing; different EIA reports made available to the public and submitted to the MoEF, the EIA conducted was a rapid EIA undertaken during the monsoon months. The matter is reserved for judgment before the NEAA.

3. Monitoring report of the Eastern Regional Office dated 25 May 2010: On 25 May 2010, Dr V.P. Upadhyay (Director 'S') of the Eastern Regional office of the MoEF submitted its report to the MoEF, which

listed various violations in para 2 of the monitoring report. They observed:

1. 'M/s Vedanta Alumina Limited has already proceeded with construction activity for expansion project without obtaining environmental clearance as per provisions of EIA Notification, 2006 that amounts to violation of the provisions of the Environment Protection Act.'

2. 'The project has not established piezometers for monitoring of ground water quality around red mud and ash disposal ponds; thus, the condition no. 5 of Specific Condition of the clearance letter is being violated.'

3. 'The condition no. 1 of the General Conditions of environmental clearance has been violated by starting expansion activities without prior approval from the ministry.'

Furthermore, all bauxite for the refinery was to be sourced from mines which have already obtained environmental clearance. The report listed fourteen mines from which bauxite was being sourced by the project proponents. However out of these, eleven had not been granted a mining licence, while two had only received terms of reference (ToR), and only one had received clearance.

Violations Under the Forest Conservation Act

The Saxena Committee has gone into great detail highlighting the various instances of violations under the Forest (Conservation) Act, 1980. All these violations—coupled with the resultant impact on the ecology and biodiversity of the surrounding area—further condemn the actions of the project proponent. Not only are these violations of a repeating nature but they are instances of willful concealment of information by the project proponent.

Decision on Stage-II Clearance

The Saxena Committee's evidence as reviewed by the FAC and read by me as well is compelling. The violations of the various legislations, especially the Forest (Conservation) Act, 1980, the Environment (Protection) Act, 1986, and the FRA, 2006, appear to be too egregious to be glossed over. Furthermore, a mass of new and incriminating evidence has come to light since the apex court delivered its judgment on 8 August 2008. Therefore, after careful consideration of the facts at hand, due deliberation over all the reports submitted and while upholding the recommendation of the FAC, I have come to the following considerations:

1. The Stage-II forest clearance for the OMC and Sterlite bauxite mining project on Niyamgiri Hills in the Lanjigarh, Kalahandi, and Rayagada districts of Odisha cannot be granted. Stage-II forest clearance, therefore, stands rejected.
2. Since the forest clearance is being rejected, the environmental clearance for this mine is inoperable.
3. It appears that the project proponent is sourcing bauxite from a large number of mines in Jharkhand for the 1 MT alumina refinery that are not in possession of valid environmental clearance. This matter is being examined separately.
4. Further, a show-cause notice is being issued by the MoEF to the project proponent as to why the environmental clearance for the 1 MTPA alumina refinery should not be cancelled.
5. A show-cause notice is also being issued to the project proponent as to why the ToRs for the EIA report for the expansion from 1 MT to 6 MT should not be withdrawn. Meanwhile, the ToR and the appraisal process for the expansion stands suspended.

Separately, the MoEF is in the process of examining what penal action should be initiated against the project proponents for the violations of various laws as documented exhaustively by the Saxena Committee.

On the issues raised by the Odisha state government, I must point out that while customary rights of the Primitive Tribal Groups are not recognized in the National Forest Policy, 1988, they are an integral part of the FRA, 2006. An Act passed by Parliament has greater sanctity than a policy statement. This is apart from the fact that the FRA came into force eighteen years after the National Forest Policy. On the other points raised by the state government officials, on the procedural aspects of the FRA, 2006, I expect that the joint committee set up by the MoEF and the Ministry of Tribal Affairs would give them due consideration. The state government officials were upset with the observations made by the Saxena Committee on their role in implementing the FRA, 2006.

Whether state government officials have connived with the violations is a separate issue and is not relevant to my decision. I am prepared to believe that the state government officials were attempting to discharge their obligations to the best of their abilities and with the best of intentions. The state government could well contest many of the observations made by the Saxena Committee. But this will not fundamentally alter the fact that serious violations of various laws have indeed taken place.

The primary responsibility of any ministry is to enforce the laws that have been passed by Parliament. For the MoEF, this means enforcing the Forest (Conservation) Act, 1980, the Environmental (Protection Act), 1986, the Forest Rights Act, 2006, and other laws. It is in this spirit that this decision has been taken.

Finally, in view of the enormous interest and concern that has been generated both nationally and internationally, I feel it is incumbent on me to make this final decision available to the public in full. All supporting documentation is also being made available on the ministry website.

Speaking Order on the POSCO Integrated Steel Plant Project at Jagatsinghpur, Odisha

2 May 2011

On 31 January 2011, I had announced that the final forest clearance for the POSCO project in Odisha would be given after the receipt of certain categorical assurances from the state government.[5]

On 13 April 2011, the state government communicated these assurances to MoEF. On 14 April 2011 because of two supposed *palli sabha* resolutions I received from the POSCO Pratirodha Sangram Samiti, I referred the matter back to the state government.[6] On 29 April 2011, the state government responded to my letter of 14 April 2011.[7]

The Government of Odisha in its latest reply dated 29 April 2011 has stated the following:

1. The two palli sabha[8] resolutions—of Dhinkia dated 21 February 2011 and of Gobindpur dated 23 February 2011—are not valid documents in terms of mandatory provisions of law under the Odisha Grama Panchayat Act, 1964 and FRA, 2006. Such resolutions can neither be relied on nor be acted upon.

2. Palli sabha of 3,445 voters of Dhinkia, only sixty-nine persons have allegedly signed the so-called palli sabha resolution of 25 February 2011, and of 1,907 voters of Gobindpur, only sixty-four persons have allegedly signed the palli sabha resolution of 23 February 2011. This clearly shows that the 'resolutions' are invalid.

3. The two 'resolutions' purported to have been passed by the palli sabha are not available in the book (recorded by the gram panchayat secretary and signed by the sarpanch) and are, therefore, fake ones.

4. Stringent action for violation of provisions of Odisha Grama Panchayat Act, 1964 will be taken against Sisir Mohapatra, sarpanch, Dhinkia who has overstepped the jurisdiction vested in him and misutilized his official position to serve the interest of POSCO Pratirodha Sangram Samiti (PPSS) of which he is the secretary.

I have gone through various provisions of the Odisha Grama Panchayat Act, 1964, Forest Rights Act, 2006 and Forest Rights Rules, 2007. The main issue here is whether the two supposed palli sabha resolutions that I received from the POSCO Pratirodha Sangram Samiti, and that were sent on 14 April to the Odisha government for disposal according to law, are legally valid documents or not.

According to Rule 4(2) of the Forest Rights Rules, 2007, the quorum of the gram sabha meeting shall not be less than two-thirds of all members of such a gram sabha. As per the report of the Odisha government, the number of members was far less than the prescribed quorum.

Further, according to Rule 3(1) of the Forest Rights Rules, 2007, the gram sabhas should be convened by the gram panchayat, whereas in this case these seem to have been convened by the sarpanch without the authority of the gram panchayat. Rule 20(a) of the Odisha Grama Panchayat Rules, 1968, which has also authorized only the gram panchayat to convene the palli sabha.

Lastly, as per the requirements of Rule 26 of the Odisha Grama Panchayat Rules, the proceedings of the palli sabha should be recorded in a book specially maintained for this purpose. In the instant case, as per the report of the district collector, the resolutions under question are not available in that book.

For these reasons, and based on the information provided by the state government, I have no option but to come to the conclusion that there has been no legally valid resolution of the gram sabha claiming recognition of forest rights as required under Section 6(1) of the FRA, 2006.

I now have three options available to me—seek further legal opinion on what the state government has stated, institute an independent inquiry into the claims and counter-claims being made by the state government and the PPSS, or repose trust in what the state government has so categorically asserted.

I have already examined the legal issues, therefore, that there is nothing to be gained by seeking further legal opinion. Similarly the facts of the case, in particular the lack of signatures of two-thirds of the village adult population on the resolution passed by the sarpanch, are too obvious to require any further enquiry or verification

I have, therefore, decided to follow the third route because the primary responsibility for implementing the FRA, 2006 is that of the state government through the institutions of the gram sabha, sub-divisional officer (SDO), and the district collector. I must respect the reports from the SDO and the collector. Their views and also of the state government must prevail unless there is overwhelming and clinching evidence to the contrary.[9] Therefore, I hold that there has been no valid claim for recognition of forest rights in Dhinkia and Gobindpur as required under the FRA, 2006.

Faith and trust in what the state government says is an essential pillar of cooperative federalism which is why I rejected the second option. Beyond a point, the bona fides of a democratically elected state government cannot always be questioned by the central government.

I am conscious of the fact that the memorandum of understanding (MoU) between the state government and POSCO expired last year and has yet to be renewed. This MoU had provisions for the export of iron ore which made me deeply uncomfortable with this project. I would expect that the revised MoU between the state and POSCO would be negotiated in such a manner that exports of raw material are completely avoided. In addition, the appeal of the state government against the decision of the Odisha High Court striking down the allocation of the Khandadhar iron ore mines to POSCO is still pending in the Supreme Court. I could well have waited for the MoU to be renewed and for a final decision of the Supreme Court, but that would have smacked of filibustering. I would now hope that the new MoU would be negotiated by the state government in such a way that exports of iron ore are completely avoided.

Therefore, in view of the state government's latest communication of 29 April 2011, final approval is accorded to the state government for diversion of 1,253 ha of forest land in favour of POSCO. This approval would, however, be subject to the condition that, in addition to the conditions already imposed on compensatory afforestation, payment of NPV, etc., POSCO would also bear the cost of regeneration of an equivalent amount of open, degraded forest land in a district to be determined and indicated by the state government.

I also expect that the state government would immediately pursue action, under the Odisha Grama Panchayat Act, 1964, against the sarpanch, Dhinkia, for what it has categorically said are 'fraudulent' acts. If no action is taken forthwith, I believe that the state government's arguments will be called into serious question.

I want to address the question of whether my decision will weaken the implementation of the FRA, 2006. To these critics I would answer that it was at my personal insistence that in August 2009, the MoEF made adherence to the FRA, 2006 an essential pre-requisite for allowing diversion of forest land for non-forestry purposes under the Forest (Conservation) Act, 1980. I was under no obligation or pressure to do so except my own commitment to FRA, 2006. The implementation of both the FRA, 2006 and the August 2009 guideline is a learning and an evolving process since we are still in largely uncharted territory. The MoEF will continue to upgrade and improve the process to ensure compliance with the law in letter and in spirit. The environment and forest clearance process for the POSCO project has generated huge interest both in India and abroad. As I had pointed out in my decision of 31 January 2011, the POSCO project itself has considerable economic, technological, and strategic significance for both the state and the country. At the same time, laws on the environment and forests must be implemented seriously. In this case, the sixty conditions imposed as part of my decision of 31 January 2011 provide a package of measures to ensure that the project will not be detrimental from an ecological and local livelihoods point of view. I would expect both the state and POSCO to be extra-sensitive on this score.

This has not been an easy decision to take and it will, I know, be both welcomed and criticized. That is perhaps inevitable given the complex nature of the issues involved. But what I want to be clearly appreciated is that all along I have tried to uphold the principle of due process. I believe as minister my responsibility is not just to do the right thing, but to do the thing right.

Letter to Chief Minister of Maharashtra Ashok Chavan on the Navi Mumbai Airport

18 JUNE 2009
I have just received your response to my letter of 17 June 2009 regarding the proposed location of the international airport at Navi Mumbai. I am very happy that you share my concerns regarding the protection of mangroves. I am also very happy that you have reiterated the commitment of the Government of Maharashtra to implement the project with minimal effects on the environment.

You have raised a number of issues in your letter on the background to the selection of this particular location. I am having the matter examined in detail. I will revert to you on the points that you have made after I have checked up all the facts. Meanwhile, I would request you to have the ToR for the EIA submitted to us as soon as possible. I assure you that these ToR will be considered expeditiously and in a most professional manner.

Letter to Chief Minister of Maharashtra Ashok Chavan on protecting Mangroves in the Navi Mumbai Airport Project Area

10 NOVEMBER 2009
You may recall our discussions on your proposal for building a new international airport in Navi Mumbai and the concern I had expressed to you regarding the destruction of over 350 acres of mangrove forests as a result of this proposed project.

I have now come to understand that Gujarat Ecology Commission has been very successful in restoring mangroves. Over last ten years, Gujarat is the only state where the area under mangroves has increased and it has increased very substantially almost six-fold. The Gujarat Ecology Commission appears to have done excellent work in this area and I feel that the expertise that they have developed can be usefully utilized by City and Industrial Development Corporation of Maharashtra (CIDCO) to see how damage to mangroves could be minimized and also to see how mangroves can be restored in Navi Mumbai and elsewhere.

Letter to Prime Minister Apprising Him on the Facts Related to the Navi Mumbai Airport and Mining in the Tadoba-Andhari Tiger Reserve

21 JANUARY 2010

I understand that both Sharad Pawar and Praful Patel have met with you regarding my stand on the Navi Mumbai Airport and the Adani coal mining project in the buffer of the Tadoba-Andhari Tiger Reserve. I wish to place before you some facts that might *not* have been brought to your attention.

The Coastal Regulation Zone (CRZ) Notification, 1991 was amended as per the Prime Minister's Office's advice on 6 January 2009. This amendment said 'development of greenfield airport at Navi Mumbai shall be undertaken subject to detailed scientific study for incorporating adequate environmental safeguard measures required for neutralizing damage to coastal environment as may be appropriate to the Navi Mumbai region'. This amendment does not automatically mean permission to build the airport. It makes the construction of an airport a permissible activity but on the basis of certain conditions being fulfilled to the satisfaction of the MoEF.

The proposed location for the Navi Mumbai Airport will involve submergence of 400 acres of mangroves and water area. I wrote to the chief minister, Maharashtra, as soon as I took over on this issue. We subsequently met and the ToRs for the EIA were issued, at my instance, to CIDCO on 4 August 2009. I had also suggested to CIDCO to engage the best international consultants for environmental management from countries like the Netherlands and the US. I had also told the chief minister that the EIA must include the impact on river diversions, which are being proposed as part of this project. We are awaiting this EIA and we are hoping that it will be a solid, credible, and professional job.

Since the airport project involves loss of mangroves, I contacted the Gujarat Ecology Commission (GEC) on my own initiative since it has done outstanding work on mangroves restoration in Gujarat over the last decade. You will be happy to know that based on my constant prodding, the GEC has submitted a report to CIDCO on mangroves restoration. The Maharashtra government was blissfully unaware of what the GEC had accomplished. I have encouraged the GEC to be proactive in Navi Mumbai.

The coal mining project will severely disrupt tiger habitats and corridors and also destroy hundreds of acres of rich teak and other forests. I had sent a technical team to the project site and have shared the report of the team with Praful Patel. I am visiting Tadoba on 27 January to make my own field-level assessment.

Sir, I wish to assure that my attitude on all projects is positive and I always tried to find a constructive middle way. There are instances when I am forced to say 'no' but my approach has been to find a 'yes, but' option whenever possible. I hope you will not mind my putting these facts before you because I do not want you to get the impression that I am becoming a stumbling block to faster economic growth and infrastructure expansion.

Letter to Minister of State (Independent Charge) for Civil Aviation Praful Patel, Countering Claims Made During an Interview on the Delays Caused by the Environment Ministry in Moving Ahead with the Navi Mumbai Airport

3 July 2010
I have read about your TV interview on the Navi Mumbai airport and the so-called 'delaying' role of the MoEF. I wish to bring the following facts for your kind consideration:

1. The MoEF first received a proposal for developing a greenfield airport at Navi Mumbai on 27 August 2007. The final amendment of CRZ Notification, 1991 making airports a permissible activity in Navi Mumbai was issued on 15 May 2009.
2. CIDCO submitted a proposal for setting up of the Navi Mumbai Airport on 22 June 2009.
3. The ToRs for conducting the EIA study were issued by the MoEF on 4 August 2009.
4. Considering the substantial environmental and coastal impacts that the new airport is likely to have, the Environmental Appraisal

Committee of the MoEF undertook a site visit on 23 December 2009. This visit could not take place earlier because of the State Assembly elections and because of the monsoon. Based on this visit, additional ToR for the environmental impact assessment were issued by the MoEF on 8 February 2010.

5. On 7 June 2010, MoEF received from the Maharashtra Pollution Control Board the report on the proceedings of the public hearings on the Navi Mumbai Airport. Along with this, a draft EIA report was also submitted.

6. On 22 June 2010, the MoEF wrote to the Maharashtra Coastal Zone Management Authority (MCZMA) asking for its recommendations on the new airport. This letter was endorsed to CIDCO as well with a request that the final EIA report be submitted to MCZMA to enable examination.

As far as next steps are concerned, the MoEF needs to receive the final EIA report from CIDCO and the final recommendations of MCZMA. The Expert Appraisal Committee of the MoEF will then consider and provide its recommendations to enable me to take an appropriate decision.

Let me clarify that the matter is not pending with MoEF. I fully understand the need for a new airport for Mumbai but at the same time I hope you will appreciate that the present proposal has substantial environmental impacts especially in the coastal area. These include loss of over 300 acres of mangroves, diversion of two rivers, levelling of an 80 m-high hill and significant coastal zone management issues.

Speaking Order on the Navi Mumbai International Airport

22 NOVEMBER 2010

I

It was in November 1997 that the Government of India first started studying the need for a second international airport for Mumbai. The MoCA constituted a committee headed by the then chairman of the Airports Authority of India. This committee submitted its report in June

2000. It recommended that the second Mumbai airport be functional by 2016–17 and identified Rewas-Mandwa as the most appropriate location for the second airport for Mumbai.

In October 2000, the Maharashtra state government wrote to MoCA suggesting that the second airport should be in Navi Mumbai and not at Rewas-Mandwa because of availability of developed infrastructure and other reasons, including the fact that Navi Mumbai is within the Mumbai Metropolitan Region.

In December 2000, the Ministry of Civil Aviation advised the Maharashtra government to carry out detailed studies on the Navi Mumbai location.

In September 2001, CIDCO submitted the techno-economic feasibility study on the Navi Mumbai Airport to MoCA.

In August 2006, the International Civil Aviation Organization (ICAO) opined that with appropriate procedures in place, simultaneous operations of both Mumbai and Navi Mumbai international airports are feasible.

In February 2007, CIDCO submitted the revised project feasibility and business plan report on the Navi Mumbai airport to the Government of India.

In July 2007, the Union Cabinet gave in-principle approval to a second international airport at Navi Mumbai.

Thereafter, the MoEF received a proposal from CIDCO for developing a greenfield airport at Navi Mumbai on 27 August 2007. This proposal was returned since it was not a permissible activity in Navi Mumbai under CRZ Notification, 1991.

Thereafter, MoCA and CIDCO approached the Government of India on 30 October 2007 to amend the CRZ Notification, 1991 to enable the new airport to come up Navi Mumbai.

In November 2007, the MoEF was asked to initiate the process of amending the CRZ Notification, 1991 to enable the construction of an airport at Navi Mumbai.

In May 2009 the Mumbai High Court allowed the prayer for amending the CRZ Notification, 1991.

The CRZ, 1991 amendment making the construction of an airport at Navi Mumbai a permissible activity in CRZ areas subject to neutralization measures being taken was finally issued on 15 May 2009.

II

On 17 June 2009, soon after taking over, I first wrote to the chief minister of Maharashtra, drawing attention to the serious environmental issues associated with the Navi Mumbai location covering: (i) loss of mangroves; (ii) diversion of the Gadhi river and the tidally influenced Ulwe water body; and (iii) removal of a hill.

On 22 June 2009, CIDCO submitted a proposal to the MoEF seeking approval for the ToRs for carrying out the EIA.

The ToRs for the EIA were issued by the MoEF on 4 August 2009.

Considering the environmental issues involved, the EAC of the MoEF undertook a site visit on 23 December 2009. The visit could not take place earlier because of State Assembly elections and also because of the monsoon. Based on this site visit, additional ToR for the EIA were issued by the MoEF on 8 February 2010.

The public hearing for the project was held on 5 May 2010 as per the EIA Notification, 2006.

The final EIA for the Navi Mumbai Airport was submitted by CIDCO to the MoEF on 6 July 2010.

Thereafter, the EIA was considered by the EAC of the MoEF on 22–23 July 2010 and a number of clarifications were sought from the state government.

III

In July and August 2010, I had detailed consultations with the Maharashtra government and MoCA on the Navi Mumbai location. Three main points emerged from these interactions.

1. MoCA brought out that international airports everywhere are built with parallel runways. This ruled out the option of having just one runway at Navi Mumbai to minimize adverse environmental impact.
2. CIDCO explained that apart from its easy connectivity to Mumbai, the main advantage of Navi Mumbai is that bulk of the land needed for the project (about 66 per cent) is already in its possession (and another 12 per cent is government land), and that fresh land acquisition elsewhere will not only be expensive but also virtually impossible.

3. MoCA also insisted that strategic considerations ruled out the Kalyan location and sites like Wada and Rewas-Mundwa suffered from serious locational and other technical disadvantages.

IV

By August 2010, it was clear that, for various technical and non-technical reasons, the Navi Mumbai location has become a fait accompli. With the constraints operating at the existing airport, the urgent need for a second airport for Mumbai, a public infrastructure, is obvious. Hence, instead of going back to the drawing board and adding at least two–three years more to the assessment/land acquisition process, I decided to accept the fait accompli in good faith and to ensure that the environmental concerns are fully addressed. I also requested the BNHS [Bombay Natural History Society] to carry out a rapid assessment of the project area and its findings were communicated to CIDCO.

Between August and October 2010, guided by the EAC, MoCA, and CIDCO engaged in serious consultations on how to incorporate environmental concerns maximally in the project design. My request to them was simple—find ways to save the mangroves to the maximum extent possible and to minimize the diversion of rivers/tidally influenced water bodies, even if both involve relocation of non-aeronautical facilities.

Various options were considered. Certain parameters, however, simply could not be changed because of the nature of the site. For instance, the runways could not be moved south so as to save all mangroves since there is an existing highway and railway line that acts as a natural barrier. Also, the terminal building has to be between the two runways to maximize operating efficiency. The option of having one runway on stilts to minimize mangrove loss was ruled out on security grounds that have acquired greater significance following the horrific events of 26/11.

The EAC visited the project site on 20 October 2010 and discussed the final redesign with CIDCO on 22 October 2010. Thereafter, it finalized its recommendations which I received on 20 November 2010.

Given all constraints, the project redesign finally agreed to is a satisfactory compromise. After some initial reluctance, CIDCO has come around and agreed to major changes in the project proposal so as to minimize environmental losses. The clear pluses are:

1. Non-essential airport facilities are being shifted and as a result 245 ha of good-quality mangrove park is being developed by CIDCO.
2. The distance between the runways is being reduced from 1,800 m to 1,555 m. Because of this, the Gadhi river will not need to be diverted.
3. A new 60 ha mangrove park will be developed towards the Moha and Panvel Creek area by CIDCO.
4. Another 310 ha area on the north-east of the airport site between the Gadhi river, Mankhurd–Panvel Rail Corridor, and National Highway 4B will be declared as a 'no development' zone and CIDCO will undertake the development as mangrove park/green area after changing the sanctioned development plan of Navi Mumbai following due procedures.

By the same token, the negatives are:

1. Around 98 ha of mangroves (albeit of low quality) will be lost forever in the area where the runways are being built.
2. The tidally-influenced Ulwe water body will still need to be re-coursed but a number of safeguards have been stipulated to minimize the adverse impacts, if any, of such re-coursing.
3. The 90 m-high hill will need to be removed to enable smooth access to the runaways. The hill, admittedly, has already been quarried indiscriminately to significantly diminish its ecological value.

On mangroves, therefore, the overall picture is as follows: Before the project, the site has 161 ha of mangroves. Now, as a result of this compromise, the site area will have $(161-98)+60+245+310 = 678$ ha of mangroves. By any standard, this is a hugely positive accomplishment from an ecological point of view.

V

While giving the final environmental clearance to the Navi Mumbai Airport project, the MoEF, while accepting the recommendations of the EAC, is stipulating thirty-two specific conditions and safeguards. Prominent among these conditions and safeguards are the following:

1. CIDCO shall obtain necessary permission from the Hon. High Court of Bombay for cutting of mangroves and clearance under the Forest (Conservation) Act, 1980 as per the orders in respect of notice of motion no. 417 of 2006 in public interest litigation No. 87/2006, as required.
2. CIDCO shall rehabilitate about 3,000 families of ten settlements from seven villages falling within the airport zone as per the R&R (rehabilitation and resettlement) policy of the Government of India or the Government of Maharashtra, whichever is more beneficial to the project-affected persons.
3. The plantation and protection of mangroves by CIDCO amounting to 615 ha will be implemented in the shape of biodiversity mangrove parks well before the airport is operational.
4. A comprehensive master plan for surface drainage and flood protection, keeping in view the re-coursing of the Ulwe river will be prepared and submitted to the MoEF.
5. CIDCO will put in place a contingency plan to avoid flooding of the low-lying areas all around the airport. The need for widening and deepening the Gadhi river will be studied, if required.
6. Since the project proposal has now under gone many changes since it was first submitted, a fresh comprehensive post-project EIA report shall be prepared under the approved layout of the airport, the new hydrological scenario, altered topography, and land use. The revised EIA report should also include ecological aspects answering queries raised by the BNHS.
7. CIDCO will conduct a baseline survey of avian fauna before the start of the construction of the airport and the details will be put up every three months on the website in association with the BNHS.
8. In order to meet all the essential aeronautical requirements and the further airport expansions, no property development shall be undertaken within the proposed aeronautical airport zone area (1,160 ha).
9. A high-level advisory and monitoring committee, which should include international experts of repute, shall be constituted by CIDCO to oversee the implementation of the environmental mitigation measures. The monitoring shall be done at various stages (planning, construction, and operation) of project and all compliance reports will be put immediately in the public domain.

VI

I believe that the environmentally protective stand taken by the MoEF initially has finally paid off and a good agreement has been obtained to the optimal satisfaction of all sides concerned.

It is possible that some environmentalists may still be unhappy with the optimal solution finally reached. But I am firmly of the view that this optimization is the best possible solution that could be crafted after many weeks of negotiations. The emphasis should now be on ensuring that the commitments made by CIDCO and the conditions stipulated by the MoEF are fulfilled in their entirety in letter and spirit.

In addition, I have requested MoCA to develop the existing Juhu airport as a green lung for Mumbai city in coordination with the MoEF and the state government.

In keeping with past practice when it comes to important national projects or issues and in keeping with the MoEF's policy of full transparency and accountability, I am making this note public immediately on granting environmental clearance to the Navi Mumbai Airport project.

The detailed set of conditions under which the environmental clearance has been approved has been communicated to CIDCO and also put up on the ministry's website.

Letter to Minister of State (Independent Charge)
for Civil Aviation Praful Patel on Developing the Juhu Airport
Area as a Green Lung for Mumbai

24 NOVEMBER 2010

I have already mentioned to you the need to develop the Juhu airport area, which is owned by the Union Ministry of Civil Aviation (MoCA), as a green lung for Mumbai city. I have mentioned this in my public communication on the Navi Mumbai Airport as well, of which you have a copy. I think it is absolutely essential to develop this area as a wonder biodiversity zone for the benefit of a city that is starved of open spaces and greenery. Knowing of your deep commitment to environmental issues, I am confident that you will accept this idea. MoEF, MoCA, and the state government can work together as a team on this project.

Letter to Chief Minister of Maharashtra Prithviraj Chavan on the Adverse Impact of the Proposed Navi Mumbai Airport on the Waghavalli Lake

15 MARCH 2011

Charles Correa, the globally famed architect, met me on 10 March 2011 and told me that the proposed airport for Navi Mumbai is located right in the middle of the Waghavali Lake, which was the heart of the proposed city centre of Navi Mumbai. According to Mr Correa, the proposed airport will completely destroy the concept and the spirit of Navi Mumbai city, with whose inception he was associated. Lastly, he said that the location of the airport was in violation of Navi Mumbai's existing master plan. The above position was never informed by the Government of Maharashtra or CIDCO to my ministry during the process of obtaining EC/CRZ clearances for the Navi Mumbai Airport. I should be grateful, therefore, if you could kindly direct this matter to be looked into with due priority and the factual position in regard to Mr Correa's statement intimated to us at the earliest.

Speaking Order on the Adarsh Cooperative Housing Society, Mumbai

16 JANUARY 2011

The Ministry of Environment and Forests decision on the Adarsh Co-operative Group Housing Society building case in Mumbai is available in all its details on the ministry website. There were three options available[10]:

I. Removal of the entire structure since it is unauthorized and no clearance whatsoever under the CRZ Notification, 1991 was obtained.
II. Removal of that part of the structure in excess of the floor space index (FSI) that might have been allowed had the requisite permission be sought from the appropriate authority.
III. Recommending government takeover of the building for a public use to be determined later.

Option II was rejected since this would be tantamount to regularizing or condoning an egregious violation of the CRZ Notification, 1991. Option III was considered but rejected because: (i) even though the final use may be in public interest, it would still be tantamount to regularizing a violation of the CRZ Notification, 1991; and (ii) there would be substantial discretionary powers that would vest with the state or central government in case of takeover.

Therefore, in light of all facts, circumstances, discussion, consideration, reasoning, and analysis presented in the Adarsh Cooperative Housing Society (ACHS) dossier, I have decided on Option I. The fact that there may well be other cases of similar violations provides no ground for mitigation of the penalty attracted by such an egregious violation as that by ACHS. Any other decision would have diluted the strong precedents that have been set in judgments of the Supreme Court and different high courts.

ACHS has violated the very spirit of the CRZ Notification, 1991 by not acknowledging the need for clearance under this notification. Whether they were aware of such requirement or not is immaterial as ignorance of law can never be an excuse for non-compliance.

Finally I wish to reiterate that the CRZ Notification, 2011 published on 7 January 2011 makes no difference to ACHS-like cases. In addition to the safeguards provided for such cases in the CRZ Notification, 2011 itself, this practice is substantiated by the principle enshrined in Article 20(1) of the Constitution, which states: 'No person shall be convicted of any offence except violation of a law in force at the time of the commission of the act charged as an offence'. Thus, ACHS was in violation when the CRZ Notification, 1991 was extant, action was initiated by the MoEF when the CRZ Notification, 1991 was extant, therefore, the action against ACHS will continue to be pursued.

Speaking Order on the Forest Clearance for SAIL's Chiria Iron Ore Mines

9 FEBRUARY 2011

Background

The erstwhile privately owned Indian Iron and Steel Company (IISCO) took control of the Chiria iron ore mine complex in the Saranda Forests in the Paschimi Singhbhum district of Jharkhand in 1936. IISCO became a fully owned subsidiary of SAIL in 1978 and the final merger took place in 2006 on the premise that the mines would be made available to SAIL since it had been forced to absorb substantial losses on IISCO's account.

The Chiria mine complex covers 2,376 ha, which is about 3 per cent of the entire Saranda forest area. Of this, around 194 ha (8 per cent) has already been broken up. SAIL's proposal that has come to MoEF for forest clearance (environmental clearance has already been obtained) comprises two components: (i) renewal of permission to mine in the 194 ha already broken up; and (ii) permission to divert an additional 401 ha (17 per cent) for mining. Thus, permission is being sought for diversion of a total of 595 ha, which 25 per cent of the total Chiria mine area. The permission is being sought for a period of twenty years.

Factors Weighing in the Decision

While deciding to accord approval for SAIL proposal, I have kept the following factors in mind.

1. SAIL is a 'maharatna' public sector company with a good track record of corporate social responsibility and as such deserving of special treatment even in this era of a certain economic orthodoxy.
2. SAIL has an Rs 18,000 crore initial public offering (IPO) on the anvil, 50 per cent of whose proceeds will accrue to the Government of India. Thus, an early decision has to be taken without waiting for 'perfect' information.
3. The Hon. Prime Minister had written to the chief minister of Jharkhand in August 2007 requesting for a renewal of mining leases in Chiria in favour of SAIL in the broader national interest.
4. Forest clearances had been given to SAIL earlier in July 1998 and October 1998 for two leases in Chiria itself.
5. Chiria is essential for the future of SAIL. Over the next fifty years, around 40 per cent of the iron ore requirement of SAIL will be met from the Chiria mines. Quite apart from this, this is the only compact deposit available to SAIL.
6. Giving permission only for renewal would be grossly insufficient for SAIL's raw material requirements. Moreover, mechanization would not be possible in the leases under consideration for renewal and they would deplete by the year 2020.
7. The existing steel plants Bokaro, Burnpur, Duragapur, and Rourkela will necessarily have to be run from iron coming from

Chiria once the mines presently feeding them are depleted in 10–12 years time.

8. Chiria is in a Left-wing extremism affected region with a substantial tribal population. Corporate Social Responsibility (CSR) activities by SAIL could help in the socio-economic development of the region, particularly as far as the Ho tribal communities are concerned.

9. There is also urgency to accord approval given the long lead times involved in starting production in an area that is not easy to work in because of various factors.

Specific Conditions Governing the Decision

While approval is being given subject to the usual conditions governing forest clearance (like those relating to compensatory afforestation and NPV) there are thirteen specific conditions that are being stipulated for this approval. These are:

1. Only mining and primary and secondary crushing would take place in the forest area. Processing beneficiation, blending, stockpiling, railway sidings, infrastructure, and all township facilities will be 15 km away in non-forest land. Only conveyor systems will be used for transportation of ore.

2. A cluster management approach will be adopted for mining-related activities to avoid excessive fragmentation. Thus, the diverted area will be broken up in phases. The forest areas above their water collection points should be kept inviolate.

3. Forest roads will not be used by SAIL during night time.

4. SAIL will position a wildlife management team at Chiria from the start of operations to monitor impacts and take remedial measures as the project proceeds.

5. Over the next twenty years, only 25 per cent of the total forest area being diverted (equivalent to around 595 ha) will be broken up.

6. SAIL will make a contribution of Rs 20 crore over the next five years for programmes relating to wildlife-related and biodiversity-related programmes in the region with particular focus on the Saranda Forest Division.

7. In keeping with the guidelines issues by the Department of Public Enterprises, SAIL will earmark at least 2 per cent of net profits for CSR activities (as distinct from wildlife and biodiversity

management programmes). The CSR will include vocational and skill-development programmes for local youth to begin as the mining activities commence. Employment of local youth will be maximized in a transparent manner.

8. Proper mitigation measures to minimize soil erosion and choking of streams will be undertaken.

9. There will be zero discharge into the Koena river and steps will be taken to ensure that the river does not get polluted. This will be subject to regular field reviews by the Central Pollution Control Board. The river ecology is critical to the health of the forest.

10. The entire mine lease covering 2,376 ha will remain with SAIL as at present. Five-year plans should be prepared for land-use and tree felling will be regulated, accordingly.

11. SAIL will support the preparation of a comprehensive wildlife and biodiversity management plan by the Wildlife Institute of India, Wildlife Trust of India and the World Wildlife Fund for Nature (WWF). This study will also identify areas that should be kept inviolate in the Saranda Forests. This study should be commissioned immediately.

12. Given that in recent months, it has been permitted mining in ecologically sensitive areas (in Duarguiburu as well as in Kiriburu-Meghahatuburu), SAIL should set up a full-fledged forest management team under a full-time executive director whose sole responsibility will be forest management.

Given the ecological sensitivity of the Saranda forest area, the MoEF will assume direct responsibility and set up a multidisciplinary expert group (that would include not only ecologists but also anthropologists) to be responsible for this monitoring. The monitoring, evaluation, and compliance reports will be made available in the public domain once a quarter. This committee will pay special attention to the concerns relating to the impact of mining on elephant habitats and migratory routes.

A Final Word

The FAC is a statutory body and I have made no effort whatsoever to interfere in its functioning, On the contrary, I have gone out of my way to ensure that it functions professionally and in an independent manner. I have brought in distinguished experts from outside government as members of the FAC.

Most of the time, I have accepted the recommendations of the FAC. But there have been occasions when the FAC has recommended approval and I have exercised my judgement and rejected that particular case giving clear reasons why I am doing so. An example of this is the Renuka Dam project in Himachal Pradesh, which the FAC had recommended but that I ended up rejecting on purely ecological grounds. On the other hand, there have been two occasions when the FAC has recommended rejection and I have exercised my judgement and overturned the FAC recommendation—the first being POSCO and the second being the present Chiria case.

The FAC will continue to focus single-mindedly on forest-related, biodiversity-related issues and concerns, while as minister I will have to necessarily to take a broader view but placing on public record in a complete manner the reasons for taking that view. That has always been and will continue to be my approach.

Letter to Prime Minister on Not Permitting Mining in the Area Around the Tadoba-Andhari Tiger Reserve

4 FEBRUARY 2010

I visited Lohara and Chandrapur districts near the Tadoba-Andhari Tiger Reserve where Adani Power Ltd has been allocated a coal mine. I spent virtually a whole day interacting with various people from Lohara and Chandrapur as also seeing the proposed mining site in some detail.

Based on my field trip, I have no hesitation in saying that we should not allow the coal mining project to proceed under any circumstances. The following factors bear mention:

The proposed lease area is in an area very rich in biodiversity and rich in thick forests, particularly of teak. Asia's biggest and only gene pool of teak with more than 250 clones would simply get destroyed by this project.

The mining site falls in the corridor that connects the Tadoba–Andhari Tiger Reserve with other protected areas mainly through the eastern and southern sides, which extends to Chhattisgarh, Andhra Pradesh, and Madhya Pradesh.

The proposed project would be detrimental to wildlife outside the Tadoba-Andhari Tiger Reserve as well, particularly in the adjoining forest divisions of Brahmapuri and Chandrapur, which are geographically connected with the Tadoba-Andhari Tiger Reserve. Rail and road requirements for the project would require further diversion of forest land in a large way, leading to further habitat fragmentation.

I found a very large number of civil society organizations in Chandrapur totally opposed to this project. Chandrapur is the fourth most-polluted industrial cluster, according to a recent study carried out by the Indian Institute of Technology, Delhi for us. This pollution is already having serious public health impacts as many doctors told me in Chandrapur. I also saw for myself the poor record in environmental management of mining companies including that of Western Coalfields, a public sector coal company, which has added to public dissatisfaction. Clearly, Chandrapur's public is very conscious of environmental and ecological issues and Chandrapur must be one of the few places that observed a bandh in favour of protecting the tiger reserve.

On 7 January 2010, MoEF had already rejected the Adani's coal project and requested the Ministry of Coal to allocate an alternative coal block. This was based on a report prepared by the member-secretary, National Tiger Conservation Authority, who visited the site a couple of months back at my request. However, since Sharad Pawar and Praful Patel had met you and expressed concern at our attitude, I, myself, volunteered to visit Lohara to see what can be done. My visit only reinforced the conclusion that this project is simply not in the national interest.

Note Rejecting Proposal for Uranium Mining in Meghalaya

10 MAY 2010
The nineteenth meeting of the Standing Committee of the National Board on Wildlife took place on 1 May 2010 under the chairmanship of Minister of State (Independent Charge), Environment and Forests, Jairam Ramesh. After a detailed discussion, the Standing Committee decided to reject a proposal of the Department of Atomic Energy for exploratory drilling of uranium in Rongcheng Plateau in the Balphakram National Park South Garo Hills district of Meghalaya.

The Standing Committee took this decision keeping in view of the sentiments of the local people and a number of representations received from local civil society groups, even though the Minister of State (Independent Charge) Environment and Forests admitted that the country urgently needs to augment domestic uranium supplies. The Standing Committee also discussed a report prepared by one of its members—Dr Asad Rahmani of the BNHS—on illegal private coal mines around the Balphakram National Park and decided to press the state government for the implementation of the recommendations contained in this report, which include (i) immediate ban on all mining and road construction activity within the National Park; (ii) strict regulation of all coal mines in Garo Hills and other parts of the state; (iii) implementation of proper mining plans which will ensure that local people avail the greatest benefit from mining. Dr Rahmani's report is available on the ministry website (www.moef.nic.in).

Letter to Secretary, Department of Atomic Energy, and Atomic Energy Commission Chairman Anil Kakodkar on Objections Being Raised to the India-based Neutrino Observatory (INO) Project in the Nilgiris

8 JULY 2009

I have received a letter from B.G. Deshmukh, former cabinet secretary and former principal secretary to Prime Minister, regarding the proposed INO project in the Nilgiris. A couple of weeks ago, Dr M.R. Srinivasan had also called me regarding this project.

You know of my profound commitment to science and technology, in general and to the Department of Atomic Energy, in particular. However, I cannot ignore what Deshmukh and Dr Srinivasan (ironically, both former members of the Atomic Energy Commission) told me and I would very respectfully request you to see whether an alternative site for the INO project can be identified. The site you have identified is ecologically very, very sensitive and is very close to the Mudumalai Tiger Reserve. It will also have adverse impacts on local watersheds.

I am very well aware of the importance of INO but in my new ministerial capacity, I would be failing in my duty if I did not bring to your notice the larger environmental issues that this project raises.

Note to Secretary, Department of Atomic Energy, and Atomic Energy Commission Chairman Anil Kakodkar, Conveying the Decision to Reject the INO Project in the Nilgiris

20 NOVEMBER 2009

I have thought long and hard about the INO project. At my instance, additional member-secretary, National Tiger Conservation Authority, additional principal chief conservator of forests (PCCF) and member-secretary of the National Tiger Conservation Authority (MS-NTCA), also visited the proposed project site at Singara, Nilgiris district, Tamil Nadu, and he has given a pointed report, which is attached.

I am very sympathetic to the INO project. It is being executed by some of our finest institutions and some of our most dedicated scientists. Its significance lies not just from a theoretical physics perspective but also has great significance for experimental physics, an area in which India has been traditionally weak. I have also had an occasion to go through the environmental management plan and the environment impact assessment of the proposed observatory and I commend these reports for the level of detail and the sensitivity demonstrated to environmental issues.

I have always been a strong supporter of Indian science and would not like to do anything that would demoralize the Indian scientific community. Yet, as the minister of environment and forests, I have to be also mindful of the large number of reports that I have received against the proposed site and the very weighty reasons put forward by the Addl PCCF and MS-NTCA that would militate against Singara. I have also considered all points objectively and have come to the conclusion that the Singara site would not be advisable and that the alternative location suggested by the Addl PCCF and MS-NTCA at Suruliyar should be seriously considered by the Department of Atomic Energy. We will try to facilitate necessary approvals from our end for the alternate location. I am told that the alternative location does not present the type of problems that Singara poses and, therefore, clearances from an environmental and forestry angle should pose a serious problem.

I have taken a considerable amount of time listening to various points of view, including the view given to me by Dr R. Sukumar, a noted scientist from the Indian Institute of Science with over twenty years of experience of working in the Nilgiris Biosphere Reserve, who has clearly stated in a note prepared at my request that arguments against Singara are, to a very large extent, exaggerated, and misplaced. Even though various safeguards have been proposed in the environmental management plan and even though I have high regard and respect for Dr Sukumar, I am forced to come to the conclusion that Singara location should not be proceeded with. I have interacted with scientists involved with the INO project and I have found them to be as mindful of environmental issues as the NGOs who are against the project. However, I do think that, on balance, the decision must go against Singara.

Note on the Clearance for the INO in the Bodi West Hills Reserved Forest

[This location was agreed upon after the MoEF raised concerns about the earlier site chosen by the Department of Atomic Energy.]

18 OCTOBER 2010

The MoEF has accorded both environment and forest clearance for the proposal of the Department of Atomic Energy to set up a neutrino observatory in the Bodi West Hills Reserved Forest in Theni district of Tamil Nadu. The approval is subject to the conditions that there will be no cutting of trees and damage to forest cover, that measures will be taken to minimise the effect of tunnelling and to dispose rock debris, and that the environmental management plan prepared by the Coimbatore-based Salim Ali Centre for Ornithology and Natural History (SACON) will be fully implemented.

The neutrino observatory project is significant for India's scientific leadership. It is executed by the Tata Institute of Fundamental Research (TIFR) and twenty other scientific institutions in the country are part of the consortium. It will be a world-class laboratory for underground science, primarily neutrino physics. It will give India an edge for research relating to understanding fundamental laws of nature. This is not just a project in theoretical physics. It will also involve development of instrumentation and large-scale experiments. When completed by 2015 at an estimated cost of around Rs 1,000 crore, it will house the world's most massive magnet. Over 200 scientists would participate in this facility.

MoEF is pleased that the Department of Atomic Energy took into account its ecological concerns on an earlier proposed site at Singara and the site was changed to the Bodi West Hills.

Letter to Prime Minister Advising Against the Ken-Betwa Interlinking Stressing on the Adverse Impact to Tiger, Wildlife, and Fauna in the Panna Reserve

4 APRIL 2011

... I have been pointing out to the Ministry of Water Resources that this project will submerge the Panna Tiger Reserve in Madhya Pradesh. The total size of the Panna is now 542 sq km. The project will submerge 44 sq km, quantitatively, this may appear a small amount around 8 per cent. However, the area that is being submerged is very much in the core of the tiger reserve.

As you are aware, Panna had a troubled history and had lost its entire tiger population in 2009. Since then we have launched an ambitious tiger translocation programme and, today, we have four tigers in residence, translocated from Kanha, Pench, and Bandhavgarh. Six cubs have also been born recently. The entire habitat can sustain a tiger population of anywhere between twenty and twenty-five. Apart from tiger numbers, this is an area of rich biodiversity and forest cover. You may recall that there is another proposed hydroelectric power project in Bhutan that will have a similar deleterious impact on the Buxa Tiger Reserve in north Bengal.

Letter to Speaker Meira Kumar on Clearance for the Durgawati Project

12 APRIL 2010

We received a proposal from the Government of Bihar vide their letter dated 3 November 2009 for the release of 2,029.8002 ha of forest land including 64.75 ha of forest land already diverted for dam seat and spill way. The proposal was examined by the FAC and, on the basis of the recommendations of the FAC, I have approved the diversion of forest land for the Durgawati Reservoir. The formal order in this regard is under issue.

Letter to Union Minister for Human Resource Development Kapil Sibal on the Use of Forest Land for Setting Up Institutions

10 September 2009

The setting up of thirty central universities is indeed a landmark achievement that has been accomplished under the leadership of the chairperson, United Progressive Alliance and the Prime Minister. However, it has been brought to my notice some of the central universities are going to be situated in hundreds of acres of forest land. Knowing your personal commitment to the cause of environment and forests, I am sure you will be the first to ensure that the establishment of central universities does not lead to considerable loss of valuable forest cover. I thought I should bring this concern to your notice.

Letter to Union Minister for Human Resource Development Kapil Sibal on Clearing the Diversion of Forest Land for IIT, Mandi and Indore

2 June 2011

I have just cleared the proposals regarding diversion of forest land for campuses of IIT, Mandi and IIT, Indore, overlooking the reservations of the FAC. I would request you to direct all the new IITs and the new central universities to use the barest minimum forest land. Where the forest land is used, it must be maintained for ecological purposes and not for construction.

Letter to Chief Minister of Rajasthan Ashok Gehlot on the Construction of Dams on the Chambal

7 August 2009

Kindly refer to your letter dated 16 July 2009 regarding the proposal for construction of four dams at Rahu Ka Gaon, Gujjapura, Jaitpura, and Barsala on river Chambal downstream of Kota Barrage.

In this connection, I would like to mention that the proposal was earlier considered by the Standing Committee of National Board for Wildlife held on 12 December 2008, wherein it was rejected. However, the proposal was reconsidered by the Standing Committee in its meeting held on 17 July 2009, wherein it was rejected again as in case the proposal is permitted after survey for implementation, it would lead to the loss of 197 km of *gharial* and dolphin habitats, both of which are endangered not only in the country, but also internationally. As the Chambal river is the only river in the country having cleanest water and having great aquatic biodiversity including flagship species like gharials, dolphins, etc., it needs to be conserved as a national heritage.

Letter to Chief Minister of Karnataka B.S. Yeddyurappa Asking Him Not to Proceed with the Gundia Hydroelectric Power Project.

[The project did not have either an environmental or a forest clearance]

20 JUNE 2009

I have received information from a number of NGOs and civil society organisations that the proposed 2 × 200 MW Gundia hydroelectric project of Karnataka Power Corporation (KPC) in Hassan district is going to drown almost 1,900 acres of thick forest in the already-endangered Western Ghats along with its entire fauna. This is something that both Karnataka and our country can ill-afford. In addition, I have been informed that the foundation stone for the project was laid on 26 May 2009, even though the environmental and forestry clearance from the Government of India has *not* been obtained. I am sure you will agree with me that it would not be proper to have the foundation stone laid in anticipation of obtaining environmental and forestry clearance. I do not think that environmental clearance should be taken for granted any longer. We have to go through the process as laid down by law and we should not consider this process a routine formality.

I am well aware of the urgent need to increase Karnataka's power generating capacity but I am sure you will agree with me that this should not be at the cost of ecological security and biodiversity conservation. A balance between the two must be struck. This, I know, is Karnataka's own priority.

Letter to Chief Minister of Andhra Pradesh N. Kiran Kumar Reddy on Ecotourism Norms being Violated in the Kothaguda Reserve Forest

10 MARCH 2011

This is with reference to the project going by the name of Sri Kotla Vijaya Bhaskar Reddy (SKVBR) Botanical Garden, Night Safari and

Eco-Park, and Bird Park at the Kothaguda Reserve Forest, Hyderabad, extending to 110.87 ha. Right at the outset, this ministry has been urging the state government of Andhra Pradesh to adhere strictly to norms of what is known as 'ecotourism', which in your government's correspondence and in the original proposal seeking clearance under the Forest (Conservation) Act, 1980 is described as that type of activities that does not leave behind any permanent impact 'but for the footprints'. In the first instance, when this ministry had considered the project, on 4 August 2004, we had stipulated the following conditions:

1. No permanent construction shall be allowed to be constructed under the proposal in the forest areas. For accommodation, only temporary structures like tents/huts/collapsible structures (collapsible structures mean such structures, which can be dismantled and shifted from one place to another) shall be allowed. Cement/masonry work shall not be allowed above plinth level except in toilets. However, use of abandoned forest rest-houses can be permitted.
2. Temporary local architecture should be preferred. The tourism facilities should be environment-friendly, simple, clean, and wholesome. In this regard, the type of facilities created by the Jungle and Lodges Corporation in Karnataka is a case in point.
3. The state government shall deposit 25 per cent of the revenue generated from the project in CAMPA, which shall be ploughed back for promotion and development of forest-tourism of the area.

However, on the express request of the state government, on 12 September 2005, the conditions were relaxed to the following extent:

1. Maximum two floors (ground + one) construction will be permitted. Cement concrete construction up to plinth level shall be allowed. For construction, framed structures with cement concrete columns and beams above ground and up to first floor may be allowed. Other construction material should be eco-friendly like that made of bamboo, timber, reconstituted wood, clay, etc. However, cement concrete flooring shall be allowed for all toilets and bathrooms, on first floor.
2. Architecture of construction should be of the type that blends with the surrounding landscape; and 3.5 per cent of the revenue generated shall be utilized by the user agency for activities/works aimed at social development of local community in consultation with the state forest department.

From the above it is obvious that this ministry's permission stressed the need to avoid all extraneous developments, structures, and activities which would affect the natural ecosystem and the natural character of the forest. Your own government had in its application under Section 2 of the Forest (Conservation) Act, 1980 written eloquently at length about the philosophy and principles of eco-tourism and had even written that you would go for 'non-consumptive tourism as compared to mass tourism'. In all its letters, the state government had written that eco-park and eco-habitat, including visitor amenities does not require clearance by the Central Zoo Authority (CZA), Government of India. In the revised management plan dated 1 June 2009, visitors amenities have been described at page 43 as eco-friendly and ethnic cottages which would adhere to Government of India guidelines dated 4 August 2004 and 12 September 2005 issued by this ministry.

Such being the background, the revised management plan dated 1 June 2009 was cleared by this ministry on the assumption that the revision would cater to the advice given by the experts in the FAC and by this ministry, and that there would be no addition to the original proposal. However, I am dismayed to learn that, far from toning down the construction and making it eco-friendly, the project proponents have actually planned to construct huge concrete structures such as a large hotel with 300–400 rooms, a convention centre with a seating capacity of 2,500 people and a multiplex having a dozen screens with a multi-level parking lot for about 5,000 vehicles, which will be totally unacceptable in a forest area. Complaints have also been received from the local residents and members of Parliament that it amounts to gross violation of the letter and spirit of the forest conservation and the environmental legislations. I am also constrained to say that it suggests that the project proponents have not been entirely forthcoming and frank in the presentation of their plans and have taken advantage of the generally benign connotation of the terms such as eco-tourism, eco-friendly, ethnic, etc., as a cover for this highly intrusive and ecologically destructive approach.

In addition to the above, I have also to point out that the CZA had certified that clearance by it is not required for the night safari park, on the ground that only exotic/imported animals would be displayed, which does not come under the definition of wildlife as per the Wildlife (Protection) Act, 1972. However, on leafing through the voluminous revised management plan of 1 June 2009, it is seen that an Indian wildlife section is also proposed with species such as tiger, wolf, chee-tah, *sambhar*, gaur, blackbuck, nilgai, etc. This, I am sorry to say, sug-gests that the project proponents intend to take cover under a general permission given by this ministry with guidelines, in order to bring in components which have not been properly explained or scrutinized.

There are a number of other conditions attached to the clearances accorded by this ministry with which compliance has not been suitably assessed. In any case, construction of such large structures would be totally unacceptable, and would invite criticism and even punitive action. I am, therefore, withdrawing the forest clearance given by this ministry for this project and asking the FAC to scrutinize in detail each and every component of the proposed project so that such gross blunders can be avoided and a truly eco-friendly and nature-friendly amenity can be pro-vided to the citizens of Hyderabad. I request you to kindly issue suitable instructions to the Andhra Pradesh Forest Development Corporation and project proponents concerned to immediately suspend all construction activities, felling of trees, digging of soil and other similar activities until this ministry takes full stock of the situation and take a final decision on the matter. An official communication from this ministry will follow.

Letter to Chief Minister of Uttarakhand Ramesh Pokhriyal Nishank on the Power Project in the Bhuidar Valley

22 October 2010

I am sure you know and are well aware of the work of Chandi Prasad Bhattji in preserving and protecting the Himalayan ecosystem.

He met me recently and drew my attention to a 23.4 MW power project being proposed in the Bhuidar Valley, which is situated at the very tip of the famed Valley of Flowers. I agree with him that such a project would have serious consequences for the wonderfully rich bio-diversity in this area.

Earlier too there was a proposal to divert the Bhidarganga waters for the Vishnuprayag hydroelectric power project but thanks to the inter-vention of Indira Gandhi and Rajiv Gandhi, this proposal was dropped by the Uttar Pradesh government in September 1986.

I am sure you share the fascination of so many Indians for the Valley of Flowers and would not agree to any project that would destroy its serenity, splendour, and its riches.

'How Green is Our Growth: India Must Walk the Environment-friendly Road to Development', Opinion piece in *The Times of India* on the Occasion of World Environment Day

5 JUNE 2010

Environment and development must go hand in hand. Who can disagree with this? But what is good in theory becomes contentious in practice. Sometimes a project will receive a 'yes' from the MoEF. Sometimes, the response will be a 'yes, but' with safeguards being stipulated for the project to proceed—indeed the large majority of the projects receive one of these responses. But there will be occasions when a definitive 'no' will have to be said.

Over three decades ago, Indira Gandhi, unarguably the greatest environmentalist we have had in our political class, was loud and clear on Silent Valley. But, thereafter, such instances have been few and far between. With India now on a high economic growth trajectory and with the need to ensure that we stay on that path, safeguards, conditions, and even Silent Valley-type trade-offs are coming into increasing prominence. No longer can we take solace in what S. Radhakrishnan had once pithily summarized as the essence of our culture: 'Why look at things in terms of this or that? Why not try to have both this and that'.

How do we address such situations where deliberate and difficult choices are imperative? While I believe that no generalization is possible since each case of environmental or biodiversity impact is sui generis, certain principles and guidelines can certainly be adopted.

First, we need to move to rules-based approaches and rely less on discretion-based decision-making. A good example of this is what has been initiated for identifying the prima facie 'go–no-go' areas for coal mining. Nine major coalfields have been analysed and digitized maps showing their overlap with forest areas have been put in the public domain. The exercise is aimed to facilitate rules-based, transparent, and objective granting of forestry clearance to coal blocks based on a 'go–no-go' concept in the future. This exercise is being extended to other coalfields and other mineral sectors, particularly iron ore.

Second, we need massive institutional strengthening of the entire environmental governance system. Parliament has passed the National Green Tribunal Bill recently. This will function as a dedicated and specialized environmental court system accessible to all citizens. A national environmental protection authority to strengthen field-level monitoring and compliance capabilities is on the anvil as is the technical and organizational strengthening of the Central Pollution Control Board and its counterparts in states. In the ministry itself, steps have been taken to clean up internal processes, whether they relate to the composition of the environmental clearance committees or the process of decision-making or strengthening the scientific capacity of the ministry.

Third, we need to embrace proactive transparency in a major way going well beyond what is required under the RTI. All information from within the ministry—policies, new proposals, monitoring reports, impact assessment—is today put on the website almost immediately. Directions have also been issued to ensure that local elected bodies and local civil society groups have the information they are entitled to as a matter of right and not as a favour being done to them. The public is our best monitoring mechanism—keeping us accountable to our targets and ensuring enforcement and compliance at the grass roots, where we are weak. Such actions greatly strengthen the hand of the public in its monitoring function.

Fourth, the trade-offs, wherever they arise, must be made explicit and a larger consensus created on the best way to move ahead. In deciding on the future course of action on Bt-brinjal, for instance, we followed this approach laboriously, having a series of large, inclusive public and expert consultations before announcing a decision on its commercialization. The entire set of facts, opinions, communications, proceedings, etc., related to the decision was made public. The decision has received both bouquets and brickbats but that is inevitable.

Fifth, we have to think of innovative financial mechanisms that marry the imperatives of growth with that of ecological security. In 2002, we made a great start when the Supreme Court intervened and directed the constitution of the CAMPA. CAMPA is a 'vehicle' created to encourage reforestation, by asking project proponents to deposit with the government a certain amount equivalent to the social and economic value of the forest land being diverted for the project. A total amount of Rs 11,000 crore has been collected in this manner over the past seven years.

A more recent, but equally important example of a similar innovation is of the National Clean Energy Fund announced by the finance minister in the Budget speech this year. The underlying proposal is to levy a clean energy cess on coal, at a rate of Rs 50 per tonne. This money will be used for funding research and innovative projects in clean energy technologies and also for environmental management of critically polluted areas.

In an address at the national conference of ministers of environment and forests in New Delhi last August, the Prime Minister had rightly observed: 'We are still at early stages of industrialization and urbanization ...We can and we must walk a different road, an environment-friendly road.' We must persevere on this road in spite of the opposition it is bound to generate—only then will high growth also be sustainable and inclusive growth.

Notes

1. I have dealt with this issue in detail in chapters 7 and 9. The push by the Ministry of Environment and Forests, and its role in abandoning three projects on the upper reaches of the Ganga led to the Ministry of Power introducing the system of taking cumulative impact assessments into account while considering hydroelectric power projects.

2. The implementation of the laws and regulations has been discussed in Chapter 6.

3. Reproduced in Samar Singh (ed). 2007. *Ecological Security: The Foundation of Sustainable Development*. New Delhi: Shipra Publications.

4. Both the letters of the Odisha government and Dr Saxena's reply were put up the ministry's website.

5. Included in Annexure I of the speaking order, which was put up on the ministry's website.

6. Included in Annexure II of the speaking order, which was put up on the ministry's website.

7. Included in Annexure III of the speaking order, which was put up on the ministry's website.

8. Which, for Odisha, means gram sabha.

9. This, notwithstanding the fact that the state government has been actively canvassing for the project in question.

10. Besides the final order, the ACHS dossier included summary proceedings of the oral hearing; analysis of oral submissions; analysis of written submissions; discussions, consideration, and reasoning; and conclusions.

3 The Choices

I had come to the view that there was no gain in indulging in an 'economic growth versus ecological security' debate. It is clear that both economic growth and ecological security are both good ends. The focus has to be, instead, on how to ensure that environmental concerns are given due consideration in devising growth strategies and vice versa.

In trying to bring environmental concerns to the high table of economic growth, I believe one should try and be like Isaiah Berlin's rendition of Archilocus' fox and not be a hedgehog. There is a general acceptance that environmental concerns are important. Yet, for a country that is trying to pull hundreds of millions of its people out of poverty, the concern over conserving dense forests and putting rich reserves of coal and mineral out of reach can well seem esoteric or even anti-growth. I have, therefore, advocated reframing the environment debate—not just moving away from the growth versus environment binary—to approaching environmental issues from the perspective of livelihood, security needs, public health, farming patterns, water availability, and so on. To put it slightly differently, if you were at a negotiating table, you would want more people who think like you and have similar interests to be arguing along with you; that way you know you will be heard. Consolidating the voices that seek to infuse concerns about the environment, livelihoods, health, and faith into growth strategies is essential. The reframing of the environment debate to broaden its base is a sure way to steer the growth strategy onto a more sustainable path.

A prime example of how reframing the debate can actually help strengthen the need for giving primacy to environmental issues is in the area of public health. Air quality in most of India's urban areas is poor, and this is, in part, on account of exponential growth in vehicular traffic. As a result of poor air quality, there has been a rise in chronic respiratory ailments. In establishing the linkage through proper research and epidemiological data, there is a case for improving public transport, introducing mandatory fuel and vehicular efficiency norms, all of which will help improve the air quality and health outcomes.

Poor health outcomes impact people's productivity, affecting growth prospects. In the case of chronic health issues, and higher incidence of diseases such as cancer, it amounts to loss of productive workforce. It also means a diversion of resources, often with little or no productive value. The link between environmental protection and public health is clear, that is why I tried hard for a partnership between the Ministry of Environment and Forests on the one hand, and the Ministry of Health and Family Welfare on the other, which did not materialize.

Similarly, environmental concerns must align themselves to issues of livelihoods. The move to reclassify bamboo as a non-timber produce and give villages greater control over the sale of bamboo, which was the essence of the Menda Lekha experiment, is an example of how the issue of environmental protection must change its approach. In tying livelihoods to forest conservation and easing the relationship between local populations and forest officials, we succeed in creating a cadre that will form the first line of protection against forest and environmental degradation.

Land degradation is a basic cause for loss in agricultural productivity. Linking the need to adopt more environmentally friendly practices in agriculture, or ensuring the ecological flow in rivers to the question of agricultural productivity in a country where ensuring food security is a core political issue is a good way to ensure that the environmental aspects of the overuse of groundwater and fertilizers are addressed while devising policies. After all, who would better understand the need to conserve and recharge groundwater or the impact of climate change on the monsoons than the farmer? The efforts at environmental protection need to put these issues at the core.

This change in approach must also acknowledge that sometimes precedence must be given to other overriding priorities. A case in point is the easing of forest clearance for public works in Maoist-affected areas. Fidelity to environmental concerns cannot come at the cost of safety, security, and the need for the state to reach out with basic services to its most deprived people. The near total absence of the state or their presence in an adversarial role has given the Maoists a stranglehold in large swathes of our forest areas, particularly in central India. My decision to relax the norms for forest clearance in these areas did not mean a carte blanche to divert forests—the norms were relaxed only for public infrastructure like schools, hospitals, and roads. My decision to fast track clearance of projects in the Siang river basin, given its strategic importance in the India–China border issue or give clearances to road works along the India–China border should also be seen in this light. This is not to say that we should cut corners on environmental issues in these cases, just that it is not always a matter of balancing two competing goods; sometimes there are more factors and it is more like a juggling act.

This chapter highlights the way in which the environment debate must be recast for it to remain a relevant force in decision making. It also sheds light on the underbelly of the quest for growth, the pressures that were and will be exerted on environment administrators who seek to balance growth with environmental integrity; but, more than anything, it serves to highlight the urgent need to reframe the environment debate. I believe that reworking the environmental question through its impacts is an effective, and perhaps, the only way of ensuring that environment finds its due place in the framing of our growth strategy.

'The Hedgehog and the Fox Revisited: Some Further Reflections on the Growth-Environment Debate in India', the Lawrence Dana Pinkam Memorial Lecture, Convocation of the Asian College of Journalism (ACJ), Chennai, and World Press Freedom Day

3 MAY 2011

I am delighted to be here this evening. When I received the invitation from my friend Mr Sashi Kumar, I had only one question—will I be asked to wear those awful gowns and quirky hats associated with graduation ceremonies? On being assured of a more civilized dress code, I readily accepted.

It is actually a triple-header ballgame today as might be reported in Wikileaks—ACJ's convocation, World Press Freedom Day, and the Second Lawrence Dana Pinkham Memorial Lecture. *The Hindu* is a great institution, which commands our 'undivided' attention. ACJ has quickly established a formidable reputation for itself—I say this as a father of a young man who joined ACJ two years ago but quickly realized that he wanted to be a don and not a scribe.

This is the twentieth anniversary of the World Press Freedom Day declared by the UN General Assembly and, today, we affirm our faith in an independent media as a pillar of an open, liberal, democratic society, and respecting that independence, whatever the provocation and howsoever strong a reason afforded for some regulation every now and then, especially by the electronic media.

I know of Professor Pinkham only by reputation and clearly he was a man of great erudition, thoroughly progressive in his values as well as being unusual in having lived and worked not just in the US but also in China and India. Not many can claim that distinction—not even Mr Ram! Doing some background homework on Professor Pinkham, I discovered that he was the son-in-law of Harry Dexter White, who along with John Maynard Keynes, is considered to be the father of the Bretton Woods Institutions, especially the International Monetary Fund (IMF) and whose role is handsomely acknowledged by Robert Skidelsky in his magisterial biography of Keynes. Professor Pinkham bears a heavy cross or deserves kudos depending on which side of the fence you are for mentoring a young Mr Ram over four decades ago.

II

One of the most celebrated essays of the twentieth century was Isaiah Berlin's 'The Hedgehog and the Fox'. The noted philosopher drew upon a fragment of verse by the Greek poet Archilocus—'the fox knows many things, but the hedgehog knows one big thing'—to delve into Tolstoy's view of history. Tolstoy, of course, is of immense relevance to us in India because of his profound influence on the Mahatma. Today, I want to use this metaphor to reflect on the current debate on unbridled economic growth and environmental conservation. I suppose metaphors from the animal kingdom are only to be expected from a minister dealing with wildlife issues on a daily basis. Incidentally, the famous distinction between 'positive' and 'negative' liberty relevant to any discussion on freedom for the individual and of the press was first drawn by Berlin himself in a set of lectures at Oxford in 1958.

My point is simple—India needs to be liberated both from the 'high gross domestic product growth hedgehogs' and the 'conservation at all costs hedgehogs'. I do not exaggerate and I am not caricaturing. The population of prickly hedgehogs of both varieties is large. And even if you disagree with me on numbers, I would say that even those who are there have a disproportionately large footprint on the public discourse from either side. What India needs more of is the smooth fox—cunning and crafty—to find the balance between high growth and enduring conservation. The hedgehog is an ideological crusader supremely convinced of the rightness of the cause while the fox will admit of doubt and uncertainty. The hedgehog does not know how to make concessions to the other point of view while the fox will use linguistic qualifiers liberally—'yes, but', 'maybe', 'perhaps'. The hedgehog has feet on the accelerator but the fox works on the clutch forever changing gears to deal with varying traffic conditions.

But do not get me wrong. Hedgehogs actually have made, and continue to make great contributions. Look at the world of science and literature, which is full of people who are singularly focused and reach the Mt Everest of accomplishment in their respective fields. At the same time, what I am really driving at is that sticking to one big idea is an anathema in policymaking in an open society of astounding diversity because the hedgehog view is unresponsive and inattentive to the untidiness and complexity of real life.

III

Environmentalists just do not get it as far as economic growth is concerned. True GDP growth rates have their limitations as a measure of progress and welfare. But that is the best summary metric we have. It is imperfect but useful nevertheless as a broad indicator of how the economy is performing. Now, why should we even be bothered with sustaining high GDP growth rates, growth rates in the region of at least 8–9 per cent per year in real terms—that is, after adjusting for inflation?

Very simply, high GDP growth rates help generate revenues for the government that could then be used in programmes deemed essential.

Thus, between 2004 and 2009, the launch of the National Rural Employment Guarantee Act and the loan waiver was made possible by the average annual real GDP growth rate of 8.4 per cent. More growth means more revenues for governments. In just five years—between 2005–6 and 2010–11, for instance—the central government's gross tax revenues doubled. More revenues means increased spending on welfare programmes—I leave aside the larger and equally important question of how effectively these revenues are actually being spent.

High GDP growth rates fulfil yet another need—they help generate jobs, provided, of course, the structure of growth itself is labour-absorbing. Some informed estimates are that India's labour force will increase by anywhere between 80 million and 110 million over this decade—a staggering addition as compared to just 15 million for China. Forty per cent of these jobs in India have to be created outside the agricultural sector—that is, in industry and services. Given this demographic reality, a high GDP growth rate—especially drawing on high growth in agriculture and manufacturing—and better spread geographically across the country assumes special significance.

A high GDP growth rate requires investments—both public and private. These investments will materialize only if there is clarity and consistency in policy. Energy is a key requirement. But if environmentalists oppose hydroelectric projects on rehabilitation and resettlement grounds, coal projects on deforestation grounds and nuclear projects on risk factors, how will India generate the energy needed to sustain a high GDP growth rate. It is the height of romantic delusion—and a dangerous one at that—to think that a country of over 1.2 billion that added 18 million annually over the past decade can meet its energy requirements through solar, wind, or biomass energy. But that is exactly what most environmentalists would have us believe.

IV

Likewise, the growth-wallahs just do not get it as far as the imperative for environmental protection is concerned. Why cannot we follow the 'grow now, pay later' approach as the growth-fetishists often advocate? I would suggest four reasons why such an approach is not acceptable. First, increasingly, environmental campaigns and movements across the country are reflecting the basic livelihood concerns of tribal and other disadvantaged sections of society. Second, air and water pollution is beginning to have serious public health impacts in one state after another. Third, climate change is a reality and will affect India in a more profound manner than any other country because of our vulnerabilities across so many dimensions—monsoon, coastal areas, forests and glaciers to name just a few. Fourth, we must bequeath something to future generations since unlike in most parts of the world, population will continue to grow in India as we move to reap our demographic karma by adding at least 400–500 million by the middle of this century.

If the environmental activists do not fully appreciate the absolute essentiality of expanded wealth creation, the growth-jihadis fail to see the wider ecological context in which growth or for that matter the existence of the economic cycle and human life cycles inevitably depend. In a largely tropical country with unevenly distributed rainfall, trapping and saving water is vital for towns as much as villages. The centrality of soil conservation and of keeping the fertile land productive needs no emphasis. Less well-known but equally critical are a whole range of ecosystem services, of mangroves or of wetlands. If the growth-champions were to pause a bit, many of their premises come from an early twentieth-century delusion that technology and growth have made nature redundant.

V

Thus, this much should be self-evident and obvious—that India needs to straddle both worlds at the same time—the world of high GDP growth and the world of meaningful ecological security. But what is self-evident and obvious often tends to get forgotten. And this is where, I might add parenthetically, you media types come in. Hedgehogs make for good copy with their clarity and certainty. Foxes do not with their ambiguity and their 'on the one hand and on the other' approach.

Thus, in certain sections of the media, the growth hedgehogs are champions of a new India while the enviro-hedgehogs are Luddites intent on sabotaging India's emergence as a major world power. In some other sections, the enviro-hedgehogs are heroes (and quite frequently heroines) saving India from loot and plunder, while the growth-hedgehogs are harbingers of doom and destruction. It is interesting that the growth-hedgehogs are acclaimed largely in the English-speaking media (especially in what are called the 'pink papers') whereas the enviro-hedgehogs are the toast of the regional and vernacular media. Here is a topic for a doctoral dissertation, no less.

To get back to the question of balance, the virtue and the need for it is incontrovertible. Working the balance, however, is easier said than done. Quite often consistency becomes a casualty since a solution is sought to be found based on specific circumstances and conditions. But I feel that if there is clarity and transparency, the charge of lack of consistency can be effectively countered. And this is precisely what I have ventured to do through two specific innovations.

The first is through the practice of 'speaking orders'. It is not for me to say whether I have succeeded or not but I am encouraged by what Pratap Bhanu Mehta wrote in *The Indian Express* (a newspaper that is a growth hedgehog I might add and, therefore, not always friendly to me) on 17 February 2011:

> 'The cabinet needs to adopt a practice perfected by Jairam Ramesh: govern with what are called speaking orders. These are orders that clearly and publicly explain why certain decisions have been taken (whether the reasons are compelling or not can be debated). But at least government will not fall into the trap leaving it unclear who took decisions and why.'

In the past two years, I have issued such 'speaking orders' on public issues like Bt-brinjal, Vedanta, Posco, Jaitapur, Navi Mumbai, and Adarsh. I see it as a way of communicating to the public the contours of the middle path. Not everyone is happy, of course. But at least all motivations are in the public domain for critical analysis.

The second innovation is the system of public consultations. This began with the Bt-brinjal case, where over a thousand people attended such half-day long interactions in Bangalore, Hyderabad, Kolkata, Nagpur, Ahmedabad, Chandigarh, and Bhubaneswar. Then when the Coastal Regulation Zone (CRZ) Notification, 1991 was being redrafted, public meetings were held in Chennai, Puri, Kochi, Goa, and Mumbai. A third time I went on Bharat Darshan in search of the middle path was when the Green India Mission was being finalized and public views were sought in Guwahati, Visakhapatnam, Dehradun, Mysore, Pune, Bhopal, and Jaipur. All these public consultations were organized by the Ahmedabad-based Centre for Environment Education and all proceedings were video-graphed and put on the ministry's website. It is a back-breaking process and very often the public consultations can easily get out of hand, as I discovered on a couple of occasions since we Indians as a rule are excellent talkers but very poor listeners. But they are an important means of establishing contact with a larger constituency and for engaging them in the process of decision-making.

I think it was the late Professor Nurul Hasan who once reportedly said—Indians are a unique bunch; when confronted with a choice they will try and take both! Well, that luxury will not always be available and I am afraid that tough, unpopular choices will have to be made. Not always will conflicting objectives be reconcilable. That is why my approach has been to make the trade-offs explicit and make the choice in full public glare. This approach will work in the short-term but what I need to do is to develop a methodology that integrates the costs and benefits of environmental protection fully into our GDP calculations. What does 10 per cent annual real rate of GDP growth that is now within our grasp really mean, if we consider the costs of environmental damage, depletion of natural resources, and pollution that this growth will entail? The only way to answer these critical questions in an objective manner is to obtain clear numbers of the environmental costs that the growth process entails—that is, estimate 'green' national accounts.

In this connection, I am happy to report that we are setting up an expert group to develop a road map for India to be able to report 'green' national accounts by 2015. I have managed to convince Professor Sir Partha Dasgupta of the University of Cambridge, perhaps the world's leading luminary and expert in this field, to chair this expert group which will also have a couple of very distinguished economists. The work of this 'blue-ribbon panel' will be of great importance in our being able to follow a balance between rapid growth and conservation since, quite frankly, what we cannot measure we cannot monitor and what we cannot monitor we cannot manage.

VI

Working the balance (which, I submit, is somewhat different from the middle path that is sort of a 50:50 approach) also needs regulatory innovations. That environmental protection requires regulation is beyond doubt. That regulations and laws themselves need to keep pace with the times to reflect the unique demographic pressures and developmental imperatives we confront also cannot be denied. But can we have regulations without regulators because very often the regulators can become a source of needless harassment and corruption? We must think creatively. Of course, the growth hedgehogs would want the regulations themselves to go or be diluted or be subject to self-certification all of which are unacceptable. The enviro-hedgehogs would like an army of inspectors to police the implementation of the regulations.

A beginning is being made to move to a market-friendly system of regulation. With the help of four of the world's leading economists at the Massachusetts Institute of Technology, we have launched a pilot project in Tamil Nadu, Gujarat, and Maharashtra to implement regulations for air pollutants. This market-based system is broadly akin to how the US dealt with the acid rain problem in the late 1980s and the early 1990s through the introduction of tradable permits. It goes beyond the traditional command and control 'inspector-raj' systems, which have inherent limitations that we know. These innovative systems leverage technology and harness markets to ensure better compliance with our environmental laws and regulations. The scheme will fundamentally transform how we do pollution control. It will rely on online real-time monitoring of pollution loads of industrial units, based on which a system of 'emissions trading' will be established. Emissions trading will allow the regulator to set a cap on the aggregate level of pollution permitted, and then allow a self-regulating system to ensure that pollution does not exceed this cap.

VII

Working the balance also demands basic institutional changes. Writing in *The Indian Express* (yet again!) on 25 March 2011, Jerry Rao had this to say and I quote:

> Why does not Jairam Ramesh as part of his legacy to the country remove the power of discretionary approvals from his ministry and hand it over to an independent Environment Commission to be statutorily established and charge this commission with the tasks of granting and monitoring approvals? ... In giving up control, Ramesh will meet resistance from many in the political and bureaucratic establishment. But if he wishes to go down in Indian history as a Sher Shah, a Munro or a Curzon, this is his golden opportunity. Let's hope he grasps it.

Well, much as I admire Sher Shah, Munro, and Curzon, I am under no illusions that I will anywhere close to achieving even a very miniscule fraction of what these great men accomplished. I am also not quite sure if a medieval monarch or two imperial administrators are the best role models in our own democratic age. But a small beginning is being made. We are now in the process of setting up a National Environmental Appraisal and Monitoring Authority (NEAMA). This will be a professional, science-based autonomous entity tasked with environmental appraisals and monitoring of compliance conditions. Once appraised by NEAMA, projects would be sent with a recommendation to the Minister of Environment and Forests for approval.

This final approval by the minister is necessary to ensure that the principle of executive accountability is maintained. Jerry Rao will not like it but when the environment minister is pilloried in Parliament on some decision or the other, the minister cannot take recourse to the 'but NEAMA is totally independent of me' type of an argument. And, in any case, at least in the case of a political figure even if it is a member of the Upper House, there is some sense of public accountability totally absent in a purely technocratic body—the functioning of an independent Genetic Engineering Approval Committee (GEAC) in my own ministry prior to 2009 and whose functioning people like Jerry Rao would approve of, is a good case in point.

NEAMA will mark a major improvement over the current system (wherein the ministry does appraisal and approval of new projects) in several ways. First, NEAMA will be a full-time entity of professionals, tasked with environmental appraisals on an ongoing basis, instead of the current system of appraisals done by environmental appraisal committees that are ad hoc and meet about once a month. In this sense, it will convert a slow 'batch' process into a continuous process, bringing greater rigour in the appraisal process, while avoiding unnecessary delays. Second, the creation of NEAMA will address the 'conflict of interest' issue by separating the process of appraisal and approval. While NEAMA will be tasked with appraisal of new projects, the ministry will be responsible for the final approval. Third, NEAMA will maintain its own real-time and time-series databases on pollution loads across the country, which it will use to appraise proposed projects, instead of relying on data provided by project proponents as is the current practice. This will provide much greater objectivity in the appraisal process. Fourth, NEAMA will have a well-equipped system to ensure compliance with the conditions imposed on new projects that are granted environmental clearance.

VIII

I spoke earlier of the role of the media in eulogizing hedgehogs and giving somewhat short shrift to foxes. That is because today's media is increasingly impatient with ambiguity, is increasingly intolerant of shades of grey, seeing the world only in terms of black and white. This attitude vitiates the public discourse and debate, and does not allow for easy compromise and consensus. As I mentioned earlier, hedgehogs being more persuasive and articulate and being purveyors of a single and simple powerful message are loved by the media. But foxes are self-critical eclectic thinkers open to updating or reworking their beliefs and view of the world when faced with contrary evidence and views. Hedgehogs tend to stretch their one good idea—and the only one they have—but beyond a point, the stretch becomes counter-productive and like all stretches reaches a breaking point.

I am convinced that a 'working the balance' approach is the only way ahead. But this should not mean that we refuse to recognize that there may well be occasions when we will be faced when growth and conservation goals are irreconcilable. There are limits to this having your cake and eating it too. A coal mine bang in the middle of a very dense forest area or in a protected area like a tiger reserve is simply unacceptable and the nation has to accept that unpleasant reality. When this happens, a decision has necessarily to be taken that will displease one side or the other. Bouquets will be offered from one side and brickbats thrown from the other. And there will be no consistency—today's bouquet offerer can well and indeed has ended becoming tomorrow's brickbat hurler and vice versa.

Twenty years ago, India embarked on its historic economic reforms programme. Fiscal sustainability was one of the three pillars of this programme—the other two being abolition of industrial licensing and freeing international trade from administrative controls. Today, as we look ahead to the next two decades, we must not only be anchored in fiscal prudence but equally look the ecological sustainability of our growth trajectory. Is a 9 per cent-plus real rate of GDP growth envisaged as the target for the Twelfth Five Year Plan that will commence on 1 April 2012 environmentally acceptable? What will that growth, essential as it is, demand from our forests and our water resources, for instance? What will it take to ensure that this growth is along what is these days being called 'a low-carbon' pathway? If 100,000 MW of power capacity has to be added to ensure a 9 per cent-plus GDP growth rate, what should its fuel mix be so as to ensure that we don't end up repeating the same mistakes that the US and China have made—after all, a perennial latecomer like India does have advantages that it can learn from others?

IX

This being a convocation address, I suppose I must end with some advice to all of you youngsters about to enter that greatest temple of learning (and earning—the University of Life. The best advice I can give you in light of what I have said today is read Berlin. Be 'hedgehoggy' but develop the traits of a fox. And a fox need not be looked down upon, as we often tend to do. I can do no better to convince you of what a fox could mean when I recall that joke—blasphemous to recall in Chennai perhaps. It goes like this: 'Q: Who is the only Indian politician to have a Hollywood studio named after him? A: Rajaji, with the studio being 20th Century Fox!'

That is as good a place to end this lecture as any.

Letter to All the Chief Ministers Elucidating the Relationship Between the Joint Forest Management Committees Work and the Gram Sabhas

29 October 2010

You are well aware that joint forest management committees (JFMCs) have played an important role in forest conservation, regeneration, and management in different states of the country.

Responding to concerns raised in many quarters, I have been having a dialogue with various stakeholders on the functioning of JFMCs in the context of decentralized governance envisaged by and embodied in the Seventy-third Amendment to the Constitution of 1993 relating to panchayats and of the Panchayat (Extension to Scheduled Areas) Act, 1996 (PESA Act, 1996).

Certain strong conclusions have emerged from these interactions.

1. Existing JFMCs should function under the overall supervision and guidance of the gram sabha, and where needed, new JFMCs are to be set up by gram sabha.
2. JFMCs should be recognized as organs of the gram sabha under the relevant State Acts relating to Panchayati Raj institutions.
3. JFMCs should function as standing committees of gram panchayats for panchayats for item 6 (social forestry and farm forestry) and item 7 (minor forest produce, or MFP) listed in the Eleventh Schedule to the Constitution.
4. The manner in which the development funds of the JFMCs are used should be approved by the gram sabha.

I am writing to seek your support in putting these conclusions into effect by appropriate amendments by the state government of the relevant Acts, rules, and executive orders relating to both JFMCs and Panchayati Raj institutions.

Letter to All Chief Ministers, Union Minister for Rural Development Vilasrao Deshmukh, Union Minister for Tribal Affairs Kantilal Bhuria, and Deputy Chairman Planning Commission Montek Singh Ahluwalia on Declaring Bamboo as a Minor Forest Produce

21 MARCH 2011
You may recall that I had written to you earlier on 29 October 2010 on the need to restructure joint forest management committees (JFMCs) to address the perceptions in some circles that they need to be made more participatory and democratic. I had identified four specific action items...

I am now writing to you on a related issue of declaring and treating bamboo as minor forest produce. As you are well aware, bamboo is a traditional source of subsistence for many forest-dwelling communities of India and has immense cultural and economic significance. Bamboo is also an essential raw material for artisans and craftsmen and is the foundation of many indigenous crafts and cottage industries. Bamboo forests are distributed in around 9 million ha of forests and apart from providing sustenance to the poor, are a vital link in sustaining the stability of many ecosystems. Bamboo forests also serve as important habitats for wildlife. There is, hence, a pressing need for us to institute a system for the conservation of bamboo forests and enable the empowerment of people for sustainable use and management of this important resource.

Legal Position on Bamboo as Minor Forest Produce

The Scheduled Tribes and Other Traditional Forest Dwellers (Recognition of Forest Rights) Act, 2006 (also known as the Forest Rights Act, 2006, or FRA, 2006) has vested the 'right of ownership, access to collect, use and dispose of the minor forest produce, which has been traditionally collected within or outside village boundaries' with the Scheduled Tribes and the traditional forest dwellers.

The FRA, 2006 also defines MFP as including 'all non-timber forest produce of plant origin including bamboo ... and the like'. In the light of these legal provisions, and the significance of bamboo in the lives and livelihoods of many communities, you are requested to direct the state forest departments to treat bamboo as MFP and respect the rights accrued to communities as per the FRA, 2006.

Next Step for State Governments

The acceptance of bamboo as MFP has many consequences for the state government and the forest administration. These are identified below:

1. Areas where rights to the community forest resource (CFR) are recognized and vested under FRA, 2006:

    a. Gram sabha will issue transit passes: The forest departments must give the gram sabha the right to issue transit passes for bamboo as an MFP in areas designated as community forest resources (declared under FRA, 2006) and village forests (under Indian Forest Act, 1927).

    b. Harvesting of Bamboo: Extraction levels for bona-fide and subsistence needs of the local community will be decided by the gram sabha. The gram sabha, in consultation with the forest department, shall develop a management plan for commercial harvesting of bamboo.

2. Areas where community forest rights are not claimed or settled:

   a. Partnership with local communities: In such areas the forest department will, in partnership with the local communities, continue to design and implement management plans and working plans that ensure the sustainable use and extraction of bamboo.
   b. Revenue sharing: All revenue generated from bamboo cultivation/management will be shared with the local communities residing in the area and dependent on the land for their bona fide subsistence needs.
   c. Ensure sustainability: However, in these areas it must be made sure that the ecological integrity of the ecosystem is maintained and other relevant laws are obeyed.

3. Others:

   a. Non-forest lands/private lands: The gram sabha will issue transit passes for bamboo grown on such lands.
   b. States with little or no bamboo resources: These states may liberalize harvest and transport of bamboo by devolving authority to the gram sabha for management plans and issuance of transit passes.

However, I am sure you will agree with me that we must guard against over-exploitation. The impacts of extraction should be reviewed every three years and appropriate changes be made in the working plans and management plans to prevent over-harvesting of bamboo. A copy of these studies should be furnished to the MoEF.

All management plans should be prepared in a transparent and participatory manner and should be understood and approved by local communities. The management plan should clearly outline the felling cycle and annual harvest potential in numbers and should as far as possible plan for a diversity of uses, according to the requirements of the gram sabha concerned.

Further, it has come to our notice that there have been instances of the forest departments asking local communities for proof of bamboo being used for bona fide subsistence needs. I'm sure that you will agree with me that this is not necessary.

I am confident that you will initiate the necessary action at your end both on restructuring of JFMCs and treating bamboo as an MFP. A clear signal from you to your forest administration will be a first step and may have to be followed by relevant changes to the state laws and administrative regulations.

Letter to Prime Minister on Initiatives Taken by the Ministry to Help Counter Maoist Influence

21 MAY 2010

For quite some time, I have been thinking on how the MoEF can help in the battle against Maoist violence. I would like to bring to your attention three specific initiatives taken over the past few months.

First, a letter has been sent to the home minister. The central government has decided to give Rs 5,000 crore as a special grant to all states for forest development programmes over the next five years. We called a meeting of Left-wing Extremism (LWE)-affected states and prepared special forest development plans in the LWE-affected districts in these states. My proposal to the home minister is that he should impress on the states as part of his interactions while reviewing anti-Maoist operations the need to implement these plans in a focused manner. I have taken up the matter with the states but the home minister also doing so adds to the value.

Second, a joint committee of the MoEF and the Ministry of Tribal Affairs has been set up under the chairmanship of N.C. Saxena to see how best the forest establishment can help in the implementation of the Forest Rights Act, 2006 and also benefit from it in the process. The idea is to use the people, especially tribals who are bestowed with ownership rights as partners in sustainable forest protection and regeneration.

Third, a detailed meeting has taken place with the Minister for Panchayati Raj Kantilal Bhuria to examine how elected panchayat bodies, particularly in PESA areas, can take direct control over forestry programmes as envisaged by Rajivji in the 73rd Amendment and the PESA Act. We have decided to take some initial steps.

You have spoken about a two-track approach to combating Maoist violence. I see these three initiatives indicated above putting into practice what you have said about addressing pressing socio-economic concerns of tribals.

Letter to Deputy Chairman, Planning Commission Montek Singh Ahluwalia on Declaring the Minimum Support Price for Minor Forest Produce

11 APRIL 2011

Following a commitment I had made to the Prime Minister in a meeting to discuss PESA in which you were also present, I have written to all chief ministers on the issue of declaring bamboo as an MFP. I had sent a copy of this letter to you earlier.

Now, I seek to address a second issue that has come up frequently in the Prime Minister's meetings on PESA—namely, declaring the minimum support price (MSP) for MFP. I have discussed this subject with the member-secretary, Planning Commission, and also with Dr T. Haque, who is chairman of a committee set up by the Ministry of Panchayati Raj in August 2010 that will soon be submitting its report.

The consensus view that has emerged is the following:

1. MSP must be notified for major MFPs considered important for tribal livelihoods. Twelve such MFPs have been identified—*tendu*, bamboo, *mahuwa* flower and seed, sal leaf and seed, lac, *chironjee*, wild honey, myrobalan, tamarind, gums (*gum karaya*), and *karanj*.
2. A central committee should fix the MSP that will be benchmark for all states to follow. States can fix MSPs above the bench-mark but definitely not below it.
3. Monopoly of any kind (including by a state agency) on purchase of all MFPs, including tendu and bamboo should be removed.
4. State agencies trading in MFPs should be committed to purchasing all MFPs from the gatherers, rather than procuring only profitable MFPs. State agencies should also improve their marketing networks significantly.
5. All transportation barriers creating hurdles in the movement of MFPs must be removed.
6. Gram sabhas must be empowered to take on a more proactive role in the management and regeneration of MFPs. Forest working plans for regeneration must be prepared with the full participation of gram sabhas.
7. Value-addition of MFPs after their collection is essential. Basic value-addition units at the village level should be established.

The MoEF is more than ready to work with the Ministry of Panchayati Raj, the Ministry of Tribal Affairs and the Planning Commission to take this MFP initiative forward. Reforms in forest administration necessitated as part of this initiative will be given the highest priority.

Note to the Secretary, Environment and Director-General Forests, on Relaxing Forest Clearance Norms in Left-Wing Extremism Affected Areas

28 April 2011

The question of 'liberalizing' provisions of the Forest (Conservation) Act, 1980 for Left-wing extremism affected districts identified by the Planning Commission and the Ministry of Home Affairs has been under discussion for quite some time. We have already increased the threshold from 1 ha to 2ha for clearance by the state government itself without applying for clearance under FCA, 1980 for public infrastructure projects in these districts.

Many chief ministers have met me in this regard. Home minister, deputy chairman and member-secretary of the Planning Commission have also spoken to me. Yesterday, I was given a presentation by the state government in Gadchiroli in which Chief Minister of Maharashtra Prithviraj Chavan and his senior colleagues were present. *I am now persuaded that we should allow state governments the flexibility up to 5 ha to clear public infrastructure projects (schools, health centres, police stations, and security complexes, housing for state government employees, roads, bridges, small-scale irrigation facilities) without applying for clearance under FCA, 1980 in the sixty Left-wing extremism (LWE)-affected districts identified by the Planning Commission and the home ministry.*

Necessary procedural formalities should be completed expeditiously to give effect to this new dispensation. I should be kept informed when the formalities have been completed.

Letter to Prime Minister on Relaxation of Forest Clearance Norms in LWE-affected areas

11 May 2011

I am writing to inform you of a very significant liberalization we have just made in the application of Forest (Conservation) Act, 1980 in the sixty LWE-affected districts identified by the Planning Commission and the home ministry.

We have now permitted the state governments to clear, without reference to the central government or without application of the FCA, 1980, all proposals relating to physical and social infrastructure involving forest land up to 5 ha. This limit has been in the 1–2 ha range but now it is uniformly going to be 5 ha for projects of the state governments involving construction of schools, health centres, roads, bridges, agricultural marketing centres, police and security complexes, etc.

Letter to Prime Minister on the Recommendation of the Forest Advisory Committee to allow Jindal Steel and Power and JSW Steel to Mine in the Saranda Forests of Jharkhand

[Allowing mining in the rich dense forest area in a Maoist-affected district would be detrimental to the government's efforts to reach out to local people and to counter Maoist influence by focusing on development, especially when there exists a strong sentiment against mining since the local population receives no benefit from it. Both projects were cleared in May 2013 by the Cabinet Committee on Investments.]

6 FEBRUARY 2013

I have been keeping you informed regularly on the implementation of the Saranda Development Plan. My last letter to you on this subject was on 28 January 2013, after unfurling the National Flag at Digha gram panchayat on 26 January, an event that took place after well over a decade. There is a silent but very visible transformation going on in Saranda, which has relevance for other such areas in different states.

In one of my earlier letters dated 3 July 2012 (a copy of which I enclose), I had drawn your attention to the propaganda that is being spread that the Saranda Development Plan is only meant to serve private mining interests. I have been at great pains to counter this propaganda and dispel this impression. Many people are not convinced but I have repeatedly spoken on this issue and said that our government is sensitive to strong local sentiment against opening up this rich forest area to mining by new players.

In this context, I was most depressed to learn today that the Forest Advisory Committee of the MoEF had just given permission for the diversion of 512.43 hectare of forest land in Saranda for iron ore mining by Jindal Steel and Power and for diversion of another 998.70 hectare of forest land for mining iron and manganese ore by JSW Steel.

Sir, I think if these approvals go ahead, I would not be able to guarantee you any further success on the Saranda Development Plan and the co-operation of local people in its full and enthusiastic implementation. Ultimately it is a decision of the Government of India and of the Government of Jharkhand but it is my duty to alert you to the deeply adverse consequences this decision would have not just in Saranda but elsewhere as well.

Letter to Prime Minister on the Efforts Made by the Environment Ministry on Clearing Road Construction on the Indo-China Border

10 JUNE 2010

I have been in close touch with *raksha mantri* on clearance of sixty-three India–China border roads in Arunachal Pradesh that have been pending.

The present factual position is as follows: thirty-six roads have been given final clearance in the last couple of months. Thirteen roads have been given 'in-principle' approval but are awaiting compliance reports from the state government and/or Border Roads Organisation (BRO). Eight road proposals are still pending with the state government/BRO. Four road proposals are pending with the BRO.

Letter to Prime Minister on Fast-tracking Environmental Clearance to Aid the Development of the Siang River Basin on Account of its Strategic Importance

14 APRIL 2010

Yesterday I attended the second meeting of the Task Force on Hydroelectric Power Projects chaired by the Hon. Union Minister for Power Sushil Kumar Shinde. Deputy Chairman, Planning Commission, Minister for Water Resources, Minister for Rural Development and I were present. There were also power ministers from different states.

During the discussion on hydroelectric power projects in the Northeast, secretary (water resources) made an extremely important point which I have heard articulated for the first time. He said that in order to strengthen our negotiating position with China, overriding priority should be given to hydroelectric power projects on the Siang river. There are hydroelectric power projects on other rivers like Subansari and Dibang but from an international point of view, it is the Siang basin projects that are of strategic significance. I then asked him what the hydroelectric potential on the Siang was and he replied that it has been estimated at around 20,000 MW. When I pressed him further, he said that three specific projects with a total capacity of 11,000 MW have been identified. Further, these projects are at very preliminary stage and we have a long way to go before work begins on them.

Clearly, we should take up projects on the Siang river basin as a matter of urgent priority. If this means even more attractive rehabilitation and resettlement (R&R) packages and if this means giving additional incentives to the Arunachal Pradesh government, we should agree. We must begin work on Siang basin projects as national projects. I am prepared to put environmental and forest clearances for them on a special track given their strategic importance.

Getting this initiative off the ground at the earliest will require the Prime Minister's personal intervention.

Letter to Prime Minister on Action Taken by the Environment Ministry to Develop the Siang River Basin

14 October 2010

I had sent a note to you on 14 April 2010 on the issue of hydroelectric power projects on the Siang river in Arunachal Pradesh ... I wish to inform you of the further action that I have taken on this note.

Overriding a number of objections, on 2 August 2010, I approved the grant of the terms of reference (ToRs) for the environmental impact assessment (EIA) for the 2,700 MW Lower Siang project being executed by a private company.

While taking note of the objections, I had recorded the following:

This is an extremely important project from a strategic point of view that is essential to strengthen our negotiating/bargaining position vis-à-vis China on the Brahmaputra waters issue. There will be other such projects on the Siang. MoEF, keeping this perspective in mind, should play a proactive role for facilitating speedy implementation. Draft ToR letter to be issued immediately with corrections in the DFA.

The ToR approval letter was issued to the company on 3 August itself.

I thought it is important to bring this fact to your attention given the campaign that has been launched by some people that my position on hydroelectric power projects in Arunachal Pradesh weakens the national interest. In fact, may I take the liberty of saying that the position I have taken as articulated in the attached note as well as in the file noting reproduced above has been entirely *suo motu* without any ministry lobbying me for it.

I was also the only one to raise the Siang river issue and the fast-tracking of projects on it in the first meeting of the Group of Ministers set up under the finance minister's chairmanship to provide guidance in coordinating external interface on energy security matters that was held on 8 July 2010.

Speaking Order on the Maheshwar Hydroelectric Power Project

6 MAY 2011

In response to various representations receive on 17 February 2010, the MoEF had issued a show-cause notice[1] under Section 5 of the Environment (Protection) Act, 1986 to Shree Maheshwar Hydroelectric Power Corporation Limited (SMHPCL) due to non-compliance of various conditions in the original environmental clearance granted to the Maheshwar Hydroelectric Power project in Madhya Pradesh on 1 May 2001.

SMHPCL responded to the show cause notice on 9 March 2010 … After a detailed examination of the SMHPCL reply, a stop-work notice was issued to the company by the MoEF on 23 April 2010.

There are twenty-seven gates in the Maheshwar Hydroelectric Power project, out of which twenty-two had already been installed and operational prior to 17 February 2010. Fifteen gates are covered from the right bank and seven from the left. The remaining five gates, the construction of which was suspended by the stop work order are basically at the centre of the dam and the river. A coffer dam has been constructed through compacted boulders and loose earth materials as a temporary measure for construction of the dam

The Madhya Pradesh chief minister wrote to the Prime Minister on 28 April 2010, protesting against the stop work order. In response to this letter, the Prime Minister's Office took a meeting on 7 May 2010 based on which the MoEF agreed to modify the stop-work order of 23 April 2010 in order to permit work only on the seven gates of the dam, which were already installed because of safety requirements. However, the stop-work order continued on the installation of the last five gates of the dam where no work on installation had commenced.

Between May 2010 and December 2010, letters were exchanged between the state government and the MoEF and periodic reviews by the PMO in view of the fact that both the chief minister of Madhya Pradesh and a former chief minister of Madhya Pradesh were keen to recommence work on the project on the grounds that it will not only produce power but also supply drinking water to Indore and Dewas. I also met with the project promoters on 19 May 2010.

On 22 December 2010, I decided not to lift the stop-work order because I felt there had been little progress on the R&R. The environmental clearance was clearly predicated on the R&R proceeding *pari passu* with dam construction. But there was clear evidence that this condition had been violated. I also ruled that since the Government of Madhya Pradesh had committed to the PMO that R&R would be completed by 31 March 2011, we should wait till then before lifting the stop-work order.

I had another occasion soon to review the matter based on a letter that the MoEF received from the PMO forwarding letters written to the Prime Minister by Digvijaya Singh, former chief minister of Madhya Pradesh. On 4 January 2011, I once again reiterated my earlier decision not to lift the stop-work order in the absence of a credible guarantee that the R&R will be completed as planned, I further recorded that the resumption of work must be linked with progress on R&R since R&R schedules has slipped badly in the past.

Meanwhile, the Madhya Pradesh chief minister wrote another letter to the Prime Minister on 11 January 2011, which was forwarded to the MoEF on 31 January 2011 with a request to examine the case.

The Madhya Pradesh chief minister went on fast in Bhopal on 12 February 2011 and one of the issues he went to fast on was the alleged delay in lifting the stop-work order on the Maheshwar Hydroelectric Power project.

Based on an assurance given by the Prime Minister to Chief Minister of Madhya Pradesh Shivraj Singh Chouhan in order to get the latter to break his fast, Dr Mihir Shah, member, Planning Commission, held a meeting on 18 February 2011 on issues that the Madhya Pradesh chief minister had raised in his fast. Special secretary, MoEF wrote to the chief secretary, Madhya Pradesh, on 21 February 2011 as a follow up to this meeting.

On 17 February 2011, secretary (power), Government of India, wrote to the secretary (environment and forests), Government of India, saying that the Central Electricity Authority had opined that the erection of the remaining five gates should be allowed. The power minister spoke to me the next day to request that the stop-work order be lifted since 400 MW of relatively cheap electricity to a power-starved state was at stake.

On 1 March 211, the Government of Madhya Pradesh sent a report on the status of the R&R and claimed that 70 per cent of R&R had been completed. I was unable to understand how the figure of 70 per cent R&R completion had been arrived at since by the state government's own admission in this letter, out of nine villages to be fully submerged only one had been relocated to a developed site. The state was asked to clarify its calculations. On 13 April 2011, I once again recorded that in view of the fact that the status provided by the government of Madhya Pradesh for the villages coming under submergence is incomplete and also in view of the fact that the calculations for arriving at 70 per cent R&R completion are not at all convincing, the moratorium on construction work on the five spill way gates should continue.

On 19 April 2011, the MoEF received another communication from the state government on the status of R&R based on a review taken at the level of the chief minister of Madhya Pradesh.

The most recent review of the project was conducted by the PMO on 2 May 2011. After this meeting the Central Water Commission sent a technical report to the ministry on 4 May 2011. This CWC report recommended the installation of the balance of five radial gates to avoid damage to the existing construction in the event of a breach of the coffer dam due to monsoon floods.

In this background I am once again called upon to review the stop work order on the balance five gates of the Maheshwar Hydroelectric Power project. Twenty-two gates have been constructed. On the one hand, there are the technical reports of the CWC and the CEA with the report of the CWC being particularly categorical in its conclusions on the need to complete the remaining five gates soon before the monsoon from an engineering safety stand point. On the other, there is no denying the poor progress on R&R.

It has been suggested by those canvassing for the revocation of the stop work order that the Ministry of Environment and Forests has no *locus standii* on the R&R issue. I disagree strongly. R&R proceeding *pari passu* with dam construction was a key condition of the May 2001 environmental clearance and the Ministry of Environment and Forests is well within its rights to be concerned with this issue, as can be seen from the environmental clearance letter of 1 May 2001.

I want to mention here a conversation that the chief minister of Madhya Pradesh had with me over the phone on 16 April 2011 when I was visiting the Panna Tiger Reserve. He told me the reason why R&R has been slow is because the project affected people have begun to think that the dam project will not be completed on account of the Ministry of Environment and Forests' rigid stance, so why move at all is the attitude of the people according to the chief minister. Earlier when the project promoter had met me on 19 May 2010 he had said that the main reason for the poor progress on R&R was the obstructionist methods being adopted by local civil society groups and activists.

Thus, after considering all the facts and keeping in view the 4 May 2011 technical report of the Central Water Commission, the status report of the R&R was sent by the state government on 19 April 2011 after the chief minister's review, Chief Minister of Madhya Pradesh Shivraj Singh Chouhan's conversation with me on 16 April, the report of the Central Electricity Authority of 17 February 2011, and the conversation of the Union Power Minister Sushilkumar Shinde with me soon thereafter, and decisions taken at various meetings convened by the PMO in response to communications received by the Prime Minister from various dignitaries, including the chief minister of Madhya Pradesh and a former chief minister of Madhya Pradesh.

I have no option but to agree to the lifting of the stop-work order on the construction of the last five spillway gates. However, these gates shall not be lowered until satisfactory completion of R&R and its review. The filling up of the reservoir up to 154 m will be considered after the R&R work has been completed.

Speaking Order on Construction of a Ropeway to Ambaji Temple in Girnar Wildlife Sanctuary

2 FEBRUARY 2011

The matter of construction of a ropeway from Bhavnath Taleti to the Ambaji temple in the Girnar Wildlife Sanctuary in Junagarh has been under consideration of the MoEF for over a year. At my suggestion, a technical group of the Standing Committee of the National Board for Wildlife (NBWL) had visited this site on 21–22 December 2010. This two-person group advised against the construction of the ropeway because it could lead to the local extinction of the 'Girnari Giddh', a critically endangered species listed in Schedule I under the Wildlife (Protection) Act, 1972. I have personally visited the site on 27 January 2011. I have also had a detailed discussion on this project with the Bombay Natural History Society (BNHS), with the state government officials, with Dr Divyabhanusinh Chavda and Dr Nita Shah, who conducted the site visit and have also met with local organizations and citizens in Junagarh.

Before indicating my final decision I must place on record the following facts: The ropeway project has been hanging fire since September 1995. But it is only after the declaration of the Girnar Reserve Forest as the Girnar Wildlife Sanctuary in May 2008 that central government approval has been necessitated. Thus, for the period between 1995 and 2008, there was no need for any central government approval had the state government decided to go ahead with the project.

The declaration of the Girnar Reserve Forest as the Girnar Wildlife Sanctuary was a welcome step. This created a new habitat for the Gir lion and a population of twenty to twenty-five lions is now resident in the Girnar Wildlife Sanctuary, which covers about 180 sq km

The Girnari Giddh population that is going to be affected by the ropeway project is between 20 and 25 per cent of the total population of long-billed vultures in Gujarat but less than 10 per cent of the vulture population in the state.

Although I have received numerous representations against the ropeway on environmental grounds (primarily anticipated adverse impacts on vulture habitats), I have seen for myself strong reasons to build the ropeway. It would minimize man-animal conflict in the Girnar Wildlife Sanctuary (a new concern) and it would also provide a convenient way of transporting thousands of pilgrims daily to the holy spots on Mt Girnar. It would also put an end to socially unacceptable modes of transportation (*dolis*) that are being used presently.

Appreciating that arguments can be made both for and against the ropeway project and based on consultations I have had with all stakeholders including Dr Divyabhanusinh Chavda, Dr Nita Shah, and Dr Asad Rehmani of the BHNS, I have decided on the following course of action.

In-principle approval is being granted for the ropeway project subject to the following six specific conditions:

1. The Government of Gujarat will conduct a study to consider alternative alignment of the ropeway project, preferably along the Dattar/ Bhesan side with a view to ensure that it does not cut across prime vulture habitat and minimizes disturbance to nesting, roosting, and ranging sites of long-billed vultures and other wildlife species, and submit a report within two months.
2. The height of the ninth and tenth tower of the ropeway will be increased to avoid disturbance to vulture nesting sites located in this area.
3. A camera of high resolution will be placed on the ninth tower to monitor movement of vultures and, if required, movement of cabins of the ropeway will be regulated in such a way as to avoid any accidental collision of vultures with the cabin of the ropeway.
4. A cafeteria for vultures will be constructed at an appropriate location to be decided in consultation with experts, to provide supplemental feed to the vultures apart from attempting to divert movement of vultures away from the ropeway.
5. A cess of Rs 5 per ticket or 2 per cent of the ticket turnover revenue, whichever is higher, will be imposed. This cess amount will be given to the Gir Lion Conservation Society for conservation related activities in and around the Girnar Wildlife Sanctuary with a focus on long-billed vultures.
6. A technical monitoring group of officers from Gujarat Forest Department, local voluntary organizations concerned, BHNS, World Wildlife Fund for Nature, and experts will be set up to advise on safety protocols and to monitor implementation of the conditions governing the clearance of the ropeway project.

As per the statutory procedure, the Standing Committee of the NBWL will take a final decision based on the report submitted by the government of Gujarat.

'The Environments of the Poor: Making Sustainable Development Inclusive', Keynote Address at the Asian Development Bank Conference on 'The Environments of the Poor', New Delhi

24 NOVEMBER 2010

I am delighted that Asian Development Bank (ADB) has organized this seminar at a time when there is an intense political debate in this country on the nature of environmentalism itself. On the one side, there are those who believe that environmental issues are really a middle-class, elitist pastime, and have no relation to the development challenges that this country faces. On the other, there are many who would argue that the growing environmental movement or environmental consciousness that we are seeing today is actually the environmentalism of the poor and that it is because of the threat to livelihoods that environmental issues are coming to the forefront today.

I think, therefore, that an intellectual exercise like this seminar, which brings together different points of view and analytical work being done in different parts of the world on the links between poverty, mainstream developmental issues, and environmental issues, is opportune and very relevant. I have seen some of the papers that have been listed for this conference and I am sure these papers would have much value to add to the ongoing debate.

In the process of mainstreaming environmental issues as part of the poverty reduction agenda, it seems to me that there are three very important aspects that we have to keep in mind: The climate change aspect, which is gaining increased significance; the public health aspect, which is often neglected; and the natural resources aspect, which is also very important and often does not get the attention that it deserves. All of what I am going to say today is born out of the Indian experience.

The Poverty–Environment–Climate Link

Let us take the climate change aspect first and analyse the relationship between the environment and poverty reduction issues in the context of climate change. It is believed in many quarters in India that we have not caused the problem of global warming, so why should we take pro-active actions to address it. Our domestic actions have been dictated by our international negotiating positions. We have not really looked at an aggressive domestic agenda. Now, why do we need a domestic agenda? That is a very important question that we have to ask. The simple reason, which should be obvious to anybody, is that there is no country in the world that is going to be as profoundly affected by climate change as India. Many countries have points of vulnerability to climate change, but I cannot think of any other country in the world which has more points of vulnerability to climate change than India. Let us look at some of these points of vulnerability.

First, of course, is our dependence on monsoon. Even though less than 18 per cent of our GDP now depends on agriculture, there is no running away from the fact that variations in GDP growth are driven by variations in the performance of the monsoon. In spite of all the impressive gains that we have made in terms of diversification of our economy, the fact is that two out of three Indians still depend on agri-culture or agriculture-related occupations for employment. Therefore, there is extraordinary dependence on the monsoons, not just by the agricultural sector, but also the other sectors of the economy due to its spillover and multiplier effects. An analysis of the last fifty years data shows that 40–45 per cent of our fluctuations in GDP are on account of variations of monsoon alone. So, the monsoons are critical. What happens to the monsoon is, perhaps to my mind, the single largest determinant of prosperity in India.

The second point of vulnerability arises from the fact that we have a large population living in our coastal areas. We have a large peninsula with millions of people living on the coast who can only be classified as highly vulnerable to rising mean sea levels. Now, if there is one aspect of the Intergovernmental Panel on Climate Change that cannot be scientifically challenged and which has got a fair degree of robustness associated with it, is the fact that climate change is going to affect mean sea levels. This is almost an incontrovertible conclusion that has been arrived at. Therefore, while we are rightly concerned about Maldives, Bangladesh, and all other countries vulnerable to rise in mean sea lev-els, the fact is that there is no other country as vulnerable to it than India in terms of sheer number of lives impacted—we have 250–300 million people living on our coast starting from the Sunderbans in West Bengal, extending all the way up to Gujarat. I am talking of almost thirteen states and union territories and a large portion of the population of India.

The third point of vulnerability arises from what is predicted to happen to the Himalayan glaciers as a result of global warming. Evidence on this, of course, is somewhat mixed. I myself don't share in its entirety the gloom and doom that is spread by many climate evangelists on the future of the Himalayan glaciers. But the fact of the matter is that the health of the Himalayan glaciers is a cause for great concern. If the majority of Himalayan glaciers continue to retreat in the manner that they have been, then they are going to seriously impact water availability in the North Indian rivers which are the lifeline for almost a billion people living in India, Nepal, Bhutan, and Bangladesh.

And finally, the fourth major point of vulnerability arises from our dependence on extraction of natural resources. The fact is that India has embarked on an 8–9 per cent GDP growth drive in the last five years, which we hope to sustain over the next fifteen to twenty years at the very minimum, and this is going to call for the greater extraction of our mineral resources. More and more we are discovering that coal reserves (which are essential for power generation) and other minerals are located in our forest areas. So the more coal we produce, the more forests we destroy, and the more forests we destroy, the more we add to our greenhouse gas emissions, besides all the concomitant ecological losses.

I do not think that there is any country in the world that is as clearly and categorically vulnerable to climate change on so many dimensions: monsoons, the rising mean sea levels, the retreat of the Himalayan glaciers and the anticipated deforestation in response to the extraction of natural resources.

So, I think, to start with we need to recognize that India is profoundly impacted by climate change and that the response to this impact has to necessarily be a mix of adaptation and mitigation. Though the 'M' word (mitigation) was a taboo in India until recently, it is very important to India. Although we are a very small emitter in per capita terms, we are today the world's fourth largest emitter in absolute terms. China is at No. 1, with 23 per cent of world greenhouse gas emissions, the US giving the Chinese a run for their money at 22 per cent, the European

Union would be about 13 per cent, and India and Russia are roughly almost on a par at about 5 per cent.

Modelling studies conducted by the National Council of Applied Economic Research (NCAER) brings to light certain grave facts. It shows that the great advantage of having a denominator (that is, population) that is one billion-plus, growing by ten million every year, is that on a per capita basis, we will always have low-emission levels, but in absolute terms, if we continue our greenhouse gas emission profile, we could end up accounting for anywhere between 8.5 and 9 per cent of world's greenhouse gas emissions by 2030. As responsible global citizens of a responsible power, we should be concerned and we need to act. An increase in our international role comes with certain responsibilities. This does not mean abdicating your negotiating position. It means that you need to walk on two legs—you negotiate internationally from a position of strength, but you also work proactively on the domestic front, taking substantive policy actions.

So, I think on the climate change aspect of the link between the environmentalism and poverty reduction, it is very clear that we are vulnerable, and it is the poorer regions and communities that will bear the burden of this vulnerability. While this will call for adaptation—and adaptation would mean largely a major investment in agriculture—this will also call for a very significant investment in mitigation.

The Poverty–Environment–Public Health Link

Now let me talk about the second dimension of this link between environment and poverty reduction that is related to public health. I believe that the public health dimensions of environmental issues have been grossly neglected in this country. And this is one reason why when you talk of environmental issues you do not get the type of resonance that you need to get. When I tell my 'growth-wallah' friends 'you know environment is an important issue', they will say, 'but you know 9–10 per cent is more important'. However, if I could tell them that 'by not dealing with environment frontally you are really debilitating the Indian population, and eroding the long-term sustainability of this growth', I probably would get a better response from them. I think that we need to change the terms of the debate on environment in this country. We need to put it out fairly and squarely as a public health issue. This is not a marketing gimmick.

One of the weaknesses of our country is that we do not have a strong epidemiological network. But from whatever anecdotal evidence we have been able to gather from the various institutions and experts, I can confidently say that there is a very close connection between conventional environmental and public health issues. For example, about twenty-five years ago, the proportion of children with respiratory diseases in Bangalore, the information technology capital of India, was less than 10 per cent. But today, data seems to suggest that almost 30 per cent of people in Bangalore suffer from asthma or some other respiratory diseases. Bathinda, a prosperous agricultural region of Punjab, has today emerged as one of the major epicentres of cancer. This has been directly attributed to land degradation and, more importantly, to water contamination and water pollution.

So, when you really look at the environmental effects of many of the economic activities, whether it is in agriculture or industry, you will find that there have been very significant public health impacts, which in my view will act as a severe drag on our ability to sustain our high rate of growth for a long period of time. There is a very good analysis on Indian poverty by Anirudh Krishna from Duke University that has been released recently. Anirudh, a former Indian Administrative Service officer, has been a professor at Duke for a long time. He has done one of the most comprehensive analysis of Indian poverty. The one powerful conclusion that he has confirmed in his analysis (spread over more than a decade) is that rural expenditure on health is the primary determinant of families getting into poverty. The more you spend on health, the inability to spend on health or the debt that you incur, leads you into poverty. There is, today, a very solid body of evidence to suggest that rural indebtedness in India is driven by expenditure on health. I may be exaggerating, but I would say that at least to my mind, a very significant part of the expenditure on health would come from environment-related factors. So, I am convinced that if we can get people to see the environmental issue as a public health issue, we would get somewhere in our attempt at integrating and mainstreaming environment into the developmental process.

The Poverty–Environment–Natural Resources Link

Let me now turn into the third issue, which is the natural resources issue. I have spoken about environment in the context of climate change. I have spoken about environment in the context of public health. Let me now talk about environment in the context of natural resources. It is absolutely clear that sustaining 8–9 per cent growth over the next two decades or more will have a significant impact on our natural resources. It's going to have a significant impact on coal as I mentioned to you, on forestry, on water, and land. A primary determinant of this growth is going to be our ability to use these natural resources in a sustainable manner.

Most of the natural resources that are required to fuel economic growth in India are located in our forest areas and most of these forest areas happen to be in the poorer regions of our country. Out of the 600 districts of our country, the 188 districts in which the tribal population is a very substantial proportion, accounts for approximately 60 per cent of our forest area. Therefore, there seems to be close nexus between poverty, forests, tribal population, the availability of natural resources, and, I might add, social violence as well. It is a strong correlation. So we have to look at and address this dimension.

Poverty: An Ecological Phenomenon

The vice-president of ADB made a very important statement about the role of environmental factors in poverty. In fact, this has been a very important issue that has engaged our attention for many years. We've looked at educational poverty and health poverty, we measure poverty as consumption poverty and the NCAER does income poverty studies. But ecological poverty or the notion that poverty can arise from ecological factors, is a very important idea that we need to look at. From my experience, I can say that in many parts of India, the single most important cause of poverty is land degradation. Land degradation is caused by a variety of environmental factors—some natural, some man-made. When land degradation is arrested, we will see a dramatic impact on poverty levels.

A very good example of this is one of the most successful World Bank projects on the reclamation of sodic soils in Uttar Pradesh. In the central part of Uttar Pradesh, small farmers are mainly low-caste farmers belonging to the weaker and discriminated sections of society. This area is really the poverty bowl of India and farmers are suffering immensely because of low yields from the land that they are cultivating, since these lands are mostly wastelands and have sodic soils. A World Bank project that was designed in the 1990s to reclaim the sodic soils—I can tell you that large parts of Uttar Pradesh have been transformed by this single most important intervention which was to restore the productivity of the land, especially for the small farms cultivated by farmers belonging to the weaker sections of our society.

Ecological poverty is extremely important and must be given adequate attention. We need to make a very systematic effort to design interventions that will ensure that ecological factors do not exacerbate poverty levels. In fact, many civil society organizations in India have worked very successfully on watershed development projects, water conservation, rainwater harvesting and the intelligent use of water for agricultural purposes, all of which have had dramatic effects on poverty levels.

* * *

I would like to reiterate that, to me, environmentalism is meaningful only as environmentalism of the poor. There are, of course, lifestyle environmental issues but for the most part, livelihood environmental issues are what we are concerned with. And I think if we look at environment in the context of climate change, public health, and natural resources, we will be able to appreciate better the link between environmentalism and poverty. We really need to redefine the terms of environmental debate in our country because today environment protection is considered by many to be a drag on development.

The whole debate has been 'conservation versus growth', 'environment versus development'. I think this is a meaningless debate and if it is formulated in this fashion, environment cannot win this debate; because who can be against 9 per cent economic growth? Therefore, we have to redefine the terms of the debate on the environment and look at it in terms of poverty reduction. This is certainly a giant step forward. I look forward to working with the ADB and the NCAER on providing further operational content to this link and also making it a part of mainstream political discourses.

Notes

1. A copy of the show-cause notice, reply to the show-cause notice, stop-work order, a letter from Chief Minister of Madhya Pradesh Shivraj Singh Chouhan, and the modified stop-work order were made public along with the speaking order.

4 Beyond Clearances

In the public mind, the environment ministry was all about clearances. This was in large measure due to extensive publicity given to my flagging projects, especially big-ticket ones, for environmental violations. Reducing the ministry to merely the act of clearing, or not clearing, projects only served to buttress the ministry's image as a throwback to era of licence raj. Environment and ecological security is more than just about making case-by-case or even making policy-based assessments about measures that directly impact economic growth.

In the 1970s and even in the 1980s, before the economy was liberalized, environment and ecological security focused largely on wildlife and forests. Over the years, the attention shifted, and the environment ministry focused more on clearances. It began to take positions on issues like air pollution largely because of the Supreme Court. My endeavour was to restore the balance; it was meaningless to talk of ecological security and not consider the state of the forests, 40 per cent of which are degraded, or the state of the rivers, lakes, wetlands, and other water bodies. To my mind, it did not make sense to just focus on the tiger, and forget the elephant, or the rhinos that too were under the constant threat from poachers, or the fact that the *gharial* or the Gangetic dolphin were under threat.

These threats have been aggravated with the rising population pressures. Mindful of this, one important mindset change I sought to bring about was to nuance the goal of bringing 33 per cent of the country under forest cover. It was an idea that seemed to become part of the lore, without any real basis. On the one hand, there was constant pressure to divert more forest land for industry and development projects, and on the other was the goal of increasing the forest cover. Instead, I chose to focus on improving the health of the degraded forests—better to improve the quality of the forests we have than expend energy on what was an impossible and impractical goal. This was an important element of the Green India Mission. Improving the quality of forests had the added benefit of carbon sequestration, helping us offset the emissions that were bound to rise as the economy grew. Protecting the biodiversity-rich forests had benefits—aside from preserving our heritage, it contributed to our natural wealth and with the access and benefit-sharing protocol in place, it would provide an avenue to augment the livelihood of the people living in these areas.

Despite the focus and attention the tiger got, it was still an animal under threat. It was not just poachers that were the aggressors. Our demand for higher growth put tiger habitats, along with that of other animals and species, in danger. A country's natural health is determined in large measure by the health of its forests and wildlife. I was, therefore, keen to pilot the re-introduction of the cheetah, the only mammal to have actually become extinct in India. Despite my efforts, the project did not take off, and put me in direct confrontation with some tiger-wallahs. Long after I left the environment ministry, the idea of reintroducing the cheetah was struck down by the Supreme Court on the grounds that India should try and preserve the wildlife it has. Keen as I was on reintroducing the cheetah, this was bit of a setback.

Turning the focus on other species, I set up the Elephant Task Force, under the chairmanship of Mahesh Rangarajan, in an attempt to draw up a plan for its protection and conservation. The railways—particularly in some stretches like north Bengal—had contributed to a large number of elephant deaths. Increased human activity was leading to higher incidence of conflict with animals. Often it would result in terrible tragedies like the killing of seven elephants in north Bengal by a speeding train. In its aftermath, I was able to draw up—with the ministry of railways and the West Bengal government—a modicum of a plan that would reduce such casualties.

Environment is a complex issue in any country, but more so in India, because of the sheer scale, the competing demands, the range of deprivation, and the need for rapid economic growth. As environment minister, I needed to be more vigilant than a master juggler; there were just too many balls up in the air at any given point. Given the scale and complexity of issues, it is difficult and fool hardy to think that all issues can be addressed by one single entity—the Ministry of Environment and Forests. Not only was it necessary to get all stakeholders involved and invested in the quest for ecological security, it was also necessary to be innovative both in terms of institutions and partners. I was, to borrow the late Elinor Ostrom's coinage, in favour of a 'polycentric' approach to addressing the issues that confronted and affected the environment.

It is this realization that in some ways led to the setting up of the National Ganga River Basin Authority. We had spent a great deal of money to clean the Ganga since the mid-1980s but there was little impact. It is to improve the outcomes that this multi-stakeholder body comprising the Gangetic states, civil society, and experts was set up. While every state needed to take steps to reduce the flow of untreated municipal waste and industrial effluents into the Ganga, there was also a need to look at the Ganga as the river system it really was. Several other measures, including the focus on lake conservation, the notification of the wetlands conservation and management rules, were undertaken to address the issue of the health of our water bodies.

It was not enough to rope in the state governments, civil society, and academics; industry and markets also needed to be part of the effort to ensure ecological security. The market-based mechanism to address air pollution devised by the Massachusetts Institute of Technology–Harvard University team led by Esther Duflo was one such attempt to use the potential of markets to address environmental issues.

I was keenly aware that no effort to address the issues of ecological security would work successfully without putting people at its centre. Partnerships, required to protect our natural environment, work when people have a stake—be it collecting non-timber forest produce or running a small business. People needed to be at the core of efforts to address environmental degradation, or encroachments in forests, or declining wildlife habitat in order to achieve success. For this, I often moved beyond a narrow definition of the environment to address issues like the need for a minimum support price for minor forest produce, or a more humane and just system of relocation of people living in tiger reserves. How we engaged with the people on such basic issues could determine in large measure how they would engage on forest conservation and protection of wildlife. It is in this context that I attempted to improve the frayed relationship between people living in and around forest areas and the forest officials. The proposed amendments to the Indian Forest Act, 1927 are part of this effort, as is the recasting of the joint forest management committees.

Sometimes, environmental issues could be tackled alongside efforts for improving livelihoods. I initiated a partnership with the Defence Research and Development Organisation for sea-buckthorn cultivation, an initiative, which if implemented properly would help tackle desertification in high-altitude areas in Jammu and Kashmir and Himachal Pradesh, as well as provide income generating opportunities. Partnerships could also be about technological support for industries, such as a new leather preservation technique developed by the Central Pollution Control Board, which would use less water and less chromium and reduce the quantum of industrial waste following into the river and water bodies.

This chapter deals with work of the environment ministry, which are beyond the headline-grabbing clearances.

'Managing the Commons: From Academics to the Real World',
Address to the Thirteenth Biennial Conference of the International
Association for the Study of the Commons, Hyderabad

10 JANUARY 2011
...As I suggested to my old friend and colleague Dr Nitin Desai, after listening to this fascinating lecture by Professor Ostrom, there are many in this audience who would rather be asking questions than listening to me, but nevertheless that does not seem to be possible. This, Prof. Ostrom, is an example of institutional monoculture, all inaugural sessions have to follow a certain set pattern; there is no 'biodiversity' that is allowed here in the inaugural session. I am sorry, we do not have the opportunity to question you on a fascinating lecture that has opened up many possibilities for policy interventions.

I am delighted and privileged to be here among so many academic scholars from all over the world. It has been one of my endeavours in my ministerial positions, and particularly, in this one to bridge the gap between the academic and the 'real' world. Unfortunately, I have not always been successful because academics measure time in terms of years and decades, and those of us here in the real world measure it in months. Some of us, who work for endangered species, might even look at it in days. So, it has been very difficult to involve academics on a daily basis. In the last nineteen months in this ministry, I have made a conscious effort to involve members of academia in my work. However, to involve them in the process of decision-making, policy formulation, or policy monitoring is not always successful. The case with academics, though not true of economists, is when working with three academics, you end up with five acrimonious opinions—not always a positive result. But, nevertheless, I think this is an opportunity to listen and read a most valuable set of academic papers that are being presented at this conference. For the next three days, many of my colleagues from the state governments, state departments, and the forest department are going to be here and I am sure they will be able to carry forward the discussions into the realm of practice.

I had the privilege of listening to a thought provoking talk by Prof. Ostrom where she focused on one commons—the management of forests based on her case studies from the Tadoba–Andhari landscape in Maharashtra and the Mahananda landscape in West Bengal.

The Issue of Commons: What Have I Learnt?

In my position, one of the big challenges has been to look at commons in hierarchy. The global commons—the debate on climate change; the regional commons—issues of rivers, river management, and aquifers; and the local commons—the management of forests. I have had to grapple with all three, and I have found the writings of Prof. Ostrom, of whom I was aware even before I became the minister, most fruitful. The one phrase that has stuck with me is the need to reject 'institutional monoculture' and follow a 'polycentric approach' when it comes to dealing with the effects of these commons and ensuring that access and equity issues are addressed. I was reading a very interesting interview of Nitin Desai and being an economist, he was asked what the fundamental distinction between a commons and a public good is. He responded with what we all learn in economics: that in the commons area, we have to look at both access and equity issues, which is not the case in conventional public goods. The real challenge before me has been to reject this concept of institutional monoculture when it comes to devising solutions for issues that are rooted in access and equity. I would like to share with you what I have learned in each of these three areas—the global commons, the regional commons and the local commons.

Global Commons

Let me start with the global commons issue, the most current and contemporary of which is the debate of climate change. What I find frustrating about the debate of climate change is the complete lack of communication between the negotiators and academics. All the interesting work on climate change is taking place in the academic world. The negotiators in their world of brackets, footnotes, and fine distinctions of 'shall and will' and 'could and should', are completely oblivious to the work of Jeffrey Frankel at Harvard, Michael Spence of Stanford, Thomas Schelling of the University of Maryland or Prof. Ostrom, herself. I think this has been a great tragedy and one of my endeavours has been to get the negotiating community to look at the body of academic literature in the climate change area. Central to a successful negotiation is how we address the issue of equity. This issue, of course, is central to climate change. If you see the Cancun Agreements, the phrase that we have been successful in incorporating is 'equitable access to sustainable development'. I was not very happy with the traditional phrasing—'equitable access to carbon space'—because this conjures up a right to pollute. I know of friends in Africa and the small islands who are very wary of not just the developed world, but also of the two big developing countries, China and India. I wanted to convey the message that this does not indicate an unfettered right to pollute, but we take it as a fundamental right to a decent quality of life and standard of living, which is what governments are supposed to ensure. We have included the concept of 'equitable access to sustainable development' in the Cancun Agreements, and before Durban next year we will have an innovative way of defining equitable access.

One of the problems of the international climate change discussions has been the complete absence of any economic criteria. As our nation moves up the per capita income ladder, the notion of countries taking on greater responsibilities is non-existent in the current architecture of climate change. One of the great challenges for future climate change is not a formula but a set of formulas that will ensure equitable access to sustainable development. Without changing the 'holy grail' of the framework, we will not succeed because we cannot get an agreement among some 193 countries. But if, as Professor Ostrom has mentioned, we are going to have a variety of approaches, a diversity of solutions depending on the context; maybe we will be able to succeed and revisit the present framework a few years from now. I think the big challenge for researchers is to give operational meaning to the concept of equitable access to sustainable development.

First, we have to define what sustainable development is. Dr Nitin Desai defined it twenty-two years ago, as the 'ability of a generation to meet its consumption needs without endangering the ability of future generation to meet theirs'. We must give it an operational meaning and develop a framework that ensures equitable access, and takes into account population, per capita income and internal issues of distribution (because even as India is rightly concerned about the equality of access on an international scale, it cannot be oblivious to differences of access internally). We are world leaders when it comes to talking about international inequality but we are hesitant about dealing with domestic inequality. The inequality in access to sustainable development within India today is a very serious issue that policymakers and academics have to come to terms with. So, I would conclude by saying that Cancun revived the multilateral process that had reached a dead-end in Copenhagen, and brought about a certain degree of consensus.

One of the biggest obstacles that remains is, how to define a global goal and define equity in the achievement of this goal, without necessarily endangering the growth prospects of developing countries.

Regional Commons

River water management is a good example of a regional common, not exactly a global common and not exactly a local common. Though this applies to global commons as well, the existing trade-offs among these multiple objectives are much starker in the regional commons area. Take a river basin for example. Twenty years ago, the concept of a minimum environmental flow did not exist in our policy discourse. So, we planned a series of hydroelectric power, irrigation, and drinking water projects, and today we are finding that many of our important and ecologically sensitive river systems do not have what ecologists are now calling 'minimum environmental flow'. How do we ensure minimum environmental flow when we have multiple pressures on the river systems for the development of hydroelectric power projects and the pressure to bring drinking water to a larger population? This is an issue that is becoming increasingly important in policy discourse. I have faced severe opposition to my decision to stop the hydroelectric power projects in the upper reaches of the Ganga, in the state of Uttarakhand, some of which were at advanced stages of completion. One particular hydroelectric power project that was 40 per cent complete, where we had spent almost Rs 500 crore, had to be scrapped to conserve the minimum environmental flow of the Bhagirathi river, which has religious, cultural, and ecological significance. These are the types of conflicts and trade-offs of regional commons, of which water is the most critical.

Local Commons

Finally, we come to the issue of local commons. Prof. Ostrom had alluded to this earlier, this whole issue of how to manage our forests. We have always asked what is the best way to manage our forests. This is the wrong question that we have asked and we often come up with the wrong solutions. The question should be: What are the sets of best ways of managing our forests? We have over 70 million ha of forest cover in our country, roughly 21 per cent of the geographical area, and for the last thirty or forty years, the theology of forest planning has been that one-third of India should come under forests. But as I have asked for the last nineteen months: What is the source of this theology? I have not yet received a satisfactory answer to this basic question. This is why I think the time has come for us to make a radical shift in our approach: From the quantity to the quality of our forests. With 70 million ha of forest cover, and 40 per cent of it being open, degraded forests, the challenge before us is to improve the quality of existing forests, rather than bring one-third of India under forest cover. There is an increasing recognition of not just the ecological role that forests perform, but as our ministry publicized a few months ago, roughly 10 per cent of our annual greenhouse gas emission is absorbed by our forests. This is a substantial contribution. The carbon sequestration potential of Indian forests was estimated to be roughly 10 per cent in the mid-1990s, but as we sustain 8–9 per cent growth we will not be able to compensate for the loss of forest cover. Our estimate is that by 2020 the annual carbon sequestration potential of our Indian forests would be between 6 and 7 per cent of our annual greenhouse gas emissions. Even maintaining this level would have a major impact on our carbon sequestration levels.

Increasingly, our forests are facing not just ecological obstacles, but also social and economic obstacles. Over 200–250 million Indians depend on forests for their livelihoods, a fact that is often forgotten by the forest department, in which I include myself. I think the challenge before us in managing Indian forests, is to ensure that their ecological value be brought into public discussion. Unfortunately over the years, our laws have not been able to recognize and enshrine the age-old economic and social functions our forests perform.

Great Laws, Bad Implementation: Why?

Coming to the question of what is standing in the way of implementing the laws we have for managing our common pool of resources? It is a very interesting question and coincidentally, in recent weeks, I have been defending myself for doing just this, implementing the laws of the land. It is quite a bizarre situation where I have become newsworthy only because I am implementing the law. In most modern countries, this is considered a part of the daily duty of a minister, but here a minister implementing the laws of the land has become an endangered species that every day I make front page news. I have four points to make in this regard.

It is time for India to recognize, accept, acknowledge, and appreciate that a 9 per cent rate of economic growth will extract an ecological cost. There is a trade-off between a series of ecological and economic objectives and our task is to make these trade-offs and choices explicit. In most cases, we may be able to have both. In fact, a 1,000 years ago, Al Beruni defined India and Indian culture as very peculiar because when confronted with a choice they will choose both. It is part of our DNA, part of our culture that we can have economic growth as well as protect our environment. This is an attractive concept to have.

There is another concept I want to suggest and maybe that is why I am becoming increasingly unpopular: There are cases when you have to make a choice. Choices must be made by our society, system, and Parliament. These are tough choices. For example, Professor Ostrom showed us that the Tadoba–Andhari Tiger Reserve, which is not threatened by cattle or local encroacher, is instead at risk from a coal mine that needs to be opened up for generating power. This is a choice we have to make. Does the Indian political system want to protect the Tadoba–Andhari Tiger Reserve (which is not just a tiger reserve, but an ecosystem, a large habitat, a biodiverse landscape that we call a tiger reserve) or are we going to open it up in the name of economic growth? The answer I get from my growth colleagues who now consider us to be traitors is 'some compensatory afforestation will resolve the problem'. The flaw in this response is that destroying a natural forest that has evolved over centuries cannot be replaced by a plantation, which is a monoculture. Its ecological value simply cannot be compared with a forest with multiple ecological benefits. That's an example of a choice that we have to make.

Increasingly, we have to make these choices. Do we want water in our rivers, or do we want tunnels in our rivers? Today in many rivers in India you see only tunnels, no water. These are not technocratic or scientific choices, but political choices. What I have tried to do is bring environment in the mainstream of the political debate of our country. These are not issues that scientists or ecologists or civil society activists alone should decide. These are issues that the political system should decide. Should India introduce genetically modified brinjal, since it happens to be the centre of genetic diversity? With 3,000 varieties of genes of brinjal present, it is not a scientific issue, it is a political issue. The political system needs to decide.

Choices will have to be made and they will mean saying 'yes' in some cases, but also saying 'no'. When you are going to stop bauxite mining because it affects the livelihood security of tribal communities, you are saying no. That is a choice that the society has to make. Now, will it affect the 9 per cent growth trajectory? My view is that it will not, but the general popular belief is that it will.

Development Dynamic

So, the first thing that is standing in the way of implementation of the laws of our country is the development dynamic. I do not think anybody in his right mind would argue against the need to sustain a 9–10 per cent real rate of economic growth. But what its ecological implications are is something we need to understand better. Twenty years ago, people like Dr Nitin Desai pointed out that the economic growth of the 1980s was not fiscally sustainable. I would suggest that twenty years later, a similar question needs to be asked whether this growth is ecologically sustainable. And how do we manage this trade-off in cases where there is a direct conflict between growth and conservation objectives? We can reconcile to the maximum extent possible, but when it is not possible, how do society and society's democratic institutions deal with it?

Institutional Monoculture

My second point is the institutional monoculture that is standing in the way of implementing laws. On the one hand we have a mindset that says only the state can be a sustainable and effective guardian of common pool resources, and then, of course, we have well-meaning, well-qualified, very aggressive, vocal civil society activists, many of whom are present in the audience today, who believe that the state is the enemy of sustainable management and only 'the communities' can manage these resources. I think the time has come for us to allow for a multiplicity of institutional models, and to allow for different ways of managing a common pool resources.

Just two days ago, I released a new set of laws for managing our coastal areas. We have 7,500 km of coastline and we have one law, one institutional model for managing them. We have introduced the new law which recognizes that Goa, Sunderbans, Chilika, Lakshadweep, Andamans, the one and only island city of Mumbai, and the backwaters of Kerala are all unique ecosystems. The Coastal Zone Notification, 2011 has niches and windows that allow for a diversity of situations. One of the reasons we are ineffective in implementing the laws is because our laws are predicated on institutional monoculture. We do not allow for regional variation. India is a land of enormous ecological diversity, and we still insist on the primacy of the state. Or sometimes we sing the virtues of self-governance or empowerment as a substitute for effective good governance of the state.

I think Professor Ostrom's insights on institutional monoculture are very important. We need to have another look at our legal regime and the basis on which these legal regimes rest. As the minister of environment and forests, I am sorry to say that the Indian Forest Act of 1927 is predicated on the assumption that people who depend on forests for their daily sustenance are criminals. That is the unwritten premise. We have not challenged the intellectual edifice and to do so requires changing a whole system and recognizing that it is very important to have the local community developing an 'economic stake'. And I emphasize the phrase 'economic stake' in the assets that they are being asked to protect regionally. The very premise of many of our laws, the institutional premise of our laws and the procedural premise needs to be rerouted quite substantially and significantly.

Split Responsibility

The third problem we have in implementing laws is split responsibility. All our laws are federal and all of the management and implementation is at the stake of the local level. So, when people ask me in Parliament, 'What are you doing about air pollution?' I respond that it is state government's responsibility. Somebody asks me, 'What are you doing about forests?' Again, I respond, it is a state government's responsibility. The real issue is the laws: the Forest Conservation Act, the Forest Rights Act, and the Environment Protection Act are all national laws, as also the Water Pollution Act and the Air Pollution Act. But the responsibility for the implementation of these laws lies at the provincial and local levels. As a country, we have not devised a set of incentives that will stimulate responsible environmental governance at sub-national levels. These split responsibilities are something that we need to come to grip with. In our federal system of resource sharing, we have been able to bring some changes about.

From April this year, you will be happy to know, the sharing of resources from the central government to the provincial government will have a 2.5 per cent weight for environmental parameters. So, states that manage the environment better will receive an incentive of greater resources from the Planning Commission. And, as part of the transfer of resources, we have introduced a large grant of Rs 5,000 crore for the sustainable management of forests, visible forest cover, and the ability to demonstrable innovations in forest management. Some are making a small start, but I believe this split responsibility is in some ways a deterrent. We have recently reviewed the functioning of the Forest Rights Act, 2006, which deals with community property rights and the flaw that we have found is that while we have effectively addressed individual rights, we have not recognized forest rights of the community. One reason is the separation between passing a national law and its implementation.

Mindset

Finally, the biggest constraint in implementing the laws for managing the common pool of resources is the mindsets of those involved in managing these resources. We need to have a completely new approach. Let me give you an example: the way the US managed the environmental problem of acid rain in the mid-1980s was a market-based approach. Now Esther Duflo and Michael Greenstone from the Massachusetts Institute of Technology have prepared a paper for market-based system for managing air pollution in India, which is available on our website. The release of this paper was marked by a huge outcry from civil society activists and academics in our country, who thought I was introducing market-based principles for environmental management—they felt that environmental management could only be managed by institutions and regulations can be managed only by regulators. The notion of a market-friendly instrument to implement a regulation is still quite an anathema to many of us. I think it is important for us to let go of these old mindsets because the fact is the management of common pool resources does require regulations. The question is, do the regulations require regulators? We need to draw a distinction between the need to have regulations and the assumption that this requires an army of regulators or inspectors, who eventually are not part of the solution.

Conclusion

I apologize, for I have taken a large part of your time this evening; I debated whether to have a prepared text, but having a prepared text makes it appear that I am very scholarly, which I am not. I am not an academic scholar, but as I said right at the beginning, I am a bit of an intellectual scavenger. I read a lot of material and literature and try to extract from them lessons that are useful for policy. I think the insights that Prof. Ostrom has shared with us, will enable us to meet the management of our common pool of resources in an effective manner which will meet the objectives of efficiency and equity. I look forward to a continued association with the large community of scholars present here. I would be more than delighted to involve you in the running of my ministry with one caveat: Please give me an output in a matter of months and not take five–six years to provide the first draft of your study.

Letter to Prime Minister on Banning the Use of Plastics

3 JULY 2009

You had written to me on 8 June 2009 on the issue of checking and banning the use of plastics and tetrapaks in the Himalayas. I fully share your and Gopal Gandhi's concerns on the matter and since receiving your letter, have taken up the matter as a priority. Gopal Gandhi wrote to me separately on the same issue and I have sent him a detailed reply.

In summary the situation is as follows:

Studies have shown that plastics and plastic bags are not harmful per se. The primary problem arises largely due to ineffective waste collection and management systems in our towns and cities. Unused plastics find their way into garbage dumps and go into drains choking the drainage system as well. Some plastic bags are eaten by cows and other animals resulting in their death.

Alternatives to plastic have their limitations. Biodegradable or degradable plastics are in a nascent stage of development. Paper bags involve cutting trees and their use is limited due to certain features.

The central government has good enabling laws and rules, which allow states the autonomy to develop their own regulations in dealing with plastic waste management. The onus of implementing these rules rests with the states. Thus, a large number of efforts in this regard have been state-driven with state agencies having met with varying degrees of focus and success.

Nevertheless, given that waste management is a long-term systemic problem, which will take time and effort to resolve, some hill states have imposed a blanket ban on the use of plastic carry bags/bottles in tourist places, in order to protect the pristine beauty of these sites. These include Jammu and Kashmir, Sikkim, West Bengal, and Himachal Pradesh.

Most notably, the Government of Himachal Pradesh has taken a Cabinet decision to ban plastics all over the state with effect from 31 August 2009. This can, perhaps, be used as a model legislation for other states with significant hill cover. The Himachal Pradesh decision is noteworthy because it imposes a complete ban on plastic bags and all non-biodegradable single-use plastic items, irrespective of size of thickness of the plastic, making it easier to implement. The ban is applicable without exception throughout the state. It empowers a whole range of government officers to enforce the ban (not just the State Pollution Control Board). It clearly lists a range of penalties for different violations of the order.

Accordingly, I am writing to the chief ministers of all states that have significant hill cover, recommending that they enact legislation or issue executive orders on the lines of the Himachal Pradesh Cabinet order. I will also emphasize the need for better ongoing monitoring of the implementation of such a ban, which is sometimes lacking. In addition, I will also set up a mechanism to follow-up on the actions taken by the state governments in the matter.

The broader systemic issue of waste collection and management also needs to be addressed. This requires a coordinated approach that entails the cooperation of state governments and urban local bodies. My ministry is working on some innovative models that would involve special purpose vehicles and private players in waste management, which we believe could help improve the effectiveness of waste management in our cities. This could form part of the Jawaharlal Nehru National Urban Renewal Mission. We will come out with a detailed note on this soon.

My ministry is also considering a comprehensive revision and amendment of the Recycled Plastics Manufacture and Usage Rules, 1999 (last amended in 2003), and will come out with a draft for discussion in the next six weeks, which I will also share with you.

Letter to Prime Minister on a Report/Technical Paper 'India's Forest and Tree Cover: Contribution as a Carbon Sink' Prepared by the Indian Council of Forestry Research and Education

10 August 2009
You will be interested in seeing the report on our forests as carbon sink, which I have got prepared and which was released this morning by

Montek Singh Ahluwalia in Dehradun. We will be using this document extensively in all our international discussions on climate change. We will also be monitoring carbon sinks at regular intervals.

The main finding of the study is that India's forest and tree cover captured around 11 per cent of our greenhouse gas emissions in the year 1994, which is the last year for which internationally comparable data on greenhouse gas emissions is officially available. A new comprehensive assessment of our greenhouse gas emissions is under way and this will be available by November 2010. It will provide time series data on greenhouse gas emissions up to the year 2004. Needless to add, maintaining this 11 per cent figure will be a great challenge and that should remain our strategic objective for the forestry sector.

Letter to Prime Minister on the *State of Forest Report*

13 NOVEMBER 2009

Every two years, the MoEF brings out a *State of Forest Report* based on satellite imagery. The last one was for the year 2005, released in 2007. We are now ready to release the *State of Forest Report 2007*. This report contains a number of new features both from the point of view of methodology and monitoring. It also incorporates climate change concerns in the context of forests ... I might add here that the last report had a foreword by Prime Minister and this year's report tries to incorporate some of the concerns expressed by the Prime Minister in the foreword.

Letter to Prime Minister on the *State of Forest Report, 2009* Following its Publication and Release

1 DECEMBER 2009

Yesterday, we released the *State of Forest Report, 2009*. This was an initiative launched by Rajivji in 1985 when he established the Forest Survey of India to conduct satellite-based surveys of our forest cover once every two years. The latest survey incorporates a number of new features: (i) it makes possible assessment of changes in forest cover; (ii) it gives forest cover by altitude and forest type; (iii) it gives growing stock (number of trees) by state.

The main highlights of the survey are:

About 21 per cent of India's geographical area us under forest cover, 3 per cent of this high density forest cover, 10 per cent medium density forest cover, and 8 per cent degraded forest cover. This means that 40 per cent of India's forest cover is open and degraded forest having no worthwhile green cover. This must be the focus of our afforestation programmes.

Between 1997 and 2007, India's forest cover increased by about 0.3 million ha per year. This is commendable given that Brail lost 2.5 million ha per year during the same period. The 188 tribal districts of the country together account for some 60 per cent of the forest cover. Thus, there is an intimate link between our tribal welfare and forestry programmes, a link that we have yet to harness fully.

The Northeastern states although accounting for less than 5 per cent of the country's geographical area together account for 25 per cent of the area under forest cover.

Area under mangroves has increased impressively in Gujarat having gone up almost sixfold in the past decade. The Gujarat Ecology Commission has to be commended for this achievement.

India's forest cover absorbs about 11 per cent of our annual greenhouse gas emissions, thus, demonstrating its significant contribution to carbon sequestration. This is particularly relevant in the context of the climate change debate.

If the area above 4,000 m where no tree can grow is excluded, five states—Arunachal Pradesh, Jammu and Kashmir, Uttarakhand, and Sikkim—show a substantial increase in their forest cover.

We are now going to deploy satellite technology to monitor much more frequently changes in forest cover in sensitive areas like Western Ghats, Northeast, and the Himalayas.

Letter to Chief Minister of Delhi Sheila Dikshit, on the Death of Cheetals

9 JUNE 2010

I wonder whether you have seen today's newspaper item on the mysterious death of eight cheetals at a wildlife sanctuary in the Aravali hills in south Delhi over the weekend. I am sure that you are as concerned about this as I am. I would request you to please have the matter examined and suitable action taken.

Letter to Union Minister for Petroleum and Natural Gas Murli Deora on CNG Supply in the Areas Around Tiger Reserves

3 AUGUST 2009

It has been our endeavour to create an eco-friendly atmosphere in and around the core/critical tiger habitats of tiger reserves in the country. However, the tourism infrastructure in such areas and increasing tourism activities are causing high level of air/noise pollution due to vehicular traffic. We have issued guidelines to phase out the tourism activities from such areas to buffer zones of tiger reserves. In this context, it is strongly felt that promoting CNG-driven vehicles in these places would minimize the pollution.

There are several important tiger reserves in Madhya Pradesh (namely, Panna, Kanha, Sanjay Dubri, Bandhavgarh, Satpura, and Pench) and the districts where these reserves are located do not have any CNG supply.

I would very much appreciate if your ministry could explore the feasibility of providing CNG outlets in these districts (Panna, Mandla, Balaghat, Umaria, Hoshangabad, and Seoni) of Madhya Pradesh.

Letter to Union Minister for Petroleum and Natural Gas, Jaipal Reddy, on providing LPG to People Living in Forest Areas to Stem Deforestation

11 JUNE 2011

You will agree with me that one of the most important steps that we can take to prevent deforestation is to provide alternative cooking fuel to villagers in and around our forest areas. There are about 1.7 lakh villages in and around our forest areas and if we can have a distribution system for providing LPG, I think we would have taken a huge step forward in protecting our forests.

Some local level initiatives have been taken. In the vicinity of the Bandipur Sanctuary, for instance, some 30,000 families have been provided with LPG through the efforts of local non-governmental organizations (NGOs) and this is already having a salutary impact on forest cover. We would require about 5–6 million tonnes of LPG per year to meet cooking fuel needs of these 1.7 lakh villages.

Can we make a beginning somewhere? I would like to discuss this with you further and get something going on the ground.

Letter to Deputy Chairman Planning Commission Montek Singh Ahluwalia on the Delhi Zoo

18 MARCH 2011

I have just received your letter of 17 March 2011 written in your new avatar as a grandfather. I was very pleased to receive the letter, which reinforces my belief that grandfather-hood greens even the most single-minded advocates of high GDP growth.

Many of the suggestions you have made for improvement in the Delhi Zoo are suggestions that I have personally taken up and some of them are being implemented but not without problems. For example, I have been fighting a battle with the Ministry of Finance for the past few months to allow the Delhi Zoo to retain its gate receipts like the system we have instituted for tiger reserves. I still have not been able to get the formal approval of the Ministry of Finance for this simple mechanism. Pleased be rest assured that I will follow-up on your suggestions and the next time you go to the zoo, you will see them reflected on the ground.

Observations Made on Tigers and Tiger Experts at the Release of the Tiger Census 2010

26 MAY 2011

1. Number of tiger experts far exceeds number of tigers.
2. Tigers are sources of livelihood security for tiger experts.
3. No two tiger experts agree with each other.
4. Like tigers, tiger experts zealously guard their territory.
5. The ferocity of attacks on opponents by tiger experts is exceeded only by ferocity of attacks by tigers on prey.

6. Tiger mortality is good news for tiger experts, while tiger fertility is not.

Letter to Prime Minister on the Relocation of Populations from Tiger Reserves

7 MAY 2010

One of the urgent recommendations of the Tiger Task Force, constituted by the National Board for Wildlife (NBWL) under your chairmanship, is securing inviolate space for the tiger. This has become very crucial at this juncture for conserving and protecting the source population of this species in the core areas of tiger reserves, in view of the ongoing mortality due to man–tiger conflicts. It may be kindly recalled, this issue was also deliberated in the recent meeting of the NBWL chaired by you.

An area of 29,284.76 sq km has been identified/notified by fifteen out of seventeen tiger states (except Bihar and Uttar Pradesh) as core/critical tiger habitat, vis-à-vis the provisions of the Wildlife (Protection) Act, 1972. As of now, there are 762 villages/settlements in the core/critical tiger habitats of the country with 48,549 families.

There is hardly any scope for coexistence in the core areas, since human presence disturbs the sociology of tigers, which require a minimum inviolate space of 800–1000 sq km. Considering the ecological imperative for making the core areas inviolate through relocation of human settlements residing therein, the relocation package under Project Tiger has also been enhanced to Rs 10 lakh per family from the earlier rate of Rs 1 lakh.

Since the inception of Project Tiger in the early 1970s till now, a total of only ninety-one villages (3,602 families) have been relocated from different tiger reserves. The progress is slow for want of adequate central assistance to the tiger states.

The relocation of families residing in the core/critical tiger habitats needs to be expedited within a definite time frame, lest the enhanced relocation package would become meaningless owing to cost escalation and the increase in the number of families. Hence, an amount of at least Rs 5,000 crore is required for this process, spreading over the current and the next plan periods for relocating 48,549 families (762 villages).

I have requested the deputy chairman, Planning Commission, in this regard, and solicit your kind intervention for providing the desired allocation to the centrally sponsored scheme of Project Tiger to accomplish this task.

Letter to Prime Minister on the Elephant Task Force along with a copy of the Task Force's Report, Gajah: Securing the Future of Elephants in India.

[The report, which was submitted to the ministry and released on 31 August, 2010; it was put up on the ministry's website for public dissemination.]

18 SEPTEMBER 2010

In India, while the tiger faces a crisis of extinction, the elephant faces a crisis of attrition. It is in this background that an elephant task force had been set up some time ago in the MoEF. The task force has submitted its report and made some far-reaching recommendations. I have highlighted some of the more significant of these recommendations.

There are around 25,000 elephants in the country, both wild and captive. The bulk of them are in Kerala, Tamil Nadu, Karnataka, and Assam. Odisha, Jharkhand, and Uttarakhand are three other important states with elephant habitats. There are about 4,000 elephants in captivity, of which a third are in temples alone, like in the case of Guruvayoor. The treatment of captive elephants particularly in temples is also a very important issue. In addition, there is the Sonepur mela that takes place every year in Bihar, which provides a great boost to elephant trade. This needs to be regulated strictly.

The recommendations of the task force have been accepted and the process of implementing them has begun. Elephants have great cultural significance in our country and it is time that Project Elephant has the same visibility as Project Tiger.

Letter to Deputy Chairman, Planning Commission Montek Singh Ahluwalia on the Outlay for Project Elephant

22 OCTOBER 2010

The elephant task force constituted by the MoEF on Project Elephant has recently submitted its report titled *Gajah* on the state of elephants in India. This report represents that a renewed impetus is being given to the preservation of the elephant along with its declaration as a national heritage animal of India. I am pleased to inform you that we have issued the official notification for the same on 21 October 2010.

The task force has made many important recommendations, which the ministry in now in the process of implementing. Foremost amongst these is the proposed establishment of a dedicated National Elephant Conservation Authority. This authority will function along the lines of the National Tiger Conservation Authority (NTCA) and will ensure that a professional full-time body oversees all the planning and implementation of all programmes devised for the benefit of elephant preservation.

A central recommendation is to increase the financial outlay of Project Elephant. The report states that 'one of the major constraints in implementing various conservation measures within elephant reserves and human–elephant conflict mitigation has been the lack of funds'. To this end, the task force has recommended an increase in the total financial outlay from Rs 81.99 crore under the Eleventh Five Year Plan to Rs 600 crore under the Twelfth Five Year Plan.

I solicit your kind cooperation in enhancing the outlay of Project Elephant, as recommended by the task force in the Twelfth Five Year Plan to at least Rs 600 crore. This is critical if we are to save the Asian elephant, over 50 per cent of which are in India.

I am attaching a copy of the report for your review, which includes detailed recommendation on the financial outlay.

Letter to Union Minister of Railways Mamata Banerjee on Elephants Killed Due to Train Accidents

9 SEPTEMBER 2009

May I take this opportunity to draw your kind attention to the fact that accidental deaths of elephants are taking place due to train accident in some states. I am told that in last four years, thirty-eight wild elephants have been killed in such accidents. I have received representations requesting intervention—especially to prevent such accidental deaths in West Bengal between Siliguri and Alipurduar. I took a review meeting on 4 September with the Railway Board officers and chief wildlife wardens of the affected states, namely West Bengal, Assam, Uttarakhand, Jharkhand, Tamil Nadu, Kerala, and Odisha.

After detailed discussion with the officers, it emerged that the situation in Uttarakhand and Jharkhand has been brought under control due to proactive actions taken by the railways and the state forest departments. The situation also appears to be under control in Assam and Kerala, where joint dialogue and actions have been initiated by the two departments. However, there is a need to take more actions in West Bengal and Tamil Nadu.

I would also like to inform that my ministry had appointed an expert committee in the year 2007 to inspect the sensitive sections of the railway track in the West Bengal portion and to suggest mitigatory measures. The expert committee after due inspection has identified three as highly vulnerable sections and three more as sensitive sections. The committee suggested speed limits of 25 km per hour in two of the highly sensitive sections and construction of some civil engineering structures like erection of retaining wall, back cutting, and filling of slopes, underpasses of 5 m width, etc., at specific sites. In addition, there are general suggestions like sharing of information of elephants' presence along the railway tracks between the forest department and railways, clearing of vegetation on 30 m width on both sides of the track, organizing sensitizing programmes for drivers, guards, etc.

In the Tamil Nadu sections, graphic and shocking images of elephant victims were shown to us. There is an urgent need to widen the cuttings and reduce the slope of the sides in the section cut through an old mine area, as elephants are getting trapped between the track and the side wall of the cutting.

Girish Chandra, additional member (traffic), had attended the meeting from the Railway Board and a copy of the expert committee's report was again given to him with a request to ensure its implementation.

I request you to direct the railway authorities in West Bengal and Tamil Nadu to jointly work out a time-bound programme with state forest departments to mitigate the problem. I appeal to you to ensure that 2010 becomes a zero-elephant-casualty year in the whole country as far as the railways are concerned.

I would also request you to direct the concerned railway authorities in West Bengal to examine the recommendation of the expert committee and prepare estimates for the construction of the structures recommended by the committee.

Letter to Union Minister for Railways Mamata Banerjee on the Accidental Death of Elephants

4 AUGUST 2010

Kindly refer to my department order dated 9 September 2009 regarding accidental deaths of elephants in West Bengal between Siliguri and Alipurduar. In the meeting taken by me with the officers of the Railway Board and state forest department on 4 September 2009, three decisions were taken: (i) to issue general advisory to all the railway zones; (ii) to jointly inspect and prepare design and estimates for construction of certain civil structures to facilitate movement of elephants across the railway track; and (iii) to examine introduction of speed limit in sensitive sections. I would like to bring to your kind notice that the joint efforts of my ministry, the state forest department, and railways have worked very well in the Rajaji National Park section in Uttarakhand and the section has been made accident-free since 2001.

However, two elephants have been killed in train accidents in West Bengal since I last wrote to you. Though, the Railway Board in its letter of 30 March 2010 has issued the general advisory to railway zones concerned, the other two decisions referred to above are yet to be implemented.

My ministry has suggested the introduction of a speed limit in the two most sensitive sections falling in the Mahananda Wildlife Sanctuary and Chapramari Wildlife Sanctuary. Incidentally, the latest accident has taken place in Mahananda Wildlife Sanctuary.

I am also informed that the design and estimates of Rs 7.27 crore have been prepared by the Railway Board for the construction of civil structures. I earnestly request you to kindly direct the authorities concerned to consider imposition of a speed limit in the suggested sections. I will also be obliged if you can consider construction of the civil structures out of the Railway's budget since it has to be executed by the Ministry of Railways.

Note on the Death of Seven Elephants on Train Tracks in North Bengal on the Night of 22 September

[This note was issued from the Permanent Mission of India in New York, which served as camp office, as I was attending the High Level Meeting of the 65th session of the General Assembly on Biodiversity.]

23 September 2010

I have just seen the news of the most tragic killing of seven elephants on train tracks in north Bengal on the night of 22 September. This is not the first time that such a mishap has taken place, although the scale with it has taken place now is unprecedented, particularly in the North-East Frontier Railway. I have written a number of letters to the minister for railways and have personally held a number of meetings with officials of the Railway Board. We have discussed measures to be taken in order to avoid such tragedies, I have been reassured on more than one occasion that these measures will be put in place.

The tragedy is all the more poignant coming in the wake of the decision by the MoEF to declare the elephant as our national heritage animal, to take steps to establish a National Elephant Conservation Authority, and to implement the recommendations of the elephant task force to protect designated key elephant corridors. I will once again meet the officials of the Railway Board when I return to India on 26 September. Meanwhile, I wish to convey my deep sense of anguish at this latest incident.

Letter to Chief Minister of West Bengal Mamata Banerjee on the Death of Elephants at Banerhat

30 September 2010

I am sure you share my anguish at the most ghastly killing of seven elephants by a speeding goods train at Banerhat between Siliguri and Alipurduar at 11 pm on 22 September 2010. Presumably, the railway authorities are conducting their own investigations on this tragic incident.

We have been quite successful in mitigating elephant deaths due to speeding trains on an 18 km stretch in Rajaji National Park in Uttarakhand. Unfortunately, we have not had the same degree of success in the Northeastern Frontier Railway and we continue to witness elephant deaths on railway tracks in north Bengal and Assam. This problem has been extensively studied and a number of meetings involving the MoEF, railways, NGOs, and the state government have also been held. On 4 September 2009, I myself took such a meeting. Very recently, the director general of forests (DGF) took a meeting on 28 September 2010. I summarize below the main suggestions that have been made to address the problem in the 160 km-stretch in north Bengal:

1. The railways should seriously examine reducing train movement at night, especially of goods trains which move at unpredictable hours. The state government has recommended that the running of trains between Gulma and Rajabhatkhawa should be stopped from 6 pm to 6 am and speed restriction of a maximum of 20 km per hour (kmph) should be placed on trains running through these tracks during day time.

2. If the suggestion of the state government does not find favour with the railways for some reason, restrictions on speed (20 kmph maximum) should definitely be imposed along identified elephant corridors and other vulnerable stretches and additional vulnerable points to be identified by the MoEF.

3. No more double-tracks should be laid in the stretch concerned along the elephant corridor.

4. Elephants (especially the young ones) should be facilitated to cross the railway track quickly. For this, in some sections elevated tracks could be developed by constructing at least 40 m wide and 10 m high underpasses for elephants. Alternatively, ramps with a gentle slope could be provided where the sides of the track are steep.

5. Adequate space should be provided on either side of the tracks enabling the elephants to move aside away from the track on hearing or seeing an approaching train.

6. Trains running in this stretch should be manned only by sensitized local drivers who are well aware of this track and situations in adjacent elephant habitats. This requires large and flat level crossings, with appropriate length and width to address the needs of the herds. This needs to be done at all regular crossing points.

7. The railway control tower at Alipurduar should be operational round-the-clock for which MoEF will bear the cost.

8. All goods trains should be diverted from the killer broad gauge track to the one existing outside, south of the forest.

9. The existing broad gauge line passing outside forest areas should be strengthened and double-laned.

Letter to Chief Minister of Chhattisgarh Raman Singh on Notifying and Denotifying Elephant Reserves

25 JANUARY 2011

I was shocked to read in *The Times of India* of 16 January 2011 that the Chhattisgarh government has decided to drop Lemru from its list of notified elephant reserves and has yet to notify Badalkol Tamorpingla Elephant Reserve.

Ironically, permission was given by the MoEF in 2007 for notifying these two elephant reserves based on your request made in your letter of 28 March 2005. You had also requested for Chhattisgarh to be included in the Project Elephant, which has been done. I understand that the state government has been repeatedly assuring MoEF that the notification is under process but this has not happened.

I would like to add that Lemru and Badalkol Tamorpingla elephant reserves are already notified as either reserve or protected forests or as sanctuary. Thus, statutory clearances from the central government under the Forest (Conservation) Act, 1980 and from NBWL under Wildlife (Protection) Act, 1972 would be required for use of these areas for any non-forestry purposes.

Since elephant reserves are notified through administrative orders of the state government, a declaration of elephant reserve would not result in any additional legal restriction or scrutiny on their use for non-forestry purposes. The very idea of declaring elephant reserves is to provide focused attention to and scientific elephant management in the area for the benefit of the local people and the elephants.

I would request you once again to review your decision and notify the two elephant reserves as you had originally wanted. As you know, the elephant is now our national heritage animal.

Letter to Chief Minister of Gujarat Narendra Modi on the Great Indian Bustard

9 JUNE 2010

You are aware that the Great Indian Bustard (GIB) is a highly endangered species, and the grasslands of Kutch in Gujarat are one of the last remaining pockets that hold promise for recovery of this species. Ornithologists consider the conservation of the Indian Bustard as equally important to that of lions and tigers. In fact, the great Salim Ali proposed in 1960s that the GIB be adopted as India's National Bird.

Conservationists and researchers working in Kutch have brought to my attention the opening of areas in Abdasa grasslands in Naliya (Kutch), a prime breeding ground for the GIB, for agriculture. A researcher also forwarded a photograph that clearly shows the marking of a new agricultural plot.

I am writing to request you to immediately intervene and prevent the diversion of revenue *gauchar* land to agriculture, and to ensure that the district officials support the Naliya conservation initiatives. If we do not intervene, the possibility of the GIB going extinct in Gujarat is very real and high.

Letter to Chief Minister of Uttarakhand Ramesh Pokhriyal on the Corbett Tiger Reserve Landscape

11 July 2009
I visited Corbett recently and was delighted to see the tiger along with other wild animals in the scenic landscape. The state authorities deserve all praise for actively managing this tiger land, which happens to be the launching pad for Project Tiger way back in the early seventies.

There are some ecological concerns requiring urgent action to ensure the ecological integrity of the Corbett landscape, which are:

1. A buffer/peripheral area needs to be delineated around the core/ critical area of the Corbett Tiger Reserve, which should encompass portions of the surrounding forest divisions, namely, Lansdowne, West Tarai, and Ramnagar. This is a statutory requirement under section 38V of the Wildlife (Protection) Act, 1972, which is essential for stepping up protection in such areas, apart from providing site specific inputs to local people with central assistance under Project Tiger. As you may be aware, during the last five months as many as six tiger deaths have been reported in and around Corbett, apart from frequent instances of man–tiger conflicts. The buffer zone under the unified control of the field director would provide the desired institutional framework and funding support to address such issues.

Clarifications have already been issued regarding the buffer zone, which in any case will not have the status of a national park/wildlife sanctuary, but would be managed as a multiple use area.

2. The protection status of Corbett and the surrounding areas has to be stepped up to ensure intelligence based enforcement. This was discussed with the local officers, and under Project Tiger central assistance would be provided for strengthening protection involving local communities and procuring equipment, night vision, vehicles/ microlite for effective enforcement, and speedy communication.

3. There is considerable tourism infrastructure in the core/critical tiger habitat apart from unregulated mushrooming of private resorts in the buffer area, which is damaging its corridor value. The non-forest areas falling in the buffer zone should be accorded protection under the Environment (Protection) Act, 1986 to prevent ecologically unsustainable land uses. Further, the tourism activities in the core should also be weaned away to the buffer in a phased manner as indicated in the guidelines of Project Tiger.

I look forward to your kind intervention on the above issues and assure you of our full support to conserve the tiger.

Letter to Chief Minister of Rajasthan Ashok Gehlot on Sambar Relocation Activities in Sariska

2 DECEMBER 2010

I wish to bring to your notice two serious issues relating to Sariska. It is learnt that in the recent past, a large number of sambar have been captured and translocated from the core area of Sariska to Kumbalgarh. Such operations can have considerable ecological ramification on the predator–prey balance in the habitat. The NTCA, which is a statutory body in the context of tiger reserves, has not even been consulted in this regard. As you are aware, we are in the process of rebuilding Sariska, and considerable effort and resources have gone into the translocation of tigers. Hence, a drastic intervention involving removal of a major prey species from the core area of a tiger reserve, without any technical advice is a very serious issue. I solicit your personal intervention for enquiring into the same, while stopping any further sambar translocation from Sariska.

Another serious issue which requires your attention relates to the renovation of the Kankwari fort inside the core area of Sariska without any due permission. It is learnt that the said fort has been restored with support from the tourism department, perhaps with a view to foster tourist visitation/stay. This is a matter of serious concern as it violates the norms of inviolate space. The Government of India has been providing considerable central assistance (100 per cent under Project Tiger) for making the core area inviolate through village relocation. During the current year an amount of Rs 37.20 crore has been sanctioned, while releasing an amount of Rs 18.60 crore in this regard. The core areas need to be kept inviolate as per the Wildlife (Protection) Act, 1972 and, hence, tourism activities need to be strictly regulated for the present, with a view to foster them in a phased manner in the buffer area. Hence, I request your personal intervention in this regard as well for preventing the Kankwari fort from being put to use for tourism. The pilgrim visitation to the Pandupole temple also needs to be regulated by resorting to group transportation.

I have reviewed the situation in Sariska and have directed the Wildlife Institute of India and NTCA officials for strengthening the radio telemetry monitoring system. They would be helping the state authorities in evolving a plan for the fringe area with livelihood options.

Letter to Chief Minister of Madhya Pradesh Shivraj Singh Chouhan on the Reintroduction of Cheetahs

15 September 2010

Thank you very much indeed for your letter of 17 August 2010, agreeing in-principle to the proposal of cheetah reintroduction in Kuno-Palpur and in Nauradehi, and for giving Dr M. K. Ranjitsinh and Dr Y. Jhala of the Wildlife Institute of India an opportunity to explain the proposal in some detail. The project would be a partnership between the state and central governments and other participating agencies such as the Wildlife Institute of India, the Wildlife Trust of India, and others. The Cheetah Project would be a new project—separate from Project Tiger and others—and will have funding of its own, committed to it by the MoEF.

I am given to understand that the response of yourself and of the state authorities was very positive and that you have assured that committed and willing personnel of proven merit would be posted on the project and that they will be retained on the job for a number of years so that the training that they will receive could be taken full advantage of.

I would wish to convey our thanks to you and to the state of Madhya Pradesh. As desired by you, we will give first priority to the reintroduction programme in Kuno-Palpur and take up Nauradehi in consequence. We would now be going ahead with the project. The next stage of it would be developed by the task force which I have appointed and on which your chief wildlife warden is a member. The first task would be to carry out a detailed survey of the two sites to prepare eco-restoration plans and other requirements, and also pre-pare a detailed budget for the next three years, in collaboration with the state authorities.

With the active participation and cooperation of all parties to the project, I am sure we should be successful in implementing the project soon.

Letter to All Chief Ministers on the Man–Animal Conflict

8 October 2010

Time and again, man–animal conflicts have been reported from several states on account of wild animals like tigers and leopards straying out near human settlements. Very often, the agitated local people surround the area, resulting in a violent mob-like situation. In the recent past, there has been a very serious incident of a range officer in Rajasthan getting seriously mauled by a tiger, while attempting to tranquilize it in the presence of many local people surrounding the spot.

Since chemical immobilization or capturing through traps is not possible by an expert team in such situations, it is important for the district magistrate and other local authorities to be sensitive to the issue by taking necessary precautions to prevent a mob like situation. An instance of a straying tiger or leopard should be treated at par with any other communal violence, and adequate deployment of local police and State Armed Forces needs to be done, besides sensitizing the local population. Perhaps, to avoid lethal encounters, it is advisable to impose Section 144 of the Code of Criminal Procedure in such areas. I solicit your personal intervention in this regard for directing the district Collectors/Magistrates accordingly.

Letter to All Chief Ministers on Identifying Wetlands

23 December 2010

As you are aware, wetlands are unique and distinct ecosystems which require coordinated and concerted efforts for their conservation. Some of the major threats faced by the wetlands are various anthropogenic pressures and processes of urbanization resulting in shrinkage of areas, loss of biodiversity, conversion of wetlands to some other uses, etc. Considering all these factors, my ministry had initiated a scheme for conservation of wetlands in 1987, which includes research and developmental activities besides conservation and management activities. Under this scheme, 115 wetlands all over the country spread over twenty-four states/union territories have been identified for conservation modulated through the process of management action plan.

Now to further boost the conservation and management efforts for these wetlands, the central government has notified the Wetlands (Conservation and Management) Rules, 2010. These rules not only provide for a regulatory mechanism but also detail the activities which need to be restricted in these wetlands. I am enclosing a copy of the gazette notification of these rules.

You may notice that all the Ramsar sites stand notified. The other wetlands which are covered by the criteria laid down in these rules will have to be identified by the concerned state/union territory government, which will submit a brief proposal in respect of each wetland to the Central Wetlands Regulatory Authority (CWRA) constituted under these rules, within a maximum period of one year. The central government will notify the identified wetlands on the recommendations of the CWRA. The CWRA has also been given the powers to regulate activities in the notified wetlands.

As per the provisions contained in these rules, the state/union territory governments are required to not only identify the wetlands within their respective territories in accordance with the criteria specified under rule 3, but also to submit a brief document providing basic information for identification of such wetlands. Even in the enforcement of regulatory activities, the state/union territory governments have a major role to ensure management and wise use of wetlands through their forest department for wetlands in protected areas and nodal department/agency for the wetlands situated outside the protected areas.

The proposals for notification of new wetlands identified by the state/union territory government as per the criteria given in the rules for regulation of activities need to be sent to us immediately in batches so that activities within these wetlands are regulated as per their wise use, which is also the mission of Ramsar Convention of Wetlands, 1971 to which our country is a signatory.

I would be grateful for your cooperation in our joint effort to conserve our wetlands by issuing necessary directions to the concerned officials in your state/union territory for taking expeditious action in the matter.

Letter to Chief Minister of Uttar Pradesh Mayawati on Preserving the Gangetic Dolphin

14 JANUARY 2010

Kindly refer to your letter 2 November 2009 regarding conservation of river Ganga and Gangetic dolphins at Narora.

I am happy to inform you that the government has set up the National Ganga River Basin Authority (NGRBA) to ensure effective abatement of pollution and conservation of the river Ganga by adopting a river basin approach. In the first meeting of the NGRBA, held on 5 October 2009 under the chairmanship of the Prime Minister, it was decided that under 'Mission Clean Ganga' no untreated municipal sewage or industrial effluents will flow into the river Ganga by year 2020. The state governments, including the Government of Uttar Pradesh, have been requested to submit comprehensive proposals for prevention of pollution of river Ganga in their state.

This ministry has also constituted an expert committee under the chairmanship of Prof. R.K. Sinha of Patna University to prioritize and identify critical stretches of river Ganga and its tributaries where the Gangetic dolphins need special attention and prepare an action plan for their conservation.

Letter to Union Minister of State for Defence M.M. Pallam Raju on Coastal Pollution

13 NOVEMBER 2010

I wanted to bring your attention to a major emerging problem related to coastal pollution and seek your help on the same. The appearance of tar balls, which are a result of waste oil dumped by ships reacting with sea water, along the western coast of India is a regular phenomenon, and is causing significant adverse impact on the coastal ecology. During August 2010, tar balls appeared in large numbers on the beaches of Goa. In this regard, a note on 'the tar balls phenomenon appearing on the Goan coasts' received from the Department of Science, Technology and Environment, Government of Goa, is enclosed along with an article from National Institute of Oceanography (NIO) for reference. The note highlights that this phenomenon of tar balls, which keeps recurring is essentially the result of errant ships illegally discharging/dumping oil into sea water and escaping undetected.

I would like to take this opportunity to seek your help in tackling this issue, which affects a number of beaches in the country. In particular, there is a need for strengthening of surveillance and operational activities by the Indian Coast Guard so as to effectively check the occurrence of such phenomenon and ensuring stringent action against defaulting ships. May I request that you take up the matter with the director-general, Indian Coast Guard, and draw upon a suitable action plan to ensure this is monitored and appropriate action taken. I would appreciate if the action plan can be shared with us. We would be happy to provide any assistance from our end in the preparation of the action plan.

Letter to Union Minister of Defence A.K. Antony on the Preservation of the Nhava Island

7 DECEMBER 2009

I write to you on an environmental issue that requires your urgent attention regarding the preservation of Nhava Island in Mumbai. This is an environmentally sensitive area located in Bombay Harbour, 1.5 km away from a World Heritage site and the island containing the Elephanta caves.

Nhava's importance stems from the fact that on it are located India's oldest nautical training institute—the Training Ship Rahman and India's first Marine Museum. Nhava's unique importance is enhanced and compounded by several factors. It is virtually the only remaining green scenic area in New Bombay located on the seafront. The bulk of the other areas on the seafront were unfortunately allowed to be destroyed or taken over by other agencies. The whole of Sheva has been taken over by the Jawaharlal Nehru Port, including the area which had earlier been designated as a regional park. On Uran, is the Naval Armament Depot, a brewery, and the ONGC terminal. Some of these activities did not need a water frontage.

As New Bombay Navi Mumbai grows, its citizens will want access to the seafront, and Nhava is the only such remaining area. Additionally, for the citizens of Greater Bombay, Nhava is the only green belt accessible by sea, across and within Bombay harbour. Given the traffic congestion that plagues the city this is something that is very important and meaningful for the residents of Mumbai.

Apart from these reasons, with the exception of the area taken over by ONGC and Mazagon Docks Limited, most of the rest of Nhava is a thickly wooded area warranting preservation on that ground alone.

Equally important is the question of Elephanta. Most of the large number of visitors to Elephanta go there, not to see the caves, but mainly to have an outing, with the added attraction of a sea trip. This is putting undue pressure on the caves and threatening the remaining archaeological artefacts, both excavated and below the ground. Archaeological experts have repeatedly drawn attention to the problem. Hence, it is vital to develop other green areas across the harbour so as to divert the excess tourists from Elephanta, and Nhava is ideal for this purpose.

Recognizing the above, the late prime minister, Shrimati Indira Gandhi, had issued a series of directives in July 1980, August 1980, and August 1982 to preserve Nhava. I am enclosing copies of these directives. You will notice that she had directed that while ONGC and Mazagon Docks could go ahead with the setting up of offshore facilities, it could be only at the levels then contemplated and planned. She had clearly directed that no further expansion of activity of any of these organizations should be allowed on Nhava. She had renewed these directives in 1982.

As far back as 1995, the then minister for environment and forests had agreed to give statutory protection to Nhava under The

Environment (Protection) Act, 1986. That fell through due to a law ministry objection, which has since been resolved. We are working on this protection proposal.

There are now reports that Mazagon Docks now wish to set up additional facilities on Nhava. This would clearly be in violation of Indiraji's directive. If there is indeed such a plan may I suggest that alternative locations be considered? Your intervention in the matter will be highly appreciated.

Letter to Prime Minister on the Dandi Eco-initiative

19 JULY 2010
The MoEF has launched an Rs 25 crore eco-initiative at Dandi. This was launched by Shri Gopal Krishna Gandhi on 7 July 2010 ... The project will take two years and is a small but significant effort on our part to commemorate Dandi in an ecologically sustainable manner.

Letter to the Chairman of the High-Level Dandi Memorial Committee Gopal Krishna Gandhi

10 NOVEMBER 2010
I am glad that the 'Diva Dandi', which will be a solar illuminated structure chosen by you, is an ideal memorial to be installed in Dandi rather than any monolithic structure.

As you may be aware, the ministry has already issued the draft Ecological Sensitive Area (ESA) Notification which proposes to declare Dandi and the adjoining three villages, namely, Onjal, Matwad, and Samapor, as ESA. This notification has been translated into Gujarati and widely published through the Gujarat Ecology Commission. A dedicated NGO has been assigned to obtain comments from individual houses located in these four villages on the draft ESA Notification. A final decision on the notification would be taken after obtaining the comments within sixty days from the date of issue of the notification. This draft notification lists out certain activities that are prohibited in the area which includes industrial activities, large-scale tourism, mining, tree cutting, etc. It promotes eco-friendly activities like green belt development, horticulture, eco-friendly tourism, etc. Copy of the notification is enclosed for your ready reference.

Further, the above four villages being located in the coastal areas also attract the provisions of the Coastal Regulation Zone (CRZ) Notification, 1991. This notification also prohibits certain activities and regulates permissible activities based on the CRZ categorization of the area. Hence, it is imperative that the CRZ map of the area is prepared and necessary approval sought by the Gujarat Coastal Zone Management Authority and the concerned agencies in accordance with the CRZ Notification, 1991.

The memorial project, Green Action for National Dandi Heritage Initiative (GANDHI), initiated by my ministry through the Society of Integrated Coastal Management has been designed so as to conform to these two notifications. I hope the structures/activities proposed by the Central Public Works Department (CPWD), department of tourism, Government of Gujarat, are in conformity with the CRZ Notification, 1991 and the proposed ESA Notification.

Letter to Prime Minister on the Resolution in the Punjab Vidhan Sabha on Efforts Made By Me to Address Pollution in Water Bodies in the State

[The resolution passed unanimously on 30 September 2010 by the Punjab Vidhan Sabha stated: 'This House thanks the central environment minister, Shri Jairam Ramesh for his whole hearted assistance to the scheme to make the state of Punjab pollution free.']

7 OCTOBER 2010
I enclose a copy of a resolution passed by the Punjab Vidhan Sabha unanimously recognizing the efforts and assistance of the MoEF in addressing pollution in water bodies in the state on 30 September 2010. I also enclose a statement of river cleaning projects cleared for Punjab since May 2009 that appears to have prompted the passing of this resolution.

Letter to Chief Minister of Kerala V. S. Achuthanandan, on the Stampede at Sabarimala and the Measures to be Taken

1 FEBRUARY 2011
The recent stampede near Sabarimala resulting in the death of a large number of pilgrims is alarming, while being a cause for very serious

concern. As you may be aware, the pilgrim visitation to Sabarimala shrine has been increasing considerably over the years with the festive seasons receiving the maximum influx.

The Public Accounts Committee visited Sabarimala and made several observations / recommendations for improving the pilgrim visitation (Eighteenth Report/PAC/2005-06/Fourteenth Lok Sabha/1 December 2005). The MoEF, in consultation with the Travancore Devaswom Board (TDB) and state government, decided on evolving a holistic master plan drawn by professionals in the field, while creating a high level coordination mechanism in the state for its implementation. An amount of Rs 57 lakh (100 per cent central assistance) was released to the state for preparation of the master plan. Further, an area of 12.675 ha of forest land within the Periyar Tiger Reserve and 110.524 ha of forest land at Nilakkal has been permitted for diversion by this ministry towards implementing the said master plan. This is in addition to 126.681 ha of forest land already made available, time and again, within the Periyar Tiger Reserve for facilitating the pilgrims. The state government has also accepted the said master plan for implementation.

I had sent the member-secretary, NTCA, for a field appraisal recently. The master plan implementation is not happening in a time-bound manner. It should be appreciated that the master plan has been drawn up by a professional agency after extensive due diligence and consists of various modules, which inter alia, includes traffic and transportation, solid waste management and water supply, sanitation, amenities, and services, besides commercial, health, firefighting, energy, and communication aspects. Further, there are: landscape module, built fabric analysis module, disaster management guidelines, and a vision document up to 2050. A faithful and timely implementation of this master plan would have prevented any kind of disaster in the area. Further, there is a need for effectively monitoring the implementation of the said master plan. The TDB has not ensured sanitation in the area, and the Pamba river in its vicinity are extremely polluted with human excreta and garbage. The Pamba river cleaning programme has also not gained momentum despite the fact that an amount of Rs 18.45 crore has been sanctioned in May 2003 with a central release of Rs 378 lakhs.

The recent stampede resulting in the tragic loss of so many lives at Uppupara has reportedly occurred due to temporary blockade in the pathway near Uppupara. There has been an increased congregation of thousands of people at the said site for viewing the 'Makaravilakku', owing to the use of an extraction forest path from the Fourth Mile point on the nearby Vallakadau-Vandi Periyar Highway.

In this context, the following actions are suggested:

1. Implementation of the master plan in a time-bound manner in a project mode, by appointing a chief executive officer with a complement of executing officials, since the TDB is unable to perform the task.
2. The financial assistance for the master plan implementation project (including Pamba river cleaning) may be obtained through a donor agency, in case the TDB/state is not able to provide the funding support.
3. An independent monitoring mechanism should be created for a quarterly monitoring of the master plan implementation.
4. To avoid stampede at Uppupara in future, the vehicular route from the Fourth Mile to Uppupara should be closed, while facilitating visitation from the Sattram entry point as suggested in the master plan.

I further wish to add that non-compliance of master plan would lead to cancellation of the diversion of forest land accorded by the ministry. *Any further demand for forest land by the TDB is meaningless at this juncture since the forest land already made available to them is not being used as suggested in the master plan.*

I solicit your urgent personal intervention in the matter. The actions suggested above are in the interest of lakhs of Sabarimala pilgrims as well as biodiversity conservation in the area and hence may be considered favourably.

Letter to Deputy Chairman, Planning Commission Montek Singh Ahluwalia on a New Building for the MoEF

29 SEPTEMBER 2009

The MoEF is facing acute shortage of office accommodation. There have been a number of fires in the building as well, which has destroyed sections of the building and made it highly unsafe. There have been four fires just since I took charge of this ministry, including one in my office. Actually, Paryavaran Bhavan as it is today is a disgrace and I am ashamed to call it the home of the ministry that is promoting eco-friendly technologies.

In addition, you are aware that there has been a rapid expansion in the scope of activities of the ministry over the past few decades. New issues have been added to the ministry's activities, such as climate change. Given this expanded and more prominent mandate, it is important to present a respectable face of the ministry, which the current offices completely fail to do.

Given the rapid expansion in the ministry's activities and systems and the need for a respectable office space—a new office space for the ministry has become absolutely necessary. The ministry had, therefore, approached the Prime Minister's Office and the Ministry of Urban Development on the need for a new, safe, and dedicated building for itself. The Ministry of Urban Development has in-principle approved allotment of a suitable plot of land to the ministry in Aliganj (Jorbagh area).

It is proposed to construct a dedicated green building for the ministry on this allotted plot of land using green technology, non-conventional energy sources, and use of eco-friendly material in its construction. This will be a world-class building of which India could be proud of. The project is estimated to cost around Rs 80 crore over the next two years. The building would be named as 'Indira Paryavaran Bhavan'.

As it is a new proposal, Planning Commission approval is necessary for its inclusion and execution in the annual plans of this ministry. I would be thankful for an early approval of the proposal by the commission so that the works could be initiated at the earliest.

'Recalling Indira Gandhi—the Environmentalist', Opinion Piece in *The Hindustan Times* on the Occasion of World Environment Day

5 JUNE 2010

The first UN Conference on the Human Environment began on 5 June 1972 and it is to commemorate this historic conclave that the day is marked as World Environment Day ever since 1973. Olaf Palme was the Swedish prime minister then and, therefore, was obliged to be present. The *only* other head of state to attend was Indira Gandhi reflecting her profound commitment to environmental causes.

It was my friend Tariq Banuri, the Pakistani economist now at the United Nations, who placed Indira Gandhi's participation at the Stockholm Summit in its larger context. In a conversation, he said that four events have shaped the modern discourse on environment. The first was the publication of Rachel Carson's *Silent Spring* in 1962. The second was the publication of Paul Ehrlich's *Population Bomb* in 1968. The third was the release of *Limits to Growth* by the Club of Rome in early 1972; and the fourth was Indira Gandhi's speech at Stockholm in which environmental issues were, for the first time, situated in their larger developmental context. Folklore has it that in appreciation of her contributions the United Nations Environment Programme (UNEP) was to be located in New Delhi but bowing to a request made by Jomo Kenyatta, she agreed to its being headquartered in Nairobi.

My own appreciation of Indira Gandhi's everlasting contributions in this area has been deepened over the last year. I knew of Silent Valley, of course, and how virtually single-handedly she saved that wonderful rainforest from destruction. But Silent Valley was only one instance of her zeal. It is to her we owe the slew of legislation of the 1970s relating to the control of water and air pollution. It is to her that we owe the Wildlife (Protection) Act, 1972 and Project Tiger launched in April 1973, not just to save India's most magnificent national animal but also to save whole habitats and ecosystems. It is to her and her alone that we owe the Forest (Conservation) Act, 1980 that remarkable piece of legislation that has saved our forests from being decimated in the name of development. Her concern with the state of our coastal areas resulted finally in CRZ, 1991. That her mind was constantly on saving India's precious natural heritage is revealed by an extraordinary event—her writing to Kedar Pande, the-then chief minister of Bihar in July 1972 from Shimla, even as she was negotiating the Shimla Pact with Zulfiqar Ali Bhutto, conveying her extreme displeasure on how forests were being felled in that state.

The MoEF as we know it today celebrates with its silver jubilee in three months' time. Forests and wildlife was transferred from the Ministry of Agriculture and combined with the Department of Environment. But the Department of Environment itself was an Indira Gandhi creation, set up in 1980. Now we are about to create a separate Department of Forests and Wildlife within the MoEF, a decision taken by the Prime Minister on 18 March 2010 at the fifth meeting of the NBWL. Interestingly, this was something Indira Gandhi herself was very keen on accomplishing as revealed at that meeting by Dr M.K.

Ranjitsinh, the noted naturalist-administrator, quoting from some of her directives of the early 1970s.

To Indira Gandhi, environmental preservation meant more than pollution control or saving endangered species. She had a much broader conception and that is why she set up the Delhi Urban Arts Commission. Her aide Usha Bhagat revealed in her memoirs *Indiraji* that on getting a phone call from Mrinalini Sarabhai from Ahmedabad, she immediately contacted the chief minister of Gujarat to stop the demolition of a *pol* (old city gate) to widen a road. The memoirs also point to Indira Gandhi's abilities as an amateur ornithologist displaying her skills in the company of Malcolm McDonald, the then British high commissioner.

Heritage preservation was very much part of her approach to environmental conservation. Shyam Chainani the well-known environmentalist, in his *Heritage and Environment*, reproduces the directive issued by her in 1982 which not merely helped in ensuring protection of the wonderful Elephanta Caves near Mumbai from commercial development but also reveals how, for her, this could best be ensured by converting it into a green area. The crucial part of her directive is worth quoting in full: 'Maharashtra government should be asked to ensure that on the Nhava and Elephanta islands no commercial or building activity of any description is allowed and positive steps are taken to green them and if necessary convert them into parks with birds wildlife etc.' Today, more than ever before there is urgent need to recapture this holistic perspective on heritage preservation, conservation, and regeneration.

Only a full *intellectual* biography will unravel in the well-springs of Indira Gandhi's extraordinary contributions in the field of environment. Perhaps, this biography will draw our attention to the influence of her parents, particularly her mother who, in her own words, 'used to tell me of the links between all creatures'. Perhaps, her reading habits (by her own admission that as a child included the *Faber Book of Insects* and Maeterlinck's books on bees, ants) had something to do with it. Then, perhaps, her fascination with Tagore's poetry and her stint at Santiniketan itself moulded her thinking. Perhaps, it could be her enduring love for the wondrous ecosystem of Kashmir—the mountains, the rivers, the lakes—that she shared with her father that shaped her love for Mother Nature.

Perhaps it was her friendship with people like Dr Salim Ali that influenced her actions. Whatever it was, India owes her a debt of gratitude and today we can do no better than to resolve to use her as a talisman as we strive to sustain high economic growth *while at the same time* protecting and regenerating our environment and forests and not at their cost as is glaring in so many instances.

'Making Sustainable Prosperity Happen NOW', Address to the Parliament of Finland, Helsinki

11 April 2012

I am truly honoured to be here today and thank you for this invitation. I was last in Helsinki fourteen months ago and I am delighted to be back to this beautiful city. I see the invitation to speak to you more as a recognition of India's long tradition of trying to reconcile the imperatives of faster economic growth and environmental protection and conservation on a scale that is unparalleled anywhere.

I cannot but recall here that there were only two heads of state/government who attended the very first UN Conference on the Human Environment held almost exactly forty years ago at Stockholm—Olaf Palme had to be there as the host and the other was the India's Prime Minister Indira Gandhi, whose speech there is widely acknowledged as having broadened the environmental agenda and discourse to embrace in a most basic manner issues of poverty alleviation, economic growth, and human development.

Our two countries have always shared a warm relationship. Finland established its embassy in India in 1949 just two years after our Independence but before we had become a republic in January 1950.

Some eighty leading Finnish companies have established themselves in India and names like Nokia, Outocumpu, Wartsila, Kone, Sandvik, and Kemira are very well-known in my country. In recent years, around twenty Indian companies have invested in Finland. We are also learning considerably from your experience in the regulation of nuclear power plants. And there are non-economic areas of mutual interest as well.

The man who has made the greatest contribution to the decipherment of the still little-understood script of the Indus Valley civilization that flourished in the sub-continent over two millennia ago is D. Asko Parpola of the University of Helsinki.

II

I was privileged to be a member of the UN Secretary General's High-Level Panel on Global Sustainability that was co-chaired by President Jacob Zuma of South Africa and your former President Halja Talonnen. This came almost a quarter of a century after the report of a similar commission headed by Gro Harlem Brundtland in October 1987.

President Talonnen was a tough taskmaster and conducted all our meetings in a most business-like way. The panel submitted its report three months back and much of what I have to say today relates to some key themes covered in that report. As I said often in meetings of the panel, it is not local communities in the developing world that need to be educated about the virtues of sustainable development. They know. They care. They are actively involved. The maximum advocacy and championing is required in the US which, even while being the locomotive for the world economy, is an exemplar of a way of life that goes against the very canons of sustainability. The noted economist John Kenneth Galbraith had drawn attention to this way back in 1958 in his now largely-forgotten classic *The Affluent Society*. There is a distinction to be made between becoming an affluent society and an effluent society!

III

We have to recognize that there is intimate link between security of livelihoods and sustainability of lifestyles—both across nations and within countries. It is well-accepted that the world cannot afford the profligate consumption patterns of the rich in the world, particularly the US. Many years ago, Mahatma Gandhi had pointedly asked, 'how many worlds would India need to emulate the lifestyle of Britain?'

Gandhi's farsighted wisdom confronts us today as the world grapples with related challenges of economic growth and climate change. That the current growth model is not sustainable or equitable is well accepted. It is also increasingly evident that improving efficiency in the use of energy and materials is only one part of the solution for the future. As the noted Indian environmentalist Sunita Narain would say, this efficiency revolution is meaningless without a sufficiency revolution.

But even as the question of sustainable consumption has been on the global agenda, answers, or more accurately actions, have eluded us. What is deemed desirable in theory is considered infeasible in practice. Today countries everywhere—including my own—are hurtling madly towards the same pattern of consumption-led, GDP-measured economic growth, even as it is known that this growth is costing us the Earth.

Undoubtedly, faster economic growth is essential to lift millions out of poverty and give them a new future. The challenge is to find the economic drivers, which will acknowledge growing aspirations for a higher standard of living, and work to reinvent lifestyles that are afford-able and sustainable.

One area where such a rework is called for urgently is in address-ing the challenges posed by the migration-urbanization-transportation nexus. Rapid migration is a reality, leading to an inevitable march towards urbanization, along with a move towards 'modern' transpor-tation. What choices we make along this nexus will be critical to the sustainability of our collective future. Will we 'lock-in' to the resource-intensive urbanization and transportation model typified by America, with suburban living and fuel-guzzling private vehicles? Or will we develop newer more 'smart' models of living that allow the teaming millions moving to cities to experience a better life, while being more sensitive to the sustainability imperatives that stare at us today? We have no choice but to get this right. The onus is as much on developed countries of the world today to share good and bad practices, as it is on developing countries to get them right.

At the global level, negotiations must address the matter of shar-ing atmospheric resources or ecological space on an equitable basis, something almost the entire world except the US accepts in some form or the other. At the national level, governments must provide economic and other incentives to steer the economy towards sustain-able consumption that will, in turn, lead to sustainable prosperity. Sustainable prosperity now—the title of this address—let us remind ourselves, is our goal.

Let me take an example from climate change to illustrate my point. In his address at the G8-plus-5 meeting at Heiligendamm, Germany, in July 2007, India's Prime Minister Dr Manmohan Singh had said: 'We are determined that India's per-capita greenhouse gas emissions are not going to exceed those of developed countries even while pursuing policies of development and economic growth'.

Later that year, Chancellor Angela Merkel called for an approach based on 'per-capita emissions increasingly converging worldwide at a level compatible with our shared climate protection goal', arguing that 'such a process of long-term convergence offers all countries scope to develop. It does not overburden any, yet ensures that the necessary action on the climate issue is taken. By this means the principle that countries have shared but differing responsibilities can be translated into political and economic reality'. This formulation, which I call the 'Singh–Merkel Convergence Formula' or some variant of it, has the potential to contribute significantly to breaking the logjam in climate negotiations but with a caveat. The caveat is this: countries will converge to per capita emission levels at different levels of per capita income and this will make a difference to living standards. This requires some further thought.

IV

The new sustainable development paradigm requires us to change how well we do the three Ms—measure, model, and monitor progress. We need to rethink what we mean by economic growth.

Narrow concepts of gross national product (GNP) growth must be purposefully transformed to reflect broader quality objectives such as prosperity and well-being. The Commission on the Measurement of Economic Performance and Social Progress, chaired by Joseph Stiglitz, Amartya Sen, and Jean-Paul Fitoussi, noted in its 2009 report, that purely economic indicators say nothing about whether material well-being is bought at the expense of environmental impacts, or at the risk of overshooting critical natural system thresholds.

For this reason, a general overhaul of the GNP concept is in order. It is necessary today to create additional and more inclusive indicators that take into planetary health and human development. National accounts need to reflect these.

In this context, I am happy to share with you that we in India have made a start, along these lines. Under the chairmanship of Prof. Sir Partha Dasgupta, perhaps the world's most prominent ecological economist today, we have established an expert group to develop a framework for 'Green National Accounts' for India, and we hope to be able to report 'Green National Accounts' by the year 2015. Such efforts need to happen at a global level through coordinated action.

Another extremely valuable exercise of quantifying the economic benefits from ecosystems of various types and costs associated with their loss is a global study called The Economics of Ecosystems and Biodiversity (TEEB) supported by the UNEP, the German government, the European Commission, and other institutions. A TEEB study for India was also commissioned, which shows, among other things that 45 per cent of household income or rural and forest dwellers in India come from natural resources and ecosystem services—this is the 'GDP of the poor' which is often ignored in traditional national accounting.

Modelling and assessments are equally important so we can remain ahead of the curve and can prepare appropriate policy responses before it is too late. India for example, has set up the Indian Network for Climate Change Assessment, a network-based programme that brings together over 120 institutions and over 220 scientists from across the country to undertake scientific assessments of different aspects of climate change across sectors and regions within the country. Such work needs to be strengthened and scaled up at national, regional and global levels.

There is a major role here for inter-governmental partnerships—the IPCC, despite its shortcomings, has given us a reasonable working model, and the same principles could now be deployed for broader sustainable development assessments. The UN Secretary-General's Panel has suggested the idea of Sustainable Development Goals (SDGs) that will be applicable to all countries unlike the Millennium Development Goals (MDGs) that are applicable only to the developing countries. It will be a Herculean endeavour to develop a consensus on what these SDGs should be and what sustainable development indices should be used on a global scale. But we must make a beginning at the Rio+20 Summit to be held very soon. The idea of preparing and releasing a Global Sustainability Outlook Report every year or bi-annually is also something that the summit should endorse.

V

There is a specific aspect of the 'three Ms' that I would like to emphasize: what scientists refer to as 'planetary boundaries', 'environmental thresholds', and 'tipping points'. I am adding yet another term to the lexicon—'planetary vulnerabilities'. We are in a strange situation today—while we know that critical natural systems are under severe stress, we have only just scratched the surface in terms of our scientific understanding of the nature and extent of many of these stresses. Today, awareness is growing of the potential for passing 'tipping points' beyond which environmental change accelerates, has the potential to become self-perpetuating, and may be difficult or even impossible to reverse. The work of the Stockholm Resilience Centre on planetary boundaries, that many of you would be familiar with, is an important example of this work.

But we need to do much more and we need to do it at a scale and at a pace that this problem deserves. It is my view that, while scientific enquiry is active across many fronts, we still lack a holistic picture of where the planet is heading. In some areas, especially climate change and ozone depletion, we have good working models on coordinated cutting-edge research linked to policy. But in other areas, the science is not as well developed. More importantly, the compounding effects of various environmental, economic and social pressures are not sufficiently understood.

It is clear that the time has come to launch a major coordinated global scientific initiative, to strengthen the interface between science and policy. This should include the preparation of regular assessments of the science around such concepts as planetary vulnerabilities, in the context of sustainable development. For such an initiative to take-off and become truly meaningful, it is important, to clearly address the concerns of developing countries that this will not be used as a tool to impose ceilings on their economic growth. I am confident that we can, as a global community, address this concern and launch the road map for such a scientific initiative at the earliest.

VI

The new sustainable development paradigm also requires that all countries, in their own self-interest, take on their fair share of responsibilities, especially as they relate to the problems of the global commons. Needless to add, the prospects of faster economic growth should not be endangered on this account. But there can be no denying the need for all countries to take on commitments to which they hold themselves accountable.

Burden sharing must be founded on the simple principle that as a country becomes richer (measured in terms of per capita income), it takes on increased responsibilities. Michael Spence, the Nobel Prize winning economist has made a concrete proposal in this direction and I would strongly recommend that his proposal be examined and taken forward.

I would also add here that there are a variety of approaches to internationalizing commitments countries are willing to enshrine in domestic legislation or executive action. That there must be some form of internationalization that is both transparent and credible is indubitable. But to argue that there is only way to accomplish this is, in my view, unrealistic and ignores varying domestic political realities that each country has to contend with.

VII

Agriculture lies at the heart of sustainable development. That is why the Zuma-Tallonnen Panel has strongly echoed the call for an EverGreen Revolution in farming with its focus on increasing production and productivity, while ensuring lower input use, water conservation, and better natural resource management. As we aim towards this, it is instructive to recall what made the first Green Revolution a success. At the heart of the first Green Revolution was publicly funded collaborative research under the Consultative Group on International Agricultural Research (CGIAR).

The CGIAR system developed new rice and wheat varieties—wheat in Mexico and rice in Manila—that transformed countries beyond recognition. India, for instance, went from being the world's largest importer of food grains in the 1960s to an exporter of rice and wheat in less than four decades time. The appetite for such publicly-funded collaborations has almost completely vanished and we seem to have a touching faith in the private agri-companies to deliver the goods this time around. This faith is misplaced and has devastating social consequences as well.

It is my fervent hope that saner counsels will assert themselves sooner rather than later and we can recapture the CGIAR spirit of the 1950s and 1960s that had such a dramatic impact on the lives of millions across the world. CGIAR-type research and development networks need to be fostered in other areas like renewable energy as well.

VIII

Before I close, let me convey to you that the three fundamental pillars of India's Twelfth Five Year Plan that began ten days ago is faster, more inclusive, and sustainable growth—a powerful recognition that growth as conventionally understood will simply not do any more. It will not do any more not because of global agreements but because of domestic imperatives. Even with rapidly declining fertility rates, India's population will grow by some 300–400 million over the next three decades and this, more than anything else, makes sustainable development all the more relevant and urgent for us—after all, as the Brundtland Commission defined for us a quarter of a century ago, 'sustainable development is development that meets the needs of the present without compromising the ability of future generations to meet their own needs'.

Let me once again say how privileged I feel to have been able to speak to all of you this afternoon. What we need is a genuine dialogue, understanding and cooperation, not polemics and grandstanding, if we are to make sustainable prosperity happen in all our countries.

5 The Science Anchor

At its inception, the separate administrative set-up for environment put science at its core. To this end, the first two secretaries of the newly-minted department of environment were scientists. However, with the years, science seemed to take a back seat in the workings of ministry.

When I took charge in 2009, restoring the importance of the natural science in the workings of the ministry was one of my key goals. This was not meant to be at the cost of the social sciences or any of the other inputs that are central to addressing issues relating to the environment. My most early public formulations on the issue related to the clearance process, to bring in science and a scientific temper to decision making.

Nowhere was the need to strengthen the scientific backbone more important than in our efforts to address climate change. The scientific basis of the global conversation and negotiations on climate change was provided through the Intergovernmental Panel on Climate Change, which evaluates climate change science. Research by Indian scientists, particularly those working in the country, was conspicuously absent from this roster of works that the IPCC evaluated. As a result, despite being a region in itself, the Indian and South Asian perspective would often be missing.

The most startling case was that of the IPCC's Fourth Assessment Report's claim that the Himalayan glaciers would disappear by 2035.

Scientists who had been studying the Himalayan glaciers told me that assessing the Himalayan glaciers on the same lines as the Arctic glaciers would be incorrect, and while the health of the Himalayan glaciers was poor, it had to do with a whole lot more than global warming. I asked V.K. Raina, a geoscientist, who had been studying Himalayan glaciers since the mid-1950s, to prepare a status report, which was published officially by the Ministry of Environment and Forests in September 2009. Both of us were criticized—I was accused of being a climate change-denier and IPCC chairman R. K. Pachauri, termed the Raina report as 'voodoo science'. However, six months later, the IPCC acknowledged that it had made a serious error. The Himalayan blunder led to a review of the IPCC's workings.

The Himalayan glaciers episode prompted me to announce the establishment of the Indian Network on Climate Change Assessment (INCCA). This was to be an Indian version of the IPCC, a large consortium of Indian scientists, comprising more than 250 scientists drawn from 125 research institutions in the country, to study, assess, and disseminate information on climate change and its impacts as it affected India. In 2010, the INCCA published a 4x4 climate change assessment, which studied four sectors (agriculture, water, natural ecosystems and biodiversity, and health) across four regions (the Himalayan region, Northeast, coastal areas, and Western Ghats). It also published a greenhouse gas (GHG) emissions inventory for the year 2007, which was the most recent estimate. The detailed studies would make it possible to take better and more informed decisions. The INCCA also took up the study of black carbon or soot in detail.

The benefits that INCCA's work brought to India during negotiations apart, I believed that there was a need to develop Indian research rather than relying on global scientific data and analysis. The dependence on borrowed data, borrowed models, and borrowed research came with political, economic, and social costs. I knew that developing India's scientific capabilities would require building and investing human resources. We needed to increase the number of doctoral and post-doctoral researchers in this area. To this end, I instituted the National Environmental Science Fellows Programme, geared towards developing the next generation of researchers. I also continuously stressed on the need to publish in peer reviewed scientific journals as that would give greater credence to India's scientific output.

My engagement with scientists was not limited to the INCCA. I had earlier enlisted the Indian Space Research Organisation in providing satellite support for the assessment of forest cover. The engagement expanded to launching nano-satellites for providing data on aerosol and carbon dioxide distribution, a dedicated satellite for monitoring GHGs, and establishing an extensive network of automated weather stations and carbon monitoring towers in different climatic zones of the country.

I also sought to increase the global exposure for Indian scientists by building linkages with Indian scientists working abroad, stepping up our engagement with the IPCC, and trying to organize international scientific meetings in various institutions in the country.

In my efforts to restore the primacy of science in the workings of the environment ministry, I took every opportunity that presented itself to build linkages with the scientific community, and institutions. The Bt-brinjal moratorium had earned me, in some quarters at least, the reputation of being 'anti-science'. Perceptions notwithstanding, I kept up an engagement with scientists on the issue of biotechnology and food crops through the six national academies led by Indian National Science Academy.

I turned to the Indian Institutes of Technology (IITs) for scientific assistance on the Mission Clean Ganga. The ministry signed a memorandum of understanding (MoU) with a consortium of the seven IITs (Bombay, Delhi, Madras, Kanpur, Kharagpur, Guwahati, and Roorkee), which was tasked with developing a Ganga river basin management plan. This was the first time all seven IITs were coming together for a major national project. The consortium—led by IIT Kanpur—has since produced thirty-seven reports.

Another instance in which I reached out to the scientific community was for the environmental assessment of industrial clusters. The exercise conducted by the Central Pollution Control Board was based on the Comprehensive Environmental Pollution Index (CEPI), which had been developed by a number of prominent academic institutions led by IIT Delhi, which was also associated with the field-level assessments.

Scientific institutions were routinely roped in for inputs, especially on issues like assessing cumulative impact of projects in specific river basins in fragile ecosystems—IIT Roorkee conducted an assessment study on the Alaknanda and Bhagirathi rivers, while IIT Guwahati undertook assessments in the Northeast.

Another aspect of this effort to bring science back into the environmental decision-making process was to resurrect existing institutions. The finance minister's small but clearly earmarked budgetary allocation for the Botanical Survey of India and the Zoological Survey of India in the 2009 Budget was a step in this direction. The Botanical Survey of India was set up in 1890 and the Zoological Survey of India in 1916. These two pre-eminent research institutions are tasked with the survey and exploration of floral and faunal resources of the country, respectively. Their ultimate goal is the taxonomic identification and documentation of the country's biodiversity. In their heydays these were centres of scientific research and study, but almost a hundred years later, both institutions were a pale shadow of their former, now long-forgotten selves.

Science, sadly, had taken a backseat in these institutions. I set up a task force headed by Prof. Madhav Gadgil to recommend the revamping and restructuring of both institutions. A plan was submitted by the taskforce in January 2010.

As part of the effort to rejuvenate the environmental science community, I sought active participation of Indian scientists working abroad. My effort at every step was to push the Indian scientific community to prominence, to publish, and to communicate more with the lay public. Several scientific publications were prepared during this period—the study on black carbon, the study on the Himalayan ecosystem, to name a few. I knew that with dedicated attention, encouragement, and the right set of opportunities Indian scientists would and could deliver. I cannot say that all my efforts were successful or even long lasting but at the core of my efforts was the belief that strengthening the scientific community would lead to more accurate and effective decision-making.

This chapter deals with the efforts made to give science its due place in the environment ministry, energize Indian science and scientists, and improve linkages with the global community of scientists.

Convocation Address at IIT Guwahati

[This convocation address attracted a great deal of attention as it came in the immediate aftermath of my comment on the research quality of the faculty in the IITs.]

27 MAY 2011
... I am not without personal links with IIT Guwahati. I was taught
Applied Mechanics in 1971 and 1972 at IIT Mumbai by your first
Director Dr D.N. Buragohain who, in turn, had been a student of my
father for well over a decade. Your present Director was one year my
junior. The Chairman of your Board of Governors was my colleague
when I was in the Ministry of Power in 2008.

I was last in this campus some three years back along with a
couple of senior Tata Consultancy Services executives to see how your
institute could be the anchor of Information Technology investments
for the benefit of Assam and the Northeast. I thought much progress
was being made but I am indeed sorry to now learn that, for some
reason that initiative could not take off. I do hope that project can
be revived.

II

Today also happens to be the forty-seventh death anniversary of
India's first prime minister whose vision and leadership was responsible for India's extensive infrastructure of science and technology. It
is, therefore, only appropriate that I use this convocation address as
an opportunity of revisiting a key Nehruvian concern—that of 'scientific temper'.

Nehru's contributions to the establishment of the IITs, of the large
network of research laboratories as part of Council of Scientific and
Industrial Research (CSIR) and Defence Research and Development
Organisation, and of the atomic energy establishment are all very
well known. A number of people contributed to the idea of the first
generation of IITs—Sir Ardeshir Dalal, Nalini Ranjan Sarkar, J.C.
Ghosh, and Humayun Kabir. It was Nehru's sustained and sponta-
neous political support that translated the idea into a reality. Over
forty-five laboratories in different fields were launched during his
seventeen years in office. It was also during the last two years of his
tenure that the first steps were taken to launch India into the elec-
tronics and space era.

But more than brick and mortar—the hardware as it were—it is
Nehru's preoccupation with what he at different times called the

'scientific method', the 'scientific approach', the 'scientific outlook' and the 'scientific temper'—the software if you will—that I wish to speak about today. The phrase 'scientific temper'[1] has come to define Nehru—like the memorable 'tryst with destiny', his wonderful description of khadi as the 'livery of freedom', his moving tribute to Mahatma Gandhi that begins with 'The light has gone out of our lives...', and his call for a 'socialistic pattern of society' at Avadi in 1955.

That Nehru was wedded to the use of science in national development is evident from his work as the chairman of the National Planning Committee set up in September 1938 by the then-President of the Indian National Congress Netaji Subhas Chandra Bose at the suggestion of his friend, the distinguished astrophysicist Meghnad Saha. The committee effectively functioned till 1940 although it was formally dissolved only in 1949. Nehru assembled a fifteen-member team of businessmen, economists, scientists, and others. There were five scientists, including Meghnad Saha and J.C. Ghosh. The task of this committee was made difficult; it is generally not widely appreciated, by Mahatma Gandhi's somewhat inexplicably strong opposition to the very idea of the committee and his veto of the publication of the final reports of the committee in 1941.[2]

Nehru has little to say on science in his *Autobiography* that came out in 1936 other than to assert 'to the British we must be grateful for one splendid gift of which they were the bearers, the gift of science and its rich offspring'. His first articulation of his larger thinking on science was contained in a message sent to the silver jubilee session of the Indian Science Congress in Calcutta held in January 1938, in which he said:

> Though I have long been a slave driven by the chariot of Indian politics, with little leisure for other thoughts, my mind has often wandered to the days when as a student I haunted the laboratories of that home of science, Cambridge. And though circumstances made me part company with science, my thoughts turned to it with longing. In later years, through devious processes I arrived again at science, when I realized that science was not only a pleasant diversion and abstraction, but was of the very texture of life, without which our modern world would vanish away. Politics led me to economics, and this led me inevitably to science and the scientific approach to all our problems and to life itself. It was

science alone that could solve these problems of hunger and poverty, of insanitation and illiteracy, of superstition and deadening custom and tradition, of vast resources running to waste, of a rich country inhabited by starving people.

Nine years later, in his *The Discovery of India*, Nehru returned to this theme and it is worth quoting at some length since it was to figure in many of his speeches as prime minister:

The applications of science are inevitable and unavoidable for all countries and peoples today. But something more than its application is necessary. It is the scientific approach, the adventurous and yet critical temper of science, the search for truth and new knowledge, the refusal to accept anything without testing and trial, the capacity to change previous conclusions in the face of new evidence, the reliance on observed fact and not on pre-conceived theory, the hard discipline of the mind—all this is necessary, not merely for the application of science but for life itself and the solution of its many problems ... The scientific approach and temper are, or should be, a way of life, a process of thinking, a method of acting and associating with our fellowmen ... The scientific temper points out the way along which man should travel. It is the temper of a free man. We live in a scientific age, so we are told, but there is little evidence of this temper in the people anywhere or even in their leaders ... Science deals with the domain of positive knowledge but the temper which it should produce goes beyond that domain.

Subsequently, Nehru never lost an opportunity to drive home these sentiments. For instance, speaking at the opening of the National Physical Laboratory in New Delhi in January 1950, he had this to say (and he could have been talking of the contemporary scene as it turns out):

I often wonder if science is not going to meet the same fate as religion, that is to say, people talked in terms of religion, but they seldom behaved as religious-minded people. Religion became a set of ceremonials and forms and some kind of a ritual worship. The inner spirit left the people. Large numbers of people talk glibly about science today and yet in their lives or actions do not exhibit a trace of science ... But science is something more. It is a way of training the mind to look at life and the whole social structure ... So I stress the need for the development of a scientific mind and temper which is more important than actual discovery as it is out of this temper and method that many more discoveries will come.

III

It was at Trinity College in Cambridge that science became an integral part of his formal education when he decided to do a Natural Science Tripos—with chemistry, geology, and botany as his subjects. There is also no question that in later life Nehru, an extraordinarily well-read man, was influenced by progressive British intellectuals who wrote on science and society like Bertrand Russell,[3] P.M.S. Blackett, J.B.S. Haldane, the Huxley brothers—Julian and Aldous—A.V. Hill, and J.D. Bernal. There is also little doubt that he was impressed by what he saw in the Soviet Union during his visit there in November 1927, a time described by his biographer S. Gopal as 'the last days of its first, halcyon period'. Few know that Nehru's first literary work was *Soviet Russia: Some Random Sketches and Impressions* published in early 1928.

But in January 1957, he dug deep into our history to convey the idea that the science and the scientific method was not alien to the Indian ethos. In his customary annual address to the Indian Science Congress in Calcutta (he spoke every year in early January from 1947 to 1964 starting a tradition that has continued) he said:

> I am coming here today from Hirakud where I performed or helped in the opening ceremony of a very magnificent piece of work of Indian engineers, the great Hirakud dam ... A day before that I performed or participated in an entirely different function at Nalanda, a great university centre of 1,500 years ago in Magadha, which is now Bihar. At this place, where the ruins of the university still exist, my mind went back to the days of the Buddha ... I thought of his message which, apart from its religious significance, was a message of tolerance, a message against superstition, rituals and dogma. It was a message essentially in the scientific spirit.

Almost exactly a year later speaking to students at the University of Guwahati not far from here, Nehru once again drew attention to the Indian tradition of the scientific approach when he said:

> ...the spirit of the Upanishads and the teachings of the Buddha, basically, were the method of science: search, enquiry and applying your mind to it, and maybe something more than the mind but it was search by experience, by reasoning ... we live in an age of science very much. Almost everything you see roundabout you is a product of science and technology, which has come out of science. But I am particularly referring to

the temper of science, the mental approach, that is, not an approach of a bigot, not the approach of a closed mind, but of an open mind, of enquiry, realising a special way of thinking as it used to be in India.

There is another probable source of Indian influence on Nehru which has been little studied. In 1934, the Indian Science News Association was established in Calcutta very largely at the initiative of the eminent astrophysicist Meghnad Saha. The association founded a magazine called *Science and Culture* which, in the words of Shiv Visvanathan—the noted sociologist and science historian—'was to present some of the most forceful arguments for a society based on the scientific method'. During its heyday which was till the late 1940s, *Science and Culture* was one of the most important science policy journals in the world. Incidentally, it still comes out but it is a pale shadow of its former glorious self.

The Science and Culture Group was a remarkable galaxy of Bengalis most of whom who studied in Presidency College during 1909–11. Apart from Saha, there were Satyendranath Bose of Bose–Einstein and 'boson' fame; J.C. Ghosh, one of the key founders of the IIT system; Nikhil Ranjan Sen, the noted mathematician; J.N. Mukherjee, later to become the Director of the Indian Agricultural Research Institute; Nilratan Dhar and P. C. Mahalanobis, the physicist–statistician and founder of the Indian Statistical Institute and the man closest to Nehru among this group. It was Saha, Visvanathan has uncovered in his *Organizing for Science*, who got the then President of the Indian National Congress Netaji Subhas Chandra Bose to get Nehru appointed as chairman of the National Planning Committee instead of the distinguished engineer Sir M. Visvesvaraya.[4] The Science and Culture Group and Nehru shared many affinities on the role of science and technology in national development as well as on the social and economic achievements of the Soviet Union. But unlike the group, Nehru was more conscious of the limitations of transplanting the Soviet Union model in the Indian political and social milieu.

Nehru's return to the Upanishads and the Buddha to give an 'Indian' flavour to the concept of the scientific temper was to find resonance decades later in Amartya Sen's well-known book *The Argumentative Indian*, where he demonstrates that the method of reason and reasoning, that the method of sceptical argument, that the acceptance of heterodoxy were, at various times, a defining characteristic of Indian civilization. Like Nehru, Sen rightly refuses to see Indian traditions through the prism of modern-day religious categories. This, of course, should not be construed as a romanticization of our past, as is the normal tendency, but an acceptance of the enormous diversity of our intellectual and cultural legacy, something that has been under sustained assault by certain ideologies and forces.

Nehru's return to Indian traditions of the scientific method should also not be taken to mean that all answers can be found by excavating our past. Nehru himself was open to ideas from different sources. Immediately following Independence, he invited the British Nobel-laureate P.M.S. Blackett to advise the Government of India on the organization for defence research. In the 1950s and the early 1960s, India was a mecca for economists from all over the world who came to advise the Planning Commission on the Second and Third Five Year Plans. You name the economist of any repute and he had been in India then. An American engineer Harvey Slocum was the driving force behind the construction of the Bhakra-Nangal dam.

Nehru's recalling of Indian traditions in the scientific method should sensitize us to another aspect of Indian philosophy that has been hugely neglected. We see ourselves as essentially a spiritual civilization and indeed the world has seen India largely through the lens of spirituality. We pat ourselves on the back often by juxtaposing our spirituality with the crassly materialistic Western values. But that there has been a strong materialist trend in our own thought is beyond question, a materialist trend that Debiprasad Chattopadhyaya showed in his brilliant book *Lokayata* that was always committed to secularism, rationalism, and science-orientation. Unfortunately, the scripture-oriented view of India completed overshadowed the materialist view with grave consequences for our image of ourselves let alone the perspective of others. Chattopadhyaya's book appeared just four years before Nehru passed away and at a time when he was preoccupied with many other pressing national, regional, and international issues. I have no doubt in my mind that Nehru would have backed the book's revolutionary thesis.

IV

In 1976, through the Forty-second Amendment Part IV-A Article 51-A on Fundamental Duties got added to our Constitution. Of particular interest is Article 51-A(h), which reads: (It shall be the duty of every citizen of India) *to develop the scientific temper, humanism and the spirit of inquiry and reform.*

Soon thereafter, there was a public debate on scientific temper generated by the statement issued in July 1981 by a group of scientists and academics under the aegis of the Nehru Centre in Mumbai. This statement triggered by what it called 'a retreat from reason' and the growth of superstitious beliefs and obscurantist beliefs' had a foreword by one of Nehru's most fervent admirers P.N. Haksar. It led to a counterstatement being issued by the noted intellectual Ashish Nandy, in which he called for a 'humanistic' as opposed to a 'scientific' temper. Actually, when you read Nehru, you find that he did not position 'humanistic temper' against 'scientific temper'. Indeed, to Nehru, humanism with its respect for was very much part and parcel of scientific temper itself. Nehru himself was acutely aware of the limits of science and could in no way be accused of falling prey to scientific hubris. The philosopher Bhiku Parekh has written that though Nehru wanted to awake India from its 'deep slumber when it came to grief because it had become dogmatic, mystical, speculative, uncritical, inward-looking and addicted to undisciplined fantasy', he was equally anxious to 'avoid the positivist mistake of regarding it (science) as the only valid form of knowledge'.

In light of Nehru's frequent exhortations and in light of this constitutional obligation, where are we in regard to 'scientific temper'? India has made huge strides since the Nehru's times. Its economy is now amongst the fastest growing in the world. Its scientific and technological capability in diverse fields is widely recognized and acknowledged. Some of our institutions of higher learning have earned global accolades but really because of the quality of students and alumni I should add.

But where are we placed in regard to the development of the 'scientific temper'? Have we, individually and collectively, become more tolerant and accommodating of diversity? Have we, individually and collectively, shed ourselves of dogma and superstition, given up outmoded ways of thinking subjecting phenomena to critical enquiry? Have we, individually and collectively, opened our minds and, as Tagore prayed, not lost ourselves in the 'dreary desert sands of dead habit'? Have we, individually and collectively broken the chains of obscurantism and bigotry of whatever kind?

V

To Nehru, of course, scientific temper was something to be inculcated in society at large. But why take society? Just have a look at our institutions of higher learning—our IITs, our universities, our numerous research laboratories—and ask yourself, 'where are they in relation to the inculcation of the scientific temper?' 'Are the true values of science—the values of relentless questioning, logical argumentation and humility, for instance—being propagated?' 'Are our intellectual institutions as a whole anchored in what Sen called "internal pluralism and external receptivity"?'

During Nehru's time itself, things had not quite gone the way he wanted. J.B.S. Haldane, one of the greatest geneticists of the twentieth century emigrated from England to spend the last years of his life in India, in part, because of his admiration for Nehru. Haldane was to warn Nehru in the late 1950s that his beloved CSIR was not the Council for Scientific and Industrial Research but actually the Council for the Suppression of Independent Research! And one of his key scientific colleagues was later to give respectability to a godman who produced ash and watches from thin air.

What has gone wrong? Why have we strayed so far? How is it that we are recognized as a major power in some knowledge-based industries and, yet, when it comes to scientific temper, we are found wanting—not just ordinary citizens but scientists and engineers as well? How is it that a number of national institutions set up with a grand vision, now have become parochial? How is it we cannot have a cool and composed public debate on any issue without abuse and vitriol being hurled? Why can't we disagree, if we have to, without being disagreeable? Personally, I think Nehru set too high a standard for us. He underestimated the hold of prejudices and atavistic passions on us—passions, in the words of his cousin B.K. Nehru the noted administrator, 'that do not yield to rationality or the wider interest of the nation'. Nehru was the supreme rationalist who expected others to be so as well. His strict demarcation of private views and public positions, for instance, led him into conflict with his own colleagues on the issue of rebuilding of the Somnath Temple—Nehru was not against the reconstruction but was against the President of India being associated with it in his 'official' capacity.

It was being suggested even during Nehru's time that his obsession with the idea of a scientific temper went against the spiritual nature of our society. That Nehru was himself aware of this murmuring is borne out by the fact that he returned to this theme in his later years. On the occasion of the golden jubilee celebrations of the Indian Institute of Science in Bangalore in 1959, he stated:

> There is something in life, let us say, like goodness, like truth, something like beauty…which presumably are very important in life. And when we put it in this way, how far can science be allied, without destroying its basis, to certain fundamental values in life? If it is not concerned with life as such—if it is independent of these values—then we may make the greatest advance there divorced from these values, but presumably the ultimate result will not be good … On the other hand, we cannot merely talk of these values without science coming into the picture. These are difficult problems and certainly a little beyond my depth. But I do not myself see any essential compatibility between the temper of science, the spirit of science, the approach of science, and these higher values—provided that even in the search for these higher values the temper of science in maintained.

Clearly, Nehru's tremendous fascination for the Buddha came out this.

Nehru saw the state as *the* instrument of building the scientific temper in society. With the benefit of hindsight, it could be argued that he gave too much importance to the role of the state. But don't forget that the primacy of the state reflected the zeitgeist, reflected the times as it were, in which he functioned. Civil society organizations had yet to emerge in large numbers as they have today, although I must say that many of these organizations are dangerously anti-science and technophobic. Nehru, perhaps, did not bargain for changing political values. Where are the political leaders and parties today who will confront obscurantism? Who protested when a young woman committed sati in Rajasthan in 1986? Who called into question the frenzy surrounding the gushing forth of milk from the Ganesha idol in the nation's capital? How is it that leaders across the political divide continue to tacitly support institutions like *khap* panchayats? We had the extraordinary spectacle of a minister a couple of years ago—a physicist to boot— who wanted to introduce astrology as a subject of study in universities. Surely, scientists should not be seen as accomplices in nourishing an irrational anti-modernist culture!

It is also often overlooked by his critics that Nehru saw the state not only as the instrument but, more importantly, as the *democratic* instrument of fostering the scientific temper. The 'Left' critique of Nehru emanates from the frustration that he did not do enough to propagate the scientific temper except open laboratories and institutes. But let us not overlook the political framework which he helped establish so pains-takingly—the framework of parliamentary democracy. He never sought to coerce but instead tried to persuade. There was never any attempt at imposition. He was the 'great communicator' when he easily could have become the 'great dictator' as he himself had feared in his famous piece of 1936 that appeared under the pseudonym of Chanakya.

With the spread of education and with economic development itself, he believed that the values that animate the scientific temper would get embedded in our lives. This has turned out to be a heroic assumption and professional education, it turns out, very often has not led to a broadening of horizons but to a narrowing of outlooks. I am not suggesting that we can look to Nehru and his ideas to give us specific answers to all our contemporary questions about science. But what we can learn from a study of India's first prime minister's concerns is something about how essential it is for people like you and me especially to see as our continuing responsibility the advancement and diffusion of an open, questioning, liberal, humanistic, and rational intellectual culture, which lies at the core of the notion of the scientific temper of Jawaharlal Nehru.

VI

So, what do I tell the graduating class? I am expected to do so this being a solemn convocation address. In light of what I have pointed out earlier, the only thing that remains for me to say is try and imbibe the spirit of Nehru's scientific temper in whatever you do. You don't have to be follower of his political party to acknowledge and appreciate the true value of Nehru's obsession with the idea of a 'scientific temper'. The essence of Nehru's fixation on scientific temper was this—a ques-tioning mind, pushing the limits, not getting encumbered or structured by narrow limited concerns, not afraid to be inconsistent with changing facts and circumstances but always proceeding on the basis of objective realities, not prisoner of any dogma, modern, or archaic. And let me tell you—modern-day dogmas can be as devastating as ancient ones. I speak from experience as someone who has to confront them daily both from the 'GDP-ists' on the one hand and the 'environmentalists' on the other.

You must all be aware of how your institution came into being. Other than the Central University in Hyderabad set up in the 1970s in response to the Telangana agitation, your IIT is perhaps the only educational institution to have been a demand expressed as part of a peace accord. So, the responsibility on all of you to do something for this region of our country is that much greater. This is a region of not only great physical beauty but also a region that is rich in natural and human resources as well. One of the great tragedies of the IITs so far has been that while their contributions to the global economy have been striking and their contributions to the national economy growing, their impacts on the local economy have been conspicuously missing. It is true that IITs are national institutions and the national character reflected in the student community must also get reflected in other aspects like faculty as well. Here, too, we are faltering and across the country we see national institutions set up during Nehru's time fall prey to narrow parochialism and lose the spirit of innovation. You are new and, therefore, better placed to avoid that fate.

You will, of course, go out from here and leave your imprint else-where. Four years of your life and more in some other cases would have been spent here and I am sure you will leave with pleasant memories. I wish you all the very best in your endeavours. In these endeavours, how-ever, I hope you will spare a thought for the immediate milieu in which this institution, started with great hopes, is located and that you will become the harbingers of a transformed Northeast as well. Thank you.

Letter to Prime Minister on Setting Up a Network of Scientific and Research Institutions, and Scientists Working on Climate Change—Indian Network for Climate Change Assessment (INCCA)

12 OCTOBER 2009

You will be pleased to know that the MoEF is launching INCCA on 14 October 2009, with 127 scientific research institutions from across the country. The first output will be published in October 2010 and this will give a comprehensive picture on the impact of climate change in various sectors and various regions of our country. It would also form a basis for our National Communication to the United Nations Framework Convention on Climate Change (UNFCCC). The first National Communication had been submitted in the year June 2004. We are getting Dr R. Chidambaram to preside over the 14 October function and Dr V. Ramanathan, an international authority on black carbon, who is presently working at the University of California, San Diego, is giving a special address. INCCA will be a core contributor to the objectives of National Mission on Strategic Knowledge, which is envisaged in the National Action Plan on Climate Change.

Email to Dr Madhav Gadgil on Revamping the Botanical Survey of India and Zoological Survey of India

18 July 2009

It has been ages since we met. I have been meaning to get in touch with you ever since I took over in environment and forests.

There are many areas where I need your support and guidance.

Most immediately, you are aware that at my bidding the finance minister has given a special grant of Rs 100 crore to the Indian Council for Forestry Research and Education, Rs 15 crore to the Botanical Survey of India, and Rs 15 crore to the Zoological Survey of India. I have visited the Botanical Survey of India (BSI) and the Zoological Survey of India (ZSI) in Kolkata recently. Both these institutions need massive renewal. The Budget grants throw a lifeline and need to be utilized in a manner that will revive them.

I want to set up a committee to recommend plans, policies and programmes for the renewal of BSI and ZSI and want very much to get you to chair it. I am hoping that you will say yes to my request after which I will send you the other names I have in mind.

Apart from this, I look forward to meeting up with you soon.

Letter to Prime Minister on India's Capability in Science and Need to Break Institutional Barriers

29 October 2009

A couple of days ago, I was at ISRO in Bangalore and I was pleasantly surprised to discover the tremendous work that has been done in the area of climate change—seventy PhDs and 600 publications have resulted from this programme, which has been engaged in research on various aspects of climate change as it affects India.

The day before, I spent some time at ISRO's National Atmospheric Research Laboratory (NARL) at Tirupathi, where too I met with a number of young scientists working in this field. One interesting idea that came up at NARL was that of a climate observatory network. The first such comprehensive national observatory is at NARL, Tirupathi itself.

I mention this to show there are so many pockets of capability in our country. I find that ISRO's work has not been part of our mainstream when it comes to discussions on climate change. I will be rectifying this but all this underscores the need for breaking institutional barriers completely and work in an 'open source' mode.

Letter to The International Association of Botanical and Mycological Societies, on India Hosting the XIX International Botanical Congress

2 July 2009

I write to you to propose India's intent to bid to host the XIX International Botanical Congress to be held in 2017. It will be our privilege to host the congress in India for the first time. India has a range of qualifications which we believe would make it an appropriate host for the congress.

India is considered one of the world's seventeen 'mega diverse' countries in terms of biodiversity. With only 2.5 per cent of the world's land area, India accounts for 7.8 per cent of the recorded species of the world, including 45,500 recorded species of plants and 91,000 recorded species of animals. India is also rich in traditional and indigenous knowledge, both coded and informal. India takes its commitment to preserving biodiversity very seriously. This is not only because of India's international obligations as a signatory to the Convention on Biological Diversity and other agreements. It is also because India believes that protecting our biodiversity is a critical national priority as it is linked to local livelihoods of millions of people in the country.

India has a great tradition of science and research related to botany. The BSI, established in 1890, has been spearheading taxonomic research for the last 119 years. India has an elaborate network of organisations and a large vibrant botanical community engaged in research on various facets of plant diversity, including botanical diversity and taxonomy, ecology and the environment, conservation and restoration biology, population biology, systematic and evolutionary biology, physiology and phytochemistry, cell biology, molecular genetics, physiology and functional genomics, ethnobotany, bioinformatics, biological databases, knowledge management, etc.

The BSI itself has a repository of over 3.5 million herbarium specimens and germplasm collections of about 1.5 million plants in its chain of botanical gardens. It has over 100 scientists working in the field of plant diversity and taxonomy, ecology, phytochemistry, pharmacognosy, and conservation and restoration biology.

The opportunity to host the prestigious congregation will provide an opportunity to the large Indian botanical fraternity to exchange ideas and share their experiences, and give exceptional exposure to young botanists of the country. This will also provide an opportunity to the visiting botanists from across the globe to have first-hand experience of India's rich ecosystem, biological, cultural, and ethnic diversity.

It will be a great privilege if India is given the opportunity to host the next congress in Kolkata, where the Botanical Survey is headquartered, close to a 272-acre, Kew-type Botanical Garden set up in 1787. The Government of India will extend all possible assistance for the congress.

Letter to Committee of the International Society of Zoological Sciences President Jean-Marc Jallon on India Hosting the XXIII International Zoological Congress

2 JULY 2009

I write to you to seek your support for hosting the next XXIII International Zoological Congress, to be held in 2012, in India. It will be our privilege to host the congress in India for the first time. India has a range of qualifications which we believe would make it an appropriate host for the congress.

India is considered one of the world's seventeen 'like-minded mega diverse countries' in terms of biodiversity. With only 2.5 per cent of the world's land area, India accounts for 7.8 per cent of the recorded species of the world, including 45,500 recorded species of plants and 91,000 recorded species of animals. India is also enormously rich in traditional and indigenous knowledge, both coded and informal. India takes its commitment to preserving biodiversity very seriously. This is not only because of India's international obligations as a signatory to the Convention on Biological Diversity, Convention on Migratory Species, RAMSAR Convention, and others, but it is also because India believes that protecting biodiversity is a critical national priority as it is linked to local livelihoods of millions of people in the country.

India has a great tradition of science and research related to Zoology. The ZSI, established on 1 July 1916, has been spearheading taxonomic research for the past ninety-three years. The ZSI is a leading organization, conducting research in the field of animal taxonomy, ecology, behavioural science, conservation biology, cytotaxonomy, population studies, biological databases and resource management in protected areas. It has an excellent network and linkage with leading research institutions and universities dealing on the subjects by the zoological community, engaged in various facets of animal science including diversity and distribution, taxonomy, ecology, environmental conservation and wildlife biology, restoration biology, population ecology, systematic and evolutionary biology, physiology, cytology and cytogenetics, molecular genetics, functional genomics, bioinformatics, biological databases, knowledge on resource management in protected areas, etc.

This leading institution itself has a repository of over 4 million national zoological specimens, including over 17,000 type specimens in their natural history collections located at its headquarters in Kolkata, and a network of sixteen regional centres at different geographical regions of the country. It has over 200 scientists working in the field of animal diversity and zoo-geographical distribution, taxonomic studies, ecology, behavioural studies and conservation biology.

The opportunity to host the prestigious zoological congregation will provide an opportunity to the large Indian scientific fraternity to exchange ideas, share their experiences, and give exceptional exposure to young scientists of the country. This will also provide an opportunity to visiting zoologists from across the globe to have first-hand experience of India's rich ecosystem, biological, cultural, and ethnic diversity.

It will be a great privilege if India is given the opportunity to host the next congress at Kolkata, where the Zoological Survey headquarters is located. The Government of India will extend all possible assistance for the congress. I shall greatly appreciate receiving a favourable response in this regard from your end to take the application process forward.

Letter to Governor of West Bengal Gopal Krishna Gandhi on the Need to Revive the Botanical Survey of India and Zoological Survey of India

8 JULY 2009

I have just seen a letter that you had addressed to my predecessor Namo Narain Meena regarding the improvements required in the zoological section of the Indian Museum that is being maintained by the ZSI, Kolkata.

In fact, I had an occasion to discuss this issue both with BSI as well as ZSI, and I can assure you that we will do something soon. Incidentally, you may have noticed that yesterday the finance minister made a special one-time grant of Rs 15 crore each to BSI and ZSI for modernization. This was a fallout of my visit to both these institutions, which are part of our history and heritage and which need to be revived urgently.

Letter to Prime Minister on a Report on the Health of the Himalayan Glaciers

[This report unleashed an international debate and contributed to setting up a review of the processes adopted by the IPCC in preparing their assessment reports.]

9 NOVEMBER 2009

It is my privilege to send you a review report on the Himalayan glaciers that I had commissioned a couple of months back.

The report concludes:

Most glaciers are retreating, a few are advancing and some are retreating at a decelerating rate.

The link between global warming and retreat has yet to be established in a robust scientific manner

Quite apart from the debate on the retreat, the health of the glaciers is a matter for concern, for example, the amount of snow cover, widespread debris, etc.

North Indian rivers get more water from the monsoon than from snow melt.

Himalayan glaciers are fundamentally different from Artic glaciers since their snout (lowest point) is 3,000–4,000 m above sea level and therefore, a comparison between the two is not valid.

We have taken up a major programme for measuring, monitoring, and modelling climate change in the Himalayan glacier system in collaboration with ISRO and many other institutions. For the first time, we are also supporting The Energy and Resources Institute (TERI) to conduct a study on the impact of soot and black carbon on the glaciers.

Responding to 'The Message from the Glaciers', an Article by Oliver Schell in the 27 May 2010 issue of the New York Review of Books

15 July 2010

Orville Schell in his fine essay ('The Message from the Glaciers', *NYRB*, 27 May) has this to say about me: 'But the Indian Minister of Environment and Forests, Jairam Ramesh, recently released a report questioning whether glaciers in the region are actually melting in a precipitous manner...'

Mr Schell is right. The report I released last November, *Himalayan Glaciers: A State-of-Art Review of Glacial Studies, Glacial Retreat and Climate Change*, does not present as alarmist a position as the IPCC and other climate evangelists like Mr Al Gore have taken. Of course, the IPCC later retracted its 'prediction' of the Himalayan glaciers melting away by 2035, which this report had challenged.

But Mr Schell seems to suggest that I am less than serious on this issue. I am not. I want to reiterate what I have been saying for the past year in both India and abroad:

1. The bulk of the 10,000-odd glaciers in the Indian Himalayas that have been studied appear to be in retreat.
2. Some glaciers, like the Gangotri glacier, are retreating but at a decelerating rate.
3. Some glaciers, like the Siachen glacier, appear to be actually advancing.

4. The Himalayan glaciers are different from other glaciers (like in the Arctic) mainly because of their snout being at least three thousand meters above sea level. This may influence their behaviour.

5. Many eminent Indian scientists have challenged the evidence of the impact of black carbon on glacier retreat. This requires further study with an open mind. But black carbon cannot hijack the ongoing debate on GHGs.

6. The health of the glaciers (as evidenced by the huge presence of debris, for example) is very poor and this needs to be addressed quickly.

7. The contribution of glaciers to the water in Himalayan rivers also needs to be examined closely. Recent World Bank studies seem to indicate that glacier melt contributes about 4 per cent of the total flow of Nepal rivers, a figure that is much lower than what we commonly assume to be the case.

I am extremely concerned, as is the Government of India, about the impact of climate change on Himalayan glaciers. A National Institute of Himalayan Glaciology has been set up in Dehradun to coordinate the measurement, modelling, and monitoring (the 3-M strategy) of glacial health. A network of automated weather stations is being put in place.

Last September, we brought out a fairly detailed report, *Governance for Sustaining the Himalayan Ecosystem*, which is under implementation in the states. We are also actively pursuing joint programs in glaciology with other countries in the Himalayan eco-region, both bilaterally as well under the aegis of the Kathmandu-based international organization, International Centre for Integrated Mountain Development (ICIMOD). We need more robust science and less sensationalizing and sermonizing on the Himalayan glacier issue.

Orville Schell's reply:

The Indian environment minister, Jairam Ramesh, admonishes us that 'we need more robust science and less sensationalizing and sermonizing on the Himalayan glacier issue.' He is right. The behavior of glaciers is still incompletely understood and urgently needs more research. While some appear quite healthy, others appear to be shrinking at an alarming rate. It is also undeniable that the connection between disappearing glaciers and climate change demands as much attention as we can afford.

While we do not have definitive information about the underlying forces, there is clearly something amiss in the melting of so many major ice systems—from the Arctic and Antarctic to the various high-altitude regions around the world. Contributing to this global phenomenon are growing amounts of dust, black carbon soot, and other particulate matter in the atmosphere, along with rising temperatures and changing patterns of precipitation, strongly suggesting that human agency is a major cause.

Reluctance to be branded 'an alarmist' such as 'the IPCC and other climate evangelists like Mr. Al Gore' might understandably make some choose to delay judgment while more studies are done. But even Ramesh himself concedes he is 'extremely concerned, as is the government of India, about the impact of climate change on Himalayan glaciers.' If this is true, then one is left to wonder whether Minister Ramesh's call for prudence and restraint is responsible. But who among us delays taking out fire insurance, even when there is substantial uncertainty that our homes will burn down?

To insinuate that the scientists cited in my article are really only 'climate evangelists' calling on gullible people to believe in environmental apocalypse is probably not what Minister Ramesh really means. At least, I hope not. After all, he is a smart and persuasive man. But so too are these scientists, who have spent their lifetimes engaged in climate research. And when so many of the world's experts conclude that anthropogenic effects, such as greenhouse gas emissions and carbon soot, are most probably causing perturbations in our global climate, and that these changes are at the root of the problems that now seem to beset many glaciers, do we not have an obligation not only to listen, but also to formulate sensible courses of action?

Letter to Prime Minister on Utilizing ISRO for Monitoring GHG Emissions

11 August 2009

I met with Dr K. Kasturirangan and Dr. G. Madhavan Nair to explore how ISRO's satellite capability can be used to monitor our GHG emissions. I feel this is an area in which we can demonstrate regional and global leadership.

The following points emerged from my discussions with our two top space technology experts.

India should enter into an agreement with the Japanese Greenhouse gases Observing SATellite (GOSAT) and the European Environmental

Satellite (ENVISAT) for accessing and independently analyzing data generated by them. These missions are expected to be in operation till 2012.

India should work towards launching its own nano-satellite by end-2010 for providing data on aerosol and carbon dioxide distribution. India's own small satellite for measuring aerosols and trace gases is scheduled for launch in 2011.

India should work towards launching its own dedicated satellite for monitoring GHGs by end-2011. Plans for this, including that for sensor development, are already under finalization at ISRO.

While our satellite capability can and must be deployed for monitoring GHGs particularly, it is equally important to develop research capability for modelling and analysing the data being generated. For this, ISRO will set up an independent institution in collaboration with academic institutions like the Indian Institute of Science, Bangalore, and IIT Delhi for which the MoEF will provide the start-up funding. The Ministry of Earth Sciences has also set up a similar centre in Pune.

ISRO has developed automated weather stations. These need to be deployed in much larger numbers across the country especially in Himalayan states to monitor the health of glaciers. In addition, ISRO will establish carbon monitoring towers in different climatic zones, according to a time-schedule.

I mentioned this initiative to Montek Ahluwalia, who welcomed it enthusiastically. He felt that we should collaborate with the US. I have also shown this letter to Dr Kasturirangan and Dr Madhavan Nair and they fully endorse its contents.

Letter to the Prime Minister on his Address to the Indian Science Congress

4 JANUARY 2010

I read your speech to the Indian Science Congress with great interest. I would like to bring to your attention the actions taken by me on five specific issues.

You spoke about genetically modified crops and human safety. Right now, the case of Bt-brinjal is in front of me and I have scheduled public consultations in seven different cities of the country. I have also written to over fifty scientists both in India and abroad seeking their views.

I hope to be in a position to take a final decision by the middle of February 2010.

You spoke of Indian companies assuming a leadership role in climate change technology. I have already initiated a dialogue with the Confederation of Indian Industry (CII). I am meeting about 100 CEOs on 6 January 2010 and, thereafter, a full-day technical workshop will be held in mid-January 2010 to identify specific opportunities for leadership by Indian companies, both public and private.

You spoke of creating a new organizational culture in our scientific establishments. I had set up an expert group under the chairmanship of Dr Madhav Gadgil to suggest a detailed blueprint for revamping of BSI and ZSI. The committee's report is to be submitted in the next few days. In addition, I am establishing another expert committee to look at how to improve the scientific skills and expertise within the MoEF, which, as you well know, was originally conceived of as a science and technology ministry.

You spoke of converting the brain-drain into the brain-gain. I am in the process of setting up a global advisory group on climate change and another global advisory committee on environmental sciences comprising distinguished People of Indian Origins/Non-Resident Indians to advise the MoEF on an ongoing basis and also help build/renew institutional capacity in the country.

You spoke about a new approach to forest management. We have received a special grant of Rs100 crore in the 2009–10 Budget for modernization of the Indian Council for Forestry Research and Education (ICFRE) system. I have convened a meeting of forestry scientists from across the country on 10 January in Dehradun to formulate a specific research agenda. In addition, we have started work on inducting IT in a significant way for forest management and Mr Sam Pitroda was present when this initiative was launched.

Letter to the Planning Commission member K. Kasturirangan, on a Committee on Scientific Functions of the MoEF

5 JANUARY 2010

You are well aware that the MoEF was started as a scientific department. The first two secretaries were, in fact, distinguished scientists. But over the years the culture of administration and regulation has overtaken scientific excellence. Clearly, there is urgent need to renew the science and technology base of the MoEF.

My desire is to set up an expert group under your chairmanship to look at the scientific functions of MoEF and tell us what more needs to be done to strengthen and deepen it. I thought you would be the best person to chair this group since you will also be in a position to relate the scientific activities in MoEF with other scientific departments like the department of science and technology (DST), department of biotechnology (DBT), Ministry of Earth Sciences, and ISRO as well.

The composition for this expert group I have in mind is as follows:

1. Dr K. Kasturirangan, member, Planning Commission
2. Dr Kalpana Balakrishnan, Professor, Environmental Health Engineering, Sri Ramachandra University, Chennai
3. Dr Chandra Venkataraman, Professor, Chemical Engineering, IIT, Mumbai
4. Dr Deepak Pental, Vice Chancellor, Delhi University
5. Shri Viswanath Anand, Retd Secretary, MoEF
6. Shri M.F. Farooqui, Addl Secretary, MoEF–Convenor

I would consider it a privilege if you would agree to this suggestion and take this initiative on board under your leadership. This would, in my view, provide a whole new direction to the MoEF.

Note to Prime Minister on the Review of the New Institutions Being Set Up for Climate Change Science

14 JANUARY 2010

Today, we jointly reviewed new institution-building initiatives being taken by the MoEF, ISRO, DST, and Ministry of Earth Sciences in the area of climate change. Our objective was to ensure that there is synergy in these initiatives and that there is close coordination and cooperation among these new institutions even though we believe some amount of competition would be desirable.

ISRO has proposed the establishment of a National Institute of Climate Environmental Sciences. DST is setting up a National Institute of Himalayan Glaciology. The Ministry of Earth Sciences is planning the creation of a Centre for Climate Change Research. After the discussions with these organizations, we have arrived at a format for collaboration which will involve an element of cross-funding. ISRO's Institute will be co-funded by ISRO, MoEF, Ministry of Earth Sciences, and DST. DST's institute will be co-funded by DST, ISRO, and MoEF. The Ministry of Earth Sciences' centre will be cofounded by the Ministry of Earth Sciences and ISRO.

ISRO's proposal is awaiting the approval of the Space Commission. Last time, it was discussed in the Space Commission, it was felt that the proposal should be considered in light of initiatives being undertaken by other ministries so as to avoid duplication. We feel that there is clarity now on the mandates for the different institutes and centres and that ISRO's proposal should be approved. ISRO has developed perhaps the deepest expertise in climate change having produced over seventy doctorates and 600 technical papers in the subject over the past two decades and we are confident that its initiative will have a significant impact.

Letter to Indian National Science Academy President M. Vijayan on Biotechnology in Food Crops

22 MARCH 2010

I thank you for the opportunity you provided to Dr Kasturirangan and me to interact with the heads of the six premier scientific academies of the country—the Indian National Science Academy, National Academy of Sciences, Indian Academy of Sciences, National Academy of Agricultural Sciences, Indian National Academy of Engineering, and National Academy of Medical Sciences—on the subject of biotechnology in food crops. I found the discussion most educative and useful as I am sure did Dr Kasturirangan also.

As we had agreed, both Dr Kasturirangan and I would very much like INSA to coordinate, with the other academies, the preparation of a detailed report on the subject of biotechnology in food crops with focus on transgenic crops. I am sure the Government of India would very much like to have to the considered views and opinions of the major scientific academies of our country on this very important subject. This report could be submitted to the Planning Commission in about six months time. Meanwhile, it would also be valuable to have the collective views of the six academies on the Biotechnology Regulatory Authority Bill that is presently under discussion in the government and a copy of which I have emailed you separately. This could also be submitted to the Planning Commission in the next three months.

I look forward to a continued dialogue with you and with the other academies as well on issues of mutual interest and concern. Since INSA represents India in the InterAcademy Council (IAC), I will also soon be sending you a copy of my communication to the IAC on improvements in IPCC procedures and processes.

Letter to IPCC Chairman R.K. Pachauri on Including Research by the Indian Institute of Tropical Meteorology in the Fifth Assessment Report

30 JANUARY 2010

I am pleased to learn that the IPCC has launched the preparation of the Fifth Assessment Report (AR 5) after duly constituting the Working Groups on various aspects of climate change—the Physical Science Basis (Working Group-I); Impacts, Vulnerability, and Adaptation (Working Group-II), and Mitigation (Working Group-III). These working groups are mandated to assess the published literature worldwide after the publication of AR 4 and, perhaps, up to 2013.

I note from the chapter outlines that the subcontinental monsoon constitutes an important element of assessment in Working Group-I. The Indian Institute of Tropical Meteorology (IITM), Pune, has been working in developing climate change scenarios using level RM3 and Precis at resolution of 50 km x 50 km. There is, however, a need for more refined and downscaled climate projections such as at 25 x 25 km resolution, which can be devised from other models for intercomparisons. Recognizing the significance of the climate scenarios for the Indian region, I have pleasure in informing you that the MoEF has constituted a group comprising scientists from IITM, ISRO, and MoEF to run specific regional models for the Indian subcontinent for the monsoon.

More specifically, we plan to conduct a suite of regional model simulations to downscale the projections of climate change for the South Asian monsoon region. Further, the ensemble of regional model runs would enable better estimation of uncertainties in the monsoon projections over the South Asian region. A comprehensive analysis of the regional climate model simulations would be carried out to assess the changes in the monsoon rainfall and circulation patterns and estimate the uncertainties of the regional projections. Indeed the results would be published in peer-reviewed scientific journals.

Additionally, we are exploring the use of a global atmospheric model with high-resolution zooming capability over the South Asian monsoon region—for the AR5 regional monsoon downscaling. This work is being planned in collaboration with the Institute Pierre Simon Laplace (IPSL), France. Other international institutional collaborations are also being explored. We will be able to provide detailed inputs for AR5. I request you to include the modeling results as an exclusive input for AR5. The results could be taken on board as per established IPCC procedures.

I shall greatly appreciate if the IPCC Working Group-I is informed of this effort. The IITM-ISRO-MoEF team would also like to be associated with other modeling groups and we look forward to your facilitating this interaction.

Letter to IPCC Chairman R.K. Pachauri on the Inclusion of Indian Scientists in Bureau Meetings of the IPCC

30 JANUARY 2010

You may recall our email correspondence regarding the MoEF support to run your IPCC office in New Delhi.

I fully appreciate the background to the arrangement with which the MoEF has had with you since late 2001 by which we provide financial support to TERI to the tune of Rs 57 lakh per year at your request.

You may recall that I had raised the issue of someone from MoEF being associated with you when you attend IPCC meetings in return for our financial support. Unfortunately, for some reason or the other, there has been no direct benefit to MoEF from this financial arrangement so far. I am glad that you have readily agreed to my suggestion to have somebody from MoEF to accompany you to IPCC meetings.

Accordingly, I am now suggesting that Dr Subodh Sharma, Adviser (Climate Change), to accompany you to the next IPCC Bureau meeting on 19–20 May 2010 in Geneva. Depending on the subjects to be discussed in subsequent meetings, we will designate other officers. I take it that the travel and other expenses of the MoEF officer would be met by IPCC.

Once again I appreciate the promptness with which you have responded to my request. I see this as a way of strengthening scientific capability within the MoEF to deal and keep abreast with IPCC-related issues.

Letter to Prime Minister on the Initiatives Taken
by the Ministry in the Area of Science

15 FEBRUARY 2010
I am writing to bring to your attention some important initiatives that have been launched in recent weeks to give renewed impetus to science in the MoEF.

Global Advisory Network Group on Environmental Sciences (GANGES)

GANGES is a new forum, comprising the world's leading environmental scientists of Indian origin, established to advise the Government of India on the country's environmental sciences agenda. GANGES will focus on questions such as: What areas of environmental sciences should we focus on from a short-term, medium-term, and long-term perspective? How should the government engage on this agenda (identify priority areas, directly conduct research, support and fund outside research, etc.)? Which institutional collaborations should be undertaken in specific areas and in what way? How should academia and private sector be engaged? How should innovation in this space be stimulated, and how do we fast-track development, demonstration and dissemination?

The following scientists are part of the group:

1. Subra Suresh, School of Engineering, Massachusetts Institute of Technology, US
2. Jagadish Shukla, Department of Atmospheric, Oceanic and Earth Sciences, George Mason University, US
3. Purnendu Dasgupta, Department of Analytical and Environmental Chemistry, University of Texas, Arlington, US
4. Veerabhadran Ramanathan, University of California, San Diego, US
5. Asit Biswas, Third World Centre for Water Management, Queens University, Canada
6. Ashok Gadgil, Lawrence Berkeley National Laboratory, US

7. Pratim Biswas, Washington University in St Louis, US
8. Kamal Bawa, University of Massachusetts, Boston, US
9. Tam Sridhar, Faculty of Engineering, Monash University, Australia
10. Shankar Sastry, Dean of Engineering, University of California, Berkeley, US
11. Venkatachalam Ramaswamy, National Oceanic and Atmospheric Administration, University of Colorado, Boulder Institute, US
12. Venky Narayanamurti, Science, Technology and Public Policy Programme, Harvard Kennedy School, US

National Environmental Sciences Fellows Programme

This new programme will provide our most promising young scientists desirous of working in the forefront of environmental sciences, engineering, and technology, the opportunity to do cutting-edge research on critical environmental issues in collaboration with leading institutes and scientists in India and the world. It will provide ten young scientists under the age of thirty-five, with a generous fellowship and institutional support to undertake this research. Each fellow would be attached to an institution, which will sign an MoU with the ministry. The selection of the fellows and thrust areas for research will be done by a management committee headed by Dr K. Kasturirangan, Member, Planning Commission, and comprising eminent scientists.

This programme will allow young Indian scientists to enhance their areas of expertise under the mentorship of the leading scientists in the world today, and will help create a cadre of top-class Indian environmental scientists for the future. The knowledge emerging from the research work under this programme will help inform our environmental policy agenda, ensuring that it is based on rigorous science.

Expert Committee to Enhance the Scientific Capacity of Ministry of Environment and Forest

Scientific personnel have historically made up a large portion of the human resources of the MoEF, as it was conceived as a science-based ministry. Over the years, a number of issues and constraints have arisen related to the scientific resources and expertise of the ministry. These need to be urgently addressed. To ensure that the scientific manpower and infrastructure in the ministry remains cutting-edge, the ministry has set up an Expert Committee to take a fresh look at scientific manpower and infrastructure in the MoEF. The committee will comprise the following members:

1. Dr Kasturirangan, member, Planning Commission, Chairman
2. Dr Chandra Venkataraman, Professor, Department of Chemical Engineering, IIT Mumbai, Member
3. Dr Deepak Pental, Vice Chancellor, Delhi University, Member
4. Dr Kalpana Balakrishnan, Professor, Environmental Health Engineering, Sri Ramachandra University Chennai, Member
5. Shri Vishwanathan Anand, Retired Secretary, MoEF, Member
6. Ms Swati A Piramal, Vice Chancellor Piramal Life Sciences Limited and Director of Piramal Healthcare Limited, Member
7. Shri M.F. Farooqui, Additional Secretary, Ministry of Environment and Forest, Convenor, Action Plan to Enhance Forestry Science

On 10 January, 2010, I had a special meeting with over 100 Indian Forest Service officers with PhD degrees in forestry science. A number of decisions related to upgrading the scientific capabilities of India's forestry establishment were taken at this meeting. These included the institution of the following:

1. Forestry Fellowship Programme: To recognize outstanding contributions to forestry sciences, a forestry fellowship programme is being introduced.
2. A National Forestry Knowledge Forum: A platform where expert knowledge in various issues in forestry will be shared is being developed. This forum will facilitate virtual interactions of experts in forestry. It will be physically located in Delhi and will be open for national and international experts in the field of forestry science.
3. National Forestry Information Network: A network is being established with a robust foundation using remote sensing, geographical information system (GIS) and management information system (MIS). All land-based forestry interventions will be geo-mapped and monitored on a time scale and will be put in the public domain. The process is being guided by a core group of forestry professionals.
4. IT for fire monitoring: A programme to use satellite data for early transmission of fire signals to the mobile phones/PDAs of field

officers is being undertaken. The University of Maryland has agreed to share all active fire data obtained from TERRA and AQUA satellites of NASA every six hours for this. This will not only help in quick fire detection and reducing the response time, but has also helped in identifying fire sensitive areas.

5. National Bureau for Forest Germplasm: A Forest Genetic Resource network is being established along the lines of the Plant Genetics Resource Bureau. The objective would be to identify, characterize, and preserve the valuable germplasm of a wide number of forestry species in the country. This will protect our valuable genetic resource against extinction and exploitation.

In the Union Budget for 2009–10, the government has already made a special grant of Rs 100 crore to the ICFRE for the modernization of forestry research. This grant is being used to support some of these and other initiatives.

Indian Network for Climate Change Assessment (INCCA)

Established by the MoEF in October 2009, INCCA is a network-based programme to make science, particularly the 'three Ms'—measuring, modelling and monitoring—the essence of our policy making in the climate change space. It brings together over 120 institutions and over 220 scientists from across the country.

The first report of the INCCA—an updated emissions inventory of greenhouses gases of anthropogenic origin of India for 2007—will be released on 11 May 2010. A comprehensive '4 x 4' assessment of key sectors in India—agriculture, water, natural ecosystems, and biodiversity and health—and key geographic 'hotspots'—the Northeast, the Indian Himalayan region, the Western Ghats, and coastal areas—will be released in November 2010.

A group has also been constituted under INCCA, comprising scientists from IITM, ISRO, and MoEF, to run specific regional models for the Indian subcontinent for the monsoon in order to enable better assessment of impacts and reduction of uncertainties in monsoon projections over the South Asian region.

The '4 x 4' and the regional assessment will be provided to the IPCC as part of the input to the IPCC's Fifth Assessment Report (AR5). This is the first time that India will be providing institutional inputs to the IPCC. This has already been communicated to Chairman, IPCC. Both these initiatives will help fill an important scientific knowledge gap in the IPCC assessment, by providing robust information at the sub-regional level.

These initiatives are in keeping with the thoughts expressed in your Indian Science Congress speech of 3 January 2010.

Letter inviting Indian Scientists Working Abroad to be Part of an Advisory Network of Scientists

28 JANUARY 2010

I am writing to invite you to become part of a new advisory group that I am setting up called GANGES. The aim of this group will be to advise the Government of India on the country's environmental sciences agenda. As the Prime Minister, in his address to the Indian Science Congress on 3 January 2010 noted: 'If India has to re-emerge as a knowledge power in the twenty-first century, then it can only be through developing a strong capability in science and technology ... Indian science should have a strong outward orientation. Our science establishments should step up global alliances that will expose our scientists to the best in the world and enhance our competitiveness.'

The aim of this group therefore will be to advise on the following:

1. What should be the environmental sciences agenda for the country? What areas should we focus on from a short-term, medium-term, and long-term perspective?
2. How should the government engage on this agenda (directly conduct research, support and fund outside research, set priority areas, etc.)?
3. Which institutional collaborations should be undertaken in specific areas and in what way? How should leading academic institutions and the private sector be engaged in the environmental sciences agenda?
4. How should innovation in this space be stimulated, and how do we fast-track development, demonstration, and dissemination of scientific research to produce results for our societal needs?

GANGES would meet as a group at least twice a year. It would also stay connected as an ongoing virtual community to exchange ideas and discuss proposals with me. I would hope to provide a report to the Prime Minister on an annual basis on the work of GANGES and the progress we make on our environmental sciences agenda.

Letter to Minister for Urban Development S. Jaipal Reddy on the National Museum of Natural History

3 FEBRUARY 2010

The National Museum of Natural History (NMNH) is functioning since 1978 from the rented accommodation at FICCI Building, Barakhamba Road. The ministry has been trying since long to get a suitable piece of land for construction of exclusive complex for NMNH at Delhi. In this connection, a decision had been taken in the meeting held on April 2009 under the chairmanship of Principal Secretary to the Prime Minister to restore the land belonging to the National Zoological Park (NZP), presently used for parking of vehicles by the Indian Trade Promotion Organisation (ITPO), back to NZP and allot 6.5 acres of the land thereof to the NMNH for construction of its headquarters building. The proposal for restoration of the land is presently under consideration of Ministry of Urban Development.

In the meanwhile, you have been kind enough to allot a piece of land measuring 9,000 sq m, at Aliganj (Jorbagh), New Delhi, to the MoEF for the construction of its own office building to be named as 'Indira Paryavaran Bhavan'. It has been brought to my notice that adjacent to the plot allotted to MoEF at Aliganj, a pocket of land (2–2.5 acres approx.) exists with some very old New Delhi Municipal Council (NDMC) type-I quarters slated for redevelopment. If the land can be retrieved from NDMC and allotted to MoEF, it would be possible to construct the NMNH complex, and other infrastructural facilities like convention centres, library, etc., for offices in Lodhi Road Complex. Some offices of MoEF can also be located in the building. Besides, the space will also be used for generating solar power and geothermal heat recovery system for air-conditioning.

I shall be thankful if you could consider the matter favourably and issue necessary instructions to retrieve the land from NDMC and allot it to the ministry.

Letter to Prime Minister About *India: Greenhouse Gas Emissions 2007*, *the First Report Prepared by the INCCA*

[Till this report was published the only official emissions estimates available were for 1994. This was rather inadequate and I was keen that we should publish updated emission estimates that will enable informed decision-making and ensure transparency. India became the first developing country to publish such an updated report.]

10 MAY 2010

You are aware that we had launched an INCCA in October 2009. The first output of INCCA is being released tomorrow by Montek Singh Ahluwalia. I have great pleasure in sending you an advance copy of this communication.

The highlights are:

1. We are the first developing country to publish updated figures for emissions. We will publish our emission inventory in a two-year cycle.
2. In 2007, 38 per cent of emissions came from electricity, 22 per cent from industry, 21 per cent from agriculture, and 7.5 per cent from the regional sector.
3. The emission intensity of India's GDP based on emission inventories for 1994–2007 has declined by more than 30 per cent in this period.

Letter to Union Finance Minister Pranab Mukherjee on Budgetary Allocation for ICFRE

23 JUNE 2011

You were very gracious enough to provide for a one time grant of Rs 100 crore for the ICFRE in para 62 of your Budget Speech on 6 July 2009.

Unfortunately, I am sorry to bring to your notice that we are still a long way from utilizing this special grant. The final Expenditure Finance Committee (EFC) proposal could get approved only on 30 December 2010, almost fifteen months after you have made your announcement. Sir, this is most frustrating.

What I am writing to you now about is a fresh problem. The Rs 100 crore grant is to be utilized in three years—roughly Rs 17 crore in 2010–11, about Rs 66 crore in 2011–12, and Rs 17 crore in 2012–13. Although, Rs 66 crore for 2011–12 was agreed to by the Planning

Commission, this amount has *not* been provided for in the final BE [budget estimate].

Therefore, an additional allocation of Rs 66 crore is absolutely essential in 2011–12 in order to fulfil the commitment that you have made in your Budget Speech of July 2009. I am making an earnest appeal to you to please help us in the matter. It is not only a question of a solemn budgetary promise but is also a question relating to the very future of ICFRE.

Letter to Royal Netherlands Academy of Arts and Sciences President and Co-chair, InterAcademy Council (IAC) Amsterdam, Robbert Dijkgraaf on IPCC Review

22 MARCH 2010

At the outset, let me welcome the decision of the UN Secretary General and the Chairman of the IPCC to establish an independent review of the IPCC Assessment Process. I am also glad that the IAC, on which the Indian National Science Academy is represented, will be conducting this review.

IPCC procedures and processes have evolved over the past two decades. In many respects, the IPCC is a unique network and its contributions have been deservedly recognized by the award of the Nobel Peace Prize. While IPCC cannot be blamed for the misuse of its findings by political leaders with their own agenda or by the media in search of headlines, there certainly are areas relating to IPCC's working in which improvements can and should be made.

It is in this constructive spirit that I am sending you a note prepared by my colleagues and I for consideration of the IAC in its review.

Review of IPCC Assessment Process by InterAcademy Council:

Suggestions on Broad Elements of Review and Assessment Process

1. Treatment of Literature:

The IPCC assessment should include principally the peer-reviewed published literature. However, certain categories of information are published in special reports, papers, and annual reports of the various governments and their agencies. Further reports published by certain institutions such as World Resources Institute, Pew Centre, Lawrence

Berkeley Labs, World Bank, autonomous bodies, UN agencies, etc., also include elements of information on climate change. This information indeed is valuable, but not on a par with the scientific peer-reviewed journals. We should not ignore these but indicate the same with suitable explanations/ limitations. The compliance of extant procedures in such cases must be ensured by a separate panel of experts.

It has also been observed that inbreeding in the form of a particular type of information is repeatedly published by a single or group of authors adding to number of references as the sole source. There is complete absence of alternate literature/ information by others. In such a situation, adequate caution is required and needs to be appropriately recorded.

2. Treatment of the Emerging Messages:

The information emerging from the assessment constitutes an important input for decision and policy relevant information. While the stated procedure may appear objective but in practice falls short of the test of objectivity reflecting on the credibility as a whole. It is felt that there should be another tier of scrutiny after the review editor consisting of experts who are broad-based and even including independent experts. Enough opportunities should be given to include contrary opinions on the same conclusions. Further limitations of the conclusions drawn should be stated and with cautions against their wider acceptability and applicability indicated.

3. Geographic Balance of Inclusion of Experts:

In the preparation of the assessment, efforts should be made to enhance participation of developing country experts. Further, special mention of the absence/existence of the information from the developing countries on the relevant aspects of climate change should be included. This would enhance the appreciation and limitation of application of extant knowledge universally. Regional context, both in availability of information and applicability of results of climate change has always been an important gap and it should be adequately reflected in the assessment.

4. Summary for Policy Makers

Summary for Policy Makers (SPM) is an integral part of the IPCC reports. The existing procedures permit approval by appropriate working groups. Instances have come to notice in the past that Summary for

Policy Makers is quite at variance with the findings/emerging messages. Since the SPM constitutes a very valuable document of the assessment, there is a need to further improve the quality, accuracy, consistency and comprehensiveness of the information for use by the policymakers in an objective manner. This could possibly be considered by an independent group of experts to ensure the consistency, accuracy and robustness of the information contained in SPM. The uncertainties, adequacy, level of confidence in the findings, and absence of information for a particular region should be clearly stated.

Suggestions on Specific Elements of the IPCC Processes

Process for finalizing scope and content of reports

a. How it accommodates divergent view points?
b. How a balanced scientific view is ensured?
c. How criticism of IPCC is included? (separate chapters, sub-topics, etc.)

Suggestions for improvement: Keep a separate chapter on divergent views in each IPCC report.

a. How continuous development of science is included and given due weightage?

Suggestions for improvement: Include sub-sections in each chapter on comparative changes between AR4 and AR5 findings. Differentiate between incremental findings and major new changes. Give proper weightage to published literature on observations of climate change impacts in all sectors and regions of the world.

Selection of experts

a. How transparency is ensured in selection and rejection of a CV?
b. How strength of CV is ensured?

Suggestions for improvement: Evaluation of all the CVs by third party and its availability in each selected and rejected in public domain.

a. How new and young scientists are encouraged?

Suggestions for improvement: Keep a healthy mix of scientists above forty-five years of age and below forty-five years of age in each report.

Literature

a. How does it ensure that all (or most) published literature has been reviewed for each topic/sub-topic?

Suggestions for improvement: Include a table in each chapter indicating estimation of number of all the peer-reviewed published papers for each topics covered in that chapter and the number of cited references in that chapter. Help may be taken from journal houses (Science Direct, Elsevier, etc.) in providing subject wise listing of all peer-reviewed papers. The chapter authors should justify if their coverage is very low, and also if some view points are not included.

a. How authentic and correct coverage of contents/essence from cited papers is ensured?

b. How does it ensure that IPCC authors do not draw their own independent conclusions (promote their own ideas) using cited literature only as a means to this end?

Suggestions for improvement: Could send the draft IPCC reports to all the corresponding authors of each of the cited references (in the draft IPCC report) during the scientific review process, with a special request to verify whether contents/essence of their papers have been correctly and objectively captured.

a. What is the process for accepting grey literature? Is it more or less stringent than accepting peer-reviewed literature?

Suggestions for improvement: Grey literature may be accepted but not preferred over peer-reviewed literature. In case any grey literature is cited in IPCC report, the authors should categorically state that no relevant better literature is available. A cross-verification may also be requested from journal houses (Science Direct, Elsevier, etc.).

a. What is the percentage of cited literature in a chapter that has one of the convening lead authors/lead authors/contributing authors/review editors as a co-author? High percentage could imply in-breeding.

b. How does it ensure that IPCC authors are not promoting their own literature in IPCC reports?

Suggestions for improvement: A table could be made indicating this percentage. A cut-off may be fixed keeping in mind the indicators such as, cited peer-reviewed references in IPCC chapter/universe of all peer-reviewed paper, and the number of chapter authors/total experts in that area.

a. Whether all literature cited is made available at one place for third party review?

Suggestions for improvement: All this literature should be made available on IPCC website during the review process.

a. How does it ensure that time allocation between writing process and review process are proper? Is sufficient time provided for chapter writing?

Suggestions for improvement: Provide sufficient time to chapter authors to produce the zero order draft. Expedite review time lines through use of technology.

Transparency

a. How do we ensure wider regional observational data coverage?

Suggestions for improvement: Expand data collection from regions where information is lacking. Bring it in public domain, especially on projections. If the data cannot be brought in public domain entirely due to proprietary issues, put maximum that is possible, plus provide summary write ups for the remaining portions. All assumptions made for calibrating and running the models should anyway be brought in public domain.

a. How do we improve and ensure transparency at various stages of the process?

Suggestions for improvement: Keep the process tracking details on the IPCC website. This may include information such as list of experts to whom the IPCC reports have been sent during expert review processes, how many have responded etc. Need for confidentiality on contents during the IPCC report preparation is appreciated, but need for excessive confidentially on process is not warranted. May be introduce a 'Right to Information' system in whole IPCC and UNFCCC processes.

Review process

a. How do we ensure that draft reports are sent to experts having different scientific views?

Suggestions for improvement: Send the draft IPCC reports to all the known 'climate sceptics' during the scientific review process.

a. How does it ensure that review editors are doing a balanced and impartial job?

b. How are quality assurance/quality control ensured in the review process?

Suggestions for improvement: The basics of jurisprudence should be observed—a person cannot review output of a process he/she has been part of. IPCC should select review editors from outside the 'regular' IPCC expert domains. IPCC could even request editor-in-chiefs and editors of reputed international journals to do this job.

a. How does it ensure that government review process is authentic, and the government-nominated experts to an IPCC report are not the ones sending (government) review comments, thus vitiating the law of natural justice (one does not review one's own work)?

Suggestions for improvement: The names of government reviewers may be asked for.

a. How does it ensure that 'new' conclusions and ideas (that were not part of the original draft that had gone through the review process, and are also not supported through published literature) are not pushed in surreptitiously in the last rounds in the guise of attending to final review comments?

Suggestions for improvement: This must be avoided. Strongly adhere to deadline dates for including a reference in IPCC reports, allow no grey literature to be cited after this date in any case, the review transcripts should be sent to those who had provided review comments. In case a 'new' change has to be introduced to answer some compelling review comments, the convening lead author, corresponding lead author, and review editor have to ensure its authenticity personally.

Public dissemination of IPCC reports

a. How does it ensure that correct and authentic findings only are disseminated?

Suggestions for improvement: All presentations on the report to be made by chapter authors only and put in public domain.

a. How does it ensure that common public are informed and included in follow up process?

Suggestions for improvement: Each IPCC report may include a chapter that provides gist of that report in easy to understand language for common public along with caveats, conditions, and probabilities clearly specified. Produce documentaries, and special dissemination materials as well for wider dissemination.

Letter to M.S. Swaminathan Research Foundation, M. S. Swaminathan, on the National Centre for Sustainable Coastal Zone Management

11 JUNE 2010

As you may be aware that the ministry is in process of establishing a National Centre for Sustainable Coastal Management (NCSCM) under the World Bank-assisted Integrated Coastal Zone Management Project. The centre would serve as a policy guiding research and development institution with the central repository of information and knowledge for coastal management. The NCSCM would serve as an impartial neutral interface between coastal communities, experts, and governments and it would promote applied research education and awareness. The centre would be a nodal institute and shall be a link to identified collaborating research departments/agencies in each of the coastal states and Union Territories.

Anna University, Chennai, has agreed to provide adequate land for establishing the above centre within its campus. The MoU between Anna University and MoEF for establishing the centre, is proposed to be signed on 21 June at 9.30 am in Anna University, Chennai. We have invited the collaborating institutions from each of the coastal states and Union Territories.

You have been instrumental in guiding us in formulating the proposal for setting up of this important centre. I will be grateful if you could make it convenient to attend the above MoU signing ceremony on 21 June 2010 at 9.30 am in Anna University, Chennai.

Letter to Vice Chancellor, Anna University, on Setting Up of the NCSCM

11 JUNE 2010

This is in continuation to my earlier letter of 20 January 2010 regarding setting up of the NCSCM within Anna University, Chennai, under the World Bank assisted Integrated Coastal Zone Management Project.

During last few months we were involved in the finalization of this World Bank project. I am happy to inform you that Cabinet Committee on Economic Affairs has approved the project including establishment of the centre with a cost estimate of Rs 166 crore for five years.

I am given to understand that the MoU between Anna University and my ministry has been firmed up and is being signed on 21 June 2010. I will be personally present for the function and I have requested Prof. M.S. Swaminathan, Chairman, M.S. Swaminathan Research Foundation, and Dr K. Kasturirangan, Member, Planning Commission, to make it convenient to attend.

I am thankful to you for providing the land and other facilities required for the Centre. With your cooperation and the high standard of expertise available in Anna University, I am sure that the Centre will develop as a world class scientific and social-based set up, which will cater not only to the needs of the coastal local communities of the country but also in the South East Asian region. I look forward to the success of this Centre.

'Green is Politics: India has to Study Climate Change on its Own', Op-ed in The Hindustan Times

16 July 2014

'Himalayan glaciers will disappear by 2035'. This was the very alarming conclusions of the Nobel Prize-winning IPCC that was brought to my attention when I took over as minister for environment and forests in May 2009. Could this really be true, I wondered. I then decided to convene a series of meetings with experts from different institutions across the country. And what emerged was something different and seemed to question the IPCC's startling assertion.

Scientists who had been studying Himalayan glaciers for decades told me that: (i) Himalayan glaciers are different from Arctic glaciers since their snout (lowest point) is 3,000 m or more above sea level and so their response to global warming could well be different; (ii) Most of the 10,000-odd Himalayan glaciers on the Indian side are indeed retreating although some like the Gangotri glacier are receding at a decelerating rate and some like the Siachen glacier are, in fact, advancing; and (iii) the health of the Himalayan glaciers is very poor with the proliferation of debris.

I then encouraged V.K. Raina, a noted geoscientist, who had been studying Himalayan glaciers since the mid-1950s, to prepare a status report based on all the interactions we held. His report was published officially by the MoEF in September 2009 and unleashed a global storm. His credentials were attacked. I was myself accused of being a climate change-denier and the IPCC chairman, R.K. Pachauri, termed the Raina report as 'voodoo science'. The story finally ended on 31 March 2014, when the IPCC released a report in Yokohoma, Japan, and admitted that its findings that the Himalayan glaciers would completely disappear by 2035 were 'erroneous; and that the error was 'really serious'.

This was actually not the first time that world science had put India in the dock on climate change issues. In the early 1990s, the US government had put out a report saying that methane emissions from India's wet paddy cultivation were around 38 million tonnes per year. This figure was challenged by the distinguished Indian physicist, the late A.P. Mitra, whose painstaking field-level work subsequently established that these emissions were, in fact, much, much lower at 2–6 million tonnes per year. This is important since methane is a more lethal greenhouse gas than carbon dioxide.

These two episodes show that climate science could well have a covert political agenda and that India needs to establish its own world-class scientific and technological infrastructure in the area of climate change. This was the background to the formation of the INCCA in 2010. Almost 250 scientists from some 125 institutions became part of this research network. The INCCA published two landmark reports. The first was a 4 x 4 assessment—four sectors (agriculture, water, natural ecosystems and biodiversity, and health) and four regions (Himalayan region, Northeast, coastal areas, and Western Ghats). This analysis was not for some distant future but for the more immediate 2030s. The second was on India's GHG emissions for the year 2007, making us the first developing country to publish the latest GHG inventory at that time.

The INCCA also took on the responsibility for studying the issue of black carbon in detail. This was a case of India being proactive since it was fast becoming a subject of international discussions and India was coming into the spotlight. In early 2010, a decision was taken to establish a National Centre for Himalayan Glaciology in Dehradun and then Prime Minister Manmohan Singh spoke of the need for India to collaborate with other countries in our region. ISRO also agreed to: (i) launch nano-satellites for providing data on aerosol and carbon dioxide distribution and a dedicated satellite for monitoring greenhouse gases; and (ii) establish an extensive network of automated weather stations and carbon monitoring towers in different climatic zones of the country. The INCCA also initiated the publication of research papers. For instance, one such paper by the eminent space scientist U.R. Rao, argued that a prediction of global warming requires a relook to take into account long-term changes in global cosmic ray intensity, something that has thus far been largely ignored by the global scientific community.

Whatever be our stance in international negotiations, given our multiple vulnerabilities, both current and future, to climate change and our climatic diversities, we must develop our own capacities to measure, model and monitor its impacts. This is an area of strategic importance. Our unique vulnerabilities arise in at least four ways. First, India's fortunes are still linked in many ways to the monsoon. Second, we have a 7,000 km-long coastline and one fact that has been incontrovertibly established by science is that mean sea levels are rising and will continue to do so. Third, of course, is the importance of the Himalayan glaciers to the water security of over half a billion people in northern and eastern India. And fourth, most of our natural resources that we want to extract for rapid GDP growth like coal and iron ore happen to be in rich forest areas. Extracting these minerals on the scale envisaged will inevitably mean considerable deforestation and this, in turn, will mean a depletion of the absorption capacity of a valuable carbon sink.

To be sure, we must be intimately plugged into the global scientific community working on climate change, taking special advantage of the presence of a number of distinguished Indian diaspora scientists active in this field. But such an engagement must be from a position of domestic strength. Many of the challenges we face are unique to India (for instance, our coal has a very high ash content) for which we have to find solutions on our own. The world has been divided into sixteen bio-geographic regions, of which ten are represented in India. Thus, it is essential to establish long-term ecological observatories to study climate change in these regions on an ongoing basis.

Notes

1. A JSTOR search reveals that the term 'scientific temper' was used way back in October 1907 in the *British Medical Journal*, but not in the term that Nehru meant. The journal used it to refer to irritation or anger of scientists who are denied recognition of their works!

2. Nehru was on a different wavelength from Gandhiji on science. Earlier, in his *Autobiography* referring to the 1934 Bihar earthquake Nehru writes, 'During my tour of earthquake areas, or just before going there, I read with great shock Gandhiji's statement to the effect that the earthquake had been a punishment for the sin of untouchability. This was a staggering remark and I welcomed, and wholly agreed with, Rabindra Nath Tagore's answer to it. Anything more opposed to the scientific outlook it would be difficult to imagine.'

3. Bertrand Russell had, in fact, used the term 'scientific temper' in his essay 'On Education' that was published in 1926.

4. Saha, reportedly nominated for the Nobel Prize four times, was to turn into a bitter critic of Nehru in later years when Homi Bhabha's influence on the prime minister was at its peak. Saha also had major differences with C.V. Raman. Many of Saha's concerns, incidentally, on the transparency and accountability of our atomic energy programme and the impact of independent stand-alone research laboratories on our universities, have great relevance today. He was responsible for the idea of the Damodar Valley Corporation built along the lines of the Tennessee Valley Authority and his work in the early 1950s on reform of the Indian calendar was very significant.

6 The Executive Awakes

The tussle between economic growth and ecological security, and the attempts to strike a balance invariably becomes a discussion on clearances given to particular industrial projects. The most-effective instrument of ensuring balance is the whole host of environment laws and regulations on our statute books. Unfortunately, for the better part of their existence, these laws have been observed more in the breach.

India has among the most progressive environmental laws and regulations, but implementation remains a major issue. It was as if we were fascinated with passing laws, then equally fascinated in bypassing them. This is where the change was required, a break from the 'pass-bypass' model. It was clear to me, that as long as the laws were on the statute books, they had to be observed in both letter and spirit. The environment ministry had to ensure that it was implementing these laws for which Parliament has given it full responsibility.

If bypassing laws is an Indian pastime, then this was made possible by two enabling factors. The first enabler lay in making environment-related laws subservient to all others. Liberalization of the economy, the resultant economic growth, and the benefits it brought with it made it almost alright to cut corners on a whole host of laws, including environmental ones. The relentless quest for economic growth made it acceptable to look the other way when environmental and other such laws were being violated. I would like to stress that contrary to common perception, environmental laws do not contribute to stymieing of the economy. If that were indeed the case, then the pre-1991 planned economy era, particularly in the period before mid-1970s, should have registered high economic growth. Instead, empirical evidence points to the fact that unregulated diversion of forests prior to the enactment of the Forest (Conservation) Act, 1980 did not contribute to rapid economic growth or industrialization.

The second enabler was the apathy of the executive; the unwillingness to implement the laws, and use what instruments were readily available to ensure a measure of ecological security. The judiciary stepped into the breach and became—over the course of nearly two decades—the both the final arbiter and policymaker in the field of environment.

Executive apathy was not a one-way street. The forest administration, for instance, found itself at the frontlines of dealing with the Maoists but with little or no state support. For instance, the family of policemen who die in the line of duty receive a lump-sum payment but no such provision existed for the forest guards. Forced often to make difficult life and death choices, these forest officials would be branded as 'collaborators' should they choose survival. I recognized that one way to break the cycle of 'indifference' would be to provide a platform for forest officials to air their concerns, needs, and suggestions to improve their effectiveness to those members of government who could bring about changes. I organized a meeting of the forest officials from the Left-Wing Extremism (LWE) Maoist-affected districts, which was attended by the home minister and senior home ministry officials. I followed up on the suggestions and action points with the Prime Minister as well. I made several interventions to address the challenges that forest officials faced in discharging their duties in these difficult regions.

Breaking this cycle of apathy and loss of jurisdiction was essential to restoring public accountability of the environment ministry. It was time for change, a time for the executive to reclaim its place. One of my first interventions was to find resolution to the issue of compensatory afforestation. Funds collected in lieu of forest diversion lay locked with the Supreme Court, in what is popularly known as the Compensatory Afforestation Management and Planning Authority (CAMPA) fund. A resolution that would be acceptable to the Supreme Court and states. I was successful in breaking nearly a decade-long the logjam. This was the first salvo in the effort to reclaim executive space and ensuring accountability.

If administrative will had been lagging, the political will to go after polluters and violators of environmental norms too had been missing. I saw my job as one that firmly signalled officers that I would back them up in their efforts to bring violators to book. My protests on the manner in which Parliament was being used to push through projects where individual members had vested interest was intended to make clear that there was political will to implement the laws of the land and it could not be made subservient to other demands. No matter how powerful or well-connected they seemed, the line had been drawn—no one was above the laws of the land.

The next step was to use what instruments were available at the disposal of the administration. The Environment (Protection) Act, 1986 provided the executive with powers to punish non-compliance, yet, these provisions were among the most unutilized though there were violations. These provisions were used to address violations by tanneries along the Ganga, and by a couple of high-profile township and industrial projects.

There was another side to the story of poor implementation—the near total absence of a compliance mechanism. No matter how robust the clearance conditions are, it amounts to naught if it is not backed up by effective monitoring. Violations of norms only come to the fore when a series of complaints reach the ministry, and often taking corrective and punitive action entails stopping or shutting down projects.

I was of the view that the regulatory arm needed to be strengthened, I also believed that the ministry needed to move out of the business of appraising and approving projects. There was a need for a permanent independent body to keep a constant watch to ensure that environmental norms and conditions were not being flouted, and that the conditions laid down were delivering on ecological security without creating an obstacle to development. This was the rationale for setting up an independent and professional National Environment Assessment and Monitoring Authority. Conceived of on the lines of the Environmental Protection Agency in the US, the proposed regulatory body had to be reconfigured keeping Indian structures in mind. Wide-ranging consultations were held on the structure of the proposed authority, I also set up an expert committee to suggest ways to strengthen the monitoring function of the environment ministry.

It takes time to build institutions, to decide on the design, to ensure that we don't repeat the mistakes of the past. But India's march on the path of high economic growth required decisions in the here and now. Executive orders were used to bring in a sense of clarity and predictability in the manner in which projects were appraised. The entire process was made online so that there is greater monitoring, transparency and accountability. Making the existing appraisal and advisory committees stronger by reaching out to a larger community of experts was another way in which I sought to improve accountability of the executive. I also introduced the system of strict accreditation of agencies preparing environmental impact assessments and environmental management plans.

The other plank of strengthening the executive came in the form of the National Green Tribunal (NGT). Besides the redress function that the tribunal had, it was in a sense providing a second line of defence to the executive in ensuring that laws of the land were followed in letter and spirit. The tribunal, set up in 2010, was one of my successes in the effort to reclaim executive space. The tribunal was both authorized and expected to punish environmental violations by imposing significant monetary damages as well as issue salutary and remedial directives.

In breaking the culture of apathy that had come to characterize environmental administration, I sought to reduce discretion, improve transparency, and bring in a degree of predictability—break the law, pay the price.

This chapter deals with the efforts to ensure that the executive, which had receded to the background, reasserted its rightful place in the administration of the environment.

'The Role of the Judiciary and the Executive in the Development of Environmental Law', lecture delivered at the National Judicial Academy in Bhopal

17 OCTOBER 2010

Honourable Judges, I am honoured to be with you today. Amidst the illustrious presence of the judges of our high courts, who represent the guardians of our Constitution, I am reminded of why we need a proactive and vibrant judiciary. In point of fact, it is your fraternity that is responsible for the environmental law we have today, not just on the statute books, but in expansive precedents laid down that continue to evolve to fit all situations.

More so than any other areas, the development of this field of law has long been dependent on the intervention of legal luminaries and juridical giants. Today, I wish to acknowledge that contribution, a contribution that has been the bedrock of all environmental victories that have since been secured.

I

All laws evolve—some, more so, than others. Unfortunately the growth of environmental law has been slow, almost at a pace that many would say borders on the stunted. This is not because of a lack of legislation. We all agree that India has had comprehensive and progressive environmental legislation in place for many years. Elaborate laws on forests, wildlife, and the environment in general were enacted and have been around for almost four decades, enforced sporadically in a piecemeal manner. This is in addition to the numerous iterations that the need for environmental protection finds in our Constitution.

Despite the existence of these laws, seldom has the administration, Centre or state, stepped in to invoke the powers under these legislations to compel environmental protection. The law is seen, instead, as a labyrinth to be navigated and 'managed' rather than as rules to be complied with for the greater good. As a result we saw a lethargy set into the system; an inertia that took almost two decades to begin to thaw. There was an absence of administrative and executive will to simply enforce the existing laws, let alone over and above other more general laws, regardless of whether the situation may have demanded it.

The subservience of environmental laws to all others—in the name of rapid and unregulated development—became a phenomenon that we all silently came to terms with. True, our laws allow us to take all necessary measures for protecting and improving the quality of the environment and 'preventing, controlling, and abating' environmental pollution. We are empowered to undertake every conceivable measure to protect the environment—from the promulgation of standards to preserve environmental quality—and regulate emissions to demarcating areas in which industries, operations, or processes shall not be carried out, except with certain safeguards. Regardless of this abundance of rules and regulations, we were content to let unscrupulous individuals and organizations treat environmental concerns with reckless disregard.

A few days ago, I was shocked to learn that while the Central Government, through the Central Pollution Control Board (CPCB), enjoys the power to issue directions to remedy instances of environmental pollution (under Section 5 of the Environment (Protection) Act), a power that has been around since 1986, it has rarely invoked it to take decisive action against individuals and organizations which flout the Act. Upon further inquiry, I was told that the number of times that it has been used to direct closure of industrial and polluting units was very few. For the last two decades this has been largely due to the unequal priority enjoyed by industrial growth over conserving natural resources. This illustrates the case in point, that even with these strong standards in existence, the Central Government has often been reluctant to enact regulations that could diminish the growth of Indian industry.

This litany of laws demonstrates two things. First, that in our zeal to be a well-legislated country, we have drafted laws with little regard to their ability to be implemented. Second, that until the government develops the required will to enforce these laws, they are paper tigers to be celebrated only for their foresight and eloquent drafting.

There must emerge an understanding that environmental concerns, including the need to protect our forests and our ecosystems, are not secondary but as important as pursuing economic growth. Neither should take place at the cost of the other. Just as environmental extremism, which blindly opposes all industrialization is undesirable, environmental growth which comes at the cost of a sustainable environment for future generations is also not acceptable.

II

It is for this reason that I have always had, in this regard above all others, the greatest respect for the Indian judiciary. Verily, the development of environmental law has walked hand-in-hand with the emergence of the concept of 'public interest litigation'. For many years the judiciary was the bulwark which stood against the onslaught of repeated attacks against our natural resources and the health of our ecosystems at large.

I am one of those who believe that judicial activism has been a natural consequence of executive lethargy and executive malfeasance.

The apex court has been taking cognizance of environmental matters since in 1984, evidence was produced before it—demonstrating a linkage between environmental pollution and damage to the Taj Mahal. The following year the court admitted petitions under Article 32 to clean up the Ganges, rid Delhi of hazardous and heavy industry, close down and relocate Shriram's industrial complex in the heart of Delhi, and regulate air pollution caused by automobiles, thermal power stations, and other industries. Interestingly, all of these were cases filed by M.C. Mehta, who, at the time, constituted the entire field of environmental law practitioners.

A personality of almost equal grandeur, and one who has intrigued me personally, ever since I took charge of the ministry is T.N. Godavarman Thirumulpad. Having led a writ petition in 1995, which led the Supreme Court to ban all kinds of felling in any state without prior permission from the Union government, I am told he now lives a life away from the spotlight. Recently, though, in an interview to an environmental journal, he professed great surprise at the 'sweep of the judgment' and its ensuing consequences.

The case and the judgment were unique not just for the case law enunciated but for the fact that it allowed the Supreme Court to develop an innovative tool of convenience, an umbrella case of sorts, under which all matters relating to environment and forest could be heard in a specialized manner. Furthermore, in acknowledgement of the need for a body of experts to assist the court, the apex court established the Central Empowered Committee (CEC) and appointed senior counsels as *amicus curiae* to act as interveners on its behalf. This body, the CEC, would undertake detailed and thorough investigations of the environmental impacts of all major projects and submit their recommendations to the Supreme Court.

In doing so, the Supreme Court established a system that compensated for the administrative lacunae that were present in the environmental regime at the time. Here, I must also register a word of caution. While the role of the Supreme Court is indeed welcome in curing the inadequacies and shortcomings of administrative procedure, it must tread carefully so as not to usurp a function that genuinely vests in the executive. From time-to-time, there may be circumstances that may require the courts to intervene, but such circumstances should be the exception and not the rule. If the exercise of this power of judicial review is not observed judiciously, then it will end up reducing the role of the executive to a nullity. The executive has, no doubt, seriously neglected its functions in the enforcement of laws passed by Parliament. But the pressure should be on the executive to stand up and be counted and not on expanding the scope of judicial interventions.

III

Friends, if ever there was a country with a compelling case for a comprehensive and detailed environmental law, it is India. We have learnt little from the lessons of Bhopal, especially with regard to leaving unethical and irresponsible behaviour unchecked and unregulated. The loss caused by Bhopal was, and still continues to be, catastrophic especially considering the crippling nature of the same that left generations diseased and enfeebled. But what compounds this loss, and demonstrated our lack of readiness, in an almost offensive and demeaning fashion, is the compensation 'awarded'.

In the face of a system that lacked the expertise to face what would ultimately become the most complex litigation of its kind, the government passed the Processing of Claims Act to allow itself to represent the victims. This move itself was fraught with inadequacies concerning victim profiling and an overtly simplistic gradation of victims. The case then moved before the District Court in America and was dismissed primarily on the grounds of it being an improper forum, a ruling confirmed on appeal. Finally, the Indian Supreme Court told both sides to come to an agreement and 'start with a clean slate' in November 1988, four years after the disaster.

Eventually, Union Carbide agreed to pay $470 million for damages caused in the Bhopal disaster, 15 per cent of the original $3 billion claimed in the lawsuit. The average amount to families of the dead was $2,200.

It is argued by many in the wake of the compensation awarded that the Supreme Court adopted a very superficial manner in its determination. This is validated, in part, by the fact that the scheme of compensation and the wisdom behind the judgment had to be explained by the Government of India in an official statement.

Because India had not dealt with environmental accidents over many years, its laws had not evolved to cover them, leaving transnational corporations largely unsupervised. The tragedy proved two things: First, in the absence of a body well-equipped to tackle such a claim (even one with governmental support), a law suit would not survive. Second, that the damages paid highlight the unequal bargaining power that developing countries have against large multinational organizations operating out of developed nations. Both these lacunae can be leveraged if a proper judicial body exists to assert such compliance. In fact, one of the reasons that Union Carbide chose to set up operations in India was because India's legal system did not have a process accommodating corporate accountability. Class-action suits, a principle regulator of corporate ethics, were entirely absent.

While this disaster prompted a number of legislations, there was little fundamental change. Last year when I joined the ministry, I realized that India at this moment stands judicially unable to litigate and adjudicate major environmental claims from large-scale industrial accidents.

To remedy this, and to ensure that we are never found wanting institutionally if ever faced with a disaster of this magnitude again, we set about establishing an NGT. Once again, we drew strength for our decision from such judgements of the apex court as *M.V. Nayudu v. Andhra Pradesh Pollution Control Board*, where the court suggested the setting up of such a specialized body for environmental matters. We also relied on the recommendations made by the Law Commission of India in their 186th report.

This would not be a body that would be confined to specialized cases of accidents or absolute liability (unlike previous environmental bodies such as the National Environment Tribunal and the National Environment Appellate Authority), but would instead be a one-stop judicial forum where all manner of substantial environmental disputes could be addressed. It would be a quasi-judicial tribunal that would bring together both judicial as well as expert members to analyse and decide complex cases of environmental litigation. For the first time in the history of independent India, was there a judicial body that was required by statute, to observe the polluter-pays principle and the principle of sustainable development.

While hitherto, the courts had been largely concerned with setting right the environmental damage done, there was almost no concept of un-liquidated damages as many felt that it would lead to unjust enrichment of the petitioner party. Therefore, even if the polluting corporation was held liable, damages were limited to repairing the harm done or compensating the effected parties.

In other words, the liability was invoked to rectifying a wrong. Courts did not look upon individual compensation as the victim's due. This is because a public interest litigation (PIL) is primarily a social remedy that does not envisage enrichment. In fact, it opposes it. Thus, the incentive to litigate vis-à-vis tangible penalties is completely absent. As a result PILs only act as a limited guarantee.

The NGT, by design, has been set free from such constraints. Its mandate is to impose such high costs on non-compliance that it becomes financially unviable for the violator to repeat the offence. There is no cap on the award that can be declared against an offending party under the NGT Act. In fact, the NGT is authorized and expected to punish environmental violations by imposing significant monetary damages, in addition to the issuance of other salutary and remedial directions.

Since India does not have a codified tort law otherwise, I am certain that this body and its parent law, will bring about a new discipline to the determination of environmentally tortious claims.

IV

The gaps in policy formulation and policy implementation often require innovative thought on the part of the authorities involved. However, sometimes the government is reluctant to pursue ideas that lack in precedent. The Supreme Court, however, is unfettered by such constraints.

The best example of a Central Government innovation that required the Supreme Court's intervention to be rendered operational is the CAMPA. The CAMPA was set up to collect funds of the same name (being the Compensatory Afforestation Fund) that was accrued whenever forest land was diverted for non-forest related purposes such as building roads, hospitals, or houses. However, soon after the Central Government enacted a law to set up this authority, it became embroiled in a dispute between the Centre and the states. The states believed that the funds—since they were collected by the states—should not be deposited with nor should their use be supervised by the Central Government.

Despite attempts on both sides the debate reached an impasse. As a result, the fund languished in an escrow account created by the Supreme Court for over seven years. My colleagues and I met with the Law Minister, the CEC, the Attorney General, and the amicus curiae, to find a solution on how we could access these funds that were lying locked in this account. Indeed, one of the tasks I have taken up consciously is that of the Ministry of Environment and Forests (MoEF) working in harmony with the CEC.

My attention was drawn to an order of the Supreme Court dated 5 May 2006, according to which the Supreme Court had, on the recommendations of the CEC, directed the constitution of an ad hoc CAMPA authority to collect funds (accumulated with the states post-30 October 2002). This body was intended to function till the creation of a statutory body to replace it.

Almost Rs 10,000 crore had accumulated by this point. On 10 July 2009, we filed an affidavit before the forest bench of the Supreme Court praying for the operationalization of the ad hoc committee. The Attorney General for India, appearing on behalf of the ministry as well as the amicus curiae, urged the court in independent submissions to accept the affidavit and the suggestions made by the ad hoc CAMPA (which were further endorsed by the CEC).

As a result the forest bench allowed the prayer. This innovative model, which was originally met with scepticism from the states and other stakeholders, saw implementation only because of the joint efforts of the executive and the judiciary. Since 2009, almost all states have accepted this judgments and opened bank accounts to receive this money, along with having submitted their annual plans of operation (detailing how they intend to spend the amounts). A total of over Rs 1,000 crore will be transferred to these states (a substantial portion of which has already been disbursed) for purposes of afforestation and re-greening activities.

V

The case of Vedanta marks a watershed moment in the field of environmental law, not just for its jurisprudential value but for its importance as a precedent in terms of marrying tribal rights to environmental concerns. Vedanta demonstrated how a decision to grant forest or environment clearance was more than just the sum of its parts that it could have consequences that could wipe out entire tribal groups if not considered with a high degree of care.

When we embarked on a study of the Vedanta case, we knew that a nuanced approach had to be taken. This was a case that would require us to go beyond the black-and-white realm of compliance with environmental and or forestry conditions. We appointed an independent team of experts headed by Dr N.C. Saxena to review the project from all perspectives—forestry, wildlife, and the settlement of forest rights of the tribal populations. I also obtained an opinion from the Attorney General of India to reaffirm that the executive still had room to exercise its own decision-making powers.

The report, which was immediately made available to the public, highlighted gross and egregious violations on the part of the project proponents to secure forest clearance. It found, inter alia, that official submissions were tailored to suit the project proponents, documents were forged and there were even allegations of intimidation of local protesters. What was most disturbing was how the rights of the Dongaria Kondh, a primitive tribal group living in the area and wholly dependent on the desired forest area for their livelihood, were completely disregarded.

It also unearthed unauthorized activities taking place on the refinery area, for which the project proponents had previously been granted environmental clearance. In light of the compelling evidence presented, I—in consultation with my colleagues—was left with little choice but to direct that forest clearance not be granted and that the attendant environmental clearance that had been granted be further investigated.

Had we evaluated the Vedanta case only through the prism of so-called 'economic development', we would have lost sight of these concerns. Had we only focused on the arguments surrounding wealth creation and job opportunities, we would have forgotten that there were facets that could not be measured in such terms.

There was no doubt in my mind that development should come to the region that the benefits of economic growth should percolate to those indigent groups who needed it the most. But we could never ever allow it at the cost of our humanity.

VI

The law is written in black and white, but we need judges to humanize that law, to read in-between the absolutes, and to find solutions that balance the seemingly competing interests of growth and environmental protection. It is through the vision of certain proactive judges do we now count the precautionary principle, the polluter pays principle, the public trust doctrine, and the standard of absolute liability as part of our jurisprudence. The role of the high courts in establishing local committees (such as, the Vellore Welfare Forum Committee in Chennai) has also been instrumental. High courts of Delhi, Chennai, and Andhra Pradesh have stepped in to establish committees on a wide range of subjects. Whenever my colleagues in Delhi administration seek to take credit for the success of the implementation of CNG-run public transport vehicles, I am quick to remind them of the Supreme Court's role, which appointed the Mashelkar Committee to develop the idea.

I am personally very grateful for the judiciary. You have often been defined as the watchdog of the executive. I pray that you never falter in that role. That you ensure our institutions function transparently and efficiently. That they adhere to the rule of the law, free of arbitrariness and petty biases.

Letter to State Forest and Environment ministers About Working Together to Address Challenges, Improve Delivery of Forestry-related Programmes, and Instituting an Annual Dialogue of Forest Ministers

15 JUNE 2009

As you are probably aware, I took over as Minister of State (Independent Charge) Environment and Forests on 29 May 2009. I have been reviewing the work of our ministry in detail. During this review, many issues have cropped up in the forestry sector, some of which require the Centre and the states to work together to realize national objectives. This cooperation becomes all the more urgent in the context of issues such as, climate change.

I want to institutionalize an annual meeting of forest ministers of states. Accordingly, I propose to convene the first such meeting in this new institutionalized series on Saturday, 25 July 2009. I believe that it would be appropriate that this first meeting takes place in the campus of Forest Research Institute, Dehradun ... and your personal presence in this meeting would signal our collective commitment to putting our forestry plans and programmes on a new and firmer footing.

The broad agenda for this interaction is the following:

1. Strategies for increasing forest cover and enhancing synergies between 'Green India Mission', National Afforestation Programme, and CAMPA funds;
2. Protection of forests in the context of the implementation of The Scheduled Tribes and Other Traditional Forest Dwellers (Recognition of Forest Rights) Act, 2006';
3. Wildlife conservation, including tiger conservation and issues related to man–animal conflict;
4. Strengthening of state forest departments by modernization, infrastructure development, and capacity building of forest officials;
5. Any other important issues that the state governments may want to raise.

Letter to State Chief Ministers on Unlocking CAMPA and Related Developments and Plans

[I was conscious that many saw my efforts to break the logjam and access the CAMPA funds as a move to centralize; this letter was an effort to allay concerns.]

15 JULY 2009

I write to inform you of recent developments on the issue of the CAMPA, which has been deadlocked for seven years.

Upon assumption of office, I immediately recognized the potential of the CAMPA funds for afforestation. It was clear that the impasse on the operationalization of CAMPA could not be allowed to continue. Accordingly, I spoke to all those who could contribute to the decision-making process to involve them in charting out the best and most agreeable course of action.

Last week, we approached the Hon. Supreme Court and, on 10 July 2009, the Supreme Court issued following orders:

1. That the state CAMPA guidelines prepared by the MoEF for utilizing CAMPA funds should be notified and implemented. These guidelines envisage:

a. A state-level CAMPA Governing Body under the chairmanship of the chief minister;
b. A state-level CAMPA Steering Committee under the chairmanship of the chief secretary;
c. A state-level CAMPA Executive Committee under the chairmanship of the principal chief conservator of forests.

2. That there will be a National CAMPA Advisory Council under the chairmanship of the union minister of environment and forests for monitoring, technical assistance, and evaluation.

3. That as an interim arrangement to get CAMPA going, 10 per cent of the accumulated principal amount will be released per year (for the next five years) by the ad hoc CAMPA authority set up by the Supreme Court order of May 2006, under the chairmanship of director-general, forests, to state CAMPAs. This money will be used for projects identified by the state CAMPA that form part of the state forest department's annual plan of operations (APOs).

The state CAMPA guidelines approved by the Supreme Court seek to promote:

a. Conservation, protection, regeneration, and management of existing forests;
b. Conservation, protection, and management of wildlife and its habitat within and outside protected areas, including the consolidation of the protected areas;
c. Compensatory afforestation;
d. Environmental services, including provision of goods such as non-timber forest products, fuel, fodder, and water; and
e. Research, training, and capacity building.

The ad hoc CAMPA, as the name suggests, is a purely temporary arrangement. It will liquidate itself once all systems in states are in place and CAMPA has become fully functional in the framework contained in the Supreme Court orders of 10 July 2009. The CEC has already approached the Supreme Court for liquidating the ad hoc CAMPA. The Supreme Court has ordered that the CEC submit progress reports once every six months. It is reasonable to assume that with the Centre and states working together cohesively to implement the Supreme Court orders of 10 July 2009, the ad hoc CAMPA will wind up within the next six–twelve months and state CAMPAs will take over completely.

I am enclosing a copy of the state CAMPA guidelines, on which action may kindly be taken, along with the opening of an account. I look forward to working with you in our common endeavour for regenerating, protecting and expanding our forest cover.

Letter to Deputy Chairman Planning Commission Montek Singh Ahluwalia on Augmenting Capacity Building Efforts in the Forestry Sector

13 August 2009

I wish to bring to your kind notice the immediate need for increase in the budgetary allocation for implementation of the one component of the scheme 'Capacity Building in Forestry Sector' of this ministry, which has been recently approved by the Cabinet Committee on Economic Affairs. The component 'Indira Gandhi National Forest Academy (IGNFA)' aims to target specific needs of Indian Forest Service (IFS) officers in the endeavour of the professional and human resource development in the forestry sector.

Among other things, IGNFA, Dehradun, will be implementing the Mandatory Mid-Career Training (MCTP) for the IFS officers as per the Prime Minister's Office's directions dated 30 October 2006 (copy enclosed). These trainings, as is the case for Indian Administrative Service and Indian Police Service, are now a prerequisite for promotion of officers to certain grades in terms of the revised All India Service Pay Rules. The implementation modality of the component is time-bound. IGNFA has already finalized the calendar for organizing three phases in five batches for IFS officers during the current financial year. The IGNFA has also finalized the bids for organizing MCTs, which require an additional allocation of Rs 16 crore in 2009–10. Currently,, the IGNFA has an average plan allocation of Rs 5.51 crore, which is equivalent to last year's expenditure in IGNFA, when the MCTP was not in force. Secretary (Environment and Forests) has also written to Planning Commission, vide letter dated 28 April 2009 for additional requirement. Though provision was made in BE, however, the outlay for the current year is kept at the level of RE for the last year. The need for immediate additional outlay was brought to your kind notice during your recent visit to Dehradun on the occasion of convocation of IGNFA.

I would, therefore, request you to explore the possibility of allocating an additional amount of Rs 16.50 crore as a specific budget additionally for the component. It may also be pointed out that it will be extremely difficult to conduct MCTP of five batches of eight–six weeks duration each if the allocation is made available at RE stage.

Writing to Union Minister of Finance Pranab Mukherjee and Minister of State (Independent Charge) Department of Personnel Prithviraj Chavan on Addressing the Anomalies in Salaries and Remuneration for the Indian Forest Service

8 December 2009

I would like to draw your kind attention to one of the major decisions taken by the Government of India while accepting the recommendations of the Sixth Central Pay Commission (6th CPC) relating to the IFS, which has been implemented but not in accordance with the decision of the government.

While dealing the justification of parity among the organized Group 'A' Services with the IAS, the sixth CPC recommended:

> Whenever any IAS officer of a particular batch is posted in the Centre to a particular grade carrying a specific grade pay in pay bands (PBs) PB-3 or PB-4, grant of higher pay scale on non-functional basis to the officers belonging to batches of organized Group 'A' services that are senior by two years or more should be given by the government.

The government, through a Cabinet decision, accepted this recommendation and further extended this benefit to the IPS and the IFS in their respective state cadres. The decision is as follows: 'Accepted. This will also be applicable to the IPS and the IAS in their respective state cadres for which the relevant cadre controlling authorities will issue the orders.'

Accordingly, this ministry vetted the draft notification forwarded by the department of personnel and training (DoP&T), which was in line with the decision of the Cabinet.

Unfortunately, while notifying the above decision a deviation seems to have crept in Rule 3: Note 3 of IFS (Pay) Second Amendment Rules, 2008, in the Government of India Resolution bearing No. 1/1/2008-IC dated 29 August 2008, issued by the department of expenditure that reads as follows:

> Whenever any IAS officer of the state or joint cadre is posted at the Centre to a particular grade carrying a specific grade pay in pay band 3 or pay band 4, the members of service, who are senior to such IAS officer by two years or more and have not so far been promoted to that particular grade, shall be appointed to the same grade on non-functional basis from the date of posting of the IAS officer in that particular grade.

The MoEF has taken up the above matter with the DoP&T vide letters dated 13 September 2008 and dated 11 August 2009, but a favourable result is still awaited. It is understood that the department of expenditure under the finance ministry has some reservations in this regard.

It is pertinent here also to bring to your kind notice that but for a few deputation assignments at the Centre which are not more than 15 per cent of the total strength, the IFS is a state-borne All Indian Service like the other two All India Services. Most of the officers serve in their respective state/joint cadres for a major part of their service career. Therefore, the appointment of an officer of the IFS in a particular grade serving in a state is to be compared with the appointment of an IAS officer in that grade in that particular state cadre and not with posting of the IAS officer at the Centre as per the amended IFS Pay Rules, 2008.

You would agree that the spirit of the recommendations of the sixth CPC and the decision of the Government of India is not correctly reflected in Rule 3: Note 3 of IFS (Pay) Second Amendment Rules, 2008, by the above notification dated 29 August 2008. I earnestly request you to kindly use your good offices to cause urgent necessary action to rectify the above.

Letter to the Prime Minister on Progress Made Towards Setting Up an Environmental Regulator

17 SEPTEMBER 2009

I am pleased to send you a copy of discussion paper that was released today on the establishment of a National Environment Protection Authority (NEPA). I have sent a copy to all chief ministers, and also put it on our website. The idea is to get comments on this discussion paper by 20 October and finalize the course of legislative and other actions thereafter. I believe that the establishment of NEPA has been long overdue and is an essential pillar of effective environmental governance in our country.

Discussion Paper, 'Towards Effective Environmental Governance: Proposal for an NEPA', on the Design of an Environmental Regulator

[I shared this preliminary discussion paper with the Prime Minister. The paper was made public to encourage consultations with stakeholders and others interested in the issue.]

17 SEPTEMBER 2009

Background

This paper discusses the need for an effective model of environmental governance in India, which includes the establishment of NEPA.

The aim of this note is to invite comments from the states, civil society, and other stakeholders regarding the design of an appropriate institutional structure for best addressing the growing environmental challenges. This is an evolving document with scope for further development, keeping in view the need for expeditiously giving a practical shape to the proposal.

Rationale for a More Effective Model of Environmental Governance

The challenge of environmental management and regulation is immense in a country as large and diverse as India. Over the years, legislation has evolved. With the enactment of the Environment (Protection) Act, 1986, the various rules and notifications, and the National Environment Policy, 2006, a credible legislative and policy base has been created. But there are gaps in the institutional mechanisms and implementation has not kept pace with the legislative and policy evolution.

The judiciary has played a major role in matters related to the enforcement of environmental laws. While this has had a salutary impact, it has also brought into focus the weaknesses in the executive. Quite clearly, while our environmental laws have been progressive, implementation by government agencies has left much to be desired. The institutional structures in their current form are inadequate for responding to the emerging environmental challenges, including river cleaning, management of wastes, hazardous substance, and plastics management, dealing with chemical contamination, monitoring compliance with environmental clearances, etc. There is no suitable authority to comprehensively and effectively implement the Environment (Protection) Act, 1986.

While the number and complexity of the projects received for environmental clearance by the MoEF has increased several-fold in recent years, its capacity has remained limited. Similarly, the CPCB and the State Pollution Control Boards (SPCBs) do not seem to have the capacity or the resources to ensure compliance with various environmental regulations. This challenge is exacerbated by the increasing complexity of environmental issues we face today, requiring the interface of science, economics, law, and other social sciences. The fact that the matter of disposal of toxic waste in Bhopal's erstwhile Union Carbide India Limited plant has not been resolved even twenty-five years after the gas tragedy illustrates the point. This underscores the need to have a suitably empowered apex level authority to deal with environmental issues.

Several recent reports have called for an institutional redesign. The report of the Steering Committee on the Environment and Forests Sector for the Eleventh Five Year Plan (2007) recommended the setting up of a National Environment Clearance Authority. The report also found it critical to urgently upgrade and strengthen the pollution regulatory institutions, and recommended the repositioning of the CPCB as the Environment Protection Authority.

Similarly, the 192nd Report (2008) of the Departmental Parliamentary Standing Committee on Science and Technology and Environment and Forests on the 'Functioning of the Central Pollution Control Board (CPCB)' has strongly recommended the strengthening of the board on various counts.

A study of India's environmental regulators, particularly the SPCBs, by the Centre for Science and Environment, New Delhi (2009), has identified several weaknesses in the implementing capacities of the SPCBs and has recommended the introduction of a uniform set of guidelines and standards of operation. Kalpavriksh Environment

Action Group has also recently come out with a study titled 'Revealing the State of Monitoring and Compliance of Environmental Clearance Conditions', which brings to the fore the existing weaknesses in the current compliance mechanism.

The lacuna, in terms of an appropriate regulatory framework, was highlighted by the Madras High Court, which observed in the case of *Tamil Nadu Pollution Control Board* v. *The State Human Rights Commission* (decided on 4 November 2004):

> ... there is an urgent need for enactment of a general resolution on environmental pollution which inter alia should enable co-ordination of activities of various regulatory agencies, creation of authority or authorities with advocate powers for environmental protection, regulation of discharge of environmental pollutants and handling of hazardous substances, speedy response in the event of accidents threatening environment and deterrent punishment to those who endanger human environment safety and health.

It is noteworthy that the Prime Minister in his address during the 'National Conference of Ministers of Environment and Forests', on 18 August 2009, suggested that the government should consider the setting up of a NEPA supported by regional Environment Protection Authorities. Quite clearly, there is a need to re-assess the entire ambit of environmental governance in the country.

Basic Structure of an Effective Environmental Governance Model

To be responsive to the complex challenge of environmental management in the country, it is being proposed that the environmental governance structure be comprised around the following dimensions:

1. Legislation and Policymaking: To be the responsibility of the MoEF.
2. Regulation, Monitoring, and Enforcement: To be the responsibility of a new NEPA.
3. Adjudication: To be the responsibility of the NGT, a Bill for which has recently been introduced in Parliament. This will support the constitutional jurisdiction of the higher courts.

The SPCBs will continue to play their respective roles in environmental management. In the case of the CPCB, some functional adjustments may be required taking into account the role of the NEPA.

Key Principles for the Establishment of the NEPA

Before we look into the structural issues related to the NEPA, it may be useful to visit some of the basic principles pertinent to its design:

1. It should be a statutory body, created through the parliamentary process.
2. It will be truly autonomous of the MoEF, equipped with substantial budget, and with powers to make its own procedures.
3. It should be professionally managed, drawing upon best-in-class expertise from all relevant professional fields including applied sciences, economics, law, etc. Its board members and CEO should be appointed for a fixed tenure.
4. It should have original powers conferred upon it under the Environment (Protection) Act, 1986.
5. Its working will subscribe to the 'polluter-pays principle' and the 'precautionary principle'.

Role of the NEPA

The proposed NEPA shall be an independent statutory body with the basic mandate of effective enforcement of environmental laws. It is envisaged that the NEPA shall have specialists from the areas of physical sciences, life sciences, engineering, law, environmental economics, public health, and environmental planning and management. This will adequately equip the authority for taking various measures for protecting and improving the quality of the environment and preventing, controlling, and abating environmental pollution.

The NEPA should assume the national stewardship of enforcement and compliance. India being a country of sub-continental dimensions, the body may have regional environmental protection agencies for decentralized functioning. The portfolio of functions, flowing out from Section 3 (2) of the Environment (Protection) Act, 1986 that may be discharged by the NEPA include:

1. Environmental Impact Assessment (EIA): This will deal with EIA notification, 2006 and Coastal Regulation Zone (CRZ) Notification, 1991, and the clearances thereunder with respect to the restriction of areas in which any industries, operations or processes or class

thereof shall not be carried out or shall be carried out subject to certain safeguards.

2. Enforcement and Compliance: This will cover areas like ambient monitoring, industrial monitoring, inspection of common facilities and administrative, civil, and criminal remedial action to ensure compliance.

3. Environmental Planning and Sustainability Studies: This area will be research-and-development (R&D)-oriented and will include studies in spatial planning, carrying capacity studies, delineation of critically polluted areas, and environmental laws.

4. Environmental Health and Ecosystem Protection: This will cover areas like toxicology, water, air, and soil pollution, laboratory management, and natural resource management.

5. Sustainable Production and Waste Management: This function will look at issues like municipal solid waste, plastic waste, hazardous waste, and also the emerging area of environmental labelling (eco-labelling) of products and services.

6. Chemical Safety and Biosafety: This function would include prevention and management of chemical accidents and related information systems and would also encompass the work related to approvals presently being given by the Genetic Engineering Approval Committee (GEAC). In this context, it is mentionable that proposal for setting up a Biotechnology Regulatory Authority, which will subsume the GEAC, is under separate consideration of the Government of India.

Role of the MoEF and the Pollution Control Boards

The ministry's role in framing legislation, policymaking, framing of Acts, making of rules, coordination with the state governments and with various environmental bodies will continue along with inter-sectoral and inter-ministerial coordination and parliamentary matters. The ministry will also head and oversee the international negotiations under its charge. In addition, the ministry shall also be executing schemes like the centrally sponsored schemes for river cleaning, establishment of Common Effluent Treatment Plants (CETPs) and Treatment Storage and Disposal Facilities (TSDFs) and R&D in clean technology. The role of MoEF in regulatory functions, however, will need to be adjusted keeping in view the responsibilities being conferred on NEPA.

The CPCB will be responsible for developing national environmental standards, monitoring ambient air and water quality, conducting R&D in pollution control technology, and coordinating the functioning of the SPCBs. The SPCBs will continue to discharge their compliance and enforcement responsibilities under the existing legislations. The NEPA will provide technical guidance to the SPCBs and it may also give directions to the state boards in environmental matters.

Design Options Related to NEPA

Four options are being outlined below with regard to the proposed NEPA.

Option 1: Create a National Environment Monitoring Authority (NEMA) Focused on Compliance and Enforcement

In this model (Table 6.1), a new body, NEMA, is created. This has a focused mandate, which is to ensure effective compliance and enforcement. NEMA particularly takes over the responsibilities for monitoring compliance and effecting enforcement of environmental clearances granted by the MoEF, a function currently discharged by the MoEF's regional offices. NEMA also takes over the role of monitoring compliance with pollution standards, currently done by the CPCB. The MoEF continues to discharge all its other functions as present, including regulatory functions such as granting of environmental clearances. The CPCB also continues to discharge all its other functions. NEMA will need to be given significant teeth in terms of powers and resources to implement its mandate. It may perform functions like inspection of facilities and related functions under Sections 9, 10, 11 of Environment (Protection) Act, 1986, issue direction under Section 5, and launch criminal prosecution under Section 19 of the Act. In short, the emphasis of this option is on pointedly strengthening compliance and enforcement.

Option 2: Create a Full-Fledged NEPA that Subsumes the CPCB

In this model (Table 6.2), we create a NEPA which subsumes the CPCB within itself. In other words, the CPCB ceases to exist on NEPA's creation. Employees of CPCB will become employees of NEPA, which shall

Table 6.1 Option 1: Create a NEMA Focused on Compliance and Enforcement

Centre						NGT
	MoEF			**NEMA**		• Specialized Tribunal for Adjudication
	Core Functions	**CPCB**	**Regulatory (Env. Clearances)**	**Compliance and Enforcement**		
	• Legislation and Policy • Parliamentary Matters • Implementation of Central Schemes • Centre-State Issues • International Cooperation • Education • Centres of Excellence	• Development of Standards • Ambient Quality Monitoring • Technical Studies and Research	• Granting Environmental Clearances and CRZ Clearances	• Monitoring of Environmental Clearances (from MoEF) • Monitoring of Pollution Standards (from CPCB)		
		↔	↔	↔	↔	
State		SPCBs/PCCs	State EIAs	State CZMAs	SPCBs/PCCs	

Note: Forestry and Wildlife continue to be functions of the MoEF and are beyond the scope of this document.

Table 6.2 Option 2: Create a Full-Fledged NEPA that Subsumes the CPCB

Centre	MoEF		NEPA		NGT
	Core Functions	R&D and Technical (formerly CPCB)	Regulatory (Env. Clearances)	Compliance and Enforcement	
	• Legislation and Policy • Parliamentary Matters • Implementation of Central Schemes • Centre-State Issues • International Cooperation • Education • Centres of Excellence	• Development of Standards (from CPCB) • Ambient Quality Monitoring (from CPCB) • Technical Studies and Research (from CPCB)	• Granting Environmental Clearances and CRZ Clearances (from MoEF)	• Monitoring of Environmental Clearances (from MoEF) • Monitoring of Pollution Standards (from CPCB)	• Specialized Tribunal for Adjudication
State	SPCBs/PCCs		State EIAs State CZMAs	SPCBs/PCCs	

Note: Forestry and wildlife continue to be functions of the MoEF and are beyond the scope of this document.

have three broad functions. First, it will conduct R&D and technical studies, primarily being done by CPCB today. Second, it will perform the regulatory function of granting environmental clearances, currently being done by the MoEF. Third, it will perform functions regarding compliance and enforcement with environmental clearances and pollution standards, as explained in Option 1.

In effect, the CPCB would morph into a NEPA, with a much larger mandate than before. A key feature of this model is that the available technical manpower of CPCB and its experience in handling pollution control may be utilized as a base for the NEPA. In addition, the existing infrastructure and the six regional offices of CPCB could be upgraded to suit the needs of NEPA. This would essentially translate into a total revamp of the CPCB as well as an organizational metamorphosis in terms of technical manpower, dimensions of functions, and approach to environmental challenges. In order to re-engineer CPCB into the NEPA an amendment of the Water (Prevention and Control of Pollution) Act, 1974 may also be needed.

The alternative view is that the multifaceted environmental challenges in the country require an effective planning and management regime, which, in turn, calls for a paradigm shift in the existing business processes and capacities of the CPCB. Retrofitting the CPCB into the NEPA may be challenging.

Option 3: Create a NEPA, with a Separate CPCB Continuing to Report to the MoEF

In this model (Table 6.3) the NEPA and the CPCB continue to work independently, collaborating where necessary. Here, a NEPA is being created that has two broad functions. First, it performs the regulatory function of granting environmental clearances, currently being done by the MoEF. Second, it performs the function of compliance and enforcement of environmental clearances and pollution standards, as explained in Option 1.

The CPCB continues to exist as today, reporting directly to the MoEF, collaborating with NEPA, wherever necessary. It continues to perform the functions it performs today, except the monitoring of compliance with pollution standards and hazardous substance and waste management, that become the functions of the NEPA.

Table 6.3   Option 3: Create a NEPA, with a separate CPCB continuing to report to MoEF

Centre	MoEF		NEPA		NGT
	Core Functions	**CPCB**	**Regulatory (Env. Clearances)**	**Compliance and Enforcement**	
	• Legislation and Policy • Parliamentary Matters • Implementation of Central Schemes • Centre-State Issues • International Cooperation • Education • Centres of Excellence	• Development of Standards • Ambient Quality Monitoring • Technical Studies and Research	• Granting Environmental Clearances and CRZ Clearances (from MoEF)	• Monitoring of Environmental Clearances (from MoEF) • Monitoring of Pollution Standards (from CPCB)	• Specialized Tribunal for Adjudication
State	SPCBs/PCCs	State EIAs	State CZMAs	SPCBs/PCCs	

Note: Forestry and Wildlife continue to be functions of the MoEF and are beyond the scope of this document.

Table 6.4 Option 4: Create a NEPA, with CPCB reporting into it

Centre	MoEF		NEPA			NGT
	Core Functions	**CPCB**	**Regulatory (Env. Clearances)**		**Compliance & Enforcement**	
	• Legislation & Policy • Parliamentary matters • Implementation of Central Schemes • Centre-State Issues • International Cooperation • Education • Centres of Excellence	• Development of Standards • Ambient Quality Monitoring • Technical Studies and Research	• Granting Environmental Clearances & CRZ Clearances (from MoEF)		• Monitoring of Environmental Clearances (from MoEF) • Monitoring of Pollution Standards (from CPCB)	• Specialized Tribunal for Adjudication
State	SPCBs/PCCs		State EIAs	State CZMAs	SPCBs /PCCs	

Note: Forestry and Wildlife continue to be functions of the MoEF and are beyond the scope of this document.

Option 4: Create a NEPA, with CPCB Reporting into It

This option (Table 6.4) is a variant of Option 3, the difference being that the CPCB reports to the NEPA instead of reporting to the MoEF. The distinctiveness of Option 4 (relative to Option 3) is that it recognizes the significant synergies that the CPCB may have with the work of the NEPA.

Epilogue

This note contains a broad outline of a proposal for a redesigned institutional structure of environmental governance of India. It is clear that new ground needs to be broken and choices made if we are to enhance the quality of our environmental management and governance. This note lays out some of these choices.

We are putting this document in the public domain for comments and inputs over the next thirty days so that we can further enhance and refine this concept. At a time when there appears to be an 'institutional fatigue' for the creation of new institutions in the public sector, we need to address the legitimate question: 'Why do we need another institution?' As this note explains, it is clear that given the limitations of our current system and the increasingly complex environmental challenges we face, there is a need for an empowered, professionally managed, independent institution for environmental protection in India.

The creation of the NEPA must be seen in the context of a broader institutional re-design, which acknowledges the need for a more focused role for the MoEF and includes the creation of the NGT. This is aimed to generate enhanced outcomes in the creation of new policies, implementation of regulations, and dispensation of justice in the environmental domain in India.

Consultation with Stakeholders, Including States, followed by a study by IIT Delhi, Resulted in a Decision to Set Up the Environmental Regulator as National Environmental Assessment and Monitoring Authority (NEAMA)

[This note put out for public dissemination gives the broad contours of the proposed regulator.]

3 MAY 2011

What is the NEAMA:

1. A body to do appraisals of all projects that currently come to MoEF for clearance under the under Category 'A' of EIA notification as all the CRZ clearances proposals under the CRZ notification of 2010.
2. It shall be a fully autonomous authority. It will have administrative/ functional and financial autonomy.
3. NEAMA shall undertake full-time continuous process of appraisal of proposals for environmental clearances (instead of the batch-processing that happens currently).
4. NEAMA shall also undertake the function of 'monitoring of clearance conditions'.
5. The impact assement (IA) division and CRZ division of MoEF, along with increased specialized manpower (as identified) shall form the initial core of NEAMA.

How will NEAMA be Set Up

1. Set up as an autonomous authority, established under Section 3(3) of the Environment (Protection) Act, 1986 for implementation of EIA Notification of 2006 and subsequent amendments to the same.
2. A Cabinet note shall be moved for giving a legal foundation for NEAMA under the Environment (Protection) Act, along with other proposed amendments to Environment (Protection) Act.

Organization Structure of NEAMA

Board of Members, comprising:
1. Full-time chairman of high standing, expertise and relevant experience.
2. Eight full-time members, each in charge of a thematic area (for example, thermal power, major minerals, hydroelectric, etc.).
3. One full-time member in charge of databases.
4. One full-time member in charge of HR, administration, legal, and support functions.
5. Full-time thematic teams, with requisite technical and field expertise in each of the thematic areas.

Relationship between NEAMA and MoEF

1. The recommendation of NEAMA, along with detailed conditions and justifications, shall be put in the public domain and send to minister of environment and forests (MEF) for perusal.
2. The MEF would, in most cases, endorse the decision of the NEAMA. Accordingly, a decision would be issued by the NEAMA.

    The MEF, if in disagreement with the decision of NEAMA, may reject the decision, but in this case the MEF will need to issue a speaking order with detailed justification. One of two actions could, thereafter, be undertaken:

    a. Ministry may issue a formal order and communicate final decision to project proponent.
    b. Ministry may send the proposal back to NEAMA for reconsideration.

    The speaking order of the minister and communication with NEAMA will be in the public domain
3. A division headed by joint secretary/director-level officer at MoEF could be set up to serve as secretariat to manage relationship with NEAMA and other administrative issues.

Observations on the Supreme Court Order on Lafarge Mining, Particularly on Setting Up of an Independent Environment Regulator

7 JULY 2011

The Supreme Court on 6 July 2011 pronounced its final judgment on the LaFarge Umium Mining Case. This decision was delivered by a bench comprising the Hon. Chief Justice S.H. Kapadia, Justice Aftab Alam, and Justice K.S. Radhakrishnan. The MoEF believes this is a landmark judgment which will set the stage for further reforms in environmental governance.

The Hon. bench refused to interfere with the decision of the MoEF granting site clearance dated 18 June1999, EIA clearance dated 9 August 2001 read with revised environmental clearance dated 19 April 2010, and Stage-I forest clearance dated 22 April 2010.

Invoking the principles of sustainable development, inter-generational equity and the doctrine of proportionality, the learned bench has stated:

The word 'development' is a relative term. One cannot assume that the tribals are not aware of principles of conservation of forest. In the present case, we are satisfied that limestone mining has been going on for centuries in the area and that it is an activity which is intertwined with the culture and the unique land holding and tenure system of the Nongtrai village. On the facts of this case, we are satisfied with due diligence exercise undertaken by MoEF in the matter of forest diversion.

There are three specific features of the Judgment that the MoEF particularly welcomes:

Greater Role of National Forest Policy, 1988

The National Forest Policy, 1988 prepared under the personal leadership of the then Prime Minister Rajiv Gandhi has been a guiding principle for forest administration for over two decades. The Supreme Court has now given it a new and enhanced status by stating the following:

Time has come for this Court to declare and we hereby declare that the National Forest Policy, 1988 which lays down far-reaching principles must necessarily govern the grant of permissions under Section 2 of the Forest (Conservation) Act, 1980 as the same provides the road map to ecological protection and improvement under the Environment (Protection) Act, 1986. The principles/guidelines mentioned in the National Forest Policy, 1988 should be read as part of the provisions of the Environment (Protection) Act, 1986 read together with the Forest (Conservation) Act, 1980.

The MoEF will ensure that this direction of the Supreme Court is implemented in letter and spirit.

Independent Regulator

During the course of the hearings the learned bench mentioned the need to have an independent and professional regulator to deal with perceived infirmities in the appraisal and clearance process. While appearing for the MoEF, in this case the learned Attorney General then had the occasion to mention the intention of the MoEF to establish an independent regulator to bring about greater professionalism in the appraisal of projects vis-à-vis environment and forestry clearances. Concurring with this submission the learned bench directed as follows:

'Thus, we are of the view that under Section 3(3) of the Environment (Protection) Act, 1986, the Central Government should appoint a national regulator for appraising projects, enforcing environmental conditions for approvals and to impose penalties on polluters.'

The MoEF has already, of its own accord, initiated this process and a draft note on the establishment of an independent NEAMA has been circulated for inter-ministerial consultations and will be moved for Cabinet approval thereafter.

Directions Based on the Affidavit Filed by the MoEF

The Hon. Bench has also accepted certain recommendations made by the MoEF in its affidavit dated 29 April 2011 and has incorporated them as part of its final order. These include the following:

1. In all future cases, the User Agency (project proponents) shall comply with the office memorandum dated 26 April 2011, issued by the MoEF, which requires that all mining projects involving forests and for such non-mining projects—which involve more than 40 ha of forests—the project proponent shall submit the documents which have been enumerated in the said office memorandum.
2. If the project proponent makes a claim regarding status of the land being non-forest and if there is any doubt the site shall be inspected by the state forest department along with the regional office of the MoEF to ascertain the status of forests, based on which the certificate in this regard be issued. In all such cases, it would be desirable for the representative of state forest department to assess the Expert Appraisal Committee.
3. At present, there are six regional offices in the country. This may be expanded to at least ten. At each regional office there may be a Standing Site Inspection committee which will take up the work of ascertaining the position of the land (namely whether it is forest land or not). In each Committee there may be one non-official member who is an expert in forestry. If it is found that forest land is involved, then forest clearance will have to be applied for first.
4. Constitution of Regional Empowered Committee, under the chairmanship of the concerned Chief Conservator of Forests

(Central) and having Conservator of Forests (Central) and three non-official members to be selected from the eminent experts in forestry and allied disciplines as its members, at each of the Regional Offices of the MoEF, to facilitate detailed/in-depth scrutiny of the proposals involving diversion of forest area more than 5 hectares and up to 40 hectares and all proposals relating to mining and encroachments up to 40 hectares.

5. Creation and regular updating of a GIS based decision support database, tentatively containing interalia the district-wise details of the location and boundary of (i) each plot of land that may be defined as forest for the purpose of the Forest (Conservation) Act, 1980; (ii) the core, buffer, and eco-sensitive zone of the protected areas constituted as per the provisions of the Wildlife (Protection) Act, 1972; (iii) the important migratory corridors for wildlife; and (iv) the forest land diverted for non-forest purpose in the past in the district. The Survey of India toposheets in digital format, the forest cover maps prepared by the Forest Survey of India in preparation of the successive *State of Forest* reports and the conditions stipulated in the approvals accorded under the Forest (Conservations) Act, 1980 for each case of diversion of forest land in the district will also be part of the proposed decision support database.

6. The office memorandum dated 26 April 2011 is in continuation of an earlier office memorandum dated 31 March 2011. This earlier office memorandum clearly delineates the order of priority required to be followed while seeking environmental clearance under the Environment Impact Assessment Notification, 2006. It provides that in cases where environmental clearance is required for a project on forest land, the forest clearance shall be obtained before the grant of the environment clearance.

7. In addition, an office memorandum dated 26 April 2011 on Corporate Environmental Responsibility has also been issued by the MoEF. This office memorandum lays down the need for PSUs and other corporate entities to evolve a Corporate Environment Policy of their own to ensure greater compliance with the environmental and forestry clearance granted to them.

8. All minutes of proceedings before the Forest Advisory Committee in respect of the Forest (Conservation) Act, 1980 as well as the

minutes of proceedings of the Expert Appraisal Committee in respect of the Environment (Protection) Act, 1986 are regularly uploaded on the ministry's website even before the final approval/decision of the MoEF is obtained. This has been done to ensure public accountability. This also includes environmental clearances given under the EIA Notification of 2006 issued under the Environment (Protection) Act, 1986. Henceforth, in addition to the above, all forest clearances given under the Forest (Conservation) Act, 1980 may now be uploaded on the ministry's website.

9. Completion of the exercise undertaken by each state/UT government in compliance of this court's order dated 12 December 1996, wherein inter alia each state/UT government was directed to constitute an expert committee to identify the areas which are 'forests' irrespective of whether they are so notified, recognized or classified under any law, and irrespective of the land of such 'forest' and the areas which were earlier 'forests' but stand degraded, denuded, and cleared, culminating in preparation of geo-referenced district forest maps containing the details of the location and boundary of each plot of land that may be defined as 'forest' for the purpose of the Forest (Conservation) Act, 1980.

10. Incorporating appropriate safeguards in the environment clearance process to eliminate chance of the grant of environment clearance to projects involving diversion of forest land by considering such forest land as non-forest, a flow chart depicting, the tentative nature and manner of incorporating them proposed safeguards, to be finalized after consultation with the state/UT governments.

11. The public consultation or public hearing as it is commonly known, is a mandatory requirement of the environment clearance process and provides an effective forum for any person aggrieved by any aspect of any project to register and seek redressal of his/her grievances.

12. The MoEF will prepare a comprehensive policy for inspection, verification, and monitoring, and the overall procedure relating to the grant of forest clearances and identification of forests in consultation with the states (given that forests fall under entry 17A of the Concurrent List).

The LaFarge judgment puts in place a structure that will make the process of environmental governance more effective. The MoEF is of the view that the judiciary has played a pivotal role in environmental and forest management. It is a matter of some satisfaction for the MoEF that the NGT set up pursuant to a Supreme Court decision became operational on 4 July 2011. In addition, over Rs 2,000 crore under the CAMPA account have already been disbursed by the MoEF to states following to a Supreme Court decision of July 2009.

The MoEF will continue to work closely with the judiciary in the pursuit of sustainable development.

Letter to Union Minister of Finance Pranab Mukherjee with Comments on the Mines and Minerals (Development and Regulation) Bill, 2010

25 JUNE 2010

As you are aware, a Group of Ministers was constituted on 14 June under your chairmanship, and of which I am a member to consider the draft 'Mines and Minerals (Development and Regulation) Bill, 2010'.

I have gone through the draft Bill and have the following observations to make for your consideration.

Competitive Bidding

1. The Bill calls for competitive bidding for PL (Prospecting Licence), LAPL (Large Area Prospecting Licence) and ML (Mining Lease) as per Section 13(1) and 13(4). However, there is a proviso that competitive bidding can happen only if no existing applications for prospecting or mining is pending. This will render a competitive bidding process ineffective, since in most states, there are PLs or MLs pending for almost every piece of land where there is a possibility of ores. This proviso should be removed and all mining leases should be given by competitive bidding basis.

2. For non-notified areas, the Bill states that the first-come-first-serve principle should apply. Since there are numerous legacy applications pending, allocating concessions/mines on this basis will result in supernormal profits for mining companies. Hence, even these should be given through competitive bidding.

3. Where the risk involved is high, such as that of diamonds, the party that has won the LAPL/PL by bidding could have the first right to the ML, and competitive bidding for ML may not be necessary.

Benefits to the Mining State

To enable states to leverage the mineral resources mined in their state for industrial development within their states, there should be a proviso allowing states to restrict bidding to only those firms that will set up industry in the state. Further, a large share (for example, 75–80 per cent) of the extracted ore could be reserved for captive use.

Benefits to Local Area and Local Communities

1. The provision to share benefits with communities or people having usufruct/traditional rights in the area that is to be mined, Para 4(ix), is very commendable. However, rather than equity, other models, such as sharing annual revenue may be considered and may be easier to implement.
2. If the equity model is to be pursued, giving only equity directly to the families may not be ideal as sometimes there are very few families in these areas, and dividing equity among a few families may not be the best use of resources. An alternative is to give a good rehabilitation package to these local families, and the remaining amount from the 26 per cent equity could be used for local area development such as setting up of schools, hospitals, livelihood generation, afforestation, etc.
3. A polluter-pays principle could be laid down in the Bill, which mandates an environmental levy for pollution caused by the mining activity during the life of the project. This environmental levy should be directly used for combating local environmental degradation through the state department of environment with the information also passed on to the MoEF.

Monitoring and Closure

1. The implementation aspect of the steps highlighted in para 4(x), which relate to mine closures remains weak. Like in the case of

environmental clearance, there could be a public hearing during the time of closure of the mine to ensure community oversight. The MoEF should be engaged in this phase to ensure appropriate safeguards are maintained during closure and reforestation can be undertaken. Currently, the primary responsibility is with the Indian Bureau of Mines, which does not have the resources or the manpower to carry out the exercise.

2. A mechanism should be established to monitor compliance of the conditions laid down while granting environmental clearances. Currently, firms are required to submit written reports on their compliance efforts. However, there is no independent physical verification of this.

I request that the Group of Ministers considers these suggestions. I am marking a copy of this letter to the Minister of Mines as well.

Excerpts from the Debate in the Lok Sabha on the National Green Tribunal (NGT) Bill

30 APRIL 2010

... Sir, twenty-four Hon. members have presented their views spread over a three-day period. Broadly, the idea of having an NGT has been supported. There have been some criticisms in respect of many of the provisions of the Bill, which I will respond to as quickly as I can.

Before I respond to the criticisms, I would like to mention that the NGT Bill is one element of a revised or a reformed or a restructured approach to environmental governance. On the one side, we need an effective Environmental Protection Authority that actually monitors compliance that ensures implementation of laws, and on the other side, you have the NGT Bill, which deals with the civil dimensions of implementation of these laws. So, the NGT Bill is not an answer to the problems of environment and forest. It provides an opportunity for people to claim civil damages arising out of the non-implementation or the wrong implementation of the laws relating to the environment and forests. So, do not see this in isolation.

In the monsoon session of Parliament, I hope to bring forward a legislation to establish a National Environmental Protection Authority (NEPA). The NEPA will be charged with the responsibility of ensuring proper implementation of the laws relating to environment and forest. And a part of the implementation is to provide an opportunity for individuals of our country to claim civil damages out of the non-implementation of the laws. So, there is a judicial dimension to governance. There is an executive dimension to governance. This Bill deals only with the judicial dimension.

Sir, many members have criticized the Bill for many of its provisions. Let me say straightaway that I am going to bring forward ten amendments today, which will take care of 90 per cent of the problems that have been expressed by the Hon. members.

The most important amendment that I am going to bring forward is an amendment to Clause 18(2)(e), which will provide an opportunity for any individual—for any citizen of India—to approach the NGT. This was the criticism that was made; that it does not provide an opportunity for individuals and it provides a limited access. But I am going to bring forward this amendment today to Clause 18(2)(e), which will expand the definition of 'persons aggrieved'. So, any person aggrieved can approach the NGT.

Sir, the second important criticism that was mentioned was that this Bill does not have the foundational principles, which should govern its functioning. That is why I am going to amend Section 19(a), which will bring principles of sustainable development. Precautionary principles, polluter-pays principles, and intergenerational equity, will all be part of this amendment.

The third important amendment that I am going to bring forward is that this Act will come into force simultaneously. It would not be section by section. The entire Act will come into force at one go. This was also a criticism that had been made by some Hon. members.

The fourth amendment that I propose to bring forward is that the decisions of the NGT can be appealed in the Supreme Court. So, anybody who is aggrieved by the decision of the NGT can go to the Supreme Court. Mr. Rajiv had raised this issue that suppose this tribunal gives a decision against community rights, and the Bill as it stood today, there was no appeal against that decision. But the amendment I am going to bring forward to Section 21 will provide for an appeal to the Supreme Court on any decision of the NGT. The fifth amendment is about the place of sitting. We did not specify the territorial jurisdiction. We are now going to specify the territorial jurisdiction in the amendment as well.

The sixth amendment relates to the number of members, the judicial members, the expert members. We will have a minimum of ten judicial members, a minimum of ten expert members; and not exceeding twenty. We specified that in the Act itself.

The seventh important amendment I am going to bring forward is the amendment which will enable a deadlock to be broken so that we give the chairperson of the tribunal the authority to break the deadlock in case there is a deadlock.

Then, I am going to bring forward some other amendments in order to maintain the integrity and the credibility of the tribunal. Sir, these amendments, which I will propose at the end of my speech today, will, I believe, go a long way in assuaging the concerns of many Hon. members.

I would just like to deal with two or three significant criticisms that have been made that are not dealt with in these amendments. I propose to come back to these criticisms in the rules that we will frame. The rules will be framed; they will be put on our website; they will be laid on the table of the House; and the Hon. members of Parliament will have every opportunity of responding to these rules. So, I will not do anything without parliamentary approval of the rules that will govern this Act.

Sir, there was a criticism that Schedule I of this Bill will give an opportunity for the government to amend these Acts. That is the complete misreading of Schedule I. There are seven laws in Schedule I. We are not going to amend any law in Schedule I. Please be under no fear on this. There is not going to be an amendment of the Forest Conservation Act or amendment of the Environment (Protection) Act, 1986. Schedule I only lists those Acts for which the NGT has jurisdiction. What we are saying is that we can expand Schedule I or delete Schedule I by the government and we will lay that decision on the floor of the House. We do not want to amend the Act every time we want to do it. We want to add or delete by notification. Of course, we will be laying that notification on the table of the House. So, it is wrong as Mr Mangani Lal Mandal was trying to say or some other members were saying that this gives the power to the government to amend the Act. No. We are not going to amend any Act in Schedule I. Schedule I only says that these are the Acts for which the jurisdiction of the NGT applies.

Sir, there was also some criticism of one year and five years saying: 'in Bhopal, the effects are long-ranging and why are we limiting to five years'. I will clarify this. In the rules, it will be five years from the date the injury begins to manifest itself and the cause is attributable to the environmental damage. I will make this very clear in the rules. The Hon. members should not have any fears on this.

As far as members are concerned, we will have a selection committee. This selection committee will ensure that this does not become a parking place for retired civil servants. This is a fear that has been expressed, and I assure the hon. members that we will have a transparent selection committee.

Environmentalists, people with background in environment, will be made members of the NGT. Activists may not be members but if activists have the requisite educational qualifications, I do not see any reason why an activist should be debarred from being a member of the NGT.

So, I think regarding the rules, many of the rules that will govern the selection of members will be made clear, and I can assure the hon. members that we will not be found wanting on this score.

One or two other criticisms have come. How is this different from the previous National Environment Tribunal? I want to make it clear that the National Environment Tribunal of 1995 dealt only with hazardous chemical substances. It had limited scope, whereas this NGT deals with the Water Act, Air Act, and Environment Protection Act. It deals with the Forests Conservation Act. It also deals with the Biological Diversity Act. So, its scope is much larger. All that I am trying to accomplish by having the NGT is to provide an opportunity for people, who feel aggrieved by the non-implementation of these laws, to seek civil damages, to go to the NGT, and we have specified that the NGT should give a decision normally within six months.

So, we are trying to bring this. There are 5,600 cases in our judiciary today relating to environment. I am sure the number of cases will increase. We need specialized environmental courts. The Supreme Court has said this. The Law Commission has said this. India will be one of the few countries that will have such a specialized environmental court. I believe Australia and New Zealand are the two countries that have such specialized tribunals. I think India would be one of the few countries to have a specialized environment tribunal too.

I want to assure the Hon. members that let us give this NGT a try. If, after a couple of months, we feel the need for amending some of the provisions, we will come back to Parliament. I have a completely open mind on this. But I believe it is important to set a beginning, to start the process, and give this NGT an opportunity to perform. I will stop here.

I have also said in the past—and I want to repeat it here—that my intention is to locate the NGT in Bhopal, not in Delhi. I do not want to create another Delhi-based institution. I want to locate it in Bhopal because Bhopal was the scene of the humanity's worst industrial environmental tragedy in 1984 and by locating the NGT in Bhopal, I think our government and our Parliament would be showing some small sensitivity to that great tragedy. We can never obliterate that tragedy from our memories but by setting the NGT in Bhopal, I think we would send a signal that we mean business. It will have four benches in different parts of the country. We will expand the number of benches depending on the generosity of my senior colleague, the minister of law, who has just walked in and is sitting right next to me.

We will follow a circuit approach so that access is not difficult for ordinary people. People will not come to courts. Courts will go to people. I assure you this—the tribunal will go to the people. People will not come to the tribunal. I want to assure this and give it a chance. If, at the end of one year, I am proved wrong, I will come back to Parliament, if I am still in this post, and come for the amendment.

I think I have kept my time.

So, with these few words, I would now urge the Hon. members to extend their full support to the NGT Bill.

Excerpts from the Debate in the Rajya Sabha on the NGT Bill, 2010

5 MAY 2010

… Sir, with your permission, if I could just make a couple of very brief opening remarks before I listen to the interventions of the Hon. members. Sir, twenty-four speakers spoke in favour of this Bill in the Lok Sabha, and I responded to those interventions and moved certain very important amendments to the NGT Bill which I want to immediately place on record because there might be criticisms that Hon. members may have.

The first and the most important amendment that has been approved by the Lok Sabha is that any aggrieved party, any individual, can approach the NGT for civil damages arising out of the no implementation of laws as listed in Schedule I of the Bill. Second, in response to the concerns raised by many Hon. members I have moved an amendment and the Lok Sabha has approved the amendment that the decisions of the NGT can be appealed to in the Supreme Court. It is not the final word; you can still go to the Supreme Court and ask for a review of the decision taken by the NGT. The third amendment that was moved and approved was related to the number of judicial members, to the number of expert members, to the number of benches, and the manner of functioning of the tribunal. All I want to say is that as we envisaged it today, there will be one central tribunal in one place and there will be four benches of this tribunal. These benches will operate on a circuit bench model so that instead of people coming to the tribunal, the tribunal will make every effort to go to the people—particularly in the areas where environment and forestry laws are maximum in their non-implementation.

Sir, I also want to say here that in my reply in the Lok Sabha, I announced that it is my intention to locate the NGT in Bhopal because Bhopal is the scene of humanity's worst environmental disaster that took place twenty-six years ago. I believe that through a small step to be taken by my ministry, my government, and Parliament, Bhopal should also be known for an important step forward in a positive sense in the matters relating to the environment. Today, Bhopal is associated only with an environmental tragedy and I hope that with the establishment of NGT, Bhopal would also be known for environmental jurisprudence that would bring to individual citizens the benefits of implementation of laws relating to environment and forests. Sir, this is not an answer to our problem; this is only one aspect of environmental governance.

I am introducing this Bill today and moving it in the Rajya Sabha. In the monsoon session, I intend to introduce another Bill to establish NEPA, that would strengthen the executive's capability to implement and monitor the laws relating to environment and forests.

The NGT Bill is confined to giving to individual citizens civil damages arising out of the non-implementation of the laws. I think, this matter has become very crucial. There have been Supreme Court rulings. There has been the 186th report of the Law Commission. And, I might mention here that this report of the Law Commission was submitted in 2003 to the then law minister, who happens to be the leader of the Opposition today. So, there is certain continuity in what we are proposing, and I hope that the Hon. members of the Rajya Sabha would extend to this Bill the same support that came in the Lok Sabha. But, I do want to assure Hon. members that if there are suggestions and if there are points made, I will certainly take them into consideration while framing the rules. I will lay the rules on the table of the House before the green tribunal becomes actually operational.

Jairam Ramesh: Mr Chairman, Sir, first of all, I want to express my gratitude to the thirteen speakers who have spoken today. They have been very generous in their comments on me and fairly critical as far as the Bill is concerned. I am grateful for both those sentiments.

The Vice-Chairman (Professor P.J. Kurien): Not to the Chair?

Jairam Ramesh: I also thank the Chair, Sir, for being very indulgent to those people who made positive comments towards me.

Sir, I know I have limited time, I will not have an opportunity of responding to every individual point or criticism that has been made by the thirteen speakers. I will make it a point in the next couple of days to respond to each individual member in writing on each of the individual points that have been made. That is an assurance that I am giving in this House.

However, Sir, I would like to address some big concerns that have been raised by many Hon. members.

First of all, the Standing Committee made twelve recommendations. I have accepted ten out of the twelve recommendations. Sir, I plead guilty. Mr Bal Apte used many Latin phrases. Let me also demonstrate my knowledge of Latin. Mea culpa! Mea maxima culpa! I was at fault because we already had the National Environment Tribunal in the past. The experience was not positive. We are planning on a legislation for a NEPA. So, the National Environment Protection Tribunal was ruled out. One option that I did consider was National Environment and Forest Protection Tribunal. It was too much of a tongue-twister. Sir, I am a creature of the modern age. I plead guilty. The word 'green' in the minds of many is associated with environment and that is why I called it, instinctively, the National Green Tribunal. I am not trivializing it. But if Hon. members feel that I am trivializing it, I am more than happy to go back and think of an alternative title and come back in the Monsoon session with an alternative title. But I would request you take my word for it; let the National Green Tribunal stand and let the seriousness of this tribunal be demonstrated by its work, irrespective of the fact that it is called the National Green Tribunal.

Sir, one of the problems that we have faced is that many speakers today commented on the legislation 'as introduced in the Lok Sabha', which came to the Rajya Sabha. There is a big difference between the legislation 'as introduced in the Lok Sabha' and the legislation 'as passed by the Lok Sabha'. I wish my good friend, Mr Bal Apte, had seen the legislation somewhat carefully. Take his criticism, for example, that this NGT ignores the principle of no-fault liability. The Section 17(3) following the amendment introduced in the Lok Sabha on 30 April reads, and I quote, 'The Tribunal shall in case of an accident apply the principle of no-fault', which is exactly the sentiment expressed by Mr Bal Apte. So, there are some points that have been taken care of. The 'polluter -pays' principle, the principle of sustainable development, the principle of inter-generational equity, and the principle of no-fault have found place in the revised legislation as passed by the Lok Sabha.

Sir, my good friend, Mr Rudy, asked why the Wildlife Protection Act is not in Schedule I.

Sir, the basic purpose of this tribunal is to decide on civil cases. The Wildlife Protection Act leads us into criminal cases. But, if there are civil issues, civil damage issues, and you yourself have brought out a very colourful example of the birds and the bees, and it is perfectly within the domain of the NGT to adjudicate. But the larger issues of the Wildlife (Protection) Act, 1972 involve criminal cases. Sansar Chand is being prosecuted for a criminal offence, whereas the purpose in the NGT is to provide civil damages for the non-implementation of the environment protection laws.

Sir, many members, particularly my friends from Kerala, Bengal, and Odisha, are concerned about Schedule I. Their concern is that we have listed seven laws in Schedule I, and they feel that we have got the freedom to amend Schedule I. No, Sir. This is a complete misreading of Schedule I. Under no circumstances is the Government of India going to take the right to amend the Forest Conservation Act, which is in Schedule I. No. All that we are saying is, to add a No. 8 or a No. 9 to Schedule I, we will do it by notification. We will not amend the Act, we will do it by notification, and we will lay the notification on the table of the House. So, Schedule I law does not mean we will amend the laws in Schedule I. We will only add or subtract by notification and lay the notification on the table of the House because the process of amending the Act is very cumbersome. And, incidentally, Sir, that is one of the recommendations of the Standing Committee, which we did not accept.

Sir, I am entirely in agreement with the criticism of the Bill that five benches are insufficient for our country. Sir, Mr Bal Apte raised the question about the number of cases which are there. Sir, 5,616 cases, as available from the Manu Patra today, are pending in various courts of our country on matters relating to environment and forest. Now, it is anybody's guess how long these cases are going to continue. Sir, I faced a dilemma. On the one side, the Law Commission, the Supreme Court, Justice Bhagwati in the famous Oleum case of 1987, all of them said, set up specialized environment courts. So, the ideal situation would have been to upgrade the district and sessions courts, the high courts, the Supreme Court, but we know how difficult that is. I agree that the tribunal approach is somewhat like a bypass surgery approach. It is because in a tribunal you have more flexibility, you devise your own procedures, you can bring in outside experts and you can have speedier adjudication. We have provided, for example, a normal time limit of six months to adjudicate cases in the NGT. So, Sir, I am entirely in sympathy with this criticism that has been made. Today, anybody can go to the district and sessions courts judge and say that my leg has been damaged because of hazardous waste in the nearby water source. And he can spend the next thirty years fighting that case. So, do we want that system, or, do we want a specialized system with the prospect of a speedier redressal of the grievance? I opted for the latter, and I am entirely in agreement with the sense of the House that five benches are certainly insufficient for our country. And, I instinctively will agree with the Law Commission's recommendation, Dr Maitreyan had raised this, the Standing Committee of which he was a distinguished chairman in the past had also raised this, and I said in the Lok Sabha—and I had the advantage of the law minister sitting next to me, but today I don't have that advantage. In the Lok Sabha, I looked at the law minister and I said that one of the first things that I would go to him is for expansion of benches. I have got the financial allocation for five benches, and the House has my assurance that I will expand the network of benches.

But, let us begin with this. If the workload increases, if the caseload increases, we will expand. This is my assurance to you and this expansion can come in the first year itself.

Sir, there has been a lot of criticism on the manner of selection. I debated also on how to select and, I think, more than specifying a procedure by an Act, conventions have to develop by which we select people. Sir, it is my intention to consult the leader of the Opposition, of course, the prime minister will be involved, the law minister will be involved, and I will be involved in the selection of the chairperson of the NGT. Now, once the chairperson of the NGT is selected, we will in the rules—that I will bring forward in the monsoon session, hopefully—stipulate the procedure for selecting the judicial members and the expert members. Normally what happens is, the minister selects the chairperson and all the members. No, I do not want to do that because, Sir, I am not bringing this Bill for my tenure. I am doing this for the future. This is not a *main hoon na* principle here. It has to outlive.

V. Maitreyan: Chidambaramji only said *main hoon na*.

Jairam Ramesh: I must echo in my senior colleague that it is not a *main hoon na* principle here. We have to institutionalize the selection process. So, my approach is, we will select the chairperson of the NGT; in consultation with the NGT chairperson, we will devise a transparent set of rules which Parliament will be in the know of for selecting the judicial members and the technical members.

Sir, in response to my friend Mr Raut, I would like to say that we need technical members. Environment is a scientific topic. Environmental activism is one thing. You can be the world's greatest environmental activist. But, you need specialized knowledge, for example, to adjudicate a claim that comes to you that says that my respiratory disease has increased because of the pollution, because of the air that I am breathing. This will be one of the cases that will come before the NGT. Mr Raut, while I have the greatest respect for environmental activists; in fact, the accusation against me is that I am friendlier towards activists than any other community in this country. The fact of the matter is, when we are setting up a tribunal, we need judicial members because there are matters of law involved here; and we need technical members who can provide the scientific and technical inputs. Environment is becoming increasingly an interdisciplinary scientific issue. So, we will not rule out the activists but, all I am saying is that environmental activism will have its place and adjudication based on legal and technical criteria will have its place.

Sir, there was also a concern as to who can approach the NGT. I want to say clearly, categorically and unequivocally that anybody can approach the NGT. Not just any aggrieved person, but anybody. Any NGO, any journalist, any media organization, any social activist group, any SPCB, any state government, the central government, or anybody can approach the NGT. This is the amendment that was passed in the Lok Sabha and I want to assure the hon. members that we are not choking access to the NGT. In fact, in our country, it would be difficult for individuals to come to the NGT, to begin with. So, we will necessarily find representations being made to the NGT on behalf of individuals by NGOs, by social action groups, by activists that Mr Raut so rightly talks about.

So, in this way I think, we have opened up the doors of the NGT. But, as I said and I repeat, geographically, we need a much larger footprint for the NGT and five benches simply is not enough.

Sir, I will address two or three important points very quickly. Both Mr Apte and Mr Rudy, and many others, talked about this issue of 'substantial claim'. Now, Sir, this word 'substantial claim', I have not invented it, as Mr Apte knows. Mr Apte is a distinguished lawyer. I have not invented it; it is there in many statutes. It is a legislative device that is used in order to define what the gravity of claim is. But, in fact, if I just request the Hon. members to look at Schedule II of this Bill, this is the substantial claim. For the first time we are giving operational meaning to what is substantial claim. What is substantial claim—death; what is substantial claim—permanent, temporary or total or partial disability or any other injury of sickness. This is the substantial claim. Loss of wages is a substantial claim; damage to private property is a substantial claim. I have listed here fifteen grounds under which individuals or organizations can approach the NGT. As of now, there is no omnibus or any other category. So, this is an exhaustive list. As the tribunal gains jurisprudence experience, we will review Scheduled II. Mr Apte's criticism, while I take in the right spirit, I have tried to give, in fact, more operational meaning to what is a substantial claim. A person in a critically polluted area can come to the NGT and make a substantial claim under any of these headings. This, I think, is a big step forward. Sir, some members, both in the Rajya Sabha and the Lok Sabha, said that this fine of Rs 25 crore is a very small sum. Sir, there is some confusion on what this Rs 25 crore is. This Rs 25 crore is a fine on a party who does not implement the orders of the tribunal. Rs 25 crore is not the penalty or the damage limit which an individual can get. If a company or a party does not implement the order of the tribunal, he has to pay a fine of Rs 25 crore. So, it is only for the non-compliance of the orders of the tribunal. The tribunal is free to award any damage, there is no limit. In fact, one of the Acts in Schedule I is the Public Liability Insurance Act of 1991. As you know, Sir, the maximum you can claim under the Public Liability Insurance Act is Rs 25,000, plus Rs 12,500 or near about, for medical expenses. So, Mr Apte knows this. So, under this NGT Bill, the NGT can well award a few lakhs of rupees under the Public Liability Insurance Act, whereas today under the Public Liability Insurance Act the maximum cap is Rs 37,500. So, this is an example of how much flexibility we are bringing into the system through the NGT.

Sir, final point I want to make is that this criticism has been repeated that this is a pro-culprit Bill. To use Mr Bal Apte's language, this is a Bill that will protect the culprits and it will not protect the citizens. Sir, Bal Apte is very, very unfair. He will be unfair to me personally because in the last eleven months if anything is there, the clamour is that I have tightened up and not opened up. But, as I said, Mr Bal Apte's concern is not with an individual, it is with the system. But what this Bill does is actually contrary to what Mr Bal Apte fears. It actually puts pressure on the offenders, on the polluters, on the encroachers because it is for the first time that you are providing a legal redress to individual citizens, to NGOs, to SPCBs that actually can go to the NGT and claim civil damages.

This is not there today. It is there. It takes a long time. But, here we are providing a specialized, faster track system in order to ensure that people who are habitual offenders, habitual polluters do get the message that if in case they keep indulging in this kind of behaviour, there is a legal system to take care of people who are badly affected by the non-implementation of these laws. Sir, I have just got a note that there are two more Bills and I must finish. I would like to say that while I am grateful to the Hon. members, my request to them is...

Balavant alias Bal Apte: Before the minister completes, I have only one sentence to say that 'no fault liability' under Section 17 in respect of death is one thing and the principle of strict liability in Rylands versus Feltcher is a law of torts principle, which is missing in Section 20.

Jairam Ramesh: Sir, I will certainly look into it.

Rajiv Pratap Rudy: Fortunately, in the House, we have two *main hoon na*. Not one, but two.

Jairam Ramesh: It cannot be on the *main hoon na* principle.

Sir, I have said that while I appreciate the sentiments of the Hon. members, I would request them to give the NGT a chance to get off the ground. In the next five–six months, we hope that the five Benches will be set up in five different parts of the country. The main one anchored in Bhopal, as I mentioned, will take off. They will develop procedures of work. Case law will develop over a period of time and I think, as experience accumulates we will always have an opportunity of reviewing the functioning of these tribunals. I would be the first to come back to Parliament and seek further amendments to the NGT Act, if the need so arises.

Najma A. Heptulla: Sir, there are three questions. You said that anybody—activists, environmental activists, or anybody—can go. But, Sir, there are environmental activists and activists. They don't leave it open-ended because there is a very thin line between development and activism. So, you will have to take care of it. The second point is that you are going to bring the rules. I am very happy because for every legislation I would like that the government brings draft rules, subject to change as in the future but that rules remain with the ministry and it takes more than six months to submit the rules. I am chairman of the Committee on Subordinate Legislation, and we have seen that the rules have not been submitted for six years and the government continues to implement without the rules being submitted to Parliament. So, please take care that what rules you bring in the next session, that you have said, will be protected and they will also take care that it should not remain an open-ended tribunal, where anybody can stop and blackmail development.

Jairam Ramesh: Sir, I will just say one thing. The hon. member has my assurance with the rulings. As I have said, it will be my serious endeavour to bring it in the monsoon session of Parliament. But before that, I will have an opportunity of putting the tribunals on our website for larger public comment. Sir, the Hon. member has raised a concern. In fact, Sir, I was being criticized by some of our party colleagues for introducing a section in the Bill which provides for 'vexatious' petitions. Now, there are petitions here for the tribunal to throw out petitions which are doctored, which obviously fulfil political objectives, and, not necessarily environmental objectives. So, there is a fine dividing line that we have to draw, but my sense is that with a sensitive chairperson in the NGT, with rules and procedures properly drafted, we will be able to follow this middle path between environment and forests.

Bharat Kumar Raut: When I speak about the people and NGOs working in tribal areas, it does not mean that I am opposing the experts. I am saying, with judiciary, experts, why cannot you have some people who are working in that area that gives humane face to it and become more authentic. Thank you.

Shantaram Laxman Naik: Sir, I am on High Court jurisdiction. Since the government is constituting the tribunal, people will go to the High Court under Article 32 and also to the Supreme Court. So, what is the use of the tribunal? Thank you.

Jairam Ramesh: Sir, I don't want to get into this debate once again. But, all I want to say is—these points that had been raised earlier had been debated by the law minister who just walked in. The home minister also was very much part of this discussion. And, we debated this issue of allowing concurrent jurisdiction. In fact, it was the Hon. home minister, who is a very distinguished lawyer, who used the word 'firm shopping'. But, we should avoid 'firm shopping'. We should not give people the availability of multiple forums. That is why we chose specialization and speed versus larger network. Let us give this a chance. And, as I have said in response to the sentiments of the hon. members, we are provided for an appeal in the Supreme Court which, I think, is adequate for the purpose of our discussion.

Letter to the Prime Minister on Issues Related to Forest Administration in Left-Wing Extremism-Affected Areas

14 September 2010
You may recall that the MoEF had organized a National Conference on Forestry Administration in LWE-affected areas last month. You had yourself met with department of forest officials from the thirty-five

worst-affected LWE districts. The home minister, tribal affairs minister, deputy chairman, Planning Commission were invited to interact with the field-level forest officers of these districts to discuss their experiences and difficulties in forestry administration. Representatives from various organizations and individuals with experience of working in these areas were also invited to participate in this conference.

I wish to bring to your notice a few of the important action points that have emerged from these discussions.

Points Needing Action from MoEF

It was decided that the forest department would be more pro-active in dealing with cases where critical public infrastructure works are being taken up by the local administration in these districts and if required a special mechanism can be worked out within the ambit of the Forest (Conservation) Act, 1980 to expedite such clearances.

In the case of the Panchayat Extension to Scheduled Areas (PESA) Act, 1996, the forest department will take steps to ensure that the joint forest management committees work under the overall guidance and control of the *gram sabha* as is envisaged in the Act.

With regard to the Forest Rights Act, 2006, the forest department would actively cooperate with the nodal agency, which is the tribal welfare department, and expedite the process of settling of these rights. It was also noted that while individual rights are being settled in large numbers, the community rights of the local communities are not being done so at the same rate. This will be looked into.

The tribal communities face a lot of problems when the forest officials book criminal cases against them in the course of enforcing the Indian Forest Act, 1927. The forest officials are forced to book criminal cases for violations as per the Act due to the very low value up to which the department can compound the offence. Necessary amendment has to be made to this provision so that petty violations can be compounded at the department level, so that the tribals do not have to go through the harsh processes of criminal justice system with which they are not very familiar and which they cannot afford.

It was felt that the main Acts which deal with the rights of the tribal communities and the Forest (Conservation) Act, 1980, do not always appear to be working in consonance, leading to certain delays and some dilution in purpose. It was decided that all such areas, where there seem to be certain differences in understanding of these legislations, will be identified and necessary steps will be taken to bring all of them in harmony with each other.

The ministry, at the time of giving permissions can consider making it mandatory for companies that plan to operate in these areas to open vocational training institutes for training the local youth and employing them in their operations for a minimum period.

Points Needing Action from State Governments

There is acute shortage of personnel at the cutting-edge level and that is hampering them in taking up the regular activities of forest protection and curbing the illegal activities that take place in these remote areas. An aggressive recruitment drive needs to be taken up especially at the cutting-edge level. More youth, particularly from the local communities, need to be recruited at the field level even if it means that certain minimum qualifications need to be brought down.

The state governments should consider raising forces like community foresters or para-foresters, who are not permanent but engaged from the local communities for limited time periods on a fixed wage. These people can then be engaged in the regular forest activities being taken up by the department and also in the large-scale activities being proposed by the department like the Green India Mission and the CAMPA activities.

Minor forest produce (MFP) is one important items on which the tribal population depends on for their livelihoods. The tribals are not able to maximize their returns on this collection due to the presence of middlemen who finance them and due to the lack of proper marketing opportunities. The states should—in collaboration with the forest department and the tribal welfare ministry—take up activities like capacity building of the tribal populations in better and sustainable practices of MFP harvesting, providing the communities with institutional finance so that middle men can be done away with, provide support and policy guidelines for coming up with a minimum support price (MSP) mechanism like it is provided for agricultural produce and to provide institutionalized marketing avenues.

One very important issue that is impacting the tribal communities is that of resettlement and rehabilitation (R&R). A robust mechanism needs to be put in place to work out the issues of R&R, specific case-wise, and also ensure that the implementation of the R&R by the respective state governments is according to the laid-out plan. Strict monitoring needs to be done to ensure time bound implementation of the same.

Points that Need Action from the Planning Commission

It is extremely important that modernization of the forest department is taken up as a priority to equip them in tackling the difficult conditions of work and the special challenges encountered in these remote areas. A Central Government initiative for modernization of the forest department, especially at the cutting-edge level, on the lines of modernization of police administration scheme, would go a long way in achieving this.

In addition to the modernization of these divisional offices with new buildings for offices and residences of the personnel, sufficient vehicles need to be provided to them to improve their mobility in these difficult terrains.

Points Needing Action from the Ministry of Home Affairs, Government of India

It is noticed that there is a greater shortage of staff in these areas compared to the rest of the state due to lack of proper facilities and the increased sense of danger in these areas. Incentives to the personnel serving in these areas like life insurance, risk allowance, and other benefits, on a par with the police personnel working under similar conditions, will help in further encouraging and motivating them.

It was decided that in the next home minister's review with the chief ministers of the LWE-affected states, a session would be devoted to the issue of the modernization of the forest administration like fresh recruitments, developing the infrastructure, giving incentives to the staff, etc.

Points Needing Action from Ministry of Tribal Affairs

There was a unanimous feeling that the National Tribal Policy, which is due to be notified needs to be notified soon and the establishment of the National Tribal Advisory Council, which has been under contemplation for long, also needs to be taken up.

Although, provided with constitutional safeguards and protected by several laws, the tribal communities are still very badly affected by issues like land alienation and chronic indebtedness which push them into abject poverty. These extremely vulnerable communities are very often seen struggling to get their rights enforced by the state, which leads to a certain disenchantment with the rule of law as it exists for them. This played up by the extremist elements leads to some of the people from these communities being led astray. It was felt that administration at all levels needs to be more sensitive to these issues and strive to implement these laws strictly both in letter and spirit.

Letter to Chief Minister of Uttarakhand, Ramesh Pokhriyal Nishank on Illegal Sand Mining in Stretches of the Ganga

6 JANUARY 2010

As you may be aware that concerns have been raised regarding the deteriorating quality of water of the river Ganga due to illegal sand mining in the river stretches at Haridwar. Some of the saints are reported to have sat on a fast unto death to protest against such illegal mining. Having realized the sensitivity of the whole matter, a team of officers from my ministry had visited the site on 10 December 2009.

It has been reported by the site visit team that mining of sand is being undertaken at Missarpur and Ajitpur sites in river Ganga at Haridwar, which was observed to be suspended during the visit of the team. The mining activity—although, reported to be undertaken through an administrative order of the government of Uttarakhand—is without any formal lease granted by the state government for these mining areas.

As you may be aware, under the provisions of Mines and Minerals (Development and Regulation) Act, 1957, powers have been delegated to the respective state governments to frame rules to control illegal mining and to deal with the situation arising there from. Further, I also invite reference to my earlier letter dated 9 December 2009, wherein the requirement of obtaining prior environmental clearance to such mining projects under the provisions of EIA Notification, 2006 was highlighted. I have been informed that no proposal for environmental clearance in respect of sand mining at Missarpur and Ajitpur site in the river Ganga in Haridwar has been received in my ministry.

Since the subject of illegal mining is entirely within the domain of the state government, I would urge you to kindly have the matter looked into so that necessary instructions are issued to the concerned officers to take immediate action to stop illegal mining going on in your state, including at the sites at Missarpur and Ajitpur in Haridwar, before the situation takes any ugly turn.

Letter to Chief Minister Digamber Kamat on Violations of the CRZ Notification

22 MARCH 2010
Kindly refer to your letter dated 4 February 2010 requesting the ministry for regularizing the structures constructed in violation of CRZ Notification, 1991 of traditional inhabitants in the CRZ area in the state of Goa.

I have got the above proposal examined in detail and the opinion given by Advocate General, state of Goa, including the orders of the Hon. High Court of Bombay at Panjim bench in Writ Petition No. 2 of 2006 and other cases concerned to the above matter.

My ministry's stand is as follows:

1. As per the CRZ Notification, 1991, CRZ that is the area up to 200 metres to High Tide Line, is no development zone and in zone 'no construction shall be permitted within the zone except for repairs of existing authorized structures not exceeding Floor Space Index, existing plinth area and existing density. For permissible activities under the notification including facilities essential for such facilities'.
2. The list of violations were examined and it was found that the majority of the construction included net-mending sheds, toilets, boat repair yards, extension of the existing house where temporary structure for warehousing of fish, and other products.

   i. The above constructions are permissible under the CRZ Notification, 1991. These structures, however, have been categorized as violation since they have not obtained permission from the Goa Coastal Zone Management Authority.
   ii. The orders of the Bombay High Court with regard to jetties in writ Petition No. 142 of 2008 is relevant in this matter. The High Court in its judgment had directed the jetty owners who have constructed without seeking permission under the notification

to obtain necessary approvals from the MoEF/Goa Coastal Zone Management Authority. Accordingly, the ministry had accorded post-facto clearance to the jetties. This line of action can be considered for the above issue.

iii. Hence, the Government of Goa needs to file an affidavit on the above lines in the above Writ Petition and initiate actions accordingly, including obtaining approval from Goa Coastal Zone Management Authority for such structures.

3. With regard to the constructions between 200–500 m, as per the CRZ Notification,1991 'constructions/reconstruction of dwelling units between 200 and 500 m of High Tide Line permitted so long it is within the ambit of traditional rights and customary uses such as existing fishing villages and *gaothans*. Building permission for such construction/reconstruction will be subject to the conditions that the total number of dwelling units shall not be more than twice the number of the existing units: total covered area on all floors shall not exceed 33 per cent of the plot size, the overall height not exceeding 9 m with not more than two floors'.

The issue here is that in the CRZ area, the dwelling units have increased more than twice the existing units. The word 'existing' has been interpreted as 'structures constructed prior to 19 February 1991' by my ministry. Hence, the number of dwelling units in a said plot should not have been doubled after 19 February 1991. In this case, it needs to be ascertained if the plots—including the dwelling units that were in existence prior to 1991—and the same dweller constructed pucca house on the same plot after 1991 when his economic status improved. In such cases, it is not a violation of CRZ Notification, 1991.

With regard to the commercial structures which have come up in violation of CRZ Notification,1991, the Government of Goa may undertake a ground verification by the state agencies not involved in CRZ matters and initiate action in accordance with Environment (Protection) Act,1986 against such violations. The ground verification including the action to be initiated against the violations needs to be carried out within a period of one month from the date of receipt of this letter.

Letter to Chief Minister of Haryana B.S. Hooda on Discharge of Untreated Effluents into the Yamuna

29 December 2010

...About untreated industrial and domestic effluents from Panipat, Samalkha, and Sonepat being discharged into the Yamuna directly. This—according to the Delhi Jal Board—has led to extremely high levels of ammonia in the water leading to the shutting down of two major water treatment plants in Delhi. I understand from the CPCB that this is not the first time that such a problem has occurred. I would request you to take necessary action to ensure that the Haryana SPCB not only monitors water quality and sewage treatment but also takes stiff action against polluters. I am asking the chairman, CPCB, to be directly in touch with the chairman, Haryana SPCB, in this regard. If it is necessary, we will not hesitate to invoke Section 5 of the Environment (Protection) Act, 1986 to take action against persistent polluters.

Letter to Union Minister of Finance Pranab Mukherjee on the Implementation of Hazardous Waste (Management, Handling and Transboundary Movement) Rules, 2008

28 April 2010

You are aware that the issue of illegal import of hazardous wastes, including electronic waste, has been attracting considerable attention. I am writing to seek your assistance for improving implementation of the Hazardous Waste (Management, Handling and Transboundary Movement) Rules, 2008, under which import of such wastes is regulated.

As per these rules, every consignment of wastes listed under Schedule III of the rules is required to be accompanied by a movement document and either a pre-shipment certification from an inspection agency or a test report from an accredited laboratory. MoEF does not have any agency to enforce these provisions at the ports. Under the rules, it is the customs authorities who are mandated to verify the aforesaid documents, take random samples and initiate legal action in case of falsification of documents, mis-declaration of goods, etc.

MoEF has taken a number of initiatives to improve enforcement of these regulatory provisions, including setting up a coordination committee at the Central Government level. The committee includes representatives of the finance ministry, the Directorate General of Foreign Trade commerce ministry, shipping, the CPCB, selected SPCBs, and other experts.

It is felt that there is a need to strengthen the existing inspection and monitoring system. I would request that in order to ensure stricter vigilance at the ports, the Ministry of Finance may constitute a task force comprising officials of the Revenue Department (Customs) and the Directorate of Revenue Intelligence. Representatives of the CPCB/SPCBs may be associated for technical support to the task force. This task force may conduct frequent random inspections at the major ports. The Ministry of Finance may also undertake a time-bound programme for strengthening of laboratories at the ports and sensitization of the customs authorities to the provisions of the Hazardous Wastes Rules.

I will be grateful for your personal attention to this issue.

Speaking Order on Lavasa Corporation Ltd

[A show-cause notice issued by the ministry on 25 November 2010 to Lavasa Corporation about structures erected without seeking clearance under relevant environmental rules and regulations. It was also asked to stop further construction work in the township. Lavasa subsequently moved the Bombay High Court seeking relief.]

18 JANUARY 2011
MoEF has served the final order on the case of Lavasa Corporation Limited (LCL) to LCL on 17 January and is filing the order in the Bombay High Court this morning.

There is irrefutable evidence presented in the dossier that LCL has constructed an entire township in contravention of the Central Government's (i) Environment Impact Assessment Notification, 1994; (ii) Environment Impact Assessment Notification, 1994 as amended in 2004; and (iii) Environment Impact Assessment Notification, 2006. This evidence has been built up on the basis of (i) a site visit as directed by the Bombay High Court; (ii) analysis of oral submissions; and (iii) analysis of written submissions.

Three options were considered to deal with these violations:

I. Removal of all unauthorized structures;
II. Imposition of penalties/conditions as a prerequisite for consideration of the project on its merits, should an application be made by LCL to the MoEF;
III. Approach the Bombay High Court, where the case is being heard with Lavasa as the petitioner, for directions.

Option III was immediately rejected since the Bombay High Court in its Interim Order dated 22 December 2010 had very clearly directed the MoEF to serve a final order on LCL by 10 January 2011 (extended by the Bombay High Court to 17 January 2011). Thus an exercise of Option III would have meant a complete abdication of basic executive responsibility.

Option I was considered but rejected because of the following reasons:

1. Construction activity at LCL is spread over a large expanse (2000 ha) and not concentrated in a confined and limited (and therefore manageable) space. It has also involved landscaping.
2. Removal of structures already built may, in fact, cause further and long-term damage to the environment.
3. The presence of a waterbody in the proximity militates against the adoption of a simple and straightforward removal option.
4. Social and physical infrastructure are stated to have been built up and developed for the benefit of local communities.
5. Third-party rights already seem to have accrued on a substantial scale.

Thus, Option II has been selected. It should be clearly understood that this, in no way, diminishes the fact that LCL should have sought permissions under the three EIA Notifications but for reasons unto themselves, chose not to do so.

Thus, Lavasa has indeed contravened and violated the law. However, keeping in view the factors listed above, the MoEF is prepared to consider the project on merits if, and only if, LCL agrees to the following terms and conditions:

1. The payment of a substantial penalty for violation of environmental laws, which is incontrovertible.
2. The creation of an Environmental Restoration Fund (ERF) with a sufficiently large corpus which would be managed by an independent

body with various stakeholders under the overall supervision of the MoEF.

3. The imposition of stringent terms and conditions which will ensure that no further environmental degradation takes place and that any degradation that has already occurred would be rectified within a specified time-frame schedule.

4. The formulation of a comprehensive EIA report and comprehensive environmental management plan (EMP) for this project.

For the purposes of ensuring immediate and proper compliance with the above, LCL is further directed to:

1. Submit the detailed project report and any revisions thereof from the inception.

2. Submit all contracts with various contractors for construction and other work.

3. Submit full plans prepared in relation to the project and all modifications thereto.

4. Submit audited statements of all amounts spent directly or indirectly on the project since inception.

5. Submit information related to all contracts entered into for the purchase/acquisition/lease/transfer of lands.

6. Submit full details of future planning with detailed proposals, phase-wise.

Based on the response, and if LCL gives relevant and credible material sought to enable the MoEF to proceed further, the ministry is prepared to consider the project on merits. This will, of course, subject to the imposition of penalties and the creation of the ERF and the formulation of a comprehensive EIA report and comprehensive EMP for this project.

As an additional safeguard and to ensure compliance with the above directions the status quo order putting a halt to any constructions at Lavasa will continue to operate until the fulfilment of all the above terms and conditions.

In the meanwhile, and pending further consideration, the government of Maharashtra has been asked to:

1. Review of the State Hill Station Policy, projects approved or in the pipeline, development of comprehensive master plan and required statutory clearances;

2. Review of the constitution of the Special Planning Authority (SPA) notified for the LCL.

The MoEF is irrevocably committed to implementing the laws of the land in letter and spirit. Though every violation is a unique case in terms of its background, location, degree, and repercussions we must strive to ensure that justice is carried out by prescribing appropriate penalties and measures for restitution.

Letter to Odisha Chief Minister Naveen Patnaik on the Polavaram Project

18 AUGUST 2010

Kindly refer to your letter dated 5 August 2010, wherein withdrawal of this ministry's letter dated 28 July 2010, granting final approval of the central government, in accordance with Section 2 of the Forest (Conservation) Act, 1980 for diversion of 3,731.07 ha forest land for the Polavaram (Indira Sagar) Project of the Andhra Pradesh on inter-state river Godavari, has been requested.

The above matter has been examined in the ministry. The said final approval for diversion of the forest land is subject to compliance of several conditions by the state of Andhra Pradesh and the concerned user agency. The important among them are as below:

1. The plan approved by the Ministry of Tribal Affairs and their conditions, as reproduced below, may be followed:

   The Government of Andhra Pradesh, under the technical guidance of the Central Water Commission, shall ensure that no submergence and displacement of people, including Scheduled Tribes (STs) takes place in the territories of states of Odisha and Chhattisgarh, and the population of these two States including STs does not get adversely affected in any manner, either by changes in drainage regime or by any kind of primary/secondary displacements.

2. The project proposal should be implemented as per the technical clearance given by the Central Water Commission and the provisions/decisions of the Inter-State Agreement and Godavari Water Tribunal Award of 1980. The user agency will ensure that in no case, there should be any submergence of forest land in Odisha

and Chhattisgarh which will tantamount to violation of Forest (Conservation) Act, 1980 as no land has been diverted for submergence in Chhattisgarh and Odisha.

3. The government of Andhra Pradesh and the user agency shall ensure that the approved R&R package is implemented in a time-bound, transparent, and *pari passu* manner.

4. The government of Andhra Pradesh shall constitute a monitoring committee under the chairmanship of the Chief Secretary or any other official of higher rank and having a representative from the MoEF as its member to monitor implementation of all the aforementioned conditions in general, and implementation of R&R package/plan, in particular.

The issues raised by the Government of Odisha in the interlocutory application bearing I.A. NO.3 of 2009, pertaining to the in-principal approval accorded by this ministry for diversion of the said forest land have been duly taken care by the aforementioned conditions stipulated in the final approval for diversion of forest land accorded by this ministry vide its letter dated 28 July 2010.

This ministry through its representative in the monitoring committee to be constituted by the government of Andhra Pradesh to monitor compliance to the conditions governing diversion of the said forest land will ensure that all such conditions are complied in a time-bound, transparent, and *pari passu* manner.

Letter to Union Home Minister P. Chidambaram on Left-Wing Extremism

22 March 2010

Over the last few months, my officers and I have been in touch with different state governments on the issue of forestry administration in those areas affected by LWE. While I agree that basic attitude and approach of the forest departments in some of these areas need to change to keep it more people-friendly, it is also true that infrastructure for forestry administration itself in these areas is very weak. In my discussions, I have been encouraging state governments to formulate divisional plans according to forest divisions which can be supported by the Centre.

The divisional plans that have been prepared so far are as follows:

1. Andhra Pradesh—Bhadrachalam (South) and Narsipatnam
2. Chhattisgarh—Dantewada and North Sarguja
3. Jharkhand—Dhalbhum and Dhanbad
4. Madhya Pradesh—Balaghat (North),Balaghat (South) and Dindori
5. Maharashtra—Wadsa
6. Odisha—Rayagada
7. West Bengal—Purulia, Jhargram, and Bankura (South)

These divisional plans have been reviewed in my ministry and have broadly been approved . We were expecting some extra financial allocations this year for this purpose, but that has not materialized. However, a positive development is the recommendation of the Thirteenth Finance Commission which gave a grant-in-aid to the forestry administration to the tune of Rs 5,000 crore over the next five years to all states. The state-wise grant for the seven states, which have finalized the divisional plans are as follows:

1. Andhra Pradesh—Rs 269 crore
2. Chhattisgarh—Rs 411 crore
3. Jharkhand—Rs 151 crore
4. Madhya Pradesh—Rs 490 crore
5. Maharashtra—Rs 310 crore
6. Odisha—Rs 331 crore
7. West Bengal—Rs 79 crore

I think the Thirteen Finance Commission grants can be utilized most productively for the implementation of the divisional plans in the LWE-affected areas in these seven states. I thought I should bring this to your attention so that you can take the matter up with the chief ministers concerned in your periodic reviews and visits.

Letter to Home Minister P. Chidambaram suggesting the Idea of an Award Recognizing the Efforts of Forest Officers and Personnel

20 MARCH 2010

In India, we consider our forests a unique national treasure. Our forests hold within them a unique wildlife, flora, and fauna and are also a source of sustainable livelihoods to over 200 million people in our country. Forestry is a noble profession but at the same time it is one of the most difficult professions as well. Unfortunately, in terms of training and equipment, forestry is not as well-equipped as the other forces such as police and army. Despite these constraints, our forestry personnel all over the country have shown great courage and determination in protecting the nation's forest and wildlife. There have been many instances where they have made the supreme sacrifice and laid down their lives while protecting our forests.

It will be in the fitness of things, if the forest officers and personnel are considered for award of medals like the Indian Police Medal for Meritorious Service and Gallantry Medals given to policemen on the occasion of Republic Day and Independence Day every year.

Letter to the Prime Minister about an Advertisement brought out by the Greenpeace in Leading Newspapers

[The advertisement accused me of subverting environment norms to favour the Tata Group.]

17 DECEMBER 2010

Respected Prime Minister Sir,

Yesterday Greenpeace, an NGO, had taken out a most scurrilous advertisement in many newspapers, a copy of which I attach for the Prime Minister's perusal.

The implication in the advertisement is that I have deliberately favoured the Tata Group and given the green signal for the Dhamra Port in Odisha, which is supposedly situated on forest land. Greenpeace got my notings through a Right to Information application and has used only few lines from it.

The matter is extremely complex and I have taken a call which I did in good faith and in clear conscience. Normally industrialists attack me for stopping projects and here an NGO is attributing motives for getting a major project going.

I would not like you to have any doubts on my integrity. If there are, as the Greenpeace clearly suggests, I am more than prepared to step down. I am quite disturbed by this advertisement and I thought I should bring this to the Prime Minister's kind attention.

Letter to Parliamentary Affairs Minister Pawan Kumar Bansal on Conflict of Interest

23 December 2010

I am writing to bring to your notice serious conflict of interest issues as far as Members of Parliament are concerned vis-à-vis the MoEF.

The first category of MPs approach me on behalf of the companies they run or with which they are closely associated. This is a blatant violation of norms. I have tried to discourage this but have not entirely succeeded.

A second category of MPs approach me pleading for projects or arguing against projects that are neither in their state nor in their constituency. I find this also objectionable, especially when the same letter is signed by MPs from different states.

A third category of MPs approach me for projects that are either in their state or constituency. I can understand this and I have no problem with such representations.

I would request you to please take note of the first two categories of MPs. Serious ethics issues are involved here. I would also like you to dissuade MPs from meeting officials directly. Such meetings are often used to put pressure.

Letter to Union Minister for Steel Virbhadra Singh

28 October 2010

In today's newspapers, I read about your advice to me to be pragmatic, not dogmatic. Your advice is well taken. The problem is that all ministries want me to be automatic.

Letter to Rajya Sabha Chairman Hamid Ansari on Questions About Individual Project Clearances

25 February 2011

There is a Starred Question at position No. 4 listed against my name for Tuesday, 1 March 2011. I would be more than glad to answer this question in all its details. But I do want to raise a broader issue of whether questions regarding individual project clearances should be entertained at all in Parliament.

7 Gross to Green

One situation that often presented itself was that state chief ministers kept requesting me to tread softly on polluting industries in their states. It was not that they were averse to implementing environmental laws and regulations. Rather, it was simply that notices to units for failure to meet environmental norms were seen as increasing the cost of doing business or leading to closure of industrial units. In either case it put at risk thousands of jobs. Somewhere along the way, a perception had gained ground that observing environmental norms would exact a high political and economic cost.

This direct correlation between the cost of observing environmental norms and the cost of doing business was not based on any real calculations. Of course, a new effluent treatment system would mean incurring a cost, but the benefits to the industrial unit and to the people living in the area would outweigh the initial costs. It is common sense. But clearly loss of jobs or businesses closing down due to higher production costs cannot be countered with common sense alone.

There were occasions when the trade-off—though not based on sophisticated calculations—was clear, and the choice obvious. One of the factors that contributed to rejecting the proposal to mine bauxite in the densely forested and sacred Niyamgiri Hills was the fact its 72 million tonne ore deposit could only provide raw material to the Vedanta's alumina refinery in Lanjigarh, with its increased capacity, for a maximum of four years. Choosing between the preservation of this densely forested area and the additional cost of procuring bauxite for Vedanta was relatively easy.

But there were more instances of polluting units shutting down, shifting base, or down-scaling operations than clear-cut cases like mining the Niyamgiri Hills. What was required was sophisticated measure that would be able to make the trade-offs explicit, by assessing the cost of environmental degradation and disregard. It is one thing to argue about the importance of ensuring that air pollution is kept within certain acceptable limits and another to demonstrate what being lax on air pollution norms would mean for the economy and the much-desired for high GDP growth. The question before me was a simple one: How do we manage what we do not measure?

The idea of providing a measure of the cost of environmental degradation was not new. We were, however, hooked on to the GDP, which is a measure of income, and does not account for loss of human and natural capital. Noted economist, Partha Dasgupta had estimated that between 1970 and 2000, India's per capita GDP grew by 3 per cent a year, but the net per capita wealth, which also takes into account factors like population size and composition, education, and health, and environmental factors like, ecosystems, land, and sub-soil resources, grew at about 0.3 per cent a year.

The World Bank has a concept of 'adjusted net savings', which takes the conventionally adjusted macroeconomic saving rate and adjusts it for environmental factors like pollution, resource depletion. In 2008, our conventional savings rate was 38 per cent of the GDP, however, once adjusted for environmental factors, it was at 24 per cent of the GDP.

These studies made it clear that there was a price to pay for disregarding the impact that purely economic decisions had on the environment. It was also evident that the cost of disregarding environmental degradation would rise as industrial and economic activity increased. There is a need to realize that there are limits to growth in the business as usual mode. The natural tendency is to put off what can be tackled later, while focusing on the more immediate and obvious problem, in this case increasing economic growth to fulfil the goal of poverty eradication.

Our conventional measure of economic growth, GDP, focuses on income and suffers from extreme narrowness, and as a result, a lot of information, particularly relating to the environment, relevant for economic evaluation is not taken into consideration. To make environmental costs and benefits central to economic decision-making, it is essential to have a metric of economic growth that would take into account natural wealth and environmental degradation, a Green GDP. As it were, such a measure would make it possible to put a value to environmental degradation and the opportunity cost of avoiding such degradation. This would allow for making the trade-offs transparent and decision-making more effective.

It is with this aim in mind that I approached Partha Dasgupta, who is the world's leading expert on environmental economics, to help fashion a framework for calculating a Green GDP—a GDP adjusted for environmental costs. I set a target of 2015, by which time we would have a framework for a green national accounts in place. While it would not replace the traditional measure of GDP, it would provide a parallel assessment of the true sense of the cost of environmental degradation. The Dasgupta expert group was set up in June 2011, and it submitted its report in 2013.

Alongside, I had initiated in February 2011, the exercise of valuing the country's biodiversity and natural ecosystems by commissioning a TEEB (The Economics of Ecosystems and Biodiversity) study to be undertaken by a consortium led by Pavan Sukhdev at UNEP. This was to be an assessment of the value of the country's natural ecosystem, which would serve as an input in the calculation of Green GDP.

I had—over the span of my rather short twenty-five months in the environment ministry—worked to bring ecological security into the political and economic mainstream. This sustained effort resulted in the Thirteenth Finance Commission suggesting that the government make provision for a corpus to pay states that were taking initiatives to conserve and improve forest cover—something akin to a 'green bonus'. It also led to the Planning Commission making a serious proposal to recast the Gadgil formula to include environmental performance as an incentive to states, while transferring resources to them. India became among the first countries to embark on a comprehensive countrywide study to assess the economic value of ecosystems and biodiversity, as well as the first country to provide even a tentative framework for green national accounts. Some of these initiatives did not make it beyond the drawing board, but we were at last talking and thinking about ecological and environmental security as an essential component of growth strategy.

I am pro-growth, no matter how my critics choose to present my record as environment minister. It is, perhaps, because I now had empirical evidence of the all too-avoidable underbelly of untrammeled high growth that I was clear that presented with a choice of 9 per cent growth and a negative impact on environment and livelihood security, and 7 per cent growth with ecological security, I would opt for the latter. Of course, a 9 per cent growth with ecological security would be the ideal situation that we should be aiming for. A Green GDP would make explicit to those who didn't have benefit of my vantage point, why it was important to take environmental considerations on board while devising a growth strategy. To my mind, a green national accounting system would not only provide a more realistic picture of economic growth, but also allow for better choices and prescriptions.

This chapter deals with the various aspects of giving the measurement of growth a green hue.

'The Limits to Growth Revisited', Convocation Address, Tata Institute of Social Sciences (TISS), Mumbai

11 MAY 2011

I am delighted to be back in this beautiful campus. It is a particular privilege to be invited to the convocation being held in the platinum jubilee year of your institute. A number of distinguished men and women, including prime ministers, have been at such functions in the past and I am not sure what I have done to be included in this galaxy. ...

I cannot but help recall that I first came here in December 1974 to attend a seminar on urban planning. I remember the redoubtable Dr M.S. Gore being present. My own paper, that I must confess appears so naïve, so theoretical, and so unrealistic in retrospect, was based on my bachelor's thesis at the nearby Indian Institute of Technology (IIT) on urban modelling based on the then-fashionable systems dynamics approach developed by Jay Forrester, Dennis Meadows, and their colleagues at the Massachusetts Institute of Technology (MIT). This was a time when I believed that management science broadly defined to include game theory, operations research, systems analysis, and the like, held the keys to all problems of public policy.

My intellectual pursuits subsequently went in other directions but, today, almost thirty-seven years later I wish to return to another theme made extraordinarily popular by Meadows and his team, which is relevant to my current ministerial preoccupations. *The Limits to Growth* was, some of you might recall, the title of a highly influential book written by Dennis Meadows and his colleagues that hit the headlines in 1972. My friend Tariq Banuri, the Pakistani economist, told me last year that that the release of this study was one of four seminal events to have decisively shaped the modern global discourse on environmental issues—the other three being the publication of Rachel Carson's *Silent Spring* in 1962, Paul Ehrlich's *The Population Bomb* in 1968, and Indira Gandhi's famous speech to the first United Nations Conference on the Human Environment at Stockholm in June 1972.

The question I want to ask today in the Indian context is whether we should even worry about the limits to growth, or more precisely, about the limits to sustained high growth.

It is a good time to ask this question. But let me straightaway admit that while posing the question is easy, finding answers that will be politically acceptable—and also carry conviction with the expanding consumerist classes in our country—will be very difficult. To give a very obvious example, we are all agreed that public transportation must get overriding priority, but are we—individually and collectively—prepared to accept the fact that the rate of growth of car ownership in our country, which is following in the footsteps of that in the US and China, is a recipe for disaster? Are we prepared to change our consumption behaviour? I suspect we are not.

Anyway, why do I say it is a good time to at least pose this question of limits to growth? Between 2003–4 and 2010–11, the Indian economy has averaged an annual rate of real GDP growth of 8.5 per cent, an unprecedented achievement. The Planning Commission is setting a target of 9 per cent-plus growth rate for the Twelfth Five Year Plan that commences in April 2012. I know many social scientists knock the idea of GDP growth as a measure of progress and even some Nobel Prize-winning economists, like Amartya Sen and Joseph Stiglitz, have written eloquently on the need to shed our obsession with high GDP growth as currently defined.

But while we must acknowledge its limitations as a measure of progress and welfare, the fact remains that GDP growth is the most convenient and most widely used single index of the dynamism of a country's agricultural, industrial, and services sectors.

I entirely agree that we should not be overly obsessed with high GDP growth but neither should we ignore its criticality, particularly as an instrument to create more jobs and to generate more revenues for the government to invest in both infrastructure and social welfare programmes. Let us not forget that the Mahatma Gandhi National Rural Employment Guarantee Act, which is today the world's largest social safety net programme, would simply not have been possible without the proceeds that the growth process generates. Let us also not run away from the stark reality that over the next decade, India's labour force will increase by anywhere between 80 million and 110 million—an astoundingly staggering number—China's labour force, by contrast, will increase by just about 15 million over the same period. And it is growth alone that will create the jobs and give us the resources to invest in skill-development that is so essential to reap the 'demographic dividend'.

Let me also recall here a simple calculation often ignored by critics of GDP growth as the index of economic performance, particularly by non-economists. And this is what we are talking of compound growth rates. An economy growing at 5 per cent per year will double in 14 years and quadruple in 28 years. An economy growing at 9 per cent per year will double in roughly eight years and quadruple in sixteen years. When international comparisons have acquired importance and when high GDP growth has strategic consequences as well for India, especially vis-à-vis our neighbours, the power of compounding should not be devalued.

There is yet another reason why we need to sustain high GDP growth rates. And that is because of the need to avoid penalties imposed by financial markets on economies. With high GDP growth rates, our fiscal deficit, current account deficit and public debt numbers look manage-able, and we avoid either substantial downgrading of credit ratings or substantial capital outflows. Crucial macroeconomic indicators that are tracked by markets worldwide look good in India when judged against the backdrop of high GDP growth rates—otherwise, we could be in serious trouble.

Where will the limits to growth emanate from?

For decades, the Planning Commission has worried about the fis-cal limits to growth. In the debate on what we can or cannot achieve, the Planning Commission has always focused on macro-variables—for instance, savings and investment rates, tax:GDP ratio, debt:GDP ratio, and fiscal and current account deficits, to name some of the more prominent of them. Of late, there has been a great deal of discussion on inflation and its impact on growth. There are those who believe that high inflation is an inevitable price we have to pay in the short-term for high growth, while there is now a consensus view emerging that high inflation now is a barrier to high growth in the medium-term and, thus, needs to be tackled boldly. The recent decision of the Reserve Bank of India to hike interest rates is a powerful reflection of this new view which, in my opinion, should have been articulated forcefully much earlier.

I would suggest that the time has now come for India to look at the limits to growth not just from a macroeconomic point of view but also from an ecological point of view. Incidentally, this was one theme running through the original Club of Rome study but over the years we seem to have lost sight of it.

We do not have to subscribe to the apocalyptic vision of the Club of Rome because over the past three decades technology has undermined many of the its predictions—the most famous of which being we will run out of oil by the turn of the twentieth century. Incidentally, technology has also made nonsense of the dire predictions made in the 1960s about India becoming a food basket case. But we do ourselves no favour if we don't even try to pose the limits to growth question from an ecological perspective and then try to assess what the 9 per cent-plus growth means for our water resources, our forest wealth, and indeed for our entire and very variegated and rich biodiversity.

But why now particularly? Can't we wait for a decade, grow, and then deal with its ecological consequences? Can't we follow the American or even Chinese approach of 'harness growth gains now, bear growth pains later'?

There are many reasons why India has to be different. First, ecology in our country is not just a matter of lifestyle as it is in the developed countries, but of basic livelihoods—whether it be the protests in Lanjigarh, in Banaskantha, in Srikakulam or just a couple of days back in Aligarh, or be it campaigns like the one launched almost four decades ago by women in the hills of Uttarakhand that was immortalized in history as the Chipko Movement, or whether it be agitations like the one launched by the Narmada Bachao Andolan that was spearheaded by a feisty TISS alumni, who continues to make life uncomfortable for me I might add.

Second, already, the public health effects of development paths followed over the past have become visible—whether it be the growth of cancer in Bathinda, the impact of Endosulphan in Kasargode, or the incidence of respiratory diseases in Chandrapur. We have been guilty of neglecting these effects. Health expenditures both in urban and rural India are on the rise and are adding to the indebtedness of poor households especially. It is entirely possible that the increased health expenditures are being caused, in part at least, by the ill-effects of air and water pollution.

Third, the impacts of ecological damage on environment are better understood today than at any time in history. A whole science of ecosystem valuation and 'green' national accounting (a theme to which I will return later) have emerged, which help give us a much better idea today of how much ecological damage is being caused by the conventional growth process than ever before in the past. Just as an example, according to the World Bank data, India's Gross National Savings as a percent of GDP was around 34.3 per cent in 2008, but its 'Adjusted Net Saving' in the same year was 24.2 per cent, the difference arising due to the depletion of natural resources and pollution related damages, in addition to conventionally measured depreciation of the nation's capital assets. Several other such assessments show similar results. In the face of such rising and credible evidence, we cannot ignore the ecological cost of the growth process.

Fourth, climate change is a reality and India will be profoundly impacted by it in multiple dimensions like no other country, whether it be through (i) effects on the behaviour of the monsoon, which retains its centrality as a determinant of agricultural performance; (ii) on the health of the Himalayan glaciers which affects the water security for almost half a billion people living in the Ganga basin; (iii) on the rise of mean sea levels that directly impacts on the livelihoods of at least 7 million fishermen and their families apart from the million who live in coastal areas in thirteen states along a 7,000 km coastline; and on our forest cover, which is home to India's considerable mineral wealth, especially iron ore, bauxite and, of course, coal. Global warming threatens humanity as a whole but India stands out in terms of its vulnerabilities in diverse ways.

Finally, there is the stark reality that India will add 400–500 million more people by the middle of this century. Many advanced countries confront population declines, while it has been said that China faces the prospect of becoming old before becoming rich like the West. But the demographic momentum in its magnitude certainly is unique to India. And sustainable development, after all, is development that 'meets the needs of the present generation without compromising the ability of future generations to meet their own needs'.

If we accept that we need to be different because of these five reasons I have just outlined, then let us move ahead and go back to the original question—what are the ecological limits to sustained high growth? It is a question that we can both afford to and must ask. We can afford to ask this question, incidentally, because we are a latecomer to the sustained high GDP growth rate club, and being a latecomer means you don't have to necessarily repeat the horrendous mistakes others have made. It is essential that we ask this question, since we are in a frenzy to make up for lost time and since a large section of our population will be impacted by ecological compromises that a sustained high growth would demand.

In my view, most fundamentally we must understand what sustained high growth means for the energy sector. Economic growth requires energy to fuel it. This, in turn, requires that resources be extracted from nature or the environment to manufacture goods, provide services, and create capital. It is, therefore, crucial to understand the implications of high growth and its limits in terms of energy. Of course, this is not the only impact. High GDP growth coming from high manufacturing growth will lead to air and water pollution. Expanding urbanization will add to the damage to our already polluted rivers—which are more sewers actually. High growth will generate huge solid waste that will have to be managed in a better fashion than we have done so far. But, today, I will focus on the energy sector alone.

Growth requires energy or, more pointedly, it requires electricity. We don't have to believe in Lenin's famous equation—'Soviet power plus electricity equals Communism'—to grasp the absolute criticality of electricity for our homes, for our farms, for our factories and offices, for our schools and hospitals.

A 9 per cent-plus rate of growth will—as calculations based on past trend show—require a 7 per cent rate of growth in electricity consumption. And past trends are not always reliable since it is well-known that there is both considerable suppressed demand and a huge backlog of basic demand itself that has to be met. Here is a depressing statistic that illustrates the magnitude of the challenge ahead—more than half, around 56 per cent, of rural households are without electricity. This translates into a population of close to 400 million.

Where will this electricity come from?

Many environmentalists argue in favour of giving primacy to energy efficiency and renewable sources of energy. Now, nobody can really argue against energy efficiency and renewables. Aggregate technical and commercial losses in power distribution, for instance, for the country as a whole are over 30 per cent, whereas it should be no more than 10–15 per cent at the most. Mandatory fuel efficiency standards in the automotive sector is an idea whose time has come and I am glad to say that they are being finally notified in the next few days, although they will be mandatory only from 2015 onwards. The use of new supercritical and ultra-supercritical technology in coal-based power generation will lead to higher efficiency in coal utilization necessitating lower use of coal.

Recently, the World Bank published a detailed report that India can harness, in a cost-competitive manner, up to 60,000 MW of power capacity through renewable sources like solar, wind, and biomass, whereas our installed capacity in these areas is less than 8,000 MW.

But the question is whether a nation of 1.2 billion—and a country that will be 1.6–1.7 billion by the middle of the century—can fulfil the economic aspirations of its people only or even very substantially through efficiency improvements and renewables, important as they definitely are. My own sense, after over a quarter of century of involvement and experience in the energy sector is that the answer to this question is 'No'. Definitely in the short-run, renewables will have a limited role in the energy basket, largely on account of the absence of a commercially viable model for renewable energy.

So India, will, for the next two-three decades at least, have to depend on largely on coal, hydroelectric, and nuclear power, quite apart from using other commercial sources like natural gas, coal-bed methane, and renewable sources like wind, solar, biomass, and small hydro.

Here is where we confront the question of limits.

Coal-based power can certainly expand since we have the world's third largest reserves of coal, albeit of relatively poor quality as judged by its high ash content. But substantial coal reserves that will need to be worked upon in the future to increase coal production are located in the rich forest areas of Jharkhand, Chhattisgarh, and Odisha. How much coal do we produce and how much of these natural forests we protect is a choice that confronts us today. If we decide to exploit all of our proven coal reserves, at the current level of technology and keeping in mind usage projection, India will run out of coal in forty-five years.

Hydroelectric power can also certainly expand since less than a quarter of India's hydroelectric potential has been utilized. But new hydroelectric project sites are the subject of inter-state river disputes or are located in a few states like Arunachal Pradesh, Sikkim, and Jammu and Kashmir, where there are formidable technical and other problems. Hydroelectric power, clean as it may seem, presents its own share of ecological headaches whether it is the submerging of large tracts of forest lands for big reservoir-based dams, or the negative impact on river biodiversity in run-of-river projects.

Nuclear power is a third option, but under the most optimistic scenario cannot contribute more than 5–6 per cent of electricity supply by 2020, up from the present level of around 3 per cent. In any case, there are renewed safety and risk concerns on an aggressive nuclear power portfolio.

And, what about natural gas? Well, we also need to manufacture fertilizers at home, for which natural gas is an ideal feedstock and, thus, the amount of gas we can allocate for power generation will necessarily be circumscribed by fertilizer production plans.

Let me complicate life a little more. Power plants need water. With the multiple demands on our scarce water resources, siting of power plants in coastal areas assumes special significance. Even without tsunami, coastal locations raise their headaches what with their impact on fishermen and their families, and after the tsunami, the concerns have escalated manifold.

What I am pointing to is the need to carefully evaluate what the energy implications of the 9 per cent-plus growth target will be and then equally carefully analyse each of the energy options from the point of view of its environmental implications. Each of these options involves making tough choices—like how much of natural forest area can we afford to give up now in favour of coal mining in the expectation that over a period of time this loss of forest cover would be made up through compensatory afforestation. And choices we must make by first making the trade-offs explicit. It also means that India can not afford to turn its back on new, innovative, and non-conventional sources of energy.

In the Eleventh Five Year Plan period of 2007–8 to 2011–12, we would have added around 50,000 MW of power generating capacity. It has been estimated that during the Twelfth Plan period, 100,000 MW would need to be added. How it should be added is the real question, especially given our voluntary pledge to cut the emissions intensity of GDP by 20–25 per cent by the year 2020, on 2005 reference levels.

Please note, I say emissions intensity and not emission levels, per se. We simply cannot afford absolute cuts in emission levels at this juncture of our development and given the huge unmet demand for electricity in particular. But declines in emissions intensity—which means that for a unit of GDP you will emit less and per unit of emissions you will produce more GDP—is an eminently desirable and feasible objective to have. What we do in the electricity sector is important since it accounts for around two-fifth of our emissions of greenhouse gases and is the single largest source from which we spew carbon dioxide into the atmosphere.

Here I must also acknowledge the research being done by TISS' climate change team led by my good friend Dr T. Jayaraman. Equity is going to be one of the most basic elements of the architecture of any international agreement as and when all 194 countries can agree and TISS' continuing work on carbon budgets is very much part of giving concrete, operational meaning to the idea of equity or of equitable access to atmospheric resources as some have called it or equitable access to sustainable development, which was India's contribution to the negotiating text so as to break the deadlock at Cancun six months back. The problem with phrases like equitable access to carbon space or even equitable access to atmospheric resources is that they convey the impression that we are asserting some sort of a fundamental right to pollute, which—given our burgeoning population—scares almost everybody in the global community. But 'equitable access to sustainable development' has no such negative connotations. I have requested Dr Jayaraman to undertake the difficult task of actually operationalizing this concept so that India can take the intellectual leadership on it going forward.

There has been one very encouraging development in recent weeks. From a straightforward high, inclusive growth theme in the Eleventh Plan, the Planning Commission has now accepted that the Twelfth

Plan will be high, inclusive, and low-carbon growth. This is a huge step forward to incorporate ecological considerations into the very core of the growth process. Just two days back, the report of an expert group set up by the Planning Commission and the Ministry of Environment and Forests (MoEF) on low-carbon strategies for inclusive growth was submitted.

This report takes two GDP growth scenarios up to 2020—8 per cent and 9 per cent, and examines how they can be realized in the backdrop of our Copenhagen pledge that I just mentioned. The report suggests that with what it calls an aggressive effort, India can actually reduce its emissions intensity of GDP by around 35 per cent even while maintaining a 8–9 per cent growth trajectory. This will mean making the right investment and technology choices in different key sectors like energy, industry, transport, buildings, and forestry. But even after this, there will need to make choices and there will be trade-offs between ecological objectives and growth goals. That is why it is imperative to make these trade-offs explicit.

Another step that has been taken to make ecology an integral part of the growth process is the initiative the MoEF and the Planning Commission are launching on green national accounts. An expert group is being set up under the chairmanship of Sir Partha Dasgupta of Cambridge University—widely acknowledged to be the guru on this subject—to prepare a road map for India to estimate and publish GDP numbers that incorporate environmental costs as well.

India's coal resources are expected to run out in forty-five years. Is that the end of our dreams of inclusive and sustained economic growth? We need to aggressively grasp technology transitions within coal, hydroelectric, and nuclear. There will be technology innovation and advancements making renewable energy more viable, fresh sources of primary energy, like shale gas and improved grids. India would need to be at the forefront of these developments.

I would like to return to the beginning once again, to the *Limits to Growth*. One of the drawbacks of this influential text was that it completely ignored technological fixes and interventions, and their impact. In pushing the limits to growth, we need to actively pursue technology and innovations, both of technology and practices. In pushing forth a sustainable growth path, we need to focus far more on innovation than we do today.

I suppose since this is a convocation address, I must say something for the graduating students as well. I don't want to sound preachy though. You are all social scientists and bring a valued perspective to the problematique of economic growth and ecology. What I would like to stress to all of you is that your perspective should be free from prejudices, if not passions. I find, unfortunately, a bias against economic growth and technology in the social science fraternity at large. I would expect all of you to be tough and searching critics sensitive to larger social concerns but please do not become vociferous techno-phobes or growth-sceptics. Thanks to that outstanding symbol of technology and growth—the Internet—India is seeing the emergence of a well-networked community of neo-Luddites. But remember that even the much-reviled Luddites were very selective in their approach in the eighteenth and ninteenth centuries when the Industrial Revolution was at its peak. I wish all of you the very best.

'More Sinned Against than Sinning', Opinion Piece in *The Economic Times* on the Occasion of World Environment Day

[The piece, focusing as it does on the environment versus growth debate, also serves to stress on the need to put an economic value to ecosystems, environmental degradation.]

4 JUNE 2010
There is a general belief particularly in the 'high GDP growth first' constituency that environment and forest clearances are holding us back from moving ahead faster. The recipe that is being bandied about particularly by corporate chieftains is 'single-window, fast-track' clearances, if at all clearances are deemed unavoidable.

Some basic facts need to be understood straightaway.

First, over 95 per cent of the applications that come for environmental clearances under the Environment Protection Act, 1986 and 85 per cent of the applications for forest area diversions under the Forest Conservation Act, 1980 get approved mostly within the time frame stipulated in the two laws. This is actually an unhealthily low rate of rejections.

Second, the environmental approvals are given to the project proponents and forest clearances are given to the state government in which the project is to come up since it owns the forest land. This explains why the two approvals cannot be easily clubbed and given at the same time.

Third, the forest clearances are given by the Centre after the cases have been examined by the state government concerned. More often than not, this examination can take years because there is no real incentive for the state in the project (this happens mostly in coal where ownership of the mines is with the central government).

Fourth, the quality of the environmental impact assessments is so mediocre (often unintelligent cut-and-paste jobs) that any responsible committee with integrity will have no option but to ask for clarifications adding to the time taken.

Fifth, the very welcome intervention of the Supreme Court has made the forest clearance process (and also that of wildlife clearance under the Wildlife Protection Act, 1972) very strict and detailed. Had this not been the case, our valuable flora and fauna would have been even more endangered than they are presently.

Sixth, the project-by-project clearance approach has meant that certain fragile regions have already reached the limits of their carrying capacity thus now necessitating the need for interventions.

Seventh, with the very desirable growth of an active civil society movement and network on environmental issues, the entire approval process is always under intense public gaze and scrutiny. Industry would like to treat this process as a mere formality but increasingly the pressure from non-governmental organizations has forced the ministry to take a more critical approach and not get swayed by whatever the project proponents put forward and the pressure they bring to bear.

After twelve months on the job, I would argue that the environment and forest approval system has not acted against the interests of faster economic growth. On the contrary, I would say that if at all, it has been functioning to the detriment of ecological security. The approval system has been extraordinarily indulgent to industry. There is undoubtedly need to make the process completely transparent and professional as indeed we have set out to do these past few months. Now, all information on pending projects awaiting environment and forest clearances are available on the ministry's website and is updated regularly. Minutes of meetings are also being put into the public domain. Parikrama of Paryavaran Bhavan, like pilgrimages to Udyog Bhavan till July 1991, are unnecessary and just not needed.

And where there is an overriding national imperative, my ministry will be more than cooperative even while protecting its core concerns. In the past months, projects cleared for the Indian Army, the Border Roads Organisation and the Indo-Tibetan Border Police without abandoning core environmental objectives will bear testimony to this. A very serious and systematic effort has been mounted to clear coal mining projects in a time-bound manner, but the fact remains that 35 per cent of the mines in the nine major coalfields studied so far are in prima facie 'no go' areas from the point of view of forest conservation and biodiversity protection. And land acquisition remains a far more formidable problem for coal companies than forest clearances. On national highways, a compromise has been struck and no on-site expenditure is to take place without getting environment and forest clearances. In any case, perhaps over 99 per cent of National Highways Authority of India projects get cleared with only a small handful stuck because of their impacts on forests and wildlife habitats.

Environment and development have to go hand-in-hand. A balanced middle path has to be found. If we accept this logic, then we must acknowledge that while there will be occasions for saying a nuanced 'yes, but', there will also be occasions when a clear and firm 'no' will have to be said. That was what Chipko was all about. That was what Silent Valley was all about when India's Prime Minister had the courage to put her foot down on a prestigious hydroelectric power project in order to save a critical ecological habitat. Accelerated growth at all costs, irrespective of its environmental impacts and consequences (which can be attended to later as part of this line of thinking) is a recipe for suicide. There are no simple solutions in the environment-development business. There are only intelligent, tough, unpopular choices that have to be made necessarily on a consultative case-by-case basis without fear or favour but with a sense of public accountability.

Note for the Media on the Recommendations of the Thirteenth Finance Commission

4 MARCH 2010

[The report of the Thirteenth Finance Commission (TFC), made several significant recommendations related to environment and forests in its report.]

The TFC, in its report, has recommended an amount of Rs 5,000 crore as forest grant for the award period 2010–15. Grants for the first two years are untied and the commission has recommended that priority should be given to the preparation of working plans. Release of grants for the last three years is linked to progress in the number of approved working plans. These grants are over and above the non-plan revenue expenditure on forestry and wildlife. The report notes: 'Our environmental grants both reward past actions and incentivize future actions. The forest grant that we recommend is essentially a reward for contributing to the ecology and biodiversity of India, as well as a compensation to states for the opportunity loss on account of keeping areas under forest.'

In addition, the TFC has recommended fourteen of state-specific grants related to environment and forests, with a total outlay of Rs 2,063 crore.

The TFC has also recommended that the MoEF shall assign to the Forest Survey of India the task of developing a uniform inventory design for information on growing stock and related parameters like biodiversity and non-Timber Forest Produce (NTFP). This would help bring clarity to the role of the country's forest wealth in climate change mitigation and also help to base fiscal transfers on more robust parameters in future.

Welcoming the TFC report, Minister Jairam Ramesh noted:

It is for the first time that a Finance Commission has given such importance to environment and forests in its recommendations. That the commission has taken such a sensitive perspective on the environment and forests is particularly heartening. The recommendations are deeply thought out, generous and fair. They will make a major contribution in ensuring that the centre and states work in symmetry towards the goal of sustainable development. I would like to sincerely thank the chairman of the TFC, Dr Vijay Kelkar, and his team for their stellar work.

Excerpts from a Presentation Proposing a Reworking of the Gadgil Formula to Include Environmental Performance

[This presentation was prepared by the Planning Commission and is, in some measure, the outcome of advocacy efforts since 2009 on the need to give incentives to states that conserved their forests and to encourage states to improve the quality of the environment. I even discussed the matter with the chairman of the TFC, Vijay Kelkar. The Commission's report suggested creating a dedicated corpus of Rs 3,000 crore for the purpose.]

DECEMBER 2010

1. Environment Performance Index—to account for 2 per cent of the State Performance Criterion under the Gadgil Formula.
2. The Five Key Components of the Index—Air Quality, Water Quality, Waste Management, Forest Cover, and Climate Change—a 20 per cent weightage for each parameter.
3. Air Quality would measure as deviation of target:

   a. The amount of No_x in the air and account for one-third of 20 per cent.
   b. So_x—in the air and account for one-third of 20 per cent.
   c. RSPM [Respirable Suspended Particulate Matter]—in the air and account for one-third of 20 per cent.

4. Water Quality

   a. Treatment efficiency of sewage (treatment capacity/total sewerage generated) account for half of the 20 per cent.
   b. Total coliform count in identified local rivers one-fourth of the 20 per cent.
   c. Biochemical oxygen demand in identified local rivers—one-fourth of the 20 per cent.

5. Waste Management

   a. Collection efficiency of municipal solid waste—one-third of 20 per cent.
   b. Treatment efficiency of biomedical waste—one-third of the 20 per cent.

9. Treatment Efficiency of industrial effluents—one-third of the 20 per cent.
6. Forest Cover

   a. Increase in forest and tree cover over State of Forest Report (SFR) 2005—half of 20 per cent.

   b. Increase in quality forest cover (dense and moderately dense) over SFR 2005—half of 20 per cent.

7. Climate Change
8. Adoption of low carbon strategies

Letter to the Prime Minister on the Athirapally Hydroelectric Power Project

[This letter was written suggesting the need to compensate states that are denied key projects on environmental grounds. This was an amplification of a proposal of giving incentives to states for conserving their natural forests.]

15 JUNE 2011
For quite some time, the Kerala government and the MoEF have been at loggerheads over the 163 MW Athirapally hydroelectric project on the Chalakudy river. Understandably, the state government wants the project to go ahead, although both within the Left Democratic Front and the United Democratic Front there are some differences of opinion. But there is clear evidence that the project would be ecologically devastating and would destroy rich and valuable biodiversity. Having seen the project site myself, I am more than convinced that the project should not be implemented. However, I also feel that Kerala should be compensated either monetarily or through the allocation of greater power from the central pool. I was in Kerala on 13 June and the Chief Minister raised this issue. I promised him that I would approach you on the matter. When states are denied such projects on larger and long-term environmental considerations, they are entitled to some sort of 'green bonus'. I do hope that the Kerala Chief Minister's request will receive your favourable consideration.

Note on the TEEB Study for Valuing Natural Capital and Ecosystem Services

18 FEBRUARY 2011
… A major new programme to value the immense wealth of natural resources and biodiversity in India, the ministry is collaborating with

TEEB study. India is committed to developing a framework for green national accounts that we can implement by 2015, and the 'TEEB for India' study will be the key facilitator.

Thus, the India TEEB project aims to recognize and harness the economic valuation of biodiversity and ecosystem services. It targets action at the policymaking level, the business decision level and the awareness of citizens.

What is TEEB

TEEB is a study of The Economics of Ecosystems and Biodiversity, established by the G8 and developing country environment ministers, that studies the economics of biodiversity loss. By providing solutions to environmental degradation, TEEB aims to connect decision-makers in the fields of policy, environment conservation, and business. It visualizes a new form of economy, which quantifies natural capital and, thus, makes the ecosystem the supplier of capital, and a new entity in public and private markets.

TEEB proved that taking this 'natural capital' into account could help countries on a global level, as well as enhancing quality of life and boosting the economy at a local level. The next logical step is for countries with an interest in utilizing the potential of their natural capital and 'ecosystem services' to conduct studies of their own natural resources and implement new policies that focus on their benefits and use.

The Wealth of India's Natural Resources

With only 2.4 per cent of the world's land area, India accounts for 7–8 per cent of the world's plant and animal species. It is one of eighteen mega diverse countries and contains three global biodiversity hotspots. India shows a high degree of endemism, which is why conserving its biodiversity is essential for the future. As a developing country, our dependence on natural capital is more than that of high-income countries. Transforming these resources into other forms of wealth is essential for our development, but it must be in a sustainable manner to ensure continued growth and the survival of our resources. Our resources and ecosystem services are often undervalued, and we should tap their potential while they still exist. Studies show that a per capita increase in wealth is a result of an efficient use of produced and natural capital. It is with the twin aims of biodiversity conservation and economic growth that India TEEB is conceived.

The Partnership

MoEF is responsible for leading the project. Along with this, private donors and funds will be approached for subsequent support. The first step in this partnership was the Stakeholder's Consultation in Delhi, held on 10–11 February. This conference was held to develop a framework for assessing the economic value of India's natural resources and strengthening biodiversity conservation programmes in the country. Interested states presented conservation initiatives that had been successful at the local level—these will potentially be presented as 'best practice' examples at Conference of Parties (COP) 11.

Two groups will be created:—India TEEB Implementation Taskforce. This task force will be responsible for action countrywide and within the pilot states, and must be comprised of an institution familiar with TEEB and similar evaluation projects worldwide. They will, in turn, facilitate the creation of a TEEB India Advisory Board to provide overall guidance to the project; this will consist of members from TEEB and the ministry, from India and abroad, with significant knowledge of the economics of ecosystems and biodiversity.

The next step would be to have these stakeholder meetings in each of the states chosen to take the project forward: Himachal Pradesh, Andhra Pradesh, Andaman and Nicobar, and Arunachal Pradesh. These meetings will take place in the next two months, and will involve concerned stakeholders particular to each state. TEEB India will have a particular focus on business and ensuring livelihoods. As a measure to include business stakeholders in the process, there will be an India TEEB business conference aimed at the private sector in the next two months.

Way Forward

The task force will be responsible for the following steps:

1. A survey of biodiversity and ecosystem services coming from various biomes to the socio-economic groups that benefit from them, particularly in terms of livelihoods, health, food, water, and energy.

2. A framework of what and how to value natural resources in India.
3. Mapping ecosystem services and their values.
4. Calculating Environmental Adjusted State Domestic Product from changes in forests, fresh water, agricultural land, and carbon sequestration, (per capita natural capital), etc. This includes calculating the 'Green Domestic Product' and 'Green State Domestic Product'.
5. Another GDP to be calculated is the 'GDP of Rural and Forest Dependant Poor'.
6. These will be expected to be recalculated on a bi-annual basis.

Within the pilot states, the task force will be responsible for six steps:

1. Identify specific ecological and economic problems in the state.
2. Specify the ecosystem services and natural capital that are relevant to state policy.
3. Select appropriate methods for disseminating information.
4. Identify and assess policy options.
5. Assess distributional impacts of policy options.
6. The capacity-building exercises for economic valuation of natural resources should be at the most basic organizational level—the results of the valuation process should be owned by local panchayats and block-level institutions.

Email to Professor Partha Dasgupta Requesting Him to Head an Expert Group to Prepare a Road Map and Framework for Green National Accounts

17 MARCH 2011

I have never had the pleasure and privilege of meeting you although we have many common friends. I have met your sister on quite a few occasions in the 1990s. Of course, I have long been an admirer of your work.

I am now the MoEF and have been giving considerable thought to the issue of green accounting. I am a great believer in the philosophy that you cannot manage what you cannot monitor and you cannot monitor what you cannot measure. This subject of green accounting has been talked about but nothing much has actually materialized other than your own writings and the World Bank's recent *The Changing Wealth of Nations*.

My idea is to put together a group of wise men and women under your leadership who will help develop a road map for institutionalizing green national accounts. I am thinking of having Nitin Desai (who I believe travelled with you by ship to England over four decades ago!), Vijay Kelkar, Pronob Sen, and Bina Agarwal ... I passed this idea through Montek Ahluwalia, who said that if we could persuade you it would be an accomplishment.

Congratulations on the recent Prize honour. I am taking the liberty of attaching a lecture I gave last year, which may interest you.

Note to the Prime Minister on the Partha Dasgupta Committee to Prepare a Framework for Green GDP

7 JUNE 2011

Prime Minister will be pleased to know that Sir Partha Dasgupta has agreed to head an expert group to develop a framework for 'green' national accounts and prepare a road map for India to implement this framework by 2015. I have been pursuing him for a number of months, given that he is an acknowledged international guru on this subject and, finally, he has given his nod. I need hardly tell the Prime Minister how important this subject is for us both domestically and internationally.

Montek Ahluwalia, Kaushik Basu, and T.C.A. Anant met me a few days back to finalize the composition of the expert group. The names that have been finalized include Nitin Desai, Vijay Kelkar, Pronab Sen, Kanchan Chopra, Kirit Parekh, K. Sunadaram, Ramesh Kolli, Haripriya Gundimeda, Priya Shyamsundar, and E. Somanthan. It was also agreed that T.C.A. Anant will be the member-convenor so that the exercise is fully integrated into the [Central Statistical Office] CSO's work.

I met Dr M.S. Gill thereafter and explained to him the importance of this initiative and that the Planning Commission is fully backing it. He too agreed that this is something we should be doing. But he made one point that he would like to be assured that the Prime Minister is supporting this initiative of establishing the expert group.

I told Dr Gill that I would approach the Prime Minister in this regard and seek the Prime Minister's 'blessings' as he put it. Since Deputy Chairman, Planning Commission, has been associated with this idea from the very beginning; I am sending this note through him.

'The Way to Green GDP', Address at the India Today Conclave

18 MARCH 2011

Friends, it gives me great pleasure to be here on the tenth anniversary of the original conclave. I am also very happy that for the first time in ten years the environment figures in a session, even though it's billed as a luncheon session. I'll do my best to ensure that you keep your date with your culinary destiny.

I am supposed to speak on the way to a green GDP. Let me begin by recalling one of the most famous literary essays of all times by the philosopher Sir Isaiah Berlin, 'The Hedgehog and the Fox'. It is derived from an ancient Greek dramatist, Archilochus, who says that the fox knows many things, but the hedgehog knows one big thing. The way to a green GDP, is to ensure that it is not hijacked by one type of hedgehog—the enviro hedgehogs who know nothing but maintaining the environment in its pristine form or the growth hedgehogs who can't see beyond their GDP noses. All of us will have to become foxes. The characteristic of the fox, as Archilochus reminded us, is that the fox knows many things. Unless we are foxes we will not move to a green GDP. The issue of a green GDP is important for four reasons that have assumed special significance in India.

Increasingly, environmentalism in this country is not a matter of lifestyle but a matter of livelihood. All I can do is to recall here, contemporary India's first environmental movement—the Chipko Movement of the mid-1970s where the women of Uttarakhand hugged the trees of the hills to ensure that their forests were protected from rapacious contractors. Thus, was born modern India's environmental consciousness. We are increasingly seeing this expand to central and western India. The livelihood concerns of tribals, forest dwellers, small farmers, and small landowners who depend on the land for an occupation are increasingly finding a voice. Their concerns are increasingly coming in to conflict with the economic objectives that we have set for ourselves.

The second reason is a public health concern. Increasingly, environmental consciousness or environmental issue is not a middle-class elitist issue, but an issue of a large number of people, including the poor and the marginalized. The fact that Bhatinda has now become one of the most serious cancer epicenters is not coincidental. In places like Chembur, Bhopal, and Chandrapur—the problems of the environment are not just environmental issues, per se, but also public health issues. Ordinary people, who may not speak the language of environmentalists, speak the language of respiratory diseases, cancer and leukaemia. In the 1960s, the incidence of respiratory diseases in Bangalore, India's most dynamic city, was less than 7 per cent amongst children. Today, independent surveys have shown that the incidents of respiratory diseases are around 25 per cent amongst children in Bangalore. Public health should drive the way to a green GDP.

The third reason is climate change. We don't have to be climate evangelists but we shouldn't be climate atheists either. Climate change is here and is a reality and there is no country in the world as vulnerable to it as India. Our economy is still dependent on the monsoon. An indifferent southwest monsoon and an indifferent northeast monsoon will wreak havoc on our economic performance. We have a large coastline with a population of about 300 million people, vulnerable to tsunamis and rise in mean sea levels. We have a population of about half a billion people living in the north Indian region dependent on water security and on the health of the Himalayan glaciers which are under retreat. And we have this large mineral wealth, which we want to exploit rapidly, from the most forest-rich areas of our nation. So, there is no country in the world—not Maldives, Bangladesh, or any African country—that is going to be as affected by climate change as India.

And, finally, the sustainability argument. We have to recognize that our demographic karma will be 1.7 billion people by the year 2050. In the next 40 years, we are going to be adding 500 million people. Just the sheer base on which India's population is growing is propelling India's population to a region of 1.6–1.7 billion people by the year 2050. Therefore, it is incumbent on this generation to ask ourselves what is the natural resource base that we want to bequeath to future generations. In many countries there is no future generation to think of, as their populations have begun to decline. India is one of those few countries where the population is not only increasing but the population is also going to get younger.

Now, let me turn to the second point of where we are on this road to a green GDP. Have we any idea what this animal called green GDP means? I'm afraid that question is more difficult to answer because economists have not really grappled with this in any meaningful way. Last year the World Bank brought out a publication called *The Changing*

Wealth of Nations. They defined a concept called 'adjusted net savings', which takes the macroeconomics saving rate as conventionally defined by economics and adjusts it for environmental pollution, resource depletion, and a whole host of environment-related factors. For the year 2008, the conventionally measured savings rate for India was 38 per cent of our GDP and, according to the World Bank's estimates, the adjusted net savings rate for environmental factors is 24 per cent of GDP. So then, what does this 14 per cent difference mean in simple English? It translates roughly into a GDP growth of 2.5–3 per cent points. If India is reporting a normal, real GDP growth of 9 per cent per year, according to the adjusted net servings it is actually 6 per cent a year, if you were to take into account all environment-related factors.

There is another estimate that is being done by the world's most distinguished environmental economist—Professor Partha Dasgupta from Cambridge University. He published a paper in which he estimated that between the year 1970 and 2000, India's per capita GDP (as economists measure) grew by three per cent per year, but net per capita wealth, which he defines as growth that takes into account environmental factors as well, only grew by about 0.3 per cent per year. Normal GDP growth does not measure well-being. So, the point I want to make is that there is a very substantial gap between the economic growth of India, as measured by GDP, and the real well-being of the country as measured by economic performance after being adjusted for environmental factors.

Let me now move to the final part of my presentation. What are the next steps we need to take? What are the milestones on the way to this green GDP? First and foremost, we need to measure. I believe if you can't measure something, you can't monitor it and manage it. So, if you want to manage, you need to monitor and if you want to monitor, you need to measure. The measurement of where we are is absolutely crucial. I'm happy to say that Professor Dasgupta has agreed to chair a high-level group to work out a road map for national resource accounting for India. By the year 2015, we hope to be amongst the few countries in the world that will report both conventional economic growth and also adjusted economic growth. The G of GDP doesn't stand for gross but green. The second important aspect to the way to a green GDP is to simply enforce the laws of the land. India is fortunate enough, (almost entirely thanks to the political vision of Indira Gandhi), to have the most progressive legislation on the environment—these include the Forest Conservation Act, the Environment Protection Act, Coastal Regulation Zone, Wildlife Protection Act, and legislations to deal with hazardous waste and pollution control.

Unfortunately, Indians delight in passing laws but take greater delight in bypassing them later. Therefore, it is no surprise that even though we have the best laws of the land even from an international perspective, they have been characterized by non-observance. In no country in the world would a minister who is enforcing laws be drawing headlines. He would be regarded as doing his normal day-to-day activities. Here, I am made out to be Frankenstein, hell-bent on destroying an economic system that has been built so assiduously over the last few decades. All I am doing is asking a very simple question—here are the laws, are they being observed or not? Now if the laws are outdated it is my responsibility, it is the government's responsibility to make sure that laws are modernized. To the consternation of many people, we said that the Coastal Regulation Zone of 1991 is outdated because it is choking Mumbai city. The new Coastal Regulation Zone, 2011 recognizes the reality of India. We cannot have one coastal law for our 7,500 km of coastline. So, we treat Goa, Mumbai, Kerala, Andaman and Nicobar Islands, and Lakshadweep differently, but we have a law. Where laws are outdated or need to be modernized, let's change the laws; but we have to enforce laws too. We have to enforce laws in an accountable and transparent manner.

India needs more regulations but could certainly do with fewer regulators. India needs more laws but could do with fewer lawyers. The trick is to find a way to implement these laws in a market-friendly manner that does not lead to harassment, or rent-seeking on the part of the government. We are trying to do this but with limited success, as we have a complicated federal system. I hope in the next couple of years, we can put in place a clear, rule-based enforcement mechanism for the laws at a central and state level.

The third aspect to the way to a green GDP is that we have to make choices. The time has come for us to recognize that we have to make some choices. It's good if we can have a 9 per cent growth and do all kinds of wonderful things. That is the ideal solution and that should be our objective. But we must recognize that there will be situations where we will have to exercise choices. Those choices must be exercised publicly, democratically, and as part of the political discourse. It cannot be done unilaterally. I think the trade-off between growth and conservation should be made explicit. Let these trade-offs be made explicit in the public domain and then let's exercise those choices. In a majority of cases you will have a yes, in some cases you will have a 'yes, but' (like the Navi Mumbai Airport), and some cases it will be a simple two letters—'N-O'. Now, that no is unacceptable and an anathema to us. A 'No' to the other person is acceptable to me, but a 'No' to me is unacceptable. I think we have reached a situation where if we have to achieve our growth objectives, we will be called upon to make some tough choices. I think the sooner we recognize the need for these choices, the better off we will be.

Finally, on the way to this growth turnpike, we have to recognize there are certain limits. We can deal with environment issues through improved technology and safeguards but we cannot deal with the destruction of forests that have taken centuries to evolve. We cannot say that a eucalyptus plantation will have the same ecological value and impact. There are limits to this growth.

Is it going to be a 9 per cent growth that destroys forests, pollutes rivers, and displace livelihoods, or is it going to be a 7 per cent growth that protects forests, cleans up rivers, and conserves livelihoods? I know where my choice lies; it has to be the latter. We should try for the 9 per cent growth in a manner that protects forests, ensures clean rivers, and protects our natural resources. But if it is not possible, ladies and gentlemen, I submit to you we have to make these choices.

So, we have to chart out a way to a green GDP as no one else will do it for us. We have to do it as part of our political, industrial, and media discourse. If we have a road map in the next decade or so, India can truly claim a leadership role in green GDP. Rather than see it as a cost that we have to incur, we should see it as an opportunity and grasp the opportunities that lay ahead.

8 The Coal Saga

The toughest challenge I faced during my tenure was on the 'go–no-go' issue—it placed me right in the cross hairs of the environment versus development debate. If putting a halt to or questioning few projects on their record of adhering to environmental norms earned me the moniker of Dr No, then the 'go–no-go' imbroglio cemented it. It wasn't just the criticism that made it tough for me. It was also an instance when I had to balance my commitment to growth and the environment, in a manner that both sides won or were left equally dissatisfied.

On the one hand was my understanding that India needed to grow and it needed energy, which came primarily from coal, and on the other was the understanding that India needed to protect its forests and be more sustainable in its natural resource management. It was one of those 'practise what you preach' moments.

Though, both I personally and the ministry were targeted as obstacles to growth, the irony was that the suggestion to clearly demarcate forest areas where mining would not be allowed came from the then chairman of Coal India Limited (CIL). Perhaps, what was even more of an irony was that the announcement that no clearance proposals would be entertained in areas demarcated as 'no-go' and that CIL would not submit any proposals for the 'no-go' areas was made jointly by then Minister for Coal Shriprakash Jaiswal and I. This was agreed on as part of the six-point agenda prepared by the environment and coal ministries to expedite the forest and environment clearances for coal mining projects, while keeping environmental interests in mind. The ministries of coal and environment, and CIL agreed to work jointly on an exercise to map coal reserves and forest cover across nine major coal fields—Singrauli, IB Valley, Mand Raigarh, Sohagpur, Talcher, Vardha Valley, Hasdeo–Arand, North Karanpura, and West Bokaro—to determine areas where mining could be permitted.

However, once the exercise was completed, the coal ministry backed out, perhaps, as the areas that would remain closed to mining activity were far more than it had anticipated. For CIL, which was facing a shortfall in production, this became an opportunity to lay the blame for not meeting targets at a doorstep other than its own. The 'go–no-go' formulation became the cause of the coal shortage. Soon, I was at the receiving end of criticism from the ministers holding infrastructure portfolios. The growth card had been flashed.

Having successfully blamed the environment ministry for 'endangering growth', the coal ministry attempted to ride the public opinion, and even the opinion of many in government, to gain access to larger swathes of forest areas. In late December 2010, the coal ministry moved a Cabinet Note, which would make it almost mandatory for the environment ministry to divert forest land for each coal block allotted by the coal ministry without taking into account the effects of such diversion on environment, forests, and wildlife. Not only would acceding to such a demand be in contravention of the laws and the Supreme Court, it would also mean having to say 'yes' to every project and proposal across the board. A situation that would render the environmental legal regime meaningless. Faced with this demand, I wrote to the Prime Minister spelling out the manner in which the coal ministry was passing the blame and how unfettered access would discourage investment in development and adoption of new technology for coal extraction.

With no compromise in sight, the matter was referred to a twelve-member Group of Ministers (GoM) headed by the then finance minister, Pranab Mukherjee—whose task it was to find a solution to this imbroglio.

As the stand-off continued, I offered the GoM a compromise—the environment ministry would take the decision on each case, taking into account recommendations from the statutory Forest Advisory Committee (FAC). The decisions would be presented to the GoM, which could overrule or support my decision. To some, the compromise was akin to a Faustian bargain but my offer was an effort to maintain the integrity of the forest clearance process and the FAC while giving the Cabinet the option to reconsider decisions in the context of the country's larger energy picture.

I took a decision on four projects in the 'no-go' areas. Of these, two were given clearance, in one case, the project developer realized it was better to opt for a mine in a 'go' area and for one project, I denied the clearance, a decision that was subsequently overturned by the GoM.

The 'go–no-go' debate and compromise solution made it clear that the environmental concerns were still not central to economic decisions. But a bigger concern was that the concern for ecological security was being used as convenient excuse to not address other issues. The coal saga once again provides a good illustration of this trend of making environmental concern the scapegoat. The coal ministry blamed the 'go–no-go' classification and the comprehensive environmental pollution index for lower production. However, there was no discussion on other factors that were responsible for CIL failing to meet its production targets, something that was a regular condition. I did try to raise the issue of CIL's production practices; for example, the coal mining major has 200,000 ha of land (including 55,000 ha of forest area) in its possession, but only 25 per cent of the area had been worked upon, or that it often mined below permissible production limits. Both issues beg the same question, why did it need access to more forest areas for mining? CIL's environmental track record was abysmal—mining over and above its permissible limits in some coal blocks was par for course, or its remedial efforts to address the adverse impacts of mining virtually non-existent.

My quest was to make environmental concerns central to growth strategies but it now was beginning to look like ecological security had become the convenient scapegoat for all other failings. The 'go–no-go' imbroglio only served to remind me that twenty-five months might be almost at the half-way point in the life of a particular administration, but it was too short a time to affect a change in mindset. My quest was beginning to look like the impossible dream, only I was not ready to give up.

This chapter deals in detail with the efforts to bring in a measure of sustainability in the manner in which natural resources are exploited in our country.

Letter to Minister of State (Independent Charge) for Coal Shriprakash Jaiswal on the Efforts to Streamline Clearance of Coal Mining Projects, While Suggesting that Rich and Dense Forest Areas be Avoided for the Time Being

25 NOVEMBER 2009

With reference to your letter dated 17 August 2009, regarding systematic change in the existing procedures of forest clearance, the MoEF has taken the following steps in this regard:

1. Prospecting guidelines have been relaxed from 1 borehole per 10 sq km to 20–25 boreholes per 10 sq km for metallic ores and 15–20 boreholes for coal and lignite;
2. The forest diversion proposals, involving up to 40 ha of forest land are to be processed at regional offices level and examined by the State Advisory Group (SAG) at the state level itself;
3. Site inspection requirement of the project area by the regional offices, MoEF, has been raised from 40 ha to 100 ha;
4. Efforts are being made jointly to identify 'go' and 'no-go' areas as conceived and prepared by your ministry. So far, only one coal field, namely, the Karanpura coal field of Jharkhand, has been analysed by the Central Mine Planning and Design Institute (CMPDI) and the Forest Survey of India (FSI);
5. On pilot basis, we have permitted prospecting in three blocks with increased number of boreholes. The impact of this would be taken into account to decide the necessity, if any, to further increase number of boreholes as per the demand of the CIL and others.

These initiatives of the two ministries, I hope, will not only be able to remove the bottlenecks in a proper expansion plan and bring in suitable systematic change in forest clearance procedures but also help the MoEF to protect and preserve its existing forest cover to enable the country and the world to fight the likely adverse impact of climate change. I would also suggest that very good forest tracts be avoided in the immediate future and existing coal mines be preferred for expansion/development.

Letter to Union Minister of State (Independent Charge) for Coal Shriprakash Jaiswal on the 'Go–No-Go' Exercise

6 JANUARY 2010

As you are aware, our two ministries have been engaged in determining the forest areas, which could be diverted for coal mining, without much destruction to the ecology of the surrounds. In the preceding minister-level meeting—wherein the officers of both ministries and CIL also participated—it was decided that the CMPDI would provide to the FSI the digitized and geo-referenced map of coal fields indicating various coal blocks to be used, for super imposing the data on the forest density map of the country. This procedure brings out the areas that can be easily given out for the mining purposes, along with the areas that have dense forest growth and a rich variety of flora and fauna, which obviously require our conservation efforts.

One such exercise has been completed, though after lot of effort only we got partial data from CMPDI, Ranchi. We plan to repeat this exercise for various other coal fields as well. These are as follows:

1. Korba
2. Hasdeo Arand
3. South Karanpura
4. Singrauli
5. Jharia
6. Ranigunj

I shall be grateful if you could kindly issue suitable directions to the CIL, particularly the CMPDI for providing a digitized and eco-referenced map with respect to these coal fields, to the FSI, Dehradun, under intimation to us. I am enclosing a copy of the letter dated 13 November 2009 containing action points emerged from the preceding meeting for your ready reference.

Letter to Prime Minister on Issues Related to Environment and Forest Clearances for Coal Mines

26 MARCH 2010

I am writing to you in connection with issues relating to environment and forest clearances for coal mines, an issue on which you have repeatedly expressed grave concern.

As former minister of state (power) and as someone who has worked on the energy sector for over two decades, I am acutely conscious of the need to increase coal production in order to expand power-generating capacity. It is because of this that I have met with the minister of state (independent charge) of coal thrice in the past nine months to find a way forward without compromising on the integrity and the credibility of the environment and forest clearance process under the Environment (Protection) Act, 1986, Forest (Conservation) Act (FCA), 1980, and Wildlife (Protection) Act, 1972.

I am pleased to tell you that we have been able to resolve most issues relating to environment clearance. For instance, we have agreed to give clearance for the ultimate production capacity of a mine instead of having the coal company come repeatedly for such clearance every time production capacity is enhanced. I don't think environment clearance is such a stumbling block, unless, of course, the public hearings throw up opposition to the opening of the mine.

The real problem lies with forest clearances. As you are aware, forestry clearance is given to the state government concerned unlike the environment clearance, which is given to the project proponent. Bulk of the so-called 'delays' that the coal ministry keeps complaining about is because of the long time involved in getting the state government concerned to approve the project at its end and forward it, with all details, to the central government for final approval. States have their own problems associated with land acquisition, for instance. They also have no real great economic incentive to clear such projects expeditiously given the present formula for royalty sharing. I have found on detailed analysis that the bulk of coal mining projects are stuck with state forest departments for one reason or another. In states like Jharkhand, it can take anywhere upward of three years for the state to send the proposal, complete in all respects, to the central government for final approval. *Amongst all coal-rich states, I've faced maximum delays in Jharkhand* and I would request you to convene a special meeting with the chief minister in this regard.

I have taken three steps with MoS (I/C) Coal to expedite forest clearances. First, I have requested Coal India to create two executive Director-level positions and take two Indian Forest Service officers on deputation who can chase up projects both with the states and with the central government. Second, we have permitted more intensive prospecting by drilling lager number of boreholes per sq.km than what is permitted without obtaining approval under FCA, 1980. In three coal blocks (in Singrauli, Mand-Raigarh, and Talcher), CIL will be able to drill at least fifteen times the number of boreholes on a trial basis than it was allowed without prior permission of MoEF.

Third, and the most important, I have initiated a preliminary exercise to delineate 'go–no-go' areas for opening coal mines. Here, what has been done between the FSI and CMPDI is that digitized maps have been generated for nine of the major coal fields on which coal reserves and forest areas by density have been superimposed on each other. 'No-go' areas are those areas where *prima facie*, one can rule out any approval for a coal mine because of factors like forest density and nature of forest. 'Go' areas are those areas where, prima facie we can say that coal mining is possible but final clearance will be subject to the usual examination procedures under FCA, 1980 and Wildlife (Protection) Act, 1972. The 'go' areas should not mean that approval is automatic. For instance, it is perfectly possible that a prima facie 'go' area coal block could well be part of a protected area or an important wildlife corridor. Final approval must depend on an examination of site-specific factors by the statutory FAC. I place the results of this rough and ready 'go–no-go' analysis for nine major coal fields in different states (Table 8.1).

You will observe from the last row of the table that overall 35 per cent of the mines in these nine coal fields are in 'no-go' areas but 65 per cent are in prima facie 'go' areas. These mines should be the focus of production planning in the medium-term horizon. You will also notice that there is one important coal field in Chhattisgarh where all the mines are in the 'no-go' category and no amount of fast-tracking will help since these mines can simply not be cleared without loss of thousands of acres of dense forest and biodiversity-rich areas

I have, if you recall, also been suggesting that if the MoEF is part of the initial coal block allocation process, many subsequent 'delays' could be minimized simply because the MoEF could easily point out that the coal block being allocated is in a 'no-go' area. For instance, any officer from the MoEF would immediately raised the red flag when a coal mine in the Tadoba–Andhari Tiger habitat was allocated to a private company some years ago. The MoEF was not consulted at that time and now when the state government approaches us for clearance, we have to say no and in the process get blamed for delays.

Table 8.1 Tabular Presentation of the Analysis Undertaken by MoEF and CMPDI

S. No.	Coalfield	State	Grand Total Area (ha)	'No-Go' Mines	'No-Go' Area (ha)	'Go' Mines	'Go' Area (ha)
1	North. Karanpura	Jharkhand	6,0561	30 (48%)	308.15 (51%)	33 (52%)	29746 (49%)
2	IB Valley	Odisha, Chhattisgarh	5,1641	24 (49%)	28,686 (56%)	25 (51%)	22,955 (44%)
3	Singrauli	M.P, U.P	69,977	29 (60%)	41,106 (59%)	19 (40%)	28,871 (41%)
4	Talcher	Odisha	81,040	19 (23%)	22,296 (28%)	64 (77%)	58,744 (72%)
5	West Bokaro	Jharkhand	14,770	11 (28%)	3,905 (26%)	28 (72%)	10,865 (72%)
6	Wardha	Maharashtra	82,932	16 (14%)	38,477 (46%)	97 (86%)	44,455 (54%)
7	Mandraigarh	Chhattisgarh	118,215	51 (64%)	80,782 (68%)	29 (36%)	37,433 (32%)
8	Hasdeo	Chhattisgarh	45,883	20 (100%)	45,883 (100%)	0 (0)	0 (0)
9	Shoagpur	Chhattisgarh Madhya Pradesh	127,553	22 (20%)	28,734 (23%)	88 (80%)	98,819 (77%)
	Total		1,013,493	351 (35%)	4,85,969 (48%)	649 (65%)	527,524 (52%)

I will continue to be in regular touch with MoS (I/C) Coal and try and be as accommodative as I can within the framework of the three laws that have necessarily to guide my work. I can assure you of complete transparency and also readiness to cut needless delays in processing of cases.

Letter to Union Minister of State (Independent Charge) for Coal Shriprakash Jaiswal on Environmental and Forest Clearances for the Coal Sector

20 APRIL 2010

I refer to the ongoing discussions between our two ministries on the growth of the coal sector and increase of coal production within the environmental and forestry regulations. In this regard I would like to apprise you of the steps taken to further streamline the procedures and measures in order to reduce the time taken for environmental and forestry clearances. In particular, we have issued a circular on expansion proposals on coal projects seeking exemption from conduct of public hearing. The broad 'go–no-go' areas have also been identified with respect to nine coal fields in the country. In this context, I would like to bring to your kind attention that the Ministry of Petroleum and Natural Gas had placed coal-bed methane blocks in the country for bidding/auction only after obtaining inputs from the MoEF, from environment and forests' angle. A similar practice needs to be followed by the Ministry of Coal (MoC) before allotting coal blocks.

With regard to coal blocks that have been allotted, I may mention that granting Terms of Reference (ToR) to such projects in such locations leads to an assumption that grant of ToR implies grant of environmental clearance. ToRs are granted to coal projects to assess the project specific impacts, and if during the process of appraisal it is found that the impacts are significant, environmental clearance could be denied to such projects (that is, grant of ToR does not necessarily mean grant of environmental clearance). I would like to reiterate that even if a coal block is within a 'go' area, the individual proponents would require applying for environmental and forestry clearances as per the provisions laid out in the Environmental Impact Assessment (EIA) Notification 2006 and the FCA on the project specific impacts and with a detailed EIA and an Environmental Management Plan (EMP) study.

Another issue, which I would like to draw your attention to as far as grant of environmental clearance for captive coal blocks are concerned, is that most of the coal blocks allotted by the MoC to private companies for captive coal mining are essentially those blocks which are 'difficult', or 'problem' blocks in terms of one or more of the following characteristics:

1. Have adverse geo-mining conditions.
2. Have large areas of forest land or fall in ecologically sensitive areas.
3. Have extensive displacement (rehabilitation and resettlement) and/ or problems of land acquisition.
4. Have problems of law and order.

I understand that it is for this very reason that CIL surrendered these blocks. It may, therefore, not be feasible nor fair for the project proponents to expect 'easy' and 'fast' clearances for such 'problem' blocks from this ministry to enable them to start their coal production without suitably addressing the various environmental and socio-economic aspects of such projects. In some cases, it may not be possible to grant environmental clearances in view of the ecologically sensitive nature, biodiversity, and dense forests existing in and around such blocks.

My ministry is also receiving applications for environmental clearance for blocks for captive coal mining without completion of exploration/determination of proven and mineable reserves for which mining plans have been prepared and approved by the MoC. Since the extent of coal reserves itself has not been firmed up, the actual mining to be carried out—and impacts thereon—cannot be determined and, hence, the proponents seek environmental clearance for one or two of the coal seams or for a small area of the block for which exploration has been completed stating that they would come again when a detailed exploration has been completed for the entire block. This entails incomplete and repeated consideration of the same proposal. Another reason for repeated consideration is that some of the EIA-EMP reports furnished do not address/only partially address the issues given in the ToR and, hence, require repeated consideration. As far as environmental clearances are concerned, we would like to bring to your attention that we are still receiving proposals for environmental clearance, which are not based on the highest achievable production capacity.

I would also like to bring to your kind attention that the Coal Bearing Areas (CBA) Act, 1957 unlike the Mines and Mineral Development and Regulation (MMDR) Act, 1957 as amended in 2002 (and being further amended in 2010), does not have provisions to fix responsibility, including costs upon the project proponent for undertaking progressive and final mine closure. As a result, many of the coal projects conceived and implemented by CIL, which are open-cast projects are often compromising on mine reclamation as this is considered as an additional cost with 'no returns'. Your ministry has brought out a guideline for the coal companies of CIL. However, the CBA continues to have no provisions for 'environment' or 'environmental protection', and requires to be amended to incorporate provisions similar to the MMDR, which is being amended in 2010, so that environment is made an integral part of coal mining operations, and to fix legal responsibility along with costs upon the project proponent, namely the CMDs of the subsidiary companies of CIL to mandatorily implement mine reclamation and mine closure and for sustainable development of coal mines in the country. I also understand that the land acquired under CBA is in perpetuity since no time limit is provided for under CBA and, hence, large areas of coalfields across the country under CBA are still with CIL even after completion of coal extraction. I would like your ministry to consider incorporating a time limit of thirty years for a lease of a block acquired under CBA, and twenty years for every renewal in line with MMDR Act, 1957.

My ministry has made an exercise on the entire process of coal production. You would agree that the entire process from exploration for coal to the actual start of coal production is a long process, of which environmental clearance is but one of the steps. The MoC/CIL India require to focus on minimizing the time in respect of all the other steps as well as, such as creation of enabling infrastructure and capacity and addressing issues such as land acquisition, and R&R for meeting coal production targets over the next twenty years. Your ministry had, in fact, highlighted these as the major constraints resulting in shortfall in production and targets.

Lastly, I also suggest that CIL companies undertake an exercise of 'self monitoring' during the next three months and furnish compliance details of at least five most important environmental clearances and forest clearances per company and report the result to CIL Board, MoEF/MoC and also possibly on their website.

I look forward to discussing these issues further in our next meeting.

Letter to B.K. Chaturvedi on Reviewing the Demarcation of 'Go–No-Go' Areas

14 MAY 2010

I have seen the minutes of the meeting held under your chairmanship on 4 May 2010 on issues in the coal sector.

I refer particularly to Para 17(vi). It says 'MoEF-MoC-Planning Commission group to relook the 'no-go areas' and draw up a gradation of the areas which could be mined subject to safeguards/better technologies which are environmentally benign.'

I am not in agreement with this. We have already spent six months drawing up 'go' and 'no-go' in the nine coal fields and because results of the analysis are uncomfortable to the MoC, it does not mean that we relook at the analysis. The 'go' and 'no-go' exercise has been carried out jointly by CMPDI and the MoEF.

Perhaps we could discuss this matter further.

Letter to the Prime Minister on the 'Go–No-Go' Issue

13 JULY 2010

… The finance minister spoke to me last week saying that the MoC has taken serious objection to our analysis on the grounds that it would adversely impact on CIL's forthcoming initial public offering (IPO). I gave him a formulation to blunt the impact of the analysis on valuations, which he and the MoS (I/C) Coal approved. This has been put on our website and I attach a copy of this 'clarification'.

Sir, I would like to submit to you the following in view of the various communications the MoC appears to be sending to the Prime Minister's Office (PMO) as reported in the newspapers.

The 'go–no-go' analysis has all along been a joint exercise between the MoEF and CMPDI. This exercise was launched in August 2009 with the full knowledge of the MoS (I/C) Coal and his officials.

I had written to you on 26 March 2010 giving the preliminary results of the analysis. I had marked copies of this letter to the finance minister, Deputy Chairman, Planning Commission, and MoS (I/C) Coal. You may recall, Sir, that I had even brought maps to one meeting of the Cabinet Committee on Economic Affairs (CCEA) and had made a brief presentation on the analysis.

The ultimate statutory authority for clearances under the FCA, 1980 is the FAC in the MoEF. The FAC makes it recommendations to the MoEF. No inter-ministerial body headed by the Principal Secretary to Prime Minister, as is being sought by the MoC, can substitute for this statutory FAC. I have made clear to the finance minister that I would stoutly oppose such a body.

'Go' areas *do not* mean automatic or fast-track clearances. All it means is that the FAC will entertain and consider the applications from coal companies. 'No-go' areas are areas in which applications need not even be made in the first instance.

Sir, the initial analysis in nine major coal fields indicated a 'go' area of around 3.44 lakh ha. The MoC wanted this to be increased to around 4.5 lakh ha. Subsequently, at the instance of the PMO the analysis was revisited and the 'go' area has been increased to around 3.86 lakh ha. I have most reluctantly agreed to this keeping growth needs in mind. Now, the MoC appears to want us to abandon the very concept of 'go–no-go', which I thought was a major innovation that would help both the coal companies and the forest departments.

Sir, I am sure you will agree with me that saving our forests for long-term ecological security is far more important than rescuing an IPO. With my long and close association with the energy sector of almost three decades I am very well aware of our energy policy imperatives but a sustained denigration of what the MoEF is attempting to do to ensure a proper balance is most unfortunate.

Letter to Union Minister for Steel, Virbhadra Singh, on the Forest Clearance for Rohne Coal Block in Jharkhand

8 OCTOBER 2010

I have received your letter dated 16 September 2010 emphasizing the need for giving forestry clearance for the Rohne coal block in the North Karanpura coal field of Jharkhand. We have received the proposal from the state government and it is under examination in the ministry. However, a preliminary analysis of the forest cover in the coal block has indicated that out of 1,250 ha, total area of 688 ha, that is, 55 per cent is under forest cover. Out of this, 47 ha is very dense forest with canopy density between 40 and 70 per cent and 440 ha is low density forest with canopy density ranging between 10 and 40 per cent. Thus, this area from forest conservation point of view is not suitable for diversion to non-forest use. Hence, it is advisable that the Ministry of Steel may take up the issue to find out some alternative coal block from areas which have less forest cover.

In fact, a coal block adjoining to Rohne by the name Dip Side of Rohne has much less forest cover. Out of 1,026 ha of total block area, only 242 ha is forest land, which is 23.6 per cent and is within the acceptable limit of 30 per cent gross forest cover. The weighted forest cover is 10.9 per cent, which is marginally higher than the acceptable limit of 10 per cent. However, if the Ministry of Steel proposes to approve this block for forest clearance, MoEF will be open to consider this request.

Letter to Union Minister of State (Independent Charge) for Coal, Shriprakash Jaiswal, on the Poor Environmental Track Record of Eastern Coalfields Limited

20 December 2010
I attach a copy of letter that I have received from Shri Bansa Gopal Chowdhury, Member of Parliament (Lok Sabha). He raises very serious issues on the environmental track record of Eastern Coalfields Limited, which I hope you will examine.

Letter to Union Minister of State (Independent Charge) for Coal, Shriprakash Jaiswal, Forwarding the Complaint on Pollution Caused by Western Coalfields Ltd

3 January 2011
I am sending you a copy of a letter that I have received from Hansraj Gangaram Ahir, Member of Parliament (Lok Sabha). The matter pertains to environmental pollution being caused by Western Coalfields Limited. I would request you to please have a look at the issues raised by him.

Letter to Prime Minister on Meeting with the Coal Minister to Address Concerns about Clearances for Coal Mines

11 FEBRUARY 2011

I met with the coal minister twice in the last five days. Last evening, I have communicated the following decisions of the MoEF to him to address CIL's short term concerns.

The MoC submitted a list of fifteen projects which are awaiting final environmental clearance from the MoEF. Of these, six projects have got the clearance, four projects are awaiting detailed analysis by the National Tiger Conservation Authority, one is awaiting scrutiny by the FAC, and four projects are awaiting clarifications from the coal companies. The FAC meeting to consider the pending case will be held in early March 2011.

The MoC submitted a list of eleven projects where public hearings have been held, EMPs prepared and are awaiting consideration of the Expert Appraisal Committee (EAC) of the MoEF. Of these, seven projects will be taken up in the EAC meeting of 21 February 2011. Out of these seven projects, (i) one project is where actual production is far less than the production level for which EC was first granted in July 2003 and where EC is now sought for enhanced capacity; (ii) three projects are where actual production is far in excess of the production capacity for which EC was first granted in 2002, 2005, and 2006, respectively, and now the cases are coming up for regularization.

The MoC submitted a list of fifty-five projects that have received EC but are awaiting forest clearance, Of these, only two projects are awaiting final consideration of the FAC, which will be done in its next meeting in early-March, 2011. The remaining fifty-three projects are awaiting (i) submission of compliance reports by the respective state governments on implementation of Stage-I conditions; or (ii) compliance with Forest Rights Act (FRA), 2006 by the state government; or (iii) submission of basic proposal by the state government for Stage-I clearance. Of these fifty-three projects, nineteen are in Chhattisgarh, sixteen are in Jharkhand, fourteen in Maharashtra, and six in Odisha. I will myself meet with these four states (although, strictly speaking, this is not my job) to expedite matters at their end.

The MoEF is reviewing the status of implementation of action plans prepared by the state governments in the forty-three critically polluted areas having a Comprehensive Environmental Pollution Index (CEPI) of seventy or more, in which the seven coal field areas also figure. Of the forty-three, the moratorium on new projects has already been lifted in five areas and the moratorium in four more areas is being lifted very soon. Technical teams are visiting the seven coal field areas in the next two weeks after which a decision will be taken as far as these areas are concerned.

In Jharkhand, particularly, where the state government has expressed great difficulty in identifying government land for compensatory, afforestation, CIL will be permitted to carry out compensatory afforestation in open/degraded forest lands. This has also been permitted in the case of SAIL's Chiria iron ore mines.

I assure you, Sir, of my fullest cooperation in ensuring that coal production targets are met. But at the same time, I must reiterate that environmental regulations are not the cause of shortfalls in coal production. I vividly recall that at your behest I was personally interacting with the officials of MoC regularly throughout 2008, when I was MoS (Power), to sort out the issue of shortfalls in coal production long before environmental regulations came to be enforced strictly.

Excerpts from a Presentation Made 'On "Go" and "No-Go" Areas for Coal Mining', to GoM Set Up to Consider Environmental and Developmental Issues Relating to Coal Mining and Other Developmental Projects

7 APRIL 2011

1. During 1950–80, 4 million ha of forest area were diverted. During 1980–2010, this was reduced to 1 million ha as a result of the Indira Gandhi-inspired Forest (Conservation) Act, 1980
2. The FAC is a statutory body in the MoEF. It subjects all proposals to due diligence but *rarely* rejects proposals.
3. Fragmentation of forest areas is avoided. Good forest areas, in addition to those part of protected area network, are not sacrificed.
4. Forests having dense cover, rich biodiversity, and ecological values, are protected. In addition, importance of forests as wildlife corridors and livelihood dependence of tribal communities on forest areas are given high consideration.

Background to 'Go–no-go'

1. In the first meeting between the MoC and MoEF in June 2009, Chairman, CIL, suggested 'go–no-go' distinction to expedite forest clearances for coal mines.
2. The Chairman, CIL said 'no-go' means no clearance whereas 'go' means automatic clearance.
3. MoEF immediately clarified that 'no-go' means no clearance whereas 'go' means *faster* clearance, not automatic clearance since field assessments are needed.
4. Joint CMPDI–MoEF exercise launched in July 2009.

Joint CMPDI–MoEF Exercise

1. Nine important coal fields were studied between July 2009 and January 2010. These coal fields were selected by CIL.
2. Digitized forest maps were super-imposed on the coal block boundary.
3. The CCEA was informally informed about results of the analysis in February 2010 and detailed communication sent to the Prime Minister in March 2010, with copies to the finance minister, deputy chairman, Planning Commission, and coal minister.

Criteria for 'Go–no-go'

1. Forest cover is defined as crop having density more than 10 per cent.
2. Gross forest cover (GFC): A coal block having 30 per cent or more area under forest cover is 'no-go'.
3. Weighted forest cover (WFC): To take into account forest quality weights are assigned—0.85 to very dense forests, 0.55 to moderately dense forests , 0.25 to open forests—for calculating forest cover percentage over the whole block.
4. The cut off for WFC has been kept as 10 per cent, that is, if a block has WFC of more than 10 per cent, it is in 'no-go'.

First results of the CMPDI–MoEF Study:

206 blocks categorized as 'no go' and 396 blocks categorized as 'go' (Table 8.2).

Table 8.2 First results of the CMPDI–MoEF Study

SI no.	Coal field	Total no. of coal blocks with area		Category 'B' blocks (10% WFC & 30% GFC)	
		Blocks	Area (ha)	Blocks	Area (ha)
1	Talcher	82	80,400	68	64,000
2	IB Valley	49	51,600	26	23,600
3	Mand Raigarh	80	118,200	29	37,400
4	Sohagpur	110	127,550	88	98,800
5	Wardha	113	82,900	98	45,000
6	Singrauli	46	66,800	20	31,600
7	North Karanpura	63	60,600	39	33,500
8	West Bokaro	39	14,800	28	10,900
9	Hasdeo Arand	20	45,900	–	–
	Total	602	648,750	396	3,44,800 (53%)

PMO Intervention

1. At urging of the MoC, the PMO coordinated another exercise to free more area for coal mining.
2. 'Cluster approach' was adopted, under which isolated forest patches (no-go blocks) occurring in the midst of 'go' areas were also added to 'go' areas. This resulted in the addition of twenty-nine coal blocks, which were falling in 'no go' areas, in the 'go' (56 per cent) area.
3. Twenty-four coal blocks, already approved by the MoEF but were found to fall in the 'no go' area, were also added in the 'go' (59 per cent) area.
4. Apart from this, twenty-eight large-sized 'no go' coal blocks, identified jointly with the MoC, recommended for boundary modification to allow few more areas in the 'go' (71 per cent) area.

Thus, out of 6,48,750 ha (602 coal blocks) of forest area under consideration, coal mining becomes 'go' in 4,62,939 ha (467 coal blocks), or 71 per cent of the total area (Table 8.3).

Table 8.3 Results of the 'Cluster approach' to Free More Area for Coal Mining

Sl no.	Coal field	As per cluster approach ('A' blocks grouped with 'B' blocks)		Including existing mines of cat. 'A'		Coal block require boundary modification*	
		Blocks	Area (ha)	Blocks	Area (ha)	Blocks	Area (ha)
1	Talcher	73	69,000	75	70,200	3	6,984
2	IB Valley	32	28,000	33	30,300	2	4,642
3	Mand Raigarh	32	40,300	32	40,300	7	7,274
4	Sohagpur	94	102600	98	105,000	1	7,203
5	Wardha	101	45,800	104	48,000	4	34,986
6	Singrauli	20	31,600	26	35,800	4	11,526
7	North Karanpura	44	35,500	51	39,300	4	8,819
8	West Bokaro	29	11,100	30	11,500	3	1,105
	Total	425	363,900 56%	449	380,400 59%	28	82,539 4,62,939 ha or 71%

Harsh Ecological Realities of Coal Mining Strategy

1. One-third of coal mines are running with one type of violation or other and irrespective of whether environmental and forestry clearances are available or not.
2. No land has been returned back to any state government though they are in operation for the last forty-five years.
3. The strategy is to bring in more and more area under mining without fully exhausting the production potential of existing areas.
4. There is no systematic time-bound reclamation plan of mined-out areas.

As a result, forest given to coal companies are lost forever. Plantations are no substitute for natural forests.

Present Pendency Position for Stage-I Forest Clearance

1. Eighteen proposals of CIL awaiting forest clearance. Only one is with MoEF and seventeen are with state governments—Jharkhand (eight), Madhya Pradesh (seven), and Chhattisgarh (two).

2. Thirty-one proposals of other than CIL awaiting forest clearance. Of these, eleven are with MoEF and twenty with states—Andhra Pradesh (seven), Jharkhand (five), Madhya Pradesh (five), Chhattisgarh (two), and Maharashtra (one).
3. Of the eleven pending with the MoEF, seven are awaiting site inspection reports.

Present Pendency Position for Stage-II Forest Clearance

Forty-five proposals of CIL given Stage-I clearance and awaiting final approval—Chhattisgarh (twenty), Jharkhand (thirteen), Madhya Pradesh (eight), Maharashtra (three), and Odisha (one).

Nineteen proposals of other than CIL awaiting final approval— Jharkhand (five), Andhra Pradesh (four), Chhattisgarh (four), Odisha (three), Madhya Pradesh (one), Maharashtra (one), and West Bengal (one).

Causes of Forest Clearance Delays at the State Level-I

Receipt of incomplete proposals (for instance, usually Survey of India toposheet of forest area at 1:50,000 scale rarely submitted on time).

Identification of revenue land for compensatory afforestation—a very serious problem especially in states like Jharkhand.

Presence of protected areas at 10 km distance of forest area usually ignored in the original proposal.

Causes of Delays in Forestry Clearances at the State Level-II

Poor track record of CIL in R&R. This has led to (i) district magistrates not issuing the no-objection certificate for revenue forest land; (ii) delays in FRA compliance; and (iii) acrimony in public hearings for environmental clearances.

States see little incentive in faster clearance (other than the 13 per cent royalty on coal). The Odisha chief minister has said as much in letter to the Prime Minister.

MoEF Initiatives to Expedite Environmental and Forest Clearances

Environmental clearance now given for maximum production capacity obviates the need to get periodic approvals.

In three coal blocks (Singrauli, Mand Raigarh, and Talcher), CIL permitted to drill at least fifteen times the present level of boreholes. This will boost exploration.

CIL now permitted to carry out compensatory afforestation in open, degraded forest land in Jharkhand. This is a very significant relaxation that will be cheaper for CIL and also save two–three years at least.

MoEF Suggestion to GoM-I

MoEF is prepared to consider *revised* 'go–no-go' approach that frees 71 per cent of area in the nine coal fields as opposed to original insistence of 53 per cent.

This is a *huge* compromise keeping in view the Prime Minister's instructions.

All 'no-go' proposals will come to FAC and subject to strict scrutiny and, *if possible*, a compromise arrived at (like the Indian Farmers Fertiliser Cooperative Limited in Chhattisgarh, where dense forest area diversion has been reduced from 2,000 ha to 782 ha, a reduction of 61 per cent). Where no compromise was possible, MoEF prepared to bring to the Cabinet for consideration along with its recommendation for rejection.

CIL has 200,000 ha of land (including 55,000 ha of forest area) in its possession. The GoM should ask why production targets cannot be met from this area.

The GoM may also deliberate on issue relating to state incentives for faster clearance at state level.

Issue of CEPI

MoC has also raised issue of CEPI and its impact on coal production because of moratorium.

Forty-three critically polluted areas identified based on CEPI. 7 coal fields in this forty-three.

In some projects, production is far in excess of level cleared environmentally (Table 8.4). In some others, production is considerably lower than the level cleared for (Table 8.5).

Table **8.4**   Some Projects in CEPI Areas (where production is in excess of limit in the environment clearance)

Project	Production limit set in EC (mtpa)	Present Production (mtpa)
Samaleshwari OS (MCL)	5	10.76
Basundhara (W) (MCL)	2.4	6.67
Belpahar (MCL)	4.50	6.55

Table **8.5**   Some Projects in CEPI Areas (where production is below limit set by the environment clearance)

Project	Production limit set in EC (mtpa)	Present Production (mtpa)
Hingula – II (MCL)	12	8.83
Kulda OPC (MCL)	10	3.43
Gajranbahal OCP (MCL)	10	Yet to start
Bharatpur OCP Exp. (MCL)	20	10.91
Bhubaneshwari OCP Exp. (MCL)	10	4

Lifting of Moratorium

1. Moratorium already lifted in Angul–Talcher.
2. Technical assessment of remediation plans in Chandrapur, Singrauli, Jharia, IB Valley, and Raniganj in progress, and hopefully moratorium will be lifted by end-April. Korba will take longer because the state has not submitted any remediation plan.

Letter to the Prime Minister on the Presentation Made before the GoM

8 APRIL 2011

The presentation[1] was made in order to find a solution as per your instructions. The highlights of the compromise that I have suggested are as follows:

1. The 'go' area in the nine coal fields that have been studied will be increased from 53 per cent to 71 per cent.

2. All 'no-go' proposals will be scrutinized by the FAC. Wherever a compromise is possible, a decision will be taken by the FAC itself. Where a compromise is not possible, the MoEF will bring a note to the Cabinet along its recommendations for rejection so that the Cabinet will have an opportunity of taking a larger developmental view either way.
3. All proposals that have been given Stage-I forest clearance prior to 31 December 2009 will be considered by FAC even if they fall in 'no-go' areas. This way, the 'go–no go' classification will not have a retrospective effect.

I believe that these suggestions open a way for a workable compromise but the problems of the coal industry are much deeper and go beyond environment and forests. I think the attempt to lay the blame for the stagnating coal production on environment and forests has been mistaken and has detracted from more urgent issues within the coal industry from being addressed.

Note to the Prime Minister on Structural Issues in the Coal Sector

10 JUNE 2011

I met the Prime Minister this morning. The Prime Minister had requested for a note on some of the structural issues I spoke about that are plaguing the coal sector.

1. Pithead stocks as on 1 April 2011 are almost 71 million tonnes (mt) as compared to about 64 mt as on 1 April 2010. Evacuation of coal from pitheads clearly has emerged as a very serious issue. MoC blames the Railways but the Chairman, Railway Board, informs me that only about 47 per cent of coal is dispatched by rail. Other modes of evacuation are road (30 per cent), merry-go-round (20 per cent), and belt and ropeway (3 per cent).
2. Many coal projects are functioning below the capacity for which they have been given EC. In the case of Mahanadhi Coalfields Limited (MCL), for instance, as compared to a production level of 144 million tonnes per year cleared environmentally, the present production from these thirty-one projects is only around 104 mt. I should also mention here that there are six projects in MCL, which are producing 13 mt per year more than the capacity for what they have been given environmental approval.

3. There is no incentive for state governments to maximize coal production. Chief ministers are saying—land is ours, forest area is ours, R&R burden is on us, pollution burden is ours, but the coal and power is for somebody else. The only incentive remains is the 13 per cent royalty rate on coal, and that too on a depressed price. There has to be an immediate revision in the rate of royalty and the basis of its calculation if we are to get state governments involved actively in the coal production.

4. Land acquisition is far more formidable challenge in the coal industry than environmental and forestry clearances. Hence, maximization of production from the land already under possession of CIL should be the primary focus—CIL already has some 200,000 ha in its possession (including about 55,000 ha of forest land).

The more domestic coal we use the more ash we produce. Today, we are producing almost 200 mt ash per year of which only about 50 per cent is utilized in cement and bricks. The balance is disposed of in ash ponds, which not only consume lots of land but are environmentally devastative. A 1,000 MW power plant today requires about 800 acres of land, and out of 800 acres, anywhere between 250 and 300 acres is for the ash pond itself. This is a colossal misuse of scarce land resources and we need, therefore, to look at complete utilization of fly ash.

Speaking Order on the Forest Clearance Proposal for the Coal Block Linked to UMPP, NTPC, and OPGC Power Plants in Odisha

JUNE 29, 2011

1. Three coal blocks (Meenakshi-A, Meenakshi-B, and Meenakshi Dipside) have been allocated to the 3,960 MW/4,000 MW Ultra Mega Power Plant (UMPP) in Odisha that is an initiative of the Central Government. Two coal blocks (Manoharpur and Manoharpur Dipside) have been allocated to the 1,320 MW power plant of the Odisha Power Generation Corporation (OPGC). One coal block (Dulanga) has been allocated to NTPC's 1,600 MW power plant. All the six coal blocks are part of the IB Valley coal field and only one (Meenakshi-A) is presently in the 'go' area, the other five being in the 'no-go' areas.

2. Since the UMPP had already advanced considerably and in response to persistent requests from it, discussions were held first with the Ministry of Power to see how the use of good quality forest land could be minimized in the UMPP-linked coal block. Based on these discussions, I wrote to the Union Minister of Power, Sushilkumar Shinde on 14 February 2011 saying that the Ministry of Power could consider the UMPP-linked coal blocks as having been approved but that this would mean the Ministry of Power giving up plans for the NTPC and OPGC power plants.[2]

3. Subsequently, NTPC and OPGC also came forward and offered substantial changes in their mining plans. OPGC made the further argument that it was the only power plant of the three from which the state would get 100 per cent power. OPGC also made a strong case for its coal block on the grounds that this would be the first power plant to be set up by the OPGC, in which the state government now has a 51 per cent stake, for almost two decades.[3]

4. To get a broader picture of the biodiversity impacts, it was decided to relook at the three projects together. Another round of discussions commenced and the final meeting took place on 27 June 2011. The picture that has emerged based on satellite imagery is as follows (Table 8.6):

Table 8.6   Mining Plans of OPGC, NTPC and UMPP

		VDF	MDF	ODF	Total
		(in hectares)			
UMPP					
	Original	0	265	248	513
	Revised	0	65	248	313
NTPC					
	Original	2	272	37	311
	Revised	0	195	35	230
OGPC					
	Original	0	622	194	816
	Revised	0	472	194	666

VDF: Very Dense Forest;
MDF: Medium Density Forest
ODF: Open, Degraded Forest

5. Thus, it will be seen that a saving in forest area to be diverted of almost 40 per cent in the case of the UMPP, 26 per cent in the case of NTPC, and 20 per cent in the case of OPGC has materialized on account of the MoEF's intervention and the cooperation received from the Ministry of Power, NTPC, and OPGC. The number of trees felled in the NTPC case falls from around 67,500 to 37,500 (a 44 per cent reduction), and in the case of OPGC, approximately 75,000 trees get saved. The numbers in regard to the UMPP have yet to be worked out but here too, the MoEF will insist on a significant reduction.

6. It also bears mention that all the power units being put up with the coal mined in these six blocks will use super-critical technology. This will result in a saving of 5–8 per cent in terms of carbon dioxide emissions from each of the generating units as compared to a comparable sub-critical 500 MW unit.

7. In view of the above two factors, all six blocks will now be considered by the FAC as 'go' areas. OPGC's proposal that is pending with the FAC will now be taken up by the FAC in its next meeting and the proposals relating to the UMPP and NTPC will be considered when they are received from the Odisha government. The additional condition that will be imposed over and above the usual conditions governing forest clearance (Net Present Value, compensatory afforestation, wildlife management plans, etc.) is that the project proponents will bear the cost of regeneration of an area of open, degraded forest land equivalent to the amount of medium-density forest land being diverted.

8. Finally, it should be pointed out that the UMPP and the NTPC power plants are both in Sundergarh district, while the OPGC power plant in Jharsuguda district. Ash disposal and water availability need special focus by the Ministry of Power in the Sundergarh district, a point reiterated to me by the state government as well.

Letter to Chief Minister of Chhattisgarh, Raman Singh, on the Proposal for Diversion of Forests to Mine the Tara Coal Block in Densely Forested Hasdeo–Arand

2 AUGUST 2010
Kindly refer to your letter dated 4 June 2010 regarding diversion of 2,301.260 ha of forest land for open-cast coal mining at Tara Coal Block of Hasdeo–Arand coal field in Chhattisgarh.

As you are aware, the project proposal submitted by the state government was put up to the FAC, a statutory committee constituted under Section 3 of the Forest (Conservation) Act, 1980. While examining the proposal, the FAC noted that the area proposed for diversion is part of a large and compact forest block very rich in species diversity, large number of trees (367 per ha), a part of unfragmented landscape and important wildlife habitat. This is one of the few patches of its kind left in the country. The FAC, therefore, decided that the whole forest block should be kept intact to derive environmental benefits and to use it as a pristine area rather than open it up for mining.

We have jointly conducted an exercise in collaboration with the CMPDI, MoC to prepare a composite map by superimposing the boundaries of various coal fields over the forest cover map of the area. This exercise has revealed that a large number of coal blocks still lie in the forest areas, which are not so rich and, therefore, could be considered for coal mining.

The MoEF is, therefore, of the considered opinion that such important un-fragmented areas as Hasdeo–Arand area need to be protected and further enriched for posterity. I may mention that a committee under the chairmanship of member (energy), Planning Commission, is working to establish a mechanism for allotting alternative coal blocks to the entrepreneurs who are allotted coal blocks in the Hasdeo-Arand coal field.

I have personally spent considerable time on this issue and I would request you to appreciate my position.

Speaking Order on Proposals to Open up Tara, Parsa East, and Kante Basan Coal Blocks in Chhattisgarh

23 June 2011

On 22 June 2011, I received the final recommendation of the FAC to reject the proposals made by the Chhattisgarh government to open up the Tara, Parsa East, and Kante Basan coal blocks in the Hasdeo–Arand forest region of the state. The FAC has been deliberating on these proposals for almost eighteen months and has considered them from time to time. On three earlier occasions—21 January 2010, 30 July 2010, and 22 October 2010—I had concurred with the FAC's recommendation and rejected the proposals. However, I now disagree with the final recommendations of the FAC for six reasons, and have decided to give Stage-I approval for these proposals.

The first reason for my rejection of the FAC recommendation arises from my understanding that these three coal blocks are clearly in the fringe and actually not in the biodiversity-rich Hasdeo–Arand forest region (a 'no-go' area). They are separated by a well-defined high hilly ridge with drainage into the Aten river, which flows towards Hariarpur in the opposite direction. It appears to be a totally different watershed. As long as the mining is restricted to the fringe area and as long as the state government does not come up with fresh applications for opening up the main Hasdeo–Arand area, I am of the opinion that permission can be accorded for Tara, Parsa East, and Kante Basan.

The second reason for my rejection of the FAC recommendation arises from the substantial changes that have been introduced in the mining plans as originally envisaged. When the project proponent is prepared to demonstrate some flexibility to accommodate our concerns, I think we should also reciprocate.

Four significant changes have been incorporated in the Tara coal block proposal to deal with our concerns: (i) medium-density forest area has been reduced from about 2,000 ha to 778 ha; (ii) total trees to be felled have been reduced from about 8.5 lakh to about 1.2 lakh; (iii) the operation period of the mine shall be reduced from forty-five years to twenty-five years; (iv) all movement of coal from the mine to the power plant situated 7 km away will be through overhead conveyor systems only. As far as Parsa East and Kante Basan are concerned, where the forest quality is poorer than Tara by the FAC's own assessment, the revised proposal envisages two phases—a fifteen-year Phase-I covering 762 ha and a subsequent fifteen-year Phase-II covering around 1,136 ha. Reclamation of the mined out area is to start from the third year onwards, thus, making it possible to link renewal for Phase-II to performance on reforestation and biodiversity management in Phase-I, which is part of the conditions governing my approval. Actually, I find the mining plan for Parsa East and Kante Basan is one, therefore, they should not be treated as separate blocks—the allocation to Rajasthan Vidyut Utpadan Nigam Limited (RVUNL) treats both as one block.

The third reason for my rejecting the FAC recommendation arises from the fact that the concerns identified relating to wildlife can, in my view, and should be taken care of through a well-prepared and well-executed wildlife management plan and programme under the aegis of an institution like the Wildlife Institute of India. Other independent institutions with expertise on elephant-related issues especially, like the Nature Conservation Foundation, Wildlife Trust of India, and the Centre for Ecological Studies at the Indian Institute of Science could also be involved the preparation and implementation of such a management plan with funds pooled from the project proponents (Indian Farmers Fertiliser Cooperative Limited and RVUNL). Such a plan should be prepared over the next four–six months and be monitored by the MoEF.

The fourth reason for my rejecting the FAC recommendation arises from the fact that these coal blocks are linked to supercritical thermal power generating stations. In fact, this is an explicit pre-condition for approval in order to remove any ambiguity on this score. Supercritical technology is absolutely essential for us in order to deal with global warming issues and concerns. With a 660/800 MW supercritical technology, anywhere from 5 to 8 per cent lower emissions of carbon dioxide will accrue over a conventional sub-critical 500 MW power plant that we have so far been putting up. Supercritical (and ultra supercritical) technology has to proliferate rapidly if we are to meet our growing energy needs in an environmentally acceptable manner.

The fifth reason for my rejecting the FAC recommendation arises from the fact that both the state governments involved—Chhattisgarh and Rajasthan (which will use the coal mined at Parsa East and Kante Basan) have been persistently following-up since their power generation plans are closely linked with these coal blocks. The chief minister of Chhattisgarh wrote to the Prime Minister on 8 July 2010 and 9 February 2011. He also wrote to me on 4 June 2010 and on 9 February 2011. The chief minister of Rajasthan wrote to the Prime Minister on 12 February 2011 and the minister for energy, Government of Rajasthan, wrote to me on 15 June 2011, 24 May 2011, 7 April 2011, 1 March 2011, and 21 February 2011.[4]

The sixth reason for my rejecting the FAC recommendation arises from the imperative to sustain the momentum generated in the Eleventh Five Year Plan in terms of capacity addition (52,000 MW or thereabouts as compared to about 21,000 MW in the Tenth Plan). The FAC's brief is to look at forest-related issues exclusively, but while the FAC has to do its due diligence with single-minded focus, as the minister I have necessarily to keep the broader developmental picture in mind and balance out different objectives and considerations.

After taking all factors into account, I am of the view that permission should be granted to opening the Tara and the Parsa East–Kante Basan coal block as proposed by the Chhattisgarh government. While granting this permission I must reiterate that any more opening of coal blocks in the main Hasdeo–Arand forest area will severely disturb the fragile ecosystem of the region. Perhaps, the Chhattisgarh government could be compensated through some sort of a 'green bonus' (either through additional central assistance or through additional allocations of power from the central pool) for not giving any further permissions for coal mining in the Hasdeo–Arand region. This green bonus policy will, of course, apply to projects in other states as well, which may not see the light of day on account of ecological factors.

Since the Parsa block of the Chhattisgarh State Electricity Board is in between the Tara and the Parsa East–Kante Basan coal block, permission for prospecting only as sought for by the state government is also hereby accorded. This block should not be worked commercially for at least the next five years till after some reclamation on portions of the two other coal block has commenced in a visible manner.

Needless to add, final Stage-II approval will be contingent on the Chhattisgarh Government demonstrating full compliance with the provisions of the FRA, 2006.

Speaking Order on Forest Clearance for Morga-II Coal Block in the Hasdeo–Arand Forests in Chhattisgarh

5 JULY 2011

The Morga-II coal block is in the core of the very biodiversity-rich Hasdeo–Arand forest area of Chhattisgarh. It was allocated in August 2006 to the Gujarat Mineral Development Corporation (GMDC). GMDC entered into a coal supply agreement with KSK Energy Ventures Limited, Hyderabad, in November 2006 to develop an 1,800 MW (3 x 600) power plant.

Morga-II is very clearly in 'no-go' area. On 23 June 2011, Stage-I approval for opening of Tara, Parsa East, and Kante Basan coal blocks in the fringes of the Hasdeo–Arand region was given. The clearance for the three coal blocks in the fringe area was given because they are not in the biodiversity-rich region of the Hasdeo–Arand forest region. They are separated by a well-defined, high hilly ridge and are in a totally different watershed. While giving this approval, I had observed, 'as long as mining is restricted to the fringe area and as long as the state government does not come up with fresh applications for opening up the main Hasdeo–Arand area, I am of the opinion that permission can be accorded for Tara, Parsa East, and Kante Basan'.

On 29 June 2011, S. Kishore and K.B. Raju, directors, KSK Energy Ventures Limited, met me and gave a representation. I explained to them that it would be virtually impossible to give forest clearance to Morga-II because it is very clearly in the main Hasdeo–Arand forest region. Moreover, the power plant does not use super-critical technology that leads to 5–8 per cent lower emissions of carbon dioxide. I also explained to them that state government forest officers had expressed their extreme reluctance to open up this block.

During this meeting, KSK Energy Ventures informed me that it has identified an alternative coal block which is in the 'go' area. This block is the Bhalumuda block in the Mand–Raigarh coal field of Chhattisgarh. CEA [Central Electricity Authority] has made a recommendation to the MoC supporting this alternative coal block.

In view of the fact that there is a clearly identified coal block and in view of the fact that KSK Energy Ventures itself sees no great difficulty in using this coal block as opposed to Morga-II, I am of the view that forest clearance for Morga-II should not be granted. In fact, KSK Energy Ventures appeared to appreciate the problems inherent in Hasdeo–Arand and expressed willingness on its own to shift the allocated coal block to Bhalumuda. It is to be hoped that the MoC will make the alternative coal block allocation given the flexibility that the MoEF is demonstrating in allowing some coal block allocated five–six years ago in forest-rich areas to be mined in view of developmental imperatives.[5]

Letter Responding to the Issues Raised by Shashi Ruia, Chairman of Essar, in his Letter to the Prime Minister

17 MARCH 2010

I have just received your letter of 12 March enclosing a copy of a letter that you have received from Shashi Ruia, chairman, Essar, regarding expeditious forest clearance for Essar's 2 x 600 MW power project in Singrauli. The coal mine in question is the Mahan coal block in the Singrauli coal field, in the Sidhi district of Madhya Pradesh.

The proposal for forest clearance was first received by the MoEF on 8 January 2008. It was considered by the FAC, on 23 July 2008, 10 October 2008, 20 July 2009, and most recently on 12 December 2009. The reason why it has been taking time is because the proposal involves diversion of 1,182.35 ha of excellent forest land. The area has dense vegetation and very good biodiversity as well. The last FAC meeting decided to send a technical team of experts to the coal mine area to assess the impact before taking a final decision. I am sure you will agree with me that this is a reasonable process to adopt in such sensitive cases.

Shashi Ruia has also mentioned in his letter that other coal-mining projects in the vicinity have been cleared while his project is awaiting clearance. I would like to state clearly that the MoEF has not cleared any coal-mining lease in this unfragmented area spread over 20,000 ha of dense forest land with rich wildlife values. With regard to the UMPP project at Sasan and the Amelia North project of Jaypee, which Shashi Ruia refers to in his letter, it has been clarified that Sasan is in an already fragmented and broken area in the northern part of Singrauli Coalfields having many coal projects of Northern Coalfields Limited, a subsidiary of CIL. Amelia North project involves lower number of trees and is also on the northern periphery of the unfragmented area. It is pertinent to mention that even these two projects have been accorded only first stage approval and not final approval. I would like to also inform you that I am personally familiar with this area and, therefore, whatever I have to say is based on actual personal knowledge.

Shashi Ruia says that the coal mine should be cleared because 65 per cent of the power plant is ready. I cannot, Sir, agree to this logic. I have repeatedly raised my objection to such fait accompli arguments in Cabinet meetings, if you will kindly recall.

Note to Principal Secretary to the Prime Minister T.K.A. Nair following Meeting with Shashi Ruia, Chairman of Essar on 12 May 2010

13 May 2010

Yesterday, Shashi Ruia, Chairman, Essar Group, met me in regard to his power project, which is linked with the Singrauli coalfield in the Sidhi district of Madhya Pradesh. I explained to him with the help of detailed maps that the Mahan coal block is in a 'no-go' area and it cannot be cleared because it will involve the destruction of high-density forests and will also destroy critical wildlife corridors and habitats. Of course, the Mahan coal block should never have been allowed in the first place but that is history now.

I also explained to Shashi Ruia the position in the nearby Sohagpur coal field, where over 70 per cent of the coal blocks are in the 'go' area. If it is possible, Ruia's power project of 2 x 600 MW, which he claims is 65 per cent complete, can get allocations from Sohagpur on a priority basis. Normally we allot coal blocks to projects, which are yet to take off, but surely here an exception can be made since the power plant is apparently going to be completed in the next six–nine months.

I would like to reiterate what I had mentioned in my letter to the Prime Minister, dated 17 March 2010. Clearance of the Mahan coal block will open up a Pandora's Box, which we should avoid at all costs.

Note to Prime Minister on a Compromise Formula, Seeking an Allocation of an Alternative Coal Block for the Essar and Hindalco Power Projects

24 MAY 2010
Senior officials from the MoEF have been interacting with Principal Secretary to the Prime Minister to further refine the concept of 'go' and 'no-go' areas as far as coal mines are concerned. On the whole, the exercise has been quite productive and we have been able to arrive at a very large degree of consensus.

However, there is one issue on which I would seek your guidance. There are power projects, which are already under implementation but whose coal mines fall in the 'no-go' area. Two examples of such projects are Essar and Hindalco in the Mahan coal block of the Singrauli coal field of Madhya Pradesh. Essar and Hindalco claim that their power projects are going to be commissioned early next year. I am finding it exceedingly difficult to accord clearance for the coal blocks. Both Ruia and Kumar Mangalam Birla have met me. I have explained to them my position. The fact is that they have gone ahead with the power plants when they did not have *final* clearance for the coal blocks.

The Adani power project in the Chandrapur coal belt is in a different category. Its coal block is in a 'no-go' area, but the power project has *not* even started. There are a number of other power projects, which are still on the drawing board and which will *not* be adversely affected by the 'go' and 'no-go' areas concept.

It is only power projects like Essar and Hindalco, which apparently are well on their way to completion, that will get affected by the 'go' and 'no-go' concept. One option would be to say we will clear the coal block even if it is in a 'no-go' area, if it is meant for a power project, which is 60–70 per cent complete. This is a fallback position that I could adopt, albeit most reluctantly, if the Prime Minister so directs. But I would still plead for an alternative coal linkage.

Speaking Order on Allocation of the Mahan Coal Block in Madhya Pradesh to Essar and Hindalco

8 JULY 2011

I

On 12 April 2006, the Union Ministry of Coal allocated the Mahan Coal Block in the Singrauli coal field in Madhya Pradesh to Essar Power Limited and Hindalco Industries Limited. The allocation letter says that the coal extracted is meant for captive use in the 1,200 MW power plant of Essar and the 650 MW power plant of Hindalco. EC was given to the Mahan coal block on 23 December 2008.

The FAC has considered this proposal four times—on 23 July 2008, 10 October 2008, 20 July 2009, and 11 December 2009. It was unable to arrive at a final decision given the complexity of the issues involved.[6] Thereafter, in January–February 2010, the Mahan coal block was identified as being in the 'no-go' zone based on the joint exercise carried out by the MoEF and CMPDI of the MoC.

II

On 17 March 2010, I wrote to the Hon. Prime Minister in response to a letter he had received from Essar and Hindalco on which my comments had been sought.[7] On 12 May 2010, Shashi Ruia met me, followed by

Kumar Mangalam Birla on 21 May 2010. I reiterated to them the points made in my letter to the Prime Minister and the difficulty the MoEF has in giving forest clearance to the Mahan coal block.[8]

On 24 May 2010, I proposed a 'compromise' formula suo moto to the Hon. Prime Minister by which the MoEF would consider clearing a coal block even if it is a 'no-go' area if it is meant for a power project, which is over 60–70 per cent complete.[9] Based on my 24 May 2010 communication to the Prime Minister, an inter-ministerial exercise was carried out by the PMO.[10] On 16 August 2010, Shashi Ruia wrote once again to the Prime Minister and me.[11] On 15 January 2011, Shashi Ruia and Kumar Mangalam Birla wrote to the finance minister asking for a quick decision on the Mahan coal block.[12]

III

There are three factors weighing in favour of clearing the proposal.

1. The Mahan coal block was allocated in 2006 before the 'go–no-go' issue came to the fare.
2. Substantial investments to the tune of about Rs 3,600 crore (reported by an inter-ministerial team set up by the PMO in July 2010)[13] appear to have already been made in the power plants linked with the Mahan coal block.
3. The Madhya Pradesh chief minister has personally spoken to me twice on clearing the proposal (most recently on 30 June 2011) on the grounds that it will boost economic activity in the state. This was one of the issues on which he went on a fast on 13 February 2011 alleging discrimination against Madhya Pradesh by the central government.

IV

But there are also four factors weighing against clearing it.

1. The coal block is undoubtedly in a biodiversity-rich area. It will destroy good natural forest cover and interfere with wildlife habitats. Clearing this coal block would open the doors for allowing other coal block to be mined, albeit those that have already been allocated in 2006 or 2007. This would fragment an area very rich in forest cover—both in terms of quantity and quality.

2. The power plants do not have the redeeming feature of being super-critical units that generate 5–8 per cent lesser emissions of carbon dioxide. Essar's plants are sub-critical 600 MW units and Hindalco's are sub-critical 125 MW units.

3. The FAC has not given it clearance since 2008 even before the 'go–no-go' issue gained prominence.

V

In a final effort to find a compromise, I met Shashi Ruia on 28 June 2011 and asked him to submit an alternative mining plan that would reduce the amount of forest area that will be diverted. I explained our concerns in some detail and also discussed some conditions under which clearance would stand a chance. An alternative mining plan was submitted to the MoEF on 30 June 2011.[14] One option presented in the alternative mining plan proposes a reduction of about 104 ha of good quality forest area. Essar argues that since the MoEF had already secured a reduction of 110 ha of good quality forest area in 2008 as part of the environmental clearance, the total saving should be reckoned at about 214 ha (or roughly 15 per cent of the original area proposed by Essar and about 18 per cent of the mining area approved).

By Essar's own admission,[15] the Mahan coal block will meet the coal requirements of the two 600 MW units for fourteen years only. There is no coal linkage for the balance life, which could extend for another ten–fifteen years at least. I am not entirely clear why such a good quality forest area should be broken up for such a partial requirement. Sal is the predominant species in the forest. Sal is a good coppice but is very difficult to grow through raising plantations. Moreover, a third 600 MW unit is planned as part of Phase-II of the project for which the coal linkage has yet to be firmed up.

On 7 July 2011, I received a report prepared by a sub-committee of the FAC after a field-visit to the Mahan coal block area.[16] The FAC sub-committee found that the quality of the forest and tree cover is much higher than that being claimed by Essar, Hindalco, and the state government. Some of the ecological issues identified by the sub-committee can be managed, for example, those relating to wildlife habitats and corridors. But there are some other ecological issues that are critical on which we have no clarity as of now. To my mind, point

No. (iv) on page 4 of the sub-committee's report is perhaps the most crucial—the fact that the Mahan coal block is located in catchment area of the Rihand Reservoir and that there is a high degree of probability of excessive siltation due to denudation of the slopes and hills when they are mined for coal. Of course, the Rihand Reservoir is under threat not just from the proposed Mahan coal block but from other coal blocks that have been allocated in the vicinity. This is a larger issue for the state government to consider. Implicit in the recommendation of the FAC sub-committee to withhold permission for forest clearance is the need to carry out more detailed EIA studies.

In this backdrop, I am unable to agree to consider the Mahan coal block for Stage-I clearance. However, in keeping with the proposal I had myself made to the GoM on 7 April 2011 to resolve issues relating to the coal blocks in the 'no-go' areas, the Mahan coal block is, therefore, being submitted to the GoM for its consideration with a recommendation that an alternative coal linkage be provided for the two power plants. The MoEF has identified the Sohagpur coal field in the Shahdol district as a possible alternative linkage.

Notes

1. A copy of the presentation was sent to the Prime Minister along with this letter.

2. This letter was made public as Annexure I of the speaking order,

3. The letter from Minister of Energy, Government of Odisha on this issue was included as Annexure-II of the speaking order.

4. Copies of these letters were made public as annexures to the speaking order.

5. The representation given to me by KSK Energy Ventures Ltd is at Annexure-I. My communication to Principal Secretary to Prime Minister supporting the alternative allocation is at Annexure-II.

6. The observations made by the FAC at each of these meetings are as Annexure-I.

7. A copy of Shashi Ruia's letter to the Prime Minister and my response is as Annexure-II. The letter has been included in this chapter.

8. A copy of a communication sent to the Principal Secretary to the Prime Minister on 13 May 2010, following my meeting with Shashi Ruia, was made public as Annexure III of the speaking order, and has been included in this chapter.

9. A copy of this communication was made public as Annexure-IV and has been included in this chapter.

10. The conclusions of this inter-ministerial exercise was included as Annexure-V of the speaking order.

11. A copy of this letter is as Annexure-VI in the speaking order.

12. Copies of these letters were made public along with the speaking order, as Annexure-VII.

13. The investment amount reported by the inter-ministerial team set up by the PMO is part of Annexure V of the speaking order.

14. The details of the alternative mining plan was included as Annexure-VIII.

15. The communication from Essar is part of the speaking order dossier as Annexure-IX.

16. This report was made public as Annexure-X.

9 Energy Dilemmas

The quest for high economic growth and the goal of eradicating poverty in our lifetime both require a manifold increase in energy consumption. Some 400 million people are still without access to electricity, while countless more have limited access. Our energy requirements are of a dimension that doesn't allow for easy options. The need to sustain economic growth coupled with our demographic realities leave no option for us but to rely on coal as the mainstay of our energy basket.

There is then the other side of the story—India's vulnerability to climate change, the need to address growing carbon emissions and air pollution (our domestic coal though low in sulphur content has high ash content), and preserve the forests as carbon sinks requires that we diversify and tap alternative sources of energy, such as solar, wind, and biomass as well as nuclear power.

Despite the advantages from a climate change and public health standpoint, the 'environment-friendly' alternative energy resources are not without environmental hazards and pitfalls.

Environmentalists are united in their opposition to the use of fossil fuels, like coal. However, they are not so united in their choice of alternative energy sources. They advocate the use of renewable sources like wind, solar, and biomass. They are even tolerant of small hydropower projects. Most environmentalists are opposed to or at best ambiguous about nuclear power. The lack of a unified voice pushing for alternative energy sources meant that sector was riddled by years of poor planning as well as bad policy choices and incentives.

I realized the extent of the difficulty that poor planning and policies with little relevance to ground realities presented in harnessing of alternative sources of energy in the course of my interactions with different stakeholders. As a result, environmental groups, the constituency that should have been most supportive of harnessing alternative energy sources, were the ones who were opposed to it. A clear case is the hydroelectric power sector. India's hydroelectricity potential is largely untapped both in the Himalayan hill states but more so in the Northeast Hydroelectricity accounts for roughly 17 per cent of the electricity generated in the country. However, the policy adopted both by the central and state governments to harness this potential was destroying the rivers as in the case of the upper reaches of the Ganga and creating concerns in the river's downstream as in the case of Assam as well as destroying biodiversity.

Unfortunately, the planning of power projects did not take into account the carrying capacity of the river, pushing the situation to a dangerous limit. Even though India had harnessed only 35 per cent of its hydroelectric power potential, it would appear that we had not done a good job of it. The upper reaches of the Ganga had more hydroelectric power projects that it could support. The river's ecological flow was at peril, endangering the river and the life it supported. I had to take the difficult decision of abandoning three hydroelectric power projects on the upper reaches of the Ganga, despite the fact that substantial expenditure had already been incurred by the NHPC in its Lohari Nag Pala project. The decision also did not find favour with the Uttarakhand Government, which felt that its 'development options' were being foreclosed. Similarly, the development of hydroelectric power projects in Arunachal Pradesh was met with huge protests in Assam. Once again, it was a case of poor groundwork—the impact of power projects in downstream Assam had not been taken into consideration. I was again, in a manner of speaking, the bearer of bad news. I made a case for stepping back and revisiting the hydropower projects in the Northeast.

My decision to push the government to scrap three hydroelectric power projects on the Bhagirathi river contributed to me being branded me as anti-development especially in Uttarakhand. However, it was not without benefits. Both this decision, and my advice to the Prime Minister to consider revisiting hydroelectric power projects in the Northeast led to the institutionalization of the practice of undertaking cumulative impact assessment for river basins. This practice would help assess and quantify the river basins capacity to support power projects and provide an assessment of the safeguards required. In time, I suggested that the practice be followed for thermal power plants as well.

The nuclear option, was another energy source that had recently opened up to us. But the public faith in the regulatory mechanism was poor. The Jaitapur Nuclear Power Park that came up for environmental clearance before me, was the subject of protests. Given my stance on other issues, environmentalists and anti-nuclear supporters expected me to deny clearance. I cleared the Jaitapur project, because it met the environmental norms, I even specified special conditions as precaution. It was a decision that made many environmentalists unhappy, charging me with abandoning the cause of the environment. It was an unfair charge.

Nuclear safety was beyond my remit, but I did understand that there was a need to present the facts to the people. I had consistently maintained the need for a strong and independent regulatory authority, and the doubts raised about the safety of nuclear plants following the Fukushima incident only served to underscore my conviction. I went beyond the scope of my mandate and raised the issue of a need for an independent regulator with the Prime Minister. I also made a point to meet with the chairman and officials of the Finnish Nuclear Regulatory Authority, during a visit to Helsinki, to understand the structure of the organization and the lessons we could draw from the Finnish authority. I have always maintained that independent regulatory oversight can go a long way in allaying the concerns of the public.

The desirability of renewable and nuclear sources for power notwithstanding harnessing these sources presented several problems. India would need to rework its approach to setting up projects, and take extra measures to reach out to the public. In the meantime, coal would continue to be the mainstay of our energy basket. This meant equal focus would have to be given to ensure that emissions and pollution from coal-based thermal power plants. This would require opting for better supercritical technology and reducing the emission intensity of thermal plants would be controlled. The good news was that NTPC, which is the biggest operator of coal-based plants in the country , had a good track record with regard to emission intensity of its plants.

Nuclear power accounts for barely 3.5 per cent of our energy supply. Even if the concerns about safety—which have heightened in the post-Fukusima era—are addressed and an aggressive nuclear power generation plan is adopted, its share is unlikely to go beyond 5 per cent by 2030. The issues relating to hydropower require to be addressed in a careful and considered manner. Harnessing solar and wind power must be the focus, something I sought to encourage in my ministerial capacity. But it requires a change in mindset. We cannot treat renewable energy sourced from solar and wind in the same way that we approach fossil fuel-based energy.

There is another aspect of India's energy dilemma. It requires us to be more aggressive about energy efficiency. It took us more than five years to put in place mandatory fuel efficiency standards for cars. As the junior power minister for power in the United Progressive Alliance-I government, I was involved with the Bureau of Energy Efficiency's efforts to introduce standards for fuel efficiency. Given the obvious environmental impacts, I raised the issue almost as soon as I took over as environment minister. My interactions only served to re-affirm what I already knew that India's energy requirements, and the fact that the world is yet to find an effective way to decouple emissions and economic growth, meant that we will continue to rely on coal for energy. But that should not preclude efforts to pursue cleaner energy options, focusing on technology and efficiency measures.

This chapter deals with the challenges of harnessing renewable and nuclear sources of power and the efforts made to control emissions from coal-based power plants.

Letter to Union Minister for Power Sushilkumar Shinde
Reiterating Issues Relating to Improving Environmental Integrity
of Power Projects Raised at the Meeting of State Power Ministers

30 JUNE 2009

First of all I would like to thank you for inviting me to the meeting of power ministers of state governments on 23 June 2009. It was a useful experience for me.

You may recall that I had raised a number of issues in my intervention and I would like to highlight some of the important ones for your further consideration:

1. My experience is that there are many instances of projects not adhering to the conditions stipulated during the environmental and forestry clearance. Unfortunately the monitoring systems for compliance are very weak but there is a need to ensure that projects fulfil their obligations when it comes to environment and forests. Perhaps, CEA could conduct an annual assessment;

2. There is a strong tendency for projects to start and have their foundation stones laid even before environmental and forestry clearances are obtained. This reduces such clearances to a mere formality, which, certainly, is not the intention of our government;

3. The Environmental Impact Assessments (EIAs) are often carried out very routinely. There is enough professional expertise available in our country which can be mobilized for carrying out rigorous analysis of projects;

4. There are some areas in the power-cum-coal sector which have already emerged as environmental 'hotspots'. Singarauli, Korba, and Talcher are examples that come readily to my mind. Water and land have emerged as serious binding constraints and new ways of optimizing their use have to be put into practice.

5. As far as hydroelectric projects are concerned, we need to carry out cumulative impact assessments on a basin-basis and not just assessment of individual projects. This is particularly true in the mega projects that are underway in states like Arunachal Pradesh and Sikkim.

I would also urge you to direct public sector units (PSUs), like NTPC, NHPC, North Eastern Electric Power Corporation Limited, and SJVN Limited to show greater sensitivity to environmental concerns at the highest level. I am aware of what they have done but I am sure you will agree with me when I say that much more needs to be done quickly, particularly in the context of climate change.

Finally, let me reassure you that the Ministry of Environment and Forests will not, in any way, delay environment and forestry clearances. We will implement laws in a business-like and transparent manner. Together we can, I am sure, demonstrate how the twin challenges of adding to power capacity quickly and of enhancing ecological security demonstrably can go hand-in-hand.

Speaking Order on Nuclear Power Corporation of India Limited, Jaitapur Nuclear Power Park

28 November 2010

The NPCIL has sought environmental clearance for 6 x 1, 650 MW power generating complex to be implemented in phases at village Madban in the Ratnagiri district of Maharashtra. NPCIL has signed an agreement with the French company AREVA for establishing this complex which will initially come up with two 1,650 MW units. Land acquisition is being done for the six units.

I

Over the past few months, I have been petitioned by various organizations, of which representations from the Konkan Bachao Samiti have been the most detailed. These petitions have argued that environmental clearance should not be given because of a variety of reasons including the following:

1. Nuclear power is extremely risky and hazardous.
2. The cost of generating power at Madban will be very high.
3. There is no clarity on waste storage and disposal and use of spent fuel.
4. Local ecology (mud flats, mangroves, and sealife particularly) will be adversely affected.
5. The environmental impact assessment carried out is grossly inadequate.
6. Safety record of the AREVA reactors are highly questionable.
7. There is no urgency to accord environmental approval.

The Konkan Bachao Samiti (KBS) has made ideological, economic, safety, and environmental arguments. I have met with the KBS personally thrice and also arranged for its members to interact with the NPCIL on two separate occasions. All the letters sent by the KBS to me are on www.moef.nic.in. They have been given due consideration by the Expert Appraisal Committee (EAC) of the MoEF for strategic projects. The EAC has also visited the project site on 28 October 2010.

While I respect the views of the KBS, I have made clear to its members that I am not the competent authority to pass judgement on matters related to the need, economics, and safety of nuclear power. As far as design safety is concerned, clearances are to be given by the Atomic Energy Regulatory Board (AERB). As far as fuel reprocessing and waste disposal is concerned, it is for NPCIL and AREVA to allay various public concerns.

What I have made clear to the KBS repeatedly is that the MoEF's brief is to implement the Environment (Protection) Act, 1986, the Forest (Conservation) Act, 1980, the Coastal Regulation Zone Notification, 1991 and other environmental laws and regulations that may be relevant for this project. I can take on board only the ecological objections raised by the KBS. But mindful of their seriousness, I have asked the NPCIL and its partner AREVA to address the other economic, commercial, safety, and technological issues. Indeed, I do believe that NPCIL must significantly improve and expand its public outreach programme.

II

The Bombay Natural History Society (BNHS) has submitted a detailed biodiversity assessment report to the MoEF a couple of days back. This report covers the entire Ratnagiri ecosystem in which Jaitapur is situated. The BNHS report stresses that the Jaitapur region is rich in biodiversity. The biodiversity is not so much in the project location, per se, as much as it is in the surrounding regions of around 10 km radius around the project site. The report says that the project could have impact on the rich marine species diversity and abundance (marine shell organisms, sea cucumbers, sea anemones, sea urchins, brittle star, etc.) around Ambolgad, north of Madban. Waghran, Ansure, Purnagadh, and Kasheli are other prime biodiversity areas that need to be fully protected by NPCIL.

The MoEF has indeed considered the BNHS report seriously and has stipulated a number of specific conditions as part of the environmental approval that are intended to deal with the concerns raised by it. I have also had personal discussions with the BNHS.

Is there any urgency to accord environmental approval?

The NPCIL–AREVA joint venture is significant not just from an energy generation but also from a strategic point of view. It is the first practical outcome of the Civilian Nuclear Agreement that India negotiated so successfully with the nuclear suppliers between 2005 and 2009.

Very soon, NPCIL and AREVA are to sign a General Framework Agreement as well as an Early Works Agreement. The final contracts are to be signed in the first half of 2011. A decision on environmental clearance is essential to facilitate all these agreements even though the first unit of 1,650 MW is expected to become operational only by 2018.

From an environmental point of view, nuclear energy is a cleaner option than coal. It is also significantly less land-intensive. Presently, 38 per cent of India's greenhouse gas (GHG) emissions come from the electricity generation sector, the single largest contribution. India's electricity generation has to grow at something like 7 per cent annually in order to sustain a real annual (GDP) growth rate of 9 per cent over the next decade.

But, unlike in the past, we now have to be extremely concerned about the impact of this increase in electricity generation on our emissions of carbon dioxide. The impact can be kept in check by a variety of means of which an increase in the share of nuclear energy in the fuel-mix is one critical option. Presently, nuclear energy accounts for around 2.9 per cent of our electricity generating capacity and we are looking to increase it to about 6 per cent by 2020 and possibly 13 per cent by 2030.

III

The nuclear power complex raises many questions on the carrying capacity of the ecologically sensitive region in which it is located. Ratnagiri district is in the fragile Western Ghats area. A very large number of development projects, particularly power plants, are planned here. The total power generating capacity proposed on a narrow strip of coastal land 50–90 km wide and 200 km long is around 33,000 MW (including NPCIL's own 9,900 MW). All of the other new plants are coal-based, which will add to the environmental problems in the area. The only gas-based plant is the one at Dabhol.

India must now get used to the concept of carrying capacity and cumulative EIA studies. All our EIA are individual project-based. But it is clear to me that in areas like the Western Ghats, we have to go beyond such project-wise assessments and look at the cumulative impact of the major projects that are being planned. I would like the Maharashtra Government to initiate such studies immediately through reputed independent institutions. The MoEF will collaborate in such studies. This is extremely urgent and crucial given the very large number of power plants, mining projects, port projects, and other pollution-intensive industries on the anvil, not only in Ratnagiri but also in the Sindhudurg and Raigad districts.

I have also sought advice from Dr Madhav Gadgil, one of India's most distinguished ecologists and chairman of the Western Ghats Ecology Expert Panel, which the MoEF set up in March 2010. He has said that local biodiversity management committees envisaged under the Biological Diversity Act, 2002 should be immediately activated in these three ecologically sensitive districts by the National Biodiversity Authority. He has reiterated the need for conducting the carrying capacity and cumulative impact assessment studies and recommended the establishment of long-term ecology surveillance networks in Raigad, Sindhudurg, and Ratnagiri to begin with. The MoEF will initiate follow-up action on Dr Gadgil's valuable suggestions.

IV

The temperature of the discharged cooling water has an important bearing on marine biodiversity. The specified limit at present is 7 degrees Celsius—that is the temperature differential of the discharged water with respect to the receiving water. The Central Water and Power Research Station (CWPRS), Pune, has carried out mathematical studies that revealed that transition period (October–February) is the most critical period from thermal dispersion point of view because the seasonal currents during this period are in the transition period.

Based on these studies, CWPRS has modelled that the maximum temperature rise at the outfall locations, when all the six units are operating at full power capacity will be in the range of 4 degrees Celsius and 4.9 degrees Celsius. Thus, while the specified temperature differential limit is 7 degrees Celsius, I am persuaded by the CWPRS analysis and accordingly the temperature differential limit is being reduced to and specified at 5 degrees Celsius as part of environmental clearance.

V

Keeping all relevant factors in mind, the MoEF is according environmental clearance to NPCIL's Jaitapur power complex but with a thirty-five conditions and safeguards, of which twelve are general conditions. Of the twenty-three specific conditions, the following are the most important.

1. In the next twelve months

   a. A comprehensive biodiversity conservation plan shall be prepared for the Jaitapur region within twelve months in consultation with the BNHS, the state forests and wildlife department, and local biodiversity management committees. This plan will also deal with measures needed to maintain the health of the mangroves in the creek area outside the plant site. The total mangrove area, according to the BNHS, may be around 150 ha.

   b. A monitoring committee comprising of outside experts and institutions (including the BNHS, College of Fisheries, Ratnagiri, and the Balasaheb Sawant Konkan Krishi Vidyapeeth, Dapoli) would be constituted by the NPCIL to oversee the implementation of environmental management measures stipulated as part of environmental clearance. The deliberations of the monitoring committee would be put on the website of the NPCIL on a regular basis.

   c. A special plan will be made to put in place appropriate safeguard measures to ensure that the fisheries in the sea adjoining Ambolgad are not affected adversely due to the project. BNHS and other agencies should be involved in this exercise. Kasheli is another critical area that needs to be safeguarded. A special plan for mitigating adverse impacts on fishing livelihoods in the region will also be implemented. Musakazi is an important fishing village and jetty which is less than a kilometre away from the project site. Access to fishing communities should be ensured at all times.

   d. Design of cooling water discharge system will be finalized with demonstrably adequate provision for its extension into the marine area beyond 2.2 km, if needed to minimize the adverse impact on biodiversity/coral reefs/aquatic fauna in the larger Jaitapur area.

e. NPCIL's ongoing environmental stewardship programme should be substantially strengthened with a focus on the Western Ghats since three of its power generating complexes—Tarapur, Kaiga, and now Jaitapur—are located in this ecologically sensitive region. This programme must build a network of independent scholars and sentinels for nature conservation.

2. During the finalization of the project design and the approval by the AERB, if the project undergoes such design/technology changes as compared to the one proposed at the stage of obtaining environmental clearance, which have significant impact on environmental components, the project will be brought back for its reconsideration of the MoEF.

3. The storage, disposal, and management of radioactive liquid waste emanating from the plant will be strictly treated and managed as per the guidelines and procedures prescribed by AERB/ICRP in this regard. The solid radioactive waste shall be stored above ground as per the standard EPR reactor design after it has been duly reviewed and certified by the AERB.

4. The radioactive levels in different components of the environment, including food chain, air quality, water, and soil shall be monitored regularly for radioactive levels in the surrounding areas as per AERB standards and records maintained for public scrutiny.

5. Online continuous monitoring of the temperature of the discharged cooling water shall be carried out at the discharge point. It shall be ensured that the temperature differential of the discharged water with respect to the intake water does not exceed 5 degrees Celsius at any given point of time.

6. A comprehensive EIA will be done when both units—1 and 2—are operational by 2019 and the results of this assessment feed into additional safeguards, if needed for the operation of the remaining four units. The decision to accord environmental clearance for NPCIL's Jaitapur power generating complex has been difficult. On the one hand there have been many issues raised on the preservation of marine biodiversity, an area in which India has been very weak. But at the same time, there are weighty strategic and economic reasons in favour of the grant of environmental clearance now.

A delicate balancing act has had to be done. There may well be, I have to admit, some unhappiness at my decision amongst some environmentalists active in the Western Ghats region, particularly, many of whom are instinctively and ideologically opposed to nuclear energy. But I do believe that the conditions that have been stipulated do provide the essential middle ground to reconcile the objectives of economic growth, fuel-mix diversification, global diplomacy, and environmental protection.

Like I have done earlier on important issues like Bt-brinjal, Vedanta, and the Navi Mumbai airport, I am making public my detailed reasoning for the decision being taken—in this case, environmental clearance for NPCIL's Jaitapur Nuclear Power Park.

Letter to Prime Minister on the Need for an Independent Nuclear Regulator in the Wake of Fukushima Catastrophe

28 MARCH 2011

I am writing to share with you some concerns that have arisen in my mind following the nuclear catastrophe in Japan. Before I do so, let me reiterate that I firmly believe that nuclear energy has an important role to play in our energy policy, more so in view of the fact that from a GHG emissions perspective, nuclear power plants are much better than coal or gas-based power plants.

First, given the huge drop in public confidence in nuclear energy, should we not now rethink the structure of the AERB? I have always been uncomfortable with the fact that it is so deeply embedded within the atomic energy establishment. There may well have been justifiable technical and strategic reasons for its current structure. But given the very significant expansion in nuclear power generating capacity planned between now and 2030, and also given the renewed doubts on risks, I do think we need to give serious thought to making the AERB a fully independent organization drawing its powers directly from Parliament.

Second, given that the AERB will be called upon to take on an expanded role, should we not relook at the technology diversity we are introducing into our nuclear power programme? We have indigenously designed heavy water reactors, indigenously designed fast-breeder reactors, and indigenously designed enriched uranium reactors (proposed), French reactors, Russian reactors and US/Japanese reactors (likely).

Each of the reactor types will call for a certain regulatory procedure, protocol, and capability. Regulatory expertise takes time to build up and in any case is not available easily. Gone are the days of Nehru and Bhabha when public organizations could attract, train, and retain top-flight professional expertise. It seems to me from a regulatory perspective, it makes greater sense to standardize on the 700 MW PWHRs and, perhaps, work on their upgradation to 1,000 MW, while allowing for an import window. But as things stand right now, imported reactors are going to drive our nuclear programme—is this desirable from a regulatory point of view is the question.

Third, while I agree that sites are limited, should we not relook at this concept of nuclear parks where we set up giant capacities in one location (like at Fukushima). Jaitapur will have 10,000 MW of capacity. Is this wise? The negative public perceptions at Jaitapur have been caused, in large measure, because of this capacity—two plants would have been opposed no doubt but would not have caused the same disquiet as six plants. I am well-aware of the technical and economic advantages of a nuclear park but when there is a risk perception, we should, in my view, not be dogmatic.

Fourth, should we now not take a hard second look at the continuation of Tarapur-I and Tarapur-II, the two boiling water reactors akin to the Fukushima reactors? I know that our engineers have reworked the original designs but even so in light of what happened in Japan—perhaps the world's most safety-conscious and methodical society—this question is, in my view, not irrelevant.

Sir, I raise these four questions as someone who has closely followed our nuclear programme for over quarter of a century and as someone who has some technical knowledge in this area as well. I have been publicly defending our nuclear power programme and have been engaging the Jaitapur protesters also. But I feel that it is my duty to share with you these concerns of mine.

Letter to Prime Minister on My Meeting with the Director General of the Radiation and Nuclear Safety Authority of Finland

18 MAY 2011
I was in Helsinki on 16–17 May for a meeting of the UN Global Sustainability Panel. I made use of this opportunity to spend some time

with STUK—the Radiation and Nuclear Safety Authority of Finland. STUK's experience with AREVA's EPR reactor is particularly relevant since similar reactors are being planned at Jaitapur.

I met with Jukka Laaksonen, Director General of STUK, who made the following points:

1. STUK is a completely independent body and is administered by the Ministry of Social Affairs and Health Administration. This ministry, however, is not involved in any of STUK's decisions as a regulator body.
2. STUK is authorized to give binding orders needed to ensure nuclear safety. It has a professional staff of over 300 recruited from the open market.
3. AREVA's EPR reactor, which is being put up in Finland for the first time anywhere in the world, is about four years behind schedule. The main reasons for this delay are:

   i. It's being the first of its kind and larger than any other plant built earlier;
   ii. Inadequate completion of design and engineering work prior to start of construction;
   iii. Lack of experience of the electrical utility company in managing large construction projects;
   iv. The EPR reactor will be commissioned by the end of 2013 and would have taken eight years from the start of construction to become operational. This period, however, can be cut down to six years. In this connection, STUK feels that we should observe what China is doing since the third and fourth EPR reactors are being built in China and China is planning for a five-year period of completion from the start of construction.
   v. STUK's jurisdiction extends to the entire supplier chain and not just to the main vendor. STUK also has made use of International Atomic Energy Agency's IRRS (Integrated Regulatory Review Service) to strengthen its effectiveness and its regulatory systems in a comprehensive manner. STUK strongly advised that India should also use this programme actively.
   vi. Communication, inspection, and constant interaction with suppliers is given the highest priority by STUK. STUK has a very strong inspection practice throughout the entire supplier chain

in addition to its regulatory oversight systems at the reactor site. Its philosophy is 'safety and quality have higher priority than costs and schedule'.

Laaksonen was appreciative of India's capabilities in the nuclear field and mentioned that he had been to Tarapur and personally believes that NPCIL's 540 MW CANDU (CANada Deuterium Uranium) reactor is superior to what the Canadians have been able to do. He strongly supported the policy of standardization of the reactor designs in order to build up effective regulatory capability, a point that I had made to the Prime Minister in an earlier communication. He was quite willing to assist in building up the proposed Nuclear Regulatory Authority of India and enabling it to deal with AREVA's reactors at Jaitapur given Finland's own experience over the past decade.

I attach two documents that were handed over to me by Laaksonen in which the important portions have been highlighted for the Prime Minister's perusal.

Note to Secretary (Power) on the Need for Cumulative Impact Assessments

[This note was written when I served as Minister of State (MoS) for Power in 2008–9.]

A couple of months ago, NHPC faced with some problems regarding environmental clearances for the 2,000 MW Lower Subansiri project in Arunachal Pradesh. I had subsequently spoken to MoS (Environment and Forests) S. Reghupathy and the final clearances were given, thanks to his intervention.

However, in the course of discussing this project with Reghupathy and with the-then Secretary (Power) and Joint Secretary (Hydropower), I had made a suggestion that we should go beyond the present system of project-by-project environmental assessment. If around 10,000 MW is going to be developed in the Subansiri Basin alone, then it is desirable to conduct an EIA, however, preliminary for all projects coming up in the Basin. Piecemeal EIAs will not give a full picture of the ecological load.

I had suggested that we should engage some consultant or set up an expert group for such a basin-wise EIA. An organization like NHPC would be interested only where its projects are involved and I am finding that even state governments like Arunachal Pradesh in their zeal for developing hydroelectric power projects are also hooked on to project-wise assessment and not a comprehensive assessment. The problems that are being faced in Uttarakhand now could have been avoided had such a comprehensive assessment been done in a transparent manner.

I think it is certainly the responsibility of the Ministry of Power to take a lead role in having such comprehensive EIAs carried out in ecologically sensitive regions. I am told that the Himachal Pradesh government is thinking of such an exercise.

Letter to Prime Minister on Issues Raised About Hydropower Projects in the Upper Reaches of the Ganga

1 AUGUST 2009

Professor G.D. Agrawal and Rajender Singh met me yesterday. Their main complaint is that the work on Lohari Nag Pala project on the Bhagirathi river in Uttarakhand has been resumed by NTPC. Both claimed that this violates the commitment given to them by the Ministry of Power.

Professor Agrawal has already issued a notice for going on a fast beginning 5 August. I requested him not to take this extreme step and conveyed to him the plans we have for the National Ganga River Basin Authority (NGRBA) as well as the Prime Minister's own desire to find a middle path which takes into account ecological concerns in the process of implementing power projects.

Professor Agrawal mentioned to me that he has put in a request to meet the Prime Minister. I thought I should convey to you this request so that he can have an opportunity of explaining his concerns to you directly.

Letter to Principal Secretary to Prime Minister, T.K.A. Nair, on Hydroelectric power Projects in Uttarakhand

5 JANUARY 2010

The principal secretary spoke to me this morning about follow-up action to be taken on the report submitted by the two-man committee comprising secretary (environment and forests) and secretary (power) on the future of the three hydroelectric power projects on the river Bhagirathi in Uttarakhand. This committee was set up following a decision taken at the first meeting of the NGRBA held on 5 October 2009. The report was submitted to the Prime Minister's Office on 5 December 2009.

After examining various options, my recommendation would be that the Prime Minister direct the MoEF to engage the non-official members of the NGRBA in discussions on the committee's report. The Prime Minister may also direct the MoEF to submit a note to him following this interaction.

After this interaction is over and he has received the note on it, my suggestion would be that the Prime Minister direct the Standing Committee of the NGRBA headed by the finance minister to take a final view on the committee's report.

I would also suggest that we make the committee's report public after the meeting of the Standing Committee.

The Prime Minister may direct that the process indicated above is completed by the end of January 2010.

Letter to Prime Minister on Hydroelectric Power Projects in Uttarakhand

22 JANUARY 2010

Most Esteemed Prime Minister Sir,

The Prime Minister may recall that at the first meeting of the NGRBA on 5 October 2009, it had been decided that the issues of Loharinag Pala, Pala Maneri, and Bhaironghati hydroelectric power projects in the upper reaches of the Bhagirathi in Uttarakhand would be studied by the ministries of environment and forests and power and a report submitted to NGRBA. Subsequently, on 3 December 2009, the joint report of the ministries of environment and forests and power was submitted to the PMO. Thereafter, the PMO asked us to engage the non-official members of the NGRBA in discussions on this joint report and submit a note to the Prime Minister following this interaction. In pursuance of this directive, I met with the non-official members of the NGRBA on 14 January 2010 and had a three-hour discussion with them.

The non-official members want the entire 130 km stretch from Gomukh to Uttar Kashi to be declared as an eco-sensitive zone. As against this, the joint committee of the ministries of environment and forests and power has recommended that the 55 km stretch from Gomukh to Loharinag Pala be declared as an eco-sensitive zone.

The non-official members and the joint committee are in agreement that the two-state government projects of Pala Maneri (480 MW) and Bhaironghati (381 MW) should not be proceeded with. My impression and information is that the state government would abide by this decision provided it is 'compensated' to the extent of around 860 MW.

The only difference between the two relates to Loharinag Pala (600 MW), which is being implemented by NTPC. The non-official members want this project also to be scrapped whereas the joint committee has recommended that this project be implemented.

On Loharinag Pala, the following merit consideration:

1. The work is presently under suspension from 19 February 2009. About 3 per cent of the work has been completed with a number of tunnels and other structures in varying stages of construction.
2. The implications of a release of 16 cubic metres per second (cumecs) as has been decided by the Ministry of Power means that the project will not be functioning for almost five months in a year (December–April).
3. The Uttarakhand Government would like the project to be completed because of its economic value to the state.
4. The non-official members raised a number of issues relating to the environmental clearance accorded to the Loharinag Pala project in 2005. Without getting into too much of a post-mortem, what I have agreed to do, is to have a group that includes some of the non-official members of the NGRBA to study the extent to which NTPC has complied with the terms and conditions associated with environmental clearance. The report of this group will be available in about two weeks' time. Meanwhile, keeping in view the opinions expressed by the non-official members, the MoEF will commission comprehensive EIA studies of all hydroelectric power projects on the Bhagirathi and the Alaknanda.

We now need to take a final decision on the three projects. Perhaps, the Prime Minister could call the finance minister, power minister and me soon to finalize the central government's stand to begin with.

Letter to Union Minister of Finance Pranab Mukherjee on Hydroelectric Power Projects in the Upper Reaches of the Bhagirathi River

12 FEBRUARY 2010

I am writing to you regarding the issue of Bhaironghati, Loharinag Pala, and Pala Maneri hydroelectric power projects on the river Bhagirathi in Uttarakhand.

It was decided in the first meeting of the NGRBA on 5 October 2009, held under the chairmanship of the Prime Minister, that the issue related to these projects would be examined by the MoEF and the Ministry of Power, and a report would be submitted to the authority (NGRBA) in sixty days.

Accordingly, a report has been submitted to the Prime Minister (chairperson, NGRBA) on 4 December 2009. The report is based on an on-the-spot assessment of the impact of these projects on the flow of the Bhagirathi river, the current status of their implementation and detailed interactions with local people, public representatives, prominent members of social, cultural, environmental, and religious organizations, officers of the district administration, and the government of Uttarakhand. I am enclosing a copy of this report along with a brief note for your perusal.

I have also discussed this issue on 14 January 2010 with the expert members of NGRBA and ascertained their views.

It has now been communicated by the PMO that the matter may be resolved at a meeting of the Finance Minister with the Minister of Power and the MoS (Independent Charge) for Environment and Forests and reported to the Prime Minister.

I would, therefore, request you to kindly convene a meeting at your convenience to resolve the issue relating to these projects.

Letter to Union Minister for Finance Pranab Mukherjee on the Decision Regarding the Future Course of Action on Three Projects in the Upper Reaches of the Bhagirathi River—Loharinag Pala, Pala Maneri, and Bhaironghati

20 MAY 2010

You may kindly recall that as per the Prime Minister's directive, you had convened a meeting on 25 March 2010 in which the power minister and

I participated to discuss the future of three projects on the Bhagirathi river in Uttarakhand. These projects are Loharinag Pala, Pala Maneri, and Bhaironghati.

At that meeting, the view which you summarized was that it would be prudent not to proceed with Pala Maneri and Bhaironghati projects since work on them is yet to commence. However, since the Loharinag Pala project is under implementation, the view taken in the meeting was that a technical committee should examine the implications of discontinuing the Loharinag Pala project of NTPC given the seismic and other geological conditions of the region. I am now enclosing a copy of the report of this committee which has been submitted to me just this evening.

The committee's main conclusion is the following—leaving the project incomplete may aggravate the risks of landslides in certain stretches in the project area and may increase the likely damage to the surroundings, including the National Highway, in the event of an earthquake or a landslide. However, these risks can be adequately mitigated through suitably designed comprehensive stabilization and monitoring measures. This will entail expenditure over and above the expenditure already incurred on the project and compensation against the committed expenditure. Besides these stabilization measures, periodic monitoring of slopes and openings will need to be carried out and timely preventive, monitoring and maintenance measures taken, as in any major engineering project in such an area.

I now request to kindly convene a meeting between the power minister and so that we can decide on the next steps. Subsequently, we would require a date from you for convening a meeting of the Standing Committee of NGRBA of which you are the chairman. I am marking a copy of this letter with enclosure to power minister and principal secretary to the Prime Minister as well.

Letter to Prime Minister on Hydroelectric Power Projects on the Upper Reaches of the Bhagirathi River

26 MAY 2010

Prime Minister is aware that at the first meeting of the NGRBA held on 5 October 2009 under his chairmanship, it was decided that the issue of Loharinag Pala, Pala Maneri, and Bhaironghati hydroelectric power projects in the upper reaches of the Bhagirathi river in Uttarakhand would be studied by the MoEF and Ministry of Power and a report submitted to the NGRBA.

Subsequently the joint report of the MoEF and Ministry of Power on these three projects was submitted on 3 December 2009. This committee had made the following recommendations:

(i) Considering its proximity to Gomukh and given the fact that work has not commenced, the Bhaironghati project may not be taken up. This would ensure that there is no hydroelectric power project in the first 55 km of the river Bhagirathi.

(ii) Work on the Pala Maneri project may be kept in abeyance till the completion of a comprehensive and cumulative impact assessment of all individual hydroelectric projects on the river Bhagirathi.

(iii) In view of the significant amount of work already done on it, Loharinag Pala project of NTPC may be allowed to continue, while ensuring that the Ministry of Power's commitment for minimum perennial flow is fully ensured in a transparent and accountable manner.

(iv) The Central Government may consider fully compensating Uttarakhand for the discontinuation of the Bhaironghati and Pala Maneri projects, which together amount to a total of 861 MW.

(v) The 55 km stretch from Gomukh to Loharinag Pala may be declared as an eco-sensitive zone where no development projects may be taken up.

I had submitted this committee's report to the Prime Minister on 3 December 2009. Thereafter, the Prime Minister has asked me to engage the non-official members of the NGRBA in discussions on this joint report and submit a note to the Prime Minister. I met the non-official members of the NGRBA on 14 January 2010 and submitted a note to the Prime Minister on 22 January 2010, in which I had highlighted the following points:

(i) The non-official members wanted the entire 130 km stretch from Gomukh to Uttar Kashi to be declared as eco-sensitive zone instead of just the 55 km stretch from Gomukh to Loharinag Pala.

(ii) The non-official members wanted the Loharinag Pala project also be scrapped even though about 30 per cent of the work has been completed. They underscored the importance of faith and sentiment.

The Prime Minister then asked me to discuss this matter with the finance minister and minister of power. In pursuance of the Prime Minister's directive, Finance Minister, and I met on 25 March 2010. This meeting decided that :

(i) Bhaironghati and Pala Maneri projects should not be implemented.
(ii) a technical committee be set up to examine the implications of discontinuing the Loharinag Pala project given the seismic and other geological conditions of the region, and be given time till 15 May to submit its report.

This technical committee submitted its report on 20 May and I have forwarded a copy of this report to both the finance minister and power minister. The main conclusion of this committee is the following:

'Leaving the project incomplete may aggravate the risks of landslides in certain stretches in the project area and may increase the likely damage to the surroundings, including the National Highway, in the event of an earthquake or a landslide. However, these risks can be adequately mitigated through suitably designed comprehensive stabilization and monitoring measures. This will entail expenditure over and above the expenditure already incurred on the project and compensation against the committed expenditure. Besides these stabilization measures, periodic monitoring of slopes and openings will need to be carried out and timely preventive, monitoring and maintenance measures taken, as in any major engineering project in such an area.'

With this background, I would like to submit the following for the Prime Minister's consideration:

(i) Undoubtedly questions of faith and sentiment are running high on the Bhagirathi projects. It is a fact that this is an eco-sensitive region and it is also a fact that river flow will be very severely affected by the manner in which projects have been planned and implemented.
(ii) The Pala Maneri and Bhaironghati projects are that of the state government, while Loharinag Pala is that of the central government. The state government has been saying that it would be

amenable to discontinue these two projects if the central government were to discontinue the Loharinag Pala project and if the state government received adequate compensation.

(iii)   The implications of release of 16 cumecs as has been decided by the Ministry of Power means that the Loharinag Pala project will not be functioning for almost five months in a year (December–April).

I have requested the finance minister to call both the power minister and me to firm up the Central Government's view on the future of the Loharinag Pala project. Meanwhile, I thought I should keep the Prime Minister informed considering the great political sensitivity involved in these projects. Recently, some senior Bharatiya Janata Party leaders have made statements that the ecological purity of both Bhagirathi and Alaknanda rivers should not be destroyed by the proliferation of hydroelectric power projects and the Ganga should not be treated as any other river. It will be a difficult task no doubt to decide on the future of Loharinag Pala but my personal view is that keeping all factors in mind, we would be better off abandoning this project as well.

Letter to Prime Minister on Hydroelectric Power Projects in the Northeast

14 June 2011

When I met the Prime Minister on 10 June 2011, I had mentioned to him the concerns in Assam on the downstream impacts of the Lower Subansiri hydroelectric power project being implemented by the NHPC in Arunachal Pradesh. I was in the Indian Institute of Technology (IIT) Guwahati on 27 May 2011 and a report prepared by a team from IIT Guwahati on this subject was made available to me. I am sending the Prime Minister a copy of this report with the main recommendations highlighted. The worry of IIT Guwahati and other organizations in Assam is that NHPC is not inclined to treat these recommendations seriously. I was asked to bring them to the Prime Minister's personal attention with a request that he direct the NHPC to sit down with the IIT Guwahati team with the objective of seeing how these recommendations can be implemented soon.

Letter to Union Minister for New and Renewable Energy Farooq Abdullah on His Comments on the Athirapally Hydroelectric Power Project in Kerala

16 JUNE 2010

My attention has just been drawn to the attached news item quoting you quite extensively on the Athirapally hydroelectric power project in Kerala.

I am absolutely amazed and taken aback by this news story. You have never spoken to me about this and yet the news item says that you have spoken to me about this project. Quoting you, the news item also goes to say that I am positively inclined towards clearing this project. This is completely false because:

(i) You have never spoken to me about it;
(ii) I continue to have very serious concerns (like many experts and civil society organizations in Kerala have) on the ecological devastation that would be caused by this project.

Just for your information, the project is going through the due process in the MoEF. May I please request you to issue a clarification denying that you have ever spoken to me about this project.

Email to the Deputy Chairman, Planning Commission, Montek Singh Ahluwalia, on the Emission Intensity of NTPC Power Plants

23 JULY 2009

Herewith, the emissions intensity analysis I had got done in August 2008 that you don't believe. You must not automatically think that our PSUs are inefficient. You will be disappointed but some of them are actually good.

For the purpose of analysis, only companies having generation of more than 125 BU and having at least 50 per cent fossil fuel mix have been considered.

CO_2 intensity of largest power generating companies (Table 9.1)

1. With respect to NTPC, the generation figures were inaccurate. The website shows total generation as 157 BU, whereas the actual

Table 9.1 CO_2 intensity of the largest power generating companies*

	Total generation (BU)	CO_2 intensity (gm/kWh)	Fossil (%)	Nuclear (%)	Hydro (%)	Renewable (%)	Normalised CO_2 intensity (gm/kWh)*
E.ON AG (GERMANY)	251	516.91	60.89	29.31	7.76	0.99	849
ESKOM (SOUTH AFRICA)	237	813.56	94.50	5.16	0.35	0	861
SOUTHERN CO. (USA)	232	667.98	73.13	20.85	2.51	3.30	913
HUANENG (CHINA)	216	1,218.02	100	0	0	0	1,218
NTPC LTD (INDIA)	200	819.91	100	0	0	0	820
AEP (USA)	185	823.08	89.27	8.99	0.75	0.98	922
DUKE ENERGY (USA)	182	534.66	60.09	30.49	8.36	0.62	890
VATTENFALL (SWEDEN)	167	492.04	56.99	14.27	26.98	1.35	863
TVA (USA)	155	587.1	60.91	29.49	9.60	0	964
RWE AG (GERMANY)	153	636	81.72	11.98	0.68	2.98	778
TAIWAN POWER CO. (TAIWAN)	149	512.78	54.72	25.56	5.26	3.14	937
CHINA HUADIAN (CHINA)	144	1,101.22	90.49	0	9.51	0	1,217
CHINA POWER (CHINA)	142	1,097.7	82.89	0	17.11	0	1,324
ENEL SPA (ITALY)	139	507.54	60.05	12.13	21.64	3.62	845
AES CORP (USA)	127	766.2	68.82	0	20.39	4.13	1,113

*Assumptions: i) Companies with annual power generation above 125 BU
ii) Companies having minimum fossil fuel mix of 50%

Source: CARMA.ORG: NTPC ANALYSIS

generation was 200.84 BU. The same has been correctly represented during the analysis.

2. The CO_2 intensity figures have been converted into gm/kWh for the sake of simplicity.

3. For the purpose of arriving at normalized CO_2 intensity for power generation, only generation from fossil has been factored in, since hydroelectric, nuclear, and renewable do not emit any CO_2.

4. The CO_2 intensity of NTPC is the second lowest (at 820 gm/kWh) next only to RWE AG, of Germany (at 778 gm/kWh), showing, thereby, that NTPC is one of the most efficient power producers globally (better than US, European, and South African companies).

Letter to Prime Minister on Mandatory Fuel Efficiency

[Despite persistent efforts, it took more than five years to have an agreement among the stakeholders both in and outside government. The standards were finally notified in February 2014.]

23 JULY 2009

I am writing to you once again to plead for urgent action on mandatory fuel efficiency standards.

You may well recall that I have been raising this issue with you since September 2009.

In the global debate on climate change, such a step would greatly enhance our standing. Apart from this, mandatory fuel efficiency standards are essential in themselves and it is unfortunate that we have not been able to announce them so far.

Letter to Chief Minister of Rajasthan Ashok Gehlot on Clearing Coal-based Power Projects Using Super-critical Technology

[Coal was to be the mainstay of our energy basket, the effort was then to reduce emissions and pollution from these plants, supercritical technology was one such option.]

18 MAY 2010

Kindly refer to your letter dated 6 May 2010 regarding the proposals of three super-critical technology based thermal power projects, each of 2 × 660 MW capacity, at Suratgarh, Chhabra, and Banswara, and to modify the existing procedures to ensure that these projects are cleared at the earliest.

I have got the matter examined in the ministry regarding the status of the environmental clearance of these projects. I am informed that the 2 × 660 MW thermal power plant as Unit 7 and 8 at Suratgarh, district Ganganagar as well as the expansion of Chhabra Thermal Power Plant in Baran district have been awarded Terms of Reference (ToR) in July and December 2009, respectively. The approval of the ToR begins the process of environmental assessment by the project authorities. The third project at Banswara, however, has not been referred to the ministry even for seeking ToR.

The projects are considered from environmental angle as per the provisions of EIA Notification, 2006 where the time lines for consideration of projects in the ministry have been elaborated. By and large the projects are appraised within the stipulated time of 210 days, which is inclusive of ToRs, public hearing, and appraisal at the ministry. It is desirable at this stage that coal linkage and water allocation are available for the proposed power projects. I may also add that if the projects require diversion of forest land and/or are in the proximity of wildlife protected areas, the clearances under the Forest (Conservation) Act, 1980 and the Wildlife (Protection) Act, 1972 would also be necessary.

In view of the above, you may like to direct the concerned departments to comply with these requirements for environment, forestry and wildlife clearances. I may also add that due priority is being given to the power sector projects keeping in view the increasing demand for power.

Note on Clearance for NTPC's Coal-based Thermal Power Projects Using Super-critical Technology for Coal-based Thermal Power Plants

[On 1 November, the ministry had issued an order which required power projects to have secured forest and environmental clearances for linked coal block or mine before applying for clearances for the project itself. This order meant that NTPC's projects at Nabinagar in Bihar, Sholapur and Mouda in Maharashtra would have to be kept on hold. NTPC had been pushing for a bulk-ordering programme for its technology transfer agreement with Alstom and Siemens for 660 MW and 800 MW super-critical technology. The bulk ordering programme would allow for technology transfer and indigenization.]

2 DECEMBER 2012

These are the first four projects under the bulk ordering programme for super-critical units that had been initiated when I was MoS (Power) in late-2008. These units are crucial for meeting our Copenhagen Accord commitments. There is a built-in phased manufacturing programme for indigenization in this bulk ordering portfolio. Land acquisition is at an advanced stage for these four projects.

On balance, therefore, we may make a one-time exception since NTPC is a 'maharatna' company and grant environmental clearance to (i), (iii), and (iv) [Nabinagar in Bihar, Sholapur and Mouda] for which the EAC has already made the recommendation; when recommendation is made on (i) [the fourth project], the same logic may apply for grant of environmental clearance.

I am well aware that we are deviating from a policy I myself have put in place but I feel there are weighty reasons for doing so.

Letter to Prime Minister on Reports by the World Bank on the Potential for Renewable Energy in India

28 MARCH 2011

I am sending for your information a detailed report that has just been prepared by the World Bank on renewable energy in India. It is one of the most comprehensive reports I have ever read on the subject and I think it merits very close attention by our government.

I summarize the main points that have been made in this report:

1. With about 150 GW of known resource potential, of which only about 10 per cent has been developed, renewable energy is an important part of the solution to India's energy shortage. Developing renewable energy can help India in the following ways:

   a. Increase its energy security: Renewable energy source, which are indigenous and have low marginal costs of generation, diversity supply, reduce import dependence, and mitigate fuel price volatility.

    b. Lower its carbon intensity: On an average, every 1 GW of additional renewable energy capacity reduces carbon dioxide emissions by 3.3 million tonnes (MT) a year.

    c. Reduce health impacts of thermal energy: Reduced mortality and morbidity from lower particulate concentrations estimated at 334 lives saved per MT of carbon abated.

    d. Improve regional economic development: particularly for many underdeveloped states that have the greatest potential for developing such resources.

    e. Help realize its aspirations for leadership in high-technology industries.

2. India has a severe electricity shortage. It needs massive additions in capacity to meet the demands of its rapidly growing economy. The country's overall power deficit—11 per cent in 2009—has risen steadily, from 8.4 per cent in 2006. About 100,000 villages (17 per cent) remain unelectrified, and almost 400 million Indians are without electricity coverage. India's per capita consumption is one of the lowest in the world.

3. The Integrated Energy Policy, 2006, estimates India needs to increase primary energy supply by three–four times and electricity generation by five–six times to meet the lifeline per capita consumption by 2031, and sustain economic growth at 8 per cent. The Integrated Energy Policy scenarios point to coal reserves of less than forty-five years (by 2040) at a growth rate of 5 per cent in domestic production, and an increasing reliance on coal imports.

4. Going forward, India has set ambitious targets of 40–55 GW of additional renewable energy capacity at the end of the Thirteenth Plan in 2022. The goals of the National Action Plan on Climate Change (NAPCC) may represent an additional renewable energy capacity of 40–80 GW by 2017. To achieve these goals, India needs an order of magnitude increase in renewable energy growth in the next decade. If India were to achieve a more modest target of 40 GW or 20 GW, double its wind capacity, quadruple its small hydroelectric power capacity, fully realize co-generation capacity, and increase biomass realization by a factor of five–six by 2022. These impressive targets have made creation of an enabling environment for renewable energy development particularly urgent and topical.

5. Renewable energy development is often questioned due to its high cost compared to conventional fuels. The study shows that cost differential to bring renewable energy to an economically feasible level is actually small. India could produce 62 GW of its renewable potential in wind, small hydroelectric, and biomass in an economically feasible manner, provided that the environmental premium of coal-based generation is taken into account. This represents 90 per cent of India's known technical potential in these technologies. About 85 per cent of this capacity can be harnessed at an avoided cost of Rs 5/kWh and the entire capacity can be harnessed at below Rs 6/kWh.

6. Small hydroelectric power is the most economically viable form of renewable technology, with an average economic cost of Rs 3.56/kWh. This resource is the most attractive in Andhra Pradesh, Haryana, Himachal Pradesh, Punjab, and Uttarakhand. The economic cost of biomass-generated power ranges from Rs 3.90 to Rs 5.70/kWh. However, biomass fuel availability and price fluctuation under a regulated market pose a significant risk to scaling up biomass-based generation. The generation cost of wind projects is highly sensitive to the capacity utilization factor, which is quite low at an average of about 23 per cent. The economic cost of wind power ranges between Rs 3.80 and Rs 5.20/kWh. A substantial proportion of wind capacity (about 37 GW) is available in four states of Andhra Pradesh, Gujarat, Karnataka, and Tamil Nadu. Solar is the most expensive renewable resource, with estimate unit costs of Rs 12/kWh for solar thermal and Rs 17/kWh for solar photovoltaic.

7. The financial incentives for state utilities to buy renewable power are substantial only compared with short-term power procurement cost. The feed-in tariffs for wind, small hydroelectric power, and biomass are typically lower than the short-term power purchase charges, such as trading and unscheduled interchange (UI). Re-allocating the money that would be spent on buying short-term power to investment in renewable energy can yield significant savings. However, the core of electricity procurement by utilities still rests with power purchase agreements (PPAs) with coal- and gas-fired plants. At the financial cost of coal-based generation, renewable capacity is not financially viable. About 5 GW of capacity is viable at the cost of gas-based generation; the entire capacity

of wind, biomass, and small hydropower is viable at the cost of diesel-based generation. Solar energy is not financially viable at any of these opportunity costs and will require subsidies in the short to medium term, particularly if renewable purchase obligations are enhanced rapidly in line with the targets of NAPCC.

8. Under the current planning and pricing regimes, subsidies required to achieve the government's declared goal of installing an additional 40 GW of renewable energy capacity in the next ten–twelve years would be between Rs 450 billion (for low-cost renewable energy with low diversity of renewable energy sources) and Rs 2.9 trillion (for high-cost renewable energy with high diversity of renewable energy sources). These numbers do not take into account the volatility of fossil fuel prices, which may reduce the requirement of subsidies.

9. Barriers: Significant barriers to renewable energy development remain in India. These are grouped into three categories—financial viability, support infrastructure, and regulatory approval—as follows.

   a. The cost-plus approach to tariff setting—along with the technology-specific focus—has led to incentives that hinder the economic development of India's renewable energy resources. India currently offers a wide variety of incentives, including feed-in tariffs, generation-based incentives, renewable purchase obligations, central, state, and regional capital subsidies, accelerated depreciation, and tax incentives. The lack of coordination between incentives and state programmes makes it difficult to adopt an economics-based, least-cost development approach to tapping the country's renewable energy potential.

   b. The limited availability of evacuation infrastructure and grid interconnections is one of the biggest obstacles to harnessing renewable energy potential. Much economically attractive wind and small hydropower potential remains untapped because of lack of adequate gird evacuation capacity and approach roads. The lack of good-quality data on renewable resources also remains a problem, despite heavy investment by the Ministry of New and Renewable Energy in collecting data on renewable energy. The lack of support infrastructure in the form of a strong indigenous supply chain remains a major barrier.

c. Existing mechanisms, including single-window clearances, facilitation by state nodal agencies, and simplified regulation for smaller renewable energy projects—have proved to be of limited effectiveness. In some cases, multiple bottlenecks have been replaced by single, larger, and more powerful road blocks, and significant delays remain the norm. In addition, speculative blocking of land has become common, leading to unsustainable price increases. Although the report does not address this, some experts in the Bank also believe that the lack of a framework for local benefit sharing is also a potent barrier.

10. Solutions: To reduce financial barriers, policymakers need to consider ways to bridge the higher costs that ensure least economic cost development of India's plentiful renewable resources. There is a need to simplify the numerous and overlapping financial incentives into a cogent set of synchronized policies established on a sound economic and market foundation. Policies could be based on short- and long-term national targets and broken down into state-level RPOs that are mandatory and enforced. Technology specific incentives could be supported by earmarked funding and increasingly allocated on a competitive basis.

11. India needs to make renewable energy evacuation a high transmission priority—as high a priority as village electrification. This is especially true for large-scale renewable energy plants. Dedicated funding should be allocated as part of existing programmes such as government' rural electrification initiative—Rajiv Gandhi Grameen Vidyutikaran Yojana, or new green funds.

12. Steps should also be taken to address the non-financial barriers that increase the cost of doing business, like information technology and telecommunication, clean technology and renewable energy have enormous growth potential and can transform the trillion-dollar energy markets around the world. To realize this potential, India needs to streamline bureaucratic processes for clearances and approvals through the use of light-touch regulation. State nodal agencies, which are supposed to play leading role in guiding renewable energy projects through the regulatory maze, need to be strengthened. A comprehensive capacity-building programme on emerging regulatory, legal, and financing issues to facilitate grid connected renewable energy should be structured.

I think between the Planning Commission and Ministry of New and Renewable Energy there should be a time-bound follow-up initiated to this report.

'Germany's Great Green Gamble: India has Much to Learn from Germany's Bold Energy Transformation'

[Opinion piece in *The Hindu*.]

8 September 2014

The Germans gave the word kindergarten to the world of education. To development economics they gave the term *wirtschaftswunder* that is used to describe their country's remarkable economic transformation, immediately following World War II. Now in the area of sustainable growth another typically compound German word is inviting global attention and that is *energiewende*. This refers to the profound energy transition Germany is going through. For a country dubbed as the 'sick man of Europe' at the beginning of this century, the achievement is stupendous.

Today, already something like 30 per cent of its electricity supply comes from solar and wind energy and it is actually exporting power. The goal is to increase this contribution to 50 per cent by 2030 and a staggering 80 per cent by 2050. Smaller countries in Scandinavia have similar achievements and ambitions but Germany is completely different because it is the world's pre-eminent industrial economy and has a population of slightly over 80 million. The scale of what Germany has accomplished over the past decade and a half is what gives it wider relevance, especially to large countries like India.

Presently, Germany has around 37,000 MW of installed solar energy capacity. In addition, it has another 29,000 MW of installed wind energy capacity. What has given renewables new momentum is the decision of Chancellor Angela Merkel to completely phase out Germany's present nuclear power generating capacity of about 12,000 MW by the year 2022. There has always been a strong anti-nuclear movement in Germany and this got a fresh impetus following the Fukushima catastrophe in May 2011 which prompted the Chancellor's dramatic volte face. It was a bold decision given that when Fukushima happened, Germany was getting between a fifth and a quarter of electricity supply from its nuclear power plants. It is the complete decommissioning of all such plants in eight years' time coupled with an overriding emphasis on energy efficiency that gives *energiewende* a unique dimension. However, question marks do remain on how much coal capacity Germany will end up adding to compensate for the abandonment of nuclear power.

Meeting domestic and international environmental objectives has undoubtedly been the primary motivation for this remarkable change. A legislation for promoting renewable energy was first enacted fourteen years ago. It has undergone many changes subsequently but the anchor remains the concept of a 'feed-in tariff' that depends on the technology being used. Anybody can invest in solar or wind power, sell surplus power to the grid, and get a generous income that covers both the investment and running costs and that is guaranteed regardless of demand for twenty years. The grid operator has a legal obligation to connect the installation and an obligation to accept any electricity whenever it is produced. As a result there are now close to 5 million small producers—individuals and cooperatives—-accounting for around half of the installed renewable energy capacity. This means that some 6 per cent of Germans are energy producers. This is the nearest equivalent to the mobile phone revolution. The structure of electricity generation has been thoroughly shaken up and the four big private utilities have been consistently losing market share.

However, the transition has not been without controversy. The most contentious issue is whether consumers are paying more now than they were earlier. The cost of renewables is financed out of a surcharge on the bills of consumers. Of course, many consumers have themselves turned producers but that apart, there appear be two views. One view is that German household expenditure on electricity has not changed over the past decade and that the latest increase will cost the consumer every month the equivalent of a pint of beer! But the fact remains that energy prices will continue to increase since the large-scale use of renewable sources does require extensive grid, storage and backup infrastructure. The gamble is criticized as being expensive but it cannot be denied that it is expansive. That is, perhaps, one reason why, according to some surveys, over two-thirds of Germans support *energiewiende*—which actually goes well beyond electricity generation and embraces changes in energy use in transportation and housing as well.

What about the energy transition in India? Presently, wind energy capacity is close to 22,000 MW and solar amounts to another 2,650 MW or so (nuclear is about 4,800 MW). Capacity-wise, wind and solar account for about 13 per cent of total electricity generating capacity, although contribution to actual energy supply is perhaps no more than 6 per cent. In April 2014, the Planning Commission's expert group on low carbon strategies for inclusive growth had released its final report that suggested that by 2030 the share of solar, wind, and biomass in electricity supply be tripled to around 18 per cent. Unfortunately this report has yet to get the full public attention it warrants.

The main difference with Germany, of course, is that in 2030 India's energy supply basket is projected to have an eight per cent contribution from nuclear energy as well. In terms of capacity, wind energy is recommended to increase to 120,000 MW and solar to 100,000 MW by 2030. These may look daunting goals at the moment but they are eminently feasible especially given the fact that India is more favourably endowed especially in relation to solar energy and, in some parts, even in wind energy.

The energy transition which will have to be driven by innovations in technology, regulation, and financing will bring multiple benefits. It will, of course, increase energy security and also reduce emissions of carbon dioxide. It will have significant positive impacts on public health and stimulate development in regions that have remained backward so far. The possibility of India acquiring strategic leadership in the green technology industry globally in about a decade's time also is very real, provided it is linked with a strong indigenous research and development and engineering capability. New avenues for employment will accelerate. A very recent study by the Council on Energy, Environment and Water and the National Resources Defense Council has estimated that around 24,000 jobs have been created in the last three years alone when solar capacity has increased from around 1,800 MW to 2,650 MW. In Germany, the renewables sector employs close to 400,000 people, therefore, as capacity and supply contribution expands, green employment in India too will grow substantially.

If a comprehensive valuation of benefits is done, as the expert group boldly pointed out 'even with lower GDP the low carbon strategy is worth pursuing'. In any case, the reduction in the average annual GDP growth rate by the expert group's own reckoning by the use of low carbon strategies is 0.1–0.15 percentage points. That is, instead of, say an eight per cent growth rate, you will end up having a 7.85–7.9 per cent growth rate. Surely, this is by no means any kind of disaster, especially when all the gains of green growth are reckoned and taken into account fully. India is ready for another 4G revolution—Great Green Growth Gamble.

10 Repositioning India Globally

Prime Minister Manmohan Singh's brief on our global engagement was simple: Change the perception about India. The core of this engagement related to climate change, a problem we had not created but the solution to which we should be part of. Repositioning India did not mean sacrificing national interests; it did mean that we should be proactive in the crafting of a solution.

I set myself four tasks: First, on the domestic front, to explain why climate change is a pressing issue for India and why we should take it seriously. Second, to energize the Indian scientific community to play a leadership role, and to put forward research focused on the Indian realities rather than depending on output from the West. Third, to reposition India—in terms of both style and substance—in international negotiations, where India had acquired an image of being a 'naysayer'. Fourth, to assume a pivotal role in shaping international agreements to ensure that India is best able to protecting its core economic interests.[1]

I assumed office barely six months ahead of the United Nations Framework Convention on Climate Change (UNFCCC) conference at Copenhagen. There were meetings galore in the run up to the November–December negotiations, which had been hyped as the beginning of a new era of global action on tackling climate change. I was on a virtual time clock to effectively affect an image change to reposition India. I engaged with civil society, domestic and foreign media, academics and think tanks, captains of industry, heads of state, ministers and ambassadors. I reached out to the South Asian Association for Regional Cooperation (SAARC) environment ministers to craft a regional approach, and other advanced developing countries. The aim was for the world to recognize that India was playing a proactive role. Given our naysayer image, any change that seemed positive would be welcomed by the global community. The home front proved to be a major challenge, where even the slightest attempt to abandon the shibboleths of the past were viewed with suspicion.

My first 'break' from the orthodox negotiation position came ahead of the Copenhagen summit in 2009. I had suggested two measures to counter the growing pressure on emerging economies like India (more so, China) to 'do more' to tackle climate change. First, I proposed enacting a domestic legislation—providing specific performance targets for mitigation actions in power, transport, industry, agriculture, buildings, and forestry for the year 2020 and 2030. These would not be explicit emission-reduction targets but performance targets that would lead to emission reductions.

Second, a mechanism through which the international community could be kept informed of our efforts at tackling climate change. I had suggested a format on the lines of the Trade Policy Review of the World Trade Organization (WTO) and Article IV consultations of the International Monetary Fund (IMF), a biennial detailed communication to the UNFCCC, and an annual Climate Policy Dialogue. Changing the global perception would require us to consistently remind the world of how, despite our many constraints, there was a serious domestic engagement with the issue of climate change and concrete actions were being taken. I felt that such an effort would allow us the space to determine the contours of what constituted climate action. Many colleagues across the political spectrum viewed this suggestion as a weakening of India's position on the issue and a bartering away of our sovereignty. I had a different perspective—we were not parting with any information that wasn't already freely available. India has a vibrant civil society and free press, and an active political system—each serving to ensure accountability from the government. Be it our records of parliamentary debates and discussions or media reports or published material from civil society, each of these imposes a check on the government. So, why not use this freely available information to be proactive in promoting transparency, allowing us to the demand the same of others.

In the international imagination, India and China would often be clubbed together, on account of their large populations, growing economic strength, and being outsourcing destinations, albeit for different categories of products. In negotiations, we worked together with China under the G77 umbrella. Given that China was a larger economy and more advanced than ours, it often offered India a cover. Ahead of Copenhagen, I was concerned that Beijing would forge a separate deal, leaving New Delhi on its own. China had announced a 40–45 per cent reduction in the emission intensity of its gross domestic product. New Delhi needed to be doing something or at least seen to be doing so. This is when I decided to activate the BASIC, a grouping of four advanced developing countries—Brazil, South Africa, India, and China. Active during negotiations, I sought to give BASIC a pre-negotiation focus. The four countries, despite being differently placed on the development curve, had common interests in protecting their growth space.

The BASIC met for the first time in Beijing in late-October 2009, the four ministers worked a counter to the draft 'Danish' agreement to be discussed at Copenhagen. We also chalked out a strategy to deal with the pressure being brought to bear on our countries. Returning to Delhi, I announced an emission intensity reduction target, worked out in consultation with the Planning Commission, of 20–25 per cent from 2005 levels by 2020.

Mindful of the need to brief the political establishment, I wrote in detail to members of Parliament about India's negotiating stance, welcomed the opportunity accorded by debates and discussions in Parliament to apprise the people's representatives and through them the country. At every turn, I kept the Prime Minister abreast with the developments and my thinking of what India's next step should be. But orthodoxies run deep and thinking out of the box is a lost art, even when the ways of the past have ceased to yield any benefit. I realized this in full measure during the interactions in Parliament and from the response to my ideas in large sections of the media.

At Copenhagen, the spotlight was on transparency and the need for developing countries to do more to tackle climate change. For me, it was important to ensure that failure of Copenhagen to deliver on the much-promised climate deal was not laid at India's door step. On my return from Copenhagen, I suggested setting up an expert committee to recommend ways to transit to a low-carbon growth path. An expert group headed by Dr Kirit Parekh was set up by the Planning Commission. It included academics, industry representatives, and organizations like the Bureau of Energy Efficiency.

Aware that the pressure on countries like India was going to be relentless, I focused on fashioning an approach to ensure that our developmental goals, which would mean a rise in emissions, would not be compromised. Eschewing the traditional approach of carbon budgets, which broadly sought to determine India's share of the permissible carbon emissions, I sought to approach the issue from the development and energy access angle. This would ensure that India's development space is guaranteed without it being seen as a demand for the 'right to pollute'. I asked Arvind Subramanian, an economist with the Peterson Institute in Washington, DC (and now chief economic advisor to the finance minister), to provide the basis for what I described as the 'per capita plus' approach. However, the exercise had to be abandoned as it was seen as a deviation from India's long-held negotiating position—where equity translated as a sharp reduction in the per capita emissions of developed countries, so that they converge over a period of time with rising per capita emissions of developing countries.

The attention and criticism of the past year left me unprepared for the reaction to my attempts at Cancun in 2010 to maneuver diplomatic room for India. There was a growing demand that countries enter into a legally binding agreement, similar to the Kyoto Protocol, to tackle climate change. The iconic 1997 agreement, the Kyoto Protocol, made it legally binding for all industrialized countries to take targets to reduce emissions. The US is not a signatory to the 1997 agreement, arguing that it would never agree to a deal that did not include all major emitters particularly emerging economies like China and India. Members of the G77 bloc, like the least developed countries—which included our neighbours Bangladesh and Nepal, allies from the African countries, traditional partners like Maldives (which is part of the Alliance of Small Island States), and even BASIC partners, South Africa and Brazil—favoured a legal agreement.

At Cancun, India's maneuvering space was fast vanishing, and in a bid to regain negotiating space, to literally live and fight another day, I made an impromptu addition—'all countries must take binding commitments under appropriate legal form'—to my address to the high-level segment of the climate talks. This impromptu one-liner came in for instant criticism from influential sections of the media, who dubbed it as India committing to taking an emission reduction target; there were rare exceptions to this tidal wave of criticism. Political opponents spared no punches even when I was in Cancun, and when I returned. However, as I explained in the immediate aftermath and later to the MPs in a letter, and in Parliament, my effort at Cancun was to prevent India from being cornered. It was an effort to nip the demand for a legal agreement in the bud without appearing to be insensitive to the demands of the vulnerable developing countries. I continued to maintain, as we had in the past, that the form of a global compact should be discussed only after there was consensus on the elements that comprised the pact.

What was lost in the din of the criticism were the efforts India made by proactively putting forward proposals on contentious issues like international consultation and analysis or a global monitoring system for emission reduction measures, and on technology. The success India had in fashioning solutions to these knotty problems, thereby, emerging as a progressive dealmaker was ignored domestically.

The picture abroad was completely different—my personal role was hailed and with it India had turned the corner in the political imagination. It allowed me—in July of 2011 at the Petersberg Dialogue in Berlin—barely a fortnight before I was to relinquish charge of the ministry, an opportunity to put forward a proposal for a global monitoring system on the finances that industrialized countries were supposed to provide to developing countries to address climate change.

There were other pressures on India as well, the US, Canada, European Union (EU), and even some developing countries like Mexico wanted India to phase out using of the refrigerant gas hydroflurocarbon (HFC) and allow for its inclusion in the Montreal Protocol. Given that our industry had just completed phasing out the ozone-depleting hydrochlorofluorocarbons (HCFCs), there was no way we could agree to this demand, it was impractical let alone its implications for the Kyoto Protocol. On this, I was able to engage the US and a working group was set up to explore the possibilities of alternatives to HFCs, which, though not harmful to the ozone layer, have a high global warming quotient.

It gives me no pleasure to see my apprehensions about persisting with the old approach to negotiations come true. In the three rounds of negotiations that followed Cancun—Durban, Doha, and Warsaw—India moved away from proactive engagement and finally emerging in Lima as a free-rider with no ideas or proposals of engaging the world. In reclaiming its role of a naysayer in international negotiations, New Delhi relinquished the opportunity to actively fashion and shape the crafting of a global solution. In the process, India ended up giving more room to industrialized countries to renege on their global commitments of reducing emissions and providing finance. As we head towards Paris and the new post-2020 agreement, India has another chance at reclaiming its place as a proactive player.

India's global engagement was not limited to climate change. In the Convention on Biological Diversity—India was to host the Tenth Conference of Parties in 2012—I was able to help push through the provisions on access and benefit sharing (ABS), which were finalized and adopted in Nagoya, Japan, in 2010. As a major victim of bio-piracy, it was in our interest to have an ABS protocol, which would help ensure that benefits of natural resources and their commercial derivatives are shared with local communities, helping secure the country's biodiversity and provide livelihood benefits to people. Without it, international drug firms were just taking human genetic and other biological materials then making us pay billions of dollars to buy the vaccines.

The hard work and the trials and tribulations of carving a space for India in formulating a solution to the pressing global environmental problems seemed to be paying off. United Nations Secretary-General Ban Ki-moon set up two high level panels, one on identifying sources for climate finance and the other on sustainability. Montek Singh Ahluwalia was a member of the panel on finance. And I was invited to be a part of his global sustainability panel to provide a road map for the post-2015 world, which was to be an important input to the deliberations at the twentieth anniversary of the Rio Convention.

This chapter deals with the effort to change the global perception about India, especially in the context of climate change negotiations, through proactive participation, building links with new partners, and strengthening existing ones. It also deals with domestic challenges that such efforts presented.

Letter to Principal Scientific Adviser to the Government of India R. Chidambaram, on the Need for India to Take Climate Change Seriously, Especially the Impact on Agriculture and the Likelihood of Increased Global Pressure on India to Take Emission-Reduction Targets

12 June 2007

I have just got to know that you are the chairman of the expert committee on impacts of climate change set up by the government on 7 May 2007.

Since I had something to do with the establishment of this commit-tee along with Dr R.K. Pachauri, I thought I would take this opportu-nity of sharing with you some special concerns of mine that prompted the initiative.

The immediate backdrop was, of course, the Stern Review with which I was quite impressed. As you are aware, Nicholas Stern and his team conducted a comprehensive review on the impact of climate change in the UK and listening to his presentation in the Planning Commission made me wonder why we also should not take such an initiative.

It is true that there is an international dimension to climate change but I approached this issue from a domestic perspective. I had been to Haryana Agricultural University (HAU), Hissar, a couple of months back where I was given a presentation on wheat yields in Haryana which had been stagnating for the past few years. The vice-chancellor of the HAU, Dr J.C. Katyal, informed me that one of the reasons for this stagnation is that maximum temperatures in the crucial months of February and March have gone up by $2\,^\circ$C and that our wheat varieties are simply not suited to such temperature variations. It is this factor, more than anything else, which led me to believe that we should take climate change more seriously than we have done in the past.

For too long, we have been preoccupied with defending our posi-tion in relation to the Kyoto Protocol on the strength of our per capita greenhouse gas emissions. Anything per capita in India is low and, therefore, I have never really bought into this argument. The question we ought to be asking ourselves is: Is climate change an issue for us or not, irrespective of what our contribution is globally? Of course, now it is almost certain that in Kyoto-II, countries like China and India will not be able to get by without taking on some commitments on containing growth in GHG emissions as they did during part of Kyoto-I.

I wish you all the best and I look forward to being in touch with you on this very vital issue. I think public education is also a very important dimension of your terms of reference, to which I hope adequate atten-tion will be paid.

I attach a copy of a note that Dr Pachauri had prepared at my request in November 2006 that helped trigger new thinking on climate change.

Excerpts from a Presentation Made to the Media on India and Climate Change Focusing on Outlining India's Position and Initiatives Being Undertaken and Planned at the Domestic Level

30 JUNE 2009

India Itself is Facing Major Climatic Variability

1. Already observed adverse climatic trends in India
   a. Warming of 0.4°C in surface air temperature over the period 1901–2000.
   b. The glaciers in the Himalayas are receding.
   (Though there are a few glaciers that may be advancing as well. There is no conclusive scientific evidence as yet to suggest that the retreat of Himalayan glaciers is being caused by climate change; the retreat could be a result of natural cyclical processes.)
2. Major projected changes by the year 2100
   a. Increase in rainfall by 15–40 per cent with (high regional variability).
   b. Warming more pronounced over land areas with maximum increase in north India.
   c. Warming, relatively greater in winter and post-monsoon seasons.
   d. Increase in annual mean temperature by 3°C–6°C.

India's Emissions Growth Path

Data indicates that India's emissions growth path has been on sustainable lines; 16 per cent of the world's population but only 4.6 per cent of the global CO_2 emissions. This is validated by objective third-party studies.

World Bank Assessment

1. India is a relatively low-carbon economy.
2. Among the seventy countries studied, India ranks sixty-third for per capita emissions, forty-eighth for CO_2 emissions per unit of GDP.
3. Offsetting factor for CO_2 emissions is high

a. 30 per cent of GHG growth offset by lowering energy intensity and improving the carbon intensity of its fuel mix; Russia and China show much lower performance.

b. Achieved this despite a low initial emission level and against a backdrop of increasing CO_2 intensity worldwide between 1999–2004.

India's Position on Climate Change

The Prime Minister has stated that India's per capita emission levels will never exceed that of the per capita emission levels of developed countries.

1. India cannot and will not take on emission reduction targets because:
   a. Poverty eradication and social and economic development are the first and over-riding priorities.
   b. Each human being has equal right to global atmospheric resources (that is, principle of equity).
   c. 'Common but differentiated responsibility' is the basis for all climate-change actions.
2. India will continue to be a low-carbon economy (World Bank study).
3. India's primary focus is on 'adaptation', with specific niches for 'mitigation'.
4. India has already unveiled a comprehensive National Action Plan on Climate Change (NAPCC) whose activities are in the public domain. Work on the action-plan has been initiated.
5. Only those nationally appropriate mitigation actions (NAMAs) can be subject to international monitoring, reporting, and verification that are enabled and supported by international finance and technology transfer.
6. India wants a comprehensive approach to reducing emissions from deforestation and forest degradation (REDD) and advocates REDD+ that includes conservation, afforestation, and sustainable management of forests.
7. India advocates collaborative research in future low-carbon technology and access to intellectual property rights (IPRs) as global public goods.

Some Issues of Concern

1. Differentiation amongst developing countries sought to be introduced through:
   a. Alternative multilateral forums
   b. Parallel bilateral negotiations
2. Sectoral approaches to mitigation actions outside the Bali Action
   Plan being advocated.
3. Making all NAMAs subject to international monitoring, reporting,
   and verification.
4. Requirement for quantification of deviation from BAU.
5. Ambiguity in responsibility for finance and technology transfer.
6. Move to limit scope of Clean Development Mechanism (CDM).
7. Bill passed by the US House of Representatives, and now before the
   US Senate, proposes to impose trade penalties on countries that do
   not accept limits on global-warming pollution.

India's Proactive Contribution to Climate Change Negotiations

1. Actively involved with G77 and China to evolve common position
   on negotiations.
2. Made nine submissions to UNFCCC on finance, technology, forestry, and other areas. For example, a mechanism for technology
   transfer and development, financial architecture for climate change,
   proposal for comprehensive approach to REDD+.
3. Worked with China, Brazil, South Africa, and thirty-three other
   countries to present a joint proposal for emission reduction targets
   by Annex 1 countries in second commitment period.

India's NAPCC

It envisages India's efforts being led through eight missions, two of
which focus on 'mitigation' and five on 'adaptation'.

1. National Solar Mission: 20,000 MW of solar power by 2020
2. National Mission for Enhanced Energy Efficiency: 10,000 MW of
   energy efficiency savings by 2020
3. National Mission for Sustainable Habitat: Energy efficiency in
   residential and commercial buildings, public transport, solid waste
   management

4. National Water Mission: Water conservation, river basin management

5. National Mission for Sustaining the Himalayan Ecosystem: Conservation and adaptation practices, glacial monitoring

6. National Mission for a Green India: 6 million ha of afforestation over degraded forest lands by the end of the Twelfth Plan

7. National Mission for Sustainable Agriculture: Drought proofing, risk management, agricultural research

8. National Mission on Strategic Knowledge for Climate Change: Vulnerability assessment, research and observation, Data management.

Critical Initiatives

In addition, India has twenty-four other 'critical initiatives' on the anvil, for which detailed plans and an institutional framework is being prepared

1. Energy Efficiency in Power Generation: Supercritical technologies, Integrated Gasification Combined Cycle (IGCC) technology, natural gas-based power plants, closed-cycle three-stage nuclear power programme, efficient transmission and distribution, hydroelectric power

2. Other Renewable Energy Technologies (RET) Programmes: RETs for power generation, biomass-based pop-up generation technologies, small-scale hydropower, wind energy, grid-connected systems, RETs for transportation and industrial fuels

3 Disaster Management: Response to extreme climate events, reducing risk to infrastructure through better design, strengthening communication networks, and disaster management facilities

4. Protection of Coastal Areas: Undertake measures for coastal protection and setting up early warning systems, development of a regional ocean modelling system, high-resolution coupled ocean-atmosphere variability studies in tropical oceans, development of a high-resolution storm surge model for coastal regions, development of salinity-tolerant crop cultivars, community awareness on coastal disasters and necessary action; timely forecasting, cyclone, and flood warning systems, enhanced plantation and regeneration of mangroves and coastal forests

5. Health Sector: Provision of enhanced public health care services and assessment of increased burden of disease due to climate change

6. Creating Appropriate Capacity at Different Levels of the Government: Building capacity in the central, state and other agencies/bodies at the local level to assimilate and facilitate the implementation of the activities of the National Plan.

Letter to Principal Secretary to Prime Minister T.K.A. Nair, on Participating in the UN Secretary-General's Heads of State and Government Summit and Enhancing Bilateral Ties with the US

4 AUGUST 2009

The Permanent Mission of India to the UN, New York, has informed us that a summit of the heads of state/government has been convened by the Secretary-General of the UN Ban Ki-moon in New York on 22 September 2009 to discuss issues relating to climate change. The communication received from the office of UN Secretary-General and the modalities and arrangements for the summit as indicated are enclosed.

I had a discussion on the subject with the foreign secretary on 18 July 2009. It was felt that in the event of the Prime Minister not being able to attend the summit, I should participate in the summit. The prime minister's special envoy on climate change will accompany me to this meet.

I would also like to utilize the opportunity for enhancing bilateral cooperation with the US on various environmental and forestry management issues. The recent Indo-US MoU on cooperation in environmental protection covers many of the relevant issues. An area of focus during my visit would be cooperation on climate change. Secretary (environment and forests) could accompany me in view of the importance of the high-level summit and other bilateral engagements.

I had discussed the possibility of having such consultations with the US side during my meeting with US Secretary of State Hillary Clinton and US Special Envoy for Climate Change Todd Stern.

I await your advice on the above.

Letter to the Prime Minister on the Meetings Held in New York, Ahead of the Copenhagen Climate Change Conference

24 SEPTEMBER 2009

I have just returned from a most productive visit to New York. I attended the Greenland Dialogue organized by the Denmark Government involving thirty countries. I also spoke at Columbia University at a function organized by Jagdish Bhagwati; a public function organized by Tony Blair at the New York Public Library and attended by the UN Secretary-General; the US–India Business Council; and the South Asian Journalists Association. In addition, I had a number of bilateral meetings with the environment ministers of Japan, South Africa, Sweden, Norway, Spain, Singapore, Indonesia, and China. I attended the high-level UN Summit on Climate Change as well. My message everywhere was the following.

India has not caused the problem of global warning but is determined to be part of the solution at Copenhagen and beyond. We will be a dealmaker and not a deal-breaker, and will engage constructively and proactively. The starting point for a fair and equitable agreement is the acceptance of the developed countries of their historical responsibility and their undertaking to make credible cuts in emission of 25–40 per cent by 2020 over the 1990 reference levels.

The 'perfect' should not become the enemy of 'good' at Copenhagen. We should clinch agreements on issues where there is already a substantial consensus like forestry, adaptation finance, technology cooperation for mitigation in energy, and CDM. India has already made detailed submissions on these subjects to the UNFCCC. Forestry is of particular importance to us since 10 per cent of our GHG emissions are presently being sequestered by our forest and tree cover.

As the Prime Minister has already stated, India will always have its per capita GHG emissions below that of developed world. This is a major binding we are imposing on ourselves, fully conscious of our own responsibilities. Our per capita emissions will be around 2–2.5 tonnes of carbon dioxide equivalent by 2020 and around 3–3.5 tonnes of carbon dioxide equivalent by 2030, as compared to 1–1.2 tonnes, at present. India agrees to the aspirational goal of limiting temperature rise to 2 °C by 2050 but this should be implemented in a manner that ensures full equity and equitable burden sharing.

While India believes that the per capita approach is the only measure that ensures equity, it also appreciates the need to go beyond it especially in view of the fact that by 2020 India will, in all likelihood, become the fourth largest emitter after China, US, and the EU. That is why we are now seriously contemplating domestic legislation to take on specific performance targets for mitigation actions in power, transport, industry, agriculture, buildings, and forestry by the year 2020 and 2030. These will not be explicit emission reduction targets but will be implicit performance targets that will lead to emission reductions. Draft legislation is ready and is under consideration. Parliamentary accountability through such a law will ensure that a durable consensus on this issue is built. We are hoping to introduce this Bill sometime in November this year when Parliament reconvenes. I called this the per capita-plus approach.

India has already embarked on implementing its NAPCC, which is a mix of adaptation and mitigation measures. On those measures that will be funded internationally and supported through international technology, we will gladly agree to international monitoring, reporting, and verification (MRV). For those mitigation actions we undertake unilaterally and on our own, we would certainly consider a mechanism to ensure that the international community is kept fully abreast of what we are doing—somewhat on the lines of the Trade Policy Review of the WTO and the Article IV consultations with the IMF. We could submit a detailed communication to the UNFCCC once every two years on what we are doing and also have an annual climate policy dialogue. In any case, India's extraordinarily vibrant civil society and open media imposes a natural MRV discipline on the government for fulfilling its commitments made in Parliament. A discipline that is more effective than any international regime. We have seen how almost all countries have flouted their legal obligations under the Kyoto Protocol and these very countries are asking for credibility from countries like India.

The idea that India is not interested in an agreement at Copenhagen is just not true. We are heavily influenced by climate change—for instance, 40–45 per cent of the annual variation in our GDP growth over the past half century has been on account of yearly variations in rainfall alone. The Himalayan ecosystem, so vital for our water security, is vulnerable because of deteriorating health of its glaciers and peninsular India will be heavily influenced by increases in sea levels. We have a huge, huge stake in ensuring an agreement is reached and we will work purposefully with other countries towards this end. India's principled position that it cannot and will not take on legally binding emission cuts does not mean it will not take significant steps to reduce its own emissions.

Since monitoring GHGs is so critical, India has decided to launch its own satellite for monitoring GHGs and aerosol by 2011. Work on this project has already begun and this capability will have regional and global significance as well. India is also hosting the Global Conference on Climate Change Technology in New Delhi in mid-October 2009, which will produce a framework for technology sharing and cooperation that could be adopted at Copenhagen.

Sir, I believe that there is now a better understanding of and appreciation for India's position and policies. There have been a couple of positive reports for the very first time on India in the international press as well as positive acknowledgements by influential people like Ban Ki-Moon, Tony Blair, and Al Gore. The amplifications of our efforts was, I believe, very timely—our commitment to consider domestic legislation preceded a somewhat similar announcement made by China, thus, allowing us to be perceived as a pathbreaker, rather than a mere follower. The pressure has now been firmly put on the US to act, something that was acknowledged to me by Todd Stern, the US climate change envoy, who expressed warm sentiments on our new initiative.

Letter to Union Minister of Finance Pranab Mukherjee on G20 and Climate Finance

6 August 2009
This invites reference to the G20 proposal to set up an expert group to deliberate on issues relating to climate finance.

Climate finance is a subject matter of discussions in the UNFCCC and all parties are currently engaged in negotiating an appropriate architecture for provision of finances for addressing the needs of developing countries. Discussion on this matter in any other forum may detract from the principles of the convention and may even have implications for climate change negotiations that cover a wide spectrum of issues.

G20, which is engaged in the task of addressing global financial meltdown, may advocate a greater reliance on private sector resources including the use of the carbon markets for meeting the needs of climate. This will be an inadequate response to the global challenge of climate change.

In view of the fact that a decision has been taken to join the expert group proposed to be set up by the G20 Secretariat to discuss this issue,

I send herewith a detailed note on our views and the various aspects of climate finance for your consideration. The finance ministry may like to articulate these views during the G20 meetings.

Letter to Prime Minister with an Update on the Visit to China

27 AUGUST 2009

As you are aware I was in Beijing for four days and I have just returned from a most productive and constructive visit. I attach for your perusal two notes. The first summarizes the main points emerging from the climate change discussions while the second summaries the main points on other issues relating to environment and forests. The visit seems to have been well received and my meetings were warm and cordial. I thank you for the opportunity given to me.

Letter to China's Vice-Administrator of State Forestry Administration Zhu Lieke following a Visit to Beijing on Cooperation in Areas Related to Forestry and Wildlife

3 SEPTEMBER 2009

I am writing to express my deep sense of gratitude for the opportunity we had for meeting each other in Beijing last week. I found our discussions most useful and productive. We discussed a number of issues relating to cooperation in forestry and wildlife management. We will be sending a delegation of experts in both these areas to Beijing sometime in the first half of November 2009. This delegation would prepare an action plan for cooperation in the four areas that we had identified: (i) forests and carbon capture; (ii) management and technology of afforestation; (iii) forest survey and monitoring; and (iv) wildlife management, with particular reference to tiger conservation and protection.

Letter to China's Vice-Minister of Environmental Protection Zhou Jian on Partnership with India

3 SEPTEMBER 2009

I am writing to express my deep sense of gratitude for the opportunity we had to meet last week in Beijing. We discussed a number of issues and as we had agreed, I will be sending a delegation of experts from India to Beijing some time in late-October or early November 2009 to take forward the ideas that we had exchanged for cooperation. If you will recall, we had spoken about cooperation in the areas of (i) river and lake conservation; (ii) pollution control and monitoring; and (iii) management of hazardous and chemical wastes.

Letter to Deputy Chairman, Planning Commission Montek Singh Ahluwalia on Allocating Funds for a Grant to SAARC Institutions Dealing with Environment

[The letter was also sent to the Union Minister for External Affairs, S.M. Krishna.]

24 SEPTEMBER 2009

On the request of the SAARC Secretariat, and in consultation with the Ministry of External Affairs, this ministry has decided to host the Eighth Meeting of the South Asian Association for Regional Cooperation (SAARC) Environment Ministers in New Delhi from 19–20 October, 2009.

During this meeting, a number of key issues like afforestation, environment management and planning, sustainable habitats and waste management, land degradation, including desertification, river cleaning programme, etc., are to be discussed. One main issue relates to institutional strengthening and capacity-building. It may be appreciated that the ability of a country/region to follow the sustainable development path is determined to a large extent by the capacity of its people and its institutions as well as by its ecological and geographical conditions. Specifically, capacity-building encompasses human, scientific, technological, organizational, institutional, and resource capabilities. A fundamental goal of capacity-building is to enhance the ability to evaluate and address the crucial questions related to policy choices and modes of implementation among development options, based on an understanding of environmental potentials and limits and of needs as perceived by the people of the region concerned.

Keeping in view the importance of this issue and also as India is hosting the said meeting, it will be appropriate that we announce a one-time grant to some of the SAARC institutions whose development would be significant for this region. Accordingly, it is proposed that we may consider a one-time grant of $1 million each for capacity-building and strengthening of the SAARC Forestry Centre in Bhutan and the SAARC Coastal Management Centre in Maldives. This grant will definitely give the message to SAARC members about India's commitments in deepening cooperation to address the various environmental challenges faced by this region.

My ministry has already written to the Planning Commission to allocate the amount in the appropriate budget head.

I will be grateful if you could kindly look into the matter so that the Planning Commission could allocate approximately an amount of Rs 10 crore to this ministry at the earliest so that we are in a position to announce this at our meeting on 19–20 October, 2009.

Letter to MPs Informing Them of India's Position in the International Negotiations, Efforts Being Made by the Ministry, and the Rationale and Implication of Measures Taken

[Initially sent on 29 September to leaders of political parties, and subsequently an updated version of the letter was sent to other MPs as well.]

5 OCTOBER 2009

As you are aware, India is engaged in global climate change negotiations being conducted under the UNFCCC. The current round of negotiations will culminate in a major meeting in Copenhagen in December this year. I know that you have a keen interest in the topic of climate change and I wanted to take this opportunity to personally provide you with an update on India's position in these negotiations and other recent developments. I look forward to engaging with you and seeking the benefit of your thoughts on this issue over the next two months.

Historical Background to India's Position

India has been an active participant in international negotiations on climate change over the last two decades. The issue of climate change first entered intergovernmental discussion in 1988 when the UN General Assembly passed a resolution recognizing climate change as a 'common concern of mankind' and endorsed the setting up of the Intergovernmental Panel on Climate Change (IPCC) to evaluate the risk posed by this threat. In 1990, the UN General Assembly adopted another resolution establishing a single intergovernmental negotiating process to conduct negotiations on an international convention on climate change. Following two years of intense negotiations, the UNFCCC was formally adopted at the Earth Summit in Rio in 1992. To date, 193 countries, including India, have ratified this treaty. Under the UNFCCC, all parties have agreed to protect the climate system for the benefit of present and future generations of humankind, on the basis of 'equity' and in accordance with their 'common but differentiated responsibilities and respective capabilities'.

Noting that the largest share of historical and current global emissions of GHGs originated in developed countries, the UNFCCC called upon them to take the lead in combating climate change. Under the convention, all developed country parties (listed in Annex I of the UNFCCC) agreed to return their GHG emissions to 1990 levels by the year 2000. Subsequently, under the Kyoto Protocol in 1997, they further agreed to take on quantified emission limitation and reduction commitments to reduce their overall emissions by at least 5 per cent below 1990 levels in the commitment period 2008–12.

Recognizing that per capita emissions in developing countries are still relatively low and that their share of global emissions will grow to meet their future social and development needs, the UNFCCC required no legally binding emission-reduction commitments from the developing countries. The UNFCCC also explicitly recognized that economic and social development and poverty eradication are the first and overriding priorities of the developing country parties. Furthermore, under the convention, developed countries committed to providing new and additional financial resources, including for the transfer of technology that were needed by the developing countries to meet the 'agreed full incremental costs' of implementing any measures that the latter took to address this issue.

In 2007, following the release of the IPCC's Fourth Assessment Report, which found the warming of the climate system to be 'unequivocal', the parties to the UNFCCC decided to launch a comprehensive process to enable the full, effective and sustained implementation of the convention. Under the Bali Action Plan, it was decided to reach an agreed outcome on this by the fifteenth session of the Conference of Parties (COP 15), to be held in Copenhagen in December 2009, by addressing the following:

1. A shared vision for long-term cooperative action, including a long-term global goal for emissions reductions.
2. Enhanced national/international action on mitigation of climate change (that is, on measures to reduce GHG emissions).
3. Enhanced action on adaptation (that is, on measures to adjust to the adverse effects of climate change).
4. Enhanced action on technology development and transfer to support action on mitigation and adaptation.
5. Enhanced action on the provision of financial resources and investment to support action on mitigation, adaptation, and technology cooperation.

Key Tenets of India's Position in Climate Change Negotiations

India has a clear, credible, and consistent position in the global climate change negotiations. The key elements of India's position are as follows:

1. We expect Copenhagen to result in a cooperative global response that is fair and equitable; and in accordance with the principle of 'common but differentiated responsibilities and respective capabilities', a principle that is enshrined in the UNFCCC;
2. We believe that each human being has equal right to the global atmospheric space, which is a common property of humanity (that is, the principle of per capita equity);
3. India cannot and will not take on internationally legally binding emission-reduction targets because:
   a. The UNFCCC does not require developing countries to take on any emission reduction commitments;
   b. The primary responsibility to reduce GHG emissions, as noted in the UNFCCC, is of the developed countries given their largest share of historical and current global emissions;
   c. Our national GHG emissions are still very low, especially when considered on a per capita basis, and will naturally grow as we continue to develop;

    d. Poverty eradication, and social and economic development are our first and overriding priorities.
4. India has already unveiled a comprehensive NAPCC whose activities are in the public domain. The eight missions under this NAPCC along with twenty-four other critical initiatives/programmes are being finalized;
5. The equal per capita entitlement principle is the only legitimate internationally acknowledged measure for reflecting equity. As stated by our Prime Minister, India's per capita emission levels will never exceed the per capita emission levels of developed countries;
6. India is undertaking a series of mitigation actions on its own accord. Only those mitigation actions that are supported and enabled by international technology, financing, and capacity-building will be subject to international measurement, reporting, and verification, that is, MRV (these supported actions are called nationally appropriate mitigation actions or NAMAs in UN parlance);
7. India's primary focus is on 'adaptation' (that is, increasing the capacity to meet the adverse effects of climate change), with specific niches for 'mitigation' (that is, measures to reduce GHG emissions);
8. India wants a comprehensive agreement on REDD, and advocates REDD+ that includes conservation, afforestation, and sustainable management of forests;
9. India advocates collaborative research in future low-carbon technology and access to IPRs as global public goods.

Recent Actions by India

India has always had a principled position on the issue of climate change. There has been an attempt in some quarters to show that India's stance is a major barrier to reaching global agreement at Copenhagen. We have rejected this forcefully. Recognizing that there is a need to further elucidate India's constructive position on this issue, I have personally engaged with civil society, domestic, and foreign media, captains of industry, heads of state, ministers and ambassadors of various countries. We have also been working in close coordination with our partners in the G77 countries. I have personally visited China and my Chinese counterpart is coming to New Delhi on 21 October to continue the bilateral dialogue. We are also having a SAARC environment ministers meeting on 19–20 October, where we will be discussing, among many other issues, the subject of climate change.

As part of this ongoing effort, we have also nuanced our message to the outside world, without diluting our negotiating position, as follows:

1. India has not caused the problem of global warming but is determined to be part of the solution at Copenhagen and beyond. We will be a dealmaker, not a deal-breaker and will engage constructively and proactively. The starting point for a fair and equitable agreement is the acceptance by developed countries of the principle of per capita equity, their historical responsibility, and their undertaking to make credible cuts in GHG emissions of 25–40 per cent by 2020 over 1990 reference levels.

2. The perfect should not become the enemy of the good at Copenhagen. We should clinch agreements on issues where there is already a substantial consensus—forestry, adaptation finance, technology cooperation for mitigation in energy, and the CDM.

3. The idea that India is not interested in an agreement at Copenhagen is simply not true. India has played a constructive role in the current negotiations. We have made twelve detailed concrete proposals on key issues under negotiation to the UNFCCC in the last two years.

4. We are an extremely responsible nation as far as our commitments are concerned—as our Prime Minister has repeatedly stated, our emissions per capita will always remain below that of the developed countries. Our per capita emissions will be around 2–2.5 tonnes of carbon dioxide equivalent by 2020 and around 3–3.5 tonnes of carbon dioxide equivalent by 2030, as compared to around 1–1.2 tonnes, at present. India shares the global aspirational goal of limiting temperature rise to 2°C by 2050 but this should be implemented in a manner that ensures full equity and equitable burden-sharing and that does not adversely affect the development plans and programmes of countries like India.

5. While India believes that the per capita approach is the only measure that ensures equity, it is also aware of the seriousness of the threat that climate change poses. India is heavily influenced by climate change, for instance, 40–45 per cent of the annual variation in our GDP growth over the past half-century has been on account of yearly variations in rainfall alone. The Himalayan

ecosystem, so vital for our water security, is vulnerable because of the deteriorating health of its glaciers and peninsular India will be influenced heavily by increases in mean sea levels. That is why we are now contemplating domestic legislation to take on specific performance targets in power, transportation, industry, agriculture, buildings, forestry and other relevant sectors by a specific target year derived from the NAPCC and various Planning Commission documents. These will *not be explicit emission reduction targets but will be implicit performance targets* for mitigation and adaptation, such as, mandatory fuel efficiency standards by 2011, mandatory energy conservation-compliant building codes by 2012, 20 per cent contribution of renewables in India's energy mix by 2030, targets for energy intensity by 2020, etc., that will lead to mitigation while also realizing other development co-benefits simultaneously. We call this the *per capita plus approach*. Draft legislation in this regard is being discussed and will be made available for public discussion shortly. I look forward to having a discussion in Parliament on this in the next couple of months.

6. India has already embarked on implementing its NAPCC, which is a mix of adaptation and mitigation measures. As explained earlier, on those mitigation actions that are supported and enabled by international technology, financing, and capacity building, we will agree to international MRV. For other mitigation actions that we undertake unilaterally and on our own, or what I call nationally accountable mitigation outcomes (NAMOs), we could consider a mechanism to ensure that the international community is kept abreast of what we are doing. We could, for example, submit a detailed national communication (NATCOM) to the UNFCCC once every two years (as opposed to the present once in six years) on what we are doing, and also have a regular climate policy dialogue based on this communication with the UNFCCC. In any case, *I have gone out of my way to stress that India's vibrant civil society, free press, and parliamentary system ensure robust MRV of all of India's actions.*

7. Technology cooperation and financial transfers will need to form the basis of any international agreement, and India is playing a key role in this regard. For example, India hosting a UN High-Level Conference on Climate Change Technology Development and Transfer in New Delhi on 22–23 October 2009, which will produce

a framework for technology sharing and cooperation that could be adopted at Copenhagen.

8. I should also mention here that in two years time India will be launching its own satellite to monitor GHG emissions and the technical work for this endeavour has already begun at the Indian Space Research Organisation.

9. Our scientific and research community has also done excellent work in preparing the country's initial National Communications (NATCOM-I) to the UNFCCC, where 131 research teams collaborated to put together a comprehensive inventory of our national GHG emissions. Indeed, for our second National Communications (NATCOM-II), we are putting together an even more detailed assessment of our national GHG inventories and of the vulnerabilities that key sectors in India face from climate change. This is expected to be available by late 2010. As mentioned before, we are willing to consider increasing the frequency and scope of our national communications further to better inform the various relevant stakeholders of the actions and initiatives that India is taking on climate change.

Implications of our Recent Actions

Our recent efforts to more proactively engage the world on clarifying our position have met with very positive responses from leaders across the world, civil society, and media. I think we are making rapid progress in altering the perception of India in international fora, and the world at large, without compromising our position. As I have emphasized, we need to take actions on climate change because it affects our people's lives, not because of any international pressures. *I am very clear that any commitments we take on must be of our own accord, on our own terms, and in line with our own development priorities. The only entity to which we will be accountable for any form of commitment will be our Parliament, and Parliament alone.*

I hope this letter helps clarify for you our position and our thinking on climate change. We have a major role to play on this issue in the upcoming months and years. It is important for me and for our government that you are kept fully informed on where we stand and what we are doing, hence this letter. I look forward to discussing these issues with you further, and to your support on the matter as we take important steps in the next few weeks.

Finally, I invite you to our new-look website (www.moef.nic.in), where you will find a number of key documents that we have been bringing out on India and climate change, including a list of twenty recent initiatives we have undertaken to address issues related to climate change, a compilation of our submissions to the UNFCCC, a report estimating India's future GHG emissions profile, and the NAPCC and, indeed, on a variety of other environment and forestry-related issues.

Note to Prime Minister on India's Preparations for Copenhagen Suggesting Nuancing of Our Approach to Protect National Interest and Development Space

[This note, and several other interventions, formed the basis of a debate in the Rajya Sabha in late November.]

13 OCTOBER 2009

1. India must launch aggressive domestic actions going beyond announcement of missions. A draft domestic law on climate change management that incorporates performance targets for efficiency and intensity, and non-fossil-based energy supply by 2020 or 2030 (nationally accountable mitigation outcomes) should be made available for public discussion without necessarily having it passed by Parliament before Copenhagen. This domestic law—a 'per capita plus' approach—is essential since the convergence of per capita emissions alone is not a sustainable basis for negotiations. The performance targets in the law would be reasonable and achievable. They would not be new obligations but things we have already committed to domestically in various forums such as the Eleventh Plan, the Integrated Energy Policy, the NAPCC, etc.

2. India must take the lead in specific areas that are the building blocks of a global agreement. The technology conference scheduled for 22–23 October offers one such an opportunity. A similar leadership role on forestry and land-use change could well be taken.

3. South Asian Cooperation in Climate Change is essential even though countries like Bangladesh and Maldives may have a different view from India's. The SAARC environment ministers are

meeting in New Delhi on 20 October and a statement will be issued following the meeting. India should prepare to extend financial and technical assistance to its SAARC partners, as well as forging a common approach to dealing with climate change in the SAARC region.

4. Cooperation between India and China in climate change will also send powerful international signals, even though China will have its own agenda of which we cannot be sure of. We may set up a consultation mechanism between India and China to facilitate coordination of policies and actions. An MoU between China and India on cooperation in climate change areas is proposed to be signed in New Delhi on 21 October.

5. Bilateral engagement with important countries needs to be deepened. An MoU with Norway on climate change is proposed to be signed in New Delhi on 23 October and the EU on 6 November. Similar initiatives are needed with the US and Japan and also Australia, Brazil, and South Africa. During the Prime Minister's visit to the US in November, India should aim to sign an agreement on climate change cooperation in order to emphasize our willingness to engage constructively.

6. India should also vociferously support the 'early start fund' on adaptation finance that is being proposed for small-island nations and least developed countries. We could consider leveraging the goodwill this would generate to prevent the move to impose mitigation and finance commitments on 'advance developing countries', that is, India and China.

7. India should announce its readiness to prepare a substantially enhanced biannual national communication to the UNFCCC (as opposed to the present requirement of once in six years) and use that as a basis for a biannual climate change implementation dialogue with the UNFCCC, and if need be with key nations (parallels exist vis-à-vis the WTO and the IMF).

8. India should also be seen to be doing more comprehensive scientific work on assessing, measuring and putting into the public domain the impact of climate change on the various sectors of the economy and the various regions of the country. The initiative to launch the Indian Network of Climate Change Assessment (INCCA) proposed for 14 October is a step in this direction.

9. India should take the position that it welcomes any initiative to bring in the US into the mainstream if need be through a special mechanism but without diluting the basic Annex-I–non-Annex-I distinction of the Kyoto Protocol. If the Australian proposal of a schedule maintains this basic distinction and the nature of differential obligations is made clear, we should have no great theological objections to it. The position we will take on international mitigation commitments, only if supported by finance and technology, needs to be nuanced simply because we need to mitigate in our self-interest

10. India must listen more and speak less in negotiations, or else we will be treated with disfavour and derision by developed countries and resented by small island states and other highly vulnerable countries, which will take away from India's standing as a global power and aspirant for permanent membership to the Security Council. This is also important so that we can retain maximum flexibility and we are not used by others and deserted at the last minute. (The President of Brazil has just said that Brazil could consider emission cuts and China has got a think tank to float the idea of a peaking year). India must not stick to G77 alone and must realize that it is now embedded in the G20. India's interests, and India's interests alone, should drive our negotiations. India must be seen as pragmatic and constructive, not argumentative and polemical.

Letter to Prime Minister Informing Him on the Developments at the SAARC Environment Ministers Meet Held in New Delhi

20 October 2009

Today, we had the eighth meeting of the SAARC environment ministers. All ministers attended except for Pakistan, which was otherwise well-represented. The following important decisions were taken:

1. An annual South Asia Workshop on Climate Change Actions will be held. India will host the first meeting in early 2010.
2. In addition to each SAARC country making a statement at Copenhagen, efforts will be made to get a slot for a statement to be made on behalf of SAARC by Sri Lanka, the current chair.
3. India will establish a network of fifty SAARC weather stations in Nepal, Bhutan, and Bangladesh to begin with to monitor weather patterns.

4. India will extend a special grant of $1 million to the SAARC Forestry Centre, Thimpu, and of another $1 million to the SAARC Coastal Zone Management Centre at Male.
5. A SAARC Environment Treaty will be signed at the SAARC Summit in Thimpu in April 2010, along with an agreement to set up a Natural Disaster Rapid Response Mechanism.

In addition, the meeting gave specific directions for cooperation in pollution control and trans-boundary biodiversity conservation.

I attach a copy of the declaration issued after the meeting.

Letter to Prime Minister Informing Him about the Developments at the Climate Technology Conference in New Delhi

26 OCTOBER 2009

The New Delhi Conference on Technology and Climate Change went off quite well. We adopted a Delhi Statement on Global Cooperation on Climate Technology, a copy of which I have the privilege to attach for your perusal.

This statement was adopted in the presence of Connie Hedegaard, the Danish minister for climate and energy and, therefore, we are expecting that it would be an important contribution to the Copenhagen meeting in early December. The only disappointment I have is that we could not reach a consensus on the IPR issue which I am sure will come up in Copenhagen once again.

Intervention at the Pre-COP Meeting at Copenhagen, Denmark

[The pre-COP meeting is a good indicator of the issues that a host country wants to tackle during the conference.]

NOVEMBER 16, 2009

India is prepared to reflect in any agreement its commitment to keep its per capita emissions below that of the developed countries. India's per capita approach has drawn wide support including from two Nobel laureates, Thomas Schelling and Michael Spence, and from the German Council for Climate Change, an influential think tank. India's per capita emissions are now around 1.2 tonnes of CO_2 equivalent and are expected to be around 2–2.5 tonnes by 2020 and

3–3.5 tonnes by 2030. The per capita limit is an onerous limit that India has imposed on itself.

India has several NAMAs, which it is considering to convert to NAMOs by indicating specific performance targets in industry, energy, transport, agriculture, buildings, and forestry for the year 2020 and 2030. These NAMOs could be institutionalized through either legislative or executive action and are derived from the NAPCC.

Change and the Eleventh Five Year Plan Document.

India is prepared to submit a NATCOM once every two years to the UNFCCC covering both supported and unsupported actions and their outcomes as well as their impacts on emissions. This NATCOM could be used as a basis for international consultations with the UNFCCC. This will more than meet the demand for international reflection of domestic commitments and obligations taken on unilaterally. The format of reporting could be decided by the UNFCCC after discussions and consensus among the parties.

India will make low-carbon sustainable growth a central element of its Twelfth Plan growth strategy. This will mean taking on commitments to reduce energy to GDP intensity and corresponding emission reduction outcomes for the year 2020.

Response to Clarifications Sought by MPs in the Rajya Sabha Raised during the Calling Attention Motion on the Government's Changing Position on Climate Change

24 NOVEMBER 2009

Sir, I am grateful for the opportunity for having this Calling Attention Motion called. We have had nine speakers and the tenth one who asked a question. And, rather than respond to each individual speaker, I will just take some of the main issues that have been raised. I would like to reiterate, once again, Sir, that as the minister for environment and forests, I stand prepared for any form of discussion at any point of time on any issue relating to climate change before the Copenhagen process starts on 7 December. I also want to reiterate two other points, Sir, as a reflection of the transparency with which I believe we should conduct the running of any ministry, but particularly the ministry that I have been holding since 29 May. As I said, I have written to all the chief ministers; I have written to seventy-two MPs. Admittedly, some MPs have been left out; an anomaly which I will rectify; and in that letter, I have tried to explain in as detailed a manner as possible what the government's thinking is on climate change.

Sir, I have also at different points of time put on the website of our ministry all the documentations that we have been bringing out from time to time on climate change, both the technical aspects of climate change as well as the negotiating aspects of climate change. Sir, I have nothing to hide, and whatever criticism has been made, I will try to respond in as effective a manner as possible. I just want to recall, Sir, I was hailed by this very House as the great defender of India's sovereignty, when I, in front of the visiting US Secretary of State Hillary Clinton, said that India will not take on legally binding emission reduction cuts. The Leader of the Opposition was gracious enough to compliment me personally. Four months later, I stand here being accused of having undermined India's sovereignty and given in to American pressure. Sir, in four months, I do not think that I could have changed my position this dramatically ... (interruptions)... Please listen to me, Sir. I have listened very carefully, please listen to me. As I said, you may disagree with me. I am prepared to have a discussion with you. So, Sir, in four months' time, I have not made any deviation from what remains a non-negotiable position for me personally and for the Government of India that under no circumstances will the Government of India accept a legally binding emission reduction cut as part of any international agreement. This is written in stone; this is cast in stone. This remains a fundamental non-negotiable point for me, personally; it remains the non-negotiable for all of us who are entrusted with the responsibility of negotiating the international agreement. India, under no circumstances, will take on legally binding emission reduction cuts, which we believe is the obligation of the developed countries, including the US.

Sir, the Hon. Leader of the Opposition raised a very pertinent question and so did the opening speaker, Brinda Karat, that's why these doubts have surfaced now, and it is my duty to respond to this question clearly and categorically. Sir, what I have been trying to do in the last six months is to introduce an element of flexibility in our position why we remained anchored with the basic principles of the UNFCCC, the Kyoto Protocol, and the Bali Action Plan. I have never, never—and I would like to make this clear to my friend, my colleague, Brinda Karat—advocated India's abdication of its position on the Kyoto Protocol. I have never said this. I have always believed that Annex-I countries have a historical responsibility for fulfilling legally binding emission cuts and that the developing countries like India are obligated to take on nationally appropriate mitigation actions.

Sir, my only purpose has been to open up windows of flexibility for India because the world is changing; different countries are taking different positions. Brazil has announced emission reduction cuts; South Korea has announced emission reduction cuts; Indonesia has announced emission reduction cuts. And, my whole purpose is that India should not be isolated. That is my whole objective that the finger-pointing game should not start and the finger, the blame should not be put on India's door. So, flexibility is what I have been advocating.

Sir, Hon. member Brinda Karat said that I advocated giving up G77. I have not said that, Sir. I have said that while we have one foot in G77, we have to be mindful of other responsibilities that India has as an emerging, rising industrial power. In fact, Sir, if I may be permitted a personal word here, I went out of my way to negotiate a partnership agreement with China. The environment in our country was not conducive to an agreement with China. But, on 21 October, India and China signed a partnership agreement for collaboration on climate change. Why would I want to do it if I was an American stooge? Why would I want to sign an agreement with China knowing full well that China today is the world's largest emitter? It accounts for 23 per cent of the GHGs and India is at No. 5, at less than 5 per cent. Yet, I went to China, I spent three days in China; my Chinese counterpart and I negotiated an agreement. This was the first agreement for China, it was the first agreement for India; because we believed that China and India have common cause to resist the pressure of the developed countries to take on legally binding emission cuts.

Sir, I would like to recount a very interesting episode that had happened when we signed the MoU or the partnership agreement with China on 21 October. The Vice-Chairman of China's National Reforms and Development Commission, Xie Zhenhua, was coming out after the signing and TV journalists asked him, 'What is China going to do to ward off the pressure from America to take on legally binding cuts?' Sir, to my surprise and to the surprise of the TV interviewer, Xie Zhenhua reply was, 'Ward off pressure is the wrong word. China seeks to engage the world.' Sir, that is what we are trying to do. We are not here trying to isolate ourselves or box ourselves into a corner, we would like a country of India's size, a country of India's aspirations to have its options open while clearly recognizing the red line that we will never compromise on the issue of legally binding emission cuts. But we have to have the option open. We have to have some flexibility. And, we need to negotiate internationally not from a defensive position, but from a position of strength.

Sir, the Hon. Leader of the Opposition spoke about my proposal for domestic legislation. Sir, I have no hesitation in saying that this is a different position than what India's position was one year ago. Yes, it is a different position. It is a new idea, and my idea is that what we do domestically should be determined by us domestically in Parliament. What commitments we take on internationally is an entirely separate issue.

Sir, Sanjay Raut is not here; oh, he has just come back, Sir, he spoke about Mumbai. There is no country in the world which is as vulnerable to climate change as India. We are vulnerable because of our coastline. We are vulnerable because of the south-west and north-east monsoon. We are vulnerable because of the Himalayan glaciers. We are vulnerable because of our forest cover. There is no country in the world, which is as vulnerable to climate change as India is. My position, before I became minister and as minister, remains that it is in India's self-interest to respond creatively and aggressively to climate change as part of a domestic agenda. Sir, that is why I would like to remind the Hon. Leader of the Opposition, with whom I have spent some time to explain to him this thinking. But, I put forward the concept of a nationally accountable mitigation outcome. What does it mean by nationally accountable? To whom? To the Parliament.

I am saying: Let Parliament decide what these mitigation outcomes are. Parliament in its collective wisdom could pass a law, if that is what the government wants and if that is what Parliament wants. Let it pass a law. Let it enforce performance standards in transport, in industry, in agriculture, in buildings, in forestry, in different sectors of the economy and let us be accountable to Parliament. Sir, I do not have to remind you—there are two distinguished ministers of the previous to previous government present here—it is your government that passed the Fiscal

Responsibility and Budget Management (FRBM) Act. The FRBM Act of 2003 was passed by the National Democratic Alliance government and I am saying, do a climate change version of the FRBM Act. That is all I am saying. Take domestic obligations, report to Parliament, and let whatever gets reported to Parliament come in the public domain. Sir, the Hon. Leader of the Opposition said that now we are opening up whatever we are doing for international review. No, Sir. That is not the proposal. Whatever actions are supported by international finance and international technology will be open for international review. All those actions that are not supported by international finance and technology, which we do domestically, unilaterally on our own, we will make it open for international discussion, international consideration, and international consultations. We are an open society. We are a democratic society. We have a media that is holding us accountable. We have a civil society that holds us accountable. We do not need MRV with some international body. Any government in India goes through this MRV everyday in Parliament, in civil society, and in the media. So, all I am saying is, as an open society, as a democratic society, as a society, as a government accountable to Parliament, let us have the courage of our convictions if we think that climate change is a serious issue, which I believe it is, let us take on performance outcomes for ourselves.

Sir, I must say here that we are great at producing plans in our country. But, we are very poor in converting plans into outcomes. Sir, you ask the Indian government or an Indian civil servant or an Indian politician to produce an action plan. We will produce it very easily but what does it mean at the end? That is where China scores over us and that is what I want us to do. I want us to have the discipline to convert an action into an outcome and that outcome gets accountable to Parliament. Sir, for me Parliament is supreme. If I am accountable to Parliament I am accountable to no other body, national or international. Sir, the answer to the Hon. Leader of the Opposition is—the domestic norms is an idea of mine—it is up to the government to accept the idea of domestic legislation. That is being discussed now. Maybe we will have a comprehensive legislation. Maybe we will have part legislation. That process of discussion is on but the idea is that we convert the nationally appropriate mitigation actions, which are very general in nature to nationally accountable mitigation outcome, which is very specific, accountable, and can be monitored easily.

Sir, lot of references have been made to differing voices in the government. Sir, I cannot deny that perceptions are different. I cannot deny that there has been a certain continuity of thought and I cannot deny that some of these ideas that I have tried to bring into the public domain—not in a backhanded manner—I have tried to do it with a purpose to create a new body of thinking which will give us some flexibility, some room for manoeuvre in the international sphere and it cannot be anybody's case, Sir, that we do not need this flexibility. We need this flexibility. We need this room for manoeuvre because frankly, Sir, I am under no illusions. We have huge problems of poverty. We have huge problems of unemployment but at the same time the world recognizes India as an emerging power.

We are the fourth largest economy in the world. We will soon become the third largest economy of the world. We have aspirations of sitting in the international community of nations in a respectable manner. If we want to be accepted internationally, we should also be prepared to engage the rest of the world internationally. We should not smell a conspiracy in every attempt at engagement. This is only my request to you. If I were to do something in a hidden manner, if I were to do in a subterfuge, if I were to do in a backhanded way with nobody knowing, with the Prime Minister not knowing—there have been reports in the newspapers recently, my positions have deviated from what the Prime Minister's directive was—there is nothing farther from the truth in this. As a member of the Council of Ministers, if I flout the Prime Minister's directive, I will not last for more than two minutes. I am bound by what the Hon. Prime Minister tells me. The ultimate authority for me, as a minister, is the Prime Minister. So, for any newspaper item and for any member to believe a newspaper item which says that I have flouted the Prime Minister's directive, I categorically and comprehensively deny that. There is absolutely no truth in this rumour. But, at the same time, the caution that Amar Singh and Arun Jaitley have given, I would say that I am well aware of this that the domestic differences could be used internationally to weaken our negotiating position. I take full cognizance of this. I have, in my own way, in the last couple of weeks, tried to bring about greater coherence in our presentation and I assure the Hon. members that there will be no private enterprise in Copenhagen negotiations. We are going as representatives of the Government of India.

And, Sir, as a mark of my respect for Parliament, five months ago, I wrote a letter to the Hon. Speaker of Lok Sabha and the Chairman of the Rajya Sabha asking both of them to nominate four Hon. MPs to join me in the delegation to Copenhagen. If I have something to hide, if I have to capitulate to the Americans in Copenhagen, will I take MPs with me and capitulate? I would capitulate in solitude. I would not capitulate with MPs breathing down my neck. So, I would humbly request the Hon. members to please look at what I have said in the context of trying to introduce a small element of flexibility and to ensure that India does not earn the reputation of a deal-breaker. The Hon. Prime Minister's words to me, when I took over this ministry on 29 May were: 'We did not cause the problem of global warming. But make sure that we are a part of the solution to global warming'. And that is what I have tried to do. We have not caused the problem of global warming. But, increasingly, as N.K. Singh pointed out, if you look at the incremental emissions, India is, in absolute terms, not in per capita terms, an increasing contributor to the new stock of CO_2 in the atmosphere. So, without getting into questions of who is responsible, I entirely agree that polluter must pay. We do not have polluter must pay principle within India. How can we argue for polluter must pay internationally? Madam, for your information, I am trying to institute that the polluter-must-pay principle within India to begin with.

Rajiv Pratap Rudy: With retrospective effect?

Jairam Ramesh: Sir, today, the Hon. Chairman of the Standing Committee on Science and Technology has presented the report on the National Green Tribunal. We are going to soon come forward with a National Environmental Protection Authority. What is all this for? This is to ensure that the polluter must pay domestically. The short point is, India must negotiate from a position of strength. India must negotiate from a position of leadership and not negotiate from a position of defensiveness. We have nothing to feel defensive about. I would like to end here. I would like to respond, in writing, to each of the individual, specific points that have been raised. I will be responding to each Hon. member individually. But, let me reiterate that I stand prepared, at any point of time, to have a discussion on any issue as open a manner as possible. I have nothing to hide. I can assure Amar Singh, Arun Jaitley, and all others that it will be my endeavour to ensure that the fears, which they have expressed on the lack of coherence or cohesiveness in the government's view, will be plugged sooner or later.

Responding to Issues Raised by MPs During the Short Duration Discussion on Climate Change in the Lok Sabha

3 DECEMBER 2009

Thank you, Mr Chairman. Sir. It has been a four-hour Short Duration Discussion. I would not have minded had it been of longer duration. I am prepared to sit here as long as the House wants and I am prepared to stand here on any day to explain the government's stand on climate change.

We have had eighteen speakers today on this subject. The opening batsman was a very distinguished physicist himself and one of the tail-enders was a very distinguished mathematician. A PhD started the discussion and a PhD almost ended the discussion today. I am referring to Dr Raghuvansh Prasad Singh who has a PhD in Mathematics.

We have had some excellent interventions. I want to mention specially that today the younger members have been truly outstanding. By Indian political standards, even I am considered young, but I am not young. But I think, Shri Sandeep Dikshit, Shri Jayant Chaudhary, Shrimati Supriya Sule, and last but not least, Dr Jyoti Mirdha made truly outstanding presentations and I want to compliment them for this.

Permit me to deal with many of the important issues that have been raised today. There are policy issues that have been raised and each individual member has raised some specific issues. Today, I will deal with the larger issues of policy.

I would like to seek the indulgence of the House to respond to the specific issues of each individual member separately with the member concerned, like the Loharinag Pala issue of Dr Jyoti Mirdha, and the forestry issue of my good friend Shri Anant Kumar Hegde. My colleague from West Bengal, including Shri Panda, raised the issue of Sundarbans. So, on specific issues, if I may be permitted I will respond to each individual separately in writing.

I want to spend this evening discussing some of the larger issues of policy that have been raised. I want to begin by saying that today I found remarkable degree of agreement that climate change is a serious issue. This is very important. ... Cutting across party lines, cutting across states, there was a clear message today that climate change is a very serious issue.

On 24 November there was a Calling Attention Motion in the Rajya Sabha. In the Rajya Sabha, the issue was me. I am glad that in the Lok Sabha the issue is climate change, although some members have made some reference to me and I will respond to them to the best of my ability. So, climate change is a very serious issue for India. Forget Copenhagen for the time being. Climate change is of great significance to our country. Ever since I became the [environment] minister on 29 May, I have been trying to spread this single message that the most vulnerable country in the world to climate change is India, not Maldives, not Bangladesh, and not America, but India. There is no country that is as much impacted by climate change as India. Now, why do I say this? First, we are dependent on monsoons, the south-west monsoon and the north-east monsoon. They are the lifeline of our country. Two out of every three Indians still depend on agriculture for their livelihood. What happens to the monsoon determines what happens to our economy and what happens to our general mood. We are depressed when the monsoons fail and we are happy when the monsoons are good. Monsoons are not only part of our economy but also part of our culture and part of our civilization. Now, the uncertainty caused by climate change on the monsoon is of first and over-riding priority for India.

Second, Sir, we have the Himalayan glaciers—anywhere between 9,000 and 12,000 glaciers. There is a great deal of scientific debate on what is happening to these glaciers but we do not have to wait for perfect science. The warning signals are already there. Most of the glaciers are receding. Why are they receding? We cannot say it with 100 per cent certainty. Is it the natural process of cyclical change? Or, is it because of global warming? Scientists are still debating this issue. But what happens to the Himalayan glaciers will determine the water security of our country. That is the second point of vulnerability.

Third, we have vast critical ecological areas. My friend Shri Anant Kumar Hegde is not here. He also initiated the Short Duration Discussion. He comes from the Western Ghats. What happens to the Western Ghats will determine the future not only of Karnataka, Goa, Maharashtra, and Kerala but indeed of the entire country. Take our Northeast. The Northeast has only 4 per cent of India's geographical area but 25 per cent of our forest cover is in the Northeast. What happens? People have talked of Cherrapunji. It used to be the world's rainiest place. It no longer is. What happens to the Western Ghats? What happens to our Northeast? What happens to the Andamans? What happens to Lakshadweep? This is the third area of vulnerability.

Fourth, if you look at the map of India, if you see where the forests are located, if you see where the coal mines are, where the bauxite is, where the iron ore is, it is in the same region. The more coal we produce, the more iron ore we produce, the more forests we will have to give up. We know that giving up forests leads to higher levels of greenhouse gas emissions. There is no country in the world which has all these four dimensions of vulnerability. That is why I have been saying time and again that India, of all the 192 countries in the world, owes a responsibility not to the world but to itself, to take climate change seriously. We are not doing the world a favour. Please forget Copenhagen; forget the UN. We have to do it in our own self-interest. Our future as a society is dependent on how we respond to the climate change challenge.

Let me go to the second point. Today, the sad fact is that if you ask me what is going to be the impact of climate change on the Sunderbans, I cannot give you a good answer. I can only tell you Aila happened; Aila might happen. But I cannot give you a good answer. If you ask me what is going to be the impact of climate change on our monsoon, I can only say that there is uncertainty; monsoon in north-west India might increase, monsoon in north-east India might decrease. So, I cannot tell you. The reason for this is that so far, all the scientific studies on climate change have been done in the Western countries. India has made no investment in studying the impact of climate change on India. This is a very important point. Today, all our knowledge on climate change is derived from the Western publications.

It is derived from Western media, it is derived from Western political leaders and we have no independent source of information and data. This is a pathetic state of condition. A country like India, with its great scientific expertise, should have invested in climate change research twenty years ago. Let me give you an example of what happened twenty years ago and Dr Joshi will recall this example because he has been a distinguished minister for science and technology. In 1990, the US, a country with which I am allegedly very close to, issued a report saying that methane emissions from India's wet paddy cultivation was 38 million tonnes per year. This report caused international headlines. All the newspapers and the media went to town saying that Indian agriculture is contributing to global warming. There was one Indian scientist who disbelieved this figure. He is no more, a very distinguished physicist—Dr Joshi knew him very well—Dr A.P. Mitra, who was the director of the National Physical Laboratory. I happened to work in the PMO at that time and Dr Mitra came to me and said, 'I do not believe these numbers and I want to start my own experiment to generate my own data'. I went to the finance minister, who happens to be our Prime Minister today, and I said, 'Sir, we need to give this scientist and his team some money'. The money was sanctioned and a three-year project was started. At the end of three years, Dr Mitra and his team conclusively established that methane emissions from Indian wet paddy cultivation was not 38 MT per year, but between 2 MT and 6 MT per year and today, I must inform the Hon. members that the internationally accepted figure for methane emissions from Indian wet paddy cultivation is about 4 MT per year, which is the median of two and six. This is what we need to do.

There is a lot of sensationalism that is going on in the name of science. We must, on our own, understand what is going to happen to our own ecosystem on account of climate change. I would like to inform the House that on 14 October this year, we launched, what is called, the Indian National Network on Climate Change Assessment and I will circulate a copy of this document to all the Hon. members. We have created a network of ninety-seven research institutions in our country, 250 scientists have been brought together as a team and every year they will conduct and make public an assessment of what is happening on account of climate change. The first report will come in November 2010 and this will be a report, which will give an assessment by Indian scientists on what is going to happen because of climate change to the Sunderbans, to the Northeast, to the Western Ghats, and to our agriculture.

This is what India needs to have done twenty years ago. It did not do it for some reason. But I am not taking credit for it. I am only an instrument of policy. But what I want to say is, this is a very important step that we have taken. Forget Copenhagen; we must have our own scientific capacity to understand the impact of climate change. We are a very varied country. We can have positive effect in one region and negative effect in another region. Rainfall might increase in Punjab and Haryana but rainfall could also decrease in Assam and Meghalaya. India is very varied. So we must understand the impact of climate change in India in all its eco-diversity.

This is the second point I want to make because members have raised this issue. One of the failures on my part amongst many other failures has been a failure to communicate to each individual MP the full substance of what we have done. I thought that by putting it on our website, it becomes automatically public. I did not bargain for the reluctance of many of my colleagues to spend time on websites. I will now ensure that in the next couple of days all this literature and material will be available to you in hard copy at your residential addresses so that we can establish a constant process of communication. I have also decided that we will now place on the table of the House the many important documents that we release from time to time.

My young friend Jayant Chaudhary referred to forests. Just four days ago, we released the *State of the Forest Report in India, 2009*. This gives you the most comprehensive assessment of what is happening to forest cover in different states of the country. I have asked for the permission to lay this on the table of the House. I hope that once such documentation becomes available, many of the questions that have been raised by MPs relating to the impact of climate change would get answered. This is my second submission.

Third, let me talk a little bit about the Copenhagen process because that is the real issue that everybody wants to hear. All this is a sort of prelude; the real masala is Copenhagen. I entirely agree with my young friend Jayant Chaudhary, but my advice to him is:

Do not be too bold at such a young age. It will create many problems for you. Go with the grain of conventional thinking before you become too much of an out-of-the-box thinker. Thinking out of the box in our country does not pay in the long run. You have to be in the box and occasionally get out of the box and come back into the box.

On the international arena, when I took over as environment minister on 29 May, the Prime Minister's instructions to me were: 'India has not caused the problem of global warming. But try and make sure that India is part of the solution. Be constructive; be proactive.' That was all he told me. Then I asked myself what is India's position when it comes to international negotiations. The only position India had: 'Our per capita is very low; your per capita is very high; therefore we would not do anything.' Sir, per capita is an accident of history. It so happened that we could not control our population. That is why we get the benefit of per capita. When you divide anything by one billion, and that one billion is increasing by twelve million every year, it is no great credit for us. Our single biggest failure in the last sixty years has been our inability to control our population growth rate. Now the only position we have is: 'Do not touch us; our per capita is very low.'

It is an important point because per capita is the only instrument of ensuring equitable distribution. But it cannot be the only point. That is the point. So, when I first started looking at this international canvass, I was struck by the fact that India's position was: 'Our per capita is low and, therefore, we are entitled to pollute more till we reach your per capita levels. Since you have caused the problem, you must fix the problem'. That was, broadly speaking, our position.

Sir, this is my personal belief, and you can question my judgement but do not question my motives. My personal belief is that India must negotiate from a position of strength; that India must negotiate from a position of leadership. I agree with Dr Joshi that we must demonstrate an alternative model of growth; we must not follow the prosperity equal to pollution model of growth. I entirely agree with him. I may have political differences with him but on this I am entirely in agreement with him. It should not remain just a slogan; we have to take many important steps. So, I ask myself this question: Can we go beyond per capita? Per capita is the basic position. Our per capita is low. Our Prime Minister has said that our per capita emissions will never exceed per capita emissions of the developed world. I said that our per capita emissions will remain below that of the developed world. My friends from the Left parties accused me of compromising the Prime Minister's statement. Sir, this is English language. This is semantics. I had a similar argument in the Rajya Sabha ... (interruptions).

I have listened to you. Please listen to me, and then we can have another argument. I had a similar argument in the Rajya Sabha. To my simple mind, I do not see any difference between 'will not exceed' and 'will remain below'. It is the same thing. This is all, splitting hair on the English language. ... (interruptions)

B. Mahtab: It is a funny language. ... (interruptions)

Jairam Ramesh: The curse is that, you know, we are experts in the English language. Therefore, that is the starting position of our negotiations. The Hon. members have asked: What is the basic principles on which India is going to Copenhagen, the central principle is that per capita emissions will always remain below/never exceed per capita emissions of the developed world. But, Sir, we have to offer something more to ourselves, not to the world. Let me now use this opportunity. A lot of MPs have asked me: 'What are the non-negotiables for India at Copenhagen?' Sir, we are all patriotic. We all want to protect India's interests. I hope that much you will grant me. I am not buying a ticket to Copenhagen to sell India's interest down the drain.

Sir, I have gone out of my way to ensure transparency in this whole process. I have written to all chief ministers on 1 October, an eight-page letter on our stand on Copenhagen. I have written to eighty MPs. I should have written to all 700-odd members but I admittedly wrote to only eighty MPs on what are stand on climate change is. Sir, I wrote four months ago, to the Hon. Speaker and to the Hon. Chairman of the Rajya Sabha: 'Please nominate members of Parliament as part of the official delegation to Copenhagen'. Sir, you will be pleased to know today how jokingly, one of my colleagues, who is not here, said that I should take all those who speak today to Copenhagen. Unfortunately, Sir, I cannot do that.

The Hon. Speaker has nominated three MPs from the Lok Sabha; and the Hon. Chairman of the Rajya Sabha has nominated two MPs from the Rajya Sabha. So, five MPs are going to be part of our official delegation to Copenhagen. Not only that, in 2030, 2040, and 2050, most of us will not be around, and we are discussing what is going to happen in years when most of us will not be around. That is why, for the first time as part of our official delegation, I am taking two schoolchildren and two college-going students. We had an essay competition. Call it the new gender empowerment, all the prizes were won by girls... (interruptions) We are taking two schoolchildren and two college-going girls as part of our official delegation. Not as hangers-on but as part of our official delegation to convey to the world India's seriousness of doing something for the future generation.

Sir, we cannot have seventy-year-olds or fifty-year-olds like me, talking about future generation. We could have the younger people talking about the future generation. That is why in the composition of our delegation, I think, you will see not only political representation but also generational representation.

Sir, there was a lot of confusion and a lot of criticism on the so-called differences between what my position has been and what the Prime Minister's articulation has been. Let me say, I am a member of the Union Council of Ministers. I am a relatively junior member of the Council of Ministers and it is inconceivable that I will survive in the council if I articulate views that are different to that of the Prime Minister. You must, at least, grant me that much common sense that I will not say anything, which does not broadly correspond to what the Prime Minister believes. Occasionally, I might express it in a language that is colourful, I might express it in a language that more conservative people would not do so. But the thought, the principle, the concept, I cannot make public unless I know that the Prime Minister shares these views. That is the principle of collective responsibility and the principle of leadership.

So, what are these new ideas that we have tried to bring into our thinking? We are going to Copenhagen in a positive fame of mind. Prepare to be—and I am using a word, which my Left friends are never happy with—flexible. I will define for you what flexibility means. We are going with a positive frame of mind; and we want a comprehensive and equitable agreement at Copenhagen. I am realistic enough to know that such an agreement may not materialize. But we will work overtime with like-minded countries, with China and other countries to ensure that there is a comprehensive and equitable arrangement.

Murli Manohar Joshi: You have been to China.

Jairam Ramesh: I will come to that. Sir, I went to China over last weekend. China, South Africa, Brazil, and India have tabled a draft in Copenhagen yesterday on what the Copenhagen Agreement should look like. Denmark as the host country also has a draft. But we participated in the discussions in Beijing and we came up with what we considered to be a draft which protects our interests. Let me also say for the information of the Hon. members that in the last few months, relations between India and China have had their ups and downs. But on 21 October, India and China signed a Partnership Agreement on Climate Change. This was the first agreement for China and the first agreement for India.

Now, China and India are not comparable. China is here with 23 per cent of world GHG emissions. It is the number one emitter. India

is here with 4.7 per cent of world GHG emissions. It is number five
in the world. So, we are not in the same boat as far as emissions are
concerned. They have to do far more than what we have to do. But on
negotiations, we are in the same boat. We have a strong alliance with
China, a strong alliance with Brazil and a strong alliance with South
Africa. We are also part of G77.

At the same time, many MPs have said about *vasudhaiva kutumbakam*. What does *vasudhaiva kutumbakam* mean? It means, you do not
have hostility to anybody. So, we have to engage with everybody. Just
because we are members of G77 does not mean that we do not talk to
the US, and every time we talk to the US does not mean that we are
selling our country down the drain. So, I would like my Left friends to
please understand the geopolitical realities in which India is. We are a
developing country. We have global aspirations. We want to be recognized as a world power. But having global aspirations and assuming
global responsibilities are two sides of the same coin. So, we are talking
to everybody. We are talking to the Europeans. We are talking to the
Americans. We have this agreement with the BASIC countries.

Murli Manohar Joshi: Mr Minister, may I say a sentence? With flexibility, you will show the desired firmness.

Jairam Ramesh: No, Sir. Let me explain. I am coming to this. If you have
a little patience, I will explain to you what the contours of the flexibility
are. Sir, there are some non-negotiable issues for us at Copenhagen.
Let me categorically state what these non-negotiable issues are. My colleague, Mr Mahtab is joining me in Copenhagen. This has not been
fixed by me. This is a choice of the Speaker. He has already quoted
what I have said on the non-negotiable issues. First one is, Raghuvansh
Prasad Singhji, listen carefully (interruptions)...

Tufani Saroj: You could have taken him along.

Jairam Ramesh: Had it in been my hands I would have taken him along
... (interruptions) Only one PhD is sufficient. If two persons holding
PhD degrees are included, it will not be good.

Murli Manohar Joshi: You better drop the person holding PhD degree.

Jairam Ramesh: No Sir, no purpose will be served without you. The
first non-negotiable is that India will not accept a legally binding
emission cut. Legally we are not ready to sign any agreement that
legally binds India for reduction in emission level. I want to say this

absolutely, clearly, and categorically. There is no question of India accepting a legally binding emission reduction target. Second, there are some attempts by some countries to say that developing countries should announce when their emissions will peak. Let me say that this is the second non-negotiable for us. We will not accept under any circumstances an agreement, which includes a peaking year for India. If it said that the emission profile of the countries such as India will be at its peak till 2025 or 2030, it will be impossible for us to accept this. We will not accept this agreement. These are the two complete dark, bright red lines and there is no question of compromising on these two non-negotiable issues.

There is a third non-negotiable. Today, it is non-negotiable, but depends on the concessions that we can get from the western countries. Perhaps, we could modulate our position in consultation with China, Brazil and South Africa. We are prepared to subject all our mitigation actions, whatever we do, which is supported by international finance and technology to international review. There is nothing wrong with it as we are getting money from outside and we are getting technology from outside. The technology-giver and the money-giver is asking to account for these things and we should have no objection to that. The problem arises on the mitigation actions, which are unsupported, that is, which we are doing on our own. We certainly would not like the unsupported actions to be subject to the same type of scrutiny that the supported actions are subject to. There should be some difference between what we do on our own and what we do with outside assistance. Raghuvanshbabu, you talked about monitoring for the last five years we shall frame monitoring system where the action we take on our own is separate. We can consider this because we are a democratic country. We have a Parliament, we have a civil society, we have media, accountability in this country is more in comparison to many other countries. If we maintain transparency in our work, no one should raise any objections to it.

Hence, Dr Joshi, very early on I mooted the concept of nationally accountable mitigation outcome. I would like to tell you a little bit about the history. Under the Bali Action Plan, the responsibility of countries such as ours is regarding nationally appropriate mitigation action, it is only about action. My experience in my country is that there has been no dearth of action but it is that of results and outcome. We are experts in writing 500 pages about actions but what is the outcome and this is where we are beaten. That is why I suggested there should be nationally accountable mitigation outcomes and accountability should be to our Parliament and towards any international institution. I had hoped that you would all congratulate me that we were accountable to our Parliament. I want that whatever we do, it should be done under the law of Parliament. I want that we shall be transparent and our accountability will be towards our Parliament. We will not do so under any international agreement. We will not be accountable to any international institution. We will be accountable to our Parliament. I fail to understand why there should be any objection to it. This idea struck my mind when I was in Beijing in September.

How will this emission intensity be cut? That is the question. We are planning a series of policy measures. On some of which we will come back to Parliament. I want to assure the Hon. members of the House that we will come back to Parliament on:

1. We are going to legislate mandatory fuel efficiency standards for our vehicles by December 2011. We will come to Parliament. We will mandate mandatory fuel efficiency standards for all vehicles. This will reduce and manage the greenhouse gas emissions from our transportation section.
2. We will come back to Parliament with a model energy conservation building code and we will recommend to the states and to the municipal administrations mandatory green building codes.
3. We are going to come to Parliament with amendments to the Energy Conservation Act to introduce what we call the energy efficiency certificate which will enable energy intensity decline in our industry. We will come to Parliament. Parliament will discuss these amendments.
4. I am going to lay this report on forests on the table of the House hopefully next week. We are going to come to Parliament regularly to report on the state of our forest cover. Today, in response to the question raised by many members, our forests are absorbing 10 per cent of our annual GHG emissions.
5. We are going to ensure that increasingly more and more of our coal-based power plants of the type that are coming up in my friend, Shri Mahtab's state which is causing him great concern, will come from clean coal technology.

This does not require law. It requires us to take decisions on super-critical technology, ultra supercritical technology, coal gasification—Dr Joshi knows as when he was the minister for science and technology many of these initiatives had started. We will ensure that 50 per cent of all new capacity that is going to come will be based on clean coal technology. That will substantially reduce the CO_2 emissions from our power stations.

So, we have an action plan in transportation, industry, buildings, forestry, and in various sectors of our economy, which will ensure 20–25 per cent cut in energy intensity between 2005 and 2020. At Copenhagen if we have a successful agreement, if we have an equitable agreement, if we are satisfied with this agreement, we are prepared to do even more.

I separate domestic responsibility from international obligation. I want to be aggressive on domestic obligation and I want to be proactive on international obligation because in international obligation there is only one thing that counts.

Ultimately, when I go to Copenhagen, it is not G77 or China or America or Brazil or South Africa, it is India's interest that counts. What is in India's interest? That is what ultimately is the only deciding factor. What is in India's interest, that is what we have to do. I believe that our negotiating position is strengthened considerably if we go to Copenhagen from a position of leadership, taking these proactive measures and taking the responsibility as part of the Eleventh Five Year Plan, Twelfth Five Year Plan, and, thereafter, between 2005 and 2020, our emission intensity would reduce by 20 per cent to 25 per cent on our own, in a legally non-binding agreement and to be reflected in any international agreement.

Sir, I want to thank the Hon. members for listening to me very patiently. I know that many of your doubts may still be there but I do want to assure the Hon. members that when I used the word 'flexibility', it does not mean the sell out. Flexibility only means the ability to move to rapidly in evolving international situations. We are not living in isolation. We are living in an international community. We have to see what is happening in the world. We are a large country. Let us not be defensive about ourselves. Let not any minister who is going abroad be told: 'Do not sell the country'. It is an insult to my personal honour and dignity to be told: 'Do not go and sell the country's honour'. No government, no minister, no prime minister, and no minster for environment will do that. We are going there to get the best agreement for India and the best agreement for India internationally is what we do domestically. What we do domestically, in my view, is an obligation to our own people that we have to undertake. Now, I thank you for this opportunity.

Matter Raised with the Permission of the Chair in the Rajya Sabha, Regarding Conflicting Statements on Climate Change

[This debate in the Rajya Sabha took place on the opening day of COP 15 in Copenhagen, MPs were reacting to the 20–25 per cent emission intensity reduction target that had been voluntarily announced—the proposal had been tabled in Parliament on 3 December—as well as to media reports about unease among the official negotiators about what was perceived as a change in India's negotiating position.]

7 December, 2009
The Leader of the Opposition (Arun Jaitley): Mr Deputy Chairman, Sir, two weeks ago, this Hon. House called the attention of the minister on the issue of India's stand in the climate change negotiations. And, this House was categorically assured by the Hon. minister, in the course of the discussion, that there would be no substantial change from the stand that this country had adopted over the last seventeen years in these negotiations. The minister also said that he will take Parliament into confidence before he proceeds to Copenhagen and the country's stand is spelt out. Sir, this Calling Attention was called in the backdrop of some apprehension that the minister was not in agreement with the stand of the Government of India, which was being conventionally taken. Now, we find that the Hon. minister and the Government of India, have unilaterally altered their position substantially over what India has been saying all these years. We have now announced, without waiting for what developed countries say, that we are going to make a 20–25 per cent cut in our carbon intensity on the 2005-level till 2020. Now, this country has, consistently, followed a policy that there is a per capita principle, that is, we have as members of developing countries, we have as much share in the carbon space as a citizen of a developed country has. The Hon. minister had addressed a letter to certain MPs,

and I also received this letter, on 29 September 2009, where till 29 September, the minister has said, and I quote from his letter: 'The equal per capita entitlement principle is the only legitimate internationally acknowledged measure for reflecting equity. As stated by our Hon. Prime Minister, India's per capita emission levels will never exceed the per capita emission levels of the developed countries'. Today, Sir, what appears to be happening is that the legally binding cut, which the developed country had to face, is something that they want to get out of, as a result of which various drafts are being internationally circulated. And, as a part of those drafts, one of the suggestions being made is, 'Please go by domestic measures'. What we seemed to have done is, we completely altered our principle; irrespective of what the developed world does, we have unilaterally announced that we are going to make cuts of 20–25 per cent.

Now, Sir, our difficulty today is that a major part of this negotiation, the deal, is still to be settled. Who is going to make the entire investment involved in India, as also in the various developing countries, as far as this reduction of carbon intensity or emission intensity of 20–25 per cent over the next few years is concerned?

Sir, when the business was as usual between 1990 and 2005 … (interruptions) … Sir, I will just take a minute or two more. Between 1990 and 2005, we had in this emission intensity a 17.6 per cent cut. That was one per cent compounded annually. Now, if we are to achieve this figure, then a lot of investment would be required because it would be almost about 1.5 per cent per year which is required till 2020. Now, one of the essential aspects of this deal has to be as to who is to bear the cost. Is the cost to be borne by those who are the victims of environmental pollution or is the cost to be borne by those who have substantially polluted the environment? Now, Sir, the original understanding was that there would be substantial cuts being made by the developed countries, and today, having really bared our hands completely on the eve of negotiations, we do not know what the developed countries are going to do. Experts in the field are now indicating that the cuts will only be 3–4 per cent on the 1990 emission levels, as far as the developed countries are concerned, and we would be rendered completely helpless in a situation of this kind.

Sir, there are two or three aspects I wish to highlight. It is bad strategy for the Government of India on the eve of a crucial negotiation to bare its hands and disclose all its cards. Our disclosed cards today become the baseline of further negotiations. We have raised our own baseline which was absolutely not necessary. Second, Sir, today, we have no reciprocity in return.

Third, we are in a state of turmoil on the eve of these negotiations. The negotiations' first phase begins today itself. Our negotiators appear to be sulking. From what has appeared in the newspapers, some of them, day-before-yesterday, refused to board the flight and said, 'unless we have a clear assurance from the Government of India that we will not be really reversing our stand, we are not willing to go'. And, lastly, Sir, the question was also asked by one of our colleagues in the Question Hour as to what is the international observation or verification of our unsupported domestic actions. Sir, earlier our stand categorically was this will never be acceptable. Now, the minister has now coined a new buzzword which is flexibility. And, flexibility says, we will see, if necessary, we will allow it. His interview to one of the leading newspapers of the country almost seems to indicate that we will allow that also. Now, this is, entirely, Sir, unacceptable, and I suggest, Sir, that the government gives a categorical assurance to this House that there will be no change in India's categorical stand which has been there all these years on this subject.

...

Sitaram Yechury: I am going to give him [Jairam Ramesh] a hint of what I am going to say in Copenhagen also. The minister, Sir, had assured Parliament and the country that there are two red lines that will not be crossed. One is that there will be no binding emission cuts that will be acceptable to India. Second, is that there will be no deadline of peaking of our emissions. Now, whatever has been stated earlier and what the minister has been stating now in the media somehow seems to contradict this. Our voluntary announcement of 20–25 per cent reduction; we presume, it is on reduction in carbon intensity because it is gone by the past record of 17 per cent reduction from 1990 to 2005, which is the compound rate of 1 per cent per year. Now, whether it is emission intensity or energy intensity or carbon intensity, these three are very different concepts and impact on the country differently. We do not know what the government is talking about. But, presuming it is carbon intensity, it means that by 2020, we will have to reduce by 150 per cent of what we have reduced in the last fifteen years. What does it mean?

Today, fifty-five crore of my countrymen do not have electricity, seventy crore of my countrymen survive on biogas fuels without any carbon emission. If this 1.5 per cent reduction is to be brought about, then it will come at the expense of the two-thirds of India. Are we today prepared to widen the gap between the rich and the poor in the country as a result of this, and has it come under any pressure? That is my point. The pressure is that on the 4 December, the White House releases a press note. I am reading from it, Sir, which is a public document. It says, 'After months of diplomatic activity, there is progress being made towards a meaningful Copenhagen accord in which all countries pledge to take action against the global threat of climate change.' No Annexure-1 or Annexure-2. No division between the developed and the developing.

Following bilateral meetings with the US President and since the United States announced an emissions reduction target that reflects the progress being made in the US Congress towards comprehensive energy legislation, China and India have for the first time set targets to reduce their carbon intensity. There has also been progress in advancing the Danish proposal for an immediate, operational accord that covers all of the issues under negotiation.

The Danish proposal is document where there is no differentiation between the developed and the developing countries. Hours after this was announced, the Prime Minister of India announces that he is also going. So, the suspicion that comes up is, is this happening under pressure? Therefore, Sir, since you asked us to restrict our time, I would be brief. Article 4, para 7 of the framework convention (UNFCCC), so far clearly talks in terms of Annexure-1 and Annexure-2 countries and the responsibility of the developed world. Therefore, Sir, we want assurances from the Hon. minister. First, the per capita emission standards cannot be diluted. It cannot be given up. Second, the historical responsibility of the advanced countries must be ensured. Third, the cut-off date that has been changed from 1990 to 2005 should not be accepted, we should stick to 1990; and, our voluntary cuts must be conditional upon three things. One, that the developed countries ensure a mandatory cut in their emissions. Two, the financing of the shift to greener technologies will be provided and they take much of the burden on financing of such a transfer to greener technologies. Three, the transfer of technologies should be beyond the purview of the IPR and they should be transferred to the Third World without this IPR royalties. We want these assurances from the minister.

D. Raja: Sir, agreeing with the speakers before me, I would like to draw the attention of the House to one international climate scheme. Our government has been supporting an international climate scheme called REDD. Even though this scheme has major implications for the livelihood of crores of Adivasis and forest dwellers, the government has never publicly discussed this scheme. Even the issue was not discussed in Parliament. The proposed scheme would make it possible for companies and governments to earn tradable carbon credits from forest protection in developing countries. Our government has gone beyond this and wants afforestation and plantation projects to be eligible for carbon credit also.

Sir, as of now, the Forest Right Act, 2006 is not being properly implemented in many areas. When the government is not giving the people secure rights to their lands and forests, what can the government do to prevent companies and government agencies grabbing the same lands to earn carbon credits under this scheme? The government's afforestation programmes are already resulting in conflict, in many states, for instance in Odisha, Andhra Pradesh, and Chhattisgarh. So, my point is, the government must be very categorical and clear on what it is going to do. Replacing natural open areas with mono-cultural plantations...

Deputy Chairman: No, the subject is, 'conflicting statements' and not on this, please.

D. Raja: Sir, no, it is part of Copenhagen Summit that is beginning today. It is part of the climate scheme and the government's position. What I am trying to say is, the government cannot support this international scheme REDD. If government has anything like this, government should share what government is going to do in Copenhagen. That is what we are asking the minister. Let him respond.

Sitaram Yechury: The government should take it seriously because Mr Raja is opposing REDD! You please understand. If Mr Raja is opposing REDD, it is a serious matter.

Jairam Ramesh: Sir, I am grateful for yet another opportunity for clarifying and before I go on Thursday, I am sure there will be more opportunities of such topics raised. So, I am grateful that...

Arun Jaitley: Mr Yechury is also going to be with you. So, we are going to keep an eye on you even there.

Jairam Ramesh: Dr Swaminathan also will be there. Sir, I am grateful to the Leader of the Opposition. Today, the discussion has not been oriented towards me personally and has been substantive on issues of climate change unlike the Calling Attention Motion where I felt as if I was an accused on a trial. Sir, let me respond to whatever each of these speakers have said in as serious a manner as possible.

Deputy Chairman: And as briefly as possible.

Jairam Ramesh: Yes, as briefly as possible. But, allow me to say, Sir, that I am sometimes perplexed by the shifting stands of our distinguished Leader of the Opposition. When I meet the Leader of the Opposition outside this hall, I get one view and when he stands up and speaks as the Leader of the Opposition, I get a different view. But, Sir, that is inherent in our political system.

M. Venkaiah Naidu: It is unbecoming on the part of a leader to mention something what is being said outside. Sir, it is never done. It is never done … (interruptions) Sir, he should withdraw it… (interruptions)

Deputy Chairman: No, no, I think, in the interest of the … (interruptions) …What you discuss privately should not form a part of it … (interruptions) … What they discuss privately should not be part of this… (interruptions)

Jairam Ramesh: Sir, let me respond … (interruptions)

Deputy Chairman: Please sit down … (interruptions) … Please do not refer to your personal conversation.

S.S. Ahluwalia: One should not refer to a personal conversation. You talk only about this issue … (interruptions)

Deputy Chairman: Let us confine to what is going on inside the House.

Arun Jaitley: Since he has referred, let me clarify it. At the Major Economies Forum after the Government of India diluted its stand I felt quite happy as most of India did when the US secretary of state was here and their environment negotiator referred to our stand a diluted stand there. The minister had the courage to stand up and contradict that. We all congratulated him. So did I. But, after he shifted his position in the Lok Sabha, I categorically told him that I disagree with his stand.

Jairam Ramesh: Sir, I will not get into this any further. I will respond to the points that have been raised. Sir, let me first talk about the non-negotiables, which will continue to be non-negotiables till the 18 December 2009 and beyond. The first non-negotiable is that we will under no circumstances accept a legally, binding emission reduction cut. This is my first point.

Second, we will not reflect whatever we do, the emission intensive cut as an example. This is not an internationally legally binding commitment. This is a unilateral domestic obligation that we have taken in our own interest and we are announcing to the world that this is what we are going to do as part of the Twelfth and Thirteenth Plan and if you want us to better it, you have to reflect it internationally, you have to support us both in terms of finance and technology. This is the second non-negotiable. The third non-negotiable is—we comprehensively and categorically reject the notion of a peak year for India. We will, under no circumstances, accept any draft which suggests that India's emissions should peak by 2025, 2030, 2040, 2045. This is simply not on our agenda.

Sir, the fourth non-negotiable is this. Please bear with me. Sir, since there is a fine distinction involved here and this has caused much consternation amongst the MPs, I would like to respond to it as openly and transparently as I can. The fourth non-negotiable is—why we accept international scrutiny of supported actions? We will not accept the same level of international scrutiny and the same type of international scrutiny for the unsupported actions. So, wherever the world supports us in terms of finance and technology, they can come and verify what we are doing. But, where you are not supporting us—the bulk of our actions will be unsupported actions—we will not subject these actions to international scrutiny. However, we are in an open system. We are in a democratic system. We are accountable to Parliament. What I have stated and what the Government of India's position is, we are prepared to submit to the UNFCCC a NATCOM, say, once in two years, which will have both the supported and unsupported actions for consideration of the UNFCCC. That is all we have said, Sir. There will be a scrutiny only when we are supported financially and technologically. But, for the unsupported actions, we are only going to submit a report—of course, we will come before to Parliament with—to the UNFCC for consideration. Sir, please bear with me...

Sitaram Yechury: But then, why submitting a report?

Jairam Ramesh: Please bear with me. We have nothing to hide. Our country has nothing to hide.

Brinda Karat: Why do you want to submit a report?

Jairam Ramesh: Madam, can I please finish? We have nothing to hide. All that we do is in the public domain. We have an NAPCC. We have a 'plan' document. Everything is debated in Parliament. We come to Parliament and say that this is the extent to which our solar energy plan has gone. This is the extent to which our energy efficiency plan has been implemented. And whatever information we are putting in the public domain, we are going to give it to international consideration. What is wrong with this? I am not saying international scrutiny. International scrutiny means, international observers coming, asking questions, looking at…

S.S. Ahluwalia: You don't require any observer.

Brinda Karat: What is consideration? Please define what you mean by the word 'consideration'.

S.S. Ahluwalia: Through big boss satellite they can observe everything. They do not need to send a man here.

Jairam Ramesh: Mr Ahluwalia, please listen to me. These are not nuclear power plants we are talking about which we need to protect. These things are all in open. We are not doing anything secretly.

Sitaram Yechury: What is consideration?

Jairam Ramesh: Sir, consideration will be defined by the UNFCCC. This is all going to be based on the guidelines. What is our proposal? Our proposal is according to guidelines framed by the UNFCCC. This is our proposal. But, according to the guidelines of the UNFCCC, we will subject all the supported actions to international scrutiny. Unsupported actions will not invite international scrutiny but will be a part of our reporting to the UNFCCC. Sir, it cannot be any Hon. MP's case that what we have made public to Parliament cannot form a part of the document that we are going to submit to an intentional body. That is not the case.

Sitaram Yechury: Actually, the point is…

Jairam Ramesh: Can I finish? Then, you can seek any clarification you want. You let me finish. I am trying to explain the whole thing.

Deputy Chairman: It is not a debate; it is only clarifications.

Sitaram Yechury: Sir, it is a very important subject.

Deputy Chairman: I agree that it is important ... (interruptions) ...

Jairam Ramesh: I am trying to come clean as much as I can. I am not trying to hide anything. I feel the transparency is the best way to strengthen one's negotiating position. I would like to reassure this House, categorically, that this proposal does not mean international MRV of our unsupported actions. It does not mean that. I would like to reassure the Leader of Opposition and I would like to reassure my colleague who is coming to Copenhagen with me that this is not what it means. All that it means is, there will be a document which we will submit to the UNFCCC, which will be once in two or three years, whatever is decided, but will have a compendium of all our actions on climate change wherever the international community has supporters, financially and technologically, but will be verified. Everything else will be just there for information. And our accountability, ultimately, Sir, as I said in the Lok Sabha, is to Parliament and Parliament alone. In fact, Sir, if the Hon. Leader of the Opposition could kindly re-read the letter I have sent him, my proposal is that we convert all our national appropriate mitigation actions to a nationally accountable mitigation outcome. You may read that letter. Mr Javadekar will recall—I have spoken to him—that I would like, not NAMA, which is what the world is talking about, but NAMO. And, what is NAMO? NAMO is, to come to Parliament and tell Parliament every year that this is what we are doing in climate change. If I am not accountable to Parliament, whom am I going to be accountable to? Our primary and only accountability is to Parliament, not to any international organization. So, please, be reassured. Now, this debate is taking place in the government whether we should have a comprehensive legislation or whether we should have piecemeal legislation. Once this debate is settled, we will come back to Parliament, but I want to reassure and reiterate to the distinguished Leader of the Opposition that my accountability on all the actions on behalf of the Government of India is to Parliament, and what reports we put out to Parliament, we will make available to any international body. I do not say...

Sitaram Yechury: Sir ...

Jairam Ramesh: May I finish? (Interruptions) Whatever reports that we come to the Parliament with will be in the public domain.

(Interruptions) Sir, please, can I finish? Sir, the Hon. Leader of the Opposition talked of reciprocity. It is true that our 20–25 per cent emission intensity cut offer by 2020 is a unilateral offer, not dependent on reciprocity. Now, why did we do this? I don't mind sharing this with you, Sir. Every major country in the world has a major offer on the table. We also have an offer on the table. But, under no circumstances, our per capita emissions should exceed—I have taken your caution and not using the word 'below'—the emissions of the developed world. That is our offer on the table. I believe, our emission intensity offer, which is a unilateral offer, which is a domestic offer, which is a non-legally binding offer, strengthens our negotiating position to demand greater cuts from the West. We have to negotiate ... (interruptions) May I finish, and then you can respond to what I said.

Arun Jaitley: Since you are on the issue, you might as well just clarify this. Quite to the contrary, it demolishes your negotiating position because the moment you say that my per capita emission will be lower than yours, this is my existing offer and I am now going to further lower it by 20–25 per cent, whether you reduce or not, it means that you completely destroy the per capita equity argument which we have conventionally taken.

Jairam Ramesh: I am afraid, the Hon. Leader of the Opposition is profoundly mistaken on this. Let me say that the Chinese have offered a 40-45 per cent cut.

Brinda Karat: Their emissions are so many more times ... (interruptions)

Jairam Ramesh: Madam, we have gone through this in a Calling Attention Motion. We can have one more round of discussions on this. The Brazilians have offered a cut. The Indonesians have offered a cut. The Mexicans have offered a cut. It is true that last year we voluntarily offered our per capita emission constraint. That remains a constraint as far as we are concerned. We are not going to deviate from the per capita principle. I want to reassure the Hon. Leader of the Opposition that the two pillars of our negotiating strategy remain the per capita convergence, ultimately, which is the only equity instrument that I have pointed out in my letter, and the historical responsibility. It is because of the historical responsibility that we will refuse to take legally-binding targets of any kind.

The Hon. Leader has asked what flexibility is. Sir, whatever we have done we are not going to be in a position to better whatever we have done unless there are substantial emission cuts made by the developed countries, unless there is a substantial financial package offered by the developed countries, and unless there is a substantial liberalization of technology flows by the developed countries. This we have made amply clear. I made this clear in my statement in the Lok Sabha as well, that there is absolutely no doubt in our mind that any further movement on India's part is conditioned on three things, that is, a substantial improvement on emission cuts by the developed countries, a substantial financial package by the developed countries, and a substantial liberalization of technology flows by the developed countries. Sir, as far as the timing of the American press release is concerned, I also got to know about it; I saw it later and I can assure this House that this was not done under any foreign pressure.

Brinda Karat: Sir ... (Interruptions)

Jairam Ramesh: In fact, if Madam can bear with me, this exercise has been going on for the last couple of months. The Planning Commission, as a part of the mid-term appraisal, has consulted a large number of independent bodies, individuals, and think tanks and the consensus view that emerged as part of the mid-term appraisal was that without jeopardizing our economic growth, without jeopardizing our poverty alleviation, and without jeopardizing our electricity supply target to every household, we can take a 20–25 per cent cut in our emission intensity which means our emissions would still continue to grow, but our emission intensity would fall. I plead with the Hon. House to give some time for this to work out and I can assure the House that if this emerges as a constraint we would be the first to re-look at it. But I am confident in my mind that emission intensity will not jeopardize the prospects. The Hon. leader of the Communist Party of India (Marxist) has rightly pointed that we are going to Copenhagen with the objective of not accepting any agreement that would put a constraint on expanding electricity supply to rural households, for livelihood security, and for all the other economic objectives.

Sir, as far as the point that my distinguished colleague who is opposing REDD is concerned, the REDD proposal was made by Brazil and Indonesia, who are contributing to deforestation and who wants financial incentives to stop deforestation. India took the lead for saying that okay if you are giving financial incentives for stopping deforestation, what about giving financial incentives for reforestation. That is our REDD+ proposal. It is not secret. It is in the public domain. I have sent you a copy of what our REDD+ proposal is. It is there in the letter that I have written to you, and I want to re-assure you that if there is any REDD+ project in India, which violates the Forest Rights Act, 2006, it is simply not acceptable. I want to tell you this categorically. In fact, I do not know whether you are aware that two months ago from my ministry we have issued a guideline that henceforth all clearances under the Forest Conservation Act ... (interruptions) That all clearances under the Forests (Conservation) Act, 1980 will be given only after the Forest Rights Act, 2006 is fully implemented. In fact, this is one of the grounds in which we have issued a letter to the Odisha government on the Niyamgiri project that the Forest Rights Act, 2006 is not implemented.

Sir, let me summarize ... (interruptions) ... Let me summarize ... (interruptions) ... Sir, our negotiating team is in Copenhagen. We have over ten negotiators in Copenhagen. It is true that one or two negotiators had some questions on my statements. I have had a discussion with them. I have tried to convince them that there is no dilution of our stand and these two negotiators are going to Copenhagen in a day or two. In closing, I want to reassure this House that while stands do evolve over time in response to changing circumstances, there is a certain basic code which we are not violating. We are not violating the per capita principle. We are not going to transgress the historical responsibility... (interruptions). Actions speak louder than words.

Brinda Karat: But, now, only words are speaking ... (interruptions).

Deputy Chairman: Now, we are converting it into another Calling Attention Motion, another debate. But, there is no further scope under Zero Hour, and only because there was an understanding ... (interruptions).

Jairam Ramesh: Sir, I would suggest to the Hon. member to give a notice for Calling Attention Motion on 20 December, and I will respond to my actions, and not to my words ... (interruptions).

Deputy Chairman: 20 December is Sunday.

Jairam Ramesh: Sir, I mean, on 21 December.

Sitaram Yechury: Sir, I would suggest that instead of saying 'please submit them for their consideration to the UN', why don't you say, 'you submit them for information'? Consideration has lot of other implications.

Jairam Ramesh: Yes, we will discuss it in-flight.

Brinda Karat: Sir, what is this? He is trivializing the issue.

Jairam Ramesh: Sir, I am not trivializing ... (interruptions).

Brinda Karat: He has not answered the question on international monitoring ... (interruptions).

S.S. Ahluwalia: Sir, he is responding to the questions raised by the MPs. And, now he is answering, 'we will discuss it in-flight'. It is not a personal affair that they will discuss it in-flight. Is he taking the whole House by flight? When he is answering it, he should answer it properly. He should address the Chair, and through the Chair, he should inform the House.

V. Narayanasamy: Sir, the minister has replied to all the points.

Jairam Ramesh: Okay, I withdraw the statement. I am trying, but once in a while, a little light comments are allowed, Sir, I am trying my best. I am prepared to come tomorrow. I am prepared to come day after tomorrow. I leave on Thursday, and before that, I am prepared to come to this House on as many occasions as you want to address the doubts that you have. I want to reassure this House that there is simply no compromising on India's national interest. We have a counter draft to the Danish draft prepared by China, Brazil, South Africa, and India. Ours is the BASIC draft. I was in Beijing. I went to Beijing myself. I contributed to the BASIC draft, and we are hoping that the BASIC draft will form the basis of our negotiations. Sir, I am as patriotic and as mindful of the national honour as any other Hon. member ... (interruptions).

Brinda Karat: Sir, he has not answered any of the basic questions ... (interruptions).

Deputy Chairman: He has answered the questions.

The Leader of the Opposition (Arun Jaitley): Sir, the basic doubt we have is that what we are getting from the developed countries. We don't have a single word on this. On the reciprocity principle, the reply merely says, 'Yes, we believe in reciprocity.' We have not got a single ... (interruptions).

Jairam Ramesh: I am afraid, he has not heard it.

Arun Jaitley: The per capita principle has been completely negated, and we are completely dissatisfied with this reply.

Jairam Ramesh: I have answered every point that the Leader of the Opposition had raised.

Arun Jaitley: We are completely dissatisfied with the reply and we walk out.

(At this stage, some Hon. members left the Chamber.)

Jairam Ramesh: That is pre-planned any way.

Brinda Karat: Sir, we completely disagree with this entire thing ... (interruptions).

Speech at the High-Level Segment at the UNFCCC Climate Change Conference, COP 15, at Copenhagen

16 DECEMBER 2009

It is my privilege to speak on behalf of the Government of India. We continue to derive inspiration from the father of our nation, Mahatma Gandhi who is an icon for the environmental movement everywhere.

India is already and will be even more profoundly impacted by climate change. In many ways, we have the highest vulnerability on multiple dimensions. We have a tremendous obligation to our own people by way of both adaptation and mitigation policies and programmes. That is why we have already announced a number of ambitious measures proactively.

We have a detailed National Action Plan on Climate Change with eight focused national missions and twenty-four critical initiatives. Under this plan, we have already launched a solar energy mission aimed at 20,000 MW by 2022 and a domestic market-based mechanism for further stimulating energy efficiency in industry. Other national missions for accelerating afforestation, for promoting sustainable habitats, for expanding sustainable agriculture and for protecting the crucial Himalayan ecosystem are on the anvil. New GHG emission-reducing technologies in coal-based power generation are being deployed on a large-scale. Mandatory fuel efficiency standards in the transport sector will soon become a reality.

We have established our own version of an IPCC comprising more than 120 of our leading scientific and technological institutions to continuously measure, monitor, and model the impacts of climate change on different sectors and in different regions of our country. In addition to establishing a nation-wide climate observatory network, we are going to launch our own satellite in 2011 to monitor GHG and aerosol emissions globally.

Derived from our detailed NAPCC, we are now considering *nationally accountable mitigation outcomes* in different sectors like industry, energy, transport, building, and forests. Over the last decade we have added over 3 million ha to our forest cover and today our forest cover is sequestering close to 10 per cent of our annual GHG emissions. We will endeavour to maintain that level.

India has been a major participant in the CDM. If all our projects are approved and implemented as scheduled by 2012, carbon credits amounting to a further 10 per cent of our annual GHG emissions will be available to developed countries to enable them to meet their Kyoto Protocol commitments.

We are convinced that a low-carbon strategy is an essential aspect of sustainable development. While we already have one of the lowest emissions intensity of the economy, we will do more. We are targeting a further emissions intensity decline of 20–25 per cent by 2020 on 2005 levels. This is significant given our huge developmental imperatives.

Deeply conscious of our international responsibilities as well, we have already declared that our per capita emissions will never exceed the per capita emissions of the developed countries. We have recently unveiled projected GHG emissions profiles till the year 2030.

Aware of the need for enhanced transparency, we have suggested using the NATCOM process, in a format and frequency to be agreed to, as a mechanism to reflect internationally the nature and impact of actions taken domestically. Let me add here that India has probably the most rigorous MRV system that any government can go through—with its democratic Parliament, activist judiciary, vigilant non-governmental organizations, and watchful media.

We are transforming environmental governance systems. A judicial NGT (National Green Tribunal) and an executive National Environment Protection Authority is on the anvil. We have just announced a new generation of national ambient air quality standards that is at par with the strictest in the world.

Our entire approach to this conference is anchored in the sanctity of the troika—the UNFCCC, the Kyoto Protocol, and the Bali Action Plan. We believe that the well-known and widely accepted principles of (i) common but differentiated responsibility; and (ii) historical responsibilities are sacrosanct.

As a global goal, India subscribes to the view that the temperature increase ought not to exceed 2 °C by 2050 from mid-nineteenth century levels. But this objective must be firmly embedded in a demonstrably equitable access to atmospheric space, with adequate finance and technology available to all developing countries.

Excellencies, one of the two heads of state to address the first UN Conference on the Environment held in Stockholm thirty-seven years ago was Indira Gandhi—the other being the host prime minister. What she said on the historic occasion brought the development agenda into the mainstream of the discourse on environmental concerns. We recall that message and reiterate our resolve to be integral part of the solution to global warming—now and always.

Suo motu Statement in the Rajya Sabha Made After Returning from Copenhagen to Inform Members About COP 15 and Decisions Taken

November 22, 2009

Mr Deputy Chairman, Sir, I rise to make a suo motu statement on the COP 15 to the UNFCCC that was held in Copenhagen, Denmark, between 7 and 18 December 2009. Before I get into the statement, Sir, let me say that this is the fourth time in the last four weeks that I am speaking in some detail on the issue of climate change reflecting our government's transparency and keenness to keep Parliament fully informed at every step. It also reflects, of course, the great interest Hon. MPs themselves have taken in this important subject ... Let me reiterate that I am more than prepared to discuss this issue in Parliament at any time, in any form that the House desires and the Chairman directs.

To return to the Copenhagen Conference, there were two segments to it. The first was between 7 and 15 December that involved negotiations at the official level. The second was between the 16 and 18 December that involved a high-level segment at the ministerial level. In addition, the Danish presidency of the COP had invited ministers from all countries for informal consultations from 12 to 17 December, 2009. Heads of State or government had also been invited to the high-level segment that is during 17–18 of December 2009. Over a hundred heads of state/government participated. Our Prime Minister addressed the conference on 18 December and I had the privilege of speaking on behalf of the Government of India on 16 December. Sir, copies of both these speeches are attached to the suo motu statement.

There were two specific outcomes of the Copenhagen Conference. In Bali, Hon. members may recall in December 2007, the COP had decided to have negotiations on two parallel tracks, both of which were expected to be concluded at Copenhagen. The first tract relates to the outcome of the Bali Action Plan and the other track pertains to the commitment of the Annex-I Parties or the developed countries for the second commitment period of the Kyoto Protocol in the period extending beyond 2012. These negotiations could not be concluded, and the Copenhagen Conference, therefore, decided to continue these negotiations to be completed at the end of 2010 at COP 16 to be held in Mexico in December 2010.

In this respect, India, South Africa, Brazil, China, and other developing countries were entirely successful in ensuring that there was no violation of the mandate for the Bali Action Plan negotiations on the enhanced implementation of the UNFCCC.

Despite relentless attempts made by the developed countries, the conference succeeded in continuing the negotiations under the Kyoto Protocol for the post-2012 period. Undoubtedly, many developed countries want to see an end to the Kyoto Protocol but we have been able to thwart these attempts for the time being. The major outcome of the conference, therefore, is the fact that the negotiations under the UNFCCC will continue to proceed in two tracks as set out in the Bali road map—one relating to the long-term cooperative action for enhancing implementation of the convention and the second relating to the second commitment period of Annex-I Parties under the Kyoto Protocol.

Another decision taken by the conference relates to the Copenhagen Accord. India, along with over twenty-five countries that included Bangladesh, Maldives, Indonesia, China, Japan, South Korea, Papua New Guinea, Australia, Russia, Mexico, the US, Brazil, Colombia, Granada, South Africa, Algeria, Sudan, Gabon, Saudi Arabia, the UK, France, Germany, Spain, and the EU, was invited by the host country to assist the President of the conference in forging a consensus on several outstanding issues. The results of such informal consultations held on 17–18 December 2009, were brought by the COP president, who happens to the Danish prime minister, on his own responsibility, to the plenary of the conference for consideration on 18 December 2009. Some countries such as Cuba, Nicaragua, Venezuela, and Bolivia did not join the consensus on the draft Copenhagen Accord presented by the Danish prime minister in his capacity as the COP president. Since the conference works on the principle of consensus, the Copenhagen Accord was not adopted as an outcome of the conference. It was, however, taken note of. The contents of the Accord are not legally binding nor do they constitute a mandate for a new negotiating process under the UNFCCC.

The Copenhagen Accord deals with the various elements of the Bali Action Plan, relating to the issues of mitigation, adaptation, financing, and technology in the context of climate change. Let me present to you the highlights of the Accord.

The Accord recognizes the principle of common but differentiated responsibilities and respective capabilities of the parties in combating climate change. The Accord recognizes the need to limit the global temperature rise by 2050 to below 2 °C above pre-industrial levels. While doing so, the Accord clearly sets out the goal in the context of equity and sustainable development. This ensures that in achieving this goal, the right of the developing countries like India to have an equitable share in access to global atmospheric resources cannot be ignored, and is ensured. I might add here that this was a point repeatedly made by our Hon. Prime Minister in all his interactions.

The Copenhagen Accord does speak of 'cooperation in achieving the peaking of global and national emissions as soon as possible'. However, the Accord explicitly recognizes—this is very important—that the time frame for peaking will be longer in developing countries. It also bears in mind that 'social and economic development and poverty eradication are the first and overriding priorities of developing countries.'

The Accord, therefore, does not speak of a specific year for peaking for developing countries, which has incidentally always been on the agenda of the developed countries. This is another area of success for us at Copenhagen. This is also consistent with the position of India as outlined by our Prime Minister over two years ago that our per capita emissions will never exceed the average per capita emissions of the developed countries.

There has been insistence from the developed countries to adopt quantified emission reduction targets in the long term by the global community. A global goal of 50 per cent emissions reduction by 2050, with reference to current levels of emissions, has generally been emphasized by the Annex-I countries. And, this was reiterated relentlessly by many heads of state of Annex-I countries at Copenhagen also. Reference to such a specific numerical target in terms of emission reduction has been avoided in the Accord because of the insistence of the developing countries, particularly India, that a global goal should be expressed only in terms of limit in increase of temperature, and not in terms of a quantified emission reduction targets, Sir, let me repeat this, because of the insistence of the developing countries, particularly India, that a global goal should be expressed only in terms of limit in increase of temperature, and not in terms of a quantified emission reduction target. This is because such a target would impose in a binding commitment for the developing countries which do not have such obligations under the UNFCCC. We can be satisfied that we were able to get our way on this issue as well.

The Accord obliges the Annex-I countries to indicate their midterm emission reduction targets for 2020 by 31 January 2010 to the Secretariat. Their actions in terms of emission reduction and financing support given to developing countries for mitigation actions in developing countries will be subject to MRV as per the guidelines adopted by the COP. The MRV applies to the developed countries as well.

The mitigation actions of the developing countries—Sir, this is very important, perhaps, the most important paragraph in my statement—are to be supported by the developed countries in accordance with Article 4.7 of the UNFCCC. Mitigation actions of the developing countries will be subject to domestic measurement, domestic reporting, and domestic verification as per its internal procedures. Reports of such mitigation actions, supported or unsupported, will be made to the Secretariat through the NATCOMs, which will be made every two years. There is a provision—I expect there will be a debate on this—for international consultations and analysis for implementation of the actions reported through the NATCOMs. The guidelines for such consultations and analysis will be devised and defined in due course. We have been able—I reiterate, as forcibly as I can—to incorporate a specific provision that these 'clearly defined guidelines' will ensure that the national sovereignty is respected. This is not an empty sentiment, these are actually words written in the Accord. Hon. members, who have had an opportunity of reading the Accord would know, and let me just read out to you what the Accord says. It says that non-Annex I parties will communicate information on the implementation of their actions through the NATCOMs with provision for international consultations and analysis under clearly defined guidelines that will ensure that national sovereignty is protected. This is not an empty boast. It is respected. You can see who had a hand in drafting of this. This is not an empty boast. But this is actual text that is reflected in the Accord. This is another accomplishment for us at Copenhagen. Of course, as I have stated on earlier occasions, the supported mitigation actions will be open to international measurement, report, and verification as per guidelines adopted by the COP.

Sir, under the Accord, the developed country parties have agreed to set up a climate fund named 'Copenhagen Green Climate Fund' to provide resources approaching $30 billion during the period 2010–12 to support adaptation and mitigation.

They have also undertaken a commitment to mobilize $100 billion a year by 2020 for such purposes and a high-level panel will be set up under the guidance of the COP to review the progress of these commitments. A technology mechanism is also proposed to be established to accelerate technology development and transfer in support of adaptation and mitigation actions in the developing countries. Negotiations on the precise architecture of this mechanism are underway in the UNFCCC and, Sir, I am pleased and proud to say that many of the proposals made by India in this regard have found acceptance. Hon. members may recall that we had a high-level conference in Delhi on this issue on the 23–24 October and following the recommendations of this conference, a network of technology innovation centres has been proposed by India as a part of this mechanism.

The objectives and the implementation of the Accord will be assessed and the process of assessment will be completed by 2015 in order to consider the possibility of further strengthening the long-term goal of limiting the temperature rise to below 1.5°C. Sir, this is in response to a demand made by forty-three small island developing states which includes Maldives. Bangladesh and Nepal have also supported this idea.

Sir, a notable feature of this conference—Sir, this is the second most important paragraph in my statement—that has been widely commented on is the manner in which the BASIC group of countries coordinated their positions. Sir, the BASIC group comprises Brazil, South Africa, India, and China. Ministers of the BASIC group comprising Brazil, South Africa, India, and China had met in Beijing, as part of the pre-Copenhagen preparations, on 27–28 November 2009, to prepare for Copenhagen in a joint manner. I had attended that meeting. The Hon. members may recall that I had briefed them in my earlier interventions on the results of that meeting. The BASIC group ministers met virtually on an hourly basis right through the Copenhagen Conference. Within BASIC, India and China worked very, very closely together. I believe that the BASIC group has emerged as a powerful force in climate change negotiations and India should have every reason to feel satisfied on the role that it has played in catalyzing the emergence of this new quartet. Their unity, the unity of Brazil, South Africa, India, and China, was instrumental in ensuring that the Accord was finalized in accordance with the negotiating framework as laid out in the UNFCCC, the Bali Action Plan, and the Kyoto Protocol. We will continue to work with Brazil, South Africa, and China, as well as other countries of the G77 to ensure that the interests of the developing countries, in general, and India, in particular, are protected in the course of negotiations during 2010 and beyond. I should also mention here, Sir, that President Barack Obama interacted with the two prime ministers—Prime Minister Wen Jiabao and Prime Minister Manmohan Singh—and the two presidents—President Lula da Silva and the President Zuma—of the BASIC group, and it was at this meeting of the BASIC heads of the state and President Obama that the Copenhagen Accord was clinched to the satisfaction of all present. It was at this crucial meeting that the BASIC group was able to get agreement on its proposals on global goals, and on monitoring and verification. It was at this meeting that the formulation, defined guidelines, 'clearly defined guidelines, that will respect national sovereignty', was formulated and accepted by President Obama as well. It was able to ensure that the Copenhagen Accord was not legally binding. It was because of the BASIC group that the Copenhagen Accord was ensured to be not legally binding and that there is no mention of any new legally binding instrument in the Accord.

Sir, this is a very, very important achievement. There is no mention whatsoever of a new legally binding instrument because this was clearly the intention of many European countries and it was the intervention of Prime Minister Manmohan Singh, Prime Minister Wen Jiabao, President Zuma, and President Lula da Silva supported by President Obama that ensured that there is no mention of a new legally binding instrument in the Copenhagen Accord.

Sir, I have been somewhat detailed in this suo motu statement. I have never hidden anything from Parliament and I have been very upfront about how our thinking on climate change has to evolve and not remain frozen in time. I have repeatedly sought from both Houses, flexibility within a framework of certain non-negotiables. Earlier, I spoke to both Houses on the basis of my intentions and some Hon. members who are shaking their heads may recall that I had said, ultimately actions will speak louder than words. I had assured both Houses that we will negotiate in a manner that the national interest is not only protected but is also enhanced. Copenhagen, Sir, is not a destination but the beginning of a long process. There are indeed many risks. Sir, I would be the first to admit, there are many risks; there are many hazards; there are many threats. We have to be extraordinarily vigilant and careful, negotiating tough but negotiating always from a position of strength. For the moment, I believe that India has come out quite well at Copenhagen and we have been recognized for our constructive approach. We will continue to play such a role. We have to deepen our capacity to pursue proactive climate diplomacy internationally. We have to get down to implementing a comprehensive domestic agenda of both adaptation and mitigation, and of moving on the road to cutting our emissions intensity of GDP by 20–25 per cent by 2020 on 2005 levels, an objective that I had announced in the Lok Sabha on the 3 December. This objective is not only eminently feasible but it can also be improved upon to the benefit of our own people. We must soon unveil a road map, a detailed road map, for a low-carbon growth strategy as part of the Twelfth Five Year Plan. We must also strengthen our own scientific capacity to measure, to monitor, and to model the impacts of climate change on different sectors of our economy and in different regions of our country.

Mr Deputy Chairman, Sir, I will now be more than glad and willing to clarify any doubts and answer any questions that Hon. members may wish to raise. I see this statement as part of a continuing dialogue between our government and Hon. MPs, as a reflection of our determination to ensure accountability to Parliament. Thank you, Sir.

Response to the Questions and Clarification Raised by Members to the Suo Motu Statement

22 DECEMBER 2009

I will respond to some of the specific queries of individual members in writing. Mr Bagrodia has asked me eight or nine questions which I will respond to in writing. A number of other members have raised specific questions which I will respond to individually. But, there are some common concerns that have been expressed. First, by the Leader of the Opposition, then by my colleague Shri Yechury, and many others. So, I would rather address these common issues very, very pointedly.

Sir, the first issue that has been raised is, have we agreed to the abandonment of the Kyoto Protocol. Sir, with the greatest of respect to the Leader of the Opposition, I would reiterate the point I made in my speech, and when I interrupted him, that the Copenhagen Accord in no way spells the demise of the Kyoto Protocol. It accepts that the negotiations on the Kyoto Protocol will continue in 2010; but, I cannot disagree with him, that it provides an alternative alignment as well. But, we are committed—I want to reassure the House—to taking the negotiations forward in 2010 and which will culminate in Mexico. But, the fact is, Sir, there are attempts to thwart the Kyoto Protocol. That is what I meant that there are attempts being made. The US has not ratified the Kyoto Protocol. The entire problem on the Kyoto Protocol has been caused by the fact that there is a common and differentiated responsibility within the developed countries. The Europeans do not want to say, 'we want to take obligations different than the Americans'. So, we have to bring the US into the mainstream of international environmental negotiations because they are the world's No. 2 emitter, accounting for almost 22 per cent of the GHGs and emissions. Many countries want to leave the Kyoto Protocol. It is no secret that the country in which Kyoto is situated itself wants to leave the Kyoto Protocol, namely Japan. But, we are committed; the developing world is committed, the BASIC countries are committed. India is committed to completing these negotiations on this track and we are going to do our utmost to ensure that the emission-reduction targets for the second commitment period, which is the post-2012 period, will be negotiated with as much force as we can muster individually as well as collectively. This much I want to reassure the House. And, I want to reassure the Leader of the Opposition and Mr Yechury that, as I have repeatedly said, the troika for us—the UNFCCC, the Bali Action Plan, and the Kyoto Protocol—are sacrosanct. And, we are not moving away from it in any manner.

Sir, the second issue, which is perhaps the most contentious issue today, relates to the world international consultations and analyses. Sir, may I just spend a couple of minutes on this because I want to assuage the concerns and fears of the Leader of the Opposition and many other members.

Sir, before we went to Copenhagen, I did say that we will accept international information reporting as far as our unsupported actions are concerned. But, Sir, the fact of the matter is that when the negotiations on the Copenhagen Accord started, the issue was that it was not anything to do with India. Sir, I have to be very careful because I am now talking about decisions and statements made by heads of states and of countries with whom we have excellent relations. We want to continue with these relations. But the fact of the matter is, Sir, this issue was not directed at India. This issue was really directed at China because today, China has 23 per cent of the world greenhouse gas emissions and the world wants to bring China into the mainstream and they want to have confidence that the Chinese numbers, Chinese systems have some credibility.

I can reassure this House, Sir, at no point of time, has any government raised any doubt on our data, no government; no head of state or negotiator has raised doubts on our transparency. Never. Nobody has said that we are non-transparent. In fact, Sir, we should be showing the world the direction on transparency. There is no system as transparent as ours and I have said before in many statements that as far as MRV is concerned, the best domestic MRV in the world is in India. Between Parliament, between the media, between civil society groups there can be no better MRV. Sir, the fact of the matter is that when it came to the crunch, it looked as if the entire negotiations involving twenty-eight heads of state would break down on the issue that the US wanted to use the world 'scrutiny'. They wanted to use the word 'review'. They wanted to use the word 'verification'. Sir, we resisted that. We resisted it for almost thirty-six hours. China, India, Brazil, and South Africa collectively resisted it. We said under no circumstances will we accept the words 'review', 'scrutiny', or 'verification'. Then, we said, why not 'dialogue', why not 'discussion'? That was rejected. Then an alternative was posed to us. How about 'assessment'? We rejected it. We did not want 'assessment' and after this process of dialogues, which took a lot of time, the four countries arrived at a common phraseology, which said, 'international consultations and analysis but with clearly defined guidelines that will respect national sovereignty'. Sir, this formulation was accepted by the US.

Sir may I say that the word 'consultations' is not new in international diplomacy. We have under the Article IV of the IMF consultations that are held between the IMF and the Indian government every year. It has been going on for decades. No sovereignty has been eroded as a result of those consultations. Sir, the Leader of the Opposition has been a distinguished commerce minister. He knows that consultations take place between the WTO and the Indian Government on trade policy. No sovereignty has been eroded. In fact, unilaterally in trade policy we have been more aggressive liberalizers than we have been under the WTO framework. So, we should not fear the word 'consultations'. It is there in the IMF, it is there in the WTO and if it is there as far as climate change is concerned, I see no great sell out as far as India is concerned. We have protected ourselves by saying, 'it is within clearly defined guidelines'. Those guidelines will be defined by us. It will be defined by 194 countries who are party to the UNFCCC and the most important paragraph there, which China, India, Brazil, and South Africa insisted on is that the clearly defined guidelines should be within the framework of respecting national sovereignty.

Sir, I can understand not having consultations on nuclear power plants. There is sovereignty involved. But all the information on our emissions is already in the public domain. Sir, 40 per cent of our CO_2 emissions is from our power stations. Now, I have here, Sir, a document that was brought out last year by the Ministry of Power, which gives you information on the CO_2 emissions from every single power plant in India. This is in the public domain. This is in the website.

This project was funded by the German Government. We are having consultations on this. There are no foreign inspectors running around our power plants. All this information is in the public domain. We are having consultations. People are analysing our data. In fact, we have got encomiums for the data that we have presented. So, I think, Sir, that we should be careful. I agree. We should ensure that these guidelines do not lead to a proliferation of inspectors coming and seeing what we are doing and what we are not doing. But, the fact of the matter is, 'consultations' and 'analysis' does not mean review, scrutiny, verification, or assessment.

Let me give you one more example, because this is a very important issue that the Hon. Leader of the Opposition has raised and I want to address this directly. Sir, eighteen years ago, in 1990, the US—I had mentioned this example in Lok Sabha and I want to mention this here as well since this is an important point—put out a report which said that methane emissions from wet paddy cultivation in India is 38 MT per year and it said that wet paddy cultivation in India is a major contributor to global methane emissions. There were some Indian scientists who challenged this data. Unfortunately, the person is no more. He was a very distinguished scientist and a Fellow of the Royal Society of London, Dr A.P. Mitra. He was the Director General of the Council for Scientific and Industrial Research. He put together a team of scientists. They, actually, measured the methane emission from wet paddy cultivation. And, their conclusion was that the annual level of methane emissions from wet paddy cultivation in India was between 2 and 6 MT per year, with a median value of 4 MT per year. Sir, do you know that, today, the accepted international figure, including the US, is not 38 MT per year for methane emission from wet paddy cultivation, but it is 4 mt from wet paddy cultivation. So, I don't see why we should be defensive. We have the capacity to challenge the best scientists in the world. We have the capacity to do our own analysis. We have the capacity to do our own measurement and, as I have given you this example, how our own example can become an international standard.

Today, the numbers that we are quoting has become the internationally accepted norm as far as emissions from wet paddy cultivation are concerned. So, Sir, I agree that there is a difference between 'information' which I had committed to in this House and 'consultations' and 'analysis.' So, I plead guilty. Yes, I have moved from the word 'information' to 'consultations' and 'analysis.' I am not going to argue on that. I am not going to get into an argument on that. There has been a shift. But, Sir, that is what I meant by flexibility. When you are negotiating with these countries, when you are faced with conflicting points and counter points and the thing that I can assure the House that this was not a unilateral decision by India, this was a decision taken collectively by China, Brazil, South Africa, and India. We decided that we will not be held responsible for the failure of Copenhagen. We decided that we will not be made the blame boys as far as the failure is concerned.

A number of comments have been made on the US. Let me also say that there was a statement made by the US delegation during the negotiations. It said, 'we will not give money to countries like Bangladesh and Maldives if the issue of transparency is not settled.' The Bangladeshi delegates asked, 'why are you not settling the issue of transparency?' The Maldives delegation asked me, 'why are you not setting the issue of transparency?' So, the issue of transparency had become a big stumbling block and, Sir, frankly, of all the countries in the world, India should not feel defensive of transparency. We should be, on the other hand, in the forefront of demanding transparency from all parties, including the BASIC parties, if I may add. So, I assure the Hon. Leader of the Opposition, Shri Yechury and all other Hon. members that 'consultations' and 'analysis' means precisely consultations and analysis. We have years of experience on consultations and analysis with the IMF and the WTO. We have nothing to fear. Our sovereignty has not been eroded. On the other hand, those organizations have gained, we have also gained in the process and I want to reassure the House that when we frame these guidelines that will respect our national sovereignty. We will take the House into confidence. After all, this is going to be an exercise that is going to involve 194 countries, which are members of the UNFCCC. It will take sometime. But, I want to reassure the House that it will not be an intrusive consultations, it will not be an intrusive analysis. This much assurance I can give you on behalf of the Government of India.

Sir, the Hon. Leader of the Opposition and many Hon. members have referred to a statement made by Mr Axelrod ... who is President Obama's close adviser. If I may be permitted, Sir, a small light-hearted comment, Mr Axelrod is the Arun Jaitley of the Obama Administration. He is their topspin doctor. He has tried to give a spin to this agreement. He has tried to say that in this agreement we will hold China and India accountable. I don't want to get into Mr Axelrod's statement. I will quote Mr Axelrod's boss, Mr Obama. Mr Obama had said in a press conference, 'It will not be legally binding, but what it will do is to allow each country to show to the world what they are doing, and there will be a sense in the part of each country that we are, in this, together; and who will know who is meeting and who is not meeting the mutual obligations that have been set forth.' He gave this statement in Copenhagen after the Accord had been finalized. He then, went on to say, 'These commitments will be subject to international consultations and analysis similar to that, for example, what takes place at WTO, etc., Mr Axelrod's statement was meant for domestic consumption. He has to convince the US Congress that China and India have been brought in. He has to convince the trade unions that China and India have been controlled. I do not want to get into the statement of Mr Axelrod that has been made for purely domestic consumption. I go by what President Obama has himself said. And, nowhere has President Obama said that this record is meant to control or strangulate China and India.

Sitaram Yechury: I hope you are not saying this for domestic consumption.

Jairam Ramesh: No; no. I am saying this for parliamentary consumption. I don't make any distinction, Mr Yechury, unlike many other distinguished members of this House, in what I say in this House and what I say outside the House. It is always same. I do not make any changes. I am sorry, Sir, I am taking a little bit more time because it is a very important issue. I will conclude very shortly. I was criticized for violating a commitment that I made on the floor of the House that we will not accept peaking year. On 16 November, the prospect was for an international agreement that would mention 2020–5 as the peaking year for developing countries, like, India. This Accord does not mention a single year for peaking. That is a major accomplishment for us. It talks of global peaking, agreed. But it also talks of longer timeframe for developing countries, as the Leader of the Opposition read out. It also talks about the peaking in the context of the first and overriding priority being given to poverty eradication and livelihood security. This is not a new language. This was there in the L'Aquila Declaration. This is a language that is repeated from the L'Aquila Declaration. What I want to convey to the Hon. members is that the concept of peaking, when the Prime Minister made his commitment two years ago that all of you had applauded, which all of Indian media had applauded, which all of Indian NGOs had applauded, is that India's per capita emission will never exceed the per capita emission of the developed world. We are implicitly accepting peaking. What we are saying is that we will peak once you peak. We are not giving a specific year for peaking. What we are saying is, if you reach at a certain level of average per capita emission, we will ensure that we will never exceed that per capita emission. That, Sir, is an implicit peaking.

What we have not done in this document is to mention a specific year for peaking. So, I do not plead guilty to this charge. I have not violated any commitment that I had made. I have not accepted, the Government of India has not accepted any peaking year for developing countries. We are not going to accept it as a part of the negotiations. We will continue to insist on the longer timeframe. But, I am sure, and Hon. members will agree with me, that we should peak in the twenty-first century. Now, in which year in the twenty-first century, time alone will tell. But it should not be anybody's case that we should peak only in the twenty-second century. We should peak sometime in the twenty-first century. If we do not peak in the twenty-first century, I think, then, we are having a very serious problem for us. (Interruptions) There may not be a twenty-second century as the home minister reminds us.

Sir, many other issues have been raised on climate fund and many other issues have been raised on technology. Sir, I also want to say one point on funding. Sir, a country like India, I believe, this is my belief, this is the belief of many people, does not need any international aid. We do not want international aid. We can stand on our own feet. Green technology is an area where India can emerge as a world leader. Ten years from now, Sir, India should be selling green technology to the world. Let us not always keep talking of technology transfer, technology transfer, technology transfer. Nobody is going to transfer technology to you. Technology has to be negotiated, technology has to be bought, and technology has to be bought on commercial terms. I want to say that many Indian companies have already seen business opportunities in this. China has moved ahead. Today, of the top ten solar companies in the world, four are Chinese. Let us see this as a business opportunity. This is an opportunity for Indian technology to move ahead and I am sure that in the next couple of years, we will, actually, be selling technology rather than keep repeating the stale mantra of technology transfer all the time.

Yes, we require international financial assistance. I am not for one suggesting that we do not require international financial assistance. But, Sir, we are not in the same category as Bangladesh or Maldives or Ethiopia or Saint Lucia or Granada. There are countries in Africa, countries in small island states, countries in Asia that require assistance more urgently than us for adaptation and mitigation. A country like India should be able to stand on its own feet and say we will do what we have to do on our own. Why are we getting into this syndrome of always looking for international finance and international technology?

This is something that we should be autonomously engaged in. Sir, I know that we are running out of time, but I want to summarize by thanking the Leader of the Opposition and all other Hon. members for raising what I think are very legitimate and valid queries. I think what I will do is, I will address each of them in a written form, a frequently-asked questions form, I will circulate it to all the MPs, and I hope in the next session of Parliament, we will have another debate on this issue because these negotiations will continue all of 2010.

I will not hesitate from any discussion of any kind at any point of time simply because we have nothing to hide as far as our negotiating strategy is concerned. Thank you.

'Hard Choices at Copenhagen'

[Opinion piece in *The Hindu*.]

17 JUNE 2014
Hillary Clinton's recent memoirs reveal how during the fortnight-long Copenhagen Climate Change Conference, on 18 December 2009, US President Barack Obama and she barged into a room in which President Lula of Brazil, President Zuma of South Africa, Prime Minister Wen Jiabao of China, and Dr Manmohan Singh were meeting along with their respective delegations and started tough negotiations.

The much-touted Copenhagen Conference was heading nowhere. Presidents and prime ministers from across the world had been unable to agree to a global agreement to combat climate change. Finally, it was the Chinese Premier who convened a meeting of the BASIC group. The quartet's ministers had been working closely together both in the run-up to and at Copenhagen itself.

Holding Up an Outcome

The two presidents and two prime ministers started their confabulations at around 6 pm. All four had immediately agreed that the BASIC group should not be seen to have been responsible for the failure at Copenhagen. Just about 15 minutes into the meeting, President Obama, accompanied by Secretary Clinton and a large retinue of officials, walked into the room unannounced saying that he was actually looking for Premier Wen and then adding that he was lucky not only to have found him but also find him in the company of his BASIC colleagues. He then got down to business right away, and said that according to his impressions, there were three contentious issues holding up a successful outcome at Copenhagen: (i) a global goal for reduction of emissions by 2050; (ii) MRV of each country's actions; and (iii) the need for a legally-binding global treaty.

After he had spoken, Premier Wen, after welcoming President Obama, turned to Dr Singh. Dr Singh, who had been greeted effusively by President Obama earlier, spoke of the complexities in the three issues raised and underscored the determination of the BASIC quartet to contribute constructively to a solution that is effective and equitable. He then asked me to elaborate.

I then proceeded to explain why the acceptance of a global goal could foreclose development options for developing countries and that for the present the global goal should rest with the formulation agreed to in the Declaration of the Leaders at the Major Economies Forum (MEF) on Energy and Climate held in L'Aquila, Italy on 9 July 2009 which said, thus: 'We recognize the scientific view that the increase in global average temperature above pre-industrial levels ought not to exceed $2\,°Ce$'. Ambassador Shyam Saran also spoke up explaining in some detail why a quantitative target would not be in the interests of developing countries.

Transparency and Language

President Obama readily conceded our point. But he went on to then say that for the US, the issue of international transparency of domestic commitments was paramount and he wouldn't leave Copenhagen without arriving at a settlement on it. The transparency issue then became the topic of heated discussion. Before the Heads-of-State meeting, Mike Froman of the US, He Yafei of China, and I had been meeting to hammer out acceptable language. I tried some formulations that were not acceptable to China and some others that were unacceptable to the US. We went in for the summit meeting without having reached any agreement. He Yafei and I had, however, agreed that India and China would not accept any formulation that did not contain the following—'... while ensuring that national sovereignty is respected'.

I briefed the meeting about the differences that still existed. President Obama then asked the Sherpas to move to the corner of the room, discuss the matter further and come back. In this impromptu conclave, I suggested 'international discussion' which was vetoed by the US. I then tried 'international consultations', which was also vetoed by the Americans who said that there must be a reference to 'assessment'. I suggested 'analysis' as an alternative and my Brazilian counterpart qualified it as 'technical analysis'.

After some 10 minutes of haggling, we moved a few steps to report back to the bosses. I told President Obama that the best we could offer was 'international consultations and technical analysis which would respect national sovereignty.' I said that 'scrutiny/review/assessment' was simply unacceptable to the BASIC group.

President Obama's immediate reaction was negative. He said that 'international consultations' seems like a pointless talk shop. I then told him that there is precedent for 'international consultations' in the relations of the IMF and the WTO with member countries. President Obama immediately saw the point and instantaneously said that if there is such a precedent he would buy this formulation. That settled 'international consultations'. President Obama then said that 'technical analysis' was unacceptable. It should be 'technical review/scrutiny/assessment'. I then said that President Obama's choice of words would be politically unacceptable but we could live with 'technical analysis' since that is what the IMF and the WTO do in any case.

Then, President Obama objected to the word 'technical' in 'technical analysis' saying that it circumscribes the scope of the analysis. I consulted with Dr Singh and Premier Wen and said that we should clinch the deal by dropping our insistence on the word 'technical'. Both President Lula and President Zuma concurred. Dr Singh and Premier Wen asked me to announce it.

I then said to President Obama, 'Sir, we will agree to "international consultations and analysis" but you must agree to the reference to "respect for national sovereign"'. Again, to President Obama's eternal credit, he did not hesitate for a moment and said 'done'. That was the breakthrough moment which the entire world had been waiting for.

After the MRV issue was settled largely on account of President Obama overruling his own aides, we moved on to the legally binding global treaty issue. Dr Singh said that much more work needed to be done before any commitment to such a treaty could be made. President Obama responded by saying that he would go along with what Dr Singh was saying. He then ended the meeting with a flourish by saying—'Now I have to sell our agreement to my good friends the Europeans'.

Incidentally, there are two other accounts of this historic meeting that Secretary Clinton describes with the focus understandably on President Obama and herself. Strobe Talbott writes in his book *Fast Forward*: 'Manmohan Singh engaged with Obama but let Jairam Ramesh, his energy and environment minister, do most of the arguing. Ramesh did so with relish. He was aggressive, sometimes acerbic, but not strident'. Jeffrey Bader in his *Obama and China's Rise* also has more direct and detailed account of the Obama–BASIC Summit meeting and writes: 'India's environment minister Jairam Ramesh argued politely but aggressively with Obama over several points'.

Undoubtedly, the Obama–BASIC meeting was a watershed. It saved Copenhagen from a complete collapse and also marked the emergence of the BASIC quartet as a major force in international climate policy diplomacy. The meeting was also tense. My Chinese counterpart Xie Zhenhua was absolutely livid at the compromise arrived at on the transparency issue even though it had the support of his own Prime Minister. In an unusual outburst, he started banging the table and launched into an angry tirade which left all of us stunned. Premier Wen quietly told the interpreter not to translate. Minister Xie continued for some time prompting President Obama to ask, 'What is he saying?' Prompt came Secretary Clinton's reply, which had the whole meeting exploding with laughter leading to a lowering of the tension, 'Mr. President, I think he is congratulating us!!!' Alas, her memoirs do not have a reference to this master quip.

Letter to Prime Minister Outlining Learnings from China at Copenhagen

6 JANUARY 2010

The Copenhagen Climate Conference was perhaps the first occasion in which the Chinese played an active leadership role. The reasons for this are varied. It could be that the Chinese knew that they were under pressure from all sides since they are now the world's No. 1 GHG emitter. It could be that the Chinese wanted to exhibit a new face in the wake of the world economic crisis of 2007 and 2008, through which China emerged unscathed. An earlier manifestation of this new confidence was in the manner in which China handled the visit of President Obama.

China operated at various levels. It kept the dialogue with G77 going and took the initiative to cement the BASIC quartet. It also engaged the US closely. Even as its negotiators were talking tough in the room, its representatives were meeting with senior US officials to work out a compromise. When differences between it and the small island states came out into the open, Chinese officials opened a channel with countries like Bangladesh, Maldives, Grenada, and Jamaica at the highest levels. This is the first lesson we need to learn from Chinese strategy and tactics: Negotiate tough but in parallel keep all lines of communications open and with the really key players actually sit down separately to bridge differences. The Chinese had clearly designated officials for different groups—G77, small island states, and G20.

China was well-represented at Copenhagen both by officials of the National Development and Reforms Commission (NDRC), the agency dealing directly with climate change and by senior officials of the foreign ministry. In fact, the crucial negotiations—both in the open and backroom—were conducted by foreign ministry officials who had their own chemistry with their interlocutors. This was striking in the case of the backroom China–USA negotiations that were conducted by He Yafei and Mike Froman, both G20 Sherpas for their countries. I was present at these negotiations and what struck me was the camaraderie between the two even though neither was budging from their positions. This is the second lesson I draw from Chinese strategy and tactics—have people in your negotiating team who can reach out to 'adversaries' by virtue of their previous contacts and keep the negotiations going. It also helps if there are professional diplomats with domain expertise who can be pressed into service. I had specifically asked for Manjeev Puri from New York to join our delegation and he made a huge difference.

Of course, the Chinese were negotiating from a position of strength. Even though they have emerged as the world's No. 1 GHG emitter, their mitigation actions and plans first announced by President Hu Jintao in September 2009 have drawn wide praise as well. China's aggressive strides in solar and wind energy have been hitting the headlines over the past few months. China was able to package its mitigation actions in a manner that conveyed extreme seriousness of purpose. In contrast, whatever we tried to do was at the last minute (our emissions intensity cut target was announced on 4 December 2009) and whatever we announced became a subject of dispute at home itself even though it generated positive sentiments abroad. This, of course, reflects different political realities in India and China, but the fact remains that we were hobbled by our lack of cohesion and we had people in our negotiating team who didn't quite believe in what the Prime Minister wanted to get done. In my meetings with US Congressmen, it turned out that they were better informed about what the Chinese plan to do but as far as India was concerned they knew about our internal differences more than what our plans. This leads me to the third lesson from Chinese strategy and tactics: Have a negotiating team that is cohesive and that has clear lines of authority and make sure that whatever we are doing is projected clearly and unambiguously.

China's overtures to India specifically merit special mention. After my visit to China in the first week of September, 2009, China went out of its way to build a partnership with India. It was at China's suggestion that the two countries entered into an MoU on cooperation in climate change on 21 October 2009. The Chinese minister came to India on 21 October and spent two and a half days here. In the pre-COP meetings held in Copenhagen on 16–17 November, China sought out India very frequently. The BASIC group meeting was held in Beijing on 27–28 November to suit my schedule and at the meeting with Premier Wen Jiabao on 27 November, care was taken to give me pride of place. At Copenhagen itself, China and India met almost every two hours at the ministerial level and, of course, the two prime ministers met on 18 December. Clearly, China tried its utmost to make India comfortable both vis-à-vis itself and also as part of the BASIC grouping. It was almost as if China was wooing us. The China–India partnership in climate change has created an important niche for bilateral cooperation and my suggestion is that even though we are at different levels of emission, it is in our interests to nurture this niche even further.

Going forward, we need to gear ourselves thoroughly for 2010, which will be a crucial year for negotiations culminating in Mexico in December 2010. Specifically, I would suggest the following:

1. Reconstitution of the negotiating team to make it more cohesive and also bring in expertise from law, economics, and finance.
2. Go aggressively forward with the domestic agenda for mitigation that has already been announced both through executive and legislative action, and ensure that the implementation of this agenda is visible both at home and abroad. This will call for radical changes in the manner in which the NAPCC is being implemented covering both the eight 'missions' and twenty-four critical initiatives. The Prime Minister's Council on Climate Change will also need to be restructured.
3. Create a full-time core climate change division in the MoEF that will focus on climate science, law, policy, and economics, as well as be the pivot for international negotiations.
4. Create a full-time climate change diplomacy group in the Ministry of External Affairs that will engage in round-the-year bilateral diplomacy with key countries particularly as also with G77.
5. Take the initiative for convening a summit of BASIC in April 2010, perhaps in Washington, when all heads of state will be there for the meeting on disarmament. The Prime Minister could set the ball rolling by writing to the other three BASIC heads of state reflecting on their solidarity in Copenhagen.
6. Take the initiative for announcing special Indian assistance programmes for Bhutan, Nepal, Bangladesh, and Maldives in climate

change adaptation since these countries expressed somewhat different views on the 2°C issue wanting it to be pegged at 1.5°C. Climate change is the theme for the next SAARC Summit at Thimpu and it may not be a bad idea to announce a $100 million fund to be set up by India to support community-led adaptation measures in SAARC countries.

Given that some European countries are 'miffed' that BASIC and the US struck a deal behind their backs, perhaps, some personal diplomacy with countries like Germany—that are generally supportive of India— could be initiated. Germany will also host the pre-Mexico ministerial in June 2010. A similar effort could be mounted with Japan and France, two countries with whom we have a very close partnership in GHG-reducing power generation technologies.

Finally, while many sectors are critical to our GHG mitigation programme, two will be crucial—power and transport. We need to announce mandatory fuel efficiency standards soon well before Mexico if possible. We also need to accelerate the transition to supercritical and ultra-super-critical coal-based power generation. A decision to allow the private sector in nuclear power generation will also, in my view, help enormously since the Nuclear Power Corporation of India Limited has more than enough on its plate already.

Letter to Bangladesh Minister of Environment and Forest Hasan Mahmud, on the Sunderbans

20 JANUARY 2010
I am writing after a visit that I have just made to the Sundarbans. I came away more than convinced that Bangladesh and India should set up a Sundarbans Ecosystem Forum. This forum would provide a ministerial-level forum to discuss issues of mutual interest relating to the Sundarbans like mangrove restoration, wetland preservation, biosphere management, tiger protection, and adaptation to climate change. Over time, as we get the forum going, we could even conceive of implementing some projects in a collaborative mode.

If this idea appeals to you, I would like to convene the first meeting of the forum under our joint chairmanship in Kolkata in the first week of April 2010, with a field visit also included.

Suo Motu Statement in the Lok Sabha on the Copenhagen Accord

9 MARCH 2010

Madam Speaker, I rise to make a suo motu statement on some of the issues relating to the Copenhagen Accord in the light of recent developments. I lay the suo motu statement on the table of the House … [Interruptions]

I had last made a statement on the subject on Thursday, 3 December 2009. Following this, the Fifteenth Conference of Parties to the UNFCCC took place at Copenhagen, Denmark. On return from Copenhagen, I made a statement in the Rajya Sabha on 22 December 2009 when I briefed the Hon. members about the conference outcomes. I had also highlighted the role played by the BASIC group of countries in the negotiations relating to the Copenhagen Accord. The Accord itself was negotiated by twenty-nine countries and was taken note of by the COP on 19 December 2009.

On 23–24 January, 2010, the environment ministers of the BASIC group of countries met in New Delhi to review the Copenhagen Conference and subsequent developments. The ministers agreed to communicate, for information of the UNFCCC Secretariat, the voluntary mitigation actions of its member countries. India did so on 30 January 2010 and communicated that India will endeavour to reduce the emissions intensity of GDP by 20–25 per cent by 2020 in comparison to the 2005 level. While doing so, we have clarified that the proposed domestic actions are voluntary in nature and will not have a legally binding character. Further, these actions will be implemented in accordance with the provisions of the relevant national legislations and policies as well as the principles and relevant provisions of the UNFCCC.

On 3 February 2010, India received a letter from the Executive Secretary of the UNFCCC asking whether India wishes to be listed in the chapeau of the Copenhagen Accord. Listing in chapeau of the Accord implies that we participated in the negotiations on Copenhagen Accord and that we stand by the Accord. After careful consideration, India has agreed to such a listing. From the BASIC group, Brazil and South Africa have already communicated their association. Simultaneously, the two countries have elaborated the circumstances under which they have associated themselves with the Accord. China has expressed support to Accord in their communication addressed to UN Secretary-General. Many other countries from G77 and China group have also associated themselves with the Accord.

Madam Speaker, I am making the statement to inform the House that India has communicated its decision to the UNFCCC Secretariat with three conditions. First, the Accord is a political document and is not legally binding. It is not a template for outcomes. Second, the Copenhagen Accord is not a separate, third-track of negotiations outside the UNFCCC. Third, the purpose of the Copenhagen Accord is to bring about a consensus in the existing and ongoing, two-track multilateral negotiations process under the UNFCCC. The Accord could have value if the areas of convergence reflected in it are used to help the parties reach agreed outcomes under the UN multilateral negotiations in the two tracks. We believe that our decision to be listed reflects the role India played in giving shape to the Copenhagen Accord. This will strengthen our negotiating position on climate change.

Madam Speaker, my sincere endeavour has been to keep this House fully informed at every stage about India's stance on climate change negotiations. This reflects the government's commitment to transparency and accountability.

Letter to China's National Development and Reform Commission, Vice-Chairman Xie Zhenhua on India's Considering Listing in the Chapeau of the Copenhagen Accord

5 MARCH 2010

You may recall that the BASIC ministers discussed the matter of listing of parties in the Chapeau of Copenhagen Accord on 24 January 2010 in New Delhi, but could not take a specific decision.

Subsequently, two of the four BASIC group of countries, that is, South Africa and Brazil have associated themselves with the Accord with certain conditionalities. In the light of the development, we feel that we should revisit the issue. After having considered the matter at some length, we feel that, as one of the countries that actively participated in the negotiations on Copenhagen Accord, India should list its name in the Chapeau of the Accord on the clear understanding that the Accord is not legally binding and does not constitute a new track of negotiations. The Copenhagen Accord will remain only an input to the two track process of negotiations on climate change leading to the COP 16 meeting in Mexico in December 2010.

I am writing to you to keep you posted. I am firmly of the view that the BASIC group of countries will continue to play a very important role in the climate change negotiations in future.

Excellency, please accept the assurances of our highest consideration.

Letter to Minister of Environment and Natural Resources of Mexico Juan Rafael Elvira Quesada, on the Climate Technology Conference in India

10 MAY 2010

Let me compliment you on successful conclusion of the Petersberg Climate Dialogue jointly organized by your government, in cooperation with the Government of Germany in Bonn.

I understand that Mexico, as next COP President, is planning to organize a series of informal meetings to prepare for successful outcomes at Cancun. I trust that the informal meetings planned by Mexico will help in creating mutual confidence and resolving the issues in the run-up to COP 16.

India is willing to work with Mexico to contribute to this process. In this context, I would like to inform that India plans to organize a conference on 'Climate Technologies' in cooperation with United Nations Department of Economic and Social Affairs from 8–9 November 2010 in New Delhi. I propose that the occasion is used to organize an informal meeting of ministers to build a consensus on elements of Global Technology Mechanism. This will be an important step forward towards building consensus on issues relating to technology cooperation in the climate change negotiations.

May I request you to consider the proposal and favour me with your advice? You may recall that I had discussed this with you at Beijing.

Remarks to the Sixth Meeting of the Major Economies Forum, Held in Washington, DC

18 APRIL 2010.

I am sorry that I am unable to be present physically at the sixth meeting of MEF Leaders' Representatives. Such are the vagaries of mother nature for which no legally binding agreement with foolproof MRV can be an effective antidote!

Todd Stern had wanted me to initiate the discussion on MRV. Before I do so, I wish to make four broad points that have a vital bearing on reducing the huge 'trust deficit' that prevails in the climate change negotiating community.

First, the Copenhagen Accord is undoubtedly an important step forward. But it cannot be a separate track for negotiation. I have repeatedly said that the areas of agreement reflected in the Accord must be used to bring consensus in the on-going two-track negotiating process, which is the only process that has legitimacy. Gordian knot-cutting can well be plurilateral but ultimately negotiations must be multilateral and carried out in good faith.

Second, there must be some visible triggers that get activated very soon to ensure that Cancun does not repeat Copenhagen. One such trigger is the beginning of actual disbursement of the $10 billion promised by the developed countries for this year for vulnerable economies, small island states and least developed countries (LDCs). Another trigger could be an agreement on REDD/REDD+, provided it looks at all potential countries uniformly and does not limit itself only to forest-basin countries. Finalizing the architecture of technology cooperation is yet another confidence-building measure. All these elements should be a part of a multilateral package in two tracks that should be delivered in Cancun. In the end, a *balance* in the outcomes on all elements of the Long-term Cooperative Action [LCA] and the Kyoto Protocol (KP) tracks must be maintained with Annex-I countries immediately taking on binding commitments for truly significant GHG reductions *within* their borders.

Third, equity is the cornerstone of any international agreement that will be accepted by developing countries. The Copenhagen Accord sets a global goal and this will determine a certain global carbon budget. The implications of this budget for the carbon budgets of individual countries need to be analysed in detail, and it has to be guaranteed as part of any international agreement that development goals of economic growth are not jeopardized by such budgets. The global objective of restricting temperature rise to 2 °C by 2050 from mid-nineteenth century levels must be firmly embedded in a *demonstrably* equitable access to atmospheric space with adequate finance and technology available to *all* developing countries.

Fourth, we need to better understand this *mantra* of 'internation-ally legally-binding agreement', which some developed countries keep chanting. What does it mean in practice? What are the consequences of non-fulfilment? What are the extenuating circumstances which could allow for non-fulfilment of commitments made as part of such an agreement? What is the place for domestic accountability mechanisms in such an agreement?

Let me now turn to the MRV issue. For Annex-I parties, this is dealt with in para 4 and for non-Annex-I parties, it is contained in para 5 of the Copenhagen Accord.

Para 4 of the Copenhagen Accord reads: 'Delivery of (emission) reductions and financing by developed countries will be measured, reported, and verified in accordance with existing and any further guidelines adopted by the COP, and will ensure that accounting of such targets and finance is rigorous, robust, and transparent.'

Thus, as can be seen, para 4 enjoins the COP to develop appropri-ate guidelines for MRV of both emission reductions and financing of Annex-I parties. This is important to recall and stress since the entire focus in the MRV debate over the past year has been on developing country mitigation actions.

Now, let me turn to para 5 of the Copenhagen Accord which reads: 'Non-Annex-I parties to the Convention will implement mitigation actions, including those to be submitted to the Secretariat by non-Annex-I parties in the format given in Appendix-II by 31 January 2010, for compilation in an INF document [information document to the UNFCCC], consistent with Article 4.1 and Article 4.7 and in the con-text of sustainable development. LDCs and small island developing states may undertake actions voluntarily and on the basis of support. Mitigation actions subsequently taken and envisaged by non-Annex-I parties, including national inventory reports, shall be communicated through national communications consistent with Article 12.1(b) every two years on the basis of guidelines to be adopted by the COP. Those mitigation actions in national communications or otherwise com-municated to the Secretariat will be added to the list in Appendix-II. Mitigation actions taken by non-Annex I parties will be subject to their domestic measurement, reporting, and verification; the result of which will be reported through their national communications every two years. Non-Annex-I parties will communicate information on the implementation of their actions through NATCOMs, with provisions for international consultations and analysis under clearly defined guidelines that will ensure that national sovereignty is respected. Nationally appropriate mitigation actions seeking international support will be recorded in a registry along with relevant technology, finance, and capacity-building support. Those actions supported will be added to the list in Appendix-II. These supported nationally appropriate mitigation actions will be subject to international measurement, reporting, and verification, in accordance with guidelines adopted by the COP.'

Now, para 5 is very convoluted and needs to be 'deconstructed' and simplified. This is what I have done as shown below. Four crucial action points are embedded in para 5.

1. Mitigation actions of non-Annex-I parties to be communicated to UNFCCC Secretariat through NATCOM consistent with Article 12.1(b), every two years, *on the basis of the guidelines to be adopted by COP.*
2. Mitigation actions taken by non-Annex-I parties will be subject to their domestic measurement, reporting, and verification, the result of which will be reported through their NATCOMs every two years.
3. Non-Annex-I parties will communicate information on the implementation of their actions (NAMAs) through NATCOMs, with provisions for *international consultations and analysis under clearly defined guidelines that will ensure that national sovereignty is respected.*
4. NAMAs seeking international support will be recorded in a registry along with relevant technology, finance, and capacity-building support. They will be subject to international measurement, reporting, and verification *in accordance with guidelines adopted by COP.*

As will be observed, COP has been given explicit responsibility for developing guidelines for putting into effect action point #1 and action point #4. The responsibility for developing guidelines for action point #3 has not been explicitly given to COP but it is reasonable to assume and expect that this too will be a task for COP. We need to discuss how we are going to execute these tasks in a purposive manner.

Reiterating that mitigation actions by developing countries are *voluntary*, I would make the following suggestions to put the action points into practice:

1. International consultations and analysis as envisaged in action point #3 above must be based on country implementation reports (derived from the respective NATCOM) prepared by the individual countries themselves so as to fulfil the 'respect for national sovereignty' promise contained within action point #3 itself. A chapter/issue format for such reports can be agreed to by the COP.
2. The frequency of international consultations and analysis can be somewhat akin to the graded system adopted by the WTO for its trade policy reviews—some countries get reviewed once every two years, some others once every four years and most others once every six years or more, depending on share of world trade.
3. There has to be a multilateral anchor for the international consultations and analysis process. The Subsidiary Body on Implementation (SBI) of the UNFCCC should consider, sooner rather than later, how and where this anchor is to be set up.

I would stress that the voluntary actions of developing countries, which are the subject of such international consultations and analysis, should under no circumstances, be seen as taking on internationally legally binding commitments by these countries. It also goes without saying that domestic GHG mitigation actions, which are not supported by finance and technology under UNFCCC arrangements ('unsupported NAMAs') as part of their NATCOM will be subject to a different protocol.

These are some preliminary ideas to stimulate discussion. I am once again sorry that I am unable to be present.

Remarks at the Seventh Meeting of the Major Economies Forum in Rome

29–30 JUNE 2010
I am delighted to be able to attend this MEF meeting.

MRV

I was able to participate in the previous meeting only by video conference and I hope the suggestions I had made on operationalizing paras 4 and 5 of the Copenhagen Accord relating to MRV for both developed and developing countries were found useful by MEF participants. I wish to reiterate the main points that I had made.

Para 4 of the Accord enjoins the COP to develop appropriate guidelines for MRV of actions of developed country parties. This is important to recall and stress since the entire focus in the MRV debate over the past year has been on developing country mitigation actions. It is also important that such an MRV regime includes not only MRV of emission-reduction commitments but also MRV of the targets, timeframes, and regimes related to the transfer of finance and technology to developing countries. The MRV on finance assumes urgent importance for all of us need to know very clearly how much of the additional $30 billion pledged by the developed countries during 2010, 2011, and 2012 has materialized so far, how precisely are disbursements to take place, what the mix between bilateral and multilateral assistance is and to which countries, and for what purposes are the funds going to flow. The one area where there is some clarity is REDD+, where $4.5 billion has been pledged.

Four crucial action points are embedded in Para 5 of the Accord:

1. Mitigation actions of non-Annex-I parties to be communicated to UNFCCC Secretariat through NATCOM consistent with Article 12.1(b), every two years, *on the basis of the guidelines to be adopted by COP.*
2. Mitigation actions taken by Non-Annex-I parties will be subject to their domestic measurement, reporting, and verification, the result of which will be reported through their NATCOMs every two years.
3. Non-Annex-I parties will communicate information on the implementation of their actions (NAMAs) through NATCOMs, with provisions for *international consultations and analysis under clearly defined guidelines that will ensure that national sovereignty is respected.*
4. NAMAs seeking international support will be recorded in a registry along with relevant technology, finance, and capacity-building support. They will be subject to international measurement, reporting, and verification *in accordance with the guidelines adopted by COP.*

I had made the following suggestions to put these four action points into practice:

1. International consultations and analysis as envisaged in action point #3 must be based on country implementation reports (derived from the respective NATCOM) prepared by the individual countries

themselves so as to fulfil the 'respect for national sovereignty' promise contained within action point #3 itself. A chapter/issue format for such reports can be agreed to by the COP.

2. The frequency of international consultations and analysis can be somewhat akin to the graded system adopted by the WTO for its trade policy reviews—some countries get reviewed once every two years, some others once every four years and most others once every six years or more, depending on share of world trade.

3. There has to be a multilateral anchor for the international consultations and analysis process. The SBI of the UNFCCC should consider, sooner rather than later, how this process should be set in motion. SBI functions under the Convention to perform this kind of work and has fairly well laid-out procedures in respect of reports of both Annex-I and non-Annex-I countries. We should allow SBI to get on with this task and fulfil the expectations resulting from our current state of negotiations.

It bears repetition that the regime for MRV for non-Annex-I countries cannot be more onerous than that for the Annex-I countries either in form or content or the consideration of their actions. Non-Annex-I countries should have a regime that is subject to consideration in terms of Article 10.2(a) of the UNFCCC.

Equity

I want to emphasize that the issue of MRV cannot be seen in the absence of another critical issue in the climate change discussions—the issue of equity. Without a working paradigm for equitable access to carbon space, what exactly will be the role and nature of MRV is far from clear and cannot be agreed.

Therefore, I also want to take this opportunity to bring the issue of *equity/equitable access to the carbon space/equitable burden sharing,* which seems to be sliding out of the negotiating discourse, back into the mainstream.

MRV must include a determination of an allocative principle and an equitable allocation of carbon space. This is particularly relevant in the context of the adequacy of actions of developed countries. This is critical if we are to have an international agreement at Cancun.

The 10 June 2010 text of the Ad Hoc Working Group on Long-term Cooperative Action (AWG–LCA) text, that was rejected by most parties, had this to say in para 2: *Deep cuts in global emissions are required according to science, and as documented in the Fourth Assessment Report of the IPCC, with a view to reducing global emissions so as to maintain the increase in global temperature below [1.5][2] degrees Celsius above pre-industrial levels, and that parties should take action to meet this objective consistent with science and on the basis of equity, taking into account historical responsibilities and access to global atmospheric resources.*

I have two observations on this formulation.

First, this para has *no reference to the foundational principle of common but differentiated responsibilities (CBDR) and respective capabilities,* which is enshrined in UNFCCC. This is unacceptable. Incidentally, in this context, I must mention I have read Todd Stern's speech at Brookings some weeks back where he has given a completely new interpretation to CBDR—new to the rest of the world, that is. I think we need to understand this interpretation in some detail.

Second, this para *omits the need for a paradigm for equitable access to precede any agreement.* This is unacceptable. Any discussion on a global goal—whether for limiting temperature increase or emissions reduction—is incomplete, meaningless, and impossible in the absence of such a paradigm. *There is no substitute for the equitable access paradigm.* Unilateral pledges, for example, do not and cannot substitute for this paradigm.

Equitable access has been an integral part of previous texts in the AWG–LCA, for example in the LCA Chair's text in Copenhagen that was adopted in Copenhagen and was also in the present Chair's May 2010 text. The previous text said in two places: (i) that a goal for emissions reduction as part of the shared vision must include 'taking into account historical responsibilities and an equitable share in the atmospheric space', and (ii) that parties recognize the broad scientific view that the temperature increase should not exceed 2° or 1.5° or 1°C, preceded by a paradigm for equal access to global atmospheric resources. *I, therefore, strongly propose that all of us agree to restore these texts in the relevant two places and send the message to our negotiators.*

Moreover, *it is vital that these principles be operationalized* so that the equity paradigm in sharing atmospheric space is spelt out in practical terms. Carbon space is development space and therefore we must agree on an appropriate methodology to determine carbon space that has been used up and that can be used in future, the rights and allocations for this space between developed and developing countries, including the implications for finance and technology transfers to developing countries.

It is critical that we arrive at an operational set of formulae on equity based primarily on cumulative per capita emissions. Some scholars have also suggested that allocation of per capita emissions must be supplemented with the fact that the level of development of a country is important in determining what level of per capita emission may be appropriate. A country with low per capita income, with little infrastructure, few climate-friendly technologies, and little organizational capacity requires a higher per capita emissions entitlement compared to a developed country with well-developed infrastructure, technology, and capacity. Thus, the carbon space concept also means that poorer countries need more carbon space in order to achieve the same level of per capita income than richer countries.

The carbon budgets approach, made explicit by think tanks in Germany, UK, Brazil, China, India, and other countries, as well as the South Centre, Geneva, provides a useful basis for conceptualizing and operationalizing equity, and must be brought to the mainstream of our discussions and negotiations.

I am just coming for attending an international conference on 'Global Carbon Budgets and Equity in Climate Change' that India hosted. We had participants from Germany, UK, Brazil, and Malaysia, and the proposals on equity and carbon budgets were discussed in great detail. The BASIC group is meeting in Rio de Janeiro in late-July and we have set aside a day to have a technical workshop on equity-related issues. These are important discussions and we must now bring these concrete proposals from the margins into the core of our negotiations. *If only lip service continues to get paid to equity, and if we pay obeisance to it only in words, and think we have addressed the issue, I am afraid that no international agreement will be possible.* Therefore, after the workshop in Rio, the BASIC and other developing countries would like to bring our concrete proposals to the other members in the UNFCCC. We hope that a workshop can be organized so that negotiators can discuss how to integrate these concepts and how to operationalize the principle of equity into the negotiations and the negotiating text. *India would be delighted to host a meeting before Cancun to enable this discussion.* Hopefully, we can make tangible progress on this by Cancun and in Cancun. *Let us work together collectively to ensure that Cancun becomes an equity-based conference and not one that gives a burial to it.*

Letter to Prime Minister on the Discussions and Developments at the Fourth BASIC Meeting in Rio de Janeiro

29 July 2010

I attended the Fourth BASIC Ministerial on 25–26 July at Rio. A copy of the statement released after the meeting is attached. The important portions have been highlighted. This was the first BASIC ministerial that was preceded by a meeting of experts from BASIC countries as well. The subject chosen was equity and it will interest you to know that our stand on per capita emissions was supported only by China with Brazil and South Africa strongly against it.

The official statement apart, looking ahead, I presented three options at Rio. First, a single legally binding agreement incorporating the foundational principles of Kyoto and in which all countries enshrine their commitments with developed countries pledging absolute emission cuts and developing countries pledging relative emission cuts as in the Copenhagen Accord. The Kyoto Protocol itself would no longer exist as a separate protocol under this option.

Second, the Kyoto Protocol extends to a second commitment period and there is another legally binding agreement in which all other countries (including the US) pledge their commitments either in absolute or relative terms as the case may be along the lines already done in the Copenhagen Accord.

Third, the Kyoto Protocol extends to a second commitment period and there is another agreement in which the US takes on legally-binding commitments like other developed countries and developing countries pledge actions as in the Copenhagen Accord but not in a legally binding manner.

The BASIC group agreed that each of the options needs to be studied and discussed further at the next BASIC ministerial to be held in Beijing on 10–11 October 2010. The US is clearly in favour of the first option but might be persuaded to accept the second option. For the moment, the BASIC group is in favour of the third option (as indeed are all developing countries).

In the context of a legally binding agreement, as in options two and three, I raised two issues that we need to understand better.

The applicability of penalties for non-compliance of commitments made by developing countries; and whether any perceived non-compliance or finding of non-compliance would be used as a basis for the application of border taxes by the developed countries, for which legislation is already on the anvil in the US and the EU.

The BASIC group agreed that these two issues too need to be discussed further both amongst ourselves and with other developed countries as well.

I had a separate bilateral meeting with the Chinese minister who reiterated the Chinese government's deep appreciation of their relationship with us on climate change. Minister Xie Zhenhua mentioned that his mandate is to deepen 'partnership with India, cooperation with USA'. I mentioned to Minister Xie that the climate change partnership should be used to further dialogue in other areas as well. I am pleased to inform you, Sir, that China has, for the first time, agreed to have a technical workshop with us on issues of common interest in the area of mountain ecology (in which glaciers will also hopefully figure).

I also had a separate bilateral interaction with the Brazilian minister. Clearly we can benefit much from a closer working relationship with Brazil in the area of biofuels (ethanol) as well as forestry research and management. I have proposed that the two countries sign an operational MoU in these two areas and the idea has been accepted.

Statement Delivered at the Panel on 'The Way Forward in Achieving the Three Objectives of the Convention on Biological Diversity and the Internationally Agreed Biodiversity Goals and Targets', High-Level Meeting of the Sixty-fifth Session of the UN General Assembly

22 SEPTEMBER 2010

It is indeed an honour for me to speak at the first ever high-level event on biodiversity of the UN General Assembly at its sixty-fifth Session.

This now sets the stage for moving biodiversity and the Convention on Biological Diversity to the central place in global environmental discourse and arena, a place that it rightfully deserves, eighteen years after the birth of this convention at the Earth Summit held at Rio de Janeiro in 1992, and years after its sister convention on climate change has been getting all the headlines.

The Convention on Biological Diversity, through its three goals, sets out commitments for maintaining the world's ecological underpinnings, while pursuing economic development. The three objectives— conservation of biodiversity, sustainable use of its components, and fair and equitable sharing of benefits arising out of the use of genetic resources, are complementary and mutually reinforcing.

While the global community can take some pride in making strides towards implementation of the first two objectives, it is regrettable that the third objective relating to access and benefit sharing, or ABS as it is called, remains largely unfulfilled.

May I take this opportunity to urge the ministers of member states to provide the much-needed urgent political impetus at this stage of negotiations, to be able to arrive at a practicable and implementable ABS protocol, which provides for a balance between access and compliance provisions and which holds the sanctity of domestic legislation? As a major victim of bio-piracy in different ways, India believes that the ABS Protocol is a key missing pillar of the Convention on Biological Diversity.

Biodiversity and ecosystem services are considered largely as public goods, their loss, therefore, goes unaccounted for in the present economic system, and, therefore, can continue unabated. We hope and expect that The Economics of Ecosystems and Biodiversity study, led by Pavan Sukhdev, the final report of which would be launched at COP 10, would be able to address this anomaly. The key messages from The Economics of Ecosystems and Biodiversity reports being released in phases, including the one for local and regional policymakers, which I had the honour to release in New Delhi earlier this month, have already sharpened awareness on the value of biodiversity. I hope in due course, this study may facilitate development of cost-effective policy responses and better-informed decisions.

My government is committed to inclusion of biodiversity as an integral part of the growth process, since this is the only path whereby we can sustain high economic growth. The debate today is no longer on development versus environment, since biodiversity is an essential ingredient of inclusive growth. GDP must be redefined as Green Domestic Product and not stand for GDP.

Another important matter that is awaiting the final approval is the establishment of an Intergovernmental Panel on Biodiversity and Ecosystem Services (IPBES). The IPBES, proposed to be set on the lines of IPCC, aims to provide a science-policy interface on biodiversity, especially in the backdrop of the looming ecological crisis owing to widespread loss of biodiversity and ecosystem services.

The expectation is that this step too will motivate political action. India as you know is a mega-diverse country with very strong science base in terms of manpower and institutions. We would, therefore, be happy to host the secretariat of IPBES, as and when it is established. The IPBES secretariat could be modelled on the lines of the Global Development Network, the headquarters of which are located in New Delhi.

As you may be aware, India has offered to host the Eleventh COP to the Convention on Biological Diversity to be held in the twentieth anniversary of the Rio Summit in 2012. We are looking forward to your support in this endeavour.

A few days back, at the invitation of the UN General Assembly President Switzerland, the eleven past, present, and future presidencies of COP adopted a Geneva Ministerial Biodiversity Call for Immediate Action, which I had the honour to co-chair. We have recognized the inextricable linkages between the issues of climate change and bio-diversity loss, and have specifically proposed that implementation of voluntary REDD/REDD+ mechanisms should be done to enrich biodiversity. We look forward to clinching a forestry agreement at the forthcoming COP to the UNFCCC at Cancun.

There are also extremely important issues relating to the linkages between the Convention on Biological Diversity and the Trade-Related Aspects of Intellectual Property Rights Agreement under the WTO that need to be addressed and finalized soon.

Thank you.

Letter to Prime Minister on Deliberations Held in New York, Ahead of the Cancun Climate Change Negotiations, COP 16

27 SEPTEMBER 2010

I have just returned from a week-long trip to the UN, New York, and wish to brief you on the various meetings I had there.

Global Sustainability Panel

On 19 September, I attended the first meeting of the UN Secretary-General's high-level Global Sustainability Panel headed by the presidents of Finland and of South Africa. The panel has fifteen members from around the world and has been set up by the UN Secretary-General to deliberate on issues relating to sustainable development in their entirety. The panel is supposed to submit its report by November 2011 and this report will be used as an input into Rio 2012, when the twentieth anniversary of the Rio Earth Summit will be celebrated. It is clear to me that there are very high expectations from the Global Sustainability Panel, which is seen as a Brundtland-II, and Vijay Nambiar told me that the UN Secretary-General is expecting India to play a key role in its activities. I have offered to host the second meeting of the panel in India sometime in March–April 2011.

Major Economies Forum

On 20–21 September, I attended the meeting of the MEF convened by the US. Here, we discussed the current state of negotiations on climate change and possible outcomes at Cancun in late November–early-December. I was asked to lead the discussions. It is clear that there will be no agreement at Cancun. What is now being talked about is a set of COP decisions in different areas like finance, adaptation, mitigation, finance, technology, forestry, and MRV/ICA (measurement, reporting, verification/international consultations and analysis). The implementation of these decisions will, of course, be after Cancun is over but the expectation is that the broad architecture in these areas will be agreed to at Cancun. India is hosting a key ministerial conference on technology cooperation on 9–10 November to facilitate a meaningful decision at Cancun.

The final round of negotiations on the texts before Cancun will take place from 3–9 October at Tianjin, China. No great breakthroughs are expected there. Mexico is holding a pre-COP on 4–5 November in Mexico City, where it will most likely circulate a draft of what Cancun is expected to accomplish. It has asked India's active assistance in this regard.

Convention on Biodiversity

On 22–23 September, I attended UN meetings on the Convention on Biodiversity. Here, too, India was given considerable prominence. COP 10 is taking place in Nagoya, Japan between 15–29 October 2010, where it is expected that an ABS Protocol to the UN Convention on Biological Diversity will be finalized. India will be hosting COP 11 sometime in October 2012. There are still differences between the developed and developing countries on the ABS. Germany, France, Norway, UK, and Japan said that India's role will be crucial to success at Nagoya.

Bilateral Meetings with Key Countries

I also had a couple of important bilateral meetings. Both Germany and France are very keen on stepping up bilateral cooperation in the field of climate change and environment. France is keen on doing joint work with India on 'green national accounting', an idea that President Nicolas Sarkozy is likely to pursue during his visit to India later this year. The German minister will visit India sometime during end-March 2011 by which time we will firm up specific initiatives of mutual interest. Japan is looking forward to the Prime Minister's visit to Japan later in October and is proposing a joint statement on climate change and Biodiversity to be signed by the two prime ministers during your visit. As far as the US is concerned, I got a clear signal from my counterpart that President Obama will make increasing use of the G20 forum to discuss climate change and environmental issues. The US frustration with the UNFCCC process is very high.

I met with my Chinese counterpart twice during the week. We reviewed all the initiatives that have been taken in the field of environment, forestry, and climate change over the past year. Most recently, the two countries have organized a joint technical workshop on mountain ecology. The Chinese minister repeatedly mentioned Premier Wen Jiabao's deep appreciation for the cooperation between India and China in the field of environment and forests. The next meeting of the BASIC group will be in Beijing on 9–10 October where we will take up issues relating to equity once again and also take up issues relating to trade barriers in the name of climate change.

Luncheon with the Alliance of Small Island States (AOSIS)

On 20 September, I lunched with ministers and permanent represen-tatives of the AOSIS (Association of Small Island States). This group comprises over forty countries and has been very wary of China and India. In fact, this group wants the global goal to be limiting tempera-ture increase to 1.5°C and not 2°C as mentioned in the Copenhagen Accord. I reiterated India's great sensitivity to their interests and con-cerns. I also offered a technical assistance programme under the Indian Technical and Economic Cooperation by which we will train profes-sionals from these countries in climate change adaptation, coastal zone management, etc. This offer was highly appreciated and Permanent Representative Hardeep Puri is taking the idea forward. I also offered to the Pacific Island States an e-network in education and health along the lines of the Pan-African e-network that India is establishing. This offer too was enthusiastically received. It is extremely important for us to build and sustain close linkages with the AOSIS in different ways.

SAARC Meeting

On 21 September, I attended a meeting hosted by the Bangladesh prime minister on climate change and Millennium Development Goals involving all SAARC countries. Here, I presented the various initiatives India has taken in SAARC (like the $1 million grant to the SAARC coastal zone management centre at Male and the $1 million grant to the SAARC forestry centre at Thimphu). I also mentioned that we are setting up the National Institute for Himalayan Glaciology in Dehra Dun and intend to take up regional programmes in glaciology as well. In addition, I spoke of the Sundarbans Ecosystem Management Forum that we are setting up jointly with Bangladesh and the trilateral Mount Kailash ecosystem restoration initiative launched by India, China, and Nepal. The meeting was well attended and many people came up to me and said that they were very happy at these initiatives. The Pakistan foreign minister nodded approvingly when I spoke of regional coop-eration in glaciology and mentioned Pakistan by name. I got the sense given the SAARC Environment Agreement that was signed at Thimphu in April 2010, we must step up our activities in climate change and envi-ronmental management within SAARC. This earns us huge goodwill all over, not just in our region but elsewhere as well.

I am grateful for the opportunity you have given me to play an active role in the international arena. It has always been my endeavour to position India as an innovative, constructive, and problem-solving player. It has also been my endeavour to nuance both the substance and style of our engagement with other countries, keeping in mind the larger strategic perspective for India's role in the world community that you have yourself so forcefully articulated at different times.

Letter to Prime Minister on the International Centre for Integrated Mountain Development (ICIMOD) and Interactions in Nepal

6 October 2010

In Kathmandu, I visited ICIMOD and reaffirmed our commitment to the activities of that international organization. Between 1983 and 2006, India's contribution to ICIMOD amounted to around $1 million. In 2009, 2010, and 2011, this contribution will total to about $0.5 million. I gave this information as an index of our growing partnership. I also spoke of your own personal interest in fostering regional cooperation in environmental management.

We have already launched a unique trilateral initiative anchored in ICIMOD. This is the Mount Kailash Sacred Landscape Initiative covering some 31,000 sq km, of which 12,000 sq km is in China, 10,000 sq km in Nepal, and 9,000 sq km in India. This initiative is for eco-restoration, biodiversity conservation, and environmental management in the Sacred Landscape to be done by the countries themselves in their respective areas as part of an agreed plan of action. There are a couple of other trans-boundary landscape eco-management initiatives along our borders with Bhutan, Bangladesh, and Myanmar that ICIMOD has identified, which we are studying.

Glaciology is an area where ICIMOD has built up some expertise, which will be of use to us at the new National Institute of Himalayan Glaciology, Dehradun. Glacial lake outburst floods pose a threat in Himachal Pradesh, Uttarakhand, and Sikkim, and ICIMOD has identified where precisely these threats are in these states. We have designated the Almora-based G.B. Pant Institute of Himalayan Environment and Development to be the coordinating institution on our side for using ICIMOD's resources, capabilities, and expertise in this area.

I also met with the ministers of environment and of forests of the Government of Nepal. The minister of environment was keen on India training young scholars from Nepal in different areas of relevance to climate change (like remote sensing) to which I readily agreed. Our ambassador is following-up on this request and we will start by having two young Nepalese scientists work with some of our leading institutions on climate change issues for six months.

The minister for environment wanted India's assistance in the field of environmental law and regulations in formulation of CDM projects that are part of the Kyoto Protocol and in strengthening pollution control infrastructure. We will be responding to these requests soon.

The minister of environment of Nepal was also keen on India's support to Nepal's initiative to convene a global meet in March 2011 in Kathmandu on 'Mountain Ecosystems and Climate Change'. I assured him that we stand prepared to extend assistance in whatever manner the Government of Nepal deems appropriate.

Nepal Ministry of Forests

Nepal and India share two critical trans-border conservation landscapes—the Terai Arc Landscape and the Khangchendzonga Landscape. The minister of forests was keen on building closer institutional linkages at all levels to deal with the management of these landscapes. I visited the Chitawan National Park, which is just across the Valmiki Tiger Reserve in Bihar. I have promised to take follow-up action on this idea with focus on conservation issues. We do have a joint protocol but there is need for more serious activity on both sides.

In addition, he and I spoke of exploring the feasibility of starting a couple of projects for afforestation and upper catchment area treatment through community-based organizations and ex-servicemen cooperatives on the Bagmati, Karnali, Kosi, and Mahakali. The minister of forests of Nepal has promised to prepare a specific project proposal and send it to me by the end of this month.

Letter to the UNFCCC Executive Secretary Christiana Figueres on HFCs and CDM

26 OCTOBER 2010

I understand that the issue of CDM benefits to HFC destruction projects is currently under discussion in the Executive Board of the CDM. In this context, some concerns have emerged on the practices and methods employed by the Executive Board for consideration of the matter.

I had earlier written to the chair of the Executive Board voicing my concerns. It is now understood that the Executive Board, which has referred the matter to the 'Methodology Panel' for a technical examination, has stopped issuance of the certified emission reductions for such projects with retrospective effect. This has been applied even to those projects where verification has been completed, affecting the credibility of the commercial operations of the units as well as the methodology agreed by the parties.

I am informed that the Methodology Panel has also apparently gone beyond the brief given by the Executive Board and has asked the industrial units to furnish commercial information having no relation to the technical issues. Such technical information for consideration of methodology at the global level is already available through valid international sources. The task of technical examination need not become the basis for transgressing into matters having commercial and competitive implications.

I will appreciate if you could take up the matter urgently with the Executive Board of the CDM and advise them to take corrective actions in the interest of credibility of international agreements and agreed rules and procedures.

Letter to Union Minister for Finance Pranab Mukherjee on Climate Finance

26 NOVEMBER 2010

Mr Andrew Mitchell, the UK Secretary of State for International Development, met me yesterday and drew my attention to specific climate change finance proposals on which the Government of India has to take a final view. These are:

The Business Partnership Fund for Pro-Poor Renewables

This is a Norwegian–British–Indian trilateral initiative that will set up a £150 million ($235 million) fund for the development of the renewables sector in India. The fund will aim to leverage government funding and catalyse private sector investment in the sector. The fund will invite bids from companies to deliver off-grid renewables for a specified level of subsidy. The companies that require the lowest level of subsidy per unit will be awarded contracts, and they will be paid according to the results they deliver, with a bonus for achieving their contract in full.

The Climate Change Innovation Programme

The UK Department for International Development (DFID) has proposed a programme with a budget of £12 million ($19 million) to strengthen the resilience to the impacts of climate change, and build capacity to plan for climate change, including through supporting states in their preparation of state climate action plans. As you are aware, a number of our states are already preparing climate action plans, and others are keen to do so. These states would benefit from the technical and financial assistance that this programme will provide. I would be grateful if DEA [Department of Economic Affairs] could move this forward with DFID.

Mr Mitchell's colleagues from DFID who were present at the meeting informed me that DEA is awaiting the concurrence of the MoEF. I am writing to clearly state that in keeping with our commitment to constructively engaging with the international community on the climate change agenda, the MoEF welcomes both these proposals and supports them. I hope DEA will now take the next steps to operationalize them.

Address at the High-Level Segment at Sixteenth Conference of Parties, COP 16 in Cancun, Mexico

[This address attracted extensive media and political attention on account of the one-line addition, 'all countries must take binding commitments in appropriate legal form' I made to the written speech.]

8 December 2010

Over sixty years ago, the Green Revolution in wheat was launched from Mexico with the development of new high-yielding varieties at the International Maize and Wheat Improvement Center (popularly called CIMMYT). Today, Madame President, the word Sonora still resonates in my country.

The time is now for us to launch an EverGreen Revolution from Mexico, a revolution that will trigger innovations in low-carbon technologies for energy, transport, agriculture, and other areas. That is why yesterday, at the meeting chaired by the president of Mexico, I suggested that this Cancun meet take a decision to establish a Consultative Group on International Agricultural Research (CGIAR)-like network of which CIMMYT is a part. I am pleased that the President warmly supported this idea, which also received enthusiastic backing from Mexico's Nobel Laureate in Chemistry Mario Molina.

Last year at Copenhagen, I had spoken about India's profound vulnerabilities to climate change and had described the actions being taken by us domestically and voluntarily to respond to this challenge in a proactive manner. Let me give you a quick update on what we have done since then.

First, we have announced that we will reduce the emissions intensity of India's GDP by 20–25 per cent by the year 2020 on a 2005 reference level, through proactive policies. India's Twelfth Five Year Plan, to be launched on 1 April 2012 will have, as one of its key pillars, a low-carbon growth strategy. Detailed work on this has already begun and is available in the public domain keeping in view our deepest commitment to transparency and accountability.

Second, we have taken firm steps to diversify our energy fuel-mix; 20,000 MW of solar power generating capacity will be set up by 2022 and the present share of nuclear power in our energy mix, which is 3 per cent today, will be doubled over the next decade. A major market-based programme has been put in place to stimulate energy efficiency. We have imposed a clean energy cess on coal for funding research and development of clean energy technologies, even though coal will continue to play a key role in our future energy strategy. We have aggressively expanded the use of natural gas in our power production.

Third, we are pursuing aggressive strategies on forestry and coastal management. India's 70 million ha of forests have not only ecological, but also livelihood significance, as they support the livelihoods of 250 million people. We are launching an ambitious Green India Mission to increase the quality and quantity of forest cover in 10 million ha of land. We have also launched a major new programme on coastal zone management to address the adaptation challenges facing over 300 million people in our country that live in vulnerable areas near our coast.

Fourth, we have set up an elaborate Indian Network for Climate Change Assessment—an Indian IPCC as it were. This network of some 250 scientists and 120 research institutions has already published India's

GHG inventory for the year 2007. It has recently released a 4 x 4 assessment of climate change impacts on four key sectors and four key regions
of the country for the 2030s, a time-frame for which decisive interventions can be made now. This network is soon going to be putting in place
a programme for measuring, monitoring, and modelling the impact of
black carbon which could have climate change and public health impacts.

Fifth, we are actively engaging in partnerships with our neighbours
and other countries to deal with climate change. India and Bangladesh
will soon enter into an agreement to establish an ecosystem forum on
the Sundarbans, which is the world's largest riverine delta system. India,
Nepal, and China have started an ecosystem regeneration initiative in
the holy Mount Kailash landscape. India has financed the establishment
of a South Asian forestry centre in Bhutan and a coastal zone management centre in Maldives. We are talking to our AOSIS partners to launch
a capacity building and technical assistance programme for scholars and
experts from Small Island Developing States (SIDS) countries.

Madame President, India is constructively engaged in the process of
international negotiations. You are aware that we have made detailed
proposals on the MRV/ICA issue as well as on technology cooperation.
I am happy that these proposals have evoked considerable support.
These proposals have been made to stimulate discussion and arrive at a
consensus on both these issues.

Ecological preservation and celebration of biodiversity is embedded
in Indian culture in myriad ways. India will not only be amongst the
fastest growing economies in the world as measured by GDP—gross
domestic product—but will also be amongst the most responsible
in ensuring a high rate of growth of the real GDP—Green Domestic
Product. That is my solemn assurance to the world community today
on behalf of the Government of India. Environmental stewardship
demands responsive leadership and all countries must take binding
commitments in appropriate legal form. That is India's calling.

Letter Sent to all MPs after the Cancun Climate Change Conference

17 DECEMBER 2010

As you know, I have just returned from the UN Climate Change
Conference at Cancun. As I have mentioned to you in the past, our

accountability is to Parliament and I intend to keep Parliament fully informed on our climate change policies and negotiating positions. Hence, I want to take this opportunity to brief you on the major developments at Cancun and their implications for India.

Major Elements of the Cancun Agreements

All parties agreed on a set of decisions, known as the Cancun Agreements, for further discussion, on the two tracks of the negotiation, namely the LCA under the UNFCCC and its Kyoto Protocol. The texts of the agreements are available on the homepage of the UNFCCC (www.unfccc.int). The broad highlights of the agreed texts are as follows:

1. Shared Vision for LCA: This was a matter of intense debate, with the LDCs and AOSIS countries pushing for much more ambitious targets. In the end, a goal of restricting temperature rise to below 2°C, with a provision for review at a subsequent date was agreed upon. Significantly, the agreed final text makes no mention of either quantitative targets for emission reduction by 2050 or global peaking year, thus, protecting the interests of developing countries. Largely due to India's efforts, references to 'equity' and 'equitable access to sustainable development' were included in this section as the basis of working towards this goal.

2. Adaptation: A Cancun Adaptation Framework was agreed upon. It exhorts developing countries to prepare and implement national adaptation plans and at the same time, calls upon developed countries to provide finance, technology, and capacity-building support for the same. It also decides to establish an Adaptation Committee to promote implementation of adaptation actions.

3. Mitigation Commitments of Developed Countries: Under the Cancun Agreements, developed countries including those that are parties to Kyoto Protocol or otherwise, will list their economy wide emission-reduction targets for the period from 2013 onwards in a UNFCCC document, and implement the targets according to agreed rules. Developed countries have also agreed to increase the ambition of their targets, and enhance reporting of their mitigation targets, including their commitments relating to provision of financing, technology, and capacity-building support to developing countries.

For the first time, and on India's insistence, the agreed text calls for an 'international assessment and review' of developed country emission reduction targets, which means that there will be mandatory in-depth review of implementation of the commitments by developed countries including assessments by experts and consultations with developing countries.

4. Kyoto Protocol: At the same time, the parties to Kyoto Protocol have agreed to continue to work towards finalizing their targets for the second commitment period (post-2012 period) with the aim to ensure that there is no gap between the first and second commitment periods of the Kyoto Protocol.

5. Mitigation Actions by Developing Countries: According to the agreement, developing countries will also list their nationally appropriate mitigation actions (not mitigation commitments or targets) in a document under the Convention, and implement them with the financial, technological, and capacity building support provided by developed countries for such actions. The text also calls for 'international consultation and analysis' of developing country actions in a manner that is non-intrusive, non-punitive, facilitative, and respectful of national sovereignty. This will apply to nationally determined actions, implemented on a voluntary basis in pursuance of the domestic mitigation goal, and reported through the official national communication of the country concerned. This was a key area where India played a crucial role in mediating an agreement that was acceptable to both developed and developing countries.

6. Forestry: The agreement encourages developing countries to undertake actions on reducing emissions from deforestation and forest degradation, conservation of forest stocks, and sustainable management of forests (the latter being most relevant to India, where we are actually increasing our forest stock through sustainable forestry). It calls upon developing countries to prepare national strategies/plans for the same. The agreement also asks for full and effective participation of indigenous people and local communities in developing and implementing these strategies. An assessment of financial options to support these actions is also to be worked out.

7. Response Measures and Trade: This urges developed countries to ensure that their climate actions avoid negative consequences on developing countries. On unilateral trade measures, it notes that

measures taken to combat climate change, including unilateral ones, should not constitute a means of arbitrary or unjustifiable discrimination or a disguised restriction on international trade. Although the language is not quite perfect from our perspective, this seeks to address an important concern of India and other developing countries that climate change should not be used as an excuse to impose unilateral trade measures on developing countries.

8. Finance: It calls upon developed countries to provide 'fast start finance' of $30 billion in 2010–12 to developing countries and submit transparent information regarding the provision of these resources. The agreements also recognize the need of providing long-term finance by the developed countries and inscribe their commitment of raising $100 billion per year by 2020 for supporting adaptation and mitigation actions in developing countries. Most importantly, the parties have decided on the establishment of a Green Climate Fund as the operating entity of the financial mechanism. This was a long-pending demand of developing countries and represents one of the most notable achievements, following persistent and protracted negotiations on this issue. The fund is to be governed by a board of twenty-four members, equally represented from developed and developing countries. The World Bank will be the trustee of the fund for the initial three years when the fund is set-up and operationalized.

9. Technology Development and Transfer: The agreement decides to establish a Technology Mechanism for supporting research, development, demonstration, deployment, diffusion, and transfer of technology in the area of mitigation and adaptation. The mechanism will be governed by a Technology Executive Committee with twenty members—nine from developed countries and eleven from developing countries—and its functions will be implemented by a Climate Technology Centre and Network. India was the key player in drafting the text on the Technology Mechanism.

India's Key Contributions at Cancun

India made six specific contributions to the final agreed text, in addition to its contribution to the process over the entire period of the conference.

1. India ensured that for the first time the phrase 'equitable access to sustainable development' found mention in the shared vision text (para 6). This is critical as climate change is largely a problem caused by historical emissions, and late developers like India need this equitable access to address their development priorities and to eradicate poverty. The phrase 'equitable access to sustainable development' is superior to the phrase 'equitable access to carbon space', which connotes a fundamental 'right to pollute' that is seen today as negative and insensitive to the global challenge of climate change.

2. India ensured that the mention of 2015 as a peaking year (para 5) and the mention of a quantitative target of emissions reduction by 2050 (para 6) did not find mention in the final text. This is important as such conditionalities could have imposed emission-reduction commitments on developing countries like India too early and could compromise their development prospects.

3. India's detailed formulation on ICA of developing country mitigation actions in a manner that is non-intrusive, non-punitive, and respectful of national sovereignty was the key input that broke an important deadlock (paras 60–7) and helped achieve progress on issues relating to mitigation.

4. It was India that ensured that for the first time, developed country mitigation actions will be subject to 'international assessment and review', which means that experts, including those from developing countries, will have the right to review whether developed countries are living up to their commitments [paras 44 and 46 (d)].

5. India's formulation on technology development and transfer (paras 113–29) through a technology executive committee (TEC) and climate technology centre and networks (CTCN), formed a critical component of the final text, and a major win for developing countries.

6. Due to India's insistent efforts, the parties avoided a decision at Cancun on the phrase 'legally binding agreement'. Instead, the AWG has been requested to 'continue discussing legal options' (para 145), with the aim to reach consensus, if possible, on this issue by the next COP.

India's Major Outreach Activities at Cancun

In addition to making major contributions to the text, India was visibly and constructively engaged in the entire process at Cancun, ensuring that we spoke up for our developing country partners, showcased our proactive voluntary actions, pushed the envelope on the intellectual debate, and bridged the gaps between parties. Some significant highlights of India's outreach efforts at Cancun included the following:

1. India hosted a major side event on the importance of equity and equitable access in the climate change negotiations. This event was attended to by a full house of experts, negotiators, and civil society, and showcased India's leadership position on this key issue.

2. India hosted a press briefing on India's proactive domestic actions on addressing climate change. This was very well attended with international media from all major countries covering the event. Here I highlighted the (i) National Action Plan on Climate Change; (ii) Indian Network for Climate Change Assessment; (iii) expert group on low-carbon strategy for inclusive growth (iv) activities being undertaken by various state governments; and (v) our regional initiatives in SAARC and with countries like Nepal, Bangladesh, and Maldives.

3. India acted as the coordinator of the BASIC group comprising Brazil, South Africa, India, and China throughout the conference, and will host the next meeting of BASIC ministers in early 2011. Although the BASIC countries had different approaches on some issues, the group stayed united until the very end, and jointly welcomed the final agreements.

4. India proactively reached out to other developing countries. It offered a scholarship programme for capacity building to SIDS. India spoke for the LDCs and Africa, calling on developed countries to immediately disburse the promised 'fast start finance', even as India had voluntarily declared at Copenhagen that it will forego its claim to this money in favour of LDCs. India also hosted a lunch for the SAARC ministers where shared concerns were discussed.

5. India conducted bilateral meetings with various countries and groups where it discussed negotiating positions, tried to bridge gaps, and identified areas for broader bilateral cooperation. These included meetings with Japan, Germany, the US, UK, Australia, France, Qatar, Mexico, and groups like EU, Africa, AOSIS, and LDCs.

6. India also served as an informal ally and facilitator for the host Mexico in reaching out to countries to promote understanding of positions and reach an agreement.

7. I also attended a Public-Private Partnership Breakfast meeting hosted by the Mexican president where I called for the establishment of a CGIAR-type network of technology delivery institutions in the area of climate change. CGIAR is the Consultative Group on International Agricultural Research, and I specifically mentioned how India's high-yielding wheat varieties in the 1960s came from one of the CGIAR institutions in Mexico called CIMMYT. This suggestion was enthusiastically endorsed by Professor Mario Molina, the 1995 Nobel laureate in Environmental Chemistry and by the president of Mexico.

The Issue of Legally Binding Commitments

At the high-level segment, I made a detailed statement which highlighted India's efforts on addressing climate change. In this statement, I also said that 'all countries must take on binding commitments in an appropriate legal form'. This statement has formed the basis for much discussion at home. So, I feel that I must clarify what I intended to convey and the context in which this statement was made.

The immediate context of this statement was that there appeared to be a view being pushed by a majority of developing and developed countries at Cancun that all countries must agree to a legally binding agreement. Most countries, including our BASIC partners Brazil and South Africa, our developing country partners in AOSIS, LDCs, Africa, and four of our SAARC partners (Bangladesh, Maldives, Nepal, and Bhutan) shared this view. The only countries opposing this were the US, China, India, the Philippines, Bolivia, Cuba, Nicaragua, Saudi Arabia, and some others. It was, therefore, important for India to demonstrate that it was not completely oblivious and insensitive to the views and opinions of a large section of the global community.

It is important that a few things are understood about my statement.

First, I have called for commitments in an 'appropriate legal form' and not a legally binding commitment. This is an important distinction. My statement leaves open the need for differentiation between Annex-I (developed) countries and non-Annex-I (developing) countries. Annex-I commitments could be legally binding with penalties. Non-Annex-I actions could be purely voluntary and without penalties. Moreover, the reference to an 'appropriate legal form' is a very broad one. Indeed, even decisions of the COP to the UNFCCC are of an appropriate legal form. Similarly, commitments that our government makes to our Parliament are also, in our view, of an appropriate legal form. In fact, if you recall I had written to you way back on 5 October 2009, where I had mentioned the idea of introducing domestic legislation that will not contain explicit emission reduction targets but will have implicit performance targets for mitigation and adaptation (such as mandatory fuel efficiency standards by 2011, mandatory energy conservation-compliant building codes by 2012, 20 per cent contribution of renewables to India's energy mix by 2030, etc.). Many countries like Brazil and Mexico already have such laws, and others like China and South Africa are also considering such legislation.

Second, contrary to some misquoted references in the domestic media, I did not make any commitment on India undertaking absolute emission cuts. India has made it very clear that while it will undertake voluntary mitigation actions, including reducing the emissions intensity of its GDP by 20–25 per cent by 2020 on a 2005 reference year, India will not take on any emission cuts or agree to any peaking year for its emissions. There is no change in this position.

Third, as I have clarified repeatedly, a legally binding agreement is not acceptable to India at this stage. I made it clear that unless we have clarity on: (i) what the substance of such an agreement is, (ii) what the penalties for non-compliance are, and (iii) what the system for monitoring is, we will not be able to even consider a legally binding agreement. This position remains unchanged.

As I have stated, due to India's efforts, the phrase 'legally-binding agreement' did not find mention in the text. Instead, a loose reference to 'continue discussing legal options' was included.

My effort was to walk the thin line between safeguarding our position while showing a level of sensitivity to the view shared by the majority of countries at Cancun, including many of our developing country partners. I believe we have been able to walk this thin line effectively with this stand. This nuancing of our position will expand negotiating options for us and give us an all-round advantageous standing.

* * *

My constant effort has been to ensure that our negotiating stance on climate change is guided by three principles: (i) the need to protect our economic growth, inclusive development, and poverty eradication agenda; (ii) the pursuit of our domestic environmental policies; and (iii) the achievement of our foreign policy objectives, in particular, that India be seen as a constructive, solution-oriented player in global negotiations. I believe we have managed to accomplish these three objectives at Cancun.

As you are aware, I have never shied away from a debate in Parliament and I look forward to a detailed discussion on the Cancun Agreements and India's role in the Budget session of Parliament. We have nothing to hide, and I remain committed to keeping Parliament fully informed of all our actions and to listening carefully to the views expressed by the Hon. members.

'India's Call at the Cancun Conclave' Op-ed piece in *The Hindu*

30 JUNE 2014

'All nations must take on binding commitments in an appropriate legal form.' I added this sentence to my prepared text at the very last minute after much cogitation while addressing the UN Climate Change Conference at Cancun, Mexico, on 8 December 2010. The conference came after the much-heralded Copenhagen meet. Bouquets from all over the world and brickbats from India followed immediately. The Mexican president and foreign minister were all praise for India's pragmatism. President Mohamed Nasheed of the Maldives said that for the first time he felt confident that India was serious about addressing the special concerns of countries like his, while Chancellor Angela Merkel publicly lauded India's constructive contributions. But at home, I was pilloried by influential NGOs, by large sections of the media, and by the present finance minister in Parliament.

Explanation for the Addition

On 17 December 2010, I addressed a detailed eight-page letter to all MPs explaining the immediate context in which the impromptu addition was made. A majority of developing and developed countries were pushing for a legally binding agreement. Most countries including our BASIC quartet partners Brazil and South Africa, our developing country partners in the AOSIS, LDCs, Africa, and four of our SAARC colleagues shared this view. The opposition came mainly from the US, China, India, the Philippines, Bolivia, Cuba, Nicaragua, and Saudi Arabia. I felt it was important for India to demonstrate that it was not completely oblivious to the views and opinions of very large sections of the global community, especially those most vulnerable to the impacts of climate change.

In my letter, I explained to the MPs that (i) commitments in an 'appropriate legal form' are not a 'legally binding commitment' and that commitments made by the government to our own Parliament in the form of domestic legislation that contain performance targets for mitigation are also 'an appropriate legal form'; and (ii) the commitments did in no way imply that India was taking on absolute emission cuts or agreeing to any peaking year for its emissions. I went on to add that this deliberate nuancing of our traditional hard line position would actually expand negotiating options for us and give us an all-round advantageous standing. The MPs appreciated the detailed explanation and I was naturally more than happy when I got a written reply on 24 December 2010 from Jaswant Singh, saying: 'I would not bother overmuch about the ersatz generated on account of our rather feeble understanding of the difference between "legally binding" and an "appropriate legal form"'.

Actually, India played a crucial role in rescuing and reviving the multilateral negotiating process in Cancun. But this did not get adequate appreciation at home because of the furore over the impromptu addition. There were at least four distinctive contributions. First, it was India that ensured for the first time that developed country mitigation actions will be subject to 'international assessment and review', which means that experts including those from developing countries will have the right to review whether developed countries are living up to their commitments. Second, it was India that ensured the inclusion of the phrase 'equitable access to sustainable development'. This was superior to the phrase 'equitable access to carbon space', which somehow connotes a fundamental 'right to pollute'. Third, India's detailed formulation on 'ICA' of developing country mitigation actions in a manner that is non-intrusive, non-punitive, and respectful of national sovereignty was the key intervention that broke an acrimonious deadlock and helped take Cancun forward. Fourth, India's formulations formed the basis of the consensus reached on technology development and sharing in both mitigation and adaptation.

Substance and Style

In a meeting convened on the sidelines by the president of Mexico, Felipe Calderón, on public-private partnerships, I called for the establishment of a CGIAR-type network of technology development and dissemination institutions in the area of climate change. I specifically mentioned how India's high-yielding wheat varieties in the 1960s came from a CGIAR institution in Mexico. I recall this suggestion being endorsed enthusiastically by President Calderon and by Professor Mario Molina, the 1995 Nobel laureate.

Our negotiating stance on climate change must not be guided by dogma or inflexibility. It should be anchored in three principles: (i) the need to protect our economic growth and poverty eradication agenda; (ii) the pursuit of our domestic environmental policies; and (iii) the achievement of our foreign policy objectives. At all times, India must be seen as a constructive, a willing-to-engage and a solution-oriented player in global negotiations. Substance is as important as style in all such global meets. We may have a strong case but often lose out because of the polemical manner in which we put across our point of view, our eagerness to score debating points, our pride in the use of the English language, and the fact that we are frequently seen as not being patient listeners. We earn disrepute by being needlessly argumentative and unyielding. To make our multilateral diplomacy effective, we must keep all channels of communication—even with those with differing perspectives—open and official, and build up bilateral camaraderie. Bilateral meetings do take place on the sidelines of multilateral get-togethers but this is no substitute for substantive year-round engagement.

It is true that at times what may appear as obstructionism internationally gets applauded domestically. And political leaders in noisy and sharply competitive democracies like ours cannot afford to neglect reactions back home. But true leadership lies in walking this fine line between safeguarding what we believe is in the national interest, while showing courage to take new positions that could well enhance that interest. Negotiating positions can never be frozen, but must actually evolve over time. And our negotiation position gets immeasurably strengthened when we speak from a position of strength. You can star negatively or positively; India accomplished the latter, both at Copenhagen and at Cancun.

Low-carbon high GDP growth is not only essential but also eminently feasible through appropriate investment and technology choices and through proper pricing policies. And having faced criticism in Parliament from sections of the present ruling establishment on my arguing for India to take on mitigation responsibilities, I was more than gratified that President Pranab Mukherjee, in his address to Parliament on 9 June 2014, said: 'The government will earnestly take up mitigation works to meet the challenges posed by climate change and will closely work with the global community in this regard.' This is yet another demonstration of a fundamental maxim of parliamentary democracy—that where you stand depends on where you sit.

Letter to the Co-Chairs of the UN Secretary General's High-Level Panel on Global Sustainability

15 MAY 2011
Thank you for your letter of 2 May 2011, with your thoughts on our panel's work and seeking our inputs. At the outset, let me thank you, the panel co-chairs, as well as the Secretariat, for providing such good direction and support to the panel's work so far. I would like to start by re-emphasizing what I said at GSP 1: that our panel needs to focus on a set of *concrete* recommendations, developed in *substantial detail*, if it has to create impact, and not be relegated to the footnotes of history. I, therefore, fully share the co-chairs' view that the report must focus on the 'how', that is, on specific options to consider and how to get there. Given this context, I take this opportunity to highlight some of the concrete areas where I think the panel could focus:

Indicators/Goals

As has been discussed, how to take forward the subject of sustainability indicators/goals could be a unique 'value-addition' provided the panel. Here we must go beyond merely suggesting the need for such goals/indicators (which would be merely re-stating what several expert panels/institutions have already stated), and provide as concrete a framework as possible. The championed paper 'Sustainable Development: Proposal for a New Indicator', submitted by us (updated copy available at GSP 3) discusses in detail one approach that can be taken, and could form the basis for discussion within this panel. The paper provides possible elements of a multidimensional indicator that captures various aspects of sustainability and development, and proposes a methodology on how this can be taken forward. The panel could use this as a basis for discussion and recommendation in its report.

Universal Access to Energy

The question of energy access is at the heart of every discussion on sustainability, especially for developing countries, where a disturbingly large share of citizens do not have access to modern (and clean) sources of energy. Ensuring universal access to energy in an equitable, inclusive, and cost-effective manner is a key moral imperative of our times. The challenge before us is to ensure that this access happens rapidly, while ensuring that the sustainability related constraints are not violated. This requires tremendous innovation in both technology and policy choices that we make. What are the realistic options before us, and how should we approach this gargantuan challenge? The panel could do the groundwork for addressing this question, providing a clear road map for the global community, international organizations, nation-states, and sub-national units. The championed paper 'Universal Energy Access by 2030', submitted by us (updated copy available at GSP 3) provides a detailed assessment of various options before us, and could provide a good background for the panel to present a road map in its final report.

Equity

We all are agreed on the importance of equity in any discussion related to sustainable development, but have varying notions on what it really means. The panel could take the discourse on the question of 'equity' forward, in particular, by clearly bringing out the links between equity and sustainable development. The championed paper 'Equity in the Context of Sustainable Development', submitted by us (updated copy available at GSP 3) provides a good starting point for this.

Innovative Paradigms

There is much to learn from 'good-practices' that have been attempted across the world. As has been suggested by the co-chairs, such practices and paradigms must be emphasized both in the main body of the report, as well as in detailed appendices. India's rights-based approach in service delivery and citizen empowerment in the context of sustainable development, which was presented at the UN-GSP interaction with the International Trade Union Confederation in Madrid in April, provides one such paradigm that could be discussed in the report.

I look forward to our discussions at GSP 3.

Informal Note on Fast-start Finance, Discussed at the Petersburg Dialogue

[This conference is an initiative of the German government. An informal ministerial attended by countries representing key negotiating blocs. The annual meet, jointly hosted by the German government and the incoming president of the Conference of Parties, provides a forum to address climate change negotiations which require political resolution.]

3 July 2011

What do the Cancun Agreements Say?

The Cancun Agreements ask for fast start funds to be disbursed by 2012, and to have a 'balanced allocation between adaptation and mitigation', to include 'forestry and investments through international institutions', be 'new and additional', and be 'prioritized' to the LDCs, AOSIS, and Africa. In an effort to increase transparency, the Cancun agreements ask all countries to submit information on resources provided to the UNFCCC, but no format is specified.

What is the Factual Position?

As of 9 May 2011:

1. Twenty-one developed countries and the European Commission have publicly announced individual fast-start finance pledges

totaling nearly $28.14 billion, to meet the $30 billion commitment of the 2009 Copenhagen Accord.

2. However, many countries have not yet made public the resources that they have actually delivered or sanctioned either for 2009, or for 2010. According to reported information, of the funds pledged, $12.4 billion has been 'budgeted', but it is unclear whether these have actually been delivered, or still have to go through national approval processes.

3. There is no standard reporting procedure that will ensure transparency, or allow easy monitoring of progress.

What is Needed?

1. Establish Standardized Reporting Procedures: Indicate status of pledged fund, ensure funding is new and additional, specify investments through international institutions, avoid double counting.

2. Set Transparency Standards: At present, ad hoc reporting makes it difficult to monitor pledges, commitments, and sanctioned money.

3. Report Status of Flow of Funds: Distinguish between pledged, committed, and sanctioned/allocated money.

4. Avoid Double Counting: Ensure there is no double counting of within-country assistance [official development assistance (ODA)/export credit/climate finance] or between country associations and individual members (for example, European Commission and member countries).

5. Report 'New' and 'Additional': Develop method of determining whether funding is 'new' and 'additional'—there is currently no internationally-agreed baseline for this, and each donor country uses its own definition. Many countries are re-packaging existing ODA or previous pledges as fast-start finance.

6. Specify Nature of Finance: Whether loan, grant, export credit, etc., a significant proportion of funding has not yet been specified.

7. Specify Break-up of Allocations: Whether funds going for mitigation, adaptation or forestry.

Note on 'New' and 'Additional'

1. Only €70 million of Germany's 2010 climate finance is new.

2. Japan's pledges are previous pledges repackaged(Hatoyama
   Intitiative repackaged from Cool Earth Partnership)
3. The US is increasing investments in international assistance programmes 'that deliver significant climate co-benefits'—$226 million
   is estimated to support climate co-benefits.

Foreword to the Handbook of Climate Change and India: Development, Politics and Governance, *edited by Navroz Dubash*

When Navroz Dubash approached me to write the foreword for this
handbook, I readily accepted—it is not often that one gets asked to
introduce a tome that attempts the daunting task of capturing such a
wide range of viewpoints on climate change. At several of the climate
change related events that I have been part of, the heated debates have
often raised the temperature by 1.5°C, sometimes even more than 2°C
above normal, so Navroz's efforts are particularly admirable! More
seriously, Navroz and his team's extensive research on international
negotiations and Indian policies, governance, and laws means he is
especially well-placed to bring together such a wide selection of Indian
and other voices on the debate.

In introducing this book, I will trace broadly India's recent approach
and actions on climate change. I hope this will serve to set the context
for the perspectives, debates, and analyses that follow.

I

As I have argued ever since I took charge of the MoEF in May 2009, *I
think there is no country more vulnerable to climate change than India*, on so
many fronts. There are four points of vulnerability that are particularly
worth mentioning.

The first major point of vulnerability arises from our heavy dependence on the monsoons—our economic and agricultural systems are
closely tied to it. Two in three Indians—either directly or indirectly—
depend on agriculture for employment. An indifferent monsoon
brings down our economic performance, but more importantly, affects
low-income groups the most. An analysis of data over the last fifty
years shows that nearly half of our fluctuations in GDP are related to

variations in the monsoon. To my mind, what happens to the monsoon is the single largest determinant of prosperity in India.

The second point of vulnerability is our long coastline—one of the longest in the world; plus with one of the highest concentrations of people—250–300 million people live along the coast, and a large proportion of them are dependent on climate-sensitive livelihoods such as agriculture and fishing. A sea-level rise of even 1 m would have serious implications, and on an index of vulnerability therefore, we rank high.

The third vulnerability arises from the threat to the health of our Himalayan glaciers. While glacial movement is a highly complex phenomenon—some glaciers in India are retreating, while others are advancing or staying steady—it is unequivocal that in general, the health of our glaciers is threatened. Melting glaciers will have a direct impact on water availability to hundreds of millions people across our Gangetic belt, disrupt crop production, and affect rainfall patterns.

Our fourth major point of vulnerability is our dependence on natural resource extraction: Most of our core mining areas are in the heart of our densest forests. This simply means that the more mining we do, the more forests we destroy, the more we add to our GHG emissions, and the more we lose our biodiversity.

Therefore, I am convinced that acting on climate change is a national priority—we need to act, for our own sake, not because of or for the sake of anyone else. We need an aggressive domestic agenda that addresses these vulnerabilities—an agenda that produces substantive policy action in the short as well as medium term, and an agenda that is delinked from progress in international negotiations. The traditional Indian approach of (i) we will not do anything substantive because we have not caused the problem of global warming; and (ii) we will not do anything unless there is an international agreement makes for good polemics but does nothing for advancing our national interest. Saying that our per capita emissions will not cross the per capita emissions of developed countries is an excellent starting point but cannot be the sole element of our approach. It has to be per capita *plus*.

II

It is with this in mind that we have worked tirelessly over the last few years to strengthen our domestic actions and ensure a more robust response to climate change—both on adaptation and mitigation.

The NAPCC has accelerated our response to climate change, and provided an opportunity to integrate related sectoral issues of poverty and vulnerability, energy efficiency, sustainable development, and forestry into the development rubric. It sets up a solid base for domestic action, and allows us to negotiate internationally from a position of strength.

As part of the NAPCC, the National Mission for Enhanced Energy Efficiency is scaling-up energy efficiency actions at every level. Most notably, the Perform Achieve and Trade mechanism under this mission will get 700 of the most energy intensive industries to become more energy efficient and help reduce India's CO_2e [Carbon dioxide equivalent] emissions by 25 million tonnes per year by 2014–15. The recently launched Green India Mission will provide a bottom-up participatory approach to improve the quality of our forests, and will also help us sequester 43 million tonnes of CO_2e annually. The Jawaharlal Nehru Solar Mission will target generating 20,000 MW of solar power by 2022. Other missions have begun working as well on equally ambitious goals.

Last year, we have set up an Expert Group on Low-Carbon Strategies for Inclusive Growth. This expert group is working on sectoral road maps which will firmly integrate low-carbon growth into the mainstream of our planning process (the interim report of the group has just been released and is on our website). These road maps will be a central part of our Twelfth Five Year Plan, which comes into effect in April 2012, and whose avowed motto is faster, inclusive, and *more sustainable* growth.

The states are also doing their part. Many have initiated state-specific action plans, and the exercise will be completed in the next few months across all states.

While strengthening domestic policy actions, we are also enhancing our capabilities of rigorous scientific work, and taking major steps in bridging the gaps in Indian climate science. The Indian Network on Climate Change Assessment (INCCA)—a network of over 125 national scientific institutions has been formed to undertake scientific assessments of different aspects of climate change. In November 2010, the INCCA published a '4 x 4 assessments' of climate change in India. This study involved a comprehensive, long-term assessment of the impacts of climate change on four key sectors—agriculture, water, natural ecosystems, and biodiversity, and health, across four climate sensitive regions of India. This is the INCCA's second major publication—after the GHG emissions report in May 2010.

We have also taken initiatives in other related areas, which have not been in the mainstream of climate change discussions but are important. INCCA has launched India's Black Carbon Research Initiative, which will enhance our understanding of the effects of black carbon in the context of global warming, and its effects on glaciers through a comprehensive national-level programme. We have also taken on the issue of HFCs, which, while being a substitute for ozone-depleting CFCs, have a high global warming potential, and are therefore being seen as an emerging 'problem' for climate change. India has initiated the formation of a joint Indo-US Task Force on 'HFC phase-down'.

III

While we have stepped up our domestic actions, we have also engaged constructively and meaningfully in the international climate change negotiations. Our efforts over the last two years have constantly been to ensure that while India has not been part of the problem, India will be part of the solution and be seen to be a constructive part of the solution. Debates are all very well but when India is refashioning its place in the world community based largely on its economic performance (and not just potential) its climate change negotiating strategy—both in terms of substance and style—has to be nuanced, flexible, and responsive to changing circumstances and challenges. We have already announced our voluntary domestic commitment of reducing the emissions intensity of our GDP by 20–25 per cent by the year 2020 on a 2005 reference level.

We are intent on building trust and furthering collective multilateral action at global and regional levels. Since Copenhagen, and even more so since Cancun, India has taken on a very proactive role in international negotiations. India's contributions at Cancun were critical in the drafting of the 'Cancun agreements' at various places—for example, on the design of the technology mechanism, on introducing the phrase 'equitable access to sustainable development' and developing the concepts of 'international consultation and analysis', and 'international assessment and review'. Furthermore, India's contributions went well-beyond the negotiating text. India spoke up for its developing country partners, showcased its proactive voluntary actions, pushed the envelope on the intellectual debate, and helped bridge the gaps between parties. We will continue this proactive engagement in international negotiations, bringing parties together, while safeguarding our national economic interests. We must also demonstrate greater sensitivity to the special needs of the small island states, LDCs, and Africa.

IV

Even as we have contributed proactively to international negotiations, we have also given a new impetus to regional cooperation in climate change. SAARC has adopted cooperation on climate change as a major defining theme of its partnership. Regional initiatives through SAARC, and individually with Nepal, Bhutan, Bangladesh, and Maldives, have begun to show results. India has made grants of $1 million each to the SAARC Forestry Centre, Thimpu, Bhutan, and the SAARC Coastal Management Centre, Male, Maldives.

Our partnership as part of the BASIC group of countries, which comprises Brazil, South Africa, India, and China, is now also extending well beyond international negotiations, to include areas of collective action.

The message as far as we are concerned is very clear: *While we will continue to proactively engage in international negotiations, even playing the role of 'dealmaker' where appropriate, we will not wait to act. We will continue to aggressively pursue domestic and collaborative actions to combat climate change.*

I take this opportunity to once again congratulate Navroz and his editorial team for producing such an excellent handbook, which brings together so many views and perspectives from India; providing for an accessible information base on the issue of climate change in India. Importantly, it adds Indian voices to the global discussion, which has so far, seen only a smattering of voices from the South. I am sure the handbook will play an important role in bridging some of the gaps in understanding that exist both within India and within the international community.

Notes

1. This section will focus primarily on India's international engagements. Issues relating to energizing the Indian scientific community are addressed in Chapter 6.

A Final Word

At the end of it all, what does this book add up to, other than being a chronicle of a ministerial tenure?

High economic growth rates are essential because they generate huge revenues for the government, which can then be utilized for social welfare and infrastructure expansion programmes. Of course, it goes without saying that rapid growth alone is not enough. It must be of a nature that creates increasing productive employment opportunities. It must be inclusive so that more and more sections of society benefit visibly and tangibly from high economic growth. There is a third dimension to economic growth, that is in addition to being rapid and inclusive, it has to be ecologically sustainable as well.

That is the simple but powerful message of this book—that environment matters, and it matters here and now for us, that sustainable development is not a luxury but an overriding necessity for India, and, indeed, that sustainable development is eminently feasible. India simply cannot afford to follow the conventional 'grow now, pay later' model of development that has been adopted by most other countries, including China.

This is so for at least four compelling reasons. First, because India will add an additional 400 million or so to its current population of about 1.2 billion by the middle of this century. India, more than any other country, has to worry deeply about its future generations. Our impatience now cannot jeopardize growth prospects later. To paraphrase the Mahatma (even though Gopal Gandhi informs me that his grandfather never said those words, which have become the creed of environmentalists everywhere), our present greed cannot threaten future need.

Second, because India faces unique vulnerabilities—both current and projected—to climate change. These arise from our continued dependence on the monsoon, from the threat of an increase in mean sea levels to millions of families living along the 7,000 km-long coastline, from the dangers posed by receding Himalayan glaciers to water flows in the north Indian rivers and from the fact that most of our vital natural resources such as coal and iron ore are located in forest-rich areas and their extraction will inevitably entail loss of a vital carbon sink. Science, as encapsulated by the IPCC's Fifth Assessment Report, stresses on the dangers that climate change poses for our food security. A warming earth impacts productivity of our agriculture, impacts availability of water even in the fertile Indo-Gangetic basin, and the rising sea-levels poses the threat of loss of land and increased salinity of our paddy-cultivating areas. Disasters resulting from extreme weather events in the last few years, the periodicity and intensity of which are on the rise, serve to underscore our vulnerability. The poor and marginalized are the ones to suffer most, clearly not benefiting from the much vaunted rapid and high economic growth

Third, because the environment is increasingly becoming a public health concern. From unprecedented industrial and vehicular pollution to the dumping of chemical waste and municipal sewage in rivers and waterbodies, the build up to a public health catastrophe is already visible. People are already suffering in a variety of ways, and environmental deterioration has emerged as a major cause of illness. Poor health impacts productivity, pushes the poor into indebtedness and further poverty, and adversely affects growth.

Fourth, because most of what is called environmentalism in India is not middle-class 'lifestyle environmentalism', but actually 'livelihood environmentalism' linked to daily issues of land productivity, water availability, access to non-timber forest produce, protection of waterbodies, protection of grazing lands and pastures, preservation of sacred places, etc.

Environmental concerns are, therefore, not part of some foreign plot or conspiracy by some non-governmental organizations to keep India in a state of perpetual poverty. These are concerns that are part of our daily lives. While it is important to integrate environmental concerns into the mainstream of the process of economic growth, we must also recognize that there will be trade-offs between growth and environment, occasions when tough choices will necessarily have to be made— choices that may well involve saying 'no'. It is when you work out the integration in practice that you confront contradictions, complexities, and conflicts that cannot be brushed aside. They have to be recognized and managed sensitively as part of the democratic process.

The debate is really not one of environment versus development but really be one of adhering to rules, regulations, and laws versus taking the rules, regulations, and laws for granted. When public hearings mean having hearings without the public and having the public without hearings, it is not an 'environment versus development' issue at all. When an industrial project begins construction to expand its capacity without bothering to seek any environmental clearance as mandated by law, it is not an 'environment versus development' question, but simply one of whether laws enacted by Parliament will be respected or not. When closure notices are issued to distilleries or paper mills or sugar factories illegally discharging toxic wastes into India's most holy Ganga river, it is not a question of 'environment versus development' but again one of whether standards mandated by law are to be enforced effectively or not. When a power plant wants to draw water from a protected area or when a coal mine wants to undertake mining in the buffer zone of a tiger sanctuary, both in contravention of the laws, it is not a 'environment versus development' question but simply one of whether laws will be adhered to or not.

By all means we must make laws pragmatic. By all means, we must have market-friendly means of implementing regulations, and we must accelerate the rate of investment in labour-intensive manufacturing especially. But none of it should not become a mockery of regulations and laws. There is no denying that laws, regulations, and rules need to be reviewed from time to time, to ensure that new and emergent realities are addressed. But no review and no iteration should move away from the basic purpose and intent with which the legislations were created. In the case of environment-related laws and regulations, the aim is to create a balance in which concerns of ecological security and other needs, such as economic growth, are met in a manner that neither is put at a great disadvantage. The work of achieving that balance, precarious as it is, is a continuous one.

Maintaining the balance, carefully calibrating it to meet emergent needs requires constant vigilance. While we focus on the legal structures, we often forget the key lies in how the laws and regulations are implemented and observed. We need to be more watchful, in our approach to using our natural resources, be it forests, minerals, or water. This need to be vigilant should not at the same time be stifling, and it is for this that we need independent institutions that are transparent, accessible, and tasked with people with expertise, who are able to function without fear or favour. Compliance with laws and regulations should be the watchword at all times.

India has huge unmet development needs. But its development imperatives should not impede its engagement with the world. Developmental needs, including the goal to eradicate poverty and deprivation should not become an excuse for hanging on to outdated ideas and templates or for limited and defensive engagement with other countries. As a country that is home to both a large number of the world's rich and the poorest people, India is placed in an unique position to craft a blueprint that balances the needs of people across the economic spectrum, in a manner that addresses the imperatives of ecological security in an ever-warming world. India should not let the shibboleths of the past prevent it from assuming a leadership role in crafting the solutions of the future. As a country that sees itself as a global leader, India must step up, and engage proactively, thinking out of the box to safeguard its development space, while at the same time helping the world craft an equitable solution to global concerns like climate change and a warming planet.

Indian civilization, amongst all world civilizations, has always shown the highest respect for biodiversity in all its myriad forms. Therefore, it should not be difficult for us to become world leaders in green growth. This is an area of strategic leadership where India can show the way. Both the champions of 'growth at all costs' and the crusaders for ecological causes must work together to enable India to attain this position. Reasoned and sober dialogue must give way to the present acrimony, must give way to simplistic solutions advocated by either side.

There is an ancient Sanskrit saying, *prakrutihi rakshati rakshita* (nature protects us if we protect nature); As the edifice of India's environmental laws and regulations comes under renewed assault because of corporate interests, we ignore that piece of wisdom at our own peril.

Index

About the Author

Jairam Ramesh is Chair of the Future Earth Engagement Committee, a global research platform on environmental challenges and a member of the International Advisory Board of the Osaka-based International Environmental Technology Centre promoted by the United Nations Environment Programme. Since 2004, he has been a Member of Parliament representing Andhra Pradesh in the Rajya Sabha. He was Union Minister of State (Independent Charge) Environment and Forests from May 2009 to July 2011, the period covered in this book. He has been Union Minister of State for Commerce and Power as well as Union Cabinet Minister of Rural Development, Drinking Water and Sanitation. He is a Visiting Fellow at various academic institutions in India and abroad and is a columnist and author. He has served on the UN Secretary General's High-level Panel on Global Sustainability.